D1213001

Encyclopedia of the Ancient Maya

Encyclopedia of the Ancient Maya

EDITED BY

WALTER R. T. WITSCHEY

ROWMAN & LITTLEFIELD

Lanham • Boulder • New York • London

Published by Rowman & Littlefield
A wholly owned subsidiary of The Rowman & Littlefield Publishing Group, Inc.
4501 Forbes Boulevard, Suite 200, Lanham, Maryland 20706
www.rowman.com

Unit A, Whitacre Mews, 26-34 Stannary Street, London SE11 4AB

British Library Cataloguing in Publication Information Available

Library of Congress Cataloging-in-Publication Data

Encyclopedia of the ancient Maya / edited by Walter R. T. Witschey.
     pages cm
  Includes bibliographical references and index.
  ISBN 978-0-7591-2284-0 (cloth : alk. paper) — ISBN 978-0-7591-2286-4 (electronic)
1. Mayas—Encyclopedias. I. Witschey, Walter Robert Thurmond, 1941- editor.
  F1435.E65 2015
  972.81'01—dc23

                                                            2015032712

∞™ The paper used in this publication meets the minimum requirements of
American National Standard for Information Sciences—Permanence of
Paper for Printed Library Materials, ANSI/NISO Z39.48-1992.

Printed in the United States of America

IN MEMORIAM

Richard E. W. Adams
Mary Ricketson Bullard
Anne M. Chapman
Flora S. Clancy
William R. Coe II
T. Patrick Culbert
Bruce Dahlin
Norberto González Crespo
Craig A. Hanson
Peter D. Harrison
Christopher Jones
Barbara Kerr
Edward B. Kurjack
John M. Longyear III
Hanns J. Prem
Robert Rands
Robert J. Sharer
Andrea Joyce Stone
George E. Stuart
Richard E. Woodbury

DEDICATION: GEORGE E. STUART

With great fondness, admiration, and esteem, I dedicate this book to George E. Stuart, National Geographic staff archaeologist, senior editor, and vice president for research and exploration; Mayanist; author; generous friend; and to me a source of life-changing inspiration.

George and I met in September 1982, when I attended a Maya seminar in Washington, D.C., under the aegis of the National Geographic Society, where George worked, and the Smithsonian Institution. I recall vividly George working in front of a pivoting greenboard, chalk in his right hand and notes in his left. He talked as he drew Maya glyphs and temple-pyramids; ball-court plans, and Long Count dates. He drew a leaf-nosed bat ("*zotz*") as he explained emblem glyphs, and that the bat represented Copan.

George's reputation at National Geographic drew me to the seminar as my own interest in the ancient Maya reawakened from a lengthy nap. At age 11, my parents gave me the newly published *Gods, Graves, and Scholars* by C. W. Ceram. The tales of archaeology infected me, especially those of Edward H. Thompson dredging the sacred well at Chichen Itza and John Lloyd Stephens purchasing the ruins of Copan for $50. I marvel at both tales today. They took me to the Hieroglyphic Stairway at Copan, and to the Sacred Well, and to many other special places in the Maya region.

In 1985 I made a commitment to meet two Maya archaeologists per month for a year, take them to lunch, and learn what I could about current research in the Maya area. George was my first lunch date, in March 1985. He gave me a list of people to see and insisted I visit E. Wyllys Andrews V, director of the Middle American Research Institute at Tulane University, who later became my dissertation advisor. My wife and I took a long weekend in New Orleans May 17–20, and I talked with several faculty members at Tulane that May.

On Memorial Day, after I returned home to Richmond, Virginia, the Anthropology Department at Tulane invited me into the doctoral program. Within 24 hours, my wife and I decided to uproot our family and move to New Orleans. George had changed our lives.

For me it was a chance to convert amateur interest in the ancient Maya to modest professional competence. It provided an opportunity to learn archaeology skills, to visit Maya sites, and to excavate for new knowledge at a poorly known site. For my wife it brought an opportunity to sing grand opera with the New Orleans Opera Company. For our oldest daughter it brought exposure to Tulane, from which she graduated with a BFA. For our youngest daughter it brought a husband and a lifetime in New Orleans. For all our family it brought an intense love of New Orleans' food, music, and culture and the land of the ancient Maya. George had changed our lives.

From 1985 until his death in 2015, George was an inspiration, a friend, and a willing discussant and writer. With generosity of spirit and unbounded knowledge of the ancient Maya, he helped, inspired, and guided me at every turn, including helping to shape this volume. He and Melinda were gracious and hospitable hosts. At a remembrance of George at Boundary End Farm, I listened hard to other members of George's enormous circle of friends describe him, and two words appeared in every description of George: generosity and inspiration.

To my friend and mentor, George E. Stuart, *Dios bo'otik*. God will repay you.

WRTW

CONTENTS

THEMATIC CONTENTS

LIST OF MAPS, TABLES, AND FIGURES

MAPS

TABLES

FIGURES

PREFACE

The great joy of scholarship is the added knowledge and fresh ideas it brings forth. Each day brings new data, new discoveries, and new insights.

This is spectacularly true in the field of Maya studies. Each year brings reports of new sites, fresh discoveries at well-known sites, new translations of the ancient script, and new revelations about the Maya calendar. Some material received as recently as a few days before going to press has been included. As an archaeologist, I am especially interested in the finding of new cities, towns, and communities, and in fresh data about old ones. I delight in the translation of glyphs by epigraphers and the surprising insights they bring. I can't help but smile when those with knowledge of glyphs, calendrics, and astronomy point out a new astronomical cycle of time in the Maya script, even a new cycle previously unrecognized by modern astronomers.

The sweep of discovery and the broadening of scope in Maya studies are far longer than my own career. Knowledge of the Maya for Europeans began with the Spanish *conquistadores*, moved forward with early explorers in the 1800s, and leapt into public consciousness with John Lloyd Stephens's tales of exploration in the Maya area and with detailed calendric studies and successes as the twentieth century began, such as those by Förstemann working with the Dresden codex.

One might expect then that new discoveries in the latter half of the twentieth century would be incremental, without the blockbuster impact of earlier discoveries, such as learning how the Maya calendar worked or the discovery of Copan and Tikal. Delightfully, such was not the case.

When Frans Blom published a new map of the Maya area in 1940 at Tulane University, there were about 1,600 archaeological sites on it. Today we count more than three times that in the Electronic Atlas of Ancient Maya Sites (http://mayagis.smv.org/).

Decipherments of the ancient script have yielded exciting new discoveries. Yuri Knorosov's paper in 1952, demonstrating that Maya writing contained pronounceable syllables, was the first of many breakthroughs in what has become a torrent of new readings. This fresh approach to the glyphs struggled for a quarter century against scholarly opposition, yet has proven to be both correct and the seminal breakthrough in decipherment.

In 1958 Heinrich Berlin wrote of detecting "Emblem Glyphs" in the script and that they might carry city names or references to founding families. In 1960 Tatiana Proskouriakoff published a remarkable paper showing that monuments at Piedras Negras

carried dates that matched human lifespans. These two efforts showed that the Maya inscriptions contained genuine history, just as other such inscriptions worldwide have been
written about rulers and their feats. In the following 15 years, several Mayanists as well as
linguists began to chase the thread of phoneticism teased out by Knorosov.

December 1973 was a watershed moment for studies of decipherment. Merle Greene
Robertson hosted the first Palenque roundtable, the Primera Mesa Redonda de Palenque.
Three of its attendees—Linda Schele, Peter Mathews, and Floyd Lounsbury—proceeded
to expand our knowledge of the Maya by working out the Late Classic dynastic sequence for Palenque with ruler names and dates. A year later at Dumbarton Oaks, the
Early Classic dynasty was unraveled. By the end of the 1970s, dynastic sequences were
published for other sites. Simon Martin and Nikolai Grube have written a remarkable
dynastic compendium of subsequent work, now in its second edition (2008), *Chronicles
of the Maya Kings and Queens: Deciphering the Dynasties of the Ancient Maya*. It has become
a standard reference for the field.

In the 1970s the remarkable David Stuart entered the game.

Although he had published earlier decipherments, Stuart wrote *Ten Phonetic Syllables*
in 1987 at age 22. This paper presented readings for "scribe" and "to write" (among others), leading to the current view that scribes were members of the royal families rather
than a separate class of artisans. Stuart identified the glyph for chocolate (*ca-ca-wa*), which
led to its stunning confirmation by analysis of the residues of caffeine and theobromine
in a Rio Azul vessel labeled for chocolate. Stuart and Stephen Houston, with other colleagues, and with valuable input from native Maya speakers, blog about new decipherments as the Maya script is yielding long-held secrets.

Decipherments moved forward in the 1980s and 1990s with the recognition that the
bands of glyphs, previously called by Michael Coe the Primary Standard Sequence, around
the rim of many Maya polychrome vases were not funerary formulae but examples of
name-tagging. Such scripts were identifying the owner (usually royalty), the type of vessel
(plate, vase, bowl), the contents (maize gruel, cocoa), and often the scribe's name and his
parentage. An exceptionally large number of these painted ceramics was made available for
study by Justin Kerr, who designed and built a camera for the purpose of photographing
such vases as roll-outs on which the entire scene and script could be viewed at one glance.
With the publishing of his photographs on the web at http://www.mayavase.com/, an
enormous body of work was made available for study by many scholars.

Decipherments have led to new views of the development of the Maya culture. Emblem glyphs mentioning the "Snake Kingdom" indicate that its origins may date earlier
than expected and involve a wider area than believed. The glyphs appear at first at Dzibanche and then at Calakmul, Mexico, and they push back the dates and the locations of
early Maya settlements. This has led to and been complemented by recent work, for example at Yaxhom by Bill Ringle; at Yaxnohcah by Ivan Šprajc, Kathryn Reese-Taylor, and
Armando Anaya Hernández; and at Ichkabal by Enrique Nalda and Sandra Balanzario, all
with large Formative period settlements and monumental architecture.

During the past 15 years, Francisco Estrada-Belli has found new sites in the region
northwest of Tikal, but outside the Mirador Basin, including the Preclassic site Cival,

with very early instances of Maya elites building triadic group pyramids and Group-E astronomical configurations.

In 2014 Šprajc rediscovered La Lagunita, a "missing" site with important inscriptions whose location had been lost, and discovered Tamchen, a new site, both in southern Campeche, Mexico.

New technologies are playing an important role in Maya region discoveries, and several are presented in the encyclopedia. These especially include LiDAR remote sensing and high sensitivity laboratory analyses. Arlen and Diane Chase were pioneers in the extensive use of LiDAR for Maya site survey, producing remarkably detailed fresh information about structures, roads, extent of settlements, and field terracing at Caracol, Belize, from a 2009 flyover survey with LiDAR. In the laboratory, both trace element analysis and stable isotope analysis of bone collagen are providing new insights into the remarkable variety of diets among Maya individuals, with variation by gender, location, and class. Tooth enamel analysis reveals where an individual grew up and gives migration information.

This volume has also placed special emphasis on environmental conditions, for it has become clear that the Maya and their culture were remarkably sensitive to environmental change. Analysis of lake bed cores is providing new information about rainfall, drought, and possible climate effects on the Classic Maya collapse.

All this is simply to provide encouragement to our inquisitive readers and young explorers of all ages: the world of the ancient Maya has many opportunities for you to find new cities, find new decipherments, find new connections between royal families, and find for yourself the wonder and sophistication of the ancient Maya.

WRTW

ACKNOWLEDGMENTS

My friends and colleagues in Maya studies deserve the fullest credit for bringing their ideas and insights to this encyclopedia. Without their contributions, the work would be considerably less valuable as a compendium of modern Maya research. E. Wyllys Andrews (my patient dissertation advisor and mentor for 30 years) and George Stuart (who changed my life) provided thoughtful guidance, as did Clifford T. Brown, Ed Kurjack, David Stuart, Vicki Bricker, Mary Miller, Justin Kerr, Karl-Herbert Mayer, and many others.

The 81 authors who contributed to this volume have made it possible to bring you a fresh look at their current studies and interesting questions they seek to answer, as well as a refresher about some long known research that remains current today. They have tolerated my numerous e-mails (1,700+), surprised me with their prompt submissions, and brought me many new facts and observations about the ancient Maya culture. Every day a learning experience! A complete list of contributors and their affiliations may be found at the end of the book. Profuse thanks to them all.

There are three particular sources that are indispensable for Maya students: (a) the sixth edition of *The Ancient Maya* (2006) by Robert Sharer and Loa Traxler; (b) the eighth edition of *The Maya* (2011) by Michael D. Coe, and (c) the second edition of *Chronicle of the Maya Kings and Queens: Deciphering the Dynasties of the Ancient Maya* (2008) by Martin Simon and Nikolai Grube. They are of prime import in their comprehensive narrative coverage of the Maya.

My Tulane associates have been generous in their assistance: Geoff Braswell, Cliff Brown, Rach Cobos, Tomás Gallareta, David Hixson, Judy Maxwell, Bill Ringle, George Bey, Dirk Van Tuerenhout, Gaby Vail, and Chris Von Nagy. In addition to Rach and Tomás, thanks go to my other Mexican colleagues Antonio Benavides and Rubén Maldonado of INAH. Thanks in full measure go to those who write about the ancient Maya and their world, whose works appear in the bibliography. As in every scholarly endeavor, we stand on the shoulders of those who have been where we could not go, who have studied what we could not study, and who had insights we did not have. All of us who have contributed to the encyclopedia owe a substantial debt to them and their work that preceded our own.

Leanne Silverman, senior acquisitions editor, and Andrea O. Kendrick, assistant acquisitions editor, with Rowman & Littlefield have been most patient with my efforts to create a new encyclopedia about the ancient Maya. Their help, guidance, and encouragement have brought the project to fruition. Five anonymous reviewers devoted time and energy to reading and analyzing the manuscript. Their insights greatly improved the final version. I owe them a debt of thanks for their careful work and generous contributions.

My wife of 34 years, Joan, was especially helpful in deferring her hoped-for retirement travel plans in support of this project. She is a daily joy, a constant and encouraging companion, and a willing participant in Maya studies and travels. Carolyn Craft provided moral support when and as most needed. My Longwood colleagues, especially Ken Perkins and Chuck Ross, have helped me in a thousand ways.

To those not named here, but instrumental in the project, thank you. To all who contributed goes credit for their skilled and insightful work. All errors are mine, not theirs.

WRTW

NOTE TO THE READER

CROSS-REFERENCING

In order to facilitate the rapid and efficient location of information, and to make this book as useful a reference tool as possible, extensive cross-references have been provided. In some cases, where multiple commonly used terms occur, the encyclopedia uses "See" to direct you to an entry, for example, "**CORN**. See **DIET**." Within individual encyclopedia entries, terms that have their own entries elsewhere are in **boldface type** the first time they appear. Further cross-referencing is shown within or at the end of an entry with "See also" to take you to other topics relevant to the one you are reading.

ORTHOGRAPHY

Writing Maya languages is complicated. When the Spanish arrived in the New World, the friars tried to adapt, with varying degrees of success, their Latin alphabet to the sounds of the indigenous languages. With diligence they learned the languages and crafted successful ways to write them, but they were not linguists. They had no modern understanding of phonology. The wide variety of Mesoamerican languages included many sounds that did not occur in the languages the Spaniards knew from Europe. The Spanish sometimes used combinations of letters, such as the /-tl/ in Náhuatl, to represent single sounds that did not match a Latin letter. In other cases, they invented new letters for the new sounds they heard.

Spoken Maya uses several glottalized consonants. This sound is so rare in English that many English speakers have trouble developing the knack of using it. A prime but rare example in English is the interjection "uh-oh," a brief comment of dismay. Most English speakers can produce the glottal stop, a slamming together of the vocal cords to cut off the air stream, just after the "uh" and before the "oh." In Maya, the use or not of a glottal stop makes a difference in the meaning of a word, and requires that the glottal stops somehow be written. The Spanish friars, for example, wrote the glottalized /t/ in Maya in different ways: it could be represented by a slashed tee /ŧ/, although it was sometimes written as /th/. Similarly, the glottalized fricative /¢'/ in Maya was written as a backwards and upside-down letter "c," which was easy to write and to typeset.

In recent decades, more accurate systems of writing the sounds of Maya and other native languages have been proposed and sometimes adopted. These are usually based on simplified versions of the 126-year-old International Phonetic Alphabet. The most significant and successful of these initiatives has been the one led by the Academy of Indigenous Languages of Guatemala (http://www.almg.org.gt/), which has implemented new, more accurate orthographies for all the native languages of that country to replace the traditional letter choices from the Colonial period.

The use of multiple systems of orthography has produced multiple spellings of the same words, which creates confusion for the uninitiated. Here are some hints that should be helpful.

Maya vowels are "pure" like those in Spanish, not combined with glides like most English vowels. Maya vowels can also be long or short, which refers to the length of time the vowel is voiced, not its tone or place of articulation in the mouth. Vowels can also be "broken," which means the glottis is snapped shut briefly in the middle of pronouncing the sound. Broken vowels are usually written by doubling the letter of the vowel and inserting an apostrophe in the middle, for example, "o›o".

In the Maya languages, the letter *x* is used to indicate a sound equivalent to the *sh* in English. Thus, the Yucatec word *bix*, meaning "how," would be written in English *beesh*. Confusion surrounding the *x* in Mesoamerica is compounded because the letter has two pronunciations in Mexican Spanish spelling. The *x* can sound like a Spanish *j*, so that the place-names Xalapa and Jalapa are equivalent and sometimes interchangeable. Many speakers of American English will know how to pronounce this because it is the root of the word *jalapeño*, a kind of chili pepper popular in the United States. The *x* can also be pronounced more like an *s* as in names such as Taxco or Tuxtla. This variation in the sound of *x* evolved because of a phonological shift that took place in sixteenth-century Spanish, just as Mesoamerican Spanish was developing.

In the Maya languages, most consonants come in glottalized and unglottalized forms. When a consonant is glottalized, the glottis in the throat is momentarily shut during pronunciation. In modern orthographies, glottalization is usually marked by placing an apostrophe after the consonant, so that, for example, *k*, which is pronounced as in English, is written *k'* when glottalized. Older Colonial orthographies vary in how they show glottal stops. Manuscripts use two letters (e.g., *pp* for a glottalized *p*) or by inventing a new letter. In the older orthographies, the *k* sound was often represented by the letter *c*, while the letter *k* was reserved for the glottalized form. In the new spelling systems, *k* is used instead of *c* for the familiar unglottalized sound, and *k'* (with the apostrophe showing the glottal stop) is used for the glottalized sound.

In the traditional Mayan language orthographies, the *h* was pronounced as in English, not Spanish. In some modern spellings, this has been replaced by a *j*, which is closer to the sound in Spanish spelling. A sound like the English *w* is common in the Mayan languages. In the Colonial period, this sound was often represented by the letter *u* combined with another vowel. Today, these sounds are spelled with the letter *w*. So, for example, the Yucatec Maya word *uinal* would be spelled *winal* in the modern system. Similarly, the traditional spelling of the word *ahau* would become *ahaw* or *ajaw*.

In this encyclopedia, we have chosen ease of use over slavish consistency. For example, the argument for using the modern orthographies, such as those adopted in Guatemala, in the Maya area is compelling: they are more accurate than the older ones, and they support the post–civil war Maya cultural revitalization. Should we choose one and apply it to the writing of Maya languages outside of Guatemala, say, in Mexico? To do so would imply spelling Yucatan as Yukatan, and Chichen Itza would become Chich'e'en Itsa'. This would be using an unusual spelling for common and well-known names, and we have deliberately chosen not to add such confusion. In addition, in Mexico, maps, road signs, and official documentation generally retain the traditional spellings. Beyond that, many of the older spellings are so commonly used in the literature that we must use them here.

MAYA RULERS: OLD AND NEW NAMES

Beginning with the 1959 discovery of Emblem Glyphs by Heinrich Berlin and the 1960 observation by Tatiana Proskouriakoff that Maya inscriptions likely described major life events of mortal kings, epigraphers identified Maya rulers in inscriptions and gave them fanciful names, based on the visual appearance of their glyphs.

Decipherment of the ancient Maya script, however, has proceeded quite rapidly since 1975 and has accelerated dramatically in the past two decades. As a consequence, many of the fanciful names of kings, based on the visual appearance of their glyphs, have now been superseded by their names as written by them phonetically in hieroglyphs on their monuments. For example the king of Tikal in AD 537–562, "Double Bird" (as he was first called, based on the visual appearance of the glyphs), is now known by his name as he had it inscribed phonetically on his monuments, "Wak Chan K'awiil."

In the encyclopedia, the older names are supplied, because they were used frequently in earlier writings we still consult. Today, now that the hieroglyphs are better understood, the encyclopedia entries use the king's name based on interpretation of the glyphs, as it is understood from his contemporary inscriptions, but also give the older name. New and old names are both indexed.

ABBREVIATIONS
Date Abbreviations

Dates are written several ways in other literature about the Maya: AD, anno Domini, "in the year of our Lord," written in front of a date indicates years after year 1 in the Christian calendar. BC, "before Christ," refers to years before the year AD 1 and is written after the date. Some authors prefer to use CE, meaning "Common Era," instead of AD, and BCE, "before Common Era," instead of BC. The initialism YBP means "years before present" and is common in climatological and geological works. The abbreviation BP is used frequently in archaeology and has a special meaning. The abbreviation BP means "before present" in radiocarbon years, but "present'" does not mean "today." Present is defined as AD 1950 because that was approximately when radiocarbon dating was devised. In lower case, bp may represent uncalibrated radiocarbon years.

In this volume, we show dates as BC or AD, such as 400 BC or AD 1250.

Abbreviations for Units of Measure

Units of measure, and their (inexact) equivalents commonly used by archaeologists in the Maya region, follow:

cm	centimeter (4/10 of an inch)
m	meter (39 inches; 1.1 yard)
km	kilometer (5/8 of a mile)
m²	square meter (1.2 square yards)
ha	hectare (100 m by 100 m; 10,000 m²; 2.5 acres)
km²	square kilometer (100 ha; 250 acres)
mi	mile (1.6 kilometers)

Other Abbreviations

AD	anno Domini, "in the year of our Lord": synonym for CE, Common Era; dates in the Judeo-Christian calendar from 1 through 2015
asl, amsl	above sea level, above mean sea level; usually elevation in meters
BC	Before Christ; synonym for BCE, before the Common Era; dates in the Judeo-Christian calendar before AD 1
BCE	Before the Common Era; dates in the Judeo-Christian calendar before AD 1
BP	Before present; number of radiocarbon dating years before AD 1950
CE	Common Era; dates in the Judeo-Christian calendar from 1 to 2015
GIS	Geographic Information System
GPS	Global Positioning System (or a ground receiver for GPS signals)
IDAEH	Instituto de Antropología e Historia (Guatemalan Institute of Anthropology and History)
INAH	Instituto Nacional de Antropología e Historia (Mexican National Institute of Anthropology and History)
IHAH	Instituto Hondureño de Antropología e Historia (Honduran Institute of Anthropology and History)
LiDAR	Light Detection and Ranging (airborne remote sense data collection)
MARI	Middle American Research Institute, Tulane University
mya	million years ago
NICH	Belize National Institute of Culture and History
PARI	The Pre-Columbian Art Institute
SLAR	Side-Looking Aperture Radar
Str.	structure: a man-made construction at an ancient site
St.	stela: a plain or carved upright stone monument
T.	in Maya archaeology, Temple: usually refers to a truncated masonry pyramid with masonry or perishable upper building with room(s); in epigraphic contexts, refers to a particular glyph by T-number in the Thompson *Catalog of Maya Hieroglyphs*
ybp	years before present

CHRONOLOGY

~14,000 BC	Paleo-Indian period. First hunter/gatherers enter the Western Hemisphere, likely via the Bering Land Bridge and along the Pacific Coast.
8000 BC	Archaic period begins. Increasing sedentism among hunter/gatherer peoples. Domestication of food, medicinal, and other utilitarian plants begins.
2000 BC	Early Formative/Early Preclassic period begins. Plant domestication virtually complete. Corn (maize) is widely grown. Settled villages are common.
1800 BC	First ceramics appear in the Maya area along the Pacific coast of Chiapas, Mexico, Guatemala, and El Salvador.
1200 BC	Rise of San Lorenzo, a major Olmec center. Beginnings of complex societies.
1000 BC	Middle Formative/Middle Preclassic period begins. Complexity of social organization apparent. Rise of Nakbé and complex Maya culture. First occupation of Kaminaljuyú.
900 BC	Rise of Cival with early triadic groups and Group-E observatories. Olmec center San Lorenzo fades; Olmec center at La Venta grows powerful.
600 BC	Origins of writing in the Oaxaca Valley of central Mexico. Growth of Yaxnohcah in the Mirador Basin, Petén, Guatemala.
500 BC	La Venta and the Olmec culture give way to the epi-Olmec culture at Tres Zapotes.
400 BC	Late Formative/Late Preclassic period begins. Rise of El Mirador. Rise of the state and urban society.
353 BC	June 3: Long Count 7.0.0.0.0.
300–200 BC	Early evidence of Maya writing at San Bartolo.
200 BC	Founding of Teotihuacán in the Basin of Mexico.
36 BC	December 10: first Long Count date known, found in the Olmec region.
AD 41	September 5: Long Count 8.0.0.0.0.
AD 100	Completion of the Pyramid of the Sun at Teotihuacán.
AD 250	Early Classic period begins. Rise of Tikal.
AD 292	July 6: first instance of a Long Count date inscribed on a stone monument in the Maya lowlands, at Tikal.
AD 378	Appearance of Teotihuacán warriors on stelae at Tikal.
AD 410	Start of dynastic history at Calakmul.

AD 435   December 9: Long Count 9.0.0.0.0.
AD 537   Start of the Middle Classic Hiatus at Tikal, extending to AD 672.
AD 562   First defeat of Tikal by Calakmul and Caracol.
AD 600   Late Classic period begins in the Maya area.
AD 695   August 6: Tikal is victorious over Calakmul and regains its independence.
AD 700   Fall of Teotihuacán.
AD 800   Terminal Classic period begins. Start of the Classic Maya collapse with
          the abandonment of Maya city-states in the central and southern low-
          lands. Rise of Chichen Itza and Uxmal.
AD 822   February 6: Last dated monument at Copán.
AD 830   March 13: Long Count 10.0.0.0.0.
AD 869   August 15: Last dated monument at Tikal.
AD 909   January 18: Last dated stela with a Maya Long Count date, at Toniná.
AD 1100   Early Postclassic period begins in the northern Maya lowlands. Collapse
          of major Maya city-states to the south is complete. New political
          structures appear. Men's councils replace rule by dynastic divine kings.
AD 1200   Late Postclassic period begins. Rise of Mayapán and Tulum.
AD 1224   June 15: Long Count 11.0.0.0.0.
AD 1511   First Spanish contact with mainland. Start of smallpox epidemic in the
          Americas.
AD 1521   Colonial era begins. Cortés conquers Tenochtitlan, the Aztec capital (now
          Mexico City).
AD 1542   Spanish conquest of the northern Yucatan Peninsula.
AD 1618   September 18: Long Count 12.0.0.0.0.
AD 1697   Conquest of the last independent Maya kingdom in Petén, Guatemala.
AD 2012   December 21: Long Count 13.0.0.0.0.

NOTES ON CHRONOLOGY

Dating is a surpassingly elaborate but necessary part of studying the history and pre-history of Mesoamerica. It is obviously important for students and scholars to know when certain historical events or processes occurred. The ordering of events in time helps determine causality, and absolute dates help establish contemporaneity for events in different places.

Historical documents often aid in dating. Historical dating contributes significantly to the Mesoamerican chronological sequence, particularly to its more recent portion. Doc-uments, however, or more precisely their authors, can lie or make errors. Documentary sources can contradict each other or be ambiguous. Thus, although we often think of documentation as the strongest kind of historical evidence, it is in fact a form of testi-mony, and testimony can be refuted by circumstantial evidence when the latter is strong enough. In Mesoamerica, documentary sources provide dates for specific events around the time of the Spanish conquest.

After the conquest, the Spanish wrote accounts of preconquest native history using testimony from the indigenous peoples. The accounts sometimes describe events that took place 500 or more years before the conquest. These chronicles are invaluable in building the chronology of the Postclassic, but they suffer from ambiguities and contradictions; certainly their chronological precision and specificity declines the further back in time they reach to describe progressively older events.

In many cases, the native peoples also wrote historical chronicles, often in their own languages but in the Roman alphabet, that provide additional information, although modern scholars find some of the native histories to be confusing or opaque because of their languages, genres, or worldviews. To these documentary sources, we can add the pre-Hispanic native screenfold books, called codices. Fragments of only four Maya codices survive today.

The first main historical period recognized in Mesoamerica is the Colonial period, which began in 1521 with the fall of Tenochtitlan, the Aztec capital, and ended in 1821 with Mexican independence from Spain. In Mexico, the succeeding Republican period ended in 1910 with the start of the Mexican Revolution (1910–1920), which was succeeded by the Modern period. In the Central American portion of Mesoamerica, the chronology is generally similar, but the Colonial period was followed by a long interval of internecine warfare between Conservatives and Liberals that continued into the twentieth century.

Recent decades have seen the growth of a new history of the Maya, derived from writing on their carved stone monuments and buildings and painted on vases and tomb walls. New translations of Maya hieroglyphs have revealed a detailed history of the actions of many divine kings, whose elite scribes spelled out their family history, span of rule, conquests in war, and death. Often these actions are accompanied by Long Count dates in the Maya calendar, which can be securely tied to a corresponding date in the Christian calendar.

Archaeology provides a complementary body of circumstantial evidence that helps constrain and verify the historical chronology, and far more important, supplements the historical testimonies by extending much further back in time, covering periods for which we possess no historical information. Archaeological evidence differs radically in kind from historical documentation, which often causes problems in reconciling the two bodies of data and interpretation. The archaeological chronology of preconquest Mesoamerica, like other archaeological sequences, is mainly defined by changes in artifact types and settlement patterns.

Archaeologists use multiple techniques to build their sequences and chronologies. Fundamental techniques include stratigraphic analysis and seriation (the ordering of materials into a series using formal logic, mathematics, and statistics), while radiocarbon dating plays a more limited role than popular belief might suggest.

Radiocarbon dating remains too expensive for frequent use; more important, one should only date samples that come from excellent contexts with significant associations, because poorly chosen samples often yield anomalous results. Finally, despite improved accuracy through modern calibration techniques, radiocarbon dating remains relatively imprecise because of fundamental statistical uncertainties caused by the probabilistic nature of radioactive decay. Thus, in practice a single radiocarbon assay can date a context with about 95 percent probability to within a range of only about 150 years. Because of this imprecision, archaeologists normally use radiocarbon dates to anchor in absolute time chronologies that they build using other, more precise techniques. For the same reason, the beginning and ending dates of archaeological periods are sometimes vaguely defined and may vary by 50 or 100 years, again, because of the imprecision of radiocarbon assays or because of variations in the dating of sequences at different sites.

In the twentieth century, archaeologists who believed that cultures evolved through similar stages of development proposed a uniform periodization of Mesoamerican prehistory, and we still use some of the names of periods that they proposed. The earliest period, which began 12,000 or 14,000 years ago, is called the Paleo-Indian period, and it is believed to correspond to strongly nomadic societies dedicated to foraging and hunting. The Paleo-Indian period is contemporary with and similar in detail to the Upper Paleolithic period in Europe and elsewhere.

The Paleo-Indian period was succeeded by the Archaic period, in which hunter-gatherers, although still nomadic, focused more on gathering a wider variety of plants, hunting smaller game, fishing, and shellfishing. The primary stages of plant and animal domestication took place during the Archaic period, leading eventually to the development of horticulture, agriculture, and sedentary life. The Archaic period is essentially the same as the Mesolithic period in Europe and the Near East.

The beginning of sedentary agricultural life marks the start of the Formative period. Identified by archaeologists through the presence of pottery, the Formative period saw dramatic increases in populations and social complexity. It is usually divided into three subperiods: Early, Middle, and Late. The Formative period is also referred to as the Preclassic period, and we use both terms as synonyms.

The succeeding Classic period is the age of the great civilizations of Mesoamerica, the Maya, Zapotecs, and Teotihuacán. In the Maya area, the Classic period is defined as the time when the Maya erected monuments with Long Count dates. Although a small number of earlier Long Count dates appear on the Pacific Coast, the earliest known Long Count date in the Maya lowlands is AD 292, inscribed on Stela 29 from Tikal. The start of the Maya Classic period is therefore conventionally said to begin at AD 250 or 300. The latest Long Count dates cluster around AD 900, which therefore is considered the end of the Classic period.

The Maya Classic period is usually divided into Early and Late segments. At Tikal, these are separated by a 135-year-long hiatus between AD 537 and 672, a period when few Long Count dates were inscribed there. Some scholars have proposed a different chronological scheme that includes a Middle Classic period, but it has not garnered much support or use among Mayanists. In some parts of the Maya lowlands, mainly in part of the Petén region of northern Guatemala and adjacent northern Belize, archaeologists recognize a Protoclassic period that overlaps the end of the Formative and the beginning of the Early Classic periods. It is defined mainly by certain characteristics of the pottery artifacts.

The Maya Classic period ends with a short Terminal Classic period, the dates of which vary in different parts of the region. In the southern Maya lowlands, the Terminal Classic may begin as early as the end of the eighth century and is marked by the appearance of fine paste pottery wares (Fine Orange and Fine Gray) shortly before the Maya collapse. "Foreign" Central Mexican influence is seen at a number of southern lowland sites in this interval, most famously at Ceibal/Seibal. In the northern lowlands, the Terminal Classic begins and ends a little later and includes the later phases of major Puuc style sites such as Uxmal and Kabah.

The Postclassic period starts around AD 900 or 950 and continues until the Spanish conquest. It is divided into two or three subperiods (Early and Late or Early, Middle, and Late), depending on the region. In the Maya area, the Postclassic follows the Maya collapse and includes various cultural manifestations, particularly in the northern lowlands and the southern highlands, that exhibit varying degrees of Mexican influence, although the significance of these outside influences is hotly debated.

The names of the Formative, Classic, and Postclassic periods were originally proposed by the distinguished archaeologist and Harvard professor Gordon Willey through a specific analogy with the ancient Greek world. Today, such an idea would be considered too ethnocentric to be helpful in understanding Mesoamerican culture. Thus, these periods no longer represent stages of human cultural development, as originally conceived by the evolutionists, but the terms have survived. Today they are used only to denote chronological intervals and carry no evolutionary connotations.

To complicate matters, some of these periods have been referred to by other names in the past. For example, Julian Steward used the terms "Regional Florescent States" and "Initial Empire" for the periods we today call Classic and Postclassic, respectively. Even more confusing, today's Formative period was once called by some archaeologists the "Archaic."

In this encyclopedia, most references are to the Preclassic/Formative, the Classic, and the Postclassic, with AD 250 and AD 900 as convenient break points between them.

INTRODUCTION

The Maya region (see **Maps 2** and **3**), and the people who have occupied it since ~1000 BC, are the intriguing focus of this volume. To be encyclopedic about a people whose ancient culture spanned 2,500 years from inception to Spanish conquest is a challenge beyond the scope of this small volume. So the challenge met here is to acquaint the reader with some of the most modern research about the culture of the ancient Maya people, their cities, and their hieroglyphic writing, as well as several of the modern techniques that tell "how we know what we know" about the ancient Maya. Our goal is to bring together information from many sources, in a readable encyclopedia format suitable for high school and college student reference and research.

"Maya" as we use it today to refer to ancient and modern people and their culture has its origins at the time of the Spanish exploration and conquest, when "Maya" was synonymous with Yucatan (the northern part of the Maya region where Yucatec Maya was spoken.) Subsequently, the term was expanded in geographic scope by researchers, not the Maya themselves, to include all of the Maya region and its peoples. This unification of the people of the region under a single label has been a modern process. In ancient times, and indeed today, the Maya were and are quite culturally diverse. Researchers, however, have adopted and refined the term Maya to include the people of a certain geographic area, speaking related languages, using the Maya script in ancient times, and sharing similarities of material culture.

Our understanding of the ancient Maya is also affected by how we study them. Many of the early archaeological studies focused on monumental architecture in large Maya settlements. Large pyramids were easy to locate (by comparison with perishable dwellings) and led to the discovery of royal tombs, ball courts, palaces, and other manifestations of the elite Maya rulers and their courts. As a consequence, some early conclusions about the Maya were biased toward the elites, who made up a fraction of the total population. Today, more wide-ranging studies seek to discover the full extent of commoner populations, their activities, and especially the labor practices that provided food for individual households and cities and that supplied construction labor.

Geographically and culturally, the Maya are part of Mesoamerica. The term "Mesoamerica" has a special meaning: it is a term that seeks to avoid the difficulties of referring to modern national boundaries, or to North America and Central America, or even to Middle America. In 1943 Paul Kirchhoff wrote that the area he called "Mesoamerica" had numerous different peoples and cultures, but that they shared a number of cultural traits, which unified them into a coherent whole. See **Mesoamerica**.

Geographically, Mesoamerica extends from the Gulf of Mexico and the Caribbean to the Pacific Ocean. Kirchhoff considered the northern boundary across Mexico as a broad U-shaped line, extending more northward along the coasts, but dipping closer to the Basin of Mexico in the interior. The southern boundary runs from the Caribbean coast of western Honduras southward, encompassing both El Salvador and the Pacific coast of Nicaragua and Costa Rica. The Maya area falls within eastern Mesoamerica, extending roughly from the Isthmus of Tehuantepec at the southernmost point of the Gulf of Mexico to the western portions of El Salvador and Honduras. Kirchhoff's description serves us well today. The ancient Maya sites of Comalcalco and Copan are indicators of the western and eastern boundaries, respectively.

The Neolithic Revolution refers to the transformation of human culture in several areas of the world (Mesopotamia or the Fertile Crescent, the Indus River valley, Egypt, Peru, China, Southeast Asia, and Mesoamerica). The transformation describes the shifts away from nomadic hunting and foraging toward domestication of plants and animals and toward sedentism. The results of these changes in human society were, with considerable variation worldwide, cities and states, dense settlements, monumental architecture, war and weaponry, mathematics, technology, astronomy, writing systems, calendars, political structures, and class stratification. In the Maya area, this transformation occurred slowly. It produced an impressive array of accomplishments that intrigue modern scholars and travelers. Whether you are fascinated by the base-20 arithmetic, the sophisticated multicycle Maya calendars, the intriguing variations in how ancient scribes could write down the Maya language, or the sheer excitement of finding a stone line leading to a massive ancient pyramid in dense jungle, you join a host who read about and study the ancient Maya.

For some, the first awareness of the lost cultures of Mesoamerica came from reading tales of exploration and adventure. John Lloyd Stephens, who wrote over 170 years ago, still captivates us with his story of purchasing Copan, Honduras, for $50. Edward Thompson dredged the Sacred Well at Chichen Itza and recovered artifacts of gold, globs of incense, and the bones of sacrificial victims, which he took from the country, much to the dismay of later generations of Mexicans.

This reference tells several stories at once. In part, it covers the sweep of culture change in the Maya area, from about 1000 BC until the Spanish conquest. In part, it tells the story written down by the Maya rulers as they wished to tell it, on carved stone monuments. In part it tells the story of how we know what we know about the ancient Maya from archaeological research, laboratory analysis, and epigraphy. In part, it tells the story of the Maya environment and climate, how the Maya met its challenges, and what modern research on these topics reveals about the successes and failures of the Maya culture. It especially includes reports of modern activities by scholars currently in the field, revealing new insights about the Maya. These stories intertwine and of necessity are not in a sequential narrative in the encyclopedia entries. Wherever you delve, however, you have the opportunity to move from one topic to another, one discovery to another, and one narrative to another.

The narrative story begins with the settling of the New World near the end of the last ice age some 16,000 years ago. From multiple lines of evidence, we know that North and South America were settled by people from Asia. It is likely they used both land routes, over the Bering land bridge between Asia and North America, as well as sea routes, hugging the shoreline of the Pacific Rim. Now that sea levels are higher by 100 meters (300 feet), shoreline evidence of their sea travel and temporary shoreline camps is inundated and destroyed or inaccessible.

Only a handful of early sites are known. Tom Dillehay's research at Monte Verde, Chile, revealed a permanent Paleo-Indian settlement without evidence of domesticated plants or animals. In the anaerobic environment of a peat bog, he found well-preserved remains of hut frames; extensive use of local plants, many of which have medicinal uses in the local modern population; mastodon bones; and a variety of tools, including rarely preserved wooden needles essential for sewing hides to make clothing and hut covers.

Few Paleo-Indian sites in Mesoamerica are known, but some show connections to the early Clovis culture of North America. Mammoth kill sites are known from Central Mexico, and recently divers have begun to recover Paleo-Indian remains from inundated caves in the Yucatan Peninsula.

In the Maya area and broader Mesoamerica, evidence of subsequent Archaic period people has been found at sites in Belize, Guatemala, Honduras, and Mexico, such as at Richmond Hill, Loltun, San Andrés, Tehuacán Valley, Tlapacoya, and the Xihuatoxtla rock shelter. The most intensive research about the Archaic period has focused on the domestication of the native grass *teosinte* into the myriad varieties of maize now found in Mesoamerica. By the end of the Archaic period, most of the food and utilitarian plants known from the region had been domesticated and were providing a third of the standard diet. People had abandoned nomadism. Sedentism was the norm. The combination of lifestyle changes, from nomadic foraging to domestication and sedentism, mark the Neolithic Revolution in Mesoamerica, and by the start of the Formative/Preclassic period at 2000 BC, the region was poised to begin the suite of cultural changes that we find so intriguing today, including the creation of special places and the emergence of cities.

With the start of the Formative/Preclassic period, ceramics and public buildings appeared. Since ceramics are both fragile and heavy, they are usually associated with settled village life. Soon large differentiated residences appeared, indicating the accumulation of valuable resources (fertile lands, water access) in the hands of a powerful few, destined to become chiefs in societies with increasingly complex social and political systems.

The earliest ceramics along the Pacific coast of Chiapas, Mexico, and the adjacent coast of Guatemala are surprisingly well made, without poorer precursors. This differs from other areas, where stone vessels were gradually replaced by crude pottery vessels, which then evolved technologically over subsequent centuries or millennia. These early well-made ceramics hint at possible contact from South America, where ceramic manufacture was much older.

During the Formative, the cultural distinctions we associate with the Maya began to appear, as they did for other Mesoamerican cultures such as the Olmec, who were contiguous to the Maya area in the southern Gulf Coast region. About 1200 BC San Lorenzo Tenochtitlán, the first major Olmec site, began developing Olmec traditions of divine rulers, an array of deities, and distinctive art, including colossal head portraits of their chiefs. The first evidence of use of the Long Count calendar appears in the Olmec area. After three centuries, the dominion of San Lorenzo waned, and Olmec power was concentrated, first at La Venta and later at Tres Zapotes.

Changing views of Maya scholars have shaped our current understanding of the cultural developments in the Formative/Preclassic. The Maya architecture, calendar, and hieroglyphic writing were long held up as the highest, earliest, and most important Mesoamerican culture. Olmec discoveries in the twentieth century, their cities, sculpture, and very early Long Count dates, tarnished the opinion of some researchers of the Maya as the best and earliest culture in the region. More recently, work at Cival and in the Mirador Basin of northern Guatemala has reshaped viewpoints and opened debates about the timing of various cultural innovations. Both Nakbe and El Mirador show early evidence of sharp social stratification, strong city-state governments, and mobilization of large labor forces for well-planned civic projects with monumental architecture in the Maya area. Cival provides very early evidence of place-making, with triadic groups, and Group-E-observatories. Cultural contact between the Olmec and the Maya occurred on several fronts. Long Count dates appear on the Pacific coast of the Maya region, then appear farther northward. Portraits from Nakbe Stela 1 and the murals of San Bartolo show iconography similar to that of the Olmec. Debate continues about the extent to which the Olmec were a mother culture to the Maya, or whether they developed in parallel with the Maya.

By 100 BC, Teotihuacán, 45 kilometers from the center of modern Mexico City, was drawing population from the entire Basin of Mexico, and on its way to becoming a metropolis, with a population estimated at 80,000 to 150,000. In AD 378 in the Classic period, a Teotihuacán expedition or military incursion into the Maya area, well-documented on stelae, upset established ruling families and created new ruling dynasties. The influence of Teotihuacan on the Maya is debated, with some taking sides reflecting either an internal approach (the Maya chose to copy the Teotihuacan culture) or an external approach (Teotihuacan interacted directly with the Maya via activities such as trade or military conquest).

Such debates are an important element of discourse about the Maya and have a long history. In much of the twentieth century, the correlation between the Maya calendar and the Gregorian calendar was a subject of dispute, with matching dates as much as 250 years apart. That debate is now generally resolved to within two days. Similar discussions have dealt with whether the Maya were peaceful/peace-loving or prone to warfare, and the character of the warfare.

Maya development was dynamic, as reflected in the fortunes of its cities. El Mirador, the largest Late Formative Maya city-state, waned. In the subsequent Classic period, major cities such as Tikal, Caracol, Calakmul, and Copán, grew more powerful. Maya rulers began to use the Long Count calendar to record dates and narratives on carved stone monuments, stucco wall panels, and stairway risers. Maya kings inscribed their family trees, recorded conquests and captive-taking, and told of their alliances with other city-states.

The multipart cyclic calendar and the fully productive writing system provide historical data about the Maya, with specific dates well-anchored to the Christian calendar. Their widespread use went hand in hand with the appearance of stunningly beautiful polychrome vases, elegance in the production of portable objects and art, and monumental architecture of breathtaking beauty and size. Early Maya researchers, cognizant of European history, called this period the "Classic" in parallel with "Classical Greece." Today the Classic refers only to the time period from AD 250 to 900, which is delimited, approximately, by the first and last inscribed Long Count dates in the Maya lowlands.

Numerous great Maya cities thrived in the three centuries of the Early Classic period. Around AD 550, however, economic difficulties, perhaps due in part to the waning power and ultimate fall and destruction by fire of Teotihuacán in Central Mexico, and political problems, exacerbated by warfare between the major Maya polities, rocked the Maya region. Current studies investigate whether climatological forces played a role. Civic construction slowed greatly, and so did the erection of monuments with written royal histories. Tikal was defeated by its archrival of the Snake Kingdom, at Dzibanché or Calakmul. Long-cherished city-state alliances were broken and new ones forged.

Beginning about AD 600, the major Maya city-states began to recover, jockeying for power positions relative to their neighbors. Warfare, however, had become systemic. By the end of the Late Classic, several sites in central Guatemala, including Dos Pilas and Aguateca, had been overrun or had collapsed. It was the beginning of the Classic Maya collapse, a process that would continue for several centuries.

During the Terminal Classic, accumulated excesses brought the Maya to a tipping point. Populations were high. Demands on commoners by the ruling elite for food, tribute items, warfare, and civic construction were increasingly burdensome. Resources of land, water, fertile soil, trees, and food were strained by population pressures. Into this mix was added an array of difficult multiyear droughts. Lack of rain caused food shortages and reduced human fertility. Worse, lack of rain represented to the commoners a failure by the divine kings to properly intercede with the gods to provide for human needs, and the populace lost faith in their leadership. The social bonds between leadership and the led were broken. Once mighty Tikal became depopulated within a century. It was recaptured by relentless jungle vegetation in months and lay abandoned for 1,000 years. Many sites shared a similar fate.

The Classic Maya collapse produced complex changes. While many cities in the central Maya lowlands were abandoned to await rediscovery in the nineteenth and twentieth centuries, new cities such as Uxmal and Chichen Itza were founded, grew, and flourished in the northern Maya lowlands. Within a few short centuries, however, these new Maya cities in northern Yucatan collapsed as well. The Maya Long Count calendar was abandoned in favor of a shorter version of timekeeping that was ambiguous over long time spans, and it left an indefinite and confusing history of the era.

In Central Mexico, Teotihuacán fell about AD 650. By AD 850 or 900 the Toltec consolidated power in Central Mexico. Tula, Hidalgo, north of Mexico City, and the Maya city Chichen Itza, separated by a distance of 1,500 kilometers, are remarkably similar in iconography and architecture, fueling a continuing debate about precedence and flow of iconography among scholars.

In the Maya area of northern Yucatan, after the fall of Chichen Itza, a new regional confederation arose, with its capital at Mayapán. In the Maya highlands, several small but powerful states arose and struggled for power, the most famous being the Quiché, Cakchiquel, and Mam.

Exploration by Europeans, beginning with Christopher Columbus in 1492, resulted in another dramatic transformation of the Maya. The first Spaniards reached Yucatan in 1511. The European "gift" of smallpox came ashore with them and their successors. Hernán Cortés laid successful siege to Tenochtitlan (now central Mexico City) in 1519–1521. Within 20 years, the Montejos conquered Yucatan and established their control over the Maya in the northern part of the peninsula.

Deaths of Mesoamericans at the hands of the Spanish, by disease and by forced labor, took 90 percent of the population by 1600. With the loss of elites and commoners alike, much of the culture of ancient Mesoamerica, which had evolved over the preceding 2,500 years, was lost as well. The ancient Maya writing system was abandoned in favor of Latin letters. Books were burned by Spanish friars. Attempts were made to change agricultural practices, replacing them with European ways. The ancient polytheistic and animistic religious practices were partially extirpated, partially displaced, and partially syncretized with Catholicism. Cathedrals and churches were built atop ancient stepped pyramids. Native Americans became an unwilling source of labor and wealth to the Spaniards, as well as a curiosity for their European conquerors. Their ancient cities were mostly ignored. Those covered in jungle remained lost to view and forgotten. Amid the transport of booty and commerce, a few ancient relics and manuscripts, including three of the four extant Maya books, were transported to the Old World as collectibles or gifts to the royal court. In this context of Spanish control, the Maya nonetheless retained their ancient language, the successful *milpa* system of agriculture, the day-counting system of the calendar, and numerous elements of their ancient culture.

Thus it continued through the Colonial period. By the mid-1800s, however, the lost cities in the jungle were stimulating curiosity in other quarters. The travels of John Lloyd Stephens and Frederick Catherwood through the Maya area, published in 1841/1843, revealed long-hidden sites to modern westerners. Stephens accurately judged that the living local Native Americans were descendants of the ancient city-builders. The developing trade in chicle for chewing gum brought tales of unknown cities told by the *chicleros*, who were exploring new areas of the jungle for the chicozapote tree and its rubbery sap. As jungle expeditions continued in the Maya region, library research in the Old World rediscovered manuscripts lost for 300 years, but now newly recognized as works of native Mesoamericans. This led to recognition of the Landa manuscript, three Maya codices, knowledge of Maya astronomy, insights into the calendar, and further searches for Maya documents.

In the mid-twentieth century, astute work by Heinrich Berlin, Tatiana Proskouriakoff, and Yuri Knorosov demonstrated that the Maya hieroglyphs recorded a spoken Maya language, and that many of the texts recorded the names and birthdays of royal rulers, their places in the local dynastic sequence, their parentage, and their achievements as rulers. Today a quite high fraction of the ancient symbols and texts can be translated as well as spoken aloud in modern Yucatec or Cholan Maya, and decipherment continues.

The latter half of the twentieth century brought even better equipped researchers to Mesoamerica. They used scientific archaeological approaches, new techniques, and sophisticated equipment to peel back the jungle, peel back the earth, and peel back the mysteries of hieroglyphic writing. They revealed with increasing clarity truths about

Mesoamerica, and the Maya region in particular. Many revelations also brought new research questions and new scholarly debate about the nature of the ancient Maya. Across the variety of local landscapes, they had developed sophisticated solutions to universal human problems: sustainable subsistence techniques, faith in deities to explain the unexplainable, elaborate social and political systems and economies. In short, the revelation is about human civilization, our coming together to solve collective problems of survival. It is an intriguing story of admirable and innovative successes, but perhaps it is also a cautionary tale for the twenty-first century about resource overutilization and failure to follow sustainable practices.

FURTHER READING

Coe, Michael D. *The Maya*. 8th ed. London: Thames and Hudson, 2011.

———. *Breaking the Maya code*. (3rd ed.). London: Thames & Hudson, 2012.

Evans, Susan Toby. *Ancient Mesoamerica & Central America: Archaeology and Culture History*. 2nd ed. London: Thames & Hudson, 2008.

Kirchhoff, Paul. "Mesoamérica, sus límites geográficos, composición étnica y caracteres culturales." *Acta Americana* I, no. 1: 92–107, 1943.

———. "Mesoamerica: Its Geographic Limits, Ethnic Composition, and Cultural Character." In *Ancient Mesoamerica: Selected Readings*, edited by John Allen Graham. Palo Alto, CA: Peek Publications, 1981.

Sharer, Robert J., and Loa P. Traxler. *The Ancient Maya*. 6th ed. Stanford, CA: Stanford University Press, 2006.

Stephens, John Lloyd. *Incidents of Travel in Central America, Chiapas, and Yucatan*. London: John Murray, 1841.

———. *Incidents of Travel in Yucatan*. New York: Harper & Bros., 1843. Reprint, New York: Dover, 1963.

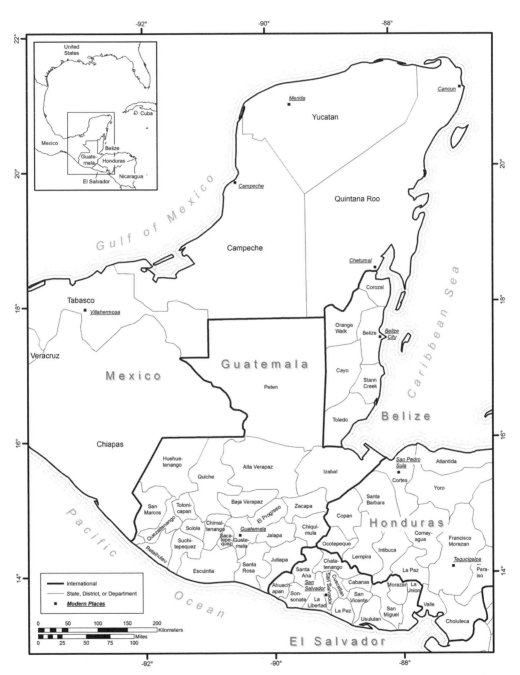

Map 1. Modern countries of the Maya area, with states, departments, districts, and selected cities. Map by Walter R. T. Witschey.

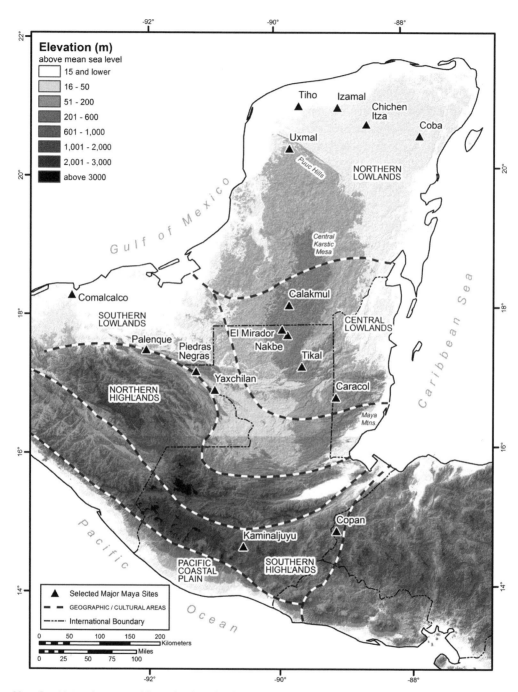

Map 2. Natural geographic and cultural subdivisions of the Maya area. The division between the lowlands and the highlands is at about the 600 m contour. Elevation data from the Shuttle Radar Topography Mission. A. Jarvis, H. I. Reuter, A. Nelson, and E. Guevara, Hole-filled seamless SRTM data V4, 2008, http://srtm.csi.cgiar.org. Map by Walter R. T. Witschey.

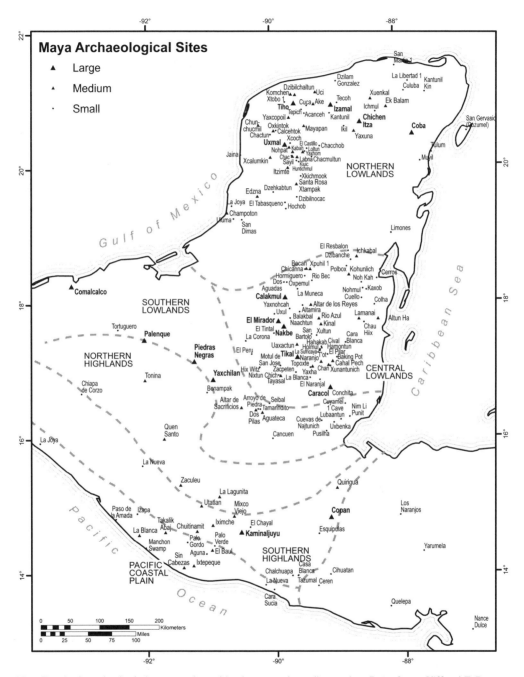

Map 3. Archaeological sites mentioned in the encyclopedia entries. Data from Clifford T. Brown and Walter R. T. Witschey, *Electronic Atlas of Ancient Maya Sites*, http://MayaGIS.smv.org. Map by Walter R. T. Witschey.

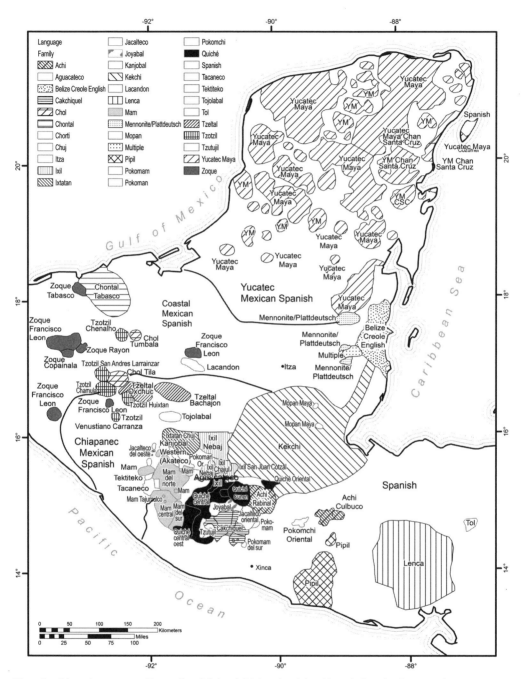

Map 4. Maya languages. Data after Michael Richards, *Atlas Lingüístico de Guatemala* (Guatemala City, Guatemala: SEPAZ, UVG, URL, USAID/G-CAP, Editorial Serviprensa, S.A.), http://pdf.usaid.gov/pdf_docs/pnadd071.pdf. 2003; *Mapa Ligüístico de Guatemala*, Academia de Lenguas Mayas de Guatemala, K'ulb'il Yol Twitz Paxil, 2014, http://www.almg.org.gt/; and Robert Longacre, "Systemic Comparison and Reconstruction," in *Handbook of Middle American Indians*, Vol. 5, *Linguistics*, ed. Norman McQuown. (Austin: University of Texas Press, 1967), 117–59. Map by Walter R. T. Witschey.

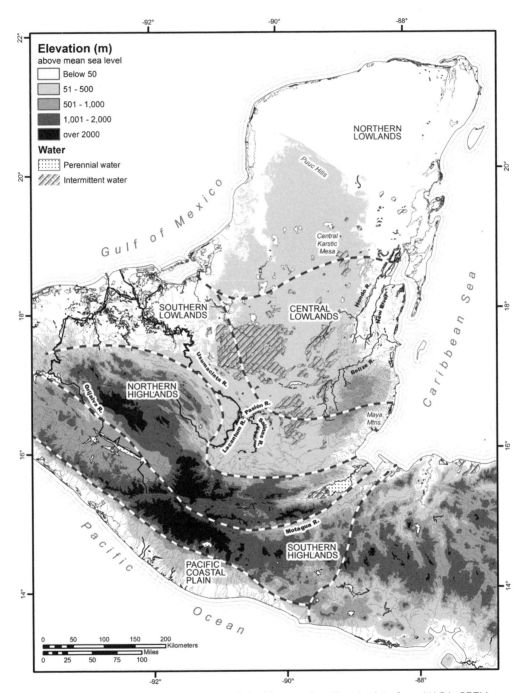

Map 5. Terrain, water bodies, and rivers of the Maya region. Terrain data from NASA, SRTM 90m Digital Elevation Model DEM, NASA Jet Propulsion Laboratory and the USGS EROS Data Center, http://srtm.usgs.gov/, http://eros.usgs.gov/. Map by Walter R. T. Witschey.

Key to lakes shown in Map 6.

1. Atitlán
2. Amatitlán
3. Ayarza
4. Atescatempa
5. Güija
6. Izabal
7. Las Pozas
8. Petexbatún
9. Rosario
10. Oquevix
11. La Gloria
12. San Diego
13. Perdida
14. Sacpuy
15. Petén Itzá
16. Salpetén
17. Macanché
18. Yaxhá
19. Almond Hill
20. Crooked Tree Lagoon
21. Honey Camp
22. Sabanita
23. Milagros
24. Bacalar
25. San José Aguilar
26. Chacan-Bata
27. San Francisco Mateos
28. La Misteriosa
29. Laguna del Cayucón
30. Jobal
31. Chacan-Lara
32. Nohbec
33. Ocom
34. Chichancanab,
35. Cobá,
36. Punta Laguna,
37. Yalahau

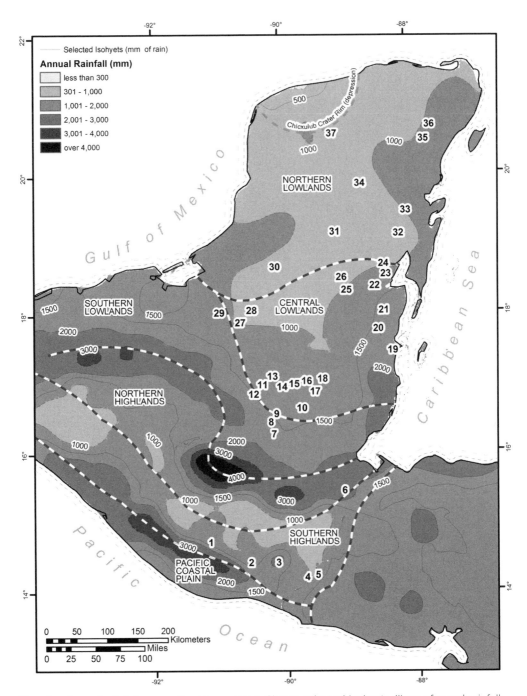

Map 6. Annual rainfall across the Maya region. Shows selected isohyets (lines of equal rainfall amounts in mm) and includes the location of the main lakes (see key) and the Chicxulub impact crater rim (zone of cenotes). Data courtesy Liseth Pérez. Map by Walter R. T. Witschey.

eKg, Early Cretaceous, Plutonic
eT, Eocene, Sedimentary
eTg, Eocene, Plutonic
g, Age unknown, Plutonic
J, Jurassic, Sedimentary
JK, Cretaceous, Sedimentary
Jv, Jurassic, Volcanic
K, Cretaceous, Sedimentary
Kg, Cretaceous, Plutonic
KT, Tertiary, Sedimentary
KTg, Tertiary, Plutonic
lD, Lower Devonian, Sedimentary
lK, Lower Cretaceous, Sedimentary
MP, Permian, Sedimentary
MPAg, Pennsylvanian, Plutonic
mT, Miocene, Sedimentary
mTvfi, Miocene, Volcanic
mTvi, Miocene, Volcanic
MZ, Mesozoic, Sedimentary
MZg, Mesozoic, Plutonic
MZsv, Mesozoic, Volcanic
MZx, Mesozoic, Metamorphic and
    undivided crystalline
nT, Neogene, Sedimentary
nTsv, Neogene, Volcanic
oT, Oligocene, Sedimentary

PAP, Permian, Sedimentary
paT, Paleocene, Sedimentary
pgT, Paleogene, Sedimentary
pKx, Pre-Cretaceous, Metamorphic and
    undivided crystalline
PZ, Paleozoic, Sedimentary
PZg, Paleozoic, Plutonic
PZMZ, Mesozoic, Sedimentary
PZvf, Paleozoic, Volcanic
PZx, Paleozoic, Metamorphic and
    undivided crystalline
Q, Quaternary, Sedimentary
Qv, Quaternary, Volcanic
Qvf, Quaternary, Volcanic
Qvm, Quaternary, Volcanic
T, Tertiary, Sedimentary
Tg, Tertiary, Plutonic
TQ, Quaternary, Sedimentary
TQv, Quaternary, Volcanic
TRg, Triassic, Plutonic
TRJ, Jurassic, Sedimentary
Tv, Tertiary, Volcanic
u, Age unknown, Plutonic
uK, Upper Cretaceous, Sedimentary
Ygn, Middle Proterozoic (pre-570 mya),
    Metamorphic and undivided crystalline

Era	Period	Epoch	Starting Date Millions of Years Ago (mya)
Cenozoic	Quaternary	Holocene	0.01
		Pleistocene	2.6
	Tertiary (Neogene)	Pliocene	5.3
		Miocene	23
	Tertiary (Paleogene)	Oligocene	33.9
		Eocene	55.8
		Paleocene	65.5
Mesozoic	Cretaceous		144
	Jurassic		208
	Triassic		245
Paleozoic	Permian		286
	Carboniferous (Pennsylvanian)		320
	Carboniferous (Mississippian)		360
	Devonian		408
	Silurian		438
	Ordovician		508
	Cambrian		570

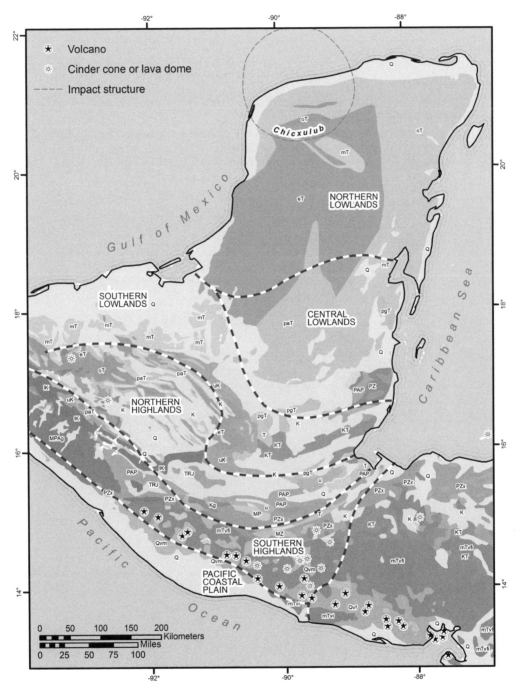

Map 7. Geologic map of the Maya region. Shows the age of exposed bedrock, including volcanoes, cinder cones, and the Chicxulub impact crater rim. Data from C. P. Garrity and D. R. Soller, *Database of the Geologic Map of North America*, 2009; adapted from a map by J. C. Reed Jr. et al., 2005, U.S. Geological Survey Data Series 424, http://pubs.usgs.gov/ds/424/. Map by Walter R. T. Witschey.

Key to the soil types shown in Map 8.

Symbol	Name	Description
RG	Regosols	Soils with very limited soil development
WR	Water Bodies	Water
LP	Leptosols	Very shallow soils over hard rock or in unconsolidated very gravelly material
GL	Gleysols	Soils with permanent or temporary wetness near the surface
FL	Fluvisols	Young soils in alluvial deposits
CM	Cambisols	Weakly to moderately developed soils
AN	Andosols	Young soils formed from volcanic deposits
PH	Phaeozems	Soils with a thick, dark topsoil rich in organic matter and evidence of removal of carbonates
LV	Luvisols	Soils with subsurface accumulation of high activity clays and high base saturation
PL	Planosols	Soils with a bleached, temporarily water-saturated topsoil on a slowly permeable subsoil
KS	Kastanozems	Soils with thick, dark brown topsoil, rich in organic matter and a calcareous or gypsum-rich subsoil
VR	Vertisols	Dark-colored cracking and swelling clays
AC	Acrisols	Soils with subsurface accumulation of low activity clays and low base saturation
AL	Alisols	Soils with subsurface accumulation of high activity clays, rich in exchangeable aluminum
NT	Nitisols	Deep, dark red, brown, or yellow clayey soils having a pronounced shiny, nut-shaped structure

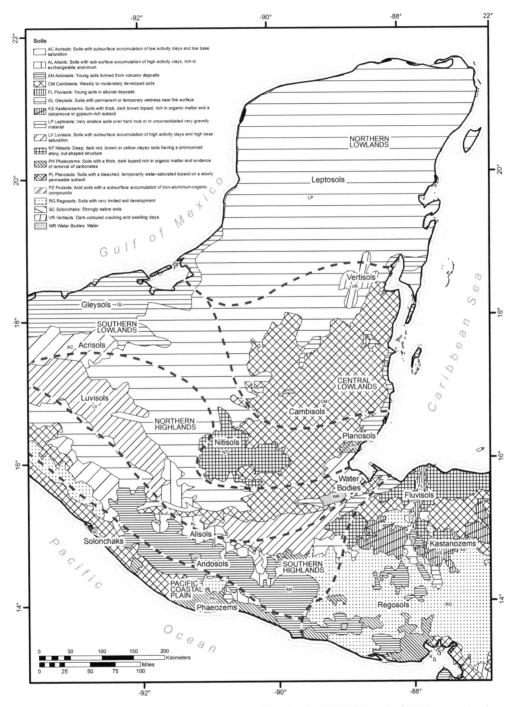

Map 8. Soils of the Maya region. Data courtesy FAO/IIASA/ISRIC/ISS-CAS/JRC, Harmonized World Soil Database (version 1.1), 2009 (Rome: FAO; Laxenburg, Austria: IIASA; and Tosha Comendant, PhD, senior scientist, Conservation Biology Institute, Databasin.org.). Map by Walter R. T. Witschey.

A

ABAJ TAKALIK
See TAKALIK ABAJ

AGUADAS

Aguadas are ponds that are widely but unevenly distributed across the Maya lowlands (see also **Maps 1–3**; **Northern Lowlands**; **Central Lowlands**; **Southern Lowlands**). Some usually hold water throughout the year, but many desiccate at the height of the dry season. Both historically and in ancient times, *aguadas* represented an essential water source in many regions. Today, the sediments within *aguadas* contain important paleoenvironmental "proxies" (biological or chemical by-products of ecosystems) that can be used to reconstruct past environmental change and Maya lifeways.

On the low-lying coastal plains many *aguadas* are **cenotes** that have accumulated deep clay plugs and no longer connect with the groundwater table. With increasing elevation in interior regions, many *aguadas* originate as limestone sinkholes that have partially filled with clay-rich sediment, effectively sealing their bottoms. The ancient Maya modified many *aguadas* to enhance their water-holding capacity by adding additional watertight lining or berms (embankments) around their edges. Other *aguadas* originated as ancient limestone (see also **Map 7**) or **chert** quarries that were often later further sealed to enhance water retention.

Aguadas functioned as reservoirs for the ancient Maya in both urban and rural settings. Today the features known as *aguadas* are distinguished from other ancient reservoirs by virtue of still holding water for at least a portion of the dry season (December–May). Thus, *aguadas* remained important water sources long after the ancient communities of which they were a part had been abandoned. Later, smaller populations continued to use these ponds for drinking water, most notably in the nineteenth and twentieth centuries wandering *chicleros* (chicle gum tappers). *Chicleros* gave names to the *aguadas* they utilized, and these names in turn came to be given to the ruins in which the ponds were situated (e.g., **San Bartolo**, La Honradez, and Pozo Maya, in the northeast Petén, Guatemala) (see also **Map 1**).

Most *aguadas* are roughly circular in shape, but many are irregularly shaped, and some are rectangular. *Aguadas* range in size from a mere 10 m across to huge features such as Aguada Maya in the Bajo La Justa, some 250 by 240 m, and the Aguada La Gondola at the Puuc region site of **Xcoch**, which had a capacity of nearly 80 million liters.

The sediments that accumulated within *aguadas* over the centuries often preserve biological and chemical materials that reflect past environmental conditions. For example, *aguadas* in which the sediments remain perennially moist preserve organic materials such as pollen. The pollen found in *aguadas* is particularly valuable for reconstructing the lifeways of ancient Maya communities because it typically reflects local **vegetation**, including plants that produce relatively little pollen, such as many agricultural crops and fruit trees that are essentially absent in the sediments of larger bodies of water such as **lakes**. For example, the Aguada Tintal near San Bartolo contains pollen indicating the cultivation of maize, cotton, and manioc as well as several kinds of fruit trees nearby. (See figure 1.) It also contains an oxidation layer indicative of drought near the end of the Late Preclassic (second century AD). However, because *aguadas* were often dredged periodically to maintain their volume, their sediment (and paleoenvironmental) records are often punctuated or incomplete.

See also BAJOS; CLIMATE; DIET; DROUGHT; GEOLOGY; GROUNDWATER; REJOLLADA; SOILS; SUBSISTENCE; WATER MANAGEMENT

Further Reading

Dunning, Nicholas P., John G. Jones, Timothy Beach, and Sheryl Luzzadder-Beach. "Physiography, Habitats, and Landscapes of the Three Rivers Region." In *Heterarchy, Political Economy, and the Ancient Maya: The Three Rivers Region of the East-central Yucatán Peninsula*, edited by Vernon L. Scarborough, Fred Valdez, and Nicholas P. Dunning, 14–24. Tucson: University of Arizona Press, 2003.

Dunning, Nicholas P., David Wahl, Timothy Beach, John G. Jones, Sheryl Luzzadder-Beach, and Carmen McCane. "The End of the Beginning: Environmental Instability and Human Response in the

Figure 1. Ezgi Akpinar-Ferrand and Andrew Miller extract a sediment core from Aguada Chintiko as part of the San Bartolo Archaeological Project. Courtesy Nicholas Dunning.

Late Preclassic East-Central Yucatan Peninsula." In *The Great Maya Droughts in Cultural Context: Case Studies in Resilience and Vulnerability*, edited by Gyles Iannone, 106–26. Boulder: University Press of Colorado, 2013.

Ferrand, Ezgi Akpinar, Nicholas P. Dunning, David L. Lentz, and John G. Jones. "Use of Aguadas as Water Management Sources in Two Southern Maya Lowland Sites." *Ancient Mesoamerica* 23, no. 1: 85–101, 2012.

Isendahl, Christian. "The Weight of Water: A New Look at Pre-Hispanic Puuc Maya Water Reservoirs." *Ancient Mesoamerica* 22, no. 1: 185–97, 2011.

Siemens, Alfred H. "Karst and the Pre-Hispanic Maya in the Southern Lowlands." In *Pre-Hispanic Maya Agriculture*, edited by Peter D. Harrison and B. L. Turner. Albuquerque: University of New Mexico Press, 1978.

■ NICHOLAS DUNNING

AGUATECA

Aguateca (16.4° N, 90.2° W) is a fortified Maya archaeological site in the department of El Petén in northern Guatemala (see also **Map 3**). It was one of two capitals in the Petexbatún kingdom; the other capital was **Dos Pilas.** The city suffered a swift and spectacular collapse around AD 810. The site was abandoned forever, resulting in the preservation of a broad range of artifacts rarely found at other Maya sites.

The site was first reported by a Guatemalan in 1957. Ian Graham followed up in 1959, returning in 1960 and 1962. In 1981 Steven Perry published a study of inscriptions at Aguateca. A Yale team based at Dos Pilas explored Aguateca in 1984. From 1990 to 1993 The Vanderbilt Petexbatún Regional Archaeological Project carried out extensive research at the site. In 1996 Takeshi Inomata, Daniela Triadan, and Erick Ponciano continued research at the site with the Aguateca Archaeological Project, encompassing fieldwork, lab work, and architectural restoration. This project ended in 2006.

Aguateca is located on the edge of a 100-m-high escarpment overlooking Laguna Petexbatún. A deep gorge runs parallel to the edge of the escarpment and divides the site in two. The escarpment and gorge provided substantial defensive advantages to the citizens of Aguateca.

The earliest substantial human presence at Aguateca dates to the Late Preclassic period (300 BC–AD 250). During the Early Classic period (AD 250–600), Aguateca was almost completely deserted. At this time the Petexbatún was dominated by a dynasty ruling from the twin capitals of Tamarindito and Arroyo de Piedra. This dynasty may have controlled the areas of Dos Pilas and Aguateca.

Aguateca was eventually pulled into Dos Pilas's orbit and gained in importance during the reign of Ucha'an K'in B'alam (AD 727–741), regent of a royal heir residing at Dos Pilas. During this reign the Aguateca-Dos Pilas kingdom recorded a victory over **Ceibal**, a large Maya city along the Río Pasión, some 22.5 km to the east/northeast of these two cities.

By AD 760 the Petexbatún kingdom suffered severe setbacks, resulting in the abandonment of Dos Pilas; Aguateca served as capital of a much smaller fiefdom for another 40 to 50 years. The last known ruler at Aguateca, Tan Te' K'inich, ruled from AD 770 to about 802. Within a few years Aguateca's multilayered yet never fully completed defensive walls were overrun and the site was hurriedly abandoned (see also **Kiuic**).

Sudden desertion of a site is a rare phenomenon in the Maya lowlands. Buildings that were hurriedly abandoned contain numerous artifacts left in place. This provides a unique opportunity to reconstruct the activities of the occupants of a building, and through these activities to get to know the inhabitants better. We know that this rapid abandonment took place in the central part of Aguateca, but not in other parts of the site.

At Aguateca four multichambered elite residences were excavated. These structures were burned at the time of abandonment. Excavations yielded 60 to 100 ceramic vessels, more than 1,000 stone tools, 20 to 60 shell ornaments, about 10 spindle whorls, and up to 300 pyrite mosaic mirror pieces, as well as various types of figurines, musical instruments, and scribal tools. The distribution of the artifacts reflects the patterns of activity and space use. These artifact assemblages were found in the spots where the original residents placed and used them. The artifacts meticulously recovered within these structures have permitted archaeologists to reconstruct the activities inside up until the last day of occupation. These discoveries also support the nicknames given to these buildings, such as the House of the Scribe (Str. M8–10) and the House of the Mirrors (Str. M8–4).

The completion of the Aguateca Archaeological Project in 2006 marked the transition of Aguateca as an active archaeological dig site to a well-maintained site open to visitors. Visitors can gain access by boat from Sayaxche, a community situated along the Pasion River, about an hour's drive south of Flores.

See also CLASSIC MAYA COLLAPSE; COBÁ, FORTIFICATIONS; PORTABLE OBJECTS; WARFARE, WARRIORS, AND WEAPONS

Further Reading

Demarest, Arthur A. *The Petexbatun Regional Archaeological Project: A Multidisciplinary Study of the Maya Collapse.* Vanderbilt Institute of Mesoamerican Archaeology. Nashville, TN: Vanderbilt University Press, 2006.

Inomata, Takeshi, and Daniela Triadan, eds. *Burned Palaces and Elite Residences of Aguateca: Excavations and Ceramics.* Monographs of the Aguateca Archaeological Project First Phase, vol. 1. Salt Lake City: University of Utah Press, 2010.

———, eds. *Life and Politics at the Royal Court of Aguateca: Artifacts, Analytical Data, and Synthesis.* Monographs of the Aguateca Archaeological Project First Phase, vol. 3. Salt Lake City: University of Utah Press, 2014.

■ DIRK VAN TUERENHOUT

ALLIANCES

The ancient Maya political landscape never produced a unified empire of political control. Instead, the picture is one of powerful city-states, linked to their smaller neighbors by geography and market forces and bonded to their more distant neighbors by mutually beneficial ties of trade, elite marriage, and pacts for offense and defense in war. These latter alliances shifted over time and space as fortunes of cities and their individual rulers waxed and waned. Archaeologists also believe that intrasite **causeways** were often the imprint of alliances between major elite families at one site.

In the seventh century, **Calakmul**, for example, had an array of smaller close-by cities under its sway, including Oxpemul, La Muñeca, Altamira, Balakbal, **Naachtun**, and Uxul. Its influence extended further beyond to the north, east, and south. Beyond this area, it established links to **Toniná**, **El Perú-Waka'**, **Dos Pilas**, **Naranjo**, **Caracol**, and **Quiriguá**. As Martin and Grube report, alliances that Calakmul forged with Caracol and Naranjo created a military juggernaut that defeated **Tikal** in AD 562. Dos Pilas, previously allied with Tikal, jumped ship to join in alliance with Calakmul. Inscriptions at Caracol make frequent mention of Calakmul and the strong military alliance between them in AD 619–636. As Tikal regained power, it conquered the rulers of El Perú-Waka' and Naranjo, a direct assault on the Calakmul alliance.

According to Kowalski, about AD 900 Lord Chahk, ruler of **Uxmal**, itself already linked to Nohpat and **Kabah** by a *sacbe*, appears to have established an alliance with **Chichen Itza**. Likewise, the double combination of a large temple-pyramid with a palace (The Great Pyramid/House of the Governor, and The Temple of the Magician/Nunnery Quadrangle) suggests a lineage alliance between two powerful families at Uxmal.

Marriage was a means of establishing economic and political alliance. Dos Pilas Hieroglyphic Bench 1 records that K'awiil Chan K'inich, a prince of Dos Pilas, married a princess of Cancuen, forging a major alliance between the two cities. At Tikal, ruler Chak Tok Ich'aak II (on the throne ca. AD 488–508) names Tzik'in Bahlam of Naranjo as his maternal grandfather, documenting a political alliance by marriage between the two cities. The murals of **Bonampak** and Stela 2 document the marriage of King Yajaw Chan Muwaan II to a royal woman from **Yaxchilan**, its larger near neighbor.

As new archaeological discoveries, especially in northern Guatemala and southern Campeche and Quintana Roo, produce new inscriptions, it becomes more clear what the alliances (and loss of alliance) meant to the Maya. They frequently carved permanent messages about marriage alliances; reciprocal city visits; royal appearances by higher-ups at smaller vassal towns; and captive-taking, sacrifice, and destruction that ended alliances and formed new ones. The near-term future of research will be to find and translate new texts that refine our understanding of these complex state-level interactions.

See also DIVINE KINGS AND QUEENS; TRADE ROUTES; WARFARE, WARRIORS, AND WEAPONS

Further Reading

Andrews, E. Wyllys, V, and William Leonard Fash, eds. *Copán: The History of an Ancient Maya Kingdom*. School of American Research advanced seminar series. Santa Fe, NM: School of American Research, 2005.

Houston, Stephen D. *Hieroglyphs and History at Dos Pilas: Dynastic Politics of the Classic Maya*. Austin: University of Texas Press, 1993.

Kowalski, Jeff K. "Lords of the Northern Maya: Dynastic History in the Inscriptions of Uxmal and Chichen Itza." *Expedition* 27, no. 3: 50–60, 1985.

Martin, Simon, and Nikolai Grube. *Chronicle of the Maya Kings and Queens: Deciphering the Dynasties of the Ancient Maya*. 2nd ed. London: Thames & Hudson, 2008.

Sabloff, Jeremy A. *Tikal: Dynasties, Foreigners & Affairs of State; Advancing Maya Archaeology*. School of American Research advanced seminar series. Santa Fe, NM: School of American Research Press, 2003.

Sharer, Robert J., and Loa P. Traxler. *The Ancient Maya*. 6th ed. Stanford, CA: Stanford University Press, 2006.

Tokovinine, Alexandre, and Vilma Fialko. "Stela 45 of Naranjo and the Early Classic Lords of Sa'aal." *The PARI Journal* 7, no. 4: 1–14, 2007.

■ WALTER R. T. WITSCHEY

ALTUN HA

The ancient town of Altun Ha (17.8° N, 88.3° W; see also **Map 3**), located in the Belize District of **Belize**, is most famous for a large, 4.42-kilogram, full-round, carved jade head of the Sun god, K'inich Ajaw, recovered from a **royal tomb** within Str. B-4. It is the largest known jade object from the Maya area.

Named for nearby Rockstone Pond, Altun Ha came to the attention of archaeologists in 1961, when villagers near the site discovered a large, carved jade pendant while quarrying there. Hamilton Anderson, then commissioner of archaeology, conducted a site visit with David Pendergast of the Royal Ontario Museum in Toronto. Pendergast subsequently spent eight field seasons at the site, and his work forms the chief body of reportage of the site. His work was followed by Joseph Palacio and Elizabeth Graham.

The site is situated in a marshy region of Belize 13 km from the Caribbean coast at an elevation of 15–20 m asl. Although the site's elites were involved in trade with the broader Maya area, several factors indicate that Altun Ha was somewhat apart from them, as demonstrated by a lack of carved stone monuments (**stelae**) and an unusual construction technique for the royal tomb within Str. B-4.

The major architectural groups occupy an area about 400 by 500 m, 20 ha. The first occupation of Altun Ha occurred in the Late Formative, about 200 BC. Notable construction began about AD 100 with a temple in the southwest near the main water source (Group E). During the Early Classic, construction began in Group A, site of the Temple of the Green Tomb (Str. A-1). About AD 550 construction began in Group B, site of the royal tomb in Str. B-4, and continued for two centuries. Following AD 750, construction quality declined, and it ended completely by AD 900. Altun Ha clearly participated in the region-wide **Classic Maya collapse**. A small population remained another century until the site was abandoned. There was a small reoccupation in the Late Postclassic.

Around Plaza A, measuring 50 by 75 m, are a number of major buildings. Str. A-1 contains a royal tomb that dates to AD 550. The structures in Group A show the typical Maya construction pattern of overbuilding in multiple eras.

Plaza B, off the south side of plaza A, is 125 by 100 m. The largest structure is B-4, within which seven tombs were found. The earliest of these, B-4/7, was a richly furnished tomb containing more than 300 jade items, eccentric flints, stingray spine bloodletters, ceramics, woven fabrics, and pelts, as well as the unreadable remains of a Maya codex. The grandeur and wealth of the tomb speak to the prosperity of Altun Ha as the Late Classic period opens. Str. B-4 has been restored to its appearance as of AD 600–650.

Today Altun Ha is readily accessible by car or bus for tourist visits, and the structures of Groups A and B may be visited easily on foot.

See also PORTABLE OBJECTS; TEXTILES AND CLOTHING; TRADE ROUTES

Further Reading

Archaeology of Altun Ha. Belize National Institute of Culture and History, Institute of Archaeology. http://nichbelize.org/ia-maya-sites/archaeology-of-altun-ha.html.

Braswell, Geoffrey E. *The Maya and Teotihuacan: Reinterpreting Early Classic Interaction.* Austin: University of Texas Press, 2004.

Pendergast, David M. "Excavations at Altun Ha." *Belize* 1970: 48–53, 1964.

———. *Altun Ha, British Honduras (Belize): The Sun God's Tomb.* Toronto, Canada: Occasional Paper 19. Royal Ontario Museum, University of Toronto Press, 1969. https://archive.org/details/altunha britishho00pend.

Pendergast, David M., and Loten H. Stanley. *Excavations at Altun Ha, Belize, 1964–1970.* Toronto: Royal Ontario Museum, 1979.

White, Christine D., David M. Pendergast, Fred J. Longstaffe, and Kimberley R. Law. "Social Complexity and Food Systems at Altun Ha, Belize: The Isotopic Evidence." *Latin American Antiquity* 12, no. 4: 371–93, 2001.

■ WALTER R. T. WITSCHEY

APOCALYPSE

The concept of "apocalypse" (from the ancient Greek "revelation") as attributed to ancient Mayas, and especially its association with the date 13.0.0.0.0 4 Ahaw 3 K'an'kin (usually correlated with December 21, 2012), is the product of confusion among twentieth-century Mayanists and the embellishment of derived interpretations in popular literature. Although the term has become a popular synonym for a future doomsday or Armageddon, there is no persuasive evidence that ancient Mayas ever predicted or prophesied anything of the kind. Instead, concepts of a future apocalypse appear to be the result of religious syncretism based on Christian beliefs, such as those expressed in Christopher Columbus's *Libro de las profecías.*

The term "apocalypse" was introduced to Maya studies by **Ernst Förstemann** in his 1906 interpretation of the Dresden codex (see also **Codices [Maya]**). He asserted that some of its calendrical texts offer "the genesis and the apocalypse of all the mythologies" and that the last page of the codex "can denote nothing but the end of the world." In 1915 Sylvanus Morley directly paraphrased his predecessor. He embellished further in *The Ancient Maya,* in which he also appropriated language from Tozzer's 1941 translation of **Diego de Landa**'s *Relación de las cosas de Yucatán.* Specifically, Morley relates an ethnohistoric account collected by Tozzer near Valladolid that referred to the destruction by floods of three previous worlds, cryptically adding about the current world that "this too will eventually be destroyed by a fourth flood." This was not an account of what *ancient* Mayas believed, but a concept articulated by missionized, Catholic Mayas of Yucatan in the early twentieth century. However, this was frequently misinterpreted. Confusion was exacerbated by Joseph Campbell's 1949 conclusion to *The Hero with a Thousand Faces,* titled "End of the Macrocosm," which cited the Dresden codex, quoted Morley, and implied that future destruction of the world by a flood was an ancient Maya belief.

Prior to Förstemann's comments, in 1897 Joseph T. Goodman had published his pioneering decipherment of the Long Count **calendar**. Goodman identified what he called a "Great Cycle" of 13 *b'ak'tuns,* for which he calculated multiple period endings, including 13.0.0.0.0 4 Ahaw 3 K'ank'in. However, despite enigmatic associations of 13.0.0.0.0 4 Ahaw 8 Kumk'u with the beginning of the current count (correlated to August 11, 3113 BC), there is little evidence that ancient Mayas counted time in successive Great Cycles or that they would have assigned any particular significance to 13.0.0.0.0 4 Ahaw 3 K'ank'in other than as a *b'ak'tun* ending similar to 9.0.0.0.0 or 10.0.0.0.0, both of which were commemorated with historical inscriptions and *b'ak'tun*-ending celebrations.

In 1951 astronomer Maud Worcester Makemson made the first association of the 13.0.0.0.0 4 Ahaw 3 K'ank'in date with catastrophe, based on her translation of a passage in the eighteenth-century *Book of Chilam Balam* of Tizimin. She erroneously correlated the date with one in the year 1752, and her book was sharply criticized, but reified this association. Makemson's association was followed by the more authoritative statement in 1966 by archaeologist Michael Coe in *The Maya*, in which, citing Goodman's Great Cycle concept, he asserted "there is a suggestion" that at the end of the current 13-*b'ak'tun* cycle, "Armageddon would overtake the degenerate peoples of the world and all creation" and that "our present universe" would "be annihilated." Coe's correlations of the specific Long Count date varied slightly, but his basic assertion was repeated in each of his popular book's eight editions.

The specific correlation of 13.0.0.0.0 4 Ahaw 3 K'ank'in with December 21, 2012, first appeared in Robert Sharer's extension of Morley's original appendix for the fourth edition of *The Ancient Maya*. After this, the date was repeated in the 1970s and 1980s by speculative authors, most notably Terence McKenna and José Argüelles, as a result of which it became a part of popular, but incorrect, lore about ancient Maya beliefs, circulating first among counterculture communities before becoming more widespread after the advent of the World Wide Web in the mid-1990s. As a result, anticipation of an apocalypse—especially as a "revelation" or metaphysical "transformation of consciousness"—built through the early 2000s until the specific date came and went. This process, referred to as the "2012 phenomenon," was accompanied by a worldwide flood of popular literature, films, and websites. It was also accompanied by an increase in syncretism among Christian, Hindu, New Age, and living Maya beliefs as well as spurious and unsupported claims about ancient traditions. This is a process known as the "pizza effect," in which externally generated concepts become integrated and presented as if they were original indigenous traditions.

Although there are two known references to 13.0.0.0.0 4 Ahaw 3 K'ank'in in seventh-century inscriptions, one on Tortuguero Monument 6 and another on Block V from Hieroglyphic Stairway 2 at **La Corona**, neither of these texts refers to a future apocalypse or catastrophic event of any kind.

Further Reading

Aveni, Anthony F. *The End of Time: The Maya Mystery of 2012*. Boulder: University Press of Colorado, 2009.

Carlson, John B., ed. *The Maya Calendar and 2012 Phenomenon Studies*. Vol. 24, *Archaeoastronomy: The Journal of Astronomy in Culture*. Austin: University of Texas Press, 2011.

Coe, Michael D. *The Maya*. New York: Praeger, 1966.

Gelfer, Joseph, ed. *2012: Decoding the Countercultural Apocalypse*. London: Equinox Publishing, 2011.

Hoopes, John W. "New Age Sympathies and Scholarly Complicities: The History and Promotion of 2012 Mythology." *Archaeoastronomy: The Journal of Astronomy in Culture* 24: 180–201, 2011.

Hoopes, John W., and Kevin Whitesides. "Seventies Dreams and 21st Century Realities: The Emergence of 2012 Mythology." *Zeitschrift für Anomalistik* 12: 50–74, 2012.

Sitler, Robert K. "The 2012 Phenomenon: New Age Appropriation of an Ancient Maya Calendar." *Nova Religio: The Journal of Alternative and Emergent Religions* 9, no. 3: 24–38, 2006.

———. "The 2012 Phenomenon Comes of Age." *Nova Religio: The Journal of Alternative and Emergent Religions* 16, no. 1: 61–87, 2012.

Stuart, David. *The Order of Days: The Maya World and the Truth about 2012.* New York: Harmony Books, 2011.

■ JOHN HOOPES

ARCHITECTURE OVERVIEW

Maya architecture includes the most modest, one-room **houses**, and the most imposing, giant temple-**pyramid** complexes. At all levels, architecture was rebuilt and overbuilt through time, always transitional, never fully permanent. Because most large Maya structures were of solid masonry, they could be easily overbuilt by the addition of a new exterior. On occasion, interior rooms were filled with masonry rubble to prevent their collapse during a new construction phase.

Building types were numerous. Large Maya sites have a central core, or multiple major core areas, defined by large plazas with surrounding monumental architecture. Included in the central core are often temple-pyramids (truncated pyramids with a perishable or masonry temple atop, sometimes serving as **royal tombs**); multistoried, multiroom **palaces**; *sacbes* (**causeways**) linking important parts of the city or linking one city with another; elite residences, with multiple rooms; one or more **ball courts** with parallel sides; **astronomical observatories**, such as E-Group configurations; **water management** features (plastered plazas, drains, collection reservoirs); and other specialized buildings, such as **council houses**, sweat baths, skull racks, and platforms for **music and dance**. As one moves outward from the center of a large city, there may be defensive walls (see also **Fortifications**), agricultural **terracing**, and smaller and smaller residences, down ultimately to the level of one-room houses built entirely of perishable materials, such as pole and thatch. Such small dwellings are difficult to find archaeologically.

The earliest well-dated lowland architecture is from Cuello, Belize. The structures, dated to ca. 1000 BC, consist of low, 25-cm-high platforms of earth and stone covered with plaster floors and supporting perishable, apparently apsidal, wooden structures.

The earliest large and complex sites in the Maya lowlands grew in the **Mirador Basin** of north-central Department of Petén, Guatemala, and to its north and east. Cival, with triadic groups and Group-E configurations, is an important early example outside the Mirador Basin. Some of these sites evolved into giant monumental ceremonial centers during the Middle and Late Formative periods (1000 BC–AD 250). The sites included **Nakbé**; **El Mirador**, the largest; Tintal; and Wakna. Residential architecture is known from both El Mirador and Nakbé. At Nakbé, early Middle Formative (ca. 800–600 BC) residential architecture included stone-faced platforms up to 2 m high featuring vertical retaining walls constructed of roughly shaped slabs of limestone and topped with floors made of limestone marl or plaster. By the end of the Middle Formative period at Nakbé (600–400 BC), massive platforms measuring 3–8 m in height and covering 40,000 m² were being constructed. One structure was 18 m tall.

Some early Maya ceremonial structures were huge. The largest structures of El Mirador, the Danta and El Tigre complexes, were among the largest buildings ever built by the ancient Maya. Other quite substantial Formative architecture is also known from sites throughout the Maya lowlands, including **Lamanai**, Belize; **Yaxuná**, Yucatan; and **Tikal**, Guatemala. The architecture of these early sites clearly foreshadowed the styles and forms of later Classic period Maya architecture, but also possessed interesting peculiarities of its own.

Solar sunrise observatories (see also **Astronomical Observatories**), called "E-groups," appear in the early Formative at Cival, and in the late Middle Formative at Nakbé. They were also constructed early in the architectural history of other sites in the Petén, such as **Uaxactún** and Tikal. An E-group is usually composed of a radial truncated pyramid with four stairways, facing a long building to the east of it. The buildings are juxtaposed so that a person standing on the pyramid and looking east will see the sunrise over the middle of the long building on the equinoxes and over the north and south corners of the long building on the solstices.

Radial pyramids, mentioned above, also appear at this time, near the end of the Middle Formative period. They are a widespread and persistent architectural form. They are square step-pyramids with approximate quadrilateral symmetry, usually having four stairways, one ascending each side. They may or may not have inset corners and a stone temple on top. Later, they occur in the "twin-pyramid complexes" of Tikal and Yaxhá as well as in E-groups and other architectural arrangements. Some of the latest Maya pyramids are radial in form, such as the Temples of Kukulcán (El Castillo) at Chichen Itza and Mayapán, dating respectively to the Terminal Classic and Late Postclassic periods.

Round structures, although rare in Classic Maya architecture, also appear in the late Middle Formative in the Maya lowlands. They too continue into the Postclassic period. Maya causeways, called *sacbes* (Yucatec Maya for "white road"), also seem to date from the late Middle Formative period. They also formed an integral element of Maya architecture and cityscapes for many centuries, until the arrival of the Spanish. These causeways represent a significant engineering achievement. They were often wide, tall, and graded, and ran straight for great distances, either connecting different parts of cities or sometimes linking distant cities with each other. El Mirador has numerous radial causeways and is linked to Nakbé by a causeway.

Toward the end of the Middle Formative period and during the succeeding Late Formative, carefully cut and squared stones began to be used in lowland Maya architecture. The advances in quarrying and masonry apparently led to the development of more elaborate architectural motifs, such as apron moldings and rounded corners on pyramids and platforms, both of which were enduring elements of the Classic architectural repertoire.

One distinctive attribute of Formative period Maya architecture is the construction of massive triadic temple-pyramids. These consist of a huge stepped pyramidal substructure, usually with inset corners, crowned by three smaller temple-pyramids facing onto a small plaza atop the base. The largest of the three temple-pyramids is set back on the substructure, while the two smaller constructions sit in front, facing each other and flanking the court.

Stucco began to be used to adorn Maya building façades during the Late Formative period, if not earlier. Thick layers of stucco were modeled into elaborate and complex designs, including monumental faces of deities. The tradition of architectural stuccoes continued throughout the pre-Columbian period.

The Classic period (AD 250–900) represents the apogee and florescence of Maya high art, including architecture. During the Classic period, corbelled vaulting was widely used to roof buildings. Inscriptions, low-relief sculpture, and modeled stucco were employed to adorn buildings. Many buildings were elaborately painted as well, although weathering long ago erased most of the paint, depriving us of information about it.

In the Early Classic period, regional styles of architecture developed. For example, in the northern lowlands of the Yucatan Peninsula, megalithic masonry is found at sites such as **Izamal**, Ake, Ikil, El Naranjal, Tepich, and many others. Some **Teotihuacán** influence from Central Mexico is seen in the architecture of several important sites, including Tikal, Copán, **Dzibilchaltún**, **Oxkintok**, and **Chunchucmil**. This influence often takes the form of *talud-tablero* platform façades.

During the later Classic period, distinctive regional styles flourished (see also ***Chenes Architectural Style***; **Petén Architectural Style**; **Puuc Architectural Style**; Río Bec; **Southern Architectural Style**; **Western Architectural Style**). Different investigators draw somewhat different geographic boundaries between the various regional styles.

The *Chenes* architectural style is typified by complex geometric mosaic sculptures on the façades of buildings, including "monster-mouth doorways" in which the iconography of the façade sculpture turns the principal doorway of a building into the symbolic mouth of a deity. *Chenes* sites are also known for their large, multistory palaces. *Chenes* sites include Chicanná, Dzibilnocac, **Edzna**, and Santa Rosa Xtampak, all in Campeche.

The Petén (Central) architectural style is found at the major sites in the heart of the Maya lowlands, in the Department of Petén in Guatemala and adjacent areas of western Belize, southern Quintana Roo, and southern Campeche (see also **Map 1**). Sites exhibiting this style include Tikal, Uaxactún, **Naranjo**, Yaxhá, **Calakmul**, **Xunantunich**, and many others. One outstanding characteristic of the style is the construction of towering temple-pyramids. The Petén architectural style also spread far to the north, following the east coast of Quintana Roo, and extended inland to the border of Campeche and Yucatan. This northern extension is referred to architecturally as the "Petén Corridor." Sites include Chachoben, Limones, Kantunilkin, and most famously, **Cobá**.

The Río Bec architectural style extends from the northern border of the Petén to the northwest and includes the type site of **Río Bec** as well as Xpuhil, **Becan**, and other sites. The southernmost Río Bec style building is found at **Naachtun**, which straddles the northern border of the Department of Petén in Guatemala. The style is defined by the presence of false towers that seem intended to mimic the giant funerary pyramids of the Petén. To the north of the Río Bec style, but overlapping it, is the *Chenes* style.

The culmination of northern Maya architecture is the **Puuc style**, centered in the region of the Puuc hills in southern Yucatan. It overlaps with *Chenes* architecture, both geographically and stylistically. The Puuc style also carries complex mosaic sculpture on the façade, but usually only above the medial molding. The engineering of these buildings is superb, and many remain well preserved. The most famous Puuc sites are located in the Puuc Hills, including **Uxmal**, **Labna**, **Sayil**, **Kabah**, Nohpat, **Oxkintok**, Chacmultun, Xkichmook, **Kiuic**, and many others. Nevertheless, the style extends over the entire northern plains and east to the border of Quintana Roo, where it intertwines with the Petén Corridor sites. In some sites, such as Uxmal, Puuc-style buildings overlie *Chenes* constructions, cementing the idea that *Chenes* is generally earlier than the final examples of the Puuc style.

The Southern architectural style includes at least **Copán**, Honduras, and nearby **Quiriguá**, Guatemala (see also **Map 2**). The style, well-preserved in the hard stone utilized, is distinguished by the particularly elegant and well-executed façade sculptures, as well as a tendency toward sculpture in the round.

The Western architectural style includes sites such as **Palenque**, in northern Chiapas, and Comalcalco in Tabasco. The style is most easily recognized by its use of mansard roofs and pierced roof combs, which convey a lightness and grace not often achieved elsewhere in the Maya area. **Comalcalco** is the westernmost major Maya site. Located on the alluvial plains of Tabasco where stone is not available, Comalcalco's buildings were constructed of fired brick. Both sites are also justly famous for their beautiful stucco work.

In the Late and Terminal Classic periods (ca. AD 800–1100) in Yucatan, a unique manifestation of Maya architecture emerged at the famous site of Chichen Itza. The style combines Puuc stylistic elements with Central Mexican motifs, such as serpent columns, warrior columns, *tzompantli* (sacrificial 'skull racks'), I-shaped ball courts, and extensive colonnades. The Central Mexican elements were once seen as evidence of a Toltec invasion from Central Mexico, but current thought emphasizes the eclectic sources of these influences.

The last flowering of Maya architecture took place during the Postclassic at **Mayapán** in central Yucatan, and at many smaller sites along the Caribbean east coast of the peninsula. This type of architecture was not well engineered. Stones were frequently not well squared, and coursing and bonding were casual at best. Typically vertical walls assumed an outward batter. Aesthetically, the style recapitulates earlier Maya elements, including radial pyramids, corbelled vaults, and stelae, but also features "Mexican" elements such as serpent temples, round temples, and colonnades. A related style emerged in the Guatemala highlands during the Postclassic, where double temples, an Aztec building type, occur and ball courts proliferated.

See also AGUADAS; CHENES ARCHITECTURAL STYLE; PETÉN ARCHITECTURAL STYLE; PUUC ARCHITECTURAL STYLE; RÍO BEC; SOUTHERN ARCHITECTURAL STYLE; WESTERN ARCHITECTURAL STYLE

Further Reading

Andrews, George F. *Pyramids and Palaces, Monsters and Masks: The Golden Age of Maya Architecture*. Vol. 1 of *The Collected Works of George F. Andrews*. Lancaster, CA: Labyrinthos, 1995.

Kowalski, Jeff K., ed. *Mesoamerican Architecture as a Cultural Symbol*. Oxford: Oxford University Press, 1999.

Kowalski, Jeff K., and Nicholas P. Dunning. "The Architecture of Uxmal: The Symbolics of Statemaking at a Puuc Maya Regional Capital." In *Mesoamerican Architecture as a Cultural Symbol*, edited by Jeff K. Kowalski. Oxford: Oxford University Press, 1999.

Miller, Mary Ellen, and Megan Eileen O'Neil. *Maya Art and Architecture.* 2nd ed. London: Thames & Hudson, 2014.

Pollock, Harry E. D. "Architecture of the Maya Lowlands." In *Handbook of Middle American Indians.* Vol. 2, *Archaeology of Southern Mesoamerica*, pt. 1, edited by Gordon R. Willey, 378–440. Austin: University of Texas Press, 1965.

Proskouriakoff, Tatiana. *An Album of Maya Architecture.* Carnegie Institution of Washington, Publication 558. Washington, DC: Carnegie Institution of Washington, 1962.

Rhyne, Charles S. *Architecture, Restoration, and Imaging of the Maya Cities of Uxmal, Kabah, Sayil, and Labná, the Puuc Region, Yucatán, México.* Reed College, 2008. http://academic.reed.edu/uxmal/.

■ CLIFFORD T. BROWN AND WALTER R. T. WITSCHEY

ART

The extraordinary range and beauty of Maya art brings to us the heart and soul of Maya beliefs and priorities. It renders for us the leading personalities of the day, the **deities** of the Maya world, and the information-filled texts of hieroglyphic writing (see also **Language and Writing Overview**). The media of Maya art include carvings in stone, bone, shell, and wood; mural painting; stucco modeling; writing; **ceramic** decoration; body deformation and decoration; and **music and dance**.

The Maya carved stone monuments, beyond ceremonial **architecture**, include elegant **stelae** on the plazas between buildings, upright pillars carrying inscriptions, ruler portraits and their stories in hieroglyphs, and dates. These sometimes accompany large, round altars or carved throne stones. The Maya also carved throne benches with backs. Important buildings, painted inside and out, carried carved or molded wall panels and wooden lintels carved with portraits and hieroglyphs. Few examples of wood carving survive; the most important and elegant are lintels from temples at **Tikal**.

Stairway risers, found at **Copán**, **Dos Pilas**, **Edzna**, **El Perú-Waka'**, **La Corona** Pusilha, **Naranjo**, Tamarindito, and **Yaxchilan** among others, were inscribed to create **hieroglyphic steps** with narratives of captive-taking, sacrifice, and genealogies. Some **ball courts** had carved centerline marker stones or carved markers high on the playing walls. The large ball court at Chichen Itza is noted for its scenes of ballplayers and human sacrifice.

Quiriguá and Copán have large stones sculpted in the round; some, called zoomorphs, are of fanciful animals.

Temple-pyramids were frequently decorated with heavy molded stucco, which, due to the Maya practice of building a new building over an older one, survive. Notable examples include the giant molded stucco masks at **Kohunlich**, the Rosalila temple at **Copán**, **Ek Balam**, Balamkú, **Holmul**, and Xultun. Roof combs on temple-pyramids such as those at Tikal and **Labna**, among others, were armatures for the creation of stucco decoration, but little survives.

Wall painting appears on interior temple walls (**Bonampak** is a famous example), on the walls of **royal tombs** (such as at **San Bartolo**), and on cave walls (such as at **Naj Tunich**). Like stelae, many carry narratives about the actions of the divine rulers.

Apparently, painted ceramics, especially polychromes from the Classic, were painted in much the same way Maya books were created: by scribes using brushes. Their content includes narrative celebrating divine rulers as well as story segments from the *Popol Vuh*. They were important funerary offerings. From the Classic and Postclassic, ceramic incense burners constituted a special class of ceramics, molded or cast into large figurines of gods, sometimes pictured in three dimensions making offerings in just the way the incense burner itself would have been used.

The four surviving Maya **codices** reveal an elaborate book-writing art form with content including astronomy, divination, and celebrating rites and rituals. The deliberate destruction of many books by the Spanish, together with the loss of others due to inhospitable climatic conditions, leaves scholars wishing for more.

The art of **weaving** had sufficient import to be portrayed in the codices. Although remains of ancient cloth are not available, illustrations, such as on the figurines from **Jaina** and on Classic Maya polychrome vases, provide a clear picture of its richness at the royal level.

The sum of these sophisticated and elegant arts portrays a Maya aesthetic from the Classic to be the equal of such art from any society on the planet.

See also CALENDAR; DIVINE KINGS AND QUEENS

Further Reading

Coe, Michael D. *Classic Maya Pottery at Dumbarton Oaks*. Washington, DC: Dumbarton Oaks, Trustees for Harvard University, 1975.

Coe, Michael D., and Justin Kerr. *The Art of the Maya Scribe*. London: Thames & Hudson, 1997.

Coe, William R., Edwin M. Shook, and Linton Satterthwaite. "The Carved Wooden Lintels of Tikal, Tikal Report No. 6." In *Tikal Reports: Numbers 1 to 11*, edited by Edwin M. Shook, Richard E. W. Adams, and Robert F. Carr. Philadelphia: University of Pennsylvania Museum of Archaeology and Anthropology, University of Pennsylvania, 1986.

Kerr, Justin. *Maya Vase Database*. Kerr Associates, 2014. http://www.mayavase.com/.

Martin, Simon, and Nikolai Grube. *Chronicle of the Maya Kings and Queens: Deciphering the Dynasties of the Ancient Maya*. 2nd ed. London: Thames & Hudson, 2008.

Miller, Mary Ellen, and Claudia Brittenham. *The Spectacle of the Late Maya Court: Reflections on the Murals of Bonampak*. William & Bettye Nowlin Series in Art, History, and Culture of the Western Hemisphere. Austin: University of Texas Press, 2013.

Miller, Mary Ellen, and Simon Martin. *Courtly Art of the Ancient Maya*. New York: Thames & Hudson, 2004.

Miller, Mary Ellen, and Megan Eileen O'Neil. *Maya Art and Architecture*. 2nd ed. London: Thames & Hudson, 2014.

Pillsbury, Joanne, Barbara Arroyo, Reiko Ishihara-Brito, and Alexandre Tokovinine, eds. *Ancient Maya art at Dumbarton Oaks*. Washington, DC: Dumbarton Oaks Research Library and Collection, 2012.

Stone, Andrea, and Marc Zender. *Reading Maya Art: A Hieroglyphic Guide to Ancient Maya Painting and Sculpture*. London: Thames & Hudson, 2011.

■ WALTER R. T. WITSCHEY

ARTIFACTS
See PORTABLE OBJECTS

ASTRONOMICAL OBSERVATORIES

Observatory is a science word, a structure erected for the express purpose of precisely observing sky phenomena, usually via a telescope housed within. Applied to archaeological remains, Maya observatories are related to celestial alignments. Three categories of astronomical orientation are recognized: entire site alignments, specialized structures, and hierophanies (see also **Astronomy**).

Because the Maya believed they were integrated into the structure of the universe, the layout of a Maya site served as a material expression of their understanding of space-time. For example, **Izapa** and La Libertad are among a number of Preclassic sites on the **Pacific Coast of Guatemala** that align with the solstices, where the sun rises and sets farthest from east and west. Several sites in Terminal Classic West Yucatan, including **Uxmal** and **Oxkintok**, point to sunrise/set positions based on 20-day intervals counted from the day the sun passed the zenith, or overhead point. This choice happened when skywatchers became aware of the special symmetry between the Maya way of counting time, in units of 20, and the way these intervals could be patterned in local **calendars** at the latitude where the cities were situated.

Specialized structures relating to sky events are often recognized by their unusual shape or arrangement compared to surrounding buildings. Their orientations have more to do with religion and politics than astronomy. Resembling the quadripartite diagrams of the Maya cosmos found in the **codices**, **Tikal**'s Classic twin **pyramid** complexes are closely oriented to the cardinal directions (see figure 2). They consist of two large radial pyramids (accessible from all four sides) positioned along a dominant east-west axis, with smaller structures located on the opposing north-south axis. Reflecting a political motivation for building orientations, inscribed stelae and altar arrangements provide information about the rulers who built them and the *k'atun* (20-year) ending celebrations that took place to honor the dynasty. Unlike most Western religious rituals (see also RITES AND RITUALS), the Maya ceremonies were conducted under the open sky; the zenith, or center of space, was believed to be the source of dynastic power. In north Yucatan, other examples in this category include the Terminal Classic Caracol of **Chichen Itza**, which, given its round shape and windows oriented to the extreme rising positions of Venus, comes closest to resembling our Western concept of an observatory. **Uxmal's** House of the Governor, also Terminal Classic and Venus oriented, is skewed from the prevailing north-south site grid. The iconography on its frieze and its carved veneer stone masks at the corners of the building contain Venus symbols and a Maya zodiacal text, thus supporting the Venus observatory hypothesis.

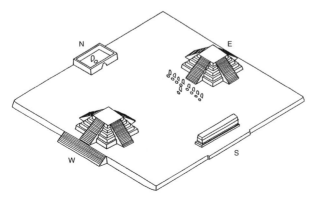

Figure 2.   Tikal Twin Pyramid Complex. There are nine known such groups at Tikal, erected on *k'atun*-ending dates, such as 9.12.0.0.0. There is one example at Yaxha and two at Zacpetén. Courtesy of Anthony F. Aveni and Hellmuth.

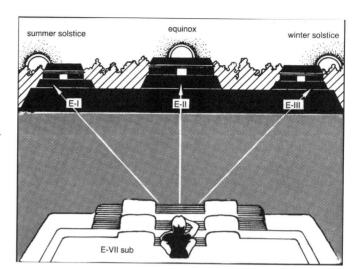

Figure 3. Uaxactún, Group E. Courtesy of Anthony F. Aveni.

Group E structures from **Classic Uaxactún** in the **Petén** also exhibit solstitial orientations (see figure 3). A radial pyramid on the west end of an open plaza overlooks a low range structure topped by three small buildings. Looking east from the pyramid, an observer sees the sun rise at the solstices over the outer pair and at the equinoxes over the central building. Alignment measurements on more than 40 examples of Group E-type structures in the **Petén** reveal orientations that suggest a calendar reform took place during the **Early Classic,** in which the Maya adapted their earlier solstice-based calendar to a zenith-based calendar, likely because the latter was more suited to the agricultural seasons in that particular area.

The hierophany, a manifestation of the sacred in the built environment, usually achieved via the subtle interplay of light and shadow, makes up the third and final category of Maya observatories. The most famous example is the Temple of Kukulcan, the Maya feathered serpent **deity**, at **Chichen Itza**. On and about the equinoxes, shadows cast by the northwest edge of this stepped-**pyramid** fall on its northern balustrade, forming diamonds of light that resemble the shadow of a descending diamondback rattlesnake. These appear attached to the sculpted open-mouthed serpent head at the base of the pyramid, thus making the phenomenon particularly attention worthy. Thousands of tourists show up on the first day of spring to share in a legacy once intended to reenact and perpetuate the ancient Maya cosmic order in an observatory that might more appropriately be called a "planetarium," or a theater in the built environment.

See also ALTUN HA; ARCHITECTURE OVERVIEW; ART; CALENDAR; CIVAL; HOLMUL; NAKBÉ; NARANJO; YAXNOHCAH

Further Reading

Aveni, Anthony F. *Skywatchers: A Revised and Updated Version of "Skywatchers of Ancient Mexico"*. Austin: University of Texas Press, 2001.
———. "Cosmology and Cultural Landscapes." In *Astronomers, Scribes and Priests: Intellectual Interchange between the Northern Maya Lowlands and Highland Mexico in the Late Postclassic Period*, edited by

Gabrielle Vail and Christine Hernandez, 115–32. Washington, DC: Dumbarton Oaks, Trustees for Harvard University, 2010.

■ ANTHONY F. AVENI

ASTRONOMY

Maya astronomy is "naked-eye" astronomy, based exclusively on what can be seen by human eye in the skies overhead, without benefit of telescopes or other devices. The ancient Maya, based on their records, observatories, and civic and **architectural** designs, were tracking the movements of the sun, the moon, and several planets, and the seasonal patterns of the stars.

From Earth, tracking the sun is straightforward. The earth's rotation in 24 hours produces the natural day-and-night phenomenon. The Maya counted whole days in their **calendars**. In a year's time, the traveling of the earth in its orbit causes the apparent location of sunrises, sunsets, whether the sun appears overhead at noon, and the background of stars to change. The Maya tracked the seasonal changes of sunrise with Group-E architectural assemblages (see also **Astronomical Observatories**), but did not use fractional days or leap days in their calendar to match the annual orbit length of 365.2422 days, as calculated by astronomers today. Equinoxes, the first days of spring and fall when the sun passes over the equator, were marked with hierophanies such as the appearance of a serpent on the west balustrade of the north stair of the Castillo at **Chichen Itza**.

The entire Maya region lies between the Tropic of Cancer at 23.4° north and the equator. As a result, there are two days each year when the sun passes directly overhead and casts no shadow. These two days split the year into two parts, the longer of which, at **Copán**, is 260 days, when the sun is to the south, and the shorter 105 days, when the sun is to the north. This split is different for more northerly sites. The *tzolk'in* calendar of 260 days may approximate the longer of these periods, but many urge that it more likely relates to the period of human gestation. Anthony Aveni notes that the Maya may have adapted their calendar from solstice observation to zenith-passage observation.

Forecasting the position of the moon is a more challenging problem. The orbit of the moon around the earth takes about 29½ days from one full moon to the next. Full moon occurs when the sun and the moon are on opposite sides of the earth. New moon occurs when the sun and moon are on the same side of the earth. First and last quarter, when half the moon is lit, occur at the midpoints, when the moon and sun are at a right angle, viewed from the earth. The Maya, counting whole days, assigned the length of each lunar month to be either 29 or 30 days. Many Maya stela **hieroglyphic inscriptions** include a lunar series of glyphs that provide the age of the moon in the current month, how long the current lunar month is (29 or 30 days), and which lunar month within a six-month interval is being recorded.

Eclipses were a frightening and powerful concept to ancient peoples, including the Maya. The moon's orbit is tilted about 5° to the orbit of the sun. Eclipses are most likely to occur when the moon passes through the plane of the sun's orbit (a node) and the earth, moon, and sun lie along a straight line. A lunar eclipse is most likely at full moon; a solar eclipse most likely at new moon. Since the tilt of the moon's orbit causes the nodes to shift along the sun's ecliptic path, repeating after 18.61 years, eclipses do not occur at precise six-month intervals, but after five or six lunar months (148 or 177/178 days). It is these intervals that the Maya tracked and that are represented in the eclipse tables of the Dresden codex (see also **Codices [Maya]**) and at **Xultun**. The Dresden codex tables show combinations of six lunar months (4 of 30 days plus 2 of 29 days = 178 days, or 3 of 29 days plus 3 of 30 days = 177 days) or five lunar months (3 of 30 days and 2 of 29 days = 148 days).

The planets drew the attention of the ancient Maya. The orbit of Venus, the third brightest object in the night sky, is inside the orbit of Earth. To us it always appears close to the sun. Venus is invisible to us as it passes in front of the sun for 14 days. Then it appears as the morning star for 240 days. As it passes behind the sun for 90 days, it is again invisible to us, then emerges as the evening star for 240 days. This cycle of 584 days was known to the Maya. They also knew that five Venus cycles (5 × 584 = 2,920 days) was equal to eight Earth years of 365 days (8 × 365 = 2,920). The heliacal rising (first rising as morning star) was of special significance to the Maya—the alignment of the Governor's Palace at **Uxmal**, for example, is aligned to the heliacal rising of Venus. Venus marked propitious times for wars to seize sacrificial captives. Venus glyphs, signifying a Tlaloc-Venus war, accompany many inscriptions of conquest by divine Maya rulers.

The Maya interest in Mars, as first shown by the work of R. W. Willson in 1924, has been extended by Harvey Bricker, Anthony Aveni, and Victoria Bricker to show that innovative Maya cycles, previously unknown in Western astronomy, were employed in the Dresden codex. The ancient Maya Mars table of 780 days matched their *tzolk'in* calendar (3 *tzolk'ins* × 260 days = 780 days). The table was subdivided into 10 blocks of 78 days, with one such block closely matching the interval of retrograde motion of Mars against the heavens. The Brickers and Aveni identify a new Maya tabulation, a two-part long and short empiric sidereal interval, visible to the Maya observer, with a seasonal pattern and including or excluding the retrograde period of Mars.

In addition to sun and moon, Venus and Mars, the Maya books and inscriptions reveal their interest in Jupiter and Saturn, the Milky Way, the Pleiades, and a sky band of constellations much like the modern zodiac.

See also DIVINE KINGS AND QUEENS; TEOTIHUACÁN (MAYA INTERACTIONS WITH); TIKAL

Further Reading

Aveni, Anthony F. *Skywatchers: A Revised and Updated Version of "Skywatchers of Ancient Mexico."* Austin: University of Texas Press, 2001.

Bricker, Harvey, and Victoria R. Bricker. *Astronomy in the Maya Codices.* Philadelphia, PA: American Philosophical Society, 2010.

Carlson, John B. *Venus-regulated Warfare and Ritual Sacrifice in Mesoamerica: Teotihuacan and the Cacaxtla "Star Wars" Connection.* Center for Archaeoastronomy Technical Publication, no. 7. College Park, MD: Center for Archaeoastronomy, 1991.

Krupp, E. C. *Echoes of the Ancient Skies: The Astronomy of Lost Civilizations.* New York: Harper & Row, 1983.

Milbrath, Susan. *Star Gods of the Maya: Astronomy in Art, Folklore, and Calendars.* Austin: University of Texas Press, 2000.

Voit, Claudia Ann. "The Venus 'Shell-over Star' Hieroglyph and Maya Warfare: An Examination of the Interpretation of a Mayan Symbol." MA thesis, Wayne State University, 2013.

■ WALTER R. T. WITSCHEY

BAJOS

A *bajo* is an area of low-lying, inundated terrain in the Maya lowlands, also known as *akalche* in some Mayan languages. *Bajo* refers most specifically to natural depressions within the interior portions of the Maya lowlands (see also **Map 2**) lying at elevations of 80 m or more above mean sea level. These depressions range in size from less than one km² to giants such as the Bajo de Ázucar and Bajo de Santa Fe, covering several hundred km². These larger *bajos* are largely the product of structural **geology**, forming in down-dropped fault blocks, whereas the smaller depressions are mainly formed by the dissolution of limestone. Today, most *bajos* desiccate in the dry season and contain low forest tolerant of **soil** moisture extremes, though some contain pockets of perennial moisture and grassy **vegetation** known as *cival*. *Bajos* account for between 40 and 60 percent of land surface areas in parts of the southern and central Maya lowlands.

Bajos in the Maya lowlands have attracted the attention of archaeologists because many large and early Maya centers (e.g., **Cival**, **El Mirador**, **Nakbé**, **Calakmul**, **Tikal**, and **Yaxnohcah**) developed along their margins. Since *bajos* have been considered inhospitable and unproductive environments, this spatial relationship has puzzled scholars. Some *bajos* exhibit paleoenvironmental evidence for former shallow **lakes** or perennial wetlands (though others do not), suggesting that these depressions experienced hydrologic changes as the result of climate drying or human-induced degradation. Thus, ancient communities may have been founded in response to environmental conditions that no longer exist within specific *bajos*.

Many *bajos* have aprons of deep, rich soil around their margins that were likely used for intensive agricultural production. These colluvial soil deposits were probably partly inadvertently produced by erosion of adjacent higher ground during the Preclassic. Some *bajos* show evidence of ancient wetland canals and field systems (see also **Water Management**), though most do not. The variability in the types of agriculture practiced in *bajos* reflects the complexity and variability of soil moisture conditions within these depressions as well as the needs and **subsistence** strategies of neighboring communities. *Bajos* were also an important source of timber for fuel and construction for the ancient Maya.

See also Aguadas; Cenote; Rejollada

Further Reading

Beach, Timothy, Sheryl Luzzadder-Beach, and Nicholas P. Dunning. "Human and Natural Impacts on Fluvial and Karst Systems in the Maya Lowlands." *Geomorphology* 101: 301–31, 2008.

Dunning, Nicholas P., Timothy Beach, and Sheryl Luzzadder-Beach. "Environmental Variability among Bajos in the Southern Maya Lowlands and Its Implications for Ancient Maya Civilization and Archaeology." In *Precolumbian Water Management: Ideology, Ritual, and Power,* edited by Lisa Joyce Lucero and Barbara W. Fash, 111–33. Tucson: University of Arizona Press, 2006.

Dunning, Nicholas P., Robert Griffin, John G. Jones, Richard Terry, Zachary Larsen, and Christopher Carr. "Life on the Edge: Tikal in a Bajo Landscape." In *Tikal: Paleoecology of an Ancient Maya City,* edited by David L. Lentz, Nicholas P. Dunning, and Vernon L. Scarborough. Cambridge, UK: Cambridge University Press, 2015.

Dunning, Nicholas P., Sheryl Luzzadder-Beach, Timothy Beach, John G. Jones, Vernon L. Scarborough, and T. Patrick Culbert. "Arising from the bajos: The evolution of neotropical landscape and the rise of Maya Civilization." *Annals of the Association of American Geographers.* 92: 267–82, 2002.

Gunn, Joel D., John E. Foss, William J. Folan, Maria del Rosario Domínguez Carrasco, and Betty B. Faust. "Bajo Sediments and the Hydraulic System of Calakmul, Campeche, Mexico." *Ancient Mesoamerica* 13: 297–315, 2002.

Hansen, Richard D., Steven Bozarth, John Jacob, David Wahl, and Thomas Schreiner. "Climatic and Environmental Variability in the Rise of Maya Civilization: A Preliminary Perspective from the Northern Petén." *Ancient Mesoamerica* 13: 273–95, 2002.

Harrison, Peter D. "The Rise of the Bajos and the Fall of the Maya." In *Social Process in Maya Prehistory,* edited by Norman Hammond, 469–508. New York: Academic Press, 1977.

Pope, Kevin O., and Bruce H. Dahlin. "Ancient Maya Wetland Agriculture: New Insights from Ecological and Remote Sensing Research." *Journal of Field Archaeology* 16: 87–106, 1989.

■ NICHOLAS DUNNING

BALL GAME/BALL COURT

A ritual and recreational ball game was played in and well beyond the Maya region, and evidence for it, archaeological remains of ball courts, may be found in ancient sites throughout Mesoamerica. From bas-relief panels (see also **Art**) and painted **ceramics**, a picture emerges that at the level of Classic Maya rulers, the ball game was of great ritual importance, perhaps as a reenactment of the Maya creation myth found in the ***Popol Vuh.*** It is unclear, however, whether elites played the game or conducted pageants of which the ball game was a part, or both (see also **Rites and Rituals**).

The first known ball court dates to 1300 BC at Paso de la Amada, in the Soconusco region of Chiapas, Mexico, on the Pacific coast. Other early courts are from the **Olmec** area, but more than 1,300 ball courts are scattered throughout Mesoamerica and beyond, from **Honduras** and **El Salvador** to Arizona.

Maya ball courts are shaped like the letter "I" with a central playing area and two end zones. Most ball courts have two parallel sides of masonry with a sloping area at ground level (bench wall), a terrace (bench), and a sloping or vertical wall above (apron), all designed to rebound the ball back into the playing area. Seating was often on top of the side walls, accessible by back stairways. The short ends were either open or had small structures to enclose them. There may be side markers on the walls at midfield, or a trio of stone markers on the centerline of the playing area. Such markers first appear in the Classic.

The largest known ball court is at **Chichen Itza** and has a playing surface 90 by 30.4 m with structures at each end. The small ball court in the Great Plaza of **Tikal**, adjacent to Temple I, by contrast, is 16 by 5.6 m with ends effectively formed by the side walls of T-I and the central acropolis. Tikal is also home to a unique triple ball court with three playing areas side-by-side, separated by common bench walls, terrace, and apron.

The bas-relief panels on the bench walls of the ball court at Chichen Itza present a grisly scene. A ball centers the picture. The image of a skull on it conveys the possibility that the ball was a rubber-wound human skull. The ball is flanked by seven ballplayers on each side. The left-central figure is elaborately dressed in ceremonial regalia, including a large quetzal-feather headdress. In his right hand he holds a large flint knife (see also **Chert**), while in his left hand he holds the decapitated head of his opponent by the hair. Opposite him, to the right of the ball, is the kneeling figure of his headless opponent with gouts of blood from the neck stump represented as serpents and water-lily plants. Just outside the ball court stands a skull rack (*tzompantli*), where the bas-relief imagery shows the heads of presumed sacrificial victims arrayed on posts.

Ballplayer regalia vary. **Chichen Itza** illustrations (from paintings and relief carvings) and effigy figurines (see also **Jaina**) of ballplayers show heavy hip pads, or yokes of stone or wood, and helmets, as well as the use of knuckle-dusters, carved hand-stones for striking the ball. Three types of carved stone artifacts are thought to be particularly associated with the ball game. Yokes appear to be stone copies of the hip protectors worn by players. They seem to be too small and heavy, however, to have actually been worn, even by athletes. They are probably stone copies of the actual wooden and/or leather apparatus. *Palmas* and *hachas* are smaller stone statues, usually anthropomorphic or zoomorphic, that seem designed to project from the front of the yokes—they have a notch appropriate to seat them on a yoke. All three types of artifacts are often beautifully carved in rare, fine-grained stone. The finest examples are works of high art, found in museums around the world.

The earliest rubber balls in **Mesoamerica** (900 BC) are from the Olmec site El Manatí, Veracruz, situated 14.5 km southeast of San Lorenzo Tenochtitlán. Balls were of solid hard rubber, or rubber wound around a calabash or human skull.

Syllabic glyphs for the Maya *pitz*, to play ball, and for ballplayer appear on ceramics, in **codices**, and in carved scenes of the ball game.

Although the precise ritual significance of the ball game, as played by elites, is still unclear, its importance to Maya rulers is demonstrated by the presence of elaborate ball courts, the portraits of rulers in sophisticated finery portrayed on ceramics, and the accompanying imagery of human sacrifice.

See also ARCHITECTURE OVERVIEW; LANGUAGE AND WRITING OVERVIEW

Further Reading

Agrinier, P. "The Ballcourts of Southern Chiapas, Mexico." In *The Mesoamerican Ballgame: International Ballgame Symposium: Selected Papers*, edited by Vernon L. Scarborough and David R. Wilcox, 175–94. Tucson: University of Arizona Press, 1991.

Colas, Pierre, and Alexander W. Voss. "A Game of Life and Death—The Maya Ball Game." In *Maya: Divine Kings of the Rainforest*, edited by Nikolai Grube, Eva Eggebrecht, and Matthias Seidel. Cologne, Germany: Könemann, 2006. Distributed by John Wilson.

Ekholm, Susanna M. "Ceramic Figurines and the Mesoamerican Ballgame." In *The Mesoamerican Ballgame*, edited by Vernon L. Scarborough and David R. Wilcox. Tucson: University of Arizona Press, 1991.

Hill, W. D., M. Blake, and J. E. Clark. "Ball Court Design Dates Back 3,400 Years." *Nature* 392, no. 6679: 878, 1998.

Kurjack, Edward B., Ruben Maldonado C., and Merle Greene Robertson. "Ballcourts of the Northern Maya Lowlands." In *The Mesoamerican Ballgame*, edited by Vernon L. Scarborough and David R. Wilcox. Tucson: University of Arizona Press, 1991.

Scarborough, Vernon L., and David R. Wilcox, eds. *The Mesoamerican Ballgame: International Ballgame Symposium: Selected Papers.* Tucson: University of Arizona Press, 1991.

Tedlock, Dennis. *Popol Vuh: The Mayan Book of the Dawn of Life.* Rev. ed. New York: Simon & Schuster, 1996.

■ WALTER R. T. WITSCHEY

BECAN

A dry moat-fortified (see also **Fortifications**) site in the state of Campeche, **Mexico**, near its border with Quintana Roo (see also **Maps 1** and **3**), Becan (18.5° N, 89.5° W) was explored as part of expeditions to the Río Bec region reported by Maurice de Périgny in 1909 and by Raymond E. Merwin in his 1913 doctoral dissertation. It was studied in detail during the expeditions of Ruppert and Denison in the 1930s. Subsequent studies between 1969 and 1971 directed by E. Wyllys Andrews IV led to major reports about Becan, including its ceramics by Joseph W. Ball, and some of its monumental structures and the defensive wall and moat by David L. Webster. Prentice M. Thomas directed a detailed survey of the site ceremonial center and settlement outside the moat.

Between 1983 and 1985 Román Piña Chán and ENAH (National School of Anthropology and History) students continued the clearing, excavating, and consolidating of monumental architecture, especially Strs. 1, 2 and 3. A decade later (1992–1994) INAH's Ricardo Bueno recommended research at the site (St. VIII and the **ball court**). Luz Evelia Campaña excavated and restored other buildings (Str. 9) during 1999–2001. In recent years, maintenance and restoration works have been supervised by INAH's Vicente Suárez A.

Becan was first occupied in the Middle Formative period about 600 BC. Its occupants constructed the defensive moat in the Early Classic, using the excavated limestone rubble to build an embankment on the interior side, perhaps in response to threats from **Calakmul**, 60 km to the southwest. These fortifications are contemporaneous with incursions at **Tikal** by **Teotihuacán**, and Teotihuacán **ceramics** appear at Becan somewhat later. Recent reevaluation of the moat indicates it also was used to store rainwater, an indispensable resource for life in a region where good water is difficult to find (see also **Water Management**).

The defenses, now badly eroded, measured 11.6 m from the bottom of the moat to the top of the inner embankment and created a 30.5-m-wide hostile area to enemies. There are seven entrance causeways across the moat, leading through the embankment, each about 3 m wide. The perimeter of the moat is 1.9 km, and encloses 25 ha and most of the major **architecture** in the ceremonial core. Becan's fortunes declined in the Early Classic, but experienced resurgence in the Late Classic.

The monumental architecture enclosed by the moat is still impressive, and much has been restored. Str. 9, for example, is more than 30 m tall. The central core is organized around three major plazas, with the architecture organized into the East Group on the highest part of the limestone outcropping; the North-Central Group with four of Becan's largest structures; and the West Group, which has a **ball court** among other structures.

Construction of major monumental architecture ended about AD 830, the time of collapse throughout much of the Maya area (see also **Classic Maya Collapse**). The site was then abandoned, as were its sister cities nearby, such as Xpuhil, that shared a similar **Río Bec** architectural style. There are no known inscriptions giving the history of Becan, and our knowledge comes primarily from the archaeological and ceramic record.

Further Reading

Ball, Joseph W., and E. Wyllys Andrews. *Preclassic Architecture at Becan, Campeche, Mexico*. Middle American Research Institute, Occasional Papers no. 3. New Orleans, LA: Middle American Research Institute, Tulane University, 1978.

Bueno Cano, Ricardo. "Excavaciones en la región Rio Bec: 1984–1985." Tesís, Escuela Nacional de Antropología e Historia, México D.F., 1989.

———. *Entre un río de robles: Un acercamiento a la arqueología de la Región Río Bec*. Colección Científica 411. Mexico, D.F., Mexico: Instituto Nacional de Antropolgía y História, 1999.

Campaña V., Luz Evelia. "Contribuciones a la historia de Becán." *Arqueología Mexicana* 75: 48–53, 2005.

Piña Chán, Román. *Cultura y ciudades mayas de Campeche*. México: Editora del Sureste/Gobierno del Estado de Campeche, 1985.

Ruppert, Karl, and John Hopkins Denison. *Archaeological Reconnaissance in Campeche, Quintana Roo, and Petén*. Carnegie Institution of Washington, Publication 543. Washington, DC: Carnegie Institution of Washington, 1943.

Suárez Aguilar, Vicente. "Labores de mantenimiento e impermeabilización en la Estructura I de Becán durante la temporada 1996." *Gaceta Universitaria* 31–32: 41–46, 1996.

———. "Trabajos de restauración llevados a cabo en Becán y Chicanná." *Gaceta Universitaria* 27–28: 50–54, 1996.

Thomas, Prentice M. *Prehistoric Maya Settlement Patterns at Becan, Campeche, Mexico*. Middle American Research Series, Publication 45. New Orleans, LA: Middle American Research Institute, Tulane University, 1981.

Webster, David. "Una Ciudad Maya Fortificada. Becán, Campeche." *Arqueología Mexicana* 18: 32–35, 1996.

Webster, David L. *Defensive Earthworks at Becan, Campeche, Mexico: Implications for Maya Warfare*. Middle American Research Institute, Publication 41. New Orleans, LA: Middle American Research Institute, Tulane University, 1976.

■ WALTER R. T. WITSCHEY, CLIFFORD T. BROWN,
AND ANTONIO BENAVIDES C.

BELIZE

The modern nation of Belize (see also **Map 1**), on the Caribbean coast of the Yucatan Peninsula, participated in the fully wider developments of the Maya region. People were in the region by Archaic times, such as at **Richmond Hill**, and Maya settlements were under way in the Middle Formative. The largest and most powerful Maya city was **Caracol**, on the western edge of the Maya Mountains, and other important ancient sites in Belize include **Lamanai, Cerros, El Pilar, Xunantunich**, Nohmul, Cuello, **Cahal Pech**, and **Altun Ha**, among many others. Most major polities collapsed as part of the ninth-century **Classic Maya collapse**, which caused most cites to the west in Guatemala to be abandoned. Some Maya continued to occupy small coastal villages for the access to marine resources through the Postclassic.

Spanish conquerors sailing along the coast chose not to settle due to the Maya resistance in Belize and the Mexican state of Quintana Roo. The first European settlers were English pirates in 1638, and there developed a slave-driven industry in logging. The last repulse of attempts by the Spanish to control the area was in 1798. Britain abolished slavery in 1838, but the effects on the local black population were small. In 1862 Belize became a Crown Colony called British Honduras. Following the Second World War, an independence movement resulted in self-governance by 1964. British Honduras was renamed Belize in 1973 and gained full independence in 1981. Queen Elizabeth II is the "head of state" for the Belizean constitutional monarchy. In practice, the prime minister and cabinet exercise executive authority in government.

The population mix of Belize continues to change rather rapidly due to an outflow of Belizeans seeking jobs, mainly in the United States, and an inflow of Spanish-speaking Central Americans from **Guatemala, Honduras**, and **El Salvador**. Chinese, Europeans, and North Americans (especially of the German-speaking Mennonite sect) add to the inflow. The ethnic mix today is about 50 percent mestizo, 25 percent Creole, 11 percent Maya, and 6 percent Garifuna.

Those who speak a modern version of the ancient Maya language number about 9 percent. The chief dialects are Yucatec Maya in the north along the borders with Guatemala and **Mexico** (Quintana Roo), and Mopan and Q'eqchi' in the southwest of the country (see also **Writing and Language Overview**; *Yucatecan Maya Languages*; **Highland Maya Languages**).

The Belize Institute for Archaeology, a part of the National Institute of Culture and History (NICH), is responsible for the administration of ancient Maya sites. Their mission is to provide research, protection, preservation, and sustainable management of Belize's cultural and archaeological resources.

Further Reading

Belize Institute of Archaeology. National Institute of Culture and History, Institute of Archaeology, 2014. http://www.nichbelize.org/ia-general/welcome-to-the-institute-of-archaeology.html. 2014.

Law, Danny. "Mayan Historical Linguistics in a New Age." *Language and Linguistics Compass* 7, no. 3: 141–56, 2013.

U.S. Central Intelligence Agency. *The World Factbook, Central America and Caribbean: Belize*. 2014. https://www.cia.gov/library/publications/the-world-factbook/geos/bh.html.

■ WALTER R. T. WITSCHEY

BONAMPAK

In the last decade of the eighth century AD, amid widespread regional warfare, King Yajaw Chan Muwaan of Bonampak and members of his court, particularly three important lords of ch'ok status, commissioned Structure 1 and the paintings within. Brought to modern attention in 1946 by Giles Healey, today these murals still form the most complete and most complex Maya painting program to survive from the first millennium AD (see also **Wall Painting**). See figure 4.

Although small **palace** structures with three doorways are common at **Yaxchilan**, within whose sphere Bonampak (16.7° N, 91.1° W) generally fell in this era, the three separate room configuration at Bonampak is novel, presumably designed to maximize wall space for painting. Three carved and thickly painted lintels over the doorways celebrate the victories of the Yaxchilan king along with the Bonampak king and his father.

A single master painter may have designed the entire program and laid down a sketch in a thin red hematite (iron ore) pigment on smooth white plaster; many others worked on the paintings, mixing pigments, especially Maya blue, for consistency from batch to

Figure 4. Reconstruction of Bonampak Room 2, North Wall, Yale University Art Gallery. Gift of Bonampak Documentation Project. Illustrated by Heather Hurst and Leonard Ashby. Courtesy of Mary Miller.

batch; painting backgrounds; layering colors to achieve a shimmering array of hues and tonalities; and using local binders in a traditional technique that is different from European fresco. Typically, two to four skilled calligraphers limned the final black outline that gives the figures dimension and yields legible texts in any one room.

Reserved panels for glyphs that were not painted, particularly in Rooms 1 and 3, give the program a sense of being unfinished. An Initial Series text in Room 1 notes two signal events, an installation in office of a person whose name does not survive in AD 790, followed by a building dedication statement in 791.

Room 1 features an enthroned (but unnamed) lord, accompanied by his family, as he receives tribute of chocolate (see also **Cacao**) and spondylus shells from 14 lords in white mantles. An unusual scene in which the three *ch'oks* are dressed on the north wall is followed by the depiction on all four walls of processions, with the three *ch'oks* dancing at the center of the south wall. Musicians play maracas, drums, trumpets, and turtle shells, while hooded performers wait their turn; on the opposite wall, regional governors, or *sajals*, stand on parade (see also **Music and Dance**). The large Initial Series text is framed by parasol bearers, hidden to the left of the text and visible at the right; the parasols alternate, effectively creating quotation marks around the written words.

The largest battle painting in the Maya region wraps around three walls of Room 2, engulfing the viewer in a depiction of scripted chaos, with warriors charging into battle toward the top and left, then attacking specific victims at the center of the large south wall, and finally, driving captives to the ground at the baseline (see also **Warfare, Warriors, and Weapons**). Named in the longest text of the battle, King Yajaw Chan Muwaan takes a prominent captive, whose foreshortened body dramatically punctuates the wall.

A masterpiece of composition, with its balanced figures and dramatically positioned dead captive along the diagonal, the north wall of Room 2 is the most frequently reproduced wall of the Bonampak paintings. King Yajaw Chan Muwaan presides over the presentation and bloodletting of captives taken in the battle; his two wives attend the scene; constellations, including the turtle—whose three bright stars across the back are known elsewhere as the belt of Orion—reign from the upper margin of the vault (see also **Astronomy**).

In all rooms, viewers would have needed to sit on the built-in bench in order to see the north wall, the wall that features the door to each room. Excavations into the bench of Room 2 in 2010 uncovered a tomb within, accompanied by elite offerings; part of the cranium had been removed (see also **Royal Tombs**). Most scholars believe that this is the burial chamber of Yajaw Chan Muwaan, who probably died during the making of the building and its paintings. Anyone sitting on the bench would thus have sat directly on the king's remains.

In Room 3, the three *ch'oks* of Room 1 dance atop an eight-level pyramid in costumes of towering feather headdresses and feathered "wings," extending from the waist; seven additional lords in similar attire dance at the base. Large yellow and red flowers may be sunflowers; hot solar **deities** preside from the upper margin. Directly at center and facing the observer as she or he walks in the door are two servants who drag a limp, dead body from the steps; a kneeling sacrificer above has removed the heart (see also **Rites and Rituals**).

The last project of the site, the paintings serve as a window into life and art on the eve of the Maya collapse.

See also ARCHITECTURE OVERVIEW; CLASSIC MAYA COLLAPSE; DIVINE KINGS AND QUEENS

Further Reading

de la Fuente, Beatriz, and Leticia Staines Cicero, eds. *La pintura mural prehispánica en México II: Área Maya—Bonampak.* 2 vols. México, D.F.: Universidad Nacional Autónoma de México, Instituto de Investigaciones Estéticas, 1998.
Houston, Stephen D. "A Splendid Predicament: Young men in Classic Maya Society." *Cambridge Archaeological Journal* 19, no. 2: 149–78, 2009.
———. "The Good Prince: Transition, Texting and Moral Narrative in the Murals of Bonampak, Chiapas, Mexico." *Cambridge Archaeological Journal* 22, no. 2: 153–75, 2012.
Miller, Mary Ellen, and Claudia Brittenham. *The Spectacle of the Late Maya Court: Reflections on the Murals of Bonampak.* William & Bettye Nowlin Series in Art, History, and Culture of the Western Hemisphere. Austin: University of Texas Press, 2013.
Roach, John. "Headless Man's Tomb Found under Maya Torture Mural." *National Geographic News*, Match 12, 2010. http://news.nationalgeographic.com/news/2010/03/100312-headless-bonampak-tomb-maya-torture-mural/.

■ MARY MILLER

BURIALS

Archaeologists and physical anthropologists study burials in order to understand culture. The different burial types of the ancient Maya represent the relationships between individual and community and are a direct reflection of culture. Burials consist of a physical and cultural context, meaning skeletal materials and the space wherein they are found must be analyzed with knowledge of Mayan **religion**, ceremony, tradition, and cultural identity. This requires the collaboration of specialists in Mayan anthropology, archaeology, and bioarchaeology. Together their expertise is combined to examine burials in terms of burial type and context, artifacts (see also **Portable Objects**) and cultural material, osteology and physical bodies, demography, and biodistance or the study of variation to understand the differences and similarities of groups.

Ancient Mayan burial types vary greatly through space and time, which makes for compelling research questions concerning cultural change and continuity. Cemeteries have been uncovered in residential and domestic areas, both in large complexes and in small family units under houses, as well as in elaborate tombs (see also **Royal Tombs**) and **temples**. Burials are also present in natural spaces such as water caverns and **caves**. These burial locales could be the original place the individual was interred (primary), or they may have been moved several times and redeposited in a different location (secondary). Archaeologists focus on these details with cultural context to investigate spatial change, social structure (see also **Class Structure**), politics, and differences among families and groups in different regions.

When a burial is uncovered in the field, it is vital to collect as much contextual data as possible. This includes the provenience of the burial, surrounding environment, archaeological context, associated artifacts, and details of the human remains. This information might include location of the burial in terms of other known sites and accessibility, and an analysis of the artifacts to determine status and time period. The items left with the body, offerings and grave goods, suggest social structure, wealth, and honor, and reflect how the individual was revered throughout life. Burial offerings of the ancient Maya included stone tools, shells, beads, **ceramics**, jade, effigies, animal remains (see also **Fauna**), and companion sacrifices.

Bioarchaeologists collect metric and nonmetric data on the skeletal remains to determine age, sex, and stature and to assess disease and trauma. These are important details for understanding the composition of the burial and for the analysis of patterns and distributions among other burials. The remains can be specifically analyzed in terms of trauma and violence to understand war and politics (see also **Warfare, Warriors, and Weapons**), or bone chemistry studies can be done to estimate **diets** and health. The remains are also examined for evidence of defleshing or modification. Ancient Maya postmortem modification included painting the remains red with cinnabar, hematite, or red ochre and replacing skeletal elements with jade and shell. Antemortem changes, such as cranial modifications and dental filings and inlays, are also explored to understand how the body was treated throughout life (see also **Physical/Biological Anthropology**).

Burials provide insight into many aspects of the ancient Mayan world, and this relies on the partnership of multiple anthropological specialists and approaches. The existence, continuation, discrepancies, and evolution of burial practices are all direct reflections of the Maya. Burials have the potential to yield opportunities in studies concerning identity, religion, ritual, politics, health, behavior, and fluctuations through time. The collection of both biological and cultural data is imperative in the quest to understand individual and collective lived experiences.

See also BONAMPAK; CACAO; CALAKMUL; CARACOL; CERRO MAYA/CERROS; CHAC II; COPÁN; DZIBILCHALTUN; ECCENTRIC LITHICS; FAUNA; GEOLOGY; HOLMUL; IXIMCHÉ; JAINA; MAYA QUEENS; MIDDLE CLASSIC HIATUS; MUSIC AND DANCE; NAJ TUNICH; OBSIDIAN; OXKINTOK; PALENQUE; PHYSICAL/BIOLOGICAL ANTHROPOLOGY; PIEDRAS NEGRAS–DYNASTIC SEQUENCE; PUSILHA; RIO AZUL; RITES OF PASSAGE; ROYAL TOMBS; SIN CABEZAS; TEOTIHUACÁN (MAYA INTERACTION WITH); TEXTILES AND CLOTHING; TRADE ROUTES; TULUM; WALL PAINTING; WARFARE, WARRIORS, AND WEAPONS; ZACUALPA; ZACULEU

Further Reading

Fitzsimmons, James L., and Shimada Izumi, eds. *Living with the Dead: Mortuary Ritual in Mesoamerica.* Tucson: University of Arizona Press, 2011.

Prufer, Keith M., and James Edward Brady. *Stone Houses and Earth Lords: Maya Religion in the Cave Context.* Mesoamerican Worlds. Boulder: University Press of Colorado, 2005.

Tiesler, Vera, and Andrea Cucina. "New Perspectives on Human Sacrifice and Ritual Body Treatment in Ancient Maya Society." In *Society for American Archaeology Annual Meeting.* New York: Springer, 2007.

White, Tim D., Michael Timothy Black, and Pieter A. Folkens. *Human Osteology.* 3rd ed. Boston: Elsevier Academic Press, 2012.

Whittington, Stephen L., and David M. Reed. *Bones of the Maya: Studies of Ancient Skeletons.* Tuscaloosa: University of Alabama Press, 2006.

■ KENDRA L. PHILMON

C

CACAO

Cacao played a significant role in the economic, ritual, and political life of the pre-Hispanic Maya, as highlighted by its presence in **iconography** and hieroglyphic captions spanning a millennium in time. The different drinks and foods containing cacao consumed by the Maya (see also **Diet**) are described in hieroglyphic texts, the most common being a frothy drink that is depicted in scenes showing life in royal courts. Cacao also served as an offering in other contexts and as a principal component in ceremonies associated with life transitions, including birth, initiation, marriage, and death. Its scientific name, *Theobroma cacao*, "food of the gods," is an apt description of the role it played within ancient Maya culture. Moreover, ethnographic research suggests that cacao—in either seed or beverage form—continues to have a place in mediating social relationships (i.e., marriage negotiations and betrothals) in some Maya communities (see also **Rites and Rituals**; **Language and Writing Overview**).

The earliest evidence for cacao use in the Maya area dates to 600–400 BC. At that time, the fruit of the plant was likely fermented to make an intoxicating drink; it was only later that techniques were developed for processing the seeds to make food and beverages in which chocolate was the principal ingredient.

Among the Classic Maya, cacao was consumed in many contexts, including elite feasting rituals held to cement social and political alliances. The codex-style Princeton Vase illustrates the final stage in the preparation of the cacao beverage—the act of frothing the cacao, which is being done by the woman at the right, who pours it from a height into another vessel (see figure 5). This scene highlights the role women played in preparing cacao for consumption, although they did not participate in the actual feasts.

Cacao seeds were also an important item of **tribute** for Classic and later Maya peoples, as well as a unit of currency. Because the tree can only be grown in very humid regions, the seeds had to be imported to those areas that were not productive for growing cacao. Cacao seeds were considered one of the most important luxury trade items (see also **Trade Routes**) and were even reproduced—and indeed, counterfeited—in other materials, including clay.

Cacao's importance in the social, ritual, and political sphere stems in part from the role it played in mythology. In the K'iche' Maya creation story related in the *Popol Vuh*,

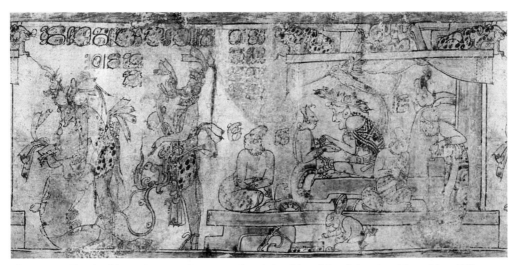

Figure 5. The frothing of cacao shown on the right side of the Princeton Vase (Kerr 511). Part of a scene depicting the Lord of the Underworld seated on his throne, surrounded by a retinue of women, one of whom is receiving a bracelet from him. In front of the raised dais, a rabbit scribe makes annotations in a screenfold codex. A second scene (to the left) depicts the decapitation of a bound prisoner. The hieroglyphic caption above this scene specifies; "It is his drinking vessel for fresh? cacao." The cacao glyph is the fourth from the left in the top row. Photo courtesy Justin Kerr.

cacao is one of the precious substances released from the mountain within which it was stored during primordial times, along with maize from which humans were formed. Its divine origin stems from the fact that it grew from the body of the Maize God, who was sacrificed by the Lords of the Underworld (see also **Deities**).

Mythological scenes featuring cacao are a common component of Classic period art. Various forms of **ceramic** vessels, found in burials throughout the Maya region, include hieroglyphic texts identifying them as the drinking vessel of a particular historical individual and specifying the type of cacao they originally contained. Studies of the contents of a number of these vessels, first carried out on residues from a lock-top jar with a cacao glyph on its rim found at **Rio Azul**, reveal the chemical signature of cacao, indicated by a combination of theobromine and caffeine. Cacao is also depicted as an offering in Postclassic sources, where it is linked to deities with associations of fertility and sustenance and also forms part of marriage rituals and bloodletting ceremonies.

Colonial sources report that cacao was grown on plantations in Yucatan and imported from Tabasco and **Honduras**. **Diego de Landa**, writing in the mid-sixteenth century, described several ceremonies involving the use of cacao, including one celebrated by plantation owners to honor the deity of merchants and cacao and another in which participants were anointed with a mixture of "virgin" water, cacao, and crushed flowers to mark their transition to puberty.

The rich mythology surrounding the production and use of cacao by Mayan speakers in different eras and regions points to its enduring importance in Maya culture. Although not used as frequently in rituals today, cacao continues to mark important life events such as birth and marriage, especially in the Guatemalan highlands, and to symbolize fertility in agricultural ceremonies practiced by Ch'orti' Maya speakers in Honduras.

See also BONAMPAK; CEREN; CERRO MAYA/CERROS; CHAC II; COMALCALCO; COTZUMAL-HUAPA; DIET; EK BALAM; MATHEMATICS; OLMEC-MAYA INTERACTIONS; PACIFIC COASTAL PLAIN; REJOLLADA; RIO AZUL; RITES AND RITUALS; TRADE ROUTES; TRIBUTE; WRITING SYSTEMS OF MESOAMERICA

Further Reading

Coe, Sophie D., and Michael D. Coe. *The True History of Chocolate*. New York: Thames & Hudson, 1996.

Grivetti, Louis Evan, and Howard-Yana Shapiro, eds. *Chocolate: History, Culture, and Heritage*. Hoboken, NJ: Wiley, 2009.

McNeil, Cameron L., ed. *Chocolate in Mesoamerica: A Cultural History of Cacao*. Gainesville: University Press of Florida, 2006.

■ GABRIELLE VAIL

CAHAL PECH

On the south side of modern San Ignacio, **Belize**, Cahal Pech (17.1° N, 89.1° W) sits atop a hill with a strategic position near the juncture of the Macal and Belize Rivers. **Ceramics** place its first occupation in the late Early Formative, but with strong growth in the Classic. It was abandoned at the end of the Classic concurrent with the **Classic Maya collapse**.

Early mentions of the site include those by Linton Satterthwaite, who made a site survey and conducted excavations in 1951, and Gordon Willey in his 1953–1955 survey of the Belize Valley. Jaime Awe, director of the National Institute of Archaeology (NICH), Belize, reports looting occurred at the site from the 1960s to the mid-1980s, halted by a joint effort of the San Ignacio community and NICH. From 1988 to 2000 Awe and Joe Ball conducted a research and reconstruction program at the site. Their reports provide a clear picture of site organization and culture history

First occupation (1200–1000 BC) led to a thriving economy in the Middle Formative, with trade bringing jade, obsidian, Caribbean shells, and **Olmec** iconography. Classic elites produced most of the standing **architecture** visible today, including tall temple-**pyramids**, multiroom range structures, and two **ball courts**, totaling about 34 major buildings. These are gathered around a central plaza about 80 m across. Occupants of Cahal Pech were utilizing nearby **caves** for ceremonies to the rain god and, apparently, human sacrifice (see also **Rites and Rituals**).

A pending research question about Cahal Pech is why it was abandoned during the Classic Maya collapse in a region in which several other sites continued to flourish for a few hundred more years.

Further Reading

Awe, Jaime. "Cahal Pech." *Archaeology* 2000 (June): 2000.

———. *Maya Cities and Sacred Caves: A Guide to the Maya Sites of Belize*. Benque Viejo del Carmen, Belize: Cubola Productions, 2007.

———. "Architectural Manifestations of Power and Prestige: Examples from the Monumental Architecture at Baking Pot, Cahal Pech, and Xunantunich." In *Research Reports in Belizean Archaeology*, 5:159–73. Belmopan, Belize: The Institute of Archaeology, National Institute of Culture and History, 2008.

Awe, Jaime, Cassandra Bill, Mark Campbell, and David Cheetham. "Early Middle Formative Occupation in the Central Maya Lowlands: Recent Evidence from Cahal Pech, Belize." *Papers from the Institute of Archaeology* 1: 1–5, 1990.

Ball, Joseph W. *Cahal Pech, the Ancient Maya, and Modern Belize: The Story of an Archaeological Park*. Ninth University Research Lecture. San Diego, CA: San Diego State University Press, 1993.

Iannone, Gyles. *Rural Complexity in the Cahal Pech Microregion*. Monograph Series, edited by Gyles Iannone and Samuel V. Connell. Los Angeles: The Cotsen Institute of Archaeology at UCLA Perspectives on Ancient Maya Rural Complexity, 2003.

Willey, Gordon R., William R. Bullard, Jr., John B. Glass, and James C. Gifford. *Prehistoric Maya Settlements in the Belize Valley*. Papers of the Peabody Museum of American Archaeology and Ethnology, vol. 54. Cambridge, MA: Peabody Museum, Harvard University, 1965.

■ WALTER R. T. WITSCHEY

CALAKMUL

From its origins in the Middle Preclassic until its abandonment in the Terminal Classic period, Calakmul (18.1° N, 89.8° W), located in the southern extreme of Campeche, **Mexico**, was one of the largest and most powerful **Maya** cities. Two of the tallest pyramidal platforms (see also **Pyramids**) ever built by the Maya—Strs. I and II—give Calakmul its modern name: "Two Mounds Close Together" (see figure 6). With 117 carved **stelae**, Calakmul has more such monuments than any other Maya site. Sadly, their texts are highly eroded and largely illegible. Thus Calakmul's importance as revealed by hieroglyphic texts is best known from other Maya cities. The lords of no Classic Maya polity—not even **Tikal**—are mentioned more times in hieroglyphic inscriptions than the "Divine Snake Lords" of Calakmul. During its heyday in the late sixth and seventh centuries AD, Calakmul exerted hegemonic domination or suzerainty over many sites up to 240 km away. Much of what we understand about Maya politics during the Late Classic is interpreted

Figure 6. Calakmul, Str. I (left) and Str. II (right). Original photo by Geoffrey Braswell, 2010.

through the lens of conflict between the two rival "superpowers," Tikal and Calakmul (see also **Warfare, Warriors, and Weapons**). The period of Snake Lord supremacy began with a defeat of Tikal in AD 562 during the **Middle Classic Hiatus**. It ended with the defeat of Calakmul by Tikal in AD 695. Nonetheless, Calakmul still remained an important royal seat, and a Divine Snake Lord was mentioned as one of four great kings in AD 849 at **Ceibal** (Seibal). Demographic decline began in the late eighth century, and Calakmul was abandoned sometime in the tenth century.

Calakmul was rediscovered by Cyrus Lundell in 1931, who gave the site its name after seeing Strs. I and II from an airplane. In later years, **Sylvanus Morley** and Charles Lindbergh used the two great mounds as navigational points of reference when charting the first commercial air route across Yucatan and Guatemala. Limited archaeological work was carried out at Calakmul by the Carnegie Institution of Washington during the 1930s. William Folan of the Universidad Autónoma de Campeche directed a major project from 1982 until 1994. Four huge structures (Strs. I, II, III, and VII) were cleared, partially excavated, and consolidated, and the city was systematically surveyed. Since 1993, excavation and consolidation has continued under the direction of Ramón Carrasco Vargas of the Instituto Nacional de Antropología e Historia. In 1989 the Calakmul Biosphere Reserve, the largest such park in Mexico, was established. Calakmul was designated a UNESCO World Heritage Site in 2002.

Calakmul is located on a karst uplift (see also **Geology**) bordered by the **Bajo** El Laberinto, a seasonal swamp and a source of water and **chert**. The great Preclassic Maya city of **El Mirador** can be seen from atop Strs. I and II. A *sacbe* (**causeway**) connecting Calakmul to El Mirador and continuing south to El Tintal has been reported but remains to be ground checked. In all, this causeway could be 68 km in length—the second longest known in the Maya region. Str. I at Calakmul is specifically aligned so as to point to one of the two great platforms at El Mirador. The central core of Calakmul is surrounded by linked ravines that channel water into 13 rectangular reservoirs. When full, these held as much as 200 million liters, providing water to the city of ca. 50,000 inhabitants throughout the year.

The center of Calakmul is dominated by a north-south plaza. Str. II forms the southern end of the plaza. Str. VII is at the north. The east and west sides form a massive astronomical commemoration group (Group-E configuration) designed to celebrate the equinoxes and solstices (see also **Astronomy**; **Astronomical Observatories**; figure 3). Str. V, a relatively low platform, is found in the southern half of the central plaza. This basic architectural template is found not only at Calakmul, but also at **Naranjo**, **Xunantunich**, and perhaps **Quiriguá**, demonstrating ties with far-flung allies. To the west and east of the main plaza are two enormous **palace** compounds called the Great and Small Acropoli. North of the plaza and behind Str. VII is an area that possibly served as a **market**. It is here that famous murals depicting Lady Nine Stone and the preparation of food and goods in a market scene have been found (see also **Wall Painting**; **Diet**).

The ancient name of the city of Calakmul was Uxte'tuun or "Three Stone Place," a reference to the mythical celestial three-stone hearth of creation. This name is echoed by the many triadic structures at the site (see also **Architecture Overview**). Another frequent toponym is Chiik Nahb, perhaps translated as "Coatimundi Pool," which may be the ancient name for the swamp. Although the city was the royal seat and capital of Divine Snake Lords (K'uhul Kaan Ajawob) during the Late Classic, that Emblem Glyph (see also **Decipherment**) was first carved at Calakmul only in AD 636. Earlier, a local Emblem Glyph whose main sign is a bat head appears on Calakmul Stelae 59 and 114, as well as on monuments at other important sites in the region. Thus, there is reason to think that the Divine Snake Lords based their kingdom somewhere else during earlier times, establishing themselves at Calakmul during their seventh-century apogee.

Centered at Calakmul, the seventh-century Snake kingdom was comprised of an inner zone defined by the secondary cities of Oxpemul, La Muñeca, Altamira, Balakbal, **Naachtun**, and Uxul. Beyond this was a zone of hegemonic control that extended into central Campeche, Quintana Roo, and northern Petén (see also **Map 1**). Finally, Calakmul had an extensive outer sphere of political influence that sometimes encompassed allies as far away as **Toniná**, **El Perú-Waka'**, **Dos Pilas**, **Naranjo**, **Caracol**, and perhaps **Quiriguá**. Although the boundaries of the Snake kingdom are not precisely known and certainly shifted over time, a rough population estimate of one to two million seems plausible for its Late Classic maximum.

The oldest pottery at Calakmul belongs to the Mamom complex, known throughout much of the Maya lowlands and dated to the late Middle Preclassic period (see also **Ceramics**; **Ceramic Analysis**). A large building decorated with stucco was discovered deeply buried within Str. II (see also **Art**). This earliest known monumental structure is contemporary with similar late Middle Preclassic platforms at **Nakbé**, then the largest site in the region and the capital of a flourishing chiefdom. During the Late Preclassic, Strs. I and II (the two largest at Calakmul) reached their current height. Although remodeled many times, these massive platforms and their superstructures dominated the city for a millennium. Substructures of Str. IV and VI that formed a large Group-E configuration also were built at this time (see also **Astronomical Observatories**). It is generally assumed that Preclassic Calakmul was first under the political sway of Nakbé and later El Mirador. Given the orientation of Str. I and the *sacbe* connecting Calakmul to it, this seems likely. It may be that several Snake Lords mentioned on ninth-century dynastic **codex-style vases** were legendary kings of El Mirador.

After about AD 150, Calakmul emerged from the collapse of El Mirador as the largest and most important site in the region. Although not yet the seat of the Snake Lords, the remarkable power and wealth of the kings of Chiik Nahb and the Bat polity is attested by massive building programs and rich royal **burials** (see also **Royal Tombs**). The oldest of these is Tomb I in Str. III, which dates to about AD 400. Three jade masks found in it are among the most ornate ever discovered in the Maya region. Another elaborate Early Classic tomb, probably also royal, was found in Str. IVb. Two stelae give us important information about the Early Classic period: Stela 114, erected in AD 435 to mark the 9.0.0.0.0 *b'ak'tun* ending, and Stela 43, which dates to AD 514. The first refers to lords of Chiik Nahb and the Bat Polity, while the second employs the regional title *k'uhul chatan winik* ("divine *Chatan* man").

The first uses of the Divine Snake Lord title date to the sixth century and appear at sites located 100–125 km northeast of Calakmul: **Dzibanché**, Polbox, and El Resbalón. It could be that the Snake Lords were based in that region at that time, or it might be that secondary lords there were merely citing their regents. Use of the full Divine Snake Lord title at Calakmul is limited to the period AD 630–731. During that century, four generations of powerful Snake kings belonging to the Yuknoom dynasty ruled from Calakmul. These were Yuknoom "Head" (AD 630–636), Yuknoom Ch'een "the Great" (AD 636–686), Yuknoom Yich'aak' K'ak' (AD 686–696), and Yuknoom Took' K'awiil (AD 702–731). Although evidence is scanty, sometime before AD 741 the rulers of Calakmul reverted back to the local Divine Bat Lord title. Although there continued to be Divine Snake Lords, we do not know where their royal court was located.

Yuknoom Ch'een the Great was the single most powerful political actor of the Late Classic period and ruled for 50 years. In AD 645, he attacked and defeated **Dos Pilas** and turned its Tikal-allied king to the side of Calakmul. With the aid of his new ally, that Dos Pilas king attacked Tikal and forced his own brother into exile. Such proxy wars, the installation of Calakmul-allied rulers, and royal rituals overseen by Yuknoom Ch'een occurred at Naranjo, El Perú-Waka', Motul de San José, Cancuen, **Piedras Negras**, and even as far away as Tabasco. When Yuknoom Ch'een the Great died he left his rivals at Tikal almost surrounded by allies of Calakmul. Nonetheless, his son and successor, Yuknoom Yich'aak' K'ak', suffered a dramatic reversal of fortune in AD 695 when he was defeated in battle by the young Jasaw Chan K'awiil, king of Tikal. This event marked the end of Calakmul supremacy and the beginning of a century-long renaissance at Tikal. Although we now know that Yuknoom Yich'aak' K'ak' was not killed in the battle, he died sometime in the ensuing seven years and was buried in Tomb IV, located beneath the floor of Str. IIb. His successor, Yuknoom Took' K'awiil, continued to maintain close ties with allies at Dos Pilas, **La Corona**, and Naranjo. He erected numerous stelae to celebrate period endings beginning in AD 702, especially in front of Str. I. He was the last Calakmul king to employ the Divine Snake Lord title, found on his final monuments dating to AD 731. An altar at Tikal may imply that Yuknoom Took' K'awiil was captured by that city a few years later in yet another battle. His death in the 730s marked the end of the Yuknoom dynasty and Calakmul as the seat of the Divine Snake Lords.

Later kings of Calakmul again used the Divine Bat title (Stelae 59 and 62). But monuments and painted pottery from other sites continued to mention Divine Snake Lords whose home is not known. In AD 736, a Divine Snake Lord—perhaps from Calakmul, perhaps not—named Wamaw K'awiil apparently made a visit to distant Quiriguá. A local Calakmul ruler named B'olon K'awiil erected several monuments (Stelae 57, 58, and possibly 88 and 62) perhaps as early as AD 751 and certainly in AD 771. These are located in the Great Acropolis, an area that continued to thrive and was largely constructed during the eighth century. B'olon K'awiil was mentioned at Toniná in AD 789. In AD 849, a Divine Snake Lord named Chan Pet was mentioned at Seibal. Of several later Calakmul monuments, only Stela 61 contains a name—Aj Took' ("[He] of the Flint")—and a **calendar** round date that probably corresponds to AD 909.

The political decline of Calakmul began in AD 695 and was well under way when the last Divine Snake Lord of the site died 35 or 40 years later. Reverting to rule by a local dynasty, Calakmul remained important, but only on a local level. The late 700s, perhaps beginning during B'olon K'awiil's rule, witnessed the beginning of a serious **drought** that particularly affected sites near the tropic/subtropic boundary (see also **Classic Maya**

Collapse). Evidence from Calakmul suggests that Terminal Classic residents lived close to functioning reservoirs. The late eighth through early tenth centuries saw a dramatic drop in population and the conversion of once sacred pyramids into residential structures. Floor assemblages recovered from Str. II and III suggest that the final abandonment was not violent. In Str. III, heavy stone *metates* were turned upside down and balanced against the inner walls of structures in order to preserve them and keep them clean for later use. Moreover, several structures show evidence of careful abandonment rituals. After the peaceful desertion of the site in the tenth century, Postclassic visitors occasionally made pilgrimages to Calakmul and left offerings in the ruined buildings.

Further Reading

Braswell, Geoffrey E., Joel D. Gunn, Maria del Rosario Domínguez Carrasco, William J. Folan, Laraine A. Fletcher, Abel Morales Lopez, and Michael D. Glascock. "Defining the Terminal Classic at Calakmul, Campeche." In *The Terminal Classic in the Maya Lowlands: Collapse, Transition, and Transformation*, edited by Arthur A. Demarest, Prudence M. Rice, and Don Stephen Rice, 162–94. Boulder: University Press of Colorado, 2005.

Folan, William J., Joyce Marcus, Sophia Pincemin, Maria del Rosario Dominguez Carrasco, Laraine A. Fletcher, and Abel Morales. "Calakmul: New Data from an Ancient Maya Capital in Campeche, Mexico." *Latin American Antiquity* 6 (December): 310–34, 1995.

Marcus, Joyce. "Maya Political Cycling and the Story of the Kaan Polity." In *The Ancient Maya of Mexico: Reinterpreting the Past of the Northern Maya Lowlands*, edited by Geoffrey E. Braswell, 88–116. Sheffield, UK: Equinox, 2012.

Martin, Simon. "Of Snakes and Bats: Shifting Identities at Calakmul." *The PARI Journal* 6, no. 2: 5–13, 2005.

Martin, Simon, and Nikolai Grube. *Chronicle of the Maya Kings and Queens: Deciphering the Dynasties of the Ancient Maya*. 2nd ed. London: Thames & Hudson, 2008.

■ GEOFFREY E. BRASWELL

CALENDAR

The workings of the ancient Maya calendar have been understood for more than a century. **Ernst Förstemann**, working with the Dresden codex (see also **Codices [Maya]**) after 1880, determined the basics of the calendar. Yet with the recent acceleration in **decipherment** of Maya hieroglyphs, new information about the calendar and its many uses has come to the fore. In addition, a question that vexed Maya scholars for many years—how to match Maya dates with those of the Gregorian calendar—is considered resolved. As a result, Maya dates found in **stela** inscriptions, on buildings, in **royal tombs**, and on **ceramics** may be directly converted to dates in the Gregorian calendar. When a Maya archaeologist says that a particular king came to power on a date certain in AD 712, we can be assured that an inscription to that effect was converted from the Maya calendar. It is common today to use online calculators to do the conversion task quickly.

The three basic components of the calendar include a Long Count that uses a modified base-20 (vigesimal) counting system. In it, days are numbered sequentially from August 11, 3114 BC, a mythological date that predates the Maya civilization. The second component is a sacred calendar of 260 days in which each day receives both a number between 1 and 13 and a day name, of which there are 20. This combination of 13 numbers with 20 day names, called a *tzolk'in*, repeats itself every 260 days. The third component of the calendar, the *haab'*, consists of 18 20-day months, with days counted from 0 to 19, plus a five-day month, to total 365 days before repeating. The *haab'* closely approximates the solar year of 365.2422 days, but the Maya calendar, which counts whole days, makes no adjustments equivalent to leap-days in the Gregorian calendar. As a result, the calendar and the solstices do not remain fixed to each other. The Maya use astronomical observations to track zenith passages, solstices, and equinoxes, and thereby the solar year (see also **Astronomy**; **Astronomical Observatories**).

Each day, by Maya reckoning, carried a Long Count, usually written with five numbers; a *tzolk'in* date consisting of a day number (1–13) followed by one of 20 day names; and a *haab'* date, consisting of a day number (0–19) and the month (one of 19). This three-part system over-determines a date, and as a result, inscriptions with a portion of the date missing can sometimes be accurately read.

In 1566 Bishop **Diego de Landa** recorded the scheme for the *tzolk'in* and *haab'* and listed the names of the days in the *tzolk'in* and the names of the months in the *haab'*, together with their hieroglyphs. The Long Count, so common on stelae in the Classic period, had fallen from use in Postclassic times.

When one combines *tzolk'in* days and numbers with *haab'* day numbers and months, they form a set of combinations that repeats every 18,980 days, approximately 52 years. This is known as a calendar round. The calendar round was used across Mesoamerica by other peoples in addition to the Maya; it is the basis of the 52-year Aztec Fire Ceremony.

One must know the Long Count date to distinguish among these half-century-long calendar rounds. By simple analogy, in the Gregorian calendar we may refer to a date as '14, and assume that such a date stands for the year 2014. If we want to refer unambiguously to a date in the nineteenth, twentieth, or twenty-first century, we must write 1814, 1914, or 2014. Most Long Count dates are written in the Maya inscriptions as a five-place number such as this: 9.9.14.17.5. We interpret this to mean 9 *b'ak'tuns* of 144,000 days each, plus 9 *k'atuns* of 7,200 days each, plus 14 *tuns* of 360 days each, plus 17 *uinals* of 20 days each, plus 5 *k'in* (5 days). This sum is 1,366,185 days from the mythical starting point of the Long Count on August 11, 3114 BC. In the inscriptions, the Long Count is often written in two columns read left-to-right top-to-bottom. It may also be written as a single column of five numbers. At the beginning of a Long Count date, one may find a glyph of introduction, ISIG or Initial Series Introductory Glyph, which translated as "the count of the *tuns* was in," for example, *haab'* month Zotz.

The 20 day names in the *tzolk'in* as recorded in the sixteenth century are Imix, Ik, Akbal, Kan, Chicchan, Cimi, Manik, Lamat, Muluc, Oc, Chuen, Eb, Ben, Ix, Men, Cib, Caban, Etznab, Cauac, and Ahau. A daily sequence runs 1 Imix, 2 Ik, 3 Akbal, 4 Kan, 5 Chicchan, 6 Cimi, 7 Manik, 8 Lamat, 9 Muluc, 10 Oc, 11 Chuen, 12 Eb, 13 Ben, 1 Ix, 2 Men, . . . until each number has been paired with each name, for a total of 260 combinations in one *tzolk'in*. The sequence then restarts at 1 Imix, 2 Ik . . . .

The 20-day months of the *haab'* recorded in the sixteenth century are Pop, Uo, Zip, Zotz, Tzec, Xul, Yaxkin, Mol, Chen, Yax, Zac, Ceh, Mac, Kankin, Muan, Pax, Kayab, Cumku, Uayeb (which has five days). The days of the month are counted from 0 to 19, with zero taken to mean the "seating" of a month. The *haab'* count runs 0 Pop, 1 Pop, 2 Pop, . . . , 19 Pop, 0 Uo, 1 Uo, 2 Uo, . . . , 19 Uo, and thus through the other months, concluding with 19 Cumku, 0 Uayeb, 1 Uayeb, 2 Uayeb, 3 Uayeb, and 4 Uayeb.

A single day in the Maya calendar is then written (in Latin letters) as Long Count, *tzolk'in* date, and *haab'* date. For example, we may say that K'ahk Uti' Witz' K'awiil, the twelfth dynastic king of **Copán**, came to the throne, according to stela he commissioned, on Long Count date 9.9.14.17.5, *tzolk'in* date 6 Chicchan, and *haab'* date 18 Kayab, which may be converted to February 5, AD 628 in the Gregorian calendar.

The Maya calendar contains several other complexities, which reveal how captivated and consumed the Maya were with counting days and astronomical cycles.

Many inscriptions include a Supplemental Series between the *tzolk'in* date and the *haab'* date. The first of the glyphs represents one of nine patron **deities** called "Lords of the Night." They form an endlessly repeating cycle of nine, much like the endlessly repeating cycle of seven days in a week of the Gregorian calendar.

Following the Lords of the Night is a sequence of glyphs designed to precisely record the lunar position. The first records the age of the current moon, from 0 (new moon) to 29 or 30 days. The precise figure for one lunar cycle is 29.5306 days, which the Maya approximated with alternating 29- and 30-day lunar months. The second records the position of this lunar month within a cycle of 6 and a cycle of 18 lunar months. The third records the length of this particular lunar month as either 29 or 30 days. The most likely purpose of this long-term counting of moon phases and cycles was to aid in forecasting lunar eclipses.

Finally, the Maya often mention several dates on a single monument, and these are frequently within the lifespan of a single individual ruler. Rather than carve lengthy Long Counts, *tzolk'ins*, and *haab's*, the Maya inserted a shorter count, a "distance number," which was to be counted in days forward or backward from the primary date in the inscription. The associated glyphs, long known as Anterior Date Indicators and Posterior Date Indicators, have been translated by David Stuart as reading "it happened" in the past or "it will happen" in the future.

As the Long Count fell into disuse at the end of the Classic, coincident with the **Classic Maya collapse**, calendar-keepers in the Postclassic adopted one innovation, called the short count. By observing that *k'atuns* could end only on particular days, they devised a cycle that repeated after each period of about 256 years. Known as the *U Kahlay Katunob*, the record of the *k'atuns*, this short count calendar system was in widespread use in the Postclassic, and was recorded by Landa.

The Maya calendar, now easy to match with dates in the Gregorian calendar, provides a detailed and specific anchor to dates for which Maya inscriptions record historical events. It also provides insight into the minds of the Maya and their fascination with integer math, use of place values, and zeroes, and their love of observational astronomy for understanding the cycles inherent in the solar system. Although much was made of the predictions of **apocalypse** attributed to the Maya and the beginning of cycle 13 (13.0.0.0.0) in December 2012, it is clear that the Maya predicted neither apocalypse nor the end of their own calendar on that date.

Further Reading

Aveni, Anthony F. *Skywatchers: A Revised and Updated Version of "Skywatchers of Ancient Mexico."* Austin: University of Texas Press, 2001.

Coe, Michael D. *Breaking the Maya: Code the 200-Year Quest to Decipher the Hieroglyphs of the Ancient Maya.* New York: First Run Features. 2008.

Freidel, David, Linda Schele, and Joy Parker. *Maya Cosmos: Three Thousand Years on the Shaman's Path.* New York: William Morrow, 1993.

Landa, Diego de. *Relación de las cosas de Yucatán* [1566]. Mexico City, D.F.: Porrua [1959]. English editions: Translated and edited by William Gates, *Yucatan before and after the Conquest, by Friar Diego de Landa* (Baltimore, MD: The Maya Society, 1937 [Reprinted by Dover, 1978]); Alfred M. Tozzer, *Landa's "Relación de las cosas de Yucatán": A Translation* (Cambridge, MA: Peabody Museum, 1941 [Reprinted by Kraus, 1966 and 1978]); Anthony R. Pagden, *The Maya: Diego de Landa's Account of the Affairs of Yucatan* (Chicago: O'Hara, 1975).

Rice, Prudence M. *Maya Calendar Origins: Monuments, Mythistory, and the Materialization of Time.* William & Bettye Nowlin Series in Art, History, and Culture of the Western Hemisphere. Austin: University of Texas Press, 2007.

Sharer, Robert J., and Loa P. Traxler. *The Ancient Maya.* 6th ed. Stanford, CA: Stanford University Press, 2006.

Van Laningham, Ivan. *Mayan Calendar Tools.* 2013. http://www.pauahtun.org/Calendar/tools.html.

■ WALTER R. T. WITSCHEY

CARACOL

Caracol (16.8° N, 89.18° W), the largest known ancient Maya site in the **Southern Lowlands**, is located in western **Belize**, Central America. Situated in the foothills of the Maya Mountains just east of the Belize border with **Guatemala**, inland and at a distance from navigable rivers, Caracol nevertheless controlled a **trade route** running between the Caribbean Sea and the Maya heartland area in the Petén of Guatemala. The site rose to prominence by brokering trade in metamorphic stone used for *manos* and *metates*, important for ancient Maya **subsistence** production. Its success was based in triumph in war (see also **Warfare, Warriors, and Weapons**), investments in landscape modification, and development of an economic system that focused on shared identity and prosperity.

Caracol was first investigated in the 1950s by Linton Satterthwaite of the University of Pennsylvania in conjunction with E. Hamilton Anderson of the Belize Department of Archaeology. In the late 1970s, Paul Healy from Trent University carried out a brief investigation of outlying agricultural features. Caracol Archaeological Project investigations, directed by Arlen Chase and Diane Chase from the University of Central Florida, have continually operated since 1985. The site has been developed for tourism by two separate projects: the first a USAID-Belize government project directed by the Chases from 1989 through 1994; the second an IDB-Belize government tourism development program directed by Jaime Awe from 2000 to 2004. While Caracol initially entered into archaeological literature because of its hieroglyphic record, it has subsequently become known for its settlement size of over 200 km² and for its anthropogenic landscape filled with constructed agricultural terraces that supported more than 100,000 people in AD 650.

Evidence of permanent settlement at Caracol dates from the Middle to Late Preclassic period (650 BC) and continues through the Terminal Classic period (approximately AD 900). Caracol established itself as a regional capital at the onset of the eighth *b'ak'tun* (ca. AD 41). At this point, the site modified an existing Group-E ritual astronomical complex in the site center (see also **Astronomical Observatories**); caches found buried within its eastern building indicate strong external trade contacts. At approximately the same time, the massive central complex known as Caana was constructed to a height of over 30 m; this complex later formed the epicentral node for Late Classic Caracol—and, even in its ruined state, rises 43.5 m above its associated plaza. See figure 7.

Caracol's hieroglyphic history derives from stone monuments (**stelae**) and stucco wall façade texts (see also **Wall Painting**). However, the recorded dynastic founding in AD 331 considerably postdated the site's initial occupation and monumental construction efforts. Two key Caracol rulers conducted successful war campaigns against the neighboring sites of **Tikal** (AD 562) and **Naranjo** (AD 631); following these conquests, the prosperity of Caracol's inhabitants increased and the population grew. Construction of road systems (**causeways**), **market** areas, and agricultural **terracing** began in the Early Classic period,

Figure 7.   The massive Caana complex (Maya for "sky place"). First built in AD 41 to a height of 30 m, it was later overbuilt; today its ruins stand 43.5 m above the plaza. This architectural complex is the epicentral node for the 200 km² ancient Maya city of Caracol, Belize. Courtesy of Arlen Chase.

but reached its greatest extent during the site's Late Classic period peak between AD 650 and 700. While all the site inhabitants shared in prosperity, as indicated by tombs, inlaid teeth, and trade items, stable isotope analysis indicates that there were differences in **diet**, with the royal members of Caracol society having greater access to both protein and maize. Ritual remains at the site, in the form of both caches and burials, are found in most of Caracol's residential groups and appear to be associated with calendric ritual (see also **Calendar**; **Rites and Rituals**). Several **royal tombs** with hieroglyphic texts have been recovered, some associated with women; death dates in these chambers do not correlate with death dates on hieroglyphic monuments, suggesting a disconnect between archaeological remains and publicly recorded history.

The latest remains at Caracol date to approximately AD 895, when epicentral buildings were burned. Human remains were left unburied in the royal **palace** compound atop Caana as well as in the plaza to its south. While the end of epicentral Caracol is associated with violence, archaeological evidence suggests that a combination of human and environmental factors, including a deviation from its organizational system based in shared prosperity, led to site abandonment.

See also Architecture Overview; Burials; Caracol-Dynastic History; Classic Maya Collapse; LiDAR; Portable Objects; Terracing; Water Management

Further Reading

Chase, Arlen, and Z. Chase Diane. Caracol Archaeological Project. http://www.caracol.org/.
———. *Investigations at the Classic Maya City of Caracol, Belize: 1985–1987*. Pre-Columbian Art Research Institute, Monograph 3. San Francisco, CA: Pre-Columbian Art Research Institute, 1987.
———, eds. *Studies in the Archaeology of Caracol, Belize*. Pre-Columbian Art Research Institute, Monograph 7. San Francisco, CA: Pre-Columbian Art Research Institute, 1994.
———. "Symbolic Egalitarianism and Homogenized Distributions in the Archaeological Record at Caracol, Belize: Method, Theory, and Complexity." *Research Reports in Belizean Archaeology* 6: 15–24, 2009.
———. "Belize Red Ceramics and Their Implications for Trade and Exchange in the Eastern Maya Lowlands." *Research Reports in Belizean Archaeology* 9: 3–14, 2012.
———. "Ancient Maya Markets and the Economic Integration of Caracol, Belize." *Ancient Mesoamerica* 25, no. 1: , 2014.
———. "Path Dependency in the Rise and Denouement of a Classic Maya City: The Case of Caracol, Belize." In *The Resilience and Vulnerability of Ancient Landscapes: Transforming Maya Archaeology through IHOPE*, edited by Arlen F. Chase and Vernon L. Scarborough, 142–54. Archaeological Papers of the American Anthropological Association, vol. 24, no. 1. Arlington, VA: American Anthropological Association, 2014.
Chase, Arlen F., Diane Z. Chase, and Michael E. Smith. "States and Empires in Ancient Mesoamerica." *Ancient Mesoamerica* 20, no. 2: 175–82, 2009.

■ARLEN F. CHASE AND DIANE Z. CHASE

CARACOL-DYNASTIC HISTORY

Caracol has the largest hieroglyphic corpus in **Belize**, consisting of 54 carved stone monuments as well as texts painted on capstones and walls in tombs, modeled in stucco on buildings, and placed on portable artifacts (see also **Decipherment**; **Portable Objects**; **Royal Tombs**; **Wall Painting**). Initial drawings and readings of these texts have been undertaken by Stephen Houston and Nikolai Grube, as well as Arlen Chase and Diane Chase. These materials reveal a lengthy written history of the site, with details about the lives of several key individuals as well as important events that affected this important Maya city. Dates associated with these texts range from AD 331 to 859. Some of the dated hieroglyphic events can be matched with archaeological signatures. Caracol's sixth- and seventh-century wars with **Tikal** and **Naranjo, Guatemala**, are followed by a marked population influx to Caracol, the construction of new **causeways** and causeway termini, and the spread of significant prosperity into most of the site's residential groups (see also **Warfare, Warriors, and Weapons**).

Currently there are 26 carved **stelae** and 28 carved altars (including **ball court** markers) known from Caracol. Five painted capstones (four with texts) and four wall panels have been found in tombs. Stucco texts are associated with five epicentral buildings, and pseudo-texts have been recovered from a building just outside Caracol's epicenter. Portable texts occur on a number of items (**ceramic**, stone, and bone) both within and outside of the site epicenter and include a ritual mace recording the childhood (*sak b'aah witzil* or "white hilltop") and adult (*? ohl k'inich*) names of perhaps Caracol's greatest ruler, K'an II. Three monuments record dates late in the Eighth Cycle, but the earliest known date associated with the site is a retrospective date that records the founding of the Caracol dynastic count in AD 331. The last monument at the site dates to AD 859, preceding abandonment of the site epicenter by several decades. However, the majority of the stone monument and modeled stucco dates refer to events that are associated with the sixth and seventh centuries. Although some scholars have argued that Calakmul was behind Caracol's success in the sixth and seventh centuries AD, we believe otherwise.

At least 13 rulers are indicated within the textual record; this is nearly half of the rulers who should be present based on succession counts. With the exception of retrospective naming of the initial ruler, Te' K'ab' Chaak or "Tree Branch Rain God," there is no direct information about the earliest rulers at the site. Eroded hieroglyphic texts can be used to reference the existence of three Caracol rulers in the late fifth and early sixth centuries. Then, in AD 553, one of Caracol's better known rulers, Yajaw Te' K'inich II (also referred to as "Lord Water"), came to power and governed for at least 40 years. Yajaw Te' K'inich II was the ruler who saw Caracol become independent from Tikal in AD 562 as a result of a "star-war." The death of Yajaw Te' K'inich II led to a complicated accession history. It appears that there was conflict over the succession, and minimally two regents are referenced in texts. The first was Knot Ahau (or Ajaw), who, according to Caracol Stela 5 acceded only to a ritual office in AD 599 and carried out rites that involved the presumably dead Yajaw Te' K'inich II, who is also referenced. Caracol Stela 1, probably erected posthumously, links a dead Yajaw Te' K'inich II to his son, K'an II (born in AD 588). Caracol Stela 3 contains history pertaining to an individual named B'atz Ek (possibly a maternal uncle), who likely mentored K'an II until his accession in AD 618. Interestingly, K'an II's texts make no reference to Knot Ahau; this silence serves to emphasize the conflict that must have existed between the two individuals.

K'an II made Naranjo, Guatemala, a second capital through a series of war events between AD 626 and 631, presumably to control Tikal territorially, given established estimates of military marching distance. Caracol controlled Naranjo until AD 680, when it broke free from Caracol in its own war of independence. K'an II died in AD 658 and was succeeded by K'ak' Ujol K'inich II (also known as "Smoke-Skull"). However, for much of the later part of the Late Classic period, Caracol's textual history is largely silent. A painted capstone date indicates that Structure A3 must have been renovated in AD 696, and Stela 21 contains a record of Caracol conflict in AD 702. Modeled stucco hieroglyphs on Caana's buildings record dates in the eighth century, but for the most part it appears that a strong dynastic kingship was not in evidence at the site during the latter part of the Late Classic period. This changed in the Terminal Classic period.

In AD 798 K'inich Joy K'awiil (also called "Hok K'awiil") recorded his accession as ruler of Caracol in texts on a series of **ball court** markers. One of the earliest stela from the Terminal Classic period, Stela 18, erected in AD 810, portrays a rearing vision serpent over a bound prisoner and suggests that **iconographic** symbolism was used to reestablish dynastic legitimacy at the site. Even though K'inich Joy K'awiil records himself as being the twenty-seventh Caracol ruler, there are suggestions that the actual dynastic line was discontinuous. On the summit of Caana, which was the location of the ruler's household, elite tombs were reentered, ritually desecrated, and then resealed, indicating changed social and political relationships during Caracol's final years. The last carved stone monument, Caracol Stela 10, was erected in AD 859; yet, based on radiocarbon **dating**, the site was not abandoned until another 40 years had passed. The textual data that are available for Caracol in the Terminal Classic period suggest that rulers may have changed approximately every 20 years and that a system of leadership, called *batabil* organization and known from the **Northern** Maya **Lowlands**, may have been in place.

In summary, Caracol is blessed with a relative abundance of textual information that covers 500 years of history and that can be conjoined with a detailed archaeological record to provide a better and richer understanding of the ancient Maya past.

See also PORTABLE OBJECTS

Further Reading

Beetz, Carl P., and Linton Satterthwaite. *The Monuments and Inscriptions of Caracol, Belize.* University Museum Monograph 45. Philadelphia: University Museum, University of Pennsylvania, 1981.

Chase, Arlen, and Z. Chase Diane. Caracol Archaeological Project. http://www.caracol.org/.

Chase, Arlen F. "Cycles of Time: Caracol in the Maya Realm, with an Appendix on 'Caracol 'Altar 21" by Stephen Houston." In *Sixth Palenque Round Table, 1986*, edited by Merle Greene Robertson, 7: 32–44. Norman: University of Oklahoma Press, 1991.

Chase, Arlen F., Nikolai Grube, and Diane Z. Chase. *Three Terminal Classic Monuments from Caracol, Belize.* Research Reports on Ancient Maya Writing. Washington, DC: Center for Maya Research, 1991.

Chase, Diane Z., and Arlen F. Chase. "Que no nos Cuentan los Jeroglíficos? Arqueología e Historia en Caracol, Belice." *Mayab* 20: 93–108, 2008.

———. "Texts and Contexts in Classic Maya Warfare: A Brief Consideration of Epigraphy and Archaeology at Caracol, Belize." In *Ancient Mesoamerican Warfare*, edited by M. Kathryn Brown and Travis W. Stanton. Walnut Creek, CA: AltaMira Press, 2003.

Grube, Nikolai. "Epigraphic Research at Caracol, Belize." In *Studies in the Archaeology of Caracol, Belize*, edited by Diane Z. Chase and Arlen Chase, 83–122. Pre-Columbian Research Institute, Monograph 7. San Francisco, CA: Pre-Columbian Research Institute, 1994.

Houston, Stephen. "Appendix II: Notes on Caracol Epigraphy and Its Significance." In *Investigations at the Classic Maya City of Caracol, Belize: 1985–1987*, edited by Arlen Chase and Diane Z. Chase, 85–100. Pre-Columbian Art Research Institute, Monograph 3. San Francisco, CA: Pre-Columbian Art Research Institute, 1987.

Martin, Simon, and Nikolai Grube. *Chronicle of the Maya Kings and Queens: Deciphering the Dynasties of the Ancient Maya*. London: Thames & Hudson, 2000.

■ ARLEN F. CHASE AND DIANE Z. CHASE

CAUSEWAY/*SACBE*

The Maya causeway is often called by its Yucatec term *sacbe,* which translates as "white road." A *sacbe* is an extended, linear, two-sided stone platform of variable height, width, and length with a constructed surface. It was used for separating and connecting various buildings, features, and locations. *Sacbes* were part of large and small centers between the late Middle Formative and the Postclassic.

Most causeways were constructed in a similar manner. After the course of the causeway had been established by removing vegetation, the ground was cleared down to the natural subsurface. Two parallel dry-laid retaining walls of cut and uncut stones were laid down, and the area in-between was filled with cobbles, gravel, and packed soil. *Sascab* or lime plaster covered the surface of a causeway. Causeways may or may not include parapets and/or drainage culverts.

There have been three main archaeological ways of classifying these constructed causeways: site layout, spatial extent, and assemblage. The site-layout approach looks at the whole settlement pattern rather than the single road. These causeway layouts are basically *linear* or *radial* (the latter term includes *triadic, cruciform,* and *dendritic* causeway systems). Some sites may have more than one layout. Linear causeway systems show no obvious hierarchy if they connect architectural groups of similar size (such as at Yo'okop). In the radial versions the center is the dominant node. **Caracol** was a centralized settlement with administrative nodes based on a dendritic transport/causeway system.

Most generalized classifications of causeways derive from the spatial dimensions. The causeways varied from 1 m up to 70 m in width, from a few meters to 100 km in length, and from ground level to 7 m in height. Standardized spatial units of length and width may have been used in some cases, like the triadic causeways at Ichmul. The length of a causeway is argued to reflect the spatial extent of social integration and interaction. The classification from length has the advantage that the height and width of a causeway may have changed along its course. Short intrasite causeways probably had a wider variety of functions. They could be used in **water management**, ceremonial processions, and demarcations of districts or defining sacred space. Longer roads would have had greater political importance, especially in areas with dispersed population where causeways unite site core and outlier. Thus, intersite causeways can be seen as integrative structures. The intersite causeways may have been a way to extend and maintain boundaries, such as the *sacbes* at **Izamal, Cobá**, and **El Mirador.**

Classification based on the assemblages formed between a causeway and other features in a local context emphasizes site-specific patterns. A causeway ended or began at different kinds of termini, such as ramps, **pyramids**, **ball courts**, range structures, plazas, domestic structures, **cenotes**, and **caves**. Causeways are also associated with *albarradas*, walls, **stelae**, boundary stones, carvings, and water sources. *Sacbes* also varied because of the nature of the terrain, such as topography, surface conditions, hydrology, and avoidance of valuable agricultural land.

A crucial aspect of the integrative functions of causeways was their use in rituals and ceremonial circuits associated with various **calendars** and the spatial divisions of a site and polity. These were performed through ritual circumambulation and periphery-center circuits, which some causeway systems are believed to reflect. Ethnohistorical data suggest that *wayeb* rituals were associated with causeway processions. The twin pyramid complexes at Tikal were located along the causeway system of the site. The pyramids are seen as being crucial nodes of *k'atun* period rituals and processions.

See also ARCHITECTURE OVERVIEW; COCHUAH REGION; GEOLOGY

Further Reading

Chase, Arlen F., and Diane Z. Chase. "Ancient Maya Causeways and Organization at Caracol, Belize." *Ancient Mesoamerica* 12, no. 2: 273–81, 2001.

Normark, Johan. "Involutions of Materiality: Operationalizing a Neo-materialist Perspective through the Causeways at Ichmul and Yo'okop." *Journal of Archaeological Method and Theory* 17, no. 2: 132–73, 2010.

Shaw, Justine M. *White Roads of the Yucatán: Changing Social Landscapes of the Yucatec Maya.* Tucson: University of Arizona Press, 2008.

Villa Rojas, Alfonso. *The Yaxuná-Cobá Causeway.* Contributions to American Archaeology, no. 9. Washington, DC: Carnegie Institution of Washington, 1934.

■ JOHAN NORMARK

CAVES

Caves are defined as humanly accessible openings in the earth, often formed in karst terrains through dissolution. Ethnohistory and ethnography document that caves and mountains are the most prominent natural features in Maya sacred landscape. For studies in sacred geography, archaeologists use an indigenous definition of cave that includes almost any type of hole that penetrates the earth: caves, rock shelters, ravines, **cenotes**, and even holes such as burrows or animal dens.

In the Amerindian geocentric view of the universe, Earth is a sacred and animate entity. The Maya believe that they originated within the earth and emerged to the earth's surface from a cave. It is often expressed in the belief in a seven-chambered cave of emergence, generally referred to by the Nahuatl term Chicomoztoc.

Caves are so important in the sacred landscape that when natural caves do not exist, artificial caves are excavated to replace them. The best-known artificial cave in Mesoamerica is the cave beneath the Pyramid of the Sun at **Teotihuacán**, but additional artificial caves have been reported at La Lagunita, Mixco Viejo, and **Zaculeu** in the Maya area. Artificial caves modeling the Chicomoztoc have been reported from **Utat-lán** and Acatzingo Viejo.

It appears that caves were used almost exclusively as places for religious ritual (see also **Rites and Rituals**). Chief among these are rituals tied to the agricultural cycle (see also **Subsistence**). Particularly important are rainmaking ceremonies, because in Maya thought rain is formed within the earth. Ethnographically indigenous groups make visits to caves to pray for rain and a good harvest on May 3, "The Day of the Cross." These rituals are especially prevalent during times of drought. The book *Heritage of Conquest* contends that as a Mesoamerican pattern, women are excluded from rituals of indigenous origin. This has been documented with regard to cave ritual among the Ch'orti', Chuj, Lacandon, Q'anjob'al, Q'eqchi', Tzeltal, and Yucatec Maya. However, the exclusion of women did not preclude them from being sacrificial victims at the Cenote of Sacrifice at **Chichen Itza**. Although this pattern is breaking down, it seems likely that caves prior to contact were seen as male-gendered space.

Natural and artificial caves are woven into the fabric of site layout. Major architectural features have been built in association with caves at La Lagunita, the High Priest Grave at Chichen Itza, **Tulum**, **Muyil**, and the central pyramid at **Xcoch**. The Petexbatún Regional Cave Survey documented the alignment of architecture with caves at **Dos Pilas**, which included the alignment of major **architecture** with large and important caves down to modest structures built over small caves. Furthermore, the alignment of architecture with artificial caves proves that the practice was deliberate.

Pilgrimage sites in Mesoamerica tend to be dedicated to rain **deities**, so not surprisingly a large number are caves. Caves that hold significance well beyond the borders of their settlements were important religiously, politically, and economically because they were the focus of the large-scale movement of people. For instance, the seventeenth-century Franciscan historian Diego López de Cogolludo states that the pre-Hispanic road (*sacbe*) system in Yucatan was constructed for use by pilgrims going to Cozumel, and markets formed around such sites as Esquipulas. **Naj Tunich**, the Cenote of Sacrifice at **Chichen Itza**, and **Loltun** are caves whose natural grandeur may contribute to their use as pilgrimage destinations. Interestingly, pilgrimage caves are generally located away from site centers but show more architectural enhancement than caves within centers.

See also BURIALS; GEOLOGY

Further Reading

Brady, James Edward. *Sources for the Study of Mesoamerican Ritual Cave Use*. 2nd ed. Department of Anthropology, Publication 1. Los Angeles: Department of Anthropology, California State University, 1999.

Brady, James Edward, and Keith M. Prufer. *In the Maw of the Earth Monster: Mesoamerican Ritual Cave Use*. Austin: University of Texas Press, 2005.

Prufer, Keith M., and James Edward Brady. *Stone Houses and Earth Lords: Maya Religion in the Cave Context*. Mesoamerican Worlds. Boulder: University Press of Colorado, 2005.

Tax, Sol. *Heritage of Conquest: The Ethnology of Middle America.* Wenner-Gren Foundation for Anthropological Research. Glencoe, IL: Free Press, 1952.

■ CRISTINA VERDUGO, TONI GONZALEZ, AND MELANIE P. SALDANA

CEIBAL

Ceibal (Seibal) (16.5° N, 90.1° W) is a large ancient Maya site located on the Río Pasión in the Petexbatún region of the Department of Petén, **Guatemala**, near the modern town of Sayaxché (see also **Map 3**).

Ceibal was first mapped by Teobert Maler in 1895. In 1961 Richard Adams undertook a few small excavations. Meanwhile, Ian Graham recorded the site's hieroglyphic inscriptions. From 1964 through 1968, Harvard University's Seibal Archaeological Project, led by Gordon Willey, conducted extensive excavations and restored some of Ceibal's **architecture**, including a Terminal Classic temple called Structure A-3. Jeremy Sabloff established Ceibal's ceramic chronology at that time. Since 2005 the Ceibal-Petexbatún Archaeological Project, directed by Takeshi Inomata and Daniela Triadan, has carried out further excavations, focusing on the site's foundation and its relationship to other Mesoamerican societies, including the **Olmec**, during the Middle Preclassic period (ca. 1000–400 BC). Inomata and colleagues have refined Sabloff's chronology through further ceramic analysis and radiocarbon dating.

Ceibal was founded surprisingly early, around 1000 BC, when the Central Plaza of Group A was created by clearing surface soils to expose a natural layer of limestone marl. Unlike contemporaneous Maya sites investigated in Belize, Ceibal did not develop gradually from a small village, but rather began as a ceremonial center. Ceibal's original public space is one of the earliest examples of the Group-E architectural complex (see also **Astronomical Observatories**), with a square platform in the west facing a long platform in the east. The first versions of these structures were carved from the natural marl. Caches of Olmec-style greenstone axes and other objects were deposited in the plaza of the E-group. Both the layout of the architecture and the caches suggest connections to sites in Chiapas, Mexico, and to the Gulf Coast Olmec center La Venta. Ceibal's earliest pottery shares some characteristics with ceramics from Chiapas and other characteristics with ceramics from early Maya sites in Belize, such as Cuello, Blackman Eddy, and **Cahal Pech**.

During the latter part of the Middle Preclassic period, Ceibal began to more closely resemble other lowland Maya sites, including **Tikal** and **Cival**. Houses were arranged around patios, large platforms were constructed in the site core, and cruciform caches were deposited in the E-group plaza. Satellite sites such as Caobal, investigated by Jessica Munson, were also built during this period. Ceibal expanded rapidly in the **Late Preclassic** (ca. 400–0 BC), and many temple-**pyramid** groups were constructed throughout the site's periphery. A large number of dismembered human sacrifice victims were deposited in the Central Plaza and in outlying groups. During the Protoclassic (or Terminal Preclassic) period (AD 0–300), Group D became an important political center, although public rituals continued at Group A (see also **Rites and Rituals**). The Early Classic saw a hiatus at the site, leaving very little evidence of construction or occupation between AD 450 and 600 (see also **Middle Classic Hiatus**).

Ceibal's Late Classic (ca. AD 600–800) elites were embroiled in the politics of the Petexbatún region, which included the twin capitals of **Dos Pilas** and **Aguateca**. In AD 735 Ceibal's king, Yich'aak B'ahlam, was captured and kept alive as a vassal, placing Ceibal under the control of the Dos Pilas dynasty. This event was commemorated on a hieroglyphic stairway in the center of Ceibal, and the monuments of earlier rulers were destroyed. Despite political turmoil, everyday life seems to have continued peacefully for the majority of Ceibal's population.

While battles among dynasties were a part of Classic Maya culture, endemic **warfare** that could destroy cities was not the norm. During the gradual **collapse** of the Classic Maya city-states, the Petexbatún region saw an unusually high rate of warfare, resulting in the partial abandonment of Dos Pilas in AD 761 and the destruction of Aguateca around AD 810. Ceibal regained independence in AD 771, when Ajaw B'ot became its first king since the capture of Yich'aak B'ahlam. Ceibal may not have been attacked during this period, but the site experienced a hiatus until AD 829, when Wat'ul K'atel took the throne. Wat'ul K'atel and his successors oversaw Ceibal's unusual Terminal Classic (ca. AD 800–900) florescence and erected many carved **stelae** that include non-Maya traits, probably indicating connections with Central Mexico and/or Yucatan. During the Terminal Classic, the royal residence was relocated from Group D to Group A, and the new palace was decorated with an elaborate stucco frieze. New trade networks allowed Ceibal's elites to import fine-paste **ceramics**, among other goods. However, not even Ceibal could survive the collapse of the Classic Maya political system, and the site was abandoned around AD 900.

See also ARCHITECTURE OVERVIEW; ART; BURIALS; PORTABLE OBJECTS

Further Reading

Burham, Melissa, and Jessica MacLellan. "Thinking Outside the Plaza: Ritual Practices in Preclassic Maya Residential Groups at Ceibal, Guatemala." *Antiquity*, no. 340: 2014. http://journal.antiquity .ac.uk/projgall/burham340.

Graham, Ian. *Seibal.* Corpus of Maya Hieroglyphic Inscriptions, vol. 7, no. 1. Cambridge, MA: Peabody Museum Press, 1996.

Inomata, Takeshi, Daniela Triadan, Kazuo Aoyama, Victor Castillo, and Hitoshi Yonenobu. "Early Ceremonial Constructions at Ceibal, Guatemala, and the Origins of Lowland Maya Civilization." *Science* 340, no. 6131: 467–71, 2013.

Munson, Jessica, and Takeshi Inomata. "Temples in the Forest: The Discovery of an Early Maya Community at Caobal, Petén, Guatemala." *Antiquity* 85, no. 328, 2011.

Willey, Gordon, ed. *Excavations at Seibal, Department of Petén.* Vols. 13–17 of *Memoirs of the Peabody Museum of Archaeology and Ethnology.* Cambridge, MA: Harvard University, 1975–1990.

■ JESSICA MACLELLAN

CENOTE

A cenote is a natural opening in karstic limestone terrain that provides access to water. It is a corruption of the Yucatec Maya word *dzonot* or *tzonot*, referring to an underground water source. The karstic limestone terrain of the Yucatan Peninsula has been partially dissolved by the percolation of rainwater carrying humic and carbonic acids through the limestone. The dissolving of the limestone has left caves and weakened areas, which sometimes collapse. The collapses take on a variety of forms, such as dry depressions in the surface; cave openings leading to water access; or outright vertical collapses of the surface into the water table that result in open wells, some 60 m or more in diameter.

Cenotes were a critical source of water for the Maya of the Northern Lowlands, since the region has no natural rivers or streams. Many Maya sites are nucleated around cenotes. Among the more notable sites with cenotes near the ceremonial center are **Chichen Itza**, **Dzibilchaltun**, and **Mayapan**.

Cenotes also carried deep religious significance for the Maya as portals to the sacred underworld. For caves with access to the water by foot, the Maya left offerings. Human sacrifice is associated with cenotes, and Edward H. Thompson recovered skeletal material from the large cenote at Chichen Itza, which is connected by **causeway** to the ceremonial center of the site.

Today cenotes are frequently under the protection of INAH in Mexico or the Institute of Archaeology in Belize. Along the coastal region of eastern Yucatan from Playa del Carmen to Tulum, tourists are able to swim or go scuba-diving in cenotes.

See also GEOLOGY; RITES AND RITUALS; WATER MANAGEMENT

Further Reading

Coggins, Clemency, and Orrin C. Shane. *Cenote of Sacrifice: Maya Treasures from the Sacred Well at Chichén Itzá*. Austin: University of Texas Press, 1984.

Explore Mexico's Cenotes. (12 image slide show). Scripps Networks Digital–Travel Channel. http://www.travelchannel.com/destinations/mexico/photos/explore-mexicos-cenotes.

Hunt, Will. "Bringing to Light Mysterious Maya Cave Rituals." *Discover*, November 12, 2014. http://discovermagazine.com/2014/dec/15-cave-of-the-crystal-maiden.

Munro, P. G, and M. L. M. Zurita. "The Role of Cenotes in the Social History of Mexico's Yucatan Peninsula." *Environment and History* 17, no. 4: 583–612, 2011.

Perry, Eugene, Luis Marin, Jana McClain, and Guadalupe Velazquez. "Ring of Cenotes (Sinkholes), Northwest Yucatan, Mexico: Its Hydrogeologic Characteristics and Possible Association with the Chicxulub Impact Crater." *Geology* 23, no. 1: 17–20, 1995.

Perry, Eugene, Guadalupe Velazquez-Oliman, and Luis Marin. "The Hydrogeochemistry of the Karst Aquifer System of the Northern Yucatan Peninsula, Mexico." *International Geology Review* 44, no. 3: 191–221, 2002.

Romey, Kristin M. "Diving the Maya Underworld." *Archaeology* 57, no. 3: 16–23, 2004.

■ WALTER R. T. WITSCHEY

CENTRAL LOWLANDS

The borders between the Central Lowlands area and its neighbors to the north and south are ill-defined; in fact some scholars simply divide the lowlands into a northern and southern part, yet the Central Lowlands have their own distinctive character (see also **Maps 2 and 6**; **Northern Lowlands**; **Southern Lowlands**). The region is bounded on the east by much of the Caribbean coast of **Belize**. On the west it grades into an area east of the Laguna de Terminos. Running north-south for 250 km is a low 350-m elevation karstic mesa, as low as 300 m asl at the north and up to 400 m high in the south. In the southwest corner of the region are the Maya Mountains of Belize, where several crests exceed 1000 m.

The karstic mesa forms a watershed divide between the east and west sides of the peninsula; to the east waters flow generally northeast via the Hondo, New, and Belize Rivers to the Caribbean, and to the west they move toward the Gulf of Mexico.

The **Mirador Basin**, an area of extensive seasonally and perennially flooded lowlands, occupies the northwest of the Central Lowlands. The Maya found the soil and water resources of the region productive and several of the great Formative Period Maya cities were here, including **Nakbé** and **El Mirador**. Most of the Department of the Petén, **Guatemala**, is encompassed here. To the south are numerous **lakes**, including the large Lake Petén Itzá, which form an east-to-west drainage basin. Grasslands on a red clay plain at 135–200 m asl dominate the southern part of the Central Lowlands with a somewhat inhospitable environment.

The Central Lowlands receive between 1,000 mm (north) and 2000 mm (south) of rainfall annually, chiefly during the rainy season from late December to late May. Together with the same high heat found to the north, the climate is favorable to productive **subsistence** endeavors.

In addition to Nakbé and El Mirador, the Central Lowlands are home to **Tikal**, **Caracol**, **Naranjo**, **Yaxhá**, **Altun Ha**, **Lamanai**, **Calakmul**, **Río Bec**, and a host of other ancient sites.

See also AGUADAS; BAJOS; GEOLOGY; WATER MANAGEMENT

Further Reading

Coe, Michael D. *The Maya*. 8th ed. London: Thames & Hudson, 2011.

Evans, Susan Toby. *Ancient Mesoamerica & Central America: Archaeology and Culture History*. 2nd ed. London: Thames & Hudson, 2008.

Sharer, Robert J., and Loa P. Traxler. *The Ancient Maya*. 6th ed. Stanford, CA: Stanford University Press, 2006.

■ WALTER R. T. WITSCHEY

CERAMIC ANALYSIS

Ceramic analysis covers the field of objects that were made of clay and fired, resulting in objects that were durable. While ceramic objects can include structural materials (e.g., bricks), traditional ceramic analysis in the Maya area concentrates on pottery vessels and figurines. The systematic and complete analysis of pottery (ceramic analysis) can tell us quite a bit about the culture that manufactured and used the vessel(s). Ceramic analysis can include analyses of style, manufacture, and use. Many archaeological ceramic reports include information about these three areas, but as technology has improved, we are able to obtain even more specialized knowledge than what is included in the typical ceramic report.

Stylistic analysis has been at the forefront of ceramic studies and has changed as paradigms in archaeology have changed. Although there is no one definition of style that can be used in ceramic analysis, style is more than something that is added onto a vessel to make it aesthetically pleasing. Some researchers use pottery vessel form and/or decoration to define culture areas (homologies) used for seriation of different sites. Other researchers see style as a functional/adaptational similarity that is a by-product of behavioral systems; style is coded and can be read to tell about past cultural systems. Still others see the style of a vessel or its decoration as a reflection of human behavior that is encased in social conditions and constraints; ethnicity and group ideology are the main foci. Regardless of the researcher's paradigm, stylistic analysis of ceramics conveys the transmission of information and the potter's cultural background.

Ceramic analysis also includes understanding how a vessel was manufactured. The manufacturing process includes the acquisition of clay, temper, and other minerals used for slips and paints; the tools used to create the objects; the building process; and the firing process. Very rarely do researchers know the exact locations where the Maya acquired their clay, temper, or minerals; however, that does not deter this kind of analysis. Mineralogical analysis utilizes techniques developed in **geology** to identify various minerals within the vessel's clay body. This type of analysis provides both qualitative and quantitative analysis, as the analyst can count (point-counting) the frequency of different minerals in the clay body and can determine if the minerals were natural to the clay or were added by the Maya (the mineral's angularity and orientation). In addition to mineralogical analysis, chemical analysis is another method used by researchers to suggest possible choices made during the manufacturing process. While there are many different techniques for chemical analysis, the two most commonly used in ceramic analysis of Maya objects are neutron activation analysis (NAA) and inductively coupled plasma spectroscopy (ICPS). NAA is a bulk method of analysis that examines the clay and temper and is often used to suggest trade patterns, as the researcher can test between local and nonlocal ceramics. On the other hand, ICPS can be targeted to examine specific clays or minerals, thus allowing the researcher to examine slips and decorative paints as well as the ceramic paste.

In addition to stylistic and technological analyses of ceramics in the Maya area, researchers analyze the use of the various excavated ceramic objects. Use analysis includes, but is not limited to, reading hieroglyphic texts, residue analysis, and contextual analysis. Some Late Classic polychrome vessels have glyphs that describe the contents of the vessels. Residue analysis suggests that the Maya used various vessels for chocolate, hallucinogens, and a wide range of other food preparations. Finally, how the Maya may have used their vessels can be interpreted from their placement in the archaeological record; however, final use does not necessarily indicate the life-history of any specific ceramic object.

By combining stylistic, technological, and use data, researchers have the ability to suggest behaviors and intentional choices of Maya potters.

See also ART; CACAO; CERAMICS; DECIPHERMENT; DIET; GEOLOGY; JAINA; PORTABLE OBJECTS; TRADE ROUTES

Further Reading

Cecil, Leslie G. "Technological Styles of Late Postclassic Slipped Pottery from the Central Petén Lakes Region, El Petén, Guatemala." PhD diss., Southern Illinois University Carbondale, 2001.

Orton, Clive, Paul Tyres, and Alan Vince. *Pottery in Archaeology*. London: Cambridge University Press, 1993.

Rice, Prudence M. *Pottery Analysis: A Sourcebook*. Chicago: University of Chicago Press, 1987.

Skibo, James M. *Pottery Function: A Use-alteration Perspective*. New York: Plenum Press, 1992.

■ LESLIE G. CECIL

CERAMICS

Throughout the history of the Maya civilization, highlands and lowlands, the Maya manufactured ceramics for various utilitarian and nonutilitarian purposes. The Maya decorated their pottery with punctations, incising, modeling, appliques, slips, and paints. All Maya pottery was hand-built and usually fired using a bonfire method; however, the excavation of kilns in **Belize** indicates that the Late Classic Maya also used kilns for firing pottery. The five time periods below represent the traditional chronological divisions used by archaeologists to discuss differences in social, political, and material culture. Within each larger time period are subdivisions (not included here): for example, Early Preclassic, Middle Preclassic, and Late Preclassic. While the temporal divisions suggest cultural continuity across the landscape, the Maya region is vast, and there are many regional differences. Because these differences cannot be fully elaborated here, what follows is a description of the general trends in paste, surface finish, and decorative modes that are characteristic of each time period.

The earliest pottery excavated in the Maya region comes from the **Pacific Coast** of **Guatemala**, **Mexico** (Chiapas), and **El Salvador**. While this pottery (the Barras, Cuadros, and Jocotal phases) is not strictly early Maya pottery, some motifs and shapes do show affinities to early Maya pottery.

*Preclassic **Highlands***: Early pottery in the Maya highlands is slipped red, black, orange, brown (streaky), and white, and most vessels have a characteristic waxy, burnished finish. Polychrome pottery is not uncommon, and the decorative motifs occur in black, white, red, yellow, and purple. Usulután pottery is distinguished by its resist pattern of wavy lines. In addition to painted decorative elements, highland pottery also exhibits incised, grooved, and fluted elements. This pottery takes the form of *tecomates*, bowls (small shoulder, medial flange, and basal break), necked jars, and vases (some footed). *Incensarios* (censer burners) appear as tall cylinders (sometimes lidded) with three prongs with modeled elements such as flanges, spikes, and masks.

*Preclassic **Lowlands***: The earliest Maya pottery was excavated from the Belize valley (**Cahal Pech**, **Cerros**, and Blackman Eddy). In general, slipped pottery from the Preclassic period exhibits a thick, waxy slip and tends to be cream, black, red, or orange. Usulutan pottery also appears in the lowlands. Polychrome pottery first occurs at the end of the Preclassic period. Decorative elements include appliqué, modeling, impressing, and incising. For the most part, the pastes of Preclassic pottery are calcite-rich; however, the earliest Preclassic pastes include volcanic ash. Vessel forms include dishes with flared sides, necked jars, bowls, and footed cylinders. By the end of the Preclassic period, censers occur and are identified by the presence of figurines (animal and human) molded to the front of a vessel and spike appliqués on small dishes. Molded animals and humans also occur on lidded bowls.

Early Classic Highlands: The waxy slips and polychrome decoration of the Preclassic period greatly diminish during the Early Classic. Slips/washes appear as light orange, buff, or white. Ceramic pastes are coarse, and vessel walls are thicker than in the previous time period. Forms include vases (vertical sides with pedestals or footed), jars, and bowls (hemispherical, basal break, basal shoulder, and basal flange). Highland pottery at the end of this time period (and into the Middle Classic) is indicative (form, paste, decoration) of **Teotihuacán** influence. Early Classic censers also show central Mexico's influence in the highlands as their form changes to a three-part (dish or hourglass receptacle, lid, and chimney) vessel. Lids and chimneys may be decorated with effigies and/or *adornos*. Ladle censers also occur.

Early Classic Lowlands: The waxy slips of the Preclassic period change to a more glossy finish in the Early Classic. Slip colors are predominantly black, cream, and orange. Polychrome pottery becomes more prevalent during this time period, and many decorative motifs are painted in red or black. Some vessels demonstrate post-firing stucco application. Vessel forms include flanged bowls/dishes with ring bases, footed cylinders, and bowls. The majority of the vessels have calcite tempering, although some volcanic ash inclusions occur. Flanged image censers and censer stands are common.

Late Classic Highlands: Ceramics of this time period are notable because they are well-fired (hard paste wares) with little decoration, appliqués, *adornos*, or slip and because of the introduction of San Juan Plumbate (characterized by ash particles and its iridescent gray surface) into the area. Forms include large globular jars with strap handles and pie crust modeled lips, bowls (hemispherical with everted rims and deep), and vases. The censer forms of the Early Classic period continue and are supplemented by flaring-sided vases with flat bottoms and spikes, ladle censers, and human effigy censers.

Late Classic Lowlands: While utilitarian, monochrome slipped, and polychrome vessels continue into this time period, it is during this period that the most elaborately decorated pottery occurs in the Maya lowlands. Cylindrical vases, bowls, jars, and footed plates are elaborately decorated with **palace** scenes; hieroglyphic texts; scenes from the ***Popol Vuh*** (Codex pottery); and numerous variations on flora, fauna, and humans (see also **Fauna**; **Vegetation**). The vast majority of these vessels have volcanic ash inclusions in the ceramic paste. Some vessels have Maya blue pigment, applied after firing. Because of the high quality of artistic and technological skills needed to manufacture these polychrome vessels, many scholars believe that there must have been artistic schools or centralized areas of production (perhaps "attached specialists"). Late Classic *incensarios* occur as bowls, basins, vases with spike appliqués, ladle censers, and effigy (animal and human) censers with modeled elements such as flanges.

Terminal Classic Highlands: This time period is difficult to define due to the lack of archaeological work in the period. In general, pottery slips are red, orange, and brown. Fine Orange occurs in this time period at sites in the coastal piedmont central highlands. Vessel forms include bowls and jars, and they are decorated with impressed fillets. The hard, well-fired pastes of the Late Classic period continue.

Terminal Classic Lowlands: The Terminal Classic period pottery is stylistically differ-ent from that of the Late Classic period. While polychrome decoration still occurs, the elaborate polychrome designs disappear in favor of monochrome slipped vessels. Some cylindrical vases exhibit modeled-carved decorative panels. In some areas Fine Orange/ Gray and Tohil Plumbate wares occur. Fine Orange/Gray ware pottery is defined by the lack of inclusions in the ceramic paste and is orange or gray in color. Tohil Plumbate is de-fined by its glassy inclusions in the ceramic paste and its iridescent gray surface. This ware continues into the Early Postclassic. Terminal Classic vessel forms include footed plates/ dishes, narrow-neck jars, shallow bowls and dishes (some with everted rims, incurved rims, or basal breaks), cylinders, and effigy urns. Many of the ceramic pastes have volcanic ash inclusions. *Incensarios* also are common in this time period and occur most frequently in the form of ladle censers, vases with spike appliqués, and cylinders with modeled faces.

Postclassic Highlands: The presence of Tohil Plumbate is a diagnostic characteristic of the Postclassic period in the Maya highlands. In addition to Tohil Plumbate, other diagnostic vessels have a monochrome slip (red, white/cream, orange-brown, brown); however, white-painted bichromes also occur. Red-and-black and red-and-white painted decoration occurs on vessels with a cream-colored slip. Decorations are incised, mold impressed, or painted. Painted motifs tend to be geometric in nature. While most pastes have volcanic ash inclusions, some pastes are micaceous in nature (possibly mined from Baja Verapaz). Forms include globular jars with strap handles, bowls (basal break or flange and tripod supports), and *comales*. Censers of this time period are represented by effigy faces on jar necks, bowls with spike appliqués, and ladle censers.

Postclassic Lowlands: While not as elaborately decorated as that of the Late Classic pe-riod, Postclassic pottery is decorated with various glyphs (and pseudo glyphs) and other zoomorphic and geometric motifs. Postclassic pottery is slipped in red, red-orange, black, cream, or pink (double slip of red and cream). While the vast majority of the Postclassic pastes contain calcite (Southern Lowlands) or dolomite (Northern Lowlands), some early Postclassic pottery has volcanic ash inclusions. Postclassic forms include footed shallow dishes/plates, narrow neck and collared jars, and restricted orifice bowls. Censers include full figure effigies (large and small) and vases with spike appliqués and other modeled elements such as flanges. The end of the Postclassic period is characterized by the presence of the Spanish, which is manifest in pottery made with local clays but Spanish forms.

See also Map 2; Architecture Overview; Central Lowlands; Ceramic Analysis; Northern Highlands; Northern Lowlands; Pacific Coastal Plain; Southern High-lands; Southern Lowlands

Further Reading

Kerr, Justin, and Barbara Kerr. *The Kerr Collections.* Electronic data set. Foundation for the Advancement of Mesoamerican Studies, Inc., 2014. http://www.famsi.org/research/kerr/index.html.

Reents-Budet, Dorie. *Painting the Maya Universe: Royal Ceramics of the Classic Period.* Durham, NC: Duke University Press, 1994.

Rice, Prudence M. "Rethinking Classic Lowland Maya Pottery Censers." *Ancient Mesoamerica* 10: 25–50, 1999.

Wetherington, Ronald K. *The Ceramics of Kaminaljuyu, Guatemala*. College Station: Pennsylvania State University Press, 1978.

■ LESLIE G. CECIL

CEREN

Ceren (13.7° N, 89.4° W) was a small village of Maya farmers that was founded as a part of the recovery from the immense Ilopango volcanic eruption, which evidently occurred in AD 535 (see also **Maps 2**, **3**, and **7**). It functioned for only a few decades and then was buried by the eruption of the nearby Loma Caldera volcanic vent. That latter eruption preserved the village and the agricultural fields to an extraordinary degree, allowing for a "clear window" into their lives. They farmed corn, beans, and squash around their houses; specialty crops in gardens; and root crops (manioc) outside of town (see also **Subsistence**). Each family built three structures: a domicile for daytime activities and sleeping; a storehouse for tools, food, and a duck tied to a post; and a kitchen. Walls and roofs were well-anchored yet flexible and therefore highly earthquake resistant. Each family had abundant space inside the walls, and an equal amount of space outside the walls and under the thatch roof eaves. Each family had a surprising abundance of possessions, including about 70 complete pottery vessels, sharp knives and scrapers of obsidian (a natural volcanic glass), a durable stone ax of jade, and other items. The obsidian knives were stored up in the thatch roof, above doorways or at corners, as a way of protecting the sharp edges and child-proofing their residences. Each kitchen had grinding stones for preparing corn gruel and tamales and a hearth for cooking as well as light in the evening after the sun set.

Each family developed a part-time **craft specialization** to produce something in greater amounts than they needed for their own consumption. They used that surplus production to exchange with other households for the things they needed but did not produce themselves. One household made grinding tools and cotton thread in excess amounts for exchange, and another made elaborately painted gourd vessels for exchange. Another household produced specialty crops such as chilies, **cacao** (chocolate), fibers from the maguey plant, and poles used for reinforcing walls. The specialization and exchange network was an increase in efficiency, as each household did not have to be economically fully self-sufficient. And importantly, the exchanges helped integrate the community socially.

Four special-purpose buildings have been excavated, and they reveal much of the richness of life in the village. The largest building, with imposing thick walls and two wide benches in the front room, was where the village elders met and resolved disputes and planned for community activities. Its function was primarily political. One household was responsible for a large sauna that seated about a dozen people. The family kept it operating with firewood and with freshwater so people exiting it could rinse off. It probably was used in a wide variety of ways, as the traditional Maya do today. Those ways include health, in helping to cure respiratory problems. Personal cleanliness is an obvious function. It must also have had religious aspects.

A religious complex of two buildings was the responsibility of another household. One of the buildings was where a shaman (diviner) practiced. Because all gender-specific items left to pay for services were used by females, we believe the diviner was a woman.

The other structure was for community celebrations, and at the moment Loma Caldera erupted the harvest ceremony was under way. It is probable that the villagers fled south on the recently discovered roadway that heads away from the eruption.

See also ARCHITECTURE OVERVIEW; CERAMICS; COUNCIL HOUSE; DIET; HOUSES; PORTABLE OBJECTS; RELIGION; TEXTILES AND CLOTHING

Further Reading

Sheets, Payson D., ed. *Before the Volcano Erupted: The Ancient Cerén Village in Central America.* Austin: University of Texas Press, 2002.
———. *The Ceren Site: An Ancient Village Buried by Volcanic Ash in Central America.* Belmont, CA: Thomson Wadsworth, 2006.

■ PAYSON SHEETS

CERRO MAYA/CERROS

Cerro Maya (18.4° N, 88.4° W) is a coastal site in Corozal District, **Belize**, situated on about 1.5 km² of land on Lowry's Point near the mouths of three rivers that empty into Chetumal Bay. The government of Belize uses the name Cerro Maya in its literature, but most publications refer to it as Cerros, the name used by David Freidel in his initial project. Locally, the term Cerros or Los Cerros refers to the profile view of the site center as seen from across the bay in Corozal Town (see also **Map 3**).

Since the earliest public building discovered to date was a 40- to 70-m-long dock, Cerro Maya probably was settled first as a trading port about 200 BC, facilitating exchange between riverine settlements on the New River, Rio Hondo, and Freshwater Creek, and coastal sites within and beyond Chetumal Bay. Current research by ceramicists Robin Robertson and Debra Walker suggests the settlers came south from what is now Quintana Roo. Besides trade, excavations in the Preclassic village settlement retrieved substantial evidence for economic lifeways that included hunting, reef and lagoon fishing, shellfish collecting, salt making, and cotton production. In addition, project paleobotanist Cathy Crane reported macrobotanical remains consistent with tree crop management of nance, cocoyol palm, and possibly cacao and achiote, as well as the cultivation of corn, beans, and squash (see also **Diet**; **Subsistence**; **Vegetation**).

Most public architecture at Cerro Maya dates to the Late Preclassic Tulix Phase (200 BC–AD 150), including a C-shaped canal that extends around the perimeter of the dispersed settlement. The canal provided drainage for the low-lying site that was repeatedly impacted by coastal windstorms, probably hurricanes (see also **Water Management**). Some occupants remained into the Early Classic Hubul Phase (AD 150–450). Migrants resettled the community in the Terminal Classic Sihnal Phase (AD 700–950), and it remained a small fishing village into the Postclassic Kanan Phase (AD 950–1532). The site is most widely known for discoveries made on a small two-tier public building, Str. 5C-2nd. There excavators revealed four impressive polychrome painted modeled façades, representing the heads of Maya deities, flanking the central outset staircase. The reburied masks were replicated for visitors in 2006 by the Belize Institute of Archaeology and are currently visible, although the paint has faded. See figure 8.

Figure 8. The most notable structure at Cerro Maya, Str. 5C-2nd, with its modeled stucco masks flanking a central stairway. The original masks have been recovered since excavation for protection; visible are replicas of them created by the Belize Institute of Archaeology. There are several interpretations of what the mask represents, including jaguars or the sun. Most agree the building layout is meant to represent the ecliptic, the astronomical backdrop through which the sun passes on its daily journey. Structure 5C-2nd probably was destroyed by a severe windstorm, as it was carefully buried by the Maya in a subsequent renovation, 5C-1st, preserving the mask to the present day. Courtesy of Debra S. Walker.

Other important finds include a rich offering (Cache 1) buried within the construction fill of Structure 6B that revealed a jade pendant and four jade heads, which may have once decorated a royal headband. Two Postclassic offerings (Caches 3 and 6) and a sacrificial **burial** (Cache 7) were discovered on the central axis atop Str. 4A, at about 20 m in height, the tallest building at the site. Cache 7 held over 75 artifacts, including copper bell anklets, jade and spondylus shell jewelry, gold alloy disks, textile remnants, and 13 chert bifaces (see also **Portable Objects**; **Rites and Rituals**; **Royal Tombs**).

Cerro Maya was first excavated between 1974 and 1981 by David Freidel, then of Southern Methodist University. Subsequently, Debra Walker ran three field seasons (1993–1995) focusing on the site's Hubul Phase collapse. Most excavated materials were exported to the United States and stored in Dallas, Texas, from 1981 until 2009, at which time they were transferred to the Florida Museum of Natural History through an agreement with the Belizean government. Selected artifacts, the digitized catalog, and a bibliography are now available online at www.flmnh.ufl.edu/cerros.

Today Cerro Maya may be visited by boat from Corozal Town (15 minutes) or by car via the hand crank ferry over the New River (about 30 minutes). Much of the site core is clear and open to view, although the canal, dispersed settlement, and major ball court group (Str. 50) require a short walk into the bush. Long sleeves and mosquito repellent are recommended.

See also ARCHITECTURE OVERVIEW; ART; TEXTILES AND CLOTHING; TRADE ROUTES

Further Reading

Cerros (Cerro Maya) Research Online Catalogue. Florida Museum of Natural History, University of Florida, 2014. http://www.flmnh.ufl.edu/cerros/.

Garber, James F. *Archaeology at Cerros, Belize, Central America*. Vol. II, *The Artifacts*. Edited by David A. Freidel. Dallas, TX: Southern Methodist University Press, 1989.

Robertson, Robin A., and David A. Freidel, eds. *Archaeology at Cerros, Belize, Central America*. Vol. I, *An Interim Report*. Dallas, TX: Southern Methodist University Press, 1986.

Scarborough, Vernon L. *Archaeology at Cerros, Belize, Central America*. Vol. III, *The Settlement System in a Late Preclassic Maya Community*. Edited by David A. Freidel. Dallas, TX: Southern Methodist University Press, 1991.

Schele, Linda, and David Freidel. *A Forest of Kings: The Untold Story of the Ancient Maya*. New York: William Morrow, 1990.

Walker, Debra S. *Sampling Cerros' Demise: A Radiometric Check on the Elusive Protoclassic*. Report to FAMSI on Grant #03064. Foundation for the Advancement of Mesoamerican Studies, Inc., 2005. http://www.famsi.org/reports/03064/index.html.

■ DEBRA S. WALKER

CHAC II

Chac II (29.2° N, 89.7° W) is 1.7 km northwest of **Sayil, Yucatan, Mexico**. The known major **architectural** and **settlement** remains, covering up to 3 km² and connected by a **causeway**, suggest that Chac was not a satellite of Sayil but an independent, earlier community dating from the Early to Late Classic periods (AD 300–800). The main Chac group consists of a three-story **palace** building to the north with 20 rooms and a "red hands" mural, and a central acropolis with two **pyramids** and multiroom range structures arranged in three distinct plaza groups. A 20-m-tall pyramid with an attached courtyard group is found to the south, and important "*witz*" groups atop steep hills are to the south and west. In addition, Chac appears to have had a significant Middle Classic (AD 400–550) occupation, with foreign ties.

Excavations at the Great Pyramid revealed five construction phases; the two earliest are Early and Middle Classic pyramids constructed in a foreign style. In addition, test pitting and horizontal exposures focused on the behavioral reconstruction of nonelite architecture. Two nonelite residential platforms located just west of central Chac have no stone vaulted buildings, but numerous perishable structures dated to the Late Classic period and earlier. Horizontal excavation revealed subfloor modular rooms arranged around small patios interconnected with corridors and even room-block substructures constructed in a foreign style. Numerous **burials** from subfloor contexts, including infants within **ceramic** vessels, were recovered in seated or flexed positions within circular-oval, stone-lined cists. These substructures with "round" burials and infant offerings resemble central Mexican residential architecture and mortuary customs.

Artifact assemblages incorporated foreign-style vessel forms and decorations, including miniature vessels, *veneneras*, a *florero*, and a *candelero* as well as ring-base thin orange ware bowls locally manufactured. Lithic artifacts included thin biface projectiles (*atlatl* dart points), and obsidian artifacts included central Mexican sources such as a bipoint from Pachuca showing **Teotihuacán**-style workmanship.

The Grecas Plaza of the Central Acropolis was a likely setting for an elite residence, with foreign ties beginning in the Early Classic. Beneath Late Classic stone-vaulted buildings are subplaza modular room structures similar to those excavated to the west, but in an elite context. These substructures revealed a variety of elite artifacts, such as a sculpted stone (the Chac Slab) with bas-relief **iconography** of a curassow, flanked by two elite figures or **deities**; painted stuccos representing **cacao** beans and malachite/turquoise necklace beads; and a possible *talud-tablero* wall segment. A deep circular cist contained ash and the remains of burned human bone, suggesting cremated burials.

Also, the nearby Gruta de Chac (Chac I) was opened, explored, and sampled, including the mapping and test excavation of a related settlement group, determining that the Chac water **cave** and the Chac (II) site were one and the same site.

See also ART; ARCHITECTURE OVERVIEW; PORTABLE OBJECTS; WATER MANAGEMENT

Further Reading

Smyth, Michael P. *A New Study of the Gruta de Chac, Yucatán, México*. Foundation for the Advancement of Mesoamerican Studies, Inc., 1998. http://www.famsi.org/reports/97011/index.html.

———. "The Teotihuacan Factor in the Yucatan: Beyond Economic Imperialism." *Journal of Anthropological Research* 64, no. 3: 395–409, 2008.

Smyth, Michael P., and David Ortegón Zapata. "Architecture, Caching, and Foreign Ritual at Chac (II), Yucatan." *Latin American Antiquity* 17, no. 2: 123–50, 2006.

———. "Foreign Lords and Early Classic Interaction at Chac, Yucatán." In *Lifeways in the Northern Maya Lowlands: New Approaches to Archaeology in the Yucatan Peninsula*, edited by Jennifer P. Mathews and Bethany A. Morrison, 119–41. Tucson: University of Arizona Press, 2006.

■ MICHAEL P. SMYTH

CHACTUN

See TAMCHEN AND CHACTUN

CHAMPOTÓN

The port city of Champotón (ancient Chakanputun or ChanPetén) (19.3° N, 90.7° W) is located along the west coast of the Yucatan Peninsula at the mouth of the Río Champotón (see also **Maps 2** and **3**). The city was one of several pre-Hispanic polities located in the Gulf Coast periphery of the Maya lowlands, extending from southern Campeche to Tabasco. The city was strategically positioned along the major maritime **trade route** linking the Maya area with greater **Mesoamerica** and the mouth of the northernmost navigable river, providing access into the interior of the Maya lowlands.

Early archaeological research at Champotón included coastal surveys by Anthony Andrews, Alberto Ruz, Jack Eaton, and Joe Ball, which documented occupations pertaining predominantly to the Postclassic period. Recent investigations by the Proyecto Champotón (directed by Dr. William Folan) and the Champotón Regional Settlement Survey (directed by Jerald Ek) have documented a much longer and more nuanced view of political, social, economic, demographic, and ecological dynamics in the region, encompassing three millennia of human occupation.

Synthesis of archaeological data from the Rio Champotón drainage reveals a pattern of regional-scale occupational continuity from the Middle Formative period through Spanish contact. The earliest occupations date to the early part of the Middle Formative period, contemporary with the earliest documented sedentary communities in the Maya lowlands. Expansion of populations took place during the late Middle Formative and Late Formative periods. By the Late Formative period, there is clear evidence of monumental public **architecture** and sociopolitical complexity.

The Classic Period was characterized by a complex pattern of demographic, economic, political, and social change. **Settlement patterns** in the Late Classic period were concentrated around the two inland centers of Ulumal and San Dimas. Based on epigraphic and archaeological data, there is strong evidence that these centers were subsumed within the political hegemony of the much larger polity of **Edzna**. By the Terminal Classic period these cities both ceased to function as important political or economic centers and fell into abandonment.

During the Terminal Classic period occupations of coastal zones expanded greatly, part of a large-scale reorientation of regional settlement. Both **ceramic** and epigraphic data reflect a change in influence from inland to coastal interaction spheres, with increasing participation in long-distance exchange networks and notable linkages with coastal cities along the Yucatan Peninsula and as far west as coastal Tabasco and Veracruz. Champotón likely began its ascent to regional dominance by this time. These changes were part of a general pattern of increasing internationalism—expressed in both cultural influence and exchange systems—that swept across Mesoamerica during the Terminal Classic/Epiclassic period.

During the Postclassic period regional populations become more concentrated in the growing city of Champotón, and the coastal port city rose to primate status within the regional political hierarchy. A Spanish expedition led by Hernández de Córdoba encountered the city in 1517. This ill-fated *entrada* met fierce opposition from local forces led by the *cacique* Moch Couoh, and the city was subsequently referred to by the Spanish as the Báhia de la Mala Pelea ("Bay of the Bad Fight"). This and subsequent Spanish expeditions provide invaluable information about the city and region, which remained occupied throughout the Colonial and modern eras.

Further Reading

Arnabar Gunam, Tomás. "El Cacicazgo de Champoton en el Siglo XVI." *Los Investigadores de la Cultura Maya* 9, no. 2: 368–80, 2001.

Eaton, Jack D., and Joseph W. Ball. *Studies on the Archaeology of Coastal Campeche, México.* Middle American Research Institute, Publication 46. New Orleans, LA: Tulane University, 1978.

Ek, Jerald D. "The Political and Economic Organization of Late Classic States in the Peninsular Gulf Coast: The View from Champotón, Campeche." In *The Ancient Maya of Mexico: Reinterpreting the Past of the Northern Maya*, edited by Geoffrey E. Braswell. Bristol, CT: Equinox Publishing Ltd., 2012.

———. "Patrones de Asentamiento y Cronología Cerámica del Período Formativo en la Cuenca del Río Champotón, Campeche." In *La Costa de Campeche en los Tiempos Prehispanicos: Una Visión 50 Años Despues*, edited by Rafael Cobos Palma. México D.F.: Universidad Nacional Autónoma de México, 2013.

———. "Resilience in Times of Political, Economic, and Social Upheaval: A Long-Term Regional Case Study of Socio-Ecological Dynamics from Champotón, Campeche." PhD diss., University at Albany, State University of New York, 2014.

Folan, William, Abel Morales, Raymundo González, José Hernández, Lynda Florey, Rosario Domínguez, Vera Tiesler Blos, D. Bolles, Roberto Ruiz, and Joel D. Gunn. "Champoton, Campeche: Su Presencia en el Desarrollo Cultural del Golfo de México y su Corredor Eco-Arqueológico." *Los Investigadores de la Cultura Maya* 11, no. 1: 64–71, 2003.

Folan, William J., Abel Morales Lopez, Raymundo González Heredia, José Antonio Hernández Trujeque, Lynda Florey Folan, Donald W. Forsyth, Vera Tiesler, María José Gómez, Aracely Hurtado Cen, Ronals Bishop, David Bolles, Geoffrey E. Braswell, Jerald D. Ek, Joel Gunn, Christopher Götz, Gerardo Vallanueva, Alicia Blanso, Tomás Arnabar Gunam, Maria del Rosario Domínguez Carrasco, and Trenton Noble. "Chakanputun, Campeche: 3,000 Años de Sustentabilidad." In *La Costa de Campeche en los Tiempos Prehispanicos: Una Visión 50 Años Despues*, edited by Rafael Cobos Palma, 257–80. México D.F., México: Universidad Nacional Autónoma de México, 2013.

Ruz Lhuillier, Alberto. *La Costa de Campeche en los Tiempos Prehispánicos.* México, D.F., México: Instituto Nacional de Antropología e Historia, 1969.

■ JERALD D. EK

CHENES ARCHITECTURAL STYLE

The Late Classic/Terminal Classic period Maya *Chenes* architectural style is named for the Maya *Ch'en*, the word for well, and is found from the **Río Bec** area just north of the **Mexico-Guatemala** border to the Puuc hills of northern Yucatan. Its purest forms are found in northern Campeche, with the Río Bec style to the south, and southern Yucatan, with the Puuc style to the north. It reflects the shared cultural values of its builders in part of the **Northern Lowlands**.

The *Chenes* style is characterized by one-story masonry buildings. ceremonial buildings, and **palaces** whose façades carry fanciful and elaborate mosaic images above and below the medial band. They often display large monster masks, with eyes, eyebrows, ear flares, jaws, and fangs, and the building entrance leads through the gaping jaw of the monster. The portals are taken to be entrances to the underworld and a suitable place for rituals by the elites of the site, such as bloodletting. Temple-**pyramids** are not common in the *Chenes* area.

Sites with typical *Chenes* architecture include Chicanná, Dzibilnocac, Hochob, Santa Rosa Xtampak, El Tabasqueño, Hormiguero, Dzehkabtun, and **Edzna**. The Monjas Group at **Chichen Itza** includes a building in the *Chenes* style. The façades of Str. II at Hochob and Str. II of Group A at Chicanná are especially good examples of monster-mouth doorways, usually regarded as images of Itzamná or the two-headed earth monster of the underworld. See figure 9.

Figure 9. At Chicanná "Serpent Mouth House," 2 km west of the larger site Becan, Str. II is a prototypical example of *Chenes*-style architecture. Photo by Walter Witschey.

See also Architecture Overview; Art; Caves; Deities; Iconography; Puuc Architectural Style; Río Bec

Further Reading

Andrews, George F. *Architectural Survey Chenes Archaeological Region: 1987 Field Season.* Austin: University of Texas, 1987. http://repositories.lib.utexas.edu/handle/2152/13490.

Gendrop, Paul. *Los Estilos Río Bec, Chenes, y Puuc en la Arquitectura Maya.* Mexico City: Universidad Nacional Autónoma de México, 1983.

Kubler, George. *The Art and Architecture of Ancient America: The Mexican, Maya, and Andean Peoples.* 3rd ed. Harmondsworth and Middlesex, UK; New York: Penguin Books, 1984.

Mendoza, Ruben G. "Chenes." In *The Oxford Encyclopedia of Mesoamerican Cultures*, edited by Davíd Carrasco. Oxford: Oxford University Press, 2001.

Pollock, H. E. D. "Architectural Notes on Some Chenes Ruins." In *Monographs and Paper in Maya Archaeology*, edited by William R. Bullard Jr., 1–88. Cambridge, MA: Harvard University, 1970.

Pollock, Harry E. D. "Architecture of the Maya Lowlands." In *Handbook of Middle American Indians.* Vol. 2, *Archaeology of Southern Mesoamerica*, pt. 1, edited by Gordon R. Willey, 378–440. Austin: University of Texas Press, 1965.

Potter, David F. "Prehispanic Architecture and Sculpture in Central Yucatan." *American Antiquity* 41, no. 4: 430–48, 1976.

————. *Maya Architecture of the Central Yucatan Peninsula.* Middle American Research Institute, Publication 44. New Orleans, LA: Middle American Research Institute, Tulane University, 1977.

■ WALTER R. T. WITSCHEY

CHERT

The naturally occurring, hard microcrystalline form of quartz (sedimentary silicon dioxide) is called chert. Due to its homogeneous nature, chert breaks in predictable conchoidal fractures. While the exact nature of its formation is disputed, chert is thought to form in several phases of microcrystallization over long periods, in either deep-sea beds or shallow pools. Chert is typically an opaque white or gray; however, the formation process determines the color, texture, and inclusions. Flint is informally synonymous with chert, distinguished by its darker color and fine grains.

Chert is found throughout the Maya lowlands within the limestone outcroppings. The durable nature of chert made it an ideal tool for cutting and chopping. Unlike obsidian, chert cannot be definitively sourced. However, the site of Colha, **Belize**, was one of the most important manufacturing and quarrying centers from the Late Preclassic through the Postclassic because of its exceptionally high quality. At Colha, large macroflakes (> 15 cm) were struck from large nodules of chert (up to 1 m in size) and transported to workshops as blanks for further reduction. Tools were produced by percussion flaking techniques using shaped hammer-stones of local limestone. The tools produced in this way included oval bifaces, tranchet bit implements, stemmed projectile points, and **eccentrics**. Mounds of debitage, broken unfinished tools, and used hammerstones attest to the nature of the chert workshops. For poorer quality chert, heat treatment was practiced to increase the workability of the stone. The exploitation of chert resulted in a depletion in the availability inversely proportional to the population increase in the Maya lowlands.

Chert held special significance because it was believed to form when the storm god **Chac** struck the ground with lightning. Chert was utilized by the Maya in many different domestic, political, and religious settings, ranging from stone architecture to small blade manufacture.

See also Craft Specialization; Geology; Iconography; Obsidian; Portable Objects

Further Reading

Andrefsky, William, Jr. *Lithics: Macroscopic Approaches to Lithic Analysis.* Cambridge, UK: Cambridge University Press, 1998.

McKillop, Heather. *The Ancient Maya: New Perspectives.* New York: W. W. Norton & Company, Inc., 2004.

Rosenfeld, Andrée. *The Inorganic Raw Materials of Antiquity.* London: Weidenfeld and Nicolson, 1965.

Shafer, Harry J., and Thomas R. Hester. "Ancient Maya Chert Workshops in Northern Belize, Central America." *American Antiquity* 48, no. 3: 519–43, 1983.

Whittaker, John C. *Flintknapping: Making and Understanding Stone Tools.* Austin: University of Texas Press, 1994.

■ RACHEL EGAN AND ALEXANDRIA HALMBACHER

CHICHEN ITZA

Chichen Itza (20.7° N, 88.6° W) is a preindustrial city located in the central area of Yucatan, **Mexico**, between the modern urban centers of Mérida and Cancun (see also **Map 3**). Before AD 900, Chichen Itza was a small community whose political center was located at the Monjas **architectural** compound, an elaborate masonry range structure with several rooms used for domestic, administrative, and political functions.

Several carved stone lintels with hieroglyphic texts were placed at different access points (see also **Decipherment**). They refer to K'ak'upakal, an important ruler, and Chichen Itza's governor around AD 850, who might have used the compound as his personal residence/government office.

The Initial Series Group and Temple of the Three Lintels are two additional architectural compounds, located south of the Monjas compound. They are spatially distant from one another and linked by a **causeway** system (*sacbe*) that provided for social cohesion among the inhabitants before AD 900 and supported the social, economic, political, and ideological foundations for the city's rise during the tenth century.

A new political and administrative architectural compound was erected at Chichen Itza after AD 900. This new compound was built on a large artificial platform known as the Great Terrace. The most important edifices located on this terrace are El Castillo, the Temple of the Warriors, and an older interior temple, Venus Platform, *Tzompantli* or skull-rack, and the Great **Ball Court**, which were built when Chichen Itza became a city in the tenth century. A major causeway (*sacbe*) extends from the Great Terrace to the Sacred Well, a **cenote** of sacrifice.

Hieroglyphic writing was not used during Chichen Itza's apogee to refer to the city´s rulers. Instead, **iconographic** elements depicting different types of serpents represent either political leaders or sovereign authorities, who seemed to have employed the generic term *Kukulkan* to refer to themselves. For instance, there exists a feathered *Kukulkan*, a scaled *Kukulkan*, and a *Kukulkan* associated with a snake with hooks in his body.

The feathered *Kukulkan* appears to descend to earth from the sky during the spring and fall equinoxes. A combination of shadows and light extending from the top to the bottom of El Castillo meets a stone-serpent head located at the base of the western side of the northern stairway of this building and creates what appears to be the body of a snake. This shadows and light phenomenon is a clear reminder that the feathered *Kukulkan* returns every six months to Chichen Itza (see also **Astronomical Observatories**; **Astronomy**).

Range structures were not built after the tenth century at Chichen Itza, and gallery-patio structures were constructed to replace them. Their form consists of a frontal-open gallery with several columns and a large back patio-quad. The frontal gallery is connected to the back patio by a single doorway. The gallery-patios were probably multipurpose structures. The frontal gallery might have been utilized for semi-public or administrative events, whereas the back patio was used for domestic functions. Gallery-patio structures are associated with temples and altars, and this architectural pattern is observed at Chichen Itza's center as well as on its periphery. An intricate road system connects the site-center with architectural compounds accommodating gallery-patio structures.

The internal organization of Chichen Itza during the tenth and eleventh centuries suggests that this urban center gained importance through its economic, political, ideological, and social activities. An example of Chichen Itza's prominence during those two centuries is the building known as El Caracol, which is located between the Monjas architectural compound and El Castillo. Due to its circular shape, height, and windows, El Caracol was probably used for astronomical horizon observations of the sun, moon, Venus, and other celestial bodies. The results of these observations were included in the hieroglyphic texts to refer to specific cosmological events during the ruler´s lifespan.

Toward the end of the eleventh century, the city of Chichen Itza collapsed as the result of prolonged and recurrent **droughts**, which also affected the entire Yucatan Peninsula. The city was consequently depopulated, with only a few residents remaining. After AD 1100, Chichen Itza was the center of religious pilgrimages, and the sinkhole known as the Sacred Cenote served this purpose. Pilgrims performed ceremonies and rituals until the Spaniards arrived in the Yucatan in the sixteenth century.

See also Architecture Overview; Art; *Chenes* Architectural Style; Puuc Architectural Style; Religion; Rites and Rituals; Warfare, Warriors, and Weapons

Further Reading

Cobos, Rafael. "Ancient Community Form and Social Complexity at Chichén Itzá, Yucatán." In *Urbanism in Mesoamerica*, edited by William T. Sanders. México, D.F., México, and University Park, PA Instituto Nacional de Antropología e Historia (México), and The Pennsylvania State University, 2003.

———. "The Relationship between Tula and Chichén Itzá: Influences or Interaction?" In *Lifeways in the Northern Maya Lowlands*, edited by Jennifer P. Mathews and Bethany A. Morrison, 173–83. Tucson: The University of Arizona Press, 2006.

———. "Multepal or Centralized Kingship? New Evidence of Governmental Organization at Chichén Itzá." In *Twin Tollans: Chichén Itzá, Tula, and the Toltecs*, edited by Jeff Karl Kowalski and Cynthia Kristan-Graham, 249–71. Washington, DC: Dumbarton Oaks, Trustees for Harvard University, 2011.

Coggins, Clemency, and Orrin C. Shane. *Cenote of Sacrifice: Maya Treasures from the Sacred Well at Chichén Itzá*. Austin: University of Texas Press, 1984.

■ RAFAEL COBOS

CHICXULUB CRATER (AND THE CENOTE ZONE)

The Chicxulub crater (21.3° N, 89.6° W) is centered near the modern village of Chicxulub, Yucatan, México, after which it is named. The Chicxulub impact crater is a geological feature underlying the modern state of Yucatan, México. It is traced at the earth's surface by an arc of a topographic depression and of karstic sinkholes, also known as the **cenote** zone, on the northwestern edge of the Yucatan Peninsula. The rest of the crater lies under the Gulf of Mexico, off the northwestern shores of the peninsula (see also **Map 7**).

Sixty-five million years ago, during the end of the Cretaceous geologic period, a bolide (asteroid or comet) struck the earth, creating an impact crater that is now known as the Chicxulub crater. The bolide struck what is now the northwestern edge of the Yucatan Peninsula where it meets the Gulf of Mexico, and the impact crater structure is buried under about a kilometer of Tertiary period limestone deposits and the sea floor. Its diameter is about 300 km. The ring of cenotes is a surface expression of the underlying structure, where preferential dissolution and collapse of the limestone overlying this structure has created a ring of sinkhole lakes, and a groundwater aquifer system that preferentially diverts groundwater flowing northwesterly through the Yucatan Peninsula. Groundwater flows around the structure sharply to the northwest and emerges as freshwater coastal springs at each end of the crater's arc.

The impact coincides with the disappearance of dinosaurs from the geologic record 65 million years ago. This site is also distinguished by a geologic gravity anomaly in a ring shape. This event was traced by scientists through a convergence of evidence, including a 65 mya iridium layer found in geologic deposits throughout the world, whose geographical distribution pointed to a catastrophic geological event centered in the Caribbean region. Other regional evidence includes shocked quartz and tsunami-like deposits. In the late 1970s and early 1980s Mexican petrochemical company scientists Antonio Camargo and Glen Penfield first suspected the existence of a ring structure based on gravitational anomaly maps and their own drilling, whose samples were considered proprietary by the company, limiting publications. Soon thereafter Alan Hildebrand and William Boynton also developed and published a hypothesis leading to this site. Two additional teams' hypotheses and evidence also converged on identifying the location in the mid-1980s and 1990s, one led by Luis Walter Alvarez in the quest to explain the disappearance of the dinosaurs, and another led by Kevin Pope, Adriana Ocampo, and others, who identified the Ring of Cenotes as the surface expression of the Chicxulub impact crater site using remotely sensed data.

Although the geologic event happened millions of years before humans or the Maya existed and ever set foot in Yucatan, the structure has influenced daily Maya life in ancient through modern times due to its strong hydrologic control of the occurrence and movement of fresh groundwater in the Yucatan region. Few surface water streams exist on the Yucatan Peninsula; therefore many Maya communities relied on, and still do rely on, wells and cenotes that tap into the groundwater that flows through this karst (fractured and dissolved limestone) environment overlying the Chicxulub crater.

See also GEOLOGY; GROUNDWATER; NORTHERN LOWLANDS

Further Reading

Alvarez, W., L. W. Alvarez, F. Asaro, and H. V. Michel. "Anomalous Iridium Levels at the Cretaceous/Tertiary Boundary at Gubbio, Italy: Negative Results of Tests for a Supernova Origin." In *Cretaceous/Tertiary Boundary Events Symposium 2, Proceedings*, edited by Tove Birkelund and W. Kegel Christensen. Copenhagen, Denmark: University of Copenhagen, 1979.

Hildebrand, Alan R., Glen T. Penfield, David A. Kring, Mark Pilkington, Antonio Camargo Zanoguera, Stein B. Jacobsen, and William V. Boynton. "Chicxulub Crater: A Possible Cretaceous/Tertiary Boundary Impact Crater on the Yucatan Peninsula, Mexico." *Geology* 19, no. 9: 867–71, 1991.

Pope, Kevin O., Adriana C. Ocampo, and Charles E. Duller. "Mexican Site for K/T Impact Crater?" *Nature* 351: 105, 1991.

Pope, Kevin O., Adriana C. Ocampo, Gary L. Kinsland, and Randy Smith. "Surface Expression of the Chicxulub Crater." *Geology* 24, no. 6: 527–30, 1996.

■ SHERYL LUZZADDER-BEACH

CHUNCHUCMIL

For nearly four decades, research has indicated that the Classic site Chunchucmil (20.6° N, 90.2° W), near the northwest Yucatan, Mexico, Gulf Coast 28 km west-northwest of Oxkintok, has been a very densely settled Maya site. A program begun there by Bruce Dahlin in 1993 and continued by Scott Hutson, David Hixson, and others has documented that the population density was even higher than originally estimated. The site shows three concentric rings of occupation from the site center, with related population estimates of 42,500 persons. The project mapped 9.4 km² of the site center plus radial transects.

The innermost ring consists of a 1 km² densely packed zone with over 10 temple-**pyramids** (8–17.5 m high) on a courtyard for **ritual** activities, streets, **causeways** (*sacbes*), a **ball court**, and a **marketplace** documented by soil tests. The temple-pyramids, thought to represent ruling elite families, are all connected by *sacbes*. Aerial reconnaissance with synthetic aperture radar shows this to be the largest group of ceremonial architecture within the surrounding 2,000-km² area. This architecture was constructed in the Early Classic, based on the recovered ceramics, although the ceramics also indicate first settlement at Chunchucmil occurred in the Middle Preclassic.

The occupation ring just beyond the site core, of houses and plazas with demarcating stone walls, has about 950 structures per km². This density drops to 350 structures per km² in the outer third ring of settlement. Beyond, settlement density falls to between 39 and 67 structures per km². The high density of urbanism has suggested new models for both place-making and political organization by the Maya.

Occupation continued into the early Late Classic, when a stone barricade wall was constructed to enclose most of the site center. At this difficult time, Chunchucmil's fortunes were falling, and there was virtually no occupation in the Terminal Classic or Postclassic.

See also FORTIFICATIONS; HOUSES; SETTLEMENT PATTERNS (NORTHERN LOWLANDS); SUBSISTENCE; WARFARE, WARRIORS, AND WEAPONS

Further Reading

Hixson, David R. "Settlement Patterns and Communication Routes of the Western Maya Wetlands: An Archaeological and Remote-sensing Survey, Chunchucmil, Yucatán, Mexico." PhD diss., Tulane University, 2011.

Hutson, Scott R., David R. Hixson, Bruce H. Dahlin, Aline Magnoni, and Daniel Mazeau. "Site and Community at Chunchucmil and Ancient Maya Urban Centers." *Journal of Field Archaeology* 33, no. 1: 19–40, 2008.

Hutson, Scott R., Aline Magnoni, Daniel Mazeau, and Travis W. Stanton. "The Archaeology of Urban Houselots at Chunchucmil, Yucatán, Mexico." In *Lifeways in the Northern Maya Lowlands: New Approaches to Archaeology in the Yucatán Peninsula*, edited by Jennifer P. Mathews and Bethany A. Morrison, 72–92. Tucson: University of Arizona Press, 2006.

■ WALTER R. T. WITSCHEY

CIVAL

Cival (17.4° N, 89.2° W), a Maya site southwest of the **Mirador Basin**, is 73 km southeast of **Nakbé**, 30 km north of **Yaxhá**, and 45 km east-northeast of **Tikal**. It was founded in the Middle Preclassic, and its early **architecture** includes Group-E configurations (see also **Astronomical Observatories**), as well as triadic groups diagnostic of the Preclassic. It was abandoned about AD 200, prior to the opening of the Classic. The central portion of the site is approximately 750 by 650 m with an east-west orientation. Francisco Estrada-Belli, as part of his investigations at **Holmul**, which began in 2000, located Cival in 2001 and noted the purely Preclassic ruins without a Classic presence.

The site center sits atop a mesa created by the Maya in 900–800 BC by leveling two hills. This major construction era, documented by radiocarbon dates, shows that the cut-and-fill operations, with some areas of fill as deep as 7 m, were completed in perhaps only 50 years. Four large structures, ranging in height from 12 m to 33 m, define north-south and east-west axes 308–m and 259–m long, respectively. The easternmost and tallest of these four structures, Group I, is a triadic group. Near the center of the intersection of axes is the observation pyramid of a Group-E configuration. The site core shows several occasions of remodeling and building, however the construction volume and effort is quite high during the initial construction phase in the Middle Preclassic, when compared with later building and remodeling.

Estrada-Belli believes that Cival and similar Middle Preclassic centers represent a new and emerging Maya concern with **astronomy** and cosmology, embodied in the creation of new places under the leadership of more active elite leadership.

Findings at Cival have sparked additional debate about the emergence of the Maya as city-builders; the characteristics that once defined the start of the Class, such as the appearance of Long Count dates and polychrome **ceramics**; and the regional changes at the end of the Late Preclassic.

See also ARCHITECTURE OVERVIEW; CALENDAR; DIVINE KINGS AND QUEENS

Further Reading

Estrada Belli, Francisco. *The First Maya Civilization: Ritual and Power before the Classic Period*. London; New York: Routledge, 2011.

Estrada-Belli, Francisco. "Lightning Sky, Rain and the Maize God: The Ideology of Preclassic Maya Rulers at Cival, Petén, Guatemala." *Ancient Mesoamerica* 17, no. 1: 57–78, 2006.

———. *Investigaciónes arqueológicas en la región de Holmul, Petén: Holmul, Cival, La Sufricaya y K'o; Informe preliminar de la temporada 2007*. Vanderbilt University, 2007. http://www.bu.edu/holmul/.

———. *Investigaciónes arqueológicas en la región de Holmul, Petén: Cival, y K'o*. Boston University, 2008. http://www.bu.edu/holmul/.

———. *Investigaciones arqueológicas en la región de Holmul, Petén: Holmul, Cival, La Sufricaya y K'o*. Foundation for the Advancement of Mesoamerican Studies Inc. (FAMSI), 2008. http://www.famsi.org/reports/07028es/07028esEstradaBelli01.pdf.

———. *Investigaciones arqueológicas en la región de Holmul, Petén: Holmul y Cival; Informe preliminar de la temporada 2013*. Boston University, 2013. http://www.bu.edu/holmul/.

Fields, Virginia M., and Dorie Reents-Budet. *Lords of Creation: The Origins of Sacred Maya Kingship.* Los Angeles, CA: Scala, in association with the Los Angeles County Museum of Art, 2005.

Skidmore, Joel. *Cival: A Preclassic Site in the News.* http://www.mesoweb.com/reports/cival.html.

■ W A L T E R   R .   T .   W I T S C H E Y

CLASS STRUCTURE

Maya society varied considerably across the 2,500-year span from Formative to Post-classic. Compounding the difficulty of analyzing class structure is the fact that until recently, archaeology in the Maya area focused on the activities of the Classic elites, the divine rulers who were responsible for and occupied the monumental masonry structures in the centers of city-states (see also **Divine Kings and Queens**). The emerging picture, which changes over the history of the ancient Maya, is that of an egalitarian society in the Early Formative. This gives way to increasing changes in status that may be the preamble to social classes, then to clear class distinctions. By the Classic, one may find evidence for a class of elites, including rulers, and members of the royal families, some of whom were scribes and artisans. Both within and below the elites were craft specialists for ceramics, sculpture, masonry, textiles, basketry, and featherwork. Class distinctions at this level are subtle, because there are few actual workshops that have been recovered archaeologically; production at the household level was common for ceramics, tools, and perishables.

As class distinctions appear, they are chiefly based, as elsewhere, on political power and differential access to resources: prime land; a good water supply; valuable minerals (see also **Obsidian**; **Subsistence**; **Water Management**). Yet as these differences appear, one is still left with the impression that Maya society primarily divided itself into commoners (nonelites) and elites. Only near the end of the Late Classic are there signs of a small, emerging middle class of artisans and craftspeople (see also **Craft Specialization**).

Commoners formed the largest fraction of the Maya populace, living in small, one-room, perishable dwellings, farming, producing the household goods they required, and paying to the elites their due and demand: foodstuffs, **textiles**, and labor.

Elites were members of one or more families or houses of leaders, from which came the divine rulers, priests and scribes, artists and artisans, and undoubtedly the managers and architects of civic building programs. Masonry dwellings are frequently associated with elites. Elites provided the group of literate members of society, keeping the **calendars**; managing **tribute**; establishing **alliances** through **trade** and intermarriage; making war (see also **Warfare, Warriors, and Weapons**); and organizing religious activities (see also **Religion**), including performance of personal dramas, acted out before their subjects, to intervene with the gods on behalf of their city and its subjects (see also **Deities and Theater**).

Exactly how the Maya organized themselves into classes is still under debate, yet current evidence suggests that a class structure that forms a continuum, without clear boundaries from commoners through the level of king, may be closest to the truth.

Further Reading

Gillespie, Susan D. "Rethinking Ancient Maya Social Organization: Replacing 'Lineage' with 'House'." *American Anthropologist* 102, no. 3: 467–84, 2000.

Grube, Nikolai, Eva Eggebrecht, Matthias Seidel, and Mark Van Stone, eds. *Maya: Divine Kings of the Rainforest*. Updated ed. Potsdam, Germany: H. F. Ullmann, 2012.

Lohse, Jon C., and Fred Valdez, eds. *Ancient Maya Commoners*. Austin: University of Texas Press, 2004.

Martin, Simon, and Nikolai Grube. *Chronicle of the Maya Kings and Queens; Deciphering the Dynasties of the Ancient Maya*. 2nd ed. London: Thames & Hudson, 2008.

Sharer, Robert J., and Loa P. Traxler. *The Ancient Maya*. 6th ed. Stanford, CA: Stanford University Press, 2006.

■ WALTER R. T. WITSCHEY

CLASSIC MAYA COLLAPSE

When Europeans first explored the interior of the Yucatan Peninsula, they came upon long abandoned cities and towns of ruined stone buildings everywhere. Most of the visible Maya cities and smaller settlements, we now know, dated to the Classic period (ca. AD 300–900). In every region the peak in number of sites, size and elaboration of public and elite construction, and lowland population was reached during the eighth century.

By about AD 800, the tradition of inscribing Classic hieroglyphic texts on stone monuments, buildings, and carved and painted polychrome **ceramics** declined, and in less than a century Classic Maya writing and Long Count dates disappeared, along with construction of large stone structures. Surveys have shown that populations in most lowland regions, in the cities and in their rural hinterlands, dropped to as little as 5 or 10 percent of the Late Classic peak (see also **Architecture Overview**; **Calendar**; **Divine Kings and Queens**; **Stelae**).

The Classic decline took generations and differed from region to region. Some of the first indications of violent conflict and site abandonment date from AD 760 to 800 in the southwest Petén at **Dos Pilas**, **Aguateca**, and nearby sites. A wave of abandonments in the west, at **Piedras Negras**, **Palenque**, and **Yaxchilan**, and in the **Central Lowlands**, at **Calakmul**, **Naranjo**, and **Yaxhá**, ended about AD 810, and some southeastern Maya sites, especially **Copán** and **Quiriguá**, collapsed about this time. A number of more centrally located cities, including **Tikal**, **Uaxactun**, **Caracol**, and **Seibal**, continued to AD 860 or 890, and many large settlements in the Northern Lowlands, such as **Dzibilchaltun**, **Ek Balam**, and Culuba, and the Puuc cities of **Uxmal**, **Sayil**, **Labna**, and **Kabah**, lasted until after AD 900. By AD 925 or 950 most or all of these had collapsed, although one huge northern city, **Chichen Itza**, may have remained a vibrant economic and political force a century or so beyond this.

The dramatic failure of Classic Maya civilization was one of the most precipitous and devastating declines in world history. But no one knows why it happened. Nearly all conceivable ecological, catastrophic, and social causes have been proposed and tested against the growing body of archaeological and hieroglyphic information. They include the supposed inability of poor tropical **soils** to support elaborate civilizations, agricultural failure brought on by reliance on shifting cultivation (see also **Subsistence**), savanna grass encroachment on overused fields, the inability of *milpa* agriculture to feed the expanding

Late Classic populations, and agricultural decline caused by an extended **drought**. Widespread peasant revolts against the nobility, invasion and conquest by Mexicanized groups (see also **Warfare, Warriors, and Weapons**), and a shift of long-distance **trade** from the interior of the Yucatan Peninsula to coastal routes have had their supporters.

Discussions of the collapse have recently become more nuanced and multicausal, combining ecological and social interpretations. Excavations in some regions have shown that the decades before major sites were abandoned were years of increasing instability and conflict. New theories emphasize and consider together the increasing role and severity of warfare; rivalry among continuously expanding noble families for ever-shrinking shares of scarce land, labor, luxury goods, and status; the failure of Classic **divine kingship** to cope with increasingly complex social, political, and economic situations; loss of crucial agricultural land to human settlement, erosion, and **soil** exhaustion; and general degradation of the landscape and natural resources by burgeoning Late Classic populations, with potential health consequences for stressed societies.

Others question whether "collapse" is the appropriate term to describe events, arguing that the processes can best be understood as transitions and transformations of Classic Maya societies as they adapted to the changing sociopolitical and economic realities of Postclassic **Mesoamerica**. Some note that despite widespread and lasting depopulation of some regions, the Maya survived, and eventually thrived, in many areas and individual settlements during the Postclassic, including the East Coast of the peninsula, the Late Postclassic city of **Mayapan**, the small, late kingdoms of the Petén Lakes region, and the **Guatemala** highlands. These authors also point out that the timing and nature of the decline of the Classic Maya varied across the lowlands, lasting as much as two centuries. Furthermore, a few Classic sites, such as **Lamanai**, in **Belize**, appear never to have been completely abandoned, although populations declined everywhere. One argument is that the Classic collapse was a continuation of a long-term process of the cycling of the relative fortunes of individual cities.

Most Maya archaeologists nevertheless continue to believe that between about AD 780 and 925, after centuries of explosive and unparalleled growth, nearly all lowland Maya cities and towns faced a crisis that destroyed most manifestations of elite culture and decimated city and hinterland alike. But despite the accumulation of new archaeological and epigraphic data in the past 50 years, all of the above carefully reasoned arguments remain hypothetical—we simply do not know which of these factors were most destabilizing, which forces most destructive.

Recent research by **climate** scientists working with archaeologists, however, has been able to chart changes in rainfall patterns (see **Map 5**) in the Maya lowlands and other areas of Mesoamerica for the past several thousand years, correlating years of **drought** and wetter weather with events in Maya history. The first results came from a core sampling of annual gypsum deposits in Lake Chichancanab, in southern Yucatan. These indicate Terminal Classic droughts from AD 770 to 870 and 920 to 1100 separated by relatively moister years. At Lake Punta Laguna, to the northeast in Quintana Roo, variations in stable oxygen isotopes in a core suggest a drought from about AD 760 to 1020, with a wetter interval from AD 890 to 950, roughly consistent with the Lake Chichancanab results.

Oxygen isotope analysis of **cave** formations from the Maya lowlands has yielded comparable but more detailed and precisely dated records of annual rainfall variation. A stalagmite from a cave at Tecoh, northern Yucatan, documented eight severe droughts between AD 800 and 950, each lasting 3 to 18 years, with moist years between them, suggesting intervals for recovery. The period from AD 950 to 1250, however, was recorded at Tecoh as a return to a wetter climate. This contrasts sharply with lake deposits farther south, including Chichancanab, which indicate the years until AD 1050 or 1100 were extremely dry, and this difference suggests regional climatic variation from north to south.

A stalagmite from Yok Balum Cave, in Belize, also subjected to oxygen isotope analysis, produced an even more detailed rainfall record. The years from AD 440 to 660, a time of vigorous population expansion in the lowlands, saw high rainfall. Then AD 660 to 1000 were years of increasing dryness, with a long drought between AD 820 and 870, and the most severe dry spell between 1020 and 1100 (this last indication similar to evidence from the Lake Chichancanab core). The most extreme short drought was recorded at AD 930.

Several proxies for rainfall variation outside the Maya lowlands—especially from the Cariaco Basin just off the coast of northern Venezuela—indicate drought at the end of the Classic period and in the century or more that followed. Their relevance for the Maya lowlands has been questioned, but they show that surrounding areas of Mesoamerica and beyond were subject to the same climatic changes at about the same time.

Closer to the Maya lowlands, a core from Manchon Swamp, a mangrove estuary on the Pacific Coast of **Guatemala** near the Mexican border, produced pollen, phytoliths, and chemical residues from mangrove peat that reflect relative rainfall over the past 6,500 years. A moist period from 850 BC to AD 750 was followed by dry and variable conditions from 750 to about 1500, including the Terminal Classic and the entire Postclassic period. Human population declined rapidly at the beginning of this span on the Pacific Coast and is invisible during the Early Postclassic (ca. AD 1000 to 1250).

Finally, bald cypress trees from a gorge 60 km north of the Toltec capital of Tula, Hidalgo, have produced a tree-ring sequence showing droughts centered at AD 810 and 860, a megadrought from AD 897 to 922, and another from AD 1149 to 1167, this last possibly encompassing the collapse of Tula.

Although different rainfall proxies in distinct regions of the Maya lowlands and areas nearby indicate variation in the timing and severity of drying events, their overall import is apparent. The period from about AD 750 to 1100 saw multiple droughts, generally increasing in severity, separated by wetter intervals. It no longer seems reasonable to argue that this extended climatic event was unrelated to the Classic Maya collapse, which spanned the years from about AD 780 to almost 950 and was followed by about two centuries of greatly reduced human population throughout the lowlands. The individual droughts within this longer span are suggested by some proxies to have occurred in pulses about 50 years apart. This, too, corresponds roughly to peak frequencies of site collapses.

The most detailed **Northern Lowland** rainfall proxy, from the Tecoh cave stalagmite, records a moist period after AD 950, following the collapse of all interior northern sites except one. This wet interval may have helped the largest city in the north, Chichen Itza, prosper for several generations after all its peers had succumbed.

The primary effect of a protracted drought would have been stress on lowland agricultural systems and the food supply. Continuing agricultural failures in affected areas could have caused many of the disruptions that either accompanied or have themselves been suggested to have caused the collapse, such as cessation of large-scale construction and inscribed royal monuments, increased elite competition, warfare, population movements, shifting trade routes, among others.

Studies of past rainfall, therefore, have identified the environmental changes, if not their causes, that forever changed Classic Maya civilization, providing the impetus for the collapse of hundreds of cities and towns and a depopulation of the lowlands lasting a thousand years. A growing body of paleoclimatological evidence also suggests that climate played a role in the success and collapse of Mesoamerican civilizations at other times, especially the end of the Maya Late Preclassic at about AD 150. What is nevertheless of greatest interest to the social scientist, given how long the Classic collapse took and how vast an area it affected, is how different regions and individual communities coped with the many natural and social stresses and changes this severe and persistent drought forced on the Maya.

See also ALTUN HA; BECAN; BELIZE; BONAMPAK; CAHAL PECH; CALAKMUL; CALENDAR; CARACOL; CEIBAL; CERRO MAYA/CERROS; CHICHEN ITZA; COPÁN; DIVINE KINGS AND QUEENS; DOS PILAS; DROUGHT; EL SALVADOR; GUATEMALA; HOLMUL; LA CORONA; MIDDLE CLASSIC HIATUS; NAACHTUN; PRIESTS; SETTLEMENT PATTERNS (CENTRAL LOWLANDS); SOILS; TAYASAL; TIKAL; VEGETATION; XCOCH; YAXCHILAN

Further Reading

Demarest, Arthur A., Prudence M. Rice, and Don Stephen Rice, eds. *The Terminal Classic in the Maya Lowlands: Collapse, Transition, and Transformation.* Boulder: University Press of Colorado, 2004.

Gill, Richardson Benedict. *The Great Maya Droughts: Water, Life, and Death.* Albuquerque: University of New Mexico Press, 2000.

Gill, Richardson B., Paul A. Mayewski, Gerald H. Haug, and Larry C. Peterson. "Drought and the Maya Collapse." *Ancient Mesoamerica* 18, no. 2: 283–302, 2007.

Kennett, D. J., S. F. M. Breitenbach, V. V. Aquino, Y. Asmerom, J. Awe, J. U. L. Baldini, P. Bartlein, B. J. Culleton, C. Ebert, C. Jazwa, M. J. Macri, N. Marwan, V. Polyak, K. M. Prufer, H. E. Ridley, H. Sodemann, B. Winterhalder, and G. H. Haug. "Development and Disintegration of Maya Political Systems in Response to Climate Change." *Science* 338, no. 6108: 788–91, 2012.

Turner, B. L., II, and Jeremy A. Sabloff. "Classic Period Collapse of the Central Maya Lowlands: Insights about Human-Environment Relationships for Sustainability." *Proceedings of the National Academy of Sciences of the United States of America* 109, no. 35: 13908–914, 2012.

Yaeger, Jason, and David A. Hodell. "The Collapse of Maya Civilization: Assessing the Interaction of Culture, Climate, and Environment." In *El Niño, Catastrophism, and Culture Change in Ancient America*, edited by Daniel H. Sandweiss and Jeffrey Quilter, 197–251. Washington, DC: Dumbarton Oaks, 2008.

■ E. WYLLYS ANDREWS

CLIMATE

The Maya cultural homeland, between 14° and 22° N latitude, is located in the tropical zone tradewind belt, where conditions in the **lowlands** are generally warm and moist. Strong solar radiation throughout the year maintains the average temperature at above 18°C (64°F) across the region, except for some **highland** areas. The climate is dominated by moist tropical weather with low atmospheric pressure, rain, cloudy skies, and high humidity during the summer wet season, and high pressure, clear skies, low humidity, and dry conditions during the winter dry season. The northeast tradewinds bring Atlantic moisture to eastern (windward) slopes, so the north and west are generally drier than southern and eastern reaches. Rainfall is about ten times higher in the Petén (over 4,000 mm/yr) than in the northern Yucatan coastal city of Progresso (under 450 mm/yr). (See **Map 5**.)

Across the Maya region in most years, there is a noticeable reduction in rainfall during August, known variously as Mid-Summer Drought, La Canícula, Veranillo, or Little Dry season, usually followed by another rainy period. During the winter dry season, rainfall occurs frequently as frontal *nortes* occur when cold air masses invade southward from North America.

Climate differs between years due to tropical cyclones (from tropical depressions to category 5 hurricanes) and large-scale teleconnections driven by the El Niño-Southern Oscillation (ENSO) system and the position of the Bermuda-Azores High pressure cell in the North Atlantic. El Niño events, which reocurr approximately every three to seven years, reduce rainfall and also the number of hurricanes affecting the Maya region. Hurricanes can bring some of the most devastating high rainfall events in the region (e.g., Hurricane Mitch in 1998), which can act as beneficial **drought** busters but are more problematic when clustered in space and time. When the Bermuda High is strong and/or located farther to the southeast, rainfall is suppressed in the Maya region. Climate disruptions, including cooling and drought, can also be triggered occasionally by large tropical volcanic eruptions (e.g., the massive Ilopango supereruption of about AD 535). See also **Ceren.**

Regional climate has changed since the last ice age. Rainfall in the **Mesoamerican** monsoon system varied in concert with other northern hemisphere monsoon systems as the position of the tropical rain belt shifted to the north and south. Rainfall in the Maya region was low during cool periods such as the Last Glacial Maximum (21,000 ybp), when mountain glaciers were found in **Guatemala** and Costa Rica, and high altitude areas were 6–7°C cooler than they are today. Rainfall was generally high during warm periods such as the Holocene when the rain belt shifted northward, increasing ecosystem productivity and agricultural potential. Rainfall in the Early Holocene (after 11,000 ybp) was highly variable. Conditions were very wet at around 9,600 ybp, followed by somewhat cooler and extremely dry conditions between 9,000 and 7,200 ybp. Regional climate became wetter and more stable centered on 6,000 ybp (7,000–4,000 ybp), followed by a millennium of drying in the northern Maya lowlands.

Climate during the ancient Maya cultural florescence was broadly similar to today, although there is evidence for major disruptions from drought. Conditions were generally moist during the pre-Classic, until a drying trend beginning at AD 100 intensified into a severe drought between AD 200 and 300. Rainfall was high during the Early Classic period (AD 300–650), but as the region became drier from AD 650 to 1000, the climate of the Terminal Classic period was characterized by multidecadal periods of persistent, severe, and/or recurrent droughts, which occurred in several-years-long pulses from AD 680 to 950. Short-lived climate extremes, including hurricanes, droughts, cold winter periods, and floods, occurred throughout the Postclassic and postconquest intervals, with different local histories across the region. The Maya region was generally wet during the Medieval Climate Anomaly, and drier and cooler during the Little Ice Age, including severe droughts in the 1390s and the 1530s and 1540s AD.

See also ALTUN HA; BECAN; BELIZE; BONAMPAK; CAHAL PECH; CALAKMUL; CALENDAR; CARACOL; CEIBAL; CERRO MAYA/CERROS; CHICHEN ITZA; CLASSIC MAYA COLLAPSE; COPÁN; DIVINE KINGS AND QUEENS; DOS PILAS; DROUGHT; EL SALVADOR; GUATEMALA; HOLMUL; LA CORONA; MIDDLE CLASSIC HIATUS; NAACHTUN; PRIESTS; SETTLEMENT PATTERNS (CENTRAL LOWLANDS); SOILS; TAYASAL; TIKAL; VEGETATION; XCOCH; YAXCHILAN

Further Reading

Frappier, Amy Benoit, James Pyburn, Aurora D. Pinkey-Drobnis, Xianfeng Wang, D. Reide Corbett, and Bruce H. Dahlin. "Two Millennia of Tropical Cyclone-induced Mud Layers in a Northern Yucatán Stalagmite: Multiple Overlapping Climatic Hazards during the Maya Terminal Classic Megadroughts." *Geophysical Research Letters* 41, no. 14: 5148–57, 2014.

García-Acosta, J., M. Pérez-Zevallos, and A. Molina del Villar. *Desastres Agrícolas en México. Catálogo Histórico.* Tomo I, *Épocas Prehispánica y Colonial.* Mexico, D. F., Mexico: Fondo de Cultura Económica and CIESAS, 2003.

Gill, Richardson Benedict. *The Great Maya Droughts: Water, Life, and Death.* Albuquerque: University of New Mexico Press, 2000.

Hodell, David A., Mark Brenner, and Jason H. Curtis. "Terminal Classic Drought in the Northern Maya Lowlands Inferred from Multiple Sediment Cores in Lake Chichancanab (Mexico)." *Quaternary Science Reviews* 24, nos. 12–13: 1413–27, 2005.

Kennett, Douglas J., Sebastian F. M. Breitenbach, V. V. Aquino, Y. Asmerom, Jaime Awe, J. U. L. Baldini, P. Bartlein, B. J. Culleton, C. Ebert, C. Jazwa, M. J. Macri, N. Marwan, V. Polyak, Keith M. Prufer, H. E. Ridley, H. Sodemann, B. Winterhalder, and Gerald H. Haug. "Development and Disintegration of Maya Political Systems in Response to Climate Change." *Science* 338, no. 6108: 788–91, 2012.

Lachniet, Matthew, and A. J. Roy. "Costa Rica and Guatemala." In *Quaternary Glaciations—Extent and Chronology, a Closer Look,* edited by J. Ehlers, P. L. Gibbard, and P. D. Hughes. Amsterdam: Elsevier, 2011.

Medina-Elizalde, Martin, Stephen J. Burns, David W. Lea, Yemane Asmerom, Lucien von Gunten, Victor Polyak, Mathias Vuille, and Ambarish Karmalkar. "High Resolution Stalagmite Climate Record from the Yucatán Peninsula Spanning the Maya Terminal Classic Period." *Earth and Planetary Science Letters* 298, nos. 1–2: 255–62, 2010.

Metcalfe, Sarah E., M. D. Jones, S. J. Davies, A. Noren, and A. MacKenzie. "Climate Variability over the Last Two Millennia in the North American Monsoon Region, Recorded in Laminated Lake Sediments from Laguna de Juanacatlán, Mexico." *The Holocene* 20, no. 8: 1195–1206, 2010.

Peterson, Larry C., and Gerald H. Haug. "Climate and the Collapse of Maya Civilization." *American Scientist* 93, no. 4: 322–29, 2005.

Webster, James W., George Brook, L. Bruce Railsback, Hai Cheng, R. Lawrence Edwards, Clark Alexander, and P. P. Reeder. "Stalagmite Evidence from Belize Indicating Significant Droughts at the Time of Preclassic Abandonment, the Maya Hiatus, and the Classic Maya collapse." *Palaeogeography, Palaeoclimatology, Palaeoecology* 250, nos. 1–4: 1–17, 2007.

■ AMY FRAPPIER

COBÁ

The gigantic Classic Maya site of Cobá (20.5° N, 87.7° W) in northern Quintana Roo, Mexico, is located 43 km from the Caribbean on two large, shallow lakes and several smaller ones. The site has numerous large ceremonial groups with temple-**pyramids**, platforms, and **ball courts**, all linked by **causeways**. The city covers 70 km², and its population peaked at about 50,000 in the Late Classic, making it comparable to **Tikal** and **Calakmul**. Its abundant freshwater supply in the lakes was clearly a major factor in its development as a regional power.

Apparently first visited by José Peon Contreras and D. Elizade of Merida in 1886, Teobert Maler then made photographs there in 1891. Following a visit by Thomas Gann in 1926, who reported the site to the Carnegie Institution of Washington, Cobá was investigated by J. Eric S. Thompson and Sylvanus Morley. The site continued to be studied in the 1970s by William Folan and in the 1980s by Antonio Benavides and Linda Manzanilla.

Cobá's tallest structure is the 42-m-high Nohoch Mul, built in the Late Classic, with a small Late Postclassic temple atop. Over 50 *sacbes* at Cobá connect ceremonial groups with each other, at lengths as short as 1 km, and with smaller neighboring polities such as Ixil, 16 km away. The longest *sacbe* built by Cobá runs westward for 100 km to **Yaxuná**, just 18 km southwest of **Chichen Itza**. Cobá took control of Yaxuna in the Late Classic, likely as a defensive move against Chichen Itza expansion. Defensive palisades at Yaxuná similar to those at **Dos Pilas** and **Aguateca** testify to siege, probably by Chichen Itza (see also **Fortifications**; **Warfare, Warriors, and Weapons**). Cobá's actions to control Yaxuná may have been part of efforts to link itself with the Puuc region.

Following settlement in the Late Formative, documented by pottery, and development in the Early Classic, Cobá kings erected at least 32 **stelae**; most are badly eroded today, frustrating efforts to construct the city's history. The earliest verifiable inscribed date at Cobá was AD 624, and another stela carries the date AD 684.

Notwithstanding the highly eroded condition of the stelae of Cobá, David Stuart suggests the following about dynastic rule.

Ruler A celebrated the half-*k'atun* ending date of 9.9.10.0.0, March 26, AD 623 according to Stela 6. ? Chan Yopaat "Ruler B" took power on 9.10.7.5.9, April 9, AD 640, as recorded on Stela 4. He celebrated the 13-*tun* anniversary of his accession on 9.11.0.5.9, January 31, AD 653, as recorded on Stela 1. He also celebrated the *k'atun*-ending of 9.12.0.0.0, July 1, AD 672, also recorded on Stela 1. Ruler C came to power on August 30, AD 682. His accession date, 9.12.10.5.12, August 30, 682, figures prominently in the historical records of **Naranjo** as the point when Lady Six Sky of **Dos Pilas** arrived in Naranjo to revitalize and reestablish the royal line. Ruler D came to power on January 18, AD 773. He celebrated the half-*k'atun* ending 9.17.10.0.0, December 2, AD 780 (see also **Divine Kings and Queens**).

Ceramic evidence shows Cobá peaked in power during the period from AD 730 to 1000 and went into decline ca. AD 1000–1200. During the latter period, the Early Postclassic, Cobá was likely conquered by Chichen Itza, then abandoned. There was a small population on the site in the Late Postclassic.

See also ARCHITECTURE OVERVIEW; CERAMICS; LAKES

Further Reading

Benavides C., Antonio. "Arquitectura doméstica en Cobá." In *Coba, Quintana Roo: Análisis de dos unidades habitacionales mayas del horizonte clásico*, edited by Linda Manzanilla, 25–67. México, D.F.: Universidad Nacional Autónoma de México, 1987.

Folan, William J., Ellen R. Kintz, and Laraine A. Fletcher. *Coba: A Classic Maya Metropolis*. Edited by Stuart Struever. Studies in Archaeology. New York: Academic Press, 1983.

Garduño Argueta, Jaime. "Introducción al patrón de asentamiento del sitio de Cobá, Quintana Roo: Tesis que para obtener el título de licenciado en antropología con especialidad en arqueología." Tesis de licenciatura, Escuela Nacional de Antropología e Historia, México, 1979.

Manzanilla, Linda, ed. *Coba, Quintana Roo: Análisis de dos unidades habitacionales mayas*. México, D.F.: Instituto de Investigaciones Antropológicas, Universidad Nacional Autónoma de México, 1987.

Stuart, David. *Notes on Accession Dates in the Inscriptions of Coba*. Mesoweb, 2010. http://www.mesoweb .com/stuart/notes/Coba.pdf.

Thompson, J. Eric S., Harry E. D. Pollock, and Jean Charlot. *A Preliminary Study of the Ruins of Coba, Quintana Roo, Mexico*. Carnegie Institution of Washington, Publication 424. Washington, DC: Carnegie Institution of Washington, 1932.

■ WALTER R. T. WITSCHEY

COCHUAH REGION

The Cochuah region (20.3° N 88.35° W at its center) is located near the center of Mexico's Yucatan Peninsula, in the west-central portion of the state of Quintana Roo and southeastern edge of the state of Yucatan. It is accessed from secondary roads leading south from the city of Valladolid or north-northwest from Chetumal. In terms of modern towns, the province extends to the south of Chunhuhub and Polyuc, to the east of Tepich, and to the north of Chikindzonot, as well as to the east of Lake Chichancanab.

Although this region is commonly left blank on maps of archaeological sites, it has actually been shown to be full of such sites. At present, 85 sites have been recorded, with the largest of these being Ichmul and Yo'okop (Okop). It is characterized by relatively little topographic variation, a paucity of surface water, and thin, reddish **soils** directly over often-exposed bedrock. **Caves** are common in the area; many contain archaeological remains.

The first outsiders to document the archaeological remains of the Cochuah region were Mason and Spinden in 1926. In 1954 Strømsvik, Pollock, and Berlin, under the auspices of the Carnegie Institution of Washington, spent six days exploring the area, visiting both Ichmul and Yo'okop. Yo'okop received further attention from amateur archaeologists Wilson, Walker, and Clapp in the late 1960s and early 1970s before a brief INAH study in the late 1990s. Since 2000, Justine Shaw and Dave Johnstone, joined by Alberto Flores and other colleagues, have worked in the region.

Ceramic dates indicate some occupations from the Middle Formative period (600/500–300 BC) until the present, although the Late Formative (300 BC–AD 250) and Terminal Classic periods (AD 750–1100) were the times when the population was greatest in the region, at levels not reached again until the late twentieth century. Following Spanish arrival in 1546, numerous churches were constructed, with the most notable being three churches in Ichmul, site of one of the first Franciscan monasteries in Yucatan.

During the Caste War (1847–1901), several forts were constructed, and key battles were fought between Maya rebels and the Mexican military. This prolonged conflict resulted in the partial abandonment of the main towns, which caused the region's infrastructure development to lag behind other portions of the peninsula until very recently.

Yo'okop (19.9° N, 88.5° W) is the most-studied site in the study area. Its extensive settlement zone has four areas of concentrated construction, Groups A–D, which contain the largest **architecture** at the site, including **temples**, **palaces**, plazas, acropoli, a sweat-bath, and a **ball court**; these groups are connected by a network of **causeways** (*sacbeob*), which was primarily constructed during the Terminal Classic. The site contains **stelae**, altars, and glyph blocks, one of which refers to a relationship with the southern site of **Calakmul**. Its Group A lies to the immediate southwest of the only body of water in the region, a culturally modified *aguada*. Ceramics indicate that it was occupied from the Middle Formative through the Postclassic; during Classic times, it had **trade** connections to the Petén and other portions of the southern lowlands.

Ichmul (20.2° N, 88.6° W) also contains a *sacbe* system, which radiates from the site core to connect to five outlying, smaller centers (San Andrés, San Cristobal, San Juan, San Pedro, and Xquerol). These roads appear to have been constructed in two phases, both of which date to the Terminal Classic. Much of the site center has been damaged by Colonial constructions, Caste War fortifications, and modern occupations, making it difficult to locate intact surface remains. Limited excavations have revealed ceramics from the Middle Formative through the Terminal Classic. Although ethnohistoric sources indicate that it was important in the Postclassic (AD 1100–1546), remains dating to this period have not been located.

Further Reading

Shaw, Justine M. "The Late to Terminal Classic Settlement Shifts at Yo'okop." In *Quintana Roo Archaeology*, edited by Justine M. Shaw and Jennifer P. Mathews, 144–57. Tucson: University of Arizona Press, 2005.

———. *White Roads of the Yucatán: Changing Social Landscapes of the Yucatec Maya*. Tucson: University of Arizona Press, 2008.

———. "Roads to Ruins: The Role of Maya Sacbeob in Ancient Maya Society." In *Highways, Byways, and Road Systems in the Pre-modern World*, edited by Susan E. Alcock, John P. Bodel, and Richard J. A. Talbert, 128–46. Chichester, UK: Wiley-Blackwell Press, 2012.

Shaw, Justine M., ed. *2,500 Years of Occupation in the Cochuah Region: Archaeological and Ethnographic Findings*. Albuquerque: University of New Mexico Press, 2014.

■ JUSTINE M. SHAW AND ALBERTO G. FLORES COLIN

CODEX

See CODICES (MAYA)

CODEX-STYLE VASES

The label *codex-style* is applied to a specific group of Maya **ceramic** vessels, characterized by fine-line monochrome black painting on a cream background with red rim and basal

Figure 10. Codex-style vase. Photo courtesy Princeton University Art Museum.

bands. Atypical codex vessels may have red figures and/or black rim and basal bands. Michael Coe called this technique codex-style, because he believed that the artists who created these vessels were painters accustomed to inscribing the folding-screen books that the Maya made from bark paper covered with stucco (see also **Codices [Maya]**). The style was created during the Late Classic period around the turn of the eighth century, and it represents some of the best work that pre-Columbian artists created. The style flourished for only a short time, possibly not more than a half a century; the technique did not undergo significant modifications. The theme presented on the vessels varies from long glyphic texts describing lineage, to single or large multiple images of **deities**, to complex mythological scenes. Because of the apparent sequence of many of these scenes, Robicsek in his book on codex-style vessels, *The Maya Book of the Dead*, further developed Coe's view that not only were the vessels painted by codex-artists, but if appropriately arranged, they may indeed represent an ancient manuscript and could be interpreted as such. By placing codex-style vases in special order, he "retrieved" several unknown ancient myths, as well as fractions of legends recorded in the *Popol Vuh*. Codex-style vessels have been found almost exclusively in Petén. Sites from which they have been recovered include **El Mirador**, **Tikal**, **Rio Azul**, and **Calakmul**. Extensive studies on the composition and origin of the vessels were carried out by Ronald Bishop and Dorie Reents-Budet. Chemical studies of them suggest that this pottery style was produced at **Nakbé** and neighboring sites. See figure 10.

See also DECIPHERMENT

Further Reading

Coe, Michael D. *The Maya Scribe and His World*. New York: The Grolier Club, 1973.

Reents-Budet, Dorie, and Ronald L. Bishop. "The Late Classic Maya 'Codex Style' Pottery." In *Primer Coloquio Internacional de Mayistas*, 775–89. México City, D.F.: Universidad Nacional Autónoma de México, Centro de Estudios Mayas Coloquio Internacional de Mayistas, 1987.

Robicsek, Francis, and Donald M. Hales. *The Maya Book of the Dead: The Ceramic Codex; The Corpus of Codex Style Ceramics of the Late Classic Period*. Charlottesville, VA; University of Virginia Art Museum, 1981. Distributed by University of Oklahoma Press.

■ FRANCIS ROBICSEK

CODICES (MAYA)

During the pre-Hispanic period, screenfold books (called codices, codex in the singular) incorporated knowledge about celestial cycles, agriculture, apiculture, and other topics; designated the appropriate days for performing rituals and **subsistence** tasks; and were used for divinatory purposes (see also **Rites and Rituals**). At the time of Spanish contact in the 1520s, dozens (or perhaps hundreds) of codices existed. Many were destroyed by Spanish friars and officials in their efforts to convert the Maya to Christianity, whereas a small number—three that are known today—were sent or taken to Europe during the Colonial period, likely as "curiosities" or examples of the idolatrous practices of the native populations. Named for the cities where they are currently housed, they include the Dresden, Madrid, and Paris codices. The Madrid codex is the longest, with 112 pages (56 leaves painted on each side), whereas the Dresden has 74 painted pages. The Paris codex appears to be only a fragment of the original; most of its 22 pages are substantially eroded.

A fourth codex of questionable origin, the Grolier, was reportedly found, along with other pre-Columbian artifacts, in a dry **cave** in Chiapas, **Mexico**, in the 1960s. Although some scholars accept it as a pre-Hispanic Maya codex, others question its authenticity, pointing to its anomalous style (which differs from the other three codices) and sloppy execution as evidence that it is of twentieth-century manufacture.

The physical manuscripts that exist today were likely painted within a century prior to the Spanish conquest. They nevertheless contain almanacs and tables that can be dated—by correlating the Maya linear **calendar** (the Long Count) with the Gregorian calendar—many centuries prior to that. Indeed, the Dresden codex's astronomical tables appear to have been initially used during the eighth to tenth centuries, suggesting that they form part of a tradition passed down from one generation of scribes to another over the centuries (see also **Astronomy**).

Astronomer-scribes like those who painted the codices may have used the walls of buildings to record and calculate celestial cycles, as suggested by recent excavations at **Xultun**, **Guatemala**. The Xultun inscriptions are contemporaneous with the use date of the eclipse table in the Dresden codex, suggesting that much of the astronomical knowledge recorded in the extant codices was initially calculated by Classic period calendrical specialists who transferred this information to screenfold books. New knowledge was then added by later scribes, as was the case with the Dresden Venus table, which was updated for use in the thirteenth century.

The Paris codex emphasizes two calendrical cycles that played a role in prophecy and perhaps also in political organization: a cycle of 13 *tun* of 360 days, and a cycle of 13 *k'atun* (20 × 360 days), or approximately 256 years. The former relates primarily to prophecies concerning the maize crop (represented by the maize deity), whereas the *k'atun* series records celestial events (eclipses, movements of the planet Venus), ruling **deities**, and prognostications pertaining to each numbered *k'atun* in the sequence spanning the years 475 to 731 CE. (See figure 11.)

The Madrid codex also focuses on celestial events and ruling deities, although its primary emphasis was on scheduling **subsistence** activities and associated rituals within a cycle of 52 years, formed by pairing the 260-day sacred cycle and the 365-day solar

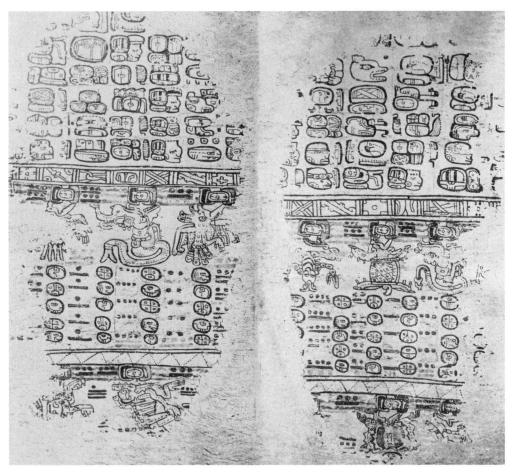

Figure 11. Two pages from the Paris codex. The Maya "zodiac" included 13 constellations, conceptualized as animals of various types. The turtle, for example, corresponded closely with the Western constellation of Orion, whereas the owl can be compared to Gemini and the rattlesnake to the Pleiades. Photograph after Rosny (1883). Courtesy of Gabrielle Vail.

year (see figure 12). The Grolier codex contains a partial Venus almanac (10 of 20 pages remain) of possible pre-Hispanic origin.

Sources from the Colonial period suggest that the Maya likely also had codices that focused on medicine, history, genealogies, and other themes, but none of these are known to have survived.

See also DECIPHERMENT; ICONOGRAPHY; LANDA, BISHOP DIEGO DE; RELIGION

Further Reading

Bricker, Harvey, and Victoria R. Bricker. *Astronomy in the Maya Codices*. Philadelphia, PA: American Philosophical Society, 2010.

Förstemann, Ernst Wilhelm. *Die Mayahandschrift der Königlichen Öffentlichen Bibliothek zu Dresden*. Leipzig: Verlag der A. Naumann'schen Lichtdruckerei, 1880.

Figure 12. Two pages from the Dresden codex Venus table. Shown are Venus in its warrior aspect at heliacal rise (middle picture on each page) and the victim of its aggression (bottom picture on each page). The upper picture on the first page shows the Moon goddess presiding over the events pictured, whereas the maize god is shown standing before the newly ascended Sun god on the following page. Photograph after Förstemann (1880). Courtesy of Gabrielle Vail.

Love, Bruce. *The Paris Codex: Handbook for a Maya Priest.* Austin: University of Texas Press, 1994.

Rosny, Louis Léon de. *Codex Cortesianus.* Manuscrit hiératique des anciens Indiens de l'Amérique centrale conservé au Musée archéologique de Madrid. Photographié et publié pour la première fois, avec une introduction et un vocabulaire de l'écriture hiératique yucatèque par Léon de Rosny. Paris: Libraires de la Société d'Ethnographie, 1883.

Vail, Gabrielle, and Anthony F. Aveni. *The Madrid Codex: New Approaches for Understanding a Pre-Hispanic Maya Manuscript.* Boulder: University Press of Colorado, 2004.

Vail, Gabrielle, and Christine Hernández. *Re-Creating Primordial Time: Foundation Rituals and Mythology in the Postclassic Maya Codices.* Boulder: University Press of Colorado, 2013.

———. *Maya Hieroglyphic Codices,* Version 5.0, March 2, 2014. Electronic data set. www.mayacodices.org.

■ GABRIELLE VAIL

COLLAPSE
See CLASSIC MAYA COLLAPSE

COMALCALCO

Ancient Comalcalco (18.3° N, 93.2° W) is located on an alluvial plain 2.5 km northeast of the modern town of that name. This ancient city flourished in the Late Classic period. The ruins stand on the east bank of the Seco River, a former tributary of the Grijalva, the major water artery of the region. Today, the area around the site comprises cattle pasture, fruit orchards, and **cacao** plantations.

Comalcalco was an important political center in the northwestern frontier of the Maya region. In ancient Mayan hieroglyphs, the city is called Joy-Chan ("knotted sky"). Discovered in 1869 by Carl Berendt, Comalcalco became famous in 1887 after the publication of Désiré Charnay's popular book describing ancient cities of the New World. In 1925 Frans Blom and Oliver LaFarge of Tulane University conducted the first significant research at the ruins.

The most important temples and a **palace** are situated in the core of the archaeological site, located in approximately 1 km² of flat terrain. Several residential areas, mostly occupied by **house** mounds and minor ceremonial structures, encircle the core. Because of the high humidity and long rainy season, excess water and an unhealthful swamp environment were constant problems. For this reason, both ceremonial and residential structures were built on artificial mounds surrounded by *bajos*. An unusual feature of urban planning is an advanced drainage system made of fired clay tubes (see also **Water Management**). The lack of native stone for construction material was another obstacle to settlement. Comalcalco is unique in that it was built using fired clay bricks rather than the limestone blocks that are typical of lowland Maya sites. It also is noteworthy that many of the bricks are decorated with graffiti consisting of various incised or painted ornaments, texts, and symbols (see also **Iconography**).

Its peripheral location on the Gulf of Mexico implies that the inhabitants of Comalcalco interacted with neighboring non–Maya peoples. Yet the **architecture**, sculptural style, and decorative motifs are similar to those developed throughout the Maya lowlands (see also **Northern Lowlands**; **Central Lowlands**; **Southern Lowlands**).

Comalcalco contains three major architectural complexes: the Great Acropolis, the North Group, and the East Acropolis. Each has precise north-south or east-west orientation. The Great Acropolis towers over the central part of the city and is an enormous pyramidal platform supporting a palace and several smaller temples. Blom discovered a small vaulted tomb made of bricks on the west side of the **palace**. The tomb is particularly interesting because of its preserved stucco relief and hieroglyphic inscriptions (see also **Royal Tombs**). The North Group contains a plaza bounded by a large **pyramid** and flanked by two parallel rows of minor temples. The Great Acropolis was connected to the North Group by a pavement made of fired bricks topped with a thick coat of lime plaster. The East Acropolis is a smaller and less complex version of the Great Acropolis. It is thought that the three principal groups were planned to have special visual lines of sight and axial alignments.

Archaeologists have found 111 smaller mounds in the 72 ha surrounding the core. This yields a settlement density of 154 structures per square kilometer, average for a Maya settlement.

Unfortunately, there are few texts describing Comalcalco's relations with its Maya neighbors. A monument at Tortuguero, the site's main regional rival, commemorates the defeat of Comalcalco in AD 649.

See also ART; PALENQUE

Further Reading

Andrews, George F., and Donald L. Hardesty. *Comalcalco, Tabasco, Mexico: Maya Art and Architecture*. Culver City, CA: Labyrinthos, 1989.

Blom, Frans Ferdinand, and Oliver La Farge. *Tribes and Temples: A Record of the Expedition to Middle America Conducted by the Tulane University of Louisiana in 1925*. New Orleans: Tulane University of Louisiana, 1926.

Charnay, Désiré. *The Ancient Cities of the New World: Being Travels and Explorations in Mexico and Central America from 1857–1882*. Translated by J. Gonino and Helen S. Conant. London: Chapman and Hall, Ltd., 1887.

Zender, Marc, Ricardo Armijo Torres, and Miriam Judith Gallegos Gómora. "Vida y Obra de Aj Pakal Tahn, un Sacerdote del Siglo VIII en Comalcalco, Tabasco, Mexico." *Los Investigadores de la Cultura Maya* 9, no. 2: 386–98, 2001.

■ MAYA AZAROVA

CONSTRUCTION TECHNIQUES
See ARCHITECTURE OVERVIEW; HOUSES

COPÁN

Copán (14.8° N, 89.1° W), a major Classic Maya city and kingdom, is famous for its exceptional **art**, **architecture**, and inscriptions (see also **Decipherment**). Its texts have provided a detailed body of information about the ancient Maya, particularly its kings of the Classic period. It ranks, with **Tikal** and **Palenque**, as one of the most extensively researched and best known of all Maya sites.

It is situated on the north bank of the Copán River in western **Honduras**, on a broad expanse of floodplain known as the Copán pocket. The Copán River flows into the Motagua, passing the nearby site of **Quiriguá**, 50 km north, on its way to the Caribbean Sea. After the abandonment of the site, the natural meandering of the Copán River cut into the site center, eroding a significant portion of the acropolis and creating a 37-m-tall by 300-m-long archaeological cross-section of its deposits, revealing four centuries of construction by 16 kings of Copán.

Copán is the easternmost major Maya site, and some scholars have conjectured that its charismatic and salient art and architecture was intended to signal the ethnic identity of the inhabitants to their non-Maya neighbors to the east. Despite its location in the hills of Honduras at an elevation of about 600 m, the site is culturally lowland, not highland, Maya. Its upland situation, however, did provide access to resources not commonly found in the lowlands. Early hieroglyphic inscriptions indicate that Copán's rulers called it Ox Witik (Three Mountain Place).

Copán was settled in the Early Formative period. Rich **burials** in what later became the residential areas of the site reveal connections to the **Olmec** and other contemporaneous Mesoamerican cultures (see also **Royal Tombs**). **Ceramics** from mortuary **caves** in hills forming the valley margins also show connections to **Mexico**. The Classic period known **dynastic sequence** started in AD 426 with Yax K'uk' Mo' who seems to have had some connection with **Teotihuacán**, and it developed through the Late Classic. Its final dated monument marks the accession of the last Copán king in AD 822, but the **Classic Maya collapse** overcame Copán before the monument was fully carved.

Copán was known to the Spaniards of the sixteenth century, and John Lloyd Stephens and Frederick Catherwood visited and purchased Copán in their travels of the 1830s. In modern times, there has been a succession of archaeological research and restoration projects at Copán under the aegis of the Instituto Hondureño de Antropología e Historia (IHAH), the Carnegie Institution of Washington, and the Peabody Museum of Harvard University. Since 1983 William Fash has directed a significant number of cross-institutional research projects at Copán that have revealed earlier structures that document the reigns of dynastic kings known from Altar Q and the **Hieroglyphic Stairway**.

The Acropolis of Copán can be divided into four sections, corresponding to the cardinal directions. In the north is a great plaza where several magnificent **stelae** with important inscriptions stand. This area was probably accessible to the public and may have had **causeways** (*sacbes*) leading to it. In the southern part of the plaza lies the great **ball court**, which carried massive macaw-head **sculptures** on its façades, perhaps alluding to the founder of the Copán dynasty, part of whose name, "K'uk' mo'," means "quetzal macaw." Temple 26 overlooks the southeast corner of the plaza, tucked just behind the ball court. The Hieroglyphic Stairway of Temple 26 bears the longest of all Maya inscriptions, excised and then carved in deep relief on the risers of the steps. The deeply carved balustrades (*alfardas*) and protruding sculptures in the middle of the stairs would have impressively memorialized the power of the dynasty for the public. The southern margin of the plaza rises steeply to the higher regions of the acropolis. Stone steps completely cover the width of this face of the acropolis, providing seating for thousands of spectators (see also **Music and Dance; Theater**). Atop this broad stair is Temple 11, not yet excavated, but the second highest structure on the acropolis. The top of the acropolis is divided into East and West Courts separated by the bulk of Temple 16, the tallest structure at the site. Excavations by Ricardo Agurcia Fasquelle within this large pyramid have revealed the remains of a carefully preserved earlier temple, named "Rosalila." Rosalila is covered with extraordinarily elaborate painted stuccoes that provide a glimpse of what many major Maya buildings might have looked like had they been preserved. The building was dedicated in AD 571 by the king known as Moon Jaguar. The West Court is dominated by the back of Temple 11 as well as by Temple 16. Altar Q was originally situated in the West Court in front of Temple 16. The East Court was surrounded by Temples 20 through 22, although Temples 20 and 21 were mostly destroyed by the meandering of the Copán River. Temple 22A may have been a **council house**, or *popol nah*, although this interpretation has been challenged. Broad stairways lead from the East and West Courts to the southern part of the acropolis. Here, Structures 29 through 32 form a palatial residential quadrangle probably built by Yax Pasaj, the last great king of Copán (see also **Palace**).

The buildings visible today on the acropolis are only the last ones built. Many earlier structures and associated **royal tombs** are buried within the acropolis, which is an entirely artificial construction composed of earlier structures and fill. Archaeologists have been able to study the earlier constructions by tunneling into the mass of the acropolis. The later structures were built of finely cut rectangular stone, quarried from the soft volcanic tuff of the surrounding hills. The masonry is carefully coursed and bonded, but the mortar used was weak, and most roof vaults collapsed long ago. The architecture is notable for integrating elaborate sculptures into façades and roofs. Some sculptures are still in situ, while others have been reassembled by archaeologists after meticulous excavation. Like other Maya architectural sculptures, those of Copán were composed of mosaics of stone blocks, but those of Copán were larger and more finely carved than most.

At Copán, unlike at other sites, the masons apparently assembled the blocks in place before carving them, rather than fabricating separate sculptural elements at workshops and then cementing them together later during construction. The Copanec method created a more refined aesthetic effect than the approach used at most other sites. In general, the sculpture of Copán, both architectural and freestanding, was more three-dimensional than most Maya art, in which low-relief carving predominates. For example, many of the **stelae** at Copán were carved in half- or three-quarters round style, a departure from the canonical Maya bas-reliefs found at most sites.

Altar Q, a square throne dedicated in AD 776, provides a retrospective account of the Copán dynasty. The altar has four Maya kings carved along each side, with each of the 16 rulers seated on his name glyph. An inscription covers the upper surface. The Altar Q texts complement a lengthy inscription of more than 2,000 glyphs on the risers of the Hieroglyphic Stairway, the longest of all Maya texts, which provides the dynastic sequence for 15 of the 16 rulers portrayed on Altar Q. The sequential portraits of the kings on Altar Q form a statement of the legitimacy and power of the sixteenth king, Yax Pasaj Chan Yopaat, as he sits beside the first king and founder of the dynasty to symbolically receive the authority to rule from him. The altar sat above a crypt with 15 sacrificed jaguars, one for each predecessor king (see also **Rites and Rituals**).

Based on the inscriptions of Copán, the dynastic sequence is well known from AD 426 through at least AD 810. Rulers 1 through 15 are mentioned on the Hieroglyphic Stairway, and Rulers 1 through 16 are carved on Altar Q. The review by Martin and Grube, summarized below, covers the highlights.

Prior to the arrival of K'inich Yax K'uk' Mo', a few inscriptions hint that the Maya actually founded Copán in the Formative. Date references span 321 BC–AD 376, including a celebration of the *k'atun*-ending date 8.6.0.0.0, December 18, AD 159. K'inich Yax K'uk' Mo' ("Radiant First Quetzal Macaw") ruled from September 5, AD 426 until ca. 435–437. He was considered the founder of the Copán dynasty in the inscriptions. On Altar Q, he appears with goggle eyes, a square shield, and a quetzal bird headdress, all indicative of connections to Central Mexico and **Teotihuacán**. The Altar Q text implies that he assumed his power at another distant site at a building called the *wi te' naah*, together with the king of **Quiriguá**, and arrived at Ox Witik (Copán) 152 days later. He is shown on the altar passing a scepter to the sixteenth ruler, Yax Pasaj Chan Yopaat, who commissioned Altar Q, in a powerful statement of legitimacy to the throne, on July 2, AD 763. Yax K'uk' Mo' was clearly an outsider who arrived at Copán to create a new political regime. With Central Mexican associations, including building the Hunal, a structure beneath Temple 16 with Teotihuacán-style *talud-tablero* architecture, Yax K'uk' Mo' may well have been leading a continued expansion by the Central Mexicans who arrived at **Tikal** in AD 378. He was buried in a vaulted crypt within the Hunal, and skeletal analysis revealed battle wounds, which he had survived, but which had not healed properly.

K'inich Popol Hol ("Mat Head," "Tok") acceded to power ca. AD 437. Popol Hol built the first ball court at Copán and elaborated his father's tomb by constructing multiple buildings over it, including those known as Yehnal, and Margarita, which served as the tomb of Popol Hol's mother, a local woman married to Yax K'uk' Mo'. He also constructed the Motmot building atop his father's Yax platform. It contains an unidentified woman's grave, with disarticulated bones interred with offerings and sacrifices, including skulls of three males, all in Teotihuacán style.

Dates of rule are not known for the next four rulers: K'ak' Ajaw ("Ruler 3"); K'altuun Hix ("Bound Stone Jaguar," "Ruler 4," "Cu-Ix,' "Ku Ix"), who built or extended the structure Papagayo over the Motmot structure, where an unusual text indicated that he was specifically quoted on the occasion; and rulers 5 and 6.

B'ahlam Nehn ("Jaguar Mirror," "Waterlily Jaguar," "Jaguar-Sun-God," "Ruler 7"), came to power August 4, AD 524 and ruled until ca. AD 532. Twenty-two days after his inauguration, B'ahlam Nehn celebrated the half-*k'atun* ending 9.4.10.0.0, August 26, AD 524. He named himself as the seventh ruler of Copán in a contemporaneous inscription. He was mentioned a decade later on Stela 16 at Caracol dated to the *k'atun*-ending celebration of 9.5.0.0.0, July 5, AD 534, by which time his successor was already in office.

Wi'Youl K'inich ("Ruler 8,""? is the Heart of the Sun God") came to power November 22, AD 532, and ruled until AD 551. Sak-lu ("Ruler 9") came to power December 28, AD 551 and ruled until AD 553.

Moon Jaguar ("Tzik B'ahlam,""Cleft-Moon Leaf-Jaguar,""Ruler 10") came to power May 24, AD 553, and ruled until his death on October 24, AD 578. In addition to mentions on the Hieroglyphic Stairway and Altar Q, Moon Jaguar erected two stelae, dated AD 554 and AD 564. He also dedicated the Rosalila temple in AD 571.

Butz' Chan ("Smoking Heavens," "Ruler 11," "Smoke Serpent," "Fire-eating Serpent") came to power November 17, AD 578, and died January 20, 628. During the reign of Butz' Chan, the population at Copán grew rapidly, as it did in other Late Classic Maya cities. At least two monuments were commissioned during his lengthy reign, including one for the celebration of the *k'atun*-ending 9.9.0.0.0, May 12, AD 613.

K'ak' Uti' Witz' K'awiil ("Smoke Imix," "Smoke-Jaguar Imix-Monster," "Smoke Jaguar," "K'ak' Nab K'awiil," "Ruler 12") was born November 11, AD 604, and came to power February 5, AD 628. He likely ruled until his death on June 15, AD 695. He lived to be titled a Five-*k'atun* Lord, surviving beyond his seventy-ninth year. A large group of monuments was carved for the *k'atun*-ending 9.11.0.0.0, October 14, AD 652. Five were widely spaced about the Copán Valley, one at Santa Rita, 12 km away. A monument at Quiriguá mentions him at the same time. In the center of Copán, he ritually razed the Papagayo structure built by Ruler 4 and erected the pyramid Mascaron above it. Subsequently Mascaron was rebuilt as Chorcha, his tomb. He clearly supervised the construction of his own tomb, since he was interred in it two days after his death.

Waxaklajuun Ubaah K'awiil ("Eighteen images of K'awiil," "18 Rabbit," "Ruler 13," "18 JOG") came to power July 2, AD 695, and ruled until death on April 29, 738. There was considerable construction development in his reign, including the Great Plaza, expansion of the Ball Court, and construction of the Hieroglyphic Stairway describing the first 12 rulers and 18 Rabbit himself. He erected numerous stelae at Copán beginning in AD 702, including markers for burning the town of Xkuy in AD 718, inaugurating the king of Quiriguá in AD 724, and linking himself to **Tikal**, **Calakmul**, and **Palenque** on a monument dated AD 731. Twice he remodeled the Great Ball Court, the second time dedicating it 6 January AD 738. In a stunning reversal for Copán, 18 Rabbit was captured and killed by his underlord, the king of Quiriguá K'ak' Tiliw' Chan Yopaat, on April 29, AD 738, in an event recorded at Quiriguá as an "axing" (beheading). From this moment, Copán may have been under the control of Quiriguá. There were no monuments, altars, or buildings erected at Copán for 17 years, while Quiriguá flourished and grew rapidly after this instantaneous shift of power.

The fourteenth ruler, K'ak' Joplaj Chan K'awiil ("K'awiil That Stokes the Sky with Fire," "Smoke Monkey," "Three Death") came to power June 7, AD 738 and ruled until his death on January 31, 749. He held the throne during the domination of Quiriguá. He is known only from other retrospective monuments, since no monuments were erected during his reign.

K'ak' Yipyaj Chan K'awiil ("K'awiil that Fills the Sky with Fire," "Ruler 15," "Smoke Shell," "Smoke Squirrel") came to power February 14, AD 749 and ruled until ca. AD 761. He appears to have ruled quietly for a time, following the death of his father, but then wrested power away from Quiriguá and resumed construction and monument carving. He doubled the length of the inscription of the Hieroglyphic Stairway to include himself; built its upper temple; and carved imagery reminiscent of the glory days of affiliation with Teotihuacán, including written passages in parallel Maya hieroglyphs and ersatz Teotihuacán writing. His stela at the foot of the stairway was dedicated on the quarter-*k'atun* date 9.16.5.0.0, April 12, AD 756.

Yax Pasaj Chan Yopaat ("First Dawned Sky Lightning God," "Yax Pac," "Madrugada," "Rising Sun," "New Sun at Horizon") came to power June 28, 763, and ruled until ca. 810. Yax Pasaj completed a variety of buildings during his reign, including Temple 11 in AD 769, and its upper levels in AD 773. He also was responsible for the last renovation and elaboration of the tomb of Yax K'uk' Mo', Temple 16. In front of it, he placed Altar Q, where he portrayed himself as the sixteenth king of Copán, receiving power directly from its founder. There are few dated monuments during this time, but several inscriptions with his name have been found in the southern 10L-32 quadrangle of the site, suggesting he built it or lived there. Ruler 16 celebrated his own second *k'atun* (40-year anniversary) and erected his last monument on the three-quarter-*k'atun* ending 9.18.15.0.0, July 24, AD 805.

Ukit Took' came to power February 6, 822. An unfinished Altar L, in the style of Altar Q, showed on its face the inauguration of Ukit Took' receiving power from his predecessor. One other side was sketched but not carved out. This incomplete monument attests to the end of kingly reign in Copán, and its fall as part of the **Classic Maya collapse**.

A visitor to Copán is struck immediately by the beauty and elegance of the visible ruins, as well as their picturesque setting in a placid valley among contorted volcanic hills. Copán is a UNESCO World Heritage site, and tourists make a significant contribution to the economy of the Honduras.

See also ARCHITECTURE OVERVIEW; ART; CALENDAR; CORBEL ARCH; DECIPHERMENT; HONDURAS; IXIMCHÉ; IXTEPEQUE; KAMINALJUYÚ; MAYA AREA; MAYA QUEENS; *POPOL VUH*; PUSILHA; SCULPTURE; SOUTHERN ARCHITECTURAL STYLE; SOUTHERN PERIPHERY; STUART, GEORGE E., AND DAVID STUART; TEOTIHUACÁN (MAYA INTERACTIONS WITH); THEATER; WARFARE, WARRIORS, AND WEAPONS; WATER MANAGEMENT; WOMEN, MEN, AND GENDER ROLES; WRITING SYSTEMS OF MESOAMERICA

Further Reading

Andrews, E. Wyllys, V, and William Leonard Fash, eds. *Copán: The History of an Ancient Maya Kingdom*. School of American Research Advanced Seminar Series. Santa Fe, NM: School of American Research, 2005.

Bell, Ellen E., Marcello A. Canuto, and Robert J. Sharer, eds. *Understanding Early Classic Copan*. Philadelphia: University Of Pennsylvania Museum of Archaeology and Anthropology, 2004.

Fash, William L. *Scribes, Warriors, and Kings: The City of Copan and the Ancient Maya*. London: Thames & Hudson, 1991.

Introducción a la arqueología de Copan, Honduras. 2 vols. and map set. Tegucigalpa, DC, Honduras: Proyecto Arqueológico Copán, Instituto Hondureño de Antropología e Historia, Secretaría de Estado en el Despacho de Cultura y Turismo, 1983.

Martin, Simon, and Nikolai Grube. *Chronicle of the Maya Kings and Queens: Deciphering the Dynasties of the Ancient Maya*. 2nd ed. London: Thames & Hudson, 2008.

Stephens, John Lloyd. *Incidents of Travel in Central America, Chiapas, and Yucatan*. London: John Murray, 1841.

■ CLIFFORD T. BROWN AND WALTER R.T. WITSCHEY

CORBEL ARCH

The corbel (corbelled) arch or vault is a roof construction technique found throughout the Maya area (**Palenque** to **Copán** and north to **Dzibilchaltun** and **Chichen Itza**). True keystone arches were seldom used by Maya builders. The corbel arch is built by adding stones to the top of a pair of facing walls. Each new course of stone is closer to the centerline of the wall pair, until the uppermost course is close enough to bridge with a capstone. (The same procedure is used by children with dominos.) The resulting ceiling is typically high, and the construction results in long narrow rooms, often found in **palace** structures such as at **Tikal**, Palenque, and **Yaxchilan**. The Maya added cross timbers for added wall-to-wall stability. While a few survive, most such beams have long vanished, but their sockets in the masonry, as at **Bonampak**, document their earlier use. Compared to a keystone arch, the corbel does not transfer roof loads to wall lines as effectively, and collapsed corbel arches are common archaeologically. It is not uncommon to find rooms whose outer walls have fallen outward, leaving a well-preserved inner wall. Subtle variations in construction highlight temporal and regional styles. In the Puuc, for example, later arches utilize boot-shaped stones whose tenons project into the wall and roof fill, and whose face is well dressed on the room interior. (See figure 13.)

See also ARCHITECTURE OVERVIEW; PUUC ARCHITECTURAL STYLE

Further Reading

Coe, Michael D. *The Maya*. 8th ed. London: Thames & Hudson, 2011.

Evans, Susan Toby. *Ancient Mesoamerica & Central America: Archaeology and Culture History*. 2nd ed. London: Thames & Hudson, 2008.

Miller, Mary Ellen, and Megan Eileen O'Neil. *Maya Art and Architecture*. 2nd ed. London: Thames & Hudson, 2014.

Figure 13. Ceremonial corbel arch astride the *sacbe* from Uxmal to Kabah. Courtesy of Walter Witschey.

Proskouriakoff, Tatiana. *An Album of Maya Architecture*. Carnegie Institution of Washington, Publication 558. Washington, DC: Carnegie Institution of Washington, 1962.

Sharer, Robert J., and Loa P. Traxler. *The Ancient Maya*. 6th ed. Stanford, CA: Stanford University Press, 2006.

■ WALTER R. T. WITSCHEY

CORN

See DIET; SUBSISTENCE

COTZUMALHUAPA

Renowned for its sculptural corpus of more than 200 stone monuments, Cotzumalhuapa (14.3° N, 91.0° W) was a major Late Classic city in southern **Guatemala**. The archaeological site is located on the fertile volcanic piedmont of the modern department of Escuintla, on the slopes of the active Fuego Volcano, at an elevation of 400–600 m above sea level. It includes the major **architectural** compounds of El Baúl, El Castillo, and Bilbao, which were previously regarded as separate sites, but are now understood as part of an extensive ancient city.

Scattered sherds provide evidence of community life dating back to the Middle Preclassic period (ca. 600 BC). By the Late Preclassic, Cotzumalhuapa was an important political and ritual center, whose leaders participated in broad networks of interaction, extending across the **Pacific coast** and **southern Guatemalan highlands**. Later constructions buried and obliterated the remains of early communities, except for deeply buried construction stages at Bilbao and El Baúl. The El Baúl Stela 1 and Bilbao Monument 42 portray standing lords engaged in ritual performance, evidencing the growing power of kings and the onset of monumentality for the commemoration of religious and political ritual (see also **Rites and Rituals**; **Divine Kings and Queens**). The obliterated glyphic cartouches of El Baúl Stela 1 contained one of the longest known Preclassic inscriptions in Mesoamerica and one of the earliest dates in the Long Count **calendar**, corresponding to AD 36 (see also **Decipherment**).

The early Cotzumalhuapa communities dwindled during the Early Classic, perhaps in response to the growth of major centers farther south. There is little evidence of influence from the highland Mexican city of **Teotihuacán**, which was strongly felt on the Pacific coastal plain between AD 400 and 650. The dominant center was Montana, which may have received an influx of Teotihuacán immigrants. Cotzumalhuapa was never abandoned, and perhaps not by coincidence, it reemerged as a dominant center after the demise of Montana. During the Late Classic period (AD 650–950) it became an extensive city, covering a minimum of 10 km². The urban layout was integrated through a complex system of **causeways** and bridges that linked together the major compounds and extended into surrounding settlements.

The El Baúl acropolis was the largest architectural compound and perhaps the royal **palace** and administrative center of the Late Classic city. In its final version it was a large, rectangular platform with two walled enclosures that may have had defensive functions (see also **Fortifications**). The entire compound covered almost 10 ha and rose 15 m above the surrounding terrain. The buildings were made of packed earth, in many cases with stone facings made from local andesite. Cobblestones were abundantly used in pavements, stairways, and building façades, while dressed stones were occasionally employed in stairways.

El Castillo was a smaller but no less important compound that may have served as the city's central plaza. The Bilbao acropolis was built in the southern part of the city, over the remains of substantial Preclassic occupation. Its size was similar to, but it was shorter than, El Baúl. Its architectural layout suggests mainly ceremonial functions, and it had an extraordinarily rich inventory of **sculptured** monuments.

No less than five causeways radiated from the El Baúl acropolis. These stone-paved avenues had variable width, typically ranging between 4 and 14 m wide. The exceptionally wide Eisen causeway reached 40 m, linking the El Baúl acropolis with an important compound located 180 m north. The 12-m-wide Lehmann causeway ran 300 m to the west, connecting the acropolis with a large **ball court**. The Gavarrete causeway was the longest, with an average width of 12 m, and extending 250 m to reach the Bilbao acropolis. Other causeways linked to settlement areas north and east of the acropolis. The Berendt causeway joined El Castillo to Bilbao, and the Habel causeway extended to Golón, a little known sector with an important array of finely carved sculptures.

Of special note are the stone bridges that span the course of several streams along the causeways. Until its destruction during tropical storm Agatha in 2010, Thompson's bridge—first reported by the noted archaeologist J. Eric S. Thompson—was the only standing pre-Columbian bridge in Mesoamerica. Its walls were built with large, undressed stones that sustained slabs over the stream. The Gavarrete causeway featured a much larger bridge over the course of the Santiago River, south of El Baúl. The retaining walls extended 30 m along the river course and originally rose to a height of 7 m, sustaining a perishable bridge. The remains of other bridges are found elsewhere in the city.

Population estimates are not available. Thick layers of recent soils cover the remains of house compounds, making them invisible on the surface. Geophysical prospection has revealed a high density of settlements around El Baúl and El Castillo, while the Bilbao sector has less dense settlements. Evidence of productive activities includes the remains of an **obsidian** workshop near El Baúl, associated with an extensive dump that contains debris from the manufacture of blades and projectile points, made of raw materials imported from **El Chayal** and San Martín Jilotepeque, in the Guatemala highlands. Representations of **cacao** in the sculptures suggest that this was an important product from ancient times and may have contributed to the city's prosperity and political sway.

The Cotzumalhuapa sculptors developed a distinctive sculptural style. The sculptures include rock carvings; freestanding **stelae**; three-dimensional sculptures; and architectural elements that include pillars, stairway blocks, wall panels, and numerous horizontally tenoned heads that projected from building façades. Elaborate reliefs represent complex scenes of interaction among several participants, often portrayed with dramatic realism. Important sculptures from El Baúl include Monument 14, a three-dimensional rampant jaguar of heroic proportions, and Monument 27, a magnificent stela that shows a gladiatorial confrontation between two masked opponents (see also **Warfare, Warriors, and Weapons**). Major sculptures from Bilbao include eight stelae that show dancing characters dressed as ball players, who perform human sacrifice and present offerings to probable ancestors and gods (see also **Music and Dance**; **Ball Game/Ball Court**). The enormous rock carving of Bilbao Monument 21 shows another scene of dance and music in a flowering place, in the presence of an enthroned goddess. The monumental El Castillo Stela 1 shows a character ascending the teeth of a gigantic maw, from which emerges the sun god (see also **Deities**). The sculptures also contain inscriptions in a local, poorly known **writing system**. The annotations generally feature circular signs combined with numerals to form **calendrical** annotations. Oversized signs and various forms or animation are frequent.

Cotzumalhuapa was probably the center of a powerful polity, whose influence extended over a large region in southern Guatemala. Surrounding sites include Palo Verde, Aguná, and many smaller sites with Cotzumalhuapa-style architecture and sculptures. Other important sites with Cotzumalhuapa sculptures include Palo Gordo, Los Cerritos Norte, La Nueva, and many others, distributed along more than 200 km along the Pacific coast. The style is also present in the highlands, with an especially strong presence in the Antigua Guatemala valley.

Since its discovery in the nineteenth century, the Cotzumalhuapa style was noted for its apparent links with various styles from the Gulf Coast, highland **Mexico**, and other regions. Early scholars interpreted the style as the product of migrant peoples. Archaeological evidence fails to support this supposition, although the style did incorporate **iconographic** motifs from Teotihuacán that were probably introduced to the coast by Early Classic migrants. The Cotzumalhuapa sculptures are strongly related with contemporary carvings from **Chichen Itza**, which place a similar emphasis on the representation of flowering places associated with dance and music, the ball game, and human sacrifice.

The city decayed around AD 950, and there was a period of stagnation during the Early Postclassic period. In the sixteenth century, Cotzumalhuapa was inhabited by the Pipil, speakers of a Nahua language that probably arrived during the Postclassic. The highland Kaqchikel kings of **Iximché** and Sololá also established settlements in the region to take advantage of its rich cacao production.

See also ARCHITECTURE OVERVIEW; ART; CERAMICS; CRAFT SPECIALIZATION

Further Reading

Chinchilla Mazariegos, Oswaldo. "The Flowering Glyphs: Animation in Cotzumalhuapa Eriting." In *Their Way of Writing: Scripts, Signs, and Pictographies in Pre-Columbian America*, edited by Elizabeth Hill Boone and Gary Urton, 43–75. Washington, DC: Dumbarton Oaks Research Library and Collection, 2011.

———. *Cotzumalguapa, la ciudad arqueológica: El Baúl-Bilbao-El Castillo*. Guatemala City, Guatemala: F&G Editores, 2012.

Parsons, Lee Allen. *Bilbao, Guatemala: An Archaeological Study of the Pacific Coast Cotzumalhuapa Region*. 2 vols. Publications in Anthropology. Milwaukee, WI: Milwaukee Public Museum, 1967–1969.

Thompson, J. Eric S. *An Archaeological Reconnaissance in the Cotzumalhuapa Region, Escuintla, Guatemala*. Contributions to American Anthropology and History, no. 44. Carnegie Institution of Washington, Publication 574. Washington, DC: Carnegie Institution of Washington, 1948.

■ OSWALDO CHINCHILLA MAZARIEGOS

COUNCIL HOUSE

From the ***Popol Vuh***, we know that one of the Late Postclassic titles of rulership was *Aj Pop* ("He of the mat"). The Maya also use *holpop*, "He at the head of the mat" for governor. The council house or *popol nah* ("mat house" in Yucatec Maya) is a distinctive architectural form with strong implications for how the Maya organized and governed themselves. The first *popol nah* recognized archaeologically was structure 10L-22a at **Copán**, built during the reign of the fourteenth ruler, K'ak' Joplaj Chan K'awiil, in AD 746, which has distinctive woven mat designs on the façade (see also **Dynastic Sequences**). In addition, the Copán council house has nine niches and glyphs representing the nine regions or neighborhoods of Copán, indicating perhaps that the lineage or region head for these barrios was the individual who was the delegate to the council house meetings.

Council houses were in use at the time of the conquest and are in use today in Maya villages. The *Chronicle of Calkini* describes them as buildings where people assembled at the doors in order to take part in a public meeting.

George J. Bey III and Rossana May Ciau report that *popol nahs* have been identified at **Ek Balam**, **Kiuic**, and **Labna** in the **Northern Lowlands** where they date to the Late and Terminal Classic. In general, a *popol nah* in that region is a structure with a long façade approached by wide steps with wide treads, a single long room, and multiple doorways to the interior room, which may have benches along the walls. One can easily picture a gathering of elders, seated and standing in the doorways to discuss community affairs.

The import of a *popol nah*, where found, is its implications for governance form: men's council. This stands in contrast to rulership by **divine king**. The archaeology of *popol nahs* suggests that they waxed and waned in favor over the centuries as governance shifted back and forth between divine king and men's council. The *popol nah* at Copán was built shortly after the thirteenth ruler, Waxaklajuun Ubaah K'awiil, was defeated and beheaded by K'ak' Tiliw' Chan Yopaat of **Quiriguá**. The timing suggests that the king of Copán was shifting governance to an earlier form, men's council, while Copán was under the control of Quiriguá.

See also ARCHITECTURE OVERVIEW

Further Reading

Encyclopedia Mesoamericana—Copan, Structure 10L-22A. Mesoweb http://www.mesoweb.com/encyc/index.asp?passcall=rightframeexact&rightframeexact=http%3A//www.mesoweb.com/encyc/view.asp%3Frecord%3D5404%26act%3Dviewexact%26view%3Dnormal%26word%3D10L-22A%26wordAND%3DCopan%2C+Structure%26redir%3Dno.

Andrews, E. Wyllys, V, and William Leonard Fash, eds. *Copán: The History of an Ancient Maya Kingdom.* School of American Research Advanced Seminar Series. Santa Fe, NM: School of American Research, 2005.

Bey, George J., III, and Rosanna May Ciau. "The Role and Realities of Popol Nahs in Northern Maya Archaeology." In *The Maya and Their Central American Neighbors: Settlement Patterns, Architecture, Hieroglyphic Texts and Ceramics*, edited by Geoffrey E. Braswell. New York: Routledge, 2014.

■ WALTER R. T. WITSCHEY

COZUMEL

Cozumel Island (20.4° N, 89.9° W), now a modern **Mexican** resort, is located 17 km east of the northern Yucatan Peninsula. The island measures 15 km wide by 45 km long, forming the eastern edge of the deep Yucatan Channel. There are numerous small Late Postclassic period structures as well as *sacbes* on Cozumel, and evidence that it was visited frequently from the mainland for pilgrimages in honor of the goddess Ixchel. Some evidence suggests that Cozumel was also a major trading entrepôt during the Postclassic period.

See also ARCHITECTURE OVERVIEW; CAUSEWAY/*SACBE*; DEITIES; RITES AND RITUALS; TRADE ROUTES

Further Reading

Freidel, David A., and Jeremy A. Sabloff. *Cozumel, Late Maya Settlement Patterns*. Orlando, FL: Academic Press, 1984.
Sabloff, Jeremy A., William L. Rathje, and Judith G. Connor. *A Study of Changing Pre-Columbian Commercial Systems: The 1972–1973 Seasons at Cozumel, Mexico; A Preliminary Report*. Cambridge, MA: Peabody Museum of Archaeology and Ethnology, Harvard University, 1975.

■ WALTER R. T. WITSCHEY

CRAFT SPECIALIZATION

Craft specialization is an important aspect of understanding the complex economic system utilized by past cultures. Often functioning as a proxy for urbanization and the flourishing of civilization, craft specialization concerns the production of goods by a certain segment of the population for use and consumption beyond the producers' households. Independent specialization occurs when there is unspecified demand for the product, while attached specialization occurs when specialists produce for elites or governing institutions in a patronage system.

Reconstructing Maya craft specialization has been problematic because there is little evidence for specialized workshops. In addition, certain crafts were perishable and do not survive in the archaeological record. Both independent and attached specialization occurred within the Maya area. The level of detail and scarcity of the resource determined if the craft was made by household specialization or via elite patronage/attached specialist. Those products, particularly jewelry or **eccentrics, flints** that were made by attached specialists (typically scribes), were of a higher quality and functioned as status symbols. The range of crafts that the ancient Maya specialized in included **ceramics, sculpture,** wood carving, painting, stonework, metalwork, **textiles,** basketry, and featherwork (see also **Wall Painting**).

Ceramics: Over time certain households specialized in ceramic forms or types for which there was greater demand. There were two methods of ceramic specialization within the Maya: household and mass production. Household production was usually tied to one or more family members, and these crafts were exchanged at local markets for utilitarian or nonlocal goods. Polychrome vessels are considered the epitome of specialization for their unique renditions of Maya narratives, ranging from historical to cosmological or mythological representations (see also **Codex-style Vases**). Polychrome vessels flourished during the Late Classic, replaced by mold-made, military-motif ceramics and Fine Orange Ware during the Postclassic. The Postclassic also marked the appearance of Plumbate ware, the only true glazed pottery found in the Americas prior to European contact.

Sculpture: Maya stone buildings were extensively carved, as were freestanding monuments (**stelae**). The extensive use of mosaics made of carved stone in façades and roof combs exhibits the great skill needed to sculpt these residences. Exterior **architecture** typically featured sculpting of propagandistic themes and elite glorification. Almost all carvings were painted in reds, yellows, blues, greens, or black depending on function and social status.

Stone Artifacts: Jade was highly prized by the Maya, as it represented a connection to the spiritual and was revered for its unique beauty. Due to the stone's hardness, those who specialized in jade work were highly specialized. It was transformed into naturally shaped cobbles, mosaics, pendants, plaques, and more. Ritual objects such as sacrificial knives, scepters, decapitators, and eccentrics (see also **Portable Objects**) were high-status markers, the finest of which were made of flint or **obsidian**.

Perishables (Textiles, Basketry, Featherwork): Textiles were often used to reaffirm trade partnerships and political alliances, particularly *patis* (woven cotton textiles of a fixed size). Finely woven cotton fabrics were elaborately embroidered, with spinning done with the use of a spindle whorl and weaving being done by belt loom, wherein one end of the warp is tied to a tree or post while the other is attached to the weaver's belt. While evidence for baskets and mats is restricted to **iconographic** representation, it is clear that baskets were essential to the traffic of goods, and mats were utilized for both practical and symbolic purposes. Feathers were used to make crests, capes, and shields, typically signifying a high-status individual. They were also used as personal ornamentation, to decorate scepters, and as embroideries.

Maya scribes had particular skills. Due to the specialized knowledge necessary for craft specialization, products created by Classic Maya elite-artists functioned to distinguish them from the nonelite populace. A unique feature of Classic Maya society was the role of Maya scribes in craft specialization. Scribes specialized in artistry, produced **codices**, painted ceramics, worked stone monuments, and much more. These elite specialists would autograph their work in order to both garner a reputation and add value to their products.

See also Altun Ha; Becan; Bonampak; Burials; Cahal Pech; Calakmul; Caracol; Ceibal; Ceren; Cerro Maya/Cerros; Chac II; Champotón; Chichen Itza; Chunchucmil; Cochuah Region; Comalcalco; Copán; Cotzumalhuapa; Dos Pilas; Dzibanché; Edzna; Ek Balam; El Mirador; El Perú-Waka'; El Pilar; Holmul; Ichkabal; Itzimte; Iximché; Izamal; Izapa; Jaina; Kabah and Nohpat; Kaminaljuyú; Kiuic; Kohunlich; Komchen; La Corona; La Lagunita; Labna; Lamanai; Mayapán; Naachtun; Naj Tunich; Nakbé; Naranjo; Nixtun Ch'ich; Noh Kah; Oxkintok; Palenque; Piedras Negras; Pusilha; Quiriguá; Rio Azul; Río Bec; San Bartolo; Sayil; Sin Cabezas;

TAKALIK ABAJ; TAMCHEN AND CHACTUN; TAYASAL; TIKAL; TONINÁ; UTATLÁN/Q'UM'ARKAJ; UXMAL; XCOCH; XUNANTUNICH; YAXCHILAN; YAXHÁ; YAXHOM; YAXNOHCAH; YAXUNA; ZAC-PETÉN; ZACUALPA; ZACULEU

Further Reading

McKillop, Heather. *The Ancient Maya: New Perspectives*. New York, NY: W. W. Norton & Company, Inc. 2004.

Sharer, Robert J. *Daily Life in Maya Civilization*. The Greenwood Press "Daily life through History" Series. Westport, CT: Greenwood Press, 1996.

Weeks, John M. *Maya Civilization*. New York: Garland Publishing, 1993.

■ ASHLEY HAMPTON

D

DANCE
See MUSIC AND DANCE

DATING

To accurately portray Maya cultural history, scholars use a variety of dating techniques to establish when events occurred. Maya researchers use most of the same techniques employed worldwide for ancient cultures.

Relative dating consists of several techniques to determine whether two or more compared things are older or younger than each other. Super-positioning, the principle that in an undisturbed archaeological context newer objects are found at the top of an excavation, and older ones are buried deeper, is used to establish site stratigraphy and relative dates for artifacts and features.

Between sites, archaeologists can compare material they excavate with the findings of earlier researchers to match material to time period. Seriation depends on the principle that cultural norms for **ceramic** and **architectural** styles change over time. Matching a pottery style in one location to a securely dated vessel from another helps establish a relative chronology. In the Maya area, archaeologists use the type-variety classification system to identify relevant time periods for potsherds they recover. Material dated with relative techniques can usually be securely dated to a period of Maya history, such as the Late Classic (see also **Ceramic Analysis**).

Absolute dating is the gold standard for chronology. Maya researchers are fortunate to recover inscriptions with dates that may be correlated with the Judeo-Christian calendar. Such absolute dates may then be used to date pottery styles and architectural styles. Dates were often recorded in the Maya Long Count and may be converted to the modern **calendar** with an accuracy of within three days. Unfortunately, Maya Long Count dates are only available in the Classic Period (see also **Decipherment**).

Researchers in the Maya area also use radiocarbon-14 dating. The most common form (isotope) of the element carbon is ^{12}C, with six protons and six neutrons. The ^{14}C isotope is unstable and decays to ^{14}N by beta decay (loss of an electron) with a half-life of about 5,700 years. Since ^{14}C is constantly formed in the upper atmosphere, its presence in the earth's carbon reservoir makes it available to plants, which in turn are eaten by animals.

In this way, all living things incorporate and constantly exchange the various isotopes of carbon, including carbon-14, with their environment.

When an organism dies, it no longer participates in the carbon exchange, and by radioactive decay, the amount of ^{14}C in the organism slowly declines, while the amount of ^{12}C remains constant. Scientists measure the ratio of ^{14}C to ^{12}C with an accelerator mass spectrometer or other instrument to determine how many years have passed since the organism died. In this way the construction posts of buildings and the charcoal of campfires, for example, may be tested to determine their absolute age.

Although other techniques for dating are employed, most Maya chronologies are based on Long Count dates, radiocarbon-14 dating, and seriation and cross-matching of artifact and architectural styles.

See also HIEROGLYPHIC STAIRWAYS; STELA

Further Reading

Burke, Heather, Claire Smith, and Larry J. Zimmerman. *The Archaeologist's Field Handbook*. Lanham, MD: AltaMira Press, 2009.
Libby, Willard F. *Radiocarbon dating*. Chicago: University of Chicago Press, 1985.
Rice, Prudence M. *Pottery Analysis: A Sourcebook*. Chicago: University of Chicago Press, 1987.

■ WALTER R. T. WITSCHEY

DECIPHERMENT

In hindsight, it is astonishing that the ancient Maya script took so long to decipher. When the Spaniards arrived in Yucatan, they not only encountered the natives there speaking Maya, but also knew they were writing their language in books. Three of these fan-folded books, **codices**, made their way to Europe shortly after the conquest and were lost from view, but were rediscovered in the 1800s. A fourth codex came to light in **Mexico** in 1965. **Diego de Landa** wrote of his experiences in Yucatan and collected detailed information about the Maya he found there in the 1500s. A fragment of his book, *Relación de las cosas de Yucatán*, survives in the Real Academia de la Historia in Madrid today.

In his book, Landa portrays writing symbols used by the Maya, with whom he spoke, and his drawing is well known today as the Landa alphabet. (See figure 26 in the sidebar.) It is an important tool in decipherment, but it is not an alphabet in the strict sense. Rather, it contains Maya symbols for the sounds of Latin letters as pronounced by the Spaniards of the sixteenth century. Landa also carefully illustrated how the symbols may be combined in order to form phrases in spoken Maya. The Maya, of course, also left behind what we know today is an enormous inventory of texts, carved on stone monuments (see also **Stelae**), inscribed on **hieroglyphic stairways**, painted on **royal tomb** walls, painted on polychrome **ceramic** vases, and etched into other **portable objects** such as bones, shells, and jades. Most of this material was discovered within the past 200 years. With this wealth of written material and an obvious target language (spoken Maya), the course of decipherment has nonetheless been a difficult one, filled with dead ends and labyrinthine turns.

After the conquest in the 1500s, nearly 200 years passed before the world awakened to the idea of ruined cities in the jungles of Mexico and **Guatemala**. The early explorer Antonio del Rio made an expedition to **Palenque** and in 1787 reported on the buildings and bas-relief **sculptures** he found. His report reached the Royal Collection of Natural History in Madrid; it was translated into English in 1822, together with a number of the drawings by Ricardo Almendáriz from his original. This is the first known instance of publication of carved-stone Maya hieroglyphs.

Juan Galindo visited Palenque in 1931 and **Copán** in 1834, and his illustrated report drew attention to the similarity between the two Maya cities. Constantine Samuel Rafinesque-Smaltz saw several of these early publications and recognized that the hieroglyphs inscribed at Palenque and those in the Dresden codex were the same (see also **Codices [Maya]**). He also decoded the Maya base-20 counting system of bar and dot numerals with a shell for zero.

Interest in the Maya burst into the consciousness of the Western world with the publication of books by John Lloyd Stephens in 1841 and 1843, who traveled through the Maya region with artist Frederick Catherwood. Stephens described the sites they visited and included Catherwood's masterful drawings made with a *camera lucida* (image projector). He also believed that the inscriptions of Palenque and those of Copán and **Quiriguá** were the same and that they matched the writing in the Dresden codex. It was clear at this time, to these men at least, that the inscriptions were in the language spoken by the living Indians of the area, the Maya.

The next player on the decipherment stage was Abbé Charles Étienne Brasseur de Bourbourg. His discoveries were remarkable. In 1855 he recorded a Maya drama, the *Rabinal Achi* (see also **Theater**). He also discovered a copy of the *Popol Vuh*, the great creation story of the Maya. In 1862 he discovered the only known copy of Landa's *Relación*, which contained not only the "alphabet" of Maya glyphs, but also glyphs for month and day names in the Maya **calendar**. He discovered a portion of the Madrid codex. His eager efforts to translate the scripts available were unfortunately completely misguided.

In 1887 the basic mechanisms of the Maya calendar were worked out by Ernst **Förstemann**, a librarian in Dresden, who became captivated by the codex in his care. To him we owe the discovery of the Long Count, the 260-day calendar tables in the Dresden codex, and tables for the appearances of Venus and eclipses of the moon. In 1905 Joseph T. Goodman suggested that Maya dates and dates in the Christian calendar could be matched day-for-day.

Alfred P. Maudslay and Teobert Maler's contributions, photographic recordings (1889–1911) of inscriptions from numerous major Maya sites, provided a rich body of texts from which decipherment could proceed—but it did not. Smaller breakthroughs continued, including decoding the glyphs for the compass points. Those focused on the Maya calendar and dates in the inscriptions paid little attention to the non-numeric content.

This bias against the inscriptions was largely due to J. Eric S. **Thompson**, who during the 50 years of his professional career (1925–1975) assumed an absolute moral and professional dominance over the field. His belief that the script would never be deciphered, since it had no phonetic content, intimidated most in the field of Maya studies. Thompson himself published a comprehensive catalog of Maya glyphs, but despaired of their translation.

In the decade of the 1950s, three scholars made a profound impact on how the glyphs were viewed and what their content might be. Their work led directly to decipherment. Yuri V. **Knorosov**, of the Institute of Ethnology, Leningrad, Russia, published an article in 1952 that was a tour de force of cryptographic analysis and understanding of languages. He interpreted Landa's alphabet as syllables, a consonant followed by a vowel, such as "ka." Instead of representing the letter "k" as most had assumed, the glyph Landa labeled "k" represents the sound "ka," as in Landa's short phrase *ma-i-n-ka-ti* represented by five syllabic glyphs. By cross-linking the Landa illustrations with Maya phrases from the Dresden codex, Knorosov demonstrated that glyphs showed the correct pronunciation for common words (turkey, dog, captured, macaw) as found in dictionaries of the Maya language.

At this time, the height of the Cold War, Thompson rejected Knorosov's premises completely, not only for their alleged connection to Marxism-Leninism, but also because they did not match his own preconceived views of the script. In any case, the Knorosov work did not circulate widely outside Russia. Thompson's objections placed a nearly insurmountable roadblock to phonetic decipherment in the paths of scholars for the next 25 years.

The other two major breaks in decipherment were made by Heinrich Berlin in 1958 and Tatiana **Proskouriakoff** in 1961. Berlin stated that he had identified glyphs that in part were universal across the Maya area, but which varied in their main portion from place to place. These he called "Emblem Glyphs." The implication was that the Maya inscriptions might be referring to specific locations or cities. The **Tikal** emblem glyph typically looked like a hair-knot; the Copán emblem glyph was a leaf-nosed bat. Today, such glyphs are read as "Holy Lord of (place)" and are known to refer to **divine kings** from the great Maya cities.

Proskouriakoff noticed a striking pattern of dated monuments from **Piedras Negras** on the Usumacinta River. In front of individual temples were groups of stelae with clear dates. Within each group, the total date range was approximately that of a human life span. The individual groups overlapped in dates, just as the life spans of grandfathers, fathers, and sons overlap. She also found that the earliest date in each group was near a glyph that looked like a tipped-up frog's head, and that the next date was always near a "toothache" glyph, a bird's head with a jaw bandage. She correctly surmised that each group of dates referred to one individual ruler; that his birth date, date of accession, and other life events were recorded; and that the groups of stelae together recorded a span of then dynastic history of Piedras Negras. This bombshell was plain evidence for all that the Maya inscriptions carried history, and that when deciphered, they would tell the stories of the great Maya rulers. The glyphs that Proskouriakoff identified could still not be pronounced, but suddenly their content meant that the Maya, like all other powerful people on the planet, had recorded their own personal histories on their monuments.

Yet the Thompson opposition to the idea of phonetic glyphs was at its peak of power. Few dared contradict him (among them David Kelley and Michael Coe). Not until 1973, two years before Thompson's death, did decipherment take wing, as a direct result of Merle Greene Robertson convening an eight-day roundtable at Palenque that included Floyd Lounsbury, Linda **Schele**, and Pater Mathews, among others. Lounsbury had provided a phonetic reading for the Emblem Glyphs, showing that they contained the Maya word for king or ruler, *ajau*. Schele had been captivated by the **art** of the glyphs and the illustrations that accompany them. Mathews had made a detailed catalog of all the glyphs known at Palenque. In a half day's work, six rulers in the Palenque **dynastic sequence** had been identified, including Lord Shield, who is buried in the rich tomb beneath the Temple of the Inscriptions. They further identified that his name, represented by a Maya war shield, was also spelled phonetically as *pa-ca-l(a)*, *pacal*, the Maya word for shield. From there it was a short leap to the identification of many occurrences at Tikal and elsewhere that stelae often included both parents' names and clear genealogical statements.

With Thompson's passing, phoneticism became a "legitimate" study; linguists also joined the action. At the center of the transition from pre-Thompson to post-Thompson thinking were Linda **Schele** and David **Stuart**.

In 1976, at the age of eight, David, son of archaeologist George Stuart, was beginning to translate glyphs. He had a Maya vocabulary at his disposal, acquired during a lengthy childhood stay at **Cobá** with his parents. Under Linda Schele's mentorship, he began translating the text on Palenque panels. He became a MacArthur Foundation Fellow in 1984 and is still the youngest person to have received such recognition. As they observed, Stuart blends anthropological linguistics, epigraphy, archaeology, ethnohistory, art history, and iconography. He has become the foremost scholar of the glyphs of our era.

By 1979 virtually all scholars of the script wholeheartedly embraced the Knorosov idea that the script was phonetic. New ideas tumbled out, such as polyvalence—one word could be represented by several different glyphs, or one glyph could represent several different words and meanings. By 1984 Peter Mathews could publish a rather complete **syllabary** of glyphs and the syllables they represented. Among epigraphers at the heart of new readings from the mid-1980s onward are Mathews, Stuart, Steve Houston, Nikolai Grube, Barbara MacLeod, and Karl Taube. These scholars produce new readings at a prodigious rate, at the same time that many new hieroglyphic texts are being unearthed by archaeologists.

A band of glyphs around the rims of many Maya vessels has yielded to decipherment, with surprising results. These bands, first identified by Michael Coe and called the Primary Standard Sequence, are now known to carry information such as the type of ceramic (dish, bowl, vase), whether it is painted or carved, the owner's name, and sometimes the intended contents (***ca-ca-o***: chocolate, *sac-ul*: corn gruel or *atole*). They often carry the name of the artist as well. This process of naming things, name-tagging, has now been also found on stelae, buildings, and **portable objects**.

The fact that Maya scribes signed their work and sometimes included their own genealogies provides direct evidence that they were far more than skilled artisans and craftsmen—they were actually members of the royal family closely related to the king himself. This positions the royal family, not priests, as long believed, as the curators of esoteric knowledge for Maya society. The royals knew and managed the calendar, **astronomy**, and the ancient script.

Today, much of the script that is phonetic can be directly read. This still leaves some individual names and other glyphs unpronounceable, yet the continuing discovery of new texts in this ancient writing system produces new phonetic parallels and new semantic details that bring vigorous life and meaning to previously undecipherable text. The story of the Maya as presented in their own words becomes richer every day.

See also Writing Systems of Mesoamerica

Further Reading

Coe, Michael D. *Breaking the Maya Code*. 3rd ed. London: Thames & Hudson, 2012.

Coe, Michael D., and Mark Van Stone. *Reading the Maya Glyphs*. 2nd ed. London: Thames & Hudson, 2005.

Houston, Stephen, Oswaldo Fernando Chinchilla Mazariegos, and David Stuart, eds. *The Decipherment of Ancient Maya Writing*. Norman: University of Oklahoma Press, 2001.

Johnson, Scott A. J. *Translating Maya Hieroglyphs*. Recovering Languages and Literacies of the Americas. Norman: University of Oklahoma Press, 2013.

Montgomery, John. *Dictionary of Maya Hieroglyphs*. New York: Hippocrene Books, 2006.

Saturno, William A., David Stuart, and Boris Beltrán. "Early Maya Writing at San Bartolo, Guatemala." *Science* 311, 5765: 1281–83, 2006.

Stuart, David. "Ten Phonetic Syllables." In *Research Reports on Ancient Maya Writing*, edited by George E. Stuart. Barnardsville, NC: Center for Maya Research, 1987.

Vail, Gabrielle, and Christine Hernández. *Re-Creating Primordial Time: Foundation Rituals and Mythology in the Postclassic Maya Codices*. Boulder: University Press of Colorado, 2013.

■ WALTER R. T. WITSCHEY

DEITIES

Maya gods were conceived in complex and multifarious ways. Most Mesoamerican peoples, including the Maya, polytheists par excellence, recognized numerous deities, and many gods were seen as having multiple aspects, incarnations, or embodiments. Many divinities show a variety of attributes, powers, or domains, which sometimes overlapped or blended, making their specific identification difficult.

This array of gods begs the question: Did the Maya really perceive gods as specific anthropomorphic beings with divine powers, or did they hold an animistic belief in the divinity of all natural objects, beings, and forces, known as '*K'uh*' in Maya? Certainly many places, such as caves, lakes, mountains, volcanoes, and objects, such as maize, idols, and chert knives, were charged with sacred meaning. The Spaniards considered this question.

The Spanish priests, and especially the friars, were obsessed with understanding Maya religion, if only to destroy it, and they were trained in theology. Of course they were ethnocentric, but their testimony is credible. The Spanish friars were in general convinced that the Maya viewed individual deities as potent individual, anthropomorphic, supernatural beings.

Some gods personified celestial bodies, such as the Sun, the Moon, Venus, and Mars. Ancestors were often deified, either specifically or generically; in many cases lineages or other kinds of descent groups had tutelary gods. Gods were related to the **Mesoamerican calendar** and its ritual cycles. Some gods had four avatars, associated with the cardinal directions and their respective colors.

In addition to early Spanish accounts such as Diego de Landa's *Relación*, information about Maya gods comes from Classic period polychrome ceramics and from iconography, as illustrated in the Postclassic period codices and other works of art.

One of the first systematic attempts to reconstruct the Maya pantheon from the gods shown in the codices was undertaken by Paul Schellhas in the late nineteenth century. Rather than try to attribute names to the gods shown in the codices, he designated them with Roman letters, starting with A. This is the origin of terms such as "God C," "God K," and "Goddess O" in Maya iconography and epigraphy. Although some have been revised, these designations are still used by scholars.

In the Early Classic the Maya make references to Chan K'uh, the Sky God, and to Kab K'uh, the Earth God. Classic period polychromes illustrate Itzamnaj, the Sky God, God D, Chac, the Storm and Rain God, God B, K'inich Ajaw, the Sun God, the Underworld Jaguar God, K'awiil, the Lightning God, God K, the Underworld God, God L, Chaac Chel, the Rainbow God, God C, Ix Sak Un, the Moon Goddess, and the Fire God.

The Maya Postclassic codices likewise refer to Itzamnaj (Ajaw Itzamnaj, Holy Lord Itzamnaj), Chac, K'inich Ajaw, and K'awiil. In addition, there are references to the Maize God-God E; Kimi, the God of Death-God A; the "God-of-All-Things"-God C; Ek Chuaj, the God of Merchants; Buluc Chabtan, the God of War and Human Sacrifice-God F; Ix Chel, the Rainbow Goddess; Goddess I; and Ix Tab, the Suicide God.

Beyond these, the Maya pantheon included the Deer God Wak Sip, the North Star God Aj Chikum Ek, Paddler Gods in the underworld, patron deities for each day, nine patron Gods of the Night, thirteen Gods of the Upper World, and Gods of the thirteen *k'atuns*.

Linda Schele and Mary Miller mention many of these and also identify the Celestial or Bicephalic Monster, the Cauac Monster, the Water-Lily Monster, the Vision Serpent, the Palenque Triad (gods GI, GII-God K, and GIII), the Headband Twins (Hero Twins from the *Popol Vuh*), the Monkey Scribes, the Paddler Gods, the Jester God that appears on royal scepters, the Maize God, the Old Gods (Gods L, N, and D), the Celestial Bird, Muan Bird, and the Water Bird. (See Figure 14.)

There is no general agreement on the number of Gods the Maya identified.

Figure 14. Classic polychrome vase. A Maya lord presents an offering to the Old God and Moon Goddess. Roll-out photo courtesy of Justin Kerr.

See also ARCHITECTURE OVERVIEW; ART; ASTRONOMICAL OBSERVATORIES; BONAMPAK; CACAO; CALENDAR; CAVES; CERRO MAYA/CERROS; CHAC II; CODEX-STYLE VASES; CODICES (MAYA); DIVINE KINGS AND QUEENS; ECCENTRIC LITHICS; EDZNA; GROUNDWATER/WATER TABLE; ICONOGRAPHY; IZAMAL; IZAPA; KABAH AND NOHPAT; MEDICINE; MUSIC AND DANCE; PETÉN ARCHITECTURAL STYLE; *POPOL VUH*; PRIESTS; PUUC ARCHITECTURAL STYLE; PYRAMID; RELIGION; RITES AND RITUALS; RITES OF PASSAGE; SAN BARTOLO; SCULPTURE; SUBSISTENCE; TAYASAL; TEXTILES AND CLOTHING; THEATER; TIKAL; UXMAL; WALL PAINTING; WOMEN, MEN, AND GENDER ROLES; WRITING SYSTEMS OF MESOAMERICA

Further Reading

Estrada-Belli, Francisco. "Lightning Sky, Rain and the Maize God: The Ideology of Preclassic Maya Rulers at Cival, Petén, Guatemala." *Ancient Mesoamerica* 17, no. 1: 57–78, 2006.

Looper, Matthew George. *To Be Like Gods: Dance in Ancient Maya Civilization*. Austin: University of Texas Press, 2009.

Milbrath, Susan. *Star Gods of the Maya: Astronomy in Art, Folklore, and Calendars*. Austin: University of Texas Press, 2000.

Miller, Mary Ellen, and Karl A. Taube. *The Gods and Symbols of Ancient Mexico and the Maya: An Illustrated Dictionary of Mesoamerican Religion*. New York: Thames & Hudson, 1993.

Schele, Linda, and Mary Ellen Miller. *The Blood of Kings: Dynasty and Ritual in Maya Art*. New York and Fort Worth, TX: G. Braziller and the Kimbell Art Museum, 1986.

Taube, Karl A. *The Major Gods of Ancient Yucatan*. Washington, DC: Dumbarton Oaks, 1992.

Tedlock, Dennis. *Popol Vuh: The Mayan Book of the Dawn of Life*. rev. ed. New York: Simon & Schuster, 1996.

Thompson, J. Eric S. *Maya History and Religion*. Norman: University of Oklahoma Press, 1970.

Tozzer, Alfred M. *Landa's "Relación de las cosas de Yucatán": A Translation*. Papers of the Peabody Museum of American Archaeology and Ethnology, vol. 18. Cambridge, MA: Harvard University, 1941.

■ WALTER R. T. WITSCHEY

DIET

The Maya diet is traditionally described as "corn, beans, squash, and chilies." This fails to satisfy in several ways. First, the Maya used corn (*zea mays*) as their single, major staple food, consuming it in multiple forms several times each day. Maize permeated every aspect of life, from domestic activities to spiritual and religious **iconography**. Second, the list ignores the rich array of other foodstuffs and condiments available and used and cultivated deliberately or acquired opportunistically. Last, the diet of Maya royalty was far more varied than that of commoners due to control of resources and **trade** goods, including foodstuffs.

There are several lines of evidence for the ancient Maya diet, including conquest-era descriptions, mentions of food in the hieroglyphic writing, archaeological remains of foodstuffs, and stable isotope analysis of human remains, and by ethnographic analogy to the diets of Maya people leading a traditional lifestyle today.

In 1517 Spaniards sailing under Francisco Hernández de Córdoba near Yucatan encountered a Maya canoe and asked for water. The Maya provided not only water but balls of ground maize (tamales?) and maize dough (*masa?*). The Spaniards landed on Cozumel, and the Maya there provided roasted and boiled birds, **cacao**, fruit of several varieties from their orchards, and honey. In Campeche, the expedition dined on bread made from maize, beans, venison, hares, partridges, doves, and likely turkeys. Some of the foods the Spanish were given by the Maya cannot be clearly identified today, but may have included mamey, sapote, papaya, and guinea pigs (see also **Fauna**; **Vegetation**).

Bishop **Diego de Landa**, writing of the Maya in 1566, said their principal **subsistence** was maize (corn, *zea mays*) of which they made a variety of foods and drinks. Landa describes several preparation steps, including the all-critical soaking of corn kernels in water mixed with lime, then grinding by hand three times. The ground corn was used to prepare breads, soups, and refreshing drinks, especially *posol* (once-ground cornmeal, sometimes fermented, in water) and *atole* (the most finely ground cornmeal, cooked in water). Landa also reported their mixing chili pepper or cacao into the corn drinks for flavoring. Beyond this strong emphasis on a variety of corn-based foods, he said the Maya made use of vegetables and of venison and of both wild and untamed birds, and fish. He added turtles, calling them meaty and tasty, with delicious eggs produced 150–200 at a time. *Balche*, an alcoholic beverage, was prepared from honey and the bark of the *balche* tree (*Lonchocarpus longistylus*). Although there is scant evidence for ancient preparation of tortillas, tamales were ubiquitous, with a variety of fillings: venison, birds, fish, squash seeds, *loroco* flowers, eggs, *chaya*, and *chipilín*.

The **codices** and inscriptions provide direct sources for diet. In the Dresden codex are mentions of tamales with iguana, turkey, deer, and fish. The Dresden also illustrates frogs, turtles, deer in snares, planting corn with a dibble stick, and numerous birds. The glyph for chocolate was deciphered in 1973 by Floyd Lounsbury. Since then, several varieties have been identified, including wild cacao, chocolate *atole*, new cacao, and fermented/sweet cacao. There are glyphs for *atole*, ripe *atole*, and bitter *atole*. A ritual drink, *sakha*, of cornmeal and water, appears in the inscriptions, sometimes connected with chocolate (see also **Rites and Rituals**). Newly uncovered murals at **Calakmul** mention vendors for tamales, *atole*, bread, corn, tamale dough, and salt.

The ratio of stable carbon and nitrogen isotopes found in bone collagen, bone apatite, and tooth enamel may be analyzed at high resolution to determine diet constituents. Maize was domesticated from the wild grass *teosinte* in the Balsa River drainage, Mexico. Isotope studies on more than 600 sets of human remains reported by Tycot reveal its early import to the Maya and other **Mesoamerican** peoples (see also **Physical/Biological Anthropology**). These studies compare animal and plant remains—white-tailed and other deer, domestic dog, armadillo, peccary, and freshwater turtle, as well as rabbit, opossum, raccoon, agouti, and tapir; fish and shellfish (in coastal and estuary areas); and maize, beans, squash, root crops, and fruits—to assess their fraction in the diet. By the Preclassic, Petén sites showed diets of approximately 70 percent maize, and typical values range from 50 to 70 percent maize in the diet. Variation in isotope ratios occurs between elites and commoners, Preclassic to Postclassic, and interior sites versus those with easier access to marine resources.

Archaeological evidence for the Maya diet comes from both dry contexts and flooded ones, such as in the Port Honduras region of Belize, where preservation may be exceptional. Foods documented include chocolate, domestic dogs raised for food, chilies, maize, squash, beans, and fish, among others. Along the coast of Yucatan at Tulum, Muyil, and other sites, fish net sinkers made from reworked potsherds are abundant and document a thriving initiative to catch fish in coastal lagoons.

Maya farmers today practicing ancient cultivation techniques intercrop corn, beans, squash, and chilies in their *milpas*. In addition, the household garden plot (*solar*) may contain several hundred species, including fruit trees that are cultivated for food, medicinal properties, ritual use, aesthetic attractiveness, and utilitarian purposes. They also hunt opportunistically, carrying a rifle with them to the *milpa*. These modern examples provide clues to ancient lifeways.

In sum, we know the major Maya crops of corn, beans, squash, and chilies were augmented with additional crops and materials gathered from the forest, including ramón, cassava, camote, macal, yam beans, piña, ayote, annona, vanilla, papaya, manioc, agaucate, and palmera. These plants were supplemented with hunted or tended birds, fish, and other animals, including chachalaca, crested guan, great curassow, ocellated turkey, and scarlet macaw; mussels, snails, crabs, conch, and skate; and turtle, iguana, cacomistle, opossum, howler monkey, spider monkey, tamandua, armadillo, rabbit, squirrel, porcupine, agouti, fox, raccoon, coati, kinkajou, jaguar, mountain lion, ocelot, margay, jaguarundi, manatee, tapir, peccary, white-tailed deer, and brocket deer.

See also CARACOL; CEREN; CERRO MAYA/CERROS; CLASSIC MAYA COLLAPSE; DECIPHERMENT; FAUNA; GEOLOGY; HOUSEHOLD PRODUCTION; ICONOGRAPHY; LABNA; LAMANAI; NORTHERN LOWLANDS; *POPOL VUH*; PHYSICAL/BIOLOGICAL ANTHROPOLOGY; REJOLLADA; RELIGION; RICHMOND HILL; RITES AND RITUALS; RITES OF PASSAGE; ROYAL TOMBS; SAN BARTOLO; SUBSISTENCE; TEXTILES AND CLOTHING; WOMEN, MEN, AND GENDER ROLES; WRITING SYSTEMS OF MESOAMERICA

Further Reading

Coe, Sophie D. *America's First Cuisines*. Austin: University of Texas Press, 1994.

Emery, Kitty F. *Dietary, Environmental, and Societal Implications of Ancient Maya Animal Use in the Petexbatun: A Zooarchaeological Perspective on the Collapse*. Institute of Mesoamerican Archaeology, no. 5 Nashville, TN: Vanderbilt University Press, 2010.

Harrison, Peter D., and B. L. Turner, eds. *Pre-Hispanic Maya Agriculture*. Albuquerque: University of New Mexico Press, 1978.

Hull, Kerry. "An Epigraphic Analysis of Classic-Period Maya Foodstuffs." In *Pre-Columbian Foodways*, edited by John Staller and Michael Carrasco, 235–56. New York: Springer, 2010.

Tykot, R. H. "Contribution of Stable Isotope Analysis to Understanding Dietary Variation among the Maya." *ACS Symposium Series* 831: 214–30, 2002.

Wiseman, Frederick M. "Agricultural and Historical Ecology of the Maya Lowlands." In *Pre-Hispanic Maya Agriculture*, edited by Peter D. Harrison and B. L. Turner, 63–115. Albuquerque: University of New Mexico Press, 1978.

■ WALTER R. T. WITSCHEY

DIVINE KINGS AND QUEENS

As Maya culture evolved in the Middle and Late Formative and Classic periods, power came to be held by kings and queens who claimed dominion over their subjects for commanding **tribute** and labor, legitimacy for their rulership role based on their ancestral bloodline, and divine power that provided them eternal life and direct connection to the gods and goddesses of the Maya world (see also **Deities**; **Dynastic Sequences**).

A review of the Maya rulers based on their own hieroglyphic inscriptions shows that far more men than women became heads of state, and that the few women who ruled often did so with a male consort or on behalf of a not-yet-mature male heir.

Maya rulers, known as a *k'uhul ajaw*, or holy lord, filled many roles. They functioned as head of state, managing power through members of an elite class with many of their own blood kin. In this role they demanded tribute to support the royal household and provide elite goods for exchange with other rulers and cities (see also **Alliances**; **Trade Routes**). They commanded the labor that constructed the monumental **architecture** in Maya cities. Maya kings also served as the head of religious activity. By their prayers, dances, offerings of incense and sacrificial victims, and their own blood, drawn and committed to the gods as a special sacrifice, they communicated both with the gods and with their own ancestors (see also **Music and Dance**; **Religion Rites and Rituals**; and **Theater**). They called upon the gods to provide rains and successful harvests. Maya kings were also the head of the military for their city-state, organizing raiding parties, waging war, taking captives, and conquering neighbor states (see also **Warfare**; **Warriors, and Weapons**).

The conjunction of these functions in a single person resulted not only in efficient control but also high risk. A good harvest and plentiful rain reinforced the power of the sitting ruler. Crop failure, or a large-scale military defeat, however, could be disastrous or fatal for the ruler and his family, resulting in overthrow and even societal collapse.

See also CALAKMUL; CARACOL; CLASSIC MAYA COLLAPSE; COBÁ; COPAN; DOS PILAS; EK BALAM; NARANJO; PALENQUE; PIEDRAS NEGRAS; QUIRIGUÁ; SUBSISTENCE; TIKAL; TONINÁ; YAXCHILAN

Further Reading

Fitzsimmons, James L. *Death and the Classic Maya Kings*. Austin: University of Texas Press, 2010.

Grube, Nikolai, Eva Eggebrecht, Matthias Seidel, and Mark Van Stone, eds. *Maya: Divine Kings of the Rainforest*. updated ed. Potsdam, Germany: H. F. Ullmann, 2012.

McAnany, Patricia A. *Living with the Ancestors: Kinship and Kingship in Ancient Maya Society*. rev. ed. Austin: University of Texas Press, 2014.

Rice, Prudence M. *Maya Political Science*. Austin: University of Texas Press, 2009.

Schele, Linda, and Mary Ellen Miller. *The Blood of Kings: Dynasty and Ritual in Maya Art*. New York and Fort Worth, TX: G. Braziller and the Kimbell Art Museum, 1986.

■ WALTER R. T. WITSCHEY

DOS PILAS

Dos Pilas (16.4° N, 90.3° W) is a Maya archaeological site in the department of El Petén in northern **Guatemala**. It was one of two capitals in the Petexbatún kingdom; the other was **Aguateca**. Home to an intrusive dynasty with origins in **Tikal**, Dos Pilas became a dominant force in the region in the early seventh century AD. Its meteoric rise to regional dominance and dramatic end occurred against the backdrop of a rivalry between two Maya superpowers: Tikal and **Calakmul**.

In 1953–1954 two brothers from Sayaxché, José and Lisandro Flores, discovered the site. In 1960 Pierre Ivanoff visited the site and dubbed it Dos Pozos. G. L. Vinson later renamed it Dos Pilas. Carlos Navarrete and Luis Luján excavated the site in the early 1960s. Yale University started research at Dos Pilas in 1984. Stephen Houston was part of this project in 1984 and 1986, publishing on the hieroglyphs and history of Dos Pilas in 1993. From 1989 through 1997 Vanderbilt University carried out investigations on a regional basis. The data thus collected, combined with the extensive written record found at the site, afford us rare insights into Maya heartland politics.

In AD 629 B'alaj Chan K'awiil, son of Tikal's ruler K'inich Muwaan Jol II, was dispatched to found a new city. This new settlement signaled its origin by using the Tikal Emblem Glyph as its own. Initially Dos Pilas was allied with Tikal in its struggle against another major kingdom, Calakmul. However, following Calakmul victories on the battlefield in AD 648 the Petexbatún kingdom realigned itself with Calakmul, its former enemy. Subsequent wars with Tikal resulted in B'alaj Chan K'awiil being ousted from Dos Pilas in AD 672 and fleeing to Aguateca. In AD 679 B'alaj Chan K'awiil took the fight to Tikal, defeating it after a major battle. At home, B'alaj Chan K'awiil concentrated his building efforts on the core of his capital. His long reign ended around AD 692.

B'alaj Chan K'awiil had two sons. Itzamnaaj B'alam was the first to succeed his father. His reign was short, as the second brother, Itzamnaaj K'awiil, acceded to the throne in AD 698. Hostilities with Tikal continued. In AD 705 Dos Pilas was victorious once more. Inscriptions recorded victories over minor opponents in AD 717 and 721. At home, this younger brother expanded a portion of the site known today as El Duende. Itzamnaaj K'awiil died in October 726. His tomb was found inside Str. L5-1. He had been laid to rest with a heavy jade collar and wristlets, surrounded by numerous fine painted **ceramics**. Around 400 pieces of shell mosaic adorned his elaborate headdress (see also **Portable Objects**; **Royal Tombs**).

Ucha'an K'in B'alam assumed the throne in January AD 727. This individual, with a track record of military achievements under the previous ruler, probably was a regent for a minor prince. **Warfare** continued unabated in the region, marked by the conquest of **Ceibal** in AD 735. Celebratory texts in the form of duplicate inscriptions at Dos Pilas and **Aguateca** confirm Aguateca's role as the twin capital in the kingdom. Ucha'an K'in B'alam died in 741.

K'awiil Chan K'inich was installed in June 746, an event reflected in inscriptions at Aguateca and Dos Pilas. His early years saw more aggression against neighbors and continued control over Ceibal. However, after 761 the king drops out of the written record, and Dos Pilas is all but abandoned. The remaining elite emerged at Aguateca, where the dynasty continued for another half century.

Dos Pilas's final days betray fear; the site witnessed an influx of refugees who built a shanty town in the center of the settlement. Range structures and a **ball court** were repurposed into components of a double defensive wall system around the site. In the process, these same structures also served as quarries, yielding precious stone blocks as construction materials to plug the gaps between buildings.

All of these frantic efforts proved to be futile. By the beginning of the ninth century, the Petexbatún cities had ceased to exist, a fate shared with other cities in the region. The identity of the attackers against Dos Pilas remains unclear; the role of warfare in the demise of this kingdom, however, is abundantly evident.

See also ALLIANCES; ART; CAVES; CEIBAL; CLASSIC MAYA COLLAPSE; COBÁ; DYNASTIC SEQUENCES; FORTIFICATIONS; HIEROGLYPHIC STAIRWAY; LA CORONA; MIDDLE CLASSIC HIATUS; MUSIC AND DANCE; NAJ TUNICH; NARANJO; PALACE; STUART, GEORGE E. AND DAVID STUART; WARFARE, WARRIORS, AND WEAPONS

Further Reading

Demarest, Arthur A. *The Petexbatun Regional Archaeological Project: A Multidisciplinary Study of the Maya Collapse.* Vanderbilt Institute of Mesoamerican Archaeology. Nashville, TN: Vanderbilt University Press, 2006.

Houston, Stephen D. *Hieroglyphs and History at Dos Pilas: Dynastic Politics of the Classic Maya.* Austin: University of Texas Press, 1993.

■ DIRK VAN TUERENHOUT

DROUGHT

Diego de Landa, writing in 1566, said,

> there would be great shortage of water, many hot spells that would wither the maize fields, from which would follow great hunger, . . . From this would come great discords, among themselves or with other towns. They also said this year would bring changes in the rule of the chiefs or the priests, because of the wars and discords.

Archbishop Diego de Landa Calderón was an early European observer of the effects of drought on the Maya people of the northern Yucatan Peninsula (see also **Northern Lowlands**; **Map 5**). His observations are all the more poignant because they are coming from the Maya themselves in a prognostication for a coming year. Subsequent studies show that drought was a haunting presence throughout the post-Columbian period, and recent work on Maya **codices** reports pre-Columbian droughts. Similarly, there is growing indirect proxy evidence for droughts in the geological records from sea and lake cores and speleothems whose range of measurement dates back thousands of years (see also **Geology**).

What might be called the "current standard interpretation" of drought visitations on the lowlands is that Maya civilization suffered periodic declines in precipitation of extended length about every 200–300 years. These were severe enough to disrupt social commerce and cause major social reorganizations. The worst of these was in the ninth century AD and was probably part of a complex set of circumstances that resulted in a systemic collapse, at least among great interior cities such as **Calakmul** and **Tikal** (see also **Classic Maya Collapse**). The ninth-century extended drought was the worst in 9,000 years according to some measures, but was not the only such event. Another extended drought is thought to have disrupted Maya lowland life in the third century AD, contributing to the transition from Preclassic to Classic social order. Other less notable droughts have been detected, such as during the sixth century. The latter appears to be traceable to an eruption of the nearby Ilopango, **El Salvador**, volcano around AD 536, which disrupted cultures worldwide (see also **Ceren**). At briefer timescales of a decade or so, the climate of the Maya lowlands appears to be susceptible to a few years of drought in every decade simply because they are located on the fluctuating boundary between the wet tropics and withering subtropics.

This standard interpretation will undoubtedly undergo significant revision in the coming years. Some reinterpretation will be due to the usual struggle between correlation and causation. Cause-and-effect relationships are always changing as new techniques refine timescales, clarifying which climate and cultural events came first. Also, how we interpret both literary and indirect evidence is heavily influenced by our own perceptions and preconceptions of both written and indirect records. In the written records, this phenomenon is compounded by the fact that both writers and readers have layers of perceptual issues that may or may not be helpful. Landa's report, for example, suggests that a drought is a climate event that unseats leaders. As we will see, interpretation of indirect data can also be bias laden.

Changing perceptions of drought in Western culture can be traced from Landa to the present and provide useful insights. Landa used drought in a general fashion to indicate diminished precipitation that caused disruption, famine, and war in Maya communities. In other words, it was a socially defined perception of drought, localized in the northwest Yucatan Peninsula. There were no specifics, such as "a 20 percent reduction in the amount of rainfall in a given year."

Since 1566 scholars have slowly refined definitions of drought. In combination with **ethnographic** studies and analysis of modern climate data, changing seasonality is an essential component of understanding drought in terms of local agricultural practices (see also **Subsistence**). Annual rainfall could remain high for a year, but if it fell at the wrong time of the year, for example in winter instead of during summer-fall, the impact on crop production could be devastating. Recognizing additional dimensions of drought is helpful. A United Nations document recognizes four types of drought: (1) meteorological (reduced rainfall), (2) agricultural (reduced soil moisture), (3) hydrological (reduced stream and **lake** levels), and (4) socioeconomic (disruption of water-dependent production of goods and services) (see also **Water Management**). This is a much more elaborate characterization of drought than Landa used, although it retains Landa's perspective about sociological impact.

Notably absent from these definitions is a direct understanding of the ethnographic view of drought. The Maya perspective on land management, a year-to-year flux of land use between cultivated fields and forest, is particularly aware of periodic droughts. Indigenous views, whether Maya or American, generally involve a Goldilocks range, a just-right amount of precipitation at the just-right time of year. Such systems are referred to in statistics as curvilinear. Western cultures are distinctly linear in their preferences, so adjusting Western science to this idea may be difficult.

Another likely change in our perceptions will result from the fact that the lake core pollen record has its own hidden biases. It has long been assumed that pollen records from sediments in lake bottoms could provide an even-handed measure of the climate as related to precipitation. There are numerous modes of pollination, however, among them wind-borne pollination and bug-bat-bird pollination. In the case of lake cores, the pollen that finds its way into lake bottom sediments is predominantly wind-borne. In the past it was assumed that wind-borne grass pollen represented drought. In a more refined view, human land management likely included fruit and nut trees that are primarily bug-bat-bird pollinators. This leads to a reinterpretation of events that may be a product of husbanding of the forest and/or drought. Correcting this bias will require formal treatments of the data that remain to be developed.

As we seek to understand the dynamic cultural changes in the Maya area, a detailed understanding of the impact and human response to drought is critical.

See also AGUADAS; CALAKMUL; CAVES; CHICHEN ITZA; CLASSIC MAYA COLLAPSE; CLIMATE; MAYAPÁN; MIDDLE CLASSIC HIATUS; NAACHTUN; SAN BARTOLO; SETTLEMENT PATTERNS (CENTRAL LOWLANDS); SOILS; TAKALIK ABAJ; UXMAL; WATER MANAGEMENT; YALAHAU REGION

Further Reading

Brenner, Mark, Michael F. Rosenmeier, David A. Hodell, and Jason H. Curtis. "Paleolimnology of the Maya Lowlands: Long-term Perspectives on Interactions among Climate, Environment, and Humans." *Ancient Mesoamerica* 13, no. 1: 141–57, 2002.

Dunning, Nicholas P., Timothy P. Beach, and Sheryl Luzzadder-Beach. "Kax and Kol: Collapse and Resilience in Lowland Maya Civilization." *Proceedings of the National Academy of Sciences USA* 109, no. 10: 3652–57, 2012.

Folan, William J., Joel Gunn, Jack D. Eaton, and Robert W. Patch. "Paleoclimatological Patterning in Southern Mesoamerica." *Journal of Field Archaeology* 10, no. 4: 453–68, 1983.

Ford, Anabel, and Ronald Nigh. "Origins of the Maya Forest Garden: Maya Resource Management." *Journal of Ethnobiology* 29, no. 2: 213–36, 2009.

Gill, Richardson Benedict. *The Great Maya Droughts: Water, Life, and Death.* Albuquerque: University of New Mexico Press, 2000.

Gunn, Joel D., William J. Folan, and Hubert R. Robichaux. "A Landscape Analysis of the Candelaria Watershed in Mexico: Insights into Paleoclimates Affecting Upland Horticulture in the Southern Yucatan Peninsula Semi-karst." *Geoarchaeology* 10, no. 1: 3–42, 1995.

Luzzadder-Beach, Sheryl, Timothy P. Beach, and Nicholas P. Dunning. "Wetland Fields as Mirrors of Drought and the Maya Abandonment." *Proceedings of the National Academy of Sciences USA* 109, no. 10: 3646–51, 2012.

■ JOEL D. GUNN

DYNASTIC SEQUENCES

Beginning in the 1970s, **decipherment** of inscriptions on **stelae**, monumental **architecture**, and an extensive inventory of **ceramics** has revealed the names and exploits of Maya rulers in several major cities. In describing their parentage, feats of battle (see also **Warfare, Warriors, and Weapons**), and longevity of rule, the ancient Maya have also shown that, like other cultures worldwide, their focus was personal, their pride was in conquest, and their story was concerned with the legitimacy of their control of power. Beginning with the breakthrough 1960 paper of Tatiana Proskouriakoff, the dynastic sequences of numerous cities dating from the Classic have been read out from their inscriptions and the inscriptions of neighboring sites. The rather steady discovery of new inscriptions refines and extends the current body of data. Sites for which histories of the rulers are known include **Calakmul, Caracol, Cobá, Copán, Dos Pilas, Ek Balam**, Motul de San Jose, **Naranjo, Palenque, Piedras Negras, Quiriguá, Tikal, Toniná**, and **Yaxchilan**.

Further Reading

Andrews, E. Wyllys, V, and William Leonard Fash, eds. *Copán: The History of an Ancient Maya Kingdom*. School of American Research Advanced Seminar Series. Santa Fe, NM: School of American Research, 2005.

Clancy, Flora S. *The Monuments of Piedras Negras, an Ancient Maya City*. Albuquerque: University of New Mexico Press, 2009.

Fields, Virginia M., and Dorie Reents-Budet. *Lords of Creation: The Origins of Sacred Maya Kingship*. Los Angeles, CA: Scala; in association with the Los Angeles County Museum of Art, 2005.

Foias, Antonia E., and Kitty F. Emery, eds. *Motul de San José: Politics, History, and Economy in a Classic Maya Polity*. Gainesville: University Press of Florida, 2012.

Graham, Ian, Peter Mathews, and Lucia Henderson. *Tonina*. Corpus of Maya Hieroglyphic Inscriptions, Peabody Museum of Archaeology and Ethnology, Harvard University, 1983–2006. https://peabody.harvard.edu/cmhi/site.php?site=Tonina.

Graham, Ian, and Eric Von Euw. *Naranjo*. Corpus of Maya Hieroglyphic Inscriptions, Peabody Museum of Archaeology and Ethnology, Harvard University, 1975–1978. https://www.peabody.harvard.edu/cmhi/site.php?site=Naranjo#loc.

Houston, Stephen D. *Hieroglyphs and History at Dos Pilas: Dynastic Politics of the Classic Maya*. Austin: University of Texas Press, 1993.

Josserand, J. Kathryn. "The Missing Heir at Yaxchilán: Literary Analysis of a Maya Historical Puzzle." *Latin American Antiquity* 18, no. 3: 295–312, 2007.

Looper, Matthew George. *Lightning Warrior: Maya Art and Kingship at Quirigua*. Linda Schele Series in Maya and Pre-Columbian Studies. Austin: University of Texas Press, 2003.

Martin, Simon. "Caracol Altar 21 Revisited: More Data on Double Bird and Tikal's Wars of the Mid-Sixth Century." *The PARI Journal* 6, no. 1: 1–9, 2005.

Martin, Simon, and Nikolai Grube. *Chronicle of the Maya Kings and Queens: Deciphering the Dynasties of the Ancient Maya*. 2nd ed. London: Thames & Hudson, 2008.

Proskouriakoff, Tatiana. "Historical Implications of a Pattern of Dates at Piedras Negras, Guatemala." *American Antiquity* 25, no. 4: 454–75, 1960.

Sabloff, Jeremy A. *Tikal: Dynasties, Foreigners & Affairs of State; Advancing Maya Archaeology*. School of American Research Advanced Seminar Series. Santa Fe, NM: School of American Research Press, 2003.

Stuart, David. *Notes on Accession Dates in the Inscriptions of Coba*. Mesoweb, 2010. http://www.mesoweb.com/stuart/notes/Coba.pdf.

Stuart, David, and George E. Stuart. *Palenque: Eternal City of the Maya*. New York: Thames & Hudson, 2008.

■ WALTER R. T. WITSCHEY

DZIBANCHÉ

The Classic period Maya site of Dzibanché (Tzibanché) (18.6° N, 88.8° W) is located in the southern part of the **Mexican** state of Quintana Roo (see also **Map 3**). It had early portraits of bound captives, perhaps the earliest in the Maya area. One inscription on a **hieroglyphic stairway** is of great interest because it recorded the name **of Yuknoom Ch'een I,** raising the possibility that the **Snake Kingdom** of K'an (**Calakmul**) may have been founded at Dzibanché in the Early Classic period (see figure 15). Important structures at the site include the Temple of the Owl; the Temple of the Lintels, from which Dzibanché gets its name "writing on wood"; and the Temple of the Captives. Just 2 km north of the ceremonial grouping called Dzibanché is a large **pyramid** known as K'inichna', "House of the Sun God," which contained two **royal tombs** with jade offerings. A small nearby group called Lamay forms a part of the total complex. Several other major sites, such as Resbalon, are found nearby, all built in the **Petén architectural** style.

See also IGHKABAL; KOHUNLICH; LA CORONA; NOH KAH

Further Reading

Martin, Simon, and Nikolai Grube. *Chronicle of the Maya Kings and Queens: Deciphering the Dynasties of the Ancient Maya.* 2nd ed. London: Thames & Hudson, 2008.

Nalda, Enrique. *Los cautivos de Dzibanché.* México, D.F.: Instituto Nacional de Antropología e Historia, 2004.

Nalda, Enrique. "Kohunlich and Dzibanché: Parallel Histories." In *Quintana Roo Archaeology*, edited by Justine M. Shaw and Jennifer P. Mathews, 228–44. Tucson: University of Arizona Press, 2005.

Velázquez García, Erik. "The Captives of Dzibanche." *The PARI Journal* 6, no. 2: 1–4, 2005.

■ CLIFFORD T. BROWN AND WALTER R. T. WITSCHEY

Figure 15. Dzibanche Str. 1. The Snake Kingdom of Calakmul may have had its origins here, according to Emblem Glyphs. Courtesy of Walter Witschey.

DZIBILCHALTUN

Dzibilchaltun (21.1° N, 89.6° W) is a site occupied from the Late Preclassic through Colonial times, situated 20 km south of the Gulf of Mexico and just north of Merida, the capital of Yucatan, **Mexico** (see also **Map 3**). Brackish lagoons behind the gulf shore and mangrove swamps there are important sources of salt. Further inland is an expanse of bare bedrock with very little **soil**, and that of poor quality. Dzibilchaltun is located just beyond the infertile area, as close to coastal resources as possible while remaining on suitably arable land.

The core of Dzibilchaltun consists of the Grand Central Plaza (see figure 16) on the east and the South Plaza on the west surrounding Cenote Xlacah, a limestone sinkhole (**cenote**) steeped in legend. Divers encountered a range of materials in the cenote, including **ceramics**, human bones, and other artifacts. The surface of Xlacah shows that the water table is some 4 m below the ground surface (see also **Groundwater/Water Table**); inhabitants of the site easily excavated wells to that depth.

Key research at Dzibilchaltun includes excavation of the Temple of the Seven Dolls and mapping of 19.4 km² by Tulane University (1950–1965), but the most interesting recent discoveries result from the exploration of the Grand Central Plaza by Mexican field teams.

The Seven Dolls complex is considered a Sun temple surrounded by elite dwellings. The massive temple was uncovered by excavating the huge **pyramidal** structure that covered it, so the building as it stands today has been stabilized but not reconstructed in any way. Although various authors doubted the reliability of the wide vaults, thick walls, wooden lintels, and broad entrances of the temple, a review of its components determined that the Temple of the Seven Dolls was structurally sound despite the use of mud mortar. It remains an exceptional example of Early Period **architecture**.

Figure 16.   Plaza at Dzibilchaltun. Photo courtesy Edward Kurjack.

The mapping of Dzibilchaltun was intended to catalog every small structure. Low heaps of gravel, considered platforms without retaining walls, are the most numerous features on the map; test pitting showed that the great majority of these were man-made. Buildings on their surfaces were made with perishable materials, so the gravel mounds probably represent construction used for only a limited period. Some 240 vaulted buildings containing an estimated 540 rooms are plotted on the map together with the definitive remains of many structures resembling the contemporary rural Maya **house**.

Surveyors encountered both single- and multiple-roomed dwellings that probably had thatched roofs. Prominent among these were the numerous remains of one-room houses with apsidal ground plans. The structures consisted of large, upright slabs forming the basal course of dry wall masonry, built in a manner similar to the technique used to build field walls. Some houses are still constructed the same way in areas where stone is plentiful. Platforms without signs of superstructures probably supported apsidal structures with wattle and daub walls and thatched roofs.

Three masonry **causeways** link the central and south plazas with architectural complexes situated about 1 km to the east, south, and west. Other causeways and buildings fill the zone within 500 m of these three masonry walkways, an area of approximately 4 km². The remainder of the map covers a cluster of peripheral complexes.

Periods of massive construction effort, political change, and religious innovation mark the Grand Central Plaza; each transformation seemed to glory in its own symbolism: **stelae** during the late Classic, the Feathered Serpent in the Postclassic, and Christian themes after the conquest (see also **Deities**; **Iconography**; **Religion**).

The history of the Grand Central Plaza begins with late Preclassic pottery from the lowest levels at Structure 45 and elsewhere. Then series of small Early Period vaulted structures were erected close to Cenote Xlacah.

Next, Late Classic construction under the direction of eighth- and ninth-century rulers opened a new chapter in site history. Earlier structures were partly demolished and buried in the course of building a greatly enlarged plaza realigned with the axial causeways. Structure 44, an elevated communal hall with 35 entrances facing north, closed the south side of the plaza.

Excavations in Str. 42 on the east side of the Grand Plaza encountered the urn burial of a ruler known as Kalom 'Uk'Uw together with a deer bone (*Mazapa pandora)* hairpin marked with his name and the Emblem Glyph for Dzibilchatun. This same individual is depicted on **Stela** 19, with a hieroglyphic date of AD 840 (see also **Decipherment**; **Royal Tombs**).

Str. 36, an Early Postclassic pyramid at the northeast corner of the Grand Plaza, marks another dramatic change. The builders broke up Stelae 9, 18, and 19 and displayed them in the lower walls of the pyramid. Some 650 carved stones that once formed a mosaic façade appeared in the rubble together with the badly battered parts of a bird-serpent-jaguar icon. This tenth-century regime change probably represents conquest by groups allied with Chichen Itza.

One architectural feature at Str. 36 is the use of inset stairs on the side retaining walls. Similar stairs were used on the last additions on the back of Str. 44 on the south side of the plaza.

Franciscan missionaries constructed a chapel on the central plaza at the end of the sixteenth century. In the process they destroyed earlier Maya sculpture and incorporated some fragments in the chapel. The cross, an example of which was with one of the Christian burials near the chapel, became the religious symbol of the new Colonial order.

See also CLASSIC MAYA COLLAPSE; CORBEL ARCH; HOUSES; KOMCHEN; SETTLEMENT PATTERNS (NORTHERN LOWLANDS); STUART, GEORGE E. AND DAVID STUART; TEOTIHUACÁN (MAYA INTERACTIONS WITH); TERRITORIAL ENTITIES; TIHO

Further Reading

Andrews, E. Wyllys, IV. "Dzibilchaltun, Lost City of the Maya." *National Geographic Magazine* 115, no. 1: 90–109, 1959.

———. "Archaeology and Prehistory in the Northern Maya Lowlands: An Introduction." In *Handbook of Middle American Indians*, Vol. 2, *Archaeology of Southern Mesoamerica*, pt. 1, edited by Gordon R. Willey, 288–330. Austin: University of Texas Press, 1980.

Andrews, E. Wyllys, IV, and E. Wyllys Andrews V. *Excavations at Dzibilchaltun, Yucatan, Mexico.* Middle American Research Institute, Publication 48. New Orleans, LA: Tulane University, 1980.

Folan, William J. *The Open Chapel of Dzibilchaltun, Yucatan.* Middle American Research Institute, Publication 26. New Orleans, LA: Tulane University, 1970.

Maldonado Cardenas, Rubén, and Susana Echeverría Castillo. "La Presencia de Chichén Itzá en el Sitio de Dzibilchaltún." *Los Investigadores de la Cultura Maya* 19: 107–22, 2010.

■ RUBÉN MALDONADO CARDENAS AND EDWARD B. KURJACK

E

ECCENTRIC LITHICS

Eccentric lithics—also referred to as eccentric flints, flaked stone symbols, or simply eccentrics—are nonutilitarian artifacts made of chipped **chert**, chalcedony, or **obsidian**. Found throughout **Mesoamerica**, eccentrics were fashioned into a wide variety of shapes, including human, natural, and supernatural figures as well as abstract symbols. In the Maya region they most commonly occur in Classic period dedicatory caches placed beneath **stelae** and altars, within public buildings, and inside elite burials (see also **Deities**; **Iconography**; **Royal Tombs**).

The first examples of Maya eccentric lithics were excavated in **Belize** during early explorations by Thomas Gann, Edward Gruning, and Thomas Joyce. Since then, they have been found mainly at sites in the **southern** and **central** Maya **Lowlands**. The simplest types are unifacially notched flakes and blades; exhausted obsidian cores also were often used. Common shapes are thought to symbolize Maya deities, serpents, scorpions, and centipedes. Others, such as lunates and trilobes, may have been inspired by **Teotihuacán** iconography. The most elaborate kind are large bifacially worked "scepters" with multiple appendages. These often depict the god K'awiil in profile and were likely meant to be hafted (see also **Deities**).

Representations in **art** suggest that some eccentrics were used in bloodletting ceremonies (see also **Rites and Rituals**). Zachary Hruby has argued that their production was an ideologically loaded, "ritualized" practice, and Gyles Iannone has associated eccentrics with an ancestor cult system that served to reinforce the status of elites. Although they were mostly manufactured locally, imported obsidian eccentrics from Teotihuacán have been found at lowland Maya sites such as **Tikal** and **Altun Ha**. The highly ornate K'awiil chert scepters from the Rosalila structure at **Copán** also were imported, probably from a workshop within the southeastern Maya region.

See also CRAFT SPECIALIZATION; TRADE ROUTES

Further Reading

Hruby, Zachary X. "Ritualized Chipped-Stone Production at Piedras Negras, Guatemala." *Archeological Papers of the American Anthropological Association* 17, no. 1: 68–87, 2007.

Joyce, Thomas Athol. "The 'Eccentric Flints' of Central America." *Journal of the Royal Anthropological Institute of Great Britain and Ireland* 62: xvii–xxvi, 1932.

■ BENIAMINO VOLTA

EDZNA

This Maya settlement 60 km southeast of Campeche city, **Mexico**, probably derives its name from *Ytzna*, a Chontal Maya toponym most likely meaning "house or place of iguanas," or alternatively "wise man" or "sorcerer." It was used in the last centuries of occupation during the Postclassic period (AD 1250–1450). The term *Ytz* has survived as a patronymic (Itzá) in many rural and urban communities of the Yucatan peninsula. Through time, Ytzna changed to Etzna and later was popularized as Edzna (19.6° N, 90.2° W).

The ancient city, however, did not have that name in previous centuries. Hieroglyphic analyses have shown that during the Late Classic period (AD 600–900) there were two Emblem Glyphs in use (see also **Decipherment**), one for downtown Edzna (represented by the rattle of the snake) and the other to manifest the political sphere of the city.

Ceramic and pollen analysis from several field seasons indicate that around 600 BC a modest agricultural community settled in the northern section of the valley. Concentration of goods and services led to building large masonry structures and a huge hydraulic system formed by 10 major canals of several kilometers each; 31 complementary canals around the core of the city; and 84 reservoirs of different dimensions and an effective use of drops and levels helping to distribute water, always from north to south (see also **Water Management**). Water availability, agricultural labors, building construction, and maintenance benefited from those works and reinforced a multilevel stratified society. A centralized government legitimized its position with its supposed relation with gods and supernatural beings (see also **Religion**). Social and political differences, improvement of **arts** and handcrafts, **writing** and a numerical system, and both regional and long-distance trade strengthened a theocratic society with a few elite members of the ruling class, some associated relatives and specialists, and many laborers (see also **Class Stratification**; **Craft Socialization**; **Divine Kings and Queens**; **Mathematics**).

The earliest monumental masonry buildings of Edzna are dated to the first centuries of our era and belong to the **Petén architectural style**. A common feature of monumental structures is the use of large stone blocks with thick stucco coatings and red paint. Many façades were covered with stucco images of gods, mythical animals, and symbols (see also **Deities and Iconography**).

During the seventh century Edzna's political structure drastically changed, and the archaeological record shows new architectonic and ceramic traditions. **Puuc** buildings and *Chenes* traits were now common, and their development lasted two or three centuries. **Sculpture** canons were also modified; the powerful governor was no longer represented alone or as the principal actor. Now **stelae** depicted several scenes, and glyphic texts and dates were shortened or disappeared. New topics were also represented: skulls, penises, and feathered serpents.

During the Late and Terminal Classic (AD 600 to 900/1000) Edzna experienced a construction and demographic boom, possibly with 30,000 inhabitants. Around AD 1000 to 1200 the city builders created new architectonic forms using sloping bases and multiple entrances formed by columns (Structure 512 and the western section of the Ambassadors Patio) similar to some buildings found at **Chichen Itza**. That resemblance speaks of a common mode of construction across different regions during the Early Postclassic. Between AD 1200 and 1400 the city waned, and buildings were eventually visited as pilgrimage sites for ceremonies where anthropomorphic censers were deposited.

Archaeologists have reported 33 stelae at Edzna, some complete, others only in fragments. Four of them were sculpted between AD 41 and 435; eleven have dates from AD 633 to 830, and the others belong to the ninth and tenth centuries. There is information about at least 10 rulers, and inscriptions connect the city with Xcalumkin, Itzimte, Altar de los Reyes, **Calakmul**, and **Piedras Negras**, among other ancient sites. Architecture, ceramics, and marine mollusks link Edzna with the western coast, the Puuc, and the Chenes regions. Other materials such as basalt, **obsidian**, and jade indicate the participation in the Mesoamerican exchange network from Michoacan to the Gulf Coast and from Central Mexico to the Motagua valley.

See also ARCHITECTURE OVERVIEW; ART; *CHENES* ARCHITECTURAL STYLE; FAUNA; PORTABLE OBJECTS; TRADE ROUTES; WARFARE, WARRIORS, AND WEAPONS

Further Reading

Benavides C, Antonio. *Edzná: A Pre-Columbian City in Campeche/Edzná: Una ciudad prehispánica de Campeche*. Arqueología de México. Mexico City and Pittsburgh, PA: Instituto Nacional de Antropología e Historia, and University of Pittsburgh, 1997.

Matheny, Ray T., Deanne L. Gurr, Donald W. Forsyth, and Hauck F. R. *Investigations at Edzná, Campeche*. Vol. 1, pt. 1, *The Hydraulic System*. Provo, UT: New World Archaeological Foundation, Brigham Young University, 1983.

Pallán Gayol, Carlos. "Secuencia dinástica, glifos emblema y topónimos en las inscripciones jeroglíficas de Edzná, Campeche, (600–900 dC): Implicaciones históricas." Tesis de Maestría, Estudios Mesoamericanos, UNAM, México, 2009.

■ ANTONIO BENAVIDES C.

EK BALAM

Ek Balam (20.9° N, 88.1° W) is one of the major sites of northern Yucatan, **Mexico** (see also **Map 3**). Located north of Valladolid and about 51 km northeast of **Chichen Itza**, it was occupied from the Middle Formative through the early Colonial period, although it was of most importance during the Late and Terminal Classic. The site was first reported by Désiré Charnay in 1886 and later visited briefly by members of the Carnegie Institution. William Ringle and George Bey directed work at the site and environs between 1985 and 1999; in 1994 Leticia Vargas and Victor Castillo of INAH began major excavations of the acropolis and other structures around the main plaza that have continued intermittently to the present.

Ek Balam lies in a zone of moderately high rainfall and generally fertile **soils**. The landscape is pockmarked by karst depressions *(rejolladas)* that may have been favored by ancient farmers. At contact, and possibly pre-Hispanically, such depressions were used for **cacao** cultivation. Water was procured from small **cenotes** (sinkholes) near the termini of the major **causeways**, some 1.8 km distant, or from a few wells cut into the bottoms of *rejolladas*. Cisterns were only rarely employed, and some may have been for maize storage, as historical documents suggest.

Most of the major **architecture** at Ek Balam is clustered around the main plaza, including the 180-m-long acropolis, a multistory **palace**, and a later range structure in the **Puuc style**. Other lesser platforms and pyramids define the remainder of the plaza; one was later modified into a **ball court**. Another was an early *popol nah* or **council house**. A number of architectural styles are present, reflecting its lengthy occupation but also external influences from the east and south. Two parallel walls encircle the central complex of structures, and a third partial wall connects several of the structures around the main plaza. These may have served to both defend and segregate the center (see also **Fortifications**).

The *Relación de Tiquibalam* states that the site was founded by Ek Balam, a foreign king coming from the east, and that he and his captains were responsible for construction of the site center. Inscriptions from the acropolis do mention the arrival of a king, presumably foreign, as well as someone or something named Ek Balam, though the context is unclear. Most texts concern the first well-attested ruler, U Cit Can Lek Tok, whose funeral chamber was opened in 2000 by Vargas and Castillo (see also **Royal Tombs**). Its entrance, an amazingly well-preserved façade of modeled stucco monsters, warriors, and winged men, is one of the masterworks of the ancient Maya. Lacadena's studies of the texts from the acropolis reveal its construction history as well as important calendrical and ritual practices (see also **Calendar**; **Decipherment**; **Iconography**; **Warfare, Warriors, and Weapons**).

The settlement of Ek Balam covers approximately 12–15 km^2, of which about 3.5 km^2 have been surveyed. This central zone is densely packed with residential groups, but with no clear neighborhood divisions; rectangular rather than apsidal **houses** are favored. Three long causeways run approximately to the north, east, and west, and two lesser ones extend to the south and southwest. Most terminate in small **pyramids**; the east and west also lead to cenotes. This arrangement suggests the practice of *wayeb*, or end-of-year rituals, as described by Bishop Diego de **Landa**.

Ek Balam apparently suffered a decline in the Terminal Classic period, perhaps at the hand of Chichen Itza, but was only partially abandoned. A small ceremonial center, the Grupo Sacrificios, was constructed just northwest of the site center and included a second ball court and a small pyramid. Another large platform was built over an existing **Puuc-style** building and was crowned with a long C-shaped structure, a feature characteristic of post-monumental occupations in Yucatan. In the Postclassic, occupation shifted to the east of the site center, and many of the remaining structures were abandoned, though a small East Coast–style temple was built in the site center. Following the conquest Ek Balam became part of the *encomienda* of the conquistador Juan Gutierrez Picón. A small *ramada* chapel was built in this eastern section to serve the remaining inhabitants.

See also ART; CLASSIC MAYA COLLAPSE; COUNCIL HOUSE; DIET; NORTHERN LOWLANDS; SCULPTURE; SUBSISTENCE; TERRITORIAL ENTITIES

Further Reading

Bey, George J., III, Craig A. Hanson, and William M. Ringle. "Classic to Postclassic at Ek Balam, Yucatan: Architectural and Ceramic Evidence for Defining the Transition." *Latin American Antiquity* 8, no. 3: 237–54, 1997.

Lacadena García-Gallo, Alfonso. "Los jeroglíficos de Ek' Balam." *Arqueología Mexicana* 13, no. 76: 64–69, 2006.

Ringle, William M., George J. Bey III, Tara Bond Freeman, Craig A. Hanson, Charles W. Houck, and J. Gregory Smith. "The Decline of the East: The Classic to Postclassic Transition at Ek Balam, Yucatán." In *The Terminal Classic in the Maya Lowlands: Collapse, Transition, and Transformation*, edited by Arthur A. Demarest, Prudence M. Rice, and Don Stephen Rice, 485–516. Boulder: University Press of Colorado, 2004.

Vargas de la Peña, Leticia, and Víctor R. Castillo Borges. "Ek' Balam: Ciudad que empieza a revelar sus secretos." *Arqueología Mexicana* 7, no. 37: 24–31, 1999.

———. "El mausoleo de Ukit Kan Le'k Tok'." *Investigadores de la Cultura Maya (Campeche, Mex.)* 9, no. 1: 145–50, 2001.

■ WILLIAM M. RINGLE

EL CHAYAL

El Chayal (14.7° N, 90.4° W) is a major **obsidian** source in the **southern Maya highlands**. Its name derives from *chay*, the Kaqchikel word for volcanic glass. The El Chayal source area is one of the largest deposits of obsidian in the North American continent. It is located about 15–30 km northeast of **Kaminaljuyú,** a large pre-Hispanic urban center in the Valley of **Guatemala** within modern Guatemala City. Obsidian from El Chayal was widely traded throughout eastern **Mesoamerica** and was the predominant variety used in the **Maya lowlands** during the Classic period.

The El Chayal source area extends for more than 300 km². Within this region, archaeologists have recorded at least 58 outcrops, five quarry-workshops, eight lithic and **ceramic** scatters, and eight sites with **architecture**. The largest quarry-workshops are found at Nance Dulce (previously called El Chayal), La Joya, and El Remudadero. Open quarrying from pits and terraces was the most common method of extraction, but tunnel mining was also practiced. Geoffrey Braswell and Michael Glascock have suggested that, although chemically distinct, the nearby outcrops of Jalapa and Sansare might be considered together with El Chayal as part of one large, complex volcanic source region.

There is much variation in color and texture among the different outcrops in the source area. The most common type of obsidian is translucent, smoky gray with black or gray banding and a smooth, brilliant surface. Other common varieties are black or reddish brown, transparent, or variegated, and some display red banding or small black specks.

El Chayal was first described by Michael Coe and Kent Flannery in 1964. Later studies were conducted by Joseph Michels and Payson Sheets. The most important and detailed project, however, was conducted recently by Edgar Suyuc and Héctor Mejía, who documented the extent of the source area and the archaeological sites associated with it.

Beginning in the Early Formative, El Chayal obsidian was traded throughout the southern highlands and into the Isthmian region (see also **Trade Routes**). With a few exceptions, it was the most common source of obsidian at lowland Maya sites during the Classic period and was also traded to the highlands and **Pacific coast** of Chiapas. It was surpassed by **Ix-tepeque** obsidian during the Terminal Classic and Early Postclassic, but again achieved wide distribution in coastal areas throughout eastern Mesoamerica during the Late Postclassic.

The increasingly wide distribution of El Chayal obsidian starting in the Middle Formative appears to be connected to the rise of the nearby center of Kaminaljuyú. Nonetheless, distinct production technologies employed in the source area imply that it was not controlled by a single entity. According to Suyuc and Mejía, there is some evidence that Kaminaljuyú controlled the exploitation of obsidian around the workshops of Nance Dulce, La Joya, and El Fiscal. In contrast, farther east, the quarry-workshops of San Antonio Este and El Remudadero may have been controlled by other groups such as the Xinca of the middle Motagua. A growing body of evidence suggests that many obsidian sources were located between—rather than at the center of—major polities. Moreover, control focused on the technological knowledge of production and exchange rather than access to raw material.

See also BURIALS; CHERT; CLASS STRUCTURE; COTZUMALHUAPA; GEOLOGY; IXTEPEQUE; OB-SIDIAN; PORTABLE OBJECTS; SAYIL; SOUTHERN HIGHLANDS; TULUM

Further Reading

Sheets, Payson D. "A Reassessment of the Precolumbian Obsidian Industry of El Chayal, Guatemala." *American Antiquity* 40, no. 1: 98–103, 1975.

Sidrys, Raymond V., John Andresen, and Derek Marcucci. "Obsidian Sources in the Maya Area." *Journal of New World Archaeology* 1, no. 5: 1–13, 1976.

Suyuc Ley, Edgar. "The Extraction of Obsidian at El Chayal, Guatemala." In *The Technology of Maya Civilization: Political Economy and Beyond in Lithic Studies*, edited by Zachary X. Hruby, Geoffrey E. Braswell, and Oswaldo Fernando Chinchilla Mazariegos, 130–39. Sheffield, UK, and Oakville, CT: Equinox Publishing, 2011.

■ BENIAMINO VOLTA

EL MIRADOR

The Maya site El Mirador (17.8° N, 89.9° W), Petén, **Guatemala**, dominated the northern Petén during the Late Formative period (see also **Map 3**). Located only a few kilometers south of the Guatemala-**Mexico** border, the site is extremely large for a Formative period site. Several *sacbes* radiate from the site core, through jungle and across the *bajos*, including one that connects to **Nakbé**; 13 km to the southeast, one running 20 km to El Tintal; and another leading toward the Classic period site **Calakmul**, 35 km to the north-northeast (see also **Causeway/sacbe**).

The remoteness of El Mirador kept it from view until 1926. Ian Graham visited and mapped it in 1962, and in 1978 Ray Matheny and Bruce Dahlin started a project that ran five years. Unexpectedly, El Mirador proved to be a Preclassic site, and formidably large. Richard Hansen began work there in 2003 with a large multidisciplinary staff. The effort has evolved into the **Mirador Basin** project and continues in 2015.

The site center is divided into two areas on an east-west axis about 2 km long. The western ceremonial area sits at the edge of an 18-m escarpment that falls away to the west to Bajo Limon and into an area of *bajos* that form the **Mirador Basin**. The largest ceremonial structure here is the Late Formative El Tigre structure, rising 56 m in a series of truncated platforms and pyramids, with temples atop. There may be Middle Classic remains unexcavated beneath. It embodies a distinctive architectural style, the triadic group associated with the Formative, with the main temple rising above an elevated plaza with two smaller flanking temples. To the southeast of El Tigre is another triadic group, Str. 34, which bears large molded stucco masks flanking the central stair. A jaguar-paw ear flare from one mask is well preserved in stucco. Farther south is the large Monos group. East of El Tigre is a plaza that contained several broken Late Formative **stelae**, including St. 2 with carved but badly eroded glyphs; all resemble similar monuments from Late Formative sites on the **Pacific coast**. The central acropolis of the western group includes a large Late Formative **palace** that was begun in the Middle Formative. A north-south wall runs along the eastern side of the western architectural complex, with the Tres Micos group at the south end. In the western group, the evidence suggests that all major architecture dates from the Formative, with a very modest reoccupation and construction in the Classic.

The western portion of El Mirador is divided from the eastern portion by the Aguada Bolocante, but is connected by a *sacbe* to the larger Danta Group to the east. Here the Danta pyramid soars 70 m, although its base begins on a low hill. The 7-m-high platform base of the temple-pyramid is nearly 305 m along its sides, with several structures on it. A second smaller platform sits on it, raising the elevation another 7 m. A third platform, supporting the Danta triadic group, rises 21 m more. It is surprising and instructive that these huge structures, among the largest ever built by the Maya, were constructed during the Formative period rather than the Classic. The impressive architecture suggests a powerful state, with strong control over substantial labor forces and over its neighbor cities.

Excavation of residential platforms reveals groupings of small houses around plazas. Mamom sherds point to a Middle Formative occupation. Late Formative pottery includes Usulatan ware, a decorated style from the Guatemala highlands. The widespread appearance of chicanel ceramics from 400 BC–AD 100 suggests that El Mirador influence was powerful and widespread.

The fortunes of El Mirador waned at the end of the Late Formative as **Tikal** grew in size and strength at the beginning of the Early Classic period. Due to its remote location in dense jungle, the site is difficult to study, and much discovery remains for future researchers.

See also ARCHITECTURE OVERVIEW; *BAJOS*; CAUSEWAY/*SACBE*; CENTRAL LOWLANDS; CODEX-STYLE VASES; CRAFT SPECIALIZATION; GUATEMALA; MIRADOR BASIN; NAACHTUN; OLMEC-MAYA INTERACTIONS; SETTLEMENT PATTERNS (CENTRAL LOWLANDS); TEOTIHUACÁN (MAYA INTERACTIONS WITH); TERRACING; TERRITORIAL ENTITIES; TIKAL; WARFARE, WARRIORS, AND WEAPONS; YAXNOHCAH (MONTEREY)

Further Reading

Dahlin, Bruce. "Ahead of Its Time?" *Journal of Social Archaeology* 9, no. 3: 341–67, 2009.

Dahlin, Bruce H. "A Colossus in Guatemala: The Preclassic Maya City of El Mirador." *Archaeology* 37, no. 5: 18–25, 1984.

Hansen, Richard D. *Excavations in the Tigre Complex, El Mirador, Petén, Guatemala*. Pt. 3. Provo, UT: New World Archaeological Foundation, Brigham Young University, 1990.

———. *An Early Maya Text from El Mirador, Guatemala*. Boundary End Archaeological Research Center—Mesoweb, 1991. http://www.mesoweb.com/bearc/cmr/37.html.

———. *Publications and Papers of the Mirador Basin Project: Project Bibliography 01–08*. Foundation for Anthropological Research and Environmental Studies (FARES), and Idaho State University, 2001–2008. http://www.fares-foundation.org/docs/Bibliography01-08.pdf.

———. *Proyecto Arqueológico Cuenca Mirador: Investigación, conservación y desarrollo en El Mirador, Petén, Guatemala: informe final temporada de Campo 2003*. 2004.

Matheny, Ray T. *El Mirador, Petén, Guatemala: Introduction*. Papers of the New World Archaeological Foundation. Provo, UT: Brigham Young University, 1993.

Matheny, Ray T., Deanne G. Matheny, and Bruce H. Dahlin. *Introduction to Investigations at El Mirador, Petén, Guatemala*. Provo, UT: New World Archaeological Foundation, Brigham Young University, 2011.

Šprajc, Ivan, and Carlos Morales-Aguilar. "Alineamientos astronómicos en el sitios arqueoógicos de Tintal, el Mirador y Nakbé, Petén, Guatemala." *Investigación y conservación en los sitios arqueologicos de la zona cultural y natural Mirador*: 123–58, 2007.

■ CLIFFORD T. BROWN AND WALTER R. T. WITSCHEY

EL PERÚ-WAKA'

Waka' (the Maya name) is located approximately 120 m above the San Pedro River in the northwest corner of the Department of Petén, **Guatemala**, at an elevation of approximately 160 m asl (see also **Map 3**). It is within the Parque Nacional Laguna Del Tigre and the **Mirador Basin**. Waka' (17.3° N, 90.4° W) sits on a high escarpment above the flood plain and extends about 1 km². The city is densely packed, with more than 900 structures known, including temple-**pyramids**, **palaces**, and elite dwellings, plus 40 **stelae** and altars. The site was first surveyed by Ian Graham in 1971, and further research began in 2003 by the Waka Research Foundation led by Héctor Escobedo, with David Freidel, Carlos Pérez, Horacio Martínez, and Juan Carlos Meléndez.

Earliest occupation occurred in the Late Formative, 300–200 BC. The site then developed rapidly in the Early Classic. Stela 15 shows a portrait of the **Teotihuacán** conquering general Siyaj K'ak', who arrived at Waka' eight days before entering **Tikal** and overthrowing the royal dynasty there. This creation of this text at Waka' also provides insight into the possible route of the military campaign to Tikal and its speed of march.

During the Late Classic (AD 600–900), Waka' was under the control of **Calakmul**, undoubtedly to secure **trade routes** to the Usumacinta River, which lasted until Tikal defeated Calakmul with the capture of King Yuknoom Yich'aak K'ak'. In AD 743 Tikal defeated Waka' and maintained control until Calakmul again defeated Tikal. Yik'in Chan K'awiil, then ruling Tikal, celebrated that victory with the carving of the wooden Lintel 3 of Temple IV, a portrait of himself as victorious king with a celestial serpent.

Documentation of the royal dynasty at Waka' includes pieces from five **royal tombs**, one of a queen from approximately AD 700–750, likely a princess from Calakmul who married into the royal family at Waka'. Another royal tomb contained two females, one pregnant, who may have themselves been offerings for a king whose royal tomb is as yet undiscovered.

Recently discovered Stela 44 dates to AD 564 and carries intriguing information about the **Middle Classic Hiatus** at Tikal, when, as believed, no carved monuments were being erected. Stanley Guenter reads the text as a dedication by King Wa'oom Uch'ab Tzi'kin to his father Chak Tok Ich'aak, who died in AD 556. Since Chak Tok Ich'aak is also the name of two Tikal rulers, researchers suspect that Waka' was controlled by Tikal at the time, and use of the name was in direct deference to Tikal. The stela had been erected, and after a century interred, as a funerary monument to Lady Ikoom, princess of Calakmul.

See also ALLIANCES; ART; HIEROGLYPHIC STAIRWAYS; LA CORONA; MAYA QUEENS

Further Reading

Escobedo, Héctor L., David Freidel, Juan Carlos Meléndez, Mary Jane Acuña, Jennifer Piehl, and Juan Carlos Pérez Calderón. *Proyecto Arqueológico El Perú Waka': Informes No. 1 (Temporada 2003) through No. 11 (Temporada 2013)*. Fundación de Investigación Arqueológica Waka', 2003–2013. http://www.mesoweb.com/informes/informes.html.

"New Monument Found at El Peru-Waka in Guatemala, Tells Story of Mayan Cleopatra." *Sci-News.com*, July 17. 2013. http://www.sci-news.com/archaeology/science-monument-el-peru-waka-guatemala-mayan-cleopatra-01233.html.

Roach, John. "Ancient Royal Tomb Discovered in Guatemala." *National Geographic News*, May 4, 2006. http://news.nationalgeographic.com/news/2006/05/0504_060504_maya_tomb.html.

Waka Research Foundation. http://www.archaeologywaka.org/faq.html.

■ WALTER R. T. WITSCHEY

EL PILAR

El Pilar (17.2° N, 89.1° W) flourished as a major Maya center for nearly two millennia beginning around 3,000 years ago. It is among the largest centers in the **Belize** River area, more than three times the size of other well-known centers such as Baking Pot or **Xunantunich** (see also **Map 3**). At its peak El Pilar was home to 15,000–20,000 people in a mosaic landscape of **houses** and gardens, as well as managed forest and agricultural fields (see also **Subsistence**).

This ancient Maya center has some 30 identified plazas in a core area of approximately 38 ha (94 acres), ranking equal with major centers of the lowland Maya region. Despite its large size, El Pilar was unexplored by archaeologists until 1983. Once discovered and mapped, the major monumental platforms and monuments were recognized as a binational asset in Belize and **Guatemala**, symbolically unified by an ancient Maya **causeway** that crosses the modern international border. (See figure 17.) Research at El Pilar has emphasized the ancient Maya people within the context of the governing elites. Multidisciplinary studies focus on where the Maya built their homes with respect to settlement patterns, when they lived there based on **ceramic** chronologies, and how they fed large populations with reference to ethnohistorical and contemporary agroforestry practices.

The major center of El Pilar was archaeologically unknown before the surveys of the Belize River Archaeological Settlement Survey (BRASS) project. Under the direction of

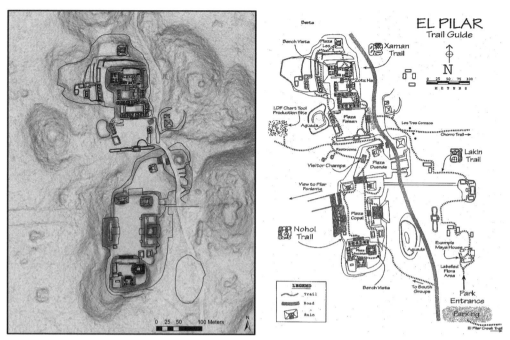

Figure 17. El Pilar central monumental architecture. Left: image developed from LiDAR remote sense data, overlain with line drawings of structures. Right: visitors' guide to the same area. Illustrations courtesy of Anabel Ford.

archaeologist Anabel Ford, the major monuments of El Pilar were mapped and shared for the first time with the archaeological world in 1984. The BRASS/El Pilar fieldwork included mapping and identification of residential sites; confirmed locations of minor centers; and gathered data on **soil**, topography, and **vegetation** critical to understanding Maya forest land use across a 1,300 km² area adjacent to El Pilar (see also **Geology**). These data provide the context for understanding the organization of the Maya political and subsistence economy. The field enterprises have been divided into stages.

The greater BRASS/El Pilar surveys of the 1983 and 1984 field seasons survey identified cultural remains within three 250-m-wide transects—one 10 km long and the other two 5 km long—traversing natural environmental zones from the riverside at 60 m to the ridgelands peaking above 300–400 m asl. Test excavations focused on stratified, random sampling of residential middens of 48 sites based on distance from the river. The environmental zones—valley, foothills, ridgelands—revealed variation in settlement size and composition, from individual farmsteads to the major center of El Pilar, and a variety of activities from basic and local household tasks to rare and exotic **obsidian** blade production.

The detailed investigation of El Pilar area Maya domestic architecture of 1990–1992 focused on the examination of Maya households, a type of research that was still in its infancy. Notable projects in the Maya area with similar concentration include the El Pilar area, the site of Kaxob, that of Chau Hiix, and Chan. A representative sample of sites tested in the survey phase was excavated. The sample totaled 10 residential units selected based on artifact assemblages. The results provided essential data on everyday life in the El Pilar area, where modest houses were located in the valley, workshops were located in the foothills; and diverse elite and farming households were related to the major center of El Pilar.

Initial research and examination of the civic monuments of El Pilar covered the decade 1993–2003. The long-term study of the major center began with (1) a detailed map of the site surroundings, (2) repair of looter damage, (3) excavations and consolidation to develop "Archaeology Under the Canopy," (4) cultural resource planning process for one resource in two countries, and (5) interpretive and educational programs on the Maya. Research on the development of complexity and the relationship of the major center of El Pilar to its landscape was a focus based on the data from the earlier surveys. Additional examination of three residential sites was undertaken to understand the variability of ancient Maya households. This included the platform above the **chert** production area, one small residential unit, and one complex compound patio unit, now consolidated as a visitor asset.

The development of the management planning and the binational park initiative has been an ongoing theme from1994 to the present. This included the promotion of cooperative management plan of El Pilar Archaeological Reserve for Maya Flora and Fauna by Belize and Guatemala, uniting the contiguous protected areas while honoring the planning processes of both nations that crossed political, economic, and cultural boundaries. This is highlighted by the ancient causeway linking El Pilar's Maya monuments as symbol of collaboration between Belize and Guatemala for the benefit of future generations of the Maya forest region.

The results of research and development at El Pilar show that it functioned as a primary administrative center for the Belize River area, about 15 km from Xunantunich and about 50 km from **Tikal**. It has expansive Maya plazas, temples, and **palaces** that were built over a course of 18 centuries, from ca. 800 BC to AD 1000. Today, El Pilar is at the heart of a 5,000-acre protected archaeological reserve for flora and **fauna**, welcoming visitors and engaging scholars (see also **Vegetation**). Large open plazas, such as Plaza Copal, and restricted palaces represented by Plaza Jobo in the north acropolis are part of a unique trail system that wanders under the canopy. El Pilar also offers visitors a glimpse into everyday life of the Maya, with the fully exposed and consolidated house site and forest garden on the east, called Tzunu'un. These aspects of El Pilar feature the ancient Maya people as well as the lifeways of the elite administration.

El Pilar is designed to be managed using the principles of "Archaeology Under the Canopy," preserving the integrity of both the forest and the ancient structures it shelters. This cultural and natural resource management approach uses the forest surrounding the site to protect structures, honoring the forest and lending a feeling of mystery and discovery for those who come for a visit.

See also SETTLEMENT PATTERNS (CENTRAL LOWLANDS)

Further Reading

Exploring Solutions Past. 2014. http://exploringsolutionspast.org/what-we-do/archaeology-under-the-canopy/el-pilar-archaeological-reserve/.

Ford, Anabel. "Adaptive Management and the Community of El Pilar: A Philosophy of Resilience for the Maya Forest." In *Of the Past, for the Future: Integrating Archaeology and Conservation*, edited by Neville Agnew and Janet Bridgland, 105–12. Washington, DC: The Getty Institute, 2006.

Ford, Anabel. "Action archaeology and the community at El Pilar." In *Anthropology: The Human Challenge*, pp. 260–262, edited by William A. Haviland, Harald E. L. Prins, Dana Walrath and Bunny McBride. Belmont, CA: Wadsworth/Cengage Learning, 2011.

———. "Afterword: El Pilar and Maya Cultural Heritage; Reflections of a Cheerful Pessimist." In *Contested Cultural Heritage: Religion, Nationalism, Erasure, and Exclusion in a Global World*, edited by Helaine Silverman, 261–65. New York: Springer, 2011.

Ford, Anabel, and M. Havrda. "Archaeology under the Canopy: Imagining the Maya of El Pilar." In *Tourism Consumption and Representation: Narratives of Place and Self*, edited by K. Meethan, A. Anderson, and S. Miles, 67–93. Wallingford, UK: CAB International, 2006.

Meerman, Jan. *Rapid Ecological Assessment: El Pilar Archaeological Reserve.* Belize Environmental Consultancies Ltd., 1998. http://biological-diversity.info/Downloads/Pilar_REA_1998.pdf.

MesoAmerican Research Center. *2014 Articles and Events.* http://www.marc.ucsb.edu/news.

Wernecke, D. Clark. "Aspects of Urban Design in an Ancient Maya Center: El Pilar, Belize." MA thesis, Florida Atlantic University, 1994.

Wernecke, Daniel Clark. "A Stone Canvas: Interpreting Maya Building Materials and Construction Technology." PhD diss., University of Texas at Austin, 2005.

Whittaker, John C., Kathryn A. Kamp, Anabel Ford, Rafael Guerra, Peter Brands, Jose Guerra, Kim Mclean, Alex Woods, Melissa Badillo, Jennifer Thornton, and Zerifeh Eiley. "Lithic Industry in a Maya Center: An Axe Workshop at El Pilar, Belize." *Latin American Antiquity* 20, no. 1: 134–56, 2009.

■ ANABEL FORD

EL SALVADOR

The modern nation of El Salvador is located on the Pacific coast of Central America, adjacent to **Guatemala** on the west and **Honduras** to the north (see also **Map 1**). The western part of El Salvador was culturally Maya in ancient times. The Maya area includes the ancient sites of Cara Sucia, Casa Blanca, Joya de **Cerén**, San Andrés, Cihuatán, and Tazumal, among others. Western El Salvador is part of the **Pacific Coastal Plain** and the **Southern Highlands** geographic regions.

Sites such as Casa Blanca show an early affinity to Maya activity along the Pacific coast in the Preclassic (500 BC–AD 250) and the Classic (AD 250–900) eras. Other sites, such as Cihuatán (AD 900–1100), were established after the **Classic Maya collapse**. Later immigration of Nahua speakers, the Pipil of central **Mexico**, formed the population encountered by the Spanish conquerors in 1524. Pedro and Gonzalo de Alvarado led the invading Spanish soldiers, but were twice defeated before final conquest in 1828. Today El Salvador is 86 percent mestizo, 13 percent white, and 1 percent Amerind, some of whom still speak Nahua.

The country is notable for its volcanoes, which form part of the Pacific Ocean "ring of fire." Four of them—Izalco, San Miguel, San Salvador, and Santa Ana—have erupted in the past century. Ilopango, which last erupted in 1880, was responsible for the founding of Ceren (Joya de Ceren) in AD 535, which was buried a few decades later after another volcanic event.

See also BALL GAME/BALL COURT; BELIZE; CERAMICS; CLASSIC MAYA COLLAPSE; DROUGHT; GUATEMALA; HONDURAS; IXTEPEQUE; IZAPA; LAKES; MAYA AREA; MESOAMERICA; SOUTHERN PERIPHERY; TIKAL

Further Reading

"List of Volcanoes in El Salvador." In *Wikipedia*, 2014. http://en.wikipedia.org/wiki/List_of_volcanoes _in_El_Salvador.

Andrews, E. Wyllys, V. *The Archaeology of Quelepa, El Salvador*. Publications of the Middle American Research Institute, no. 42 New Orleans, LA: Tulane University, 1976.

FUNDAR. Fundación Nacional de Arqueología de El Salvador (National Foundation of Archaeology of El Salvador). 2012.http://www.fundar.org.sv/e_layout.html.

Instituto Geográfico Nacional, Ingeniero Pablo Arnoldo Guzmán. *Atlas de el Salvador*. 4th ed. El Salvador, C.A.: Instituto Geográfico Nacional-Centro Nacional de Registros, Ingeniero Pablo Arnoldo Guzmán, Ministerio de Obras Públicas, 2000.

Sharer, Robert. *The Prehistory of Chalchuapa, El Salvador*. Philadelphia: University of Pennsylvania Press, 1978.

Sheets, Payson D., ed. *Before the Volcano Erupted: The Ancient Cerén Village in Central America*. Austin: University of Texas Press, 2002.

———. *The Ceren Site: An Ancient Village Buried by Volcanic Ash in Central America*. Belmont, CA: Thomson Wadsworth, 2006.

U.S. Central Intelligence Agency. *The World Factbook, Central America and Caribbean: El Salvador*. 2014 https://www.cia.gov/library/publications/the-world-factbook/geos/es.html.

■ WALTER R. T. WITSCHEY

EXOTIC FOODSTUFFS

See SUBSISTENCE; TRADE ROUTES

F

FAUNA

The Maya cultural region lies within a global biodiversity hotspot characterized by high animal species diversity and many unique species found nowhere else in the world. The region's faunal diversity is directly linked to the region's diverse biomes, which include lowland rainforest, highland cloud and montane forest, and coastal mangroves. The ancient Maya therefore had access to a broad suite of terrestrial, aquatic, and marine fauna to use as food or for other purposes (see also **Subsistence**). In the absence of major, large-bodied domesticated animals, the ancient Maya relied extensively on wild animals, which they obtained through hunting, fishing, and shellfishing. These wild resources provided the majority of their dietary animal protein and also served as pets, sources of raw materials (e.g., hides, feathers, bones, shells), and ritual items (e.g., stingray spine perforators) and sacrifices (see also **Rites and Rituals**). Although the ancient Maya had access to domesticated dogs and turkeys, they did not rely primarily on domesticated animals until the Colonial period (post-AD 1500), when Old World domesticated animals such as cows, pigs, horses, sheep, goats, and chickens were introduced to the Americas.

The available fauna varies across the Maya cultural region based on local habitat conditions (see table 1). However, some of the largest-bodied and most common prey species include ungulates such as white-tailed deer, smaller forest-dwelling brocket deer, tapirs, and peccaries, a pig-like species native to the Americas. Smaller mammals commonly targeted by both ancient and modern hunters include large rodents such as agoutis and pacas, rabbits, armadillos, coatis, kinkajous, foxes, anteaters, and various species of opossum. Monkeys are also common throughout the Maya area, but their remains are rare in archaeological deposits. Wild cats native to the region include the iconic jaguar, which figured prominently in Maya **art** and **religion**; as well as the puma, jaguarundi, and two smaller spotted cats (ocelot and margay). In coastal areas, marine mammals such as dolphins, whales, and manatees are also present, but the manatee was the only marine mammal hunted extensively by the ancient Maya.

Table 1. Faunal Species of the Maya Area

Common Name	Scientific Name (Family or Genus species)
Mammals	
opossum	Didelphidae
armadillo	Dasypus novemcinctus
anteater	Tamandua mexicana
otter	Lutra longicaudis
raccoon	Procyon lotor
coati	Nasua narica
kinkajou	Poto flavus
domestic dog	Canis lupus familiaris
grey fox	Urocyon cinereoargenteus
jaguar	Panthera onca
puma	Puma concolor
jaguarundi	Puma yagouaroundi
ocelot	Leopardus pardalis
margay	Leopardus wiedii
spider monkey	Ateles geoffroyi
howler monkey	Alouatta pigra
tapir	Tapirus bairdii
white-tailed deer	Odocoileus virginianus
brocket deer	Mazama sp.
white-lipped peccary	Tayassu pecari
collared peccary	Pecari tajacu
paca	Cuniculus paca
agouti	Dasyprocta punctata
rabbit	Sylvilagus sp.
manatee[a]	Trichechus manatus
Birds	
great curassow	Crax rubra
crested guan	Penelope purpurascens
chachalaca	Ortalis vetula
bobwhite quail	Colinus nigrogularis
ocellated turkey	Meleagris ocellata
domestic turkey	Meleagris gallopavo
quetzal	Pharomachris mocinno
scarlet macaw	Ara macao
Reptiles and Amphibians	
cane toad	Bufo marinus
crocodile	Crocodylus sp.
green iguana	Iguana iguana
Central American river turtle	Dermatemys mawii
mud/musk turtle	Kinosternidae
common slider turtle	Trachemys scripta
sea turtle[1]	Cheloniidae
fer-de-lance snake	Bothrops asper
rattlesnake	Crotalus simus
Fish	
shark[a]	Carcharhinidae
stingray[a]	Dasyatidae
sea catfish[a]	Ariidae
grouper[a]	Serranidae

Common Name	Scientific Name (Family or Genus species)
jack[a]	Carangidae
snapper[a]	Lutjanidae
parrotfish[a]	Scaridae
tropical gar	*Lepisosteus tropicus*
freshwater catfish	Ictaluridae
freshwater bass	Centrarchidae
cichlids fish	Ciclidae
Invertebrates	
apple snail	*Pomacea* sp.
jute	*Pachychilus* sp.
freshwater clam	Unionidae
conch[a]	*Strombus* sp.
olive shell[a]	*Oliva* sp.
oyster[a]	*Crassostrea* sp.
spiny oyster[a]	*Spondylus* sp.
hard-shelled clam[a]	*Mercenaria* sp.
spiny lobster[a]	Palinuridae
crab[a]	Portunidae
shrimp[a]	Penaeidae
stingless bee	*Melipona beechieii*

Note: Species mentioned in text and other common animals used by the ancient Maya.
  Species list is not exhaustive, and animal species vary geographically.

a. marine species

Bird diversity is also extremely high in the Maya region (> 700 species). Game birds including the great curassow, guan, chachalaca, quail, and ocellated turkey were commonly hunted for meat, while other birds were used primarily for their feathers. Brightly colored and long-tailed species such as quetzals and scarlet macaws were the most coveted sources of feathers, but many other species of parrots, songbirds, and raptors were likely used for similar purposes. Such feathers appear frequently in the headdresses of Maya rulers whose images are carved on **stelae** and painted on murals (see also **Wall Painting**).

Well over 200 species of reptiles and amphibians are found in the Maya area. Many of these species are small frogs, salamanders, and lizards that are not exploited by human populations. However, larger-bodied species including crocodiles, turtles, snakes, and iguanas were used by the ancient Maya. Turtles were very commonly used, especially the large Central American river turtle, which can grow to over two feet long. In coastal regions sea turtles were also hunted. Snakes are another reptile significant to the ancient Maya. Snakes appear frequently in Maya art as vision serpents that connect to the spirit world and as part of the plumed serpent **iconography** common throughout much of **Mesoamerica**. The only amphibian thought to be used by the ancient Maya is the giant cane toad. This species secretes a harmful toxin, so it was likely used for medicinal or ritual purposes rather than human consumption.

The region's **lakes**, rivers, and coastlines also provide habitat for numerous species of marine and freshwater fish. In coastal regions, reef fish such as grouper, snapper, jack, and parrotfish were heavily exploited as a food source. Marine fish were also occasionally transported to inland Maya sites, along with highly valued ritual items such as stingray spines, shark teeth, and marine seashells. The use of freshwater fish by the ancient Maya is less well understood, but the presence of **ceramic** net weights and bone fishhooks at some inland Maya sites suggests that they made use of the various freshwater fish species available for human consumption.

Mollusks or shellfish are similarly available in marine and freshwater habitats and were also consumed by the ancient Maya. Inland lakes and rivers contain edible species such as apple snail, jute, and freshwater clams. Coastal regions contain a much greater diversity of shellfish, including common species such as conchs, oysters, hard-shelled clams, and olive shells. Other aquatic invertebrates available for consumption include crabs, shrimp, and lobsters.

Prior to the Colonial period, the domestic dog and turkey were the only major domesticated animals available to the Maya. Domesticated dogs, which entered the region along with the first human settlers, were used as companions, hunters, and sacrificial victims, but they were also consumed as food. The domesticated turkey, which originated in the Central Mexican highlands, is nonlocal to the Maya area and was introduced during pre-Colonial times. In addition to the dog and turkey, the ancient Maya raised domesticated colonies of stingless bees, which were used for producing honey. Occasional captive rearing of wild species, including white-tailed deer, peccary, ocellated turkey, and quail, has also been suggested for the ancient Maya, but the use of wild animal species was the norm.

Many animal species were consumed by the ancient Maya, but meat was not the only resource obtained from animals. The need for secondary products such as hides, feathers, fats, bone, and shell also likely motivated their capture or collection. For example, thick mammal bones were used to create a vast array of tools, including needles, awls, and fishhooks, while the bony shells of turtles and armadillos were used to make bowls or instruments (e.g., rattles and drums). Personal adornments such as beads, pendants, tinklers, and ear flares were also crafted from animal bone, tooth, and shell, and ancient artwork depicts the use of feathers and animal hides (especially jaguar pelts) as clothing and ritual regalia (see also **Music and Dancing**; **Portable Objects**).

Animals and animal products also played a prominent role in Maya ritual and **religion**. Deer, dogs, turkeys, peccaries, wild cats, and other species were used as sacrificial victims and offerings to the gods during ceremonies. Whole animals were also interred in burials and ritual caches. In addition to the use of whole or live animals in ritual, the Maya also selected particular elements of species for ceremonial use. For example, stingray tail spines were employed in bloodletting ceremonies, and animal skulls were used as part of ceremonial headdresses or costumes (see also **Theater**).

Maya animal use was complex in both the number of species used and the number of ways animals were used as dietary and nondietary resources. How the Maya used and interacted with animals is also significant, because unlike most other ancient complex civilizations, the Maya relied primarily on wild rather than domesticated animal resources.

See also ART; BURIALS; CAVES; CERAMICS; DATING; DIET; EDZNA; EL PILAR; HOUSEHOLD PRODUCTION; ICONOGRAPHY; IZAPA; JAINA; LAKES; LOLTUN CAVE; MEDICINE; MUSIC AND

Dance; Pacific Coastal Plain; *Popol Vuh*; Religion; Rites and Rituals; San Bartolo; Subsistence; Trade Routes; Water Management; Zacualpa

Further Reading

Benson, Elizabeth P. *Birds and Beasts of Ancient Latin America.* Gainesville: University Press of Florida, 1997.

Emery, Kitty F. *Maya Zooarchaeology: New Directions in Method and Theory*, Cotsen Institute of Archaeology, Monograph 51. Los Angeles: Cotsen Institute of Archaeology at University of California, Los Angeles, 2004.

Hamblin, Nancy L. *Animal Use by the Cozumel Maya.* Tucson: University of Arizona Press, 1984.

Lee, Julian C. *A Field Guide to the Amphibians and Reptiles of the Maya World: The Lowlands of Mexico, Northern Guatemala, and Belize.* Ithaca, NY: Cornell University Press, 2000.

Pohl, Mary, ed. *Prehistoric Lowland Maya Environment and Subsistence Economy.* Papers of the Peabody Museum of Archaeology and Ethnology, Harvard University, vol. 77. Cambridge, MA: Peabody Museum of Archaeology and Ethnology, Harvard University: Distributed by Harvard University Press, 1985.

■ ERIN KENNEDY THORNTON

FEATHERWORK

See Fauna; Portable Objects; Trade Routes

FLORA

See Vegetation

FOREST MANAGEMENT

See Subsistence; Vegetation

FORTIFICATIONS

To fortify a city is to make an archaeological declaration that one had powerful enemies and resources to protect. In the Maya area, there are cities with strong, well-planned, well-built walls, others whose fortifications seem to have been hastily prepared, and some that are not fortified at all. Fortifications are more prevalent in the **lowlands**, where the naturally flat terrain provides little defense. In the **highlands**, many sites are easily defended because of their location in rugged terrain.

The Honduran site Los Naranjos, on the eastern Maya periphery, may have the earliest fortifications in the region. The first of two earthwork systems of ditch and rampart was constructed in the Middle Formative (800–400 BC) with a length of 1.3 km. **Becan** is surrounded by a massive ditch and rampart 1.9 km long, with a depth from ditch bottom to rampart top of 11 m. Local rulers commanded a workforce that expended some 1,000 man-years of effort to build the moat during the Late Formative. It was maintained and used well into the Classic.

In the Late Classic, **Tikal** constructed a moat and rampart defensive line 4.5 km north of the Great Plaza, running east-west for 9.5 km, with its ends terminating at swamps. Chacchob, near the Puuc hills, had a long occupation, with significant construction in the **Puuc style** in the Late Classic. A 2 km moat provides defense for the site center. Both Cuca and **Ek Balam** have two concentric stone walls enclosing the main structures of the site center. **Tulum**, occupied in the Late Postclassic, has a prominent position on cliffs overlooking the Caribbean. A massive C-shaped wall with entrance gates occupies the land side. At 3–4 m high and 8 m thick, the wall provides a formidable defense for the site center and principal elite residences. It does not, however, defend the extensive areas of residences and field walls of the more modest dwellings of the commoners.

At **Dos Pilas**, after the upheavals of the eighth century, a small populace stripped ceremonial structures of stone to quickly build defensive walls that cross platforms and ignore the original city plan. Apparently their haste in construction was to no avail, and the site was soon abandoned.

In sum, lowland fortifications, whether ditch and rampart or stone wall, seem widely scattered. Many sites have no fortifications at all. Further research is necessary to gain a full understanding of why and by whom particular sites felt sufficiently threatened to make massive defensive constructions, while other similar sites felt no need for constructed defenses.

See also AGUATECA; CHUNCHUCMIL; CIVAL; COCHUAH REGION; DOS PILAS; HOLMUL; IXIMCHÉ; MAYAPÁN; NAACHTUN; NIXTUN-CH'ICH'; Q'UM'ARKAJ; SETTLEMENT PATTERNS (NORTHERN LOWLANDS); UXMAL; WARFARE, WARRIORS, AND WEAPONS; ZACPETÉN

Further Reading

Lothrop, Samuel Kirkland. *Tulum: An Archaeological Study of the East Coast of Yucatan.* Carnegie Institution of Washington, Publication 335. Washington, DC: Carnegie Institution of Washington, 1924.

Puleston, Dennis Edward. "Defensive Earthwork at Tikal." *Expedition* 9, no. 3: 40–48, 1967.

Webster, David. "Lowland Maya Fortifications." *Proceedings of the American Philosophical Society* 120, no. 5: 361–71, 1976.

Webster, David. "Una Ciudad Maya Fortificada. Becán, Campeche." *Arqueología Mexicana* 18: 32–35, 1996.

Webster, David L. *Defensive Earthworks at Becan, Campeche, Mexico: Implications for Maya Warfare.* Middle American Research Institute, Publication 41. New Orleans, LA: Tulane University, 1976.

■ WALTER R. T. WITSCHEY

FÖRSTEMANN, ERNST WILHELM (1822–1906)

As a staff member, then Royal Librarian of the Saxony State Library in Dresden, Germany, Förstemann recognized the Dresden **codex** as a pre-Columbian Maya manuscript. In 1880 he began studying the codex, and he published about it until his death. His first efforts were to make a copy of the book, 60 copies of which were published using photo-chromo-lithography. An earlier tracing of the codex for Lord Kingsborough dates to 1825–1826. Förstemann made a second photographic copy in 1892. The reproductions by Förstemann are invaluable for Maya scholars, since the original codex suffered severe water damage during the fire-bombing of Dresden in the Second World War.

Over the course of several years with the Dresden codex, and relying on **Diego de Landa**'s *Relacion*, Förstemann determined how the Maya numerals were written (dots = one; bars = five; shell = zero, place-holder) and how the Long Count worked to count consecutive days from August 11, 3114 BC, a day named 4 Ahaw 8 Cumku. He showed the workings of the modified base-20 vigesimal counting system. He related the *tzolk'in* description in Landa to the daily almanacs in the Dresden codex. Recognizing that the codex contained the number 584, the length of the synodic cycle of Venus, he showed that the Maya understood the four parts of the Venus orbit: inferior conjunction and superior conjunction, when Venus is invisible in front of or behind the sun, and morning star and evening star, when the planet is close to the sun in the dawn or dusk sky. He also elucidated the complex lunar tables of the Dresden, which foretell eclipses.

Förstemann is credited with extracting the meaning of the **mathematics** in the Dresden codex. His work marked the beginning of a century in which Maya scholars usually focused either on the numbers and dates in the script or on deciphering its texts, but not both. In the last 40 years, however, those who analyze the script recognize that understanding the contents of an inscription requires unifying the two approaches into a coherent, single study. See also **Astronomical Observatories**; **Astronomy**; **Calendar**.

Further Reading

Codex Dresdensis—Mscr.Dresd.R.310. Saxon State Library—Dresden State and University Library (SLUB). 2013 http://digital.slub-dresden.de/werkansicht/dlf/2967/2/.

Coe, Michael D. *Breaking the Maya Code.* 3rd ed. London: Thames & Hudson, 2012.

Marhenke, Randa. *Maya Hieroglyphic Writing: The Ancient Maya Codices.* 2012 ed. Foundation for the Advancement of Mesoamerican Studies, Inc., February 15, 2012. http://www.famsi.org/mayawriting/codices/marhenke.html.

■ WALTER R. T. WITSCHEY

G

GEOLOGY

The ancient Maya occupied **lowland** and **highland** areas of what is today southern **Mexico** and northern Central America, where they exploited terrains characterized by different rock types. Local geology shaped Maya culture because it (1) provided construction material; (2) was the base rock for soil development; (3) gave rise to local water bodies; (4) led to cave formation; and (5) was the source of clay and stone used to make ceramics, tools, and art objects (see also **Map 7**).

The Maya lowlands of the Yucatan Peninsula are characterized by fossil-rich sedimentary rock called limestone (calcium carbonate, $CaCO_3$), which formed in ancient shallow seas. In some parts of the peninsula, there are local deposits of gypsum (calcium sulfate, $CaSO_4 \cdot H_2O$). The land surface in the lowland area now lies 0 to ~300 m asl. The age of exposed rock generally increases from north to south. Barrier islands on the north coast formed within the last 10,000 years, whereas surface rock in southern Petén, **Guatemala** dates to the time of the dinosaurs, more than 65 million years ago. The Maya Mountains of **Belize** are an exception on the low-lying, limestone-rich peninsula, in that they possess ancient granites that are more than 420 million years old and rise > 1,100 m asl.

The northernmost part of the Yucatan Peninsula is flat. Farther south, the processes of faulting and folding gave rise to hilly topography. The ancient Maya used limestone to build their great ceremonial centers and to carve ornate monuments with inscribed texts and illustrations called **stelae**. Crushed limestone was burned to create lime (CaO), to which water was added to make construction mortar and stucco. Lime was also used to prepare corn tortillas, a staple of the Maya **diet**. Mineral **soils** derived from the limestone bedrock are nutrient-poor, and ash from slash-and-burn agriculture helped to fertilize soils with required plant nutrients (see also **Subsistence**).

Long-term dissolution of the limestone bedrock gave rise to karst terrain, characterized by pockmarked surface rock, sinkholes, **caves**, and underground conduits that carry groundwater. Rivers and streams are features of the Southern Lowlands, but the Northern Lowlands are devoid of flowing surface waters. Numerous caves, such as Calcehtók and **Loltun**, were perceived as portals to the underworld (*Xibalba*). A ring of sinkholes (**cenotes**) in the northwest Yucatan Peninsula surrounds the site where the **Chicxulub** meteorite crashed into the ocean 65 million years ago, ending the reign of dinosaurs. Clays in the limestone lowlands were used to make polychrome pottery vessels (see also

Ceramics). A hard, silica-rich rock called **chert**, of which flint is one type, formed as nodules within the limestone and was knapped to form tools, weapons, and works of **art** (see also **Warfare, Warriors, and Weapons**).

The Maya highlands include parts of the state of Chiapas (Mexico) and much of southern Guatemala. The area is characterized by steep volcanic terrain. Faulting and volcanism in the highland region are related to plate tectonics, including passage of the Cocos Plate beneath the Caribbean Plate, and eastward sliding of the Caribbean Plate relative to the North American Plate. Earthquakes and landslides are common. The Maya highlands possess rocks of diverse ages, including Paleozoic metamorphic rocks, Paleozoic, Mesozoic and Quaternary sediments, and Tertiary and Quaternary volcanic rocks. There are 37 volcanoes in the Guatemala highlands, of which 4 remain active. Volcano Tajumulco, in southwest Guatemala, is the highest point in Central America (4,220 m asl).

The highlands possess rich volcanic soils that were exploited for agriculture by the ancient Maya. The Maya also used volcanic ash to temper their pottery. Large caldera **lakes** such as Atitlán and Ayarza were formed by volcanic eruptions and collapse of magma chambers, ca. 84,000 and ca. 20,000 years ago, respectively (see also **Map 7**). Jade from the highlands was traded widely and utilized for carvings, personal adornments, and **burial tribute** (see also **Portable Objects**). **Obsidian** was also traded and knapped to make arrowheads, spear points, knife blades, and ceremonial objects. The geology of the Maya region shaped the lifeways of the area's ancient occupants by providing construction material; generating agricultural soils; yielding clay and rock from which ceramics, tools, and art objects were fashioned; and giving rise to the water bodies that were critical to human survival.

See also Bajos; Ceramic Analysis

Further Reading

Garrity, C. P., and D. R. Soller. *Database of the Geologic Map of North America: Adapted from the Map by J. C. Reed, Jr. and Others (2005)*. U.S. Geological Survey, 2009. http://pubs.usgs.gov/ds/424/.

Hammond, Norman. "Obsidian Trade Routes in the Mayan Area." *Science* 178: 1092–93, 1972.

Hodell, David A., Rhonda L. Quinn, Mark Brenner, and George Kamenov. "Spatial Variation of Strontium Isotopes ($^{87}Sr/^{86}Sr$) in the Maya Region: A Tool for Tracking Ancient Human Migration." *Journal of Archaeological Science* 31, no. 5: 585–601, 2004.

Marshall, Jeffrey S. "Geomorphology and Physiographic Provinces of Central America." In *Central America: Geology, Resources, and Natural Hazards*, edited by Jochen Bundschuh and Guillermo E. Alvarado Induni, pp. 75–122. London and New York: Taylor and Francis, 2007.

Molnar, Peter, and Lynn R. Sykes. "Tectonics of the Caribbean and Middle America Regions from Focal Mechanisms and Seismicity." *Geological Society of America Bulletin* 80, 9: 1639–84, 1969.

■ LISETH PÉREZ AND MARK BRENNER

GROUND SURVEY TECHNIQUES

Ground survey techniques are traditionally used in Maya archaeology to record sites and features. While at one time limited to terrestrial mapping using traditional tools, these techniques now include a host of remote-sensing technologies that record features above and below ground.

Traditional ground survey in the Maya area included a range of products: sketch maps, pace-and-compass maps, contour maps, and rectified maps made with transit or alidade. Past archaeological projects throughout the Maya lowlands mapped ruined structures and features with traditional tools and transferred the information to graph paper at specific scales to be drafted by hand and then published in paper form. Although historic survey of sites was done on foot ("pedestrian survey") and the data were recorded by hand, today GPS units and transits store data points for mapping that can be placed in their digital form on computers and incorporated into GIS systems. Many published older maps from sites such as **Tikal**, **Guatemala**, and **Mayapan**, **Mexico**, now have been converted to digital format.

Even with advances in technology, due to the fact that forest cover obfuscates many sites, most mapping still is terrestrial-based and labor-intensive. Survey involves cutting systematic paths through the jungle and combing between these paths for ancient remains. These paths also function as lines of sight for the mapping instruments. For decades, these ground survey techniques constrained researchers from covering large areas and also resulted in a focus on noticeable monumental **architecture** rather than full sites. However, aerial-based and satellite-based survey methods have radically changed these limitations (see also **LiDAR**).

Remote survey methods are either terrestrial-based or above-ground. Above-ground remote-sensing surveys have tended to employ either planes or satellites, but more recently drones have also been used. Aerial survey in the Maya area started with flights by Charles Lindbergh in the early twentieth century that recorded high **pyramids** protruding through the tree canopy as well as linear features that were **causeways**. Planes are currently used in conjunction with radar (SLAR) and laser (LiDAR) survey methods. Satellites also provide data related to ground survey that range from course resolution (LANDSAT and multi- and hyper-spectral imagery) through finer resolution (CORONA and QUICKBIRD photographic images).

Terrestrial-based survey that focuses on **soils** and features below the surface is known as geophysical survey (see also **Map 7**; **Map**). These techniques are capable of mapping below-ground features, particularly if there are matrix and compositional differences in the soils and rubble. Geophysical surveys can either be active or passive; passive surveys measure inherent soil properties, while active surveys transmit elements into the soil and record a response. Ground-based remote sensing includes a host of methods—acoustic and seismic (i.e., sonar), electromagnetic (ground-penetrating radar), resistance (electrical resistivity and conductivity), magnetic survey (magnetometers), and geochemical analyses (i.e., phosphate analyses)—as well as thermal prospection, **vegetation** surveys, and metal detection. Magnetometers were successfully employed at the site of **Quiriguá**, Guatemala, to detect a buried causeway. Geochemical analyses have been used to demonstrate the existence of **markets** at Maya sites. However, ground-penetrating radar has not been very effective in the Maya area because of the high limestone content of the soil.

Besides more passive mapping techniques, active ground survey is also used to collect artifactual materials from the surface in some drier parts of the Maya area (i.e., Puuc region). In this kind of ground survey, surface materials are systematically collected using a host of sampling strategies in order to make interpretations about what is beneath the ground. In the **highlands** of Mexico, the systematic collection of surface artifacts is used in lieu of excavation to make interpretations about site history and function. This is not possible in much of the Maya area, where the overlying soil (and vegetation) obscures the below ground remains. Sometimes shovel tests and other probes, derived from contract archaeology in the United States, are used as part of this methodology to gain some idea of what is below the surface. However, for much of the Maya area, the surface-subsurface relationship needs to be established through careful excavation in order to provide reliability for surface-based interpretations.

See also BECAN; CAHAL PECH; CALAKMUL; CHAMPOTÓN; EK BALAM; EL PERÚ-WAKA'; EL PILAR; HOUSES; ICHKABAL; IXIMCHÉ; MUYIL; NIXTUN-CH'ICH'; PUSILHA; RIO AZUL; SAYIL; SUBSISTENCE; XCOCH

Further Reading

Carr, Robert F., and James E. Hazard. *Map of the Ruins of Tikal, El Petén, Guatemala.* Tikal Reports 11, Museum Monograph. Philadelphia: University Museum, University of Pennsylvania, 1961.

Comer, Douglas C., and Michael J. Harrower, eds. *Mapping Archaeological Landscapes from Space: In Observance of the 40th Anniversary of the World Heritage Convention.* SpringerBriefs in Archaeology, vol. 5. New York: Springer, 2013.

Dahlin, Bruce H., Christopher T. Jensen, Richard E. Terry, David R. Wright, and Timothy Beach. "In Search of an Ancient Maya Market." *Latin American Antiquity* 18, no. 4: 363–84, 2007.

Kvamme, Kenneth L. "Geophysical Surveys as Landscape Archaeology." *American Antiquity* 68, no. 3: 435–57, 2003.

■ ARLEN F. CHASE

GROUNDWATER/WATER TABLE

In Mesoamerica, groundwater is an important resource for enduring the dry season of the subtropics, as evidenced by ancient stone-lined wells that are found throughout settlements in the Maya world, settlements around **cenotes** (sinkhole **lakes** in collapsed limestone), human artifacts and ancient water vessels deep in water-bearing **caves**, and water wells tapping these same resources today.

Groundwater is located in the phreatic (saturated) zone in the earth's crust, below the vadose (unsaturated) zone of **soil** water. In the groundwater zone, all pore spaces between sediments are filled with water, and pressure is greater than atmospheric pressure. The top of the groundwater surface is also known as the water table. Groundwater is the second largest storehouse of freshwater in the global hydrologic system, second only to glacial ice. Groundwater is transmitted in geologic units called aquifers, whose porosity and permeability allow the movement of water through the matrices of earth material that comprise them. This material may be confined or unconfined, and groundwater may emerge under pressure as artesian springs or be exposed in lakes and sinkholes in limestone. Surface water from rainfall, riverbeds, and lakebeds may infiltrate into the ground to recharge the groundwater table. Water tables left over from past, wetter climates that are no longer recharged are known as fossil water. Once these resources are pumped out and drawn down by water wells, they may never be replaced, and ground sinking or subsidence may occur from this overuse of the resource, also known as groundwater overdraft.

Groundwater chemistry generally reflects the natural geological materials in which it resides, but it may also be contaminated by runoff from the earth's surface that infiltrates into the groundwater zone from farms, septic systems, and urban runoff. Different geologic materials will regulate the speed at which groundwater flows through them; thereby each aquifer may impose a different residence time for groundwater, ranging from days to millennia depending upon its conditions. Groundwater chemistry, in turn, may also influence landform or geomorphic processes, including creating dripstone formations in caves, known as speleothems; chemical erosion and collapse of stone such as in karst processes, forming caves and sinkholes in limestone; and aggradation of minerals in wetlands from emerging springs, such as gypsum.

For the ancient and modern Maya groundwater is a source of daily life and also a part of ritual. Water-formed and water-bearing caves connected ancient Maya rituals with the underworld where some of their **deities** resided, as evidenced by human remains, **art**, and artifacts found in caves. Ritual sacrifice was practiced in the cenotes of such ancient Maya settlements as **Chichen Itza** in Yucatan Mexico; human skeletal remains and artifacts at the bottoms of cenotes bear silent witness to these ancient practices.

See also MAP 5; MAP 7; MAP 8; RELIGION; RITES AND RITUALS; WATER MANAGEMENT

Further Reading

Luzzadder-Beach, Sheryl. "Water Resources of the Chunchucmil Maya." *Geographical Review* 90, no. 4: 493–510, 2000.

Luzzadder-Beach, Sheryl, and Timothy Beach. "Water Chemistry Constraints and Possibilities for the Ancient and Contemporary Maya Wetlands." *Journal of Ethnobiology* 28, no. 2: 211–30, 2008.

———. "Arising from the Wetlands: Mechanisms and Chronology of Landscape Aggradation in the Northern Coastal Plain of Belize." *Annals of the Association of American Geographers* 99, no. 1: 1–26, 2009.

Perry, Eugene, Luis Marin, Jana McClain, and Guadalupe Velazquez. "Ring of Cenotes (Sinkholes), Northwest Yucatan, Mexico: Its Hydrogeologic Characteristics and Possible Association with the Chicxulub Impact Crater." *Geology* 23, no. 1: 17–20, 1995.

Perry, Eugene, Guadalupe Velazquez-Oliman, and Luis Marin. "The Hydrogeochemistry of the Karst Aquifer System of the Northern Yucatan Peninsula, Mexico." *International Geology Review* 44, no. 3: 191–221, 2002.

Veni, George. "Maya Utilization of Karst Groundwater Resources." *Environmental Geology and Water Sciences* 16, no. 1: 63–66, 1990.

■ SHERYL LUZZADDER-BEACH

GUATEMALA

The modern nation of Guatemala is central to the Maya region, bordered by **Mexico** to the west and north and by **Belize**, **Honduras**, and **El Salvador** to the east. The entire southern border is the Pacific Ocean. It participates in all the geographic regions of the Maya area, from the **Central and Southern Lowlands** to the **Northern** and **Southern**

Highlands and the **Pacific Coastal Plain**. Within its borders are numerous major Maya sites, including **Nakbé**, **El Mirador, Tikal, Uaxactun, Piedras Negras, Quiriguá,** and **Kaminaljuyú**.

The earliest occupation is documented by Paleo-Indian spear points. In the Middle Preclassic, the sites of Kaminaljuyú, **Izapa**, and **Takalik Abaj** are important highland and Pacific coastal sites, while in the Central Lowlands, Nakbé has very early monumental masonry **architecture**. In the Late Preclassic El Mirador was dominant in the Central Lowlands, while Tikal began developments that would lead to its later ascendancy. Numerous sites clamor for attention in the Classic, perhaps Tikal most of all, with its rich dynastic history, incursion or invasion by **Teotihuacán**, unsuccessful defense against Calakmul, and rebound in the Late Classic (see also **Dynastic Sequences**; **Fortifications**; **Warfare, Warriors, and Weapons**). Most lowland Guatemalan sites were abandoned during the **Classic Maya collapse**, but several smaller regional polities developed in the Postclassic before the Spanish conquest. Kingdoms of note in the highlands included the K'iche', Kaqchikel, Tz'utujil, Mam, and Poqomam, and in the lowlands the Itza and the Kowoj. After the fall of Tenochtitlan to Cortés in 1521, Pedro and Gonzalo Alvarado led the 1524 conquest of Guatemala along the Pacific coast and through the highlands. By this time the march of smallpox, deadly to Native Americans, was decimating populations in Guatemala and to the southeast.

Today's Guatemalan population is about 60 percent Mestizo and European and 40 percent Maya. In addition to Spanish, 23 official Maya languages are spoken in Guatemala today.

Two of Guatemala's ancient Maya sites, Tikal and Quiriguá, are on the UNESCO list of World Heritage Sites. The protected area of the Tikal National Park covers 570 km^2. *The Electronic Atlas of Ancient Maya Sites* (http://mayagis.smv.org/) identifies more than 1,400 ancient Maya sites in the country.

Further Reading

Atlas Arqueológico de Guatemala (Organization), and Universidad de San Carlos de Guatemala, Escuela de Historia. *Atlas Arqueoláogico de Guatemala: [Revista].* 3 vols. [Guatemala]: Ministerio de Cultura y Deportes, Universidad de San Carlos de Guatemala, Escuela de Historia, 1993.

Brown, Kenneth L. "A Brief Report on Paleoindian-Archaic Occupation in the Quiche Basin, Guatemala." *American Antiquity* 45, no. 2: 313–24, 1980.

Departamento de Monumentos Prehispanicos y Coloniales. *Mapa Arqueológico de la República de Guatemala.* Guatemala C.A: Instituto Geographico Militar, Ministerio de la Defensa Nacional y Departamento de Monumentos Prehispanicos y Coloniales, Instituto de Antropología e Historia de Guatemala, 1991.

Historia, Instituto de Antropología e. *Monografías Atlas Arqueológico de Guatemala: Registro de sitios Arqueológicos del Sureste y Centro-oeste de Petén 1987–2008.* Guatemala City, Guatemala: Ministerio de Cultura y Deportes, Dirección General de Patrimonio Cultural y Natural, Instituto de Antropología e Historia, 2008. http://www.atlasarqueologico.com/index.php.

Instituto de Antropologia e Historia (IDAEH-Guatemala). Ministerio de Cultura y Deportes, 2014. http://www.mcd.gob.gt/.

U.S. Central Intelligence Agency. *The World Factbook, Central America and Caribbean: Guatemala.* 2014. https://www.cia.gov/library/publications/the-world-factbook/geos/gt.html.

■ WALTER R. T. WITSCHEY

H

HIEROGLYPHIC STAIRWAYS

The ancient Maya rulers frequently commissioned stairways for temple-**pyramids** and buildings, the risers of which carried text in the hieroglyphic script. This frequently provided a permanent reminder of the **divine king's** right to the throne, and provided the stage for the ruler to act out his many roles in front of his subjects (see also **Theater**).

The most stunning example of such a stairway by far is that on Str. 26 overlooking the **ball court** at **Copán**, which carries the longest known Maya text. In it the fifteenth ruler of Copán, K'ak'Yipyaj Chan K'awiil, recounts his ancestors. The upper two-thirds of the stairway was collapsed by an earthquake and the stones, reassembled before reading of the glyphs was as advanced as today, are not in their proper reading order.

Hieroglyphic stairways are also reported from **Ceibal**, **Dos Pilas**, **Dzibanché**, **Edzna**, **El Perú-Waka'**, **La Corona**, **Oxkintok**, **Naranjo,** Tamarindito, and **Yaxchilan**, among other sites.

See also DECIPHERMENT; LANGUAGE AND WRITING OVERVIEW

Further Reading

Andrews, E. Wyllys, V, and William Leonard Fash, eds. *Copán: The History of an Ancient Maya Kingdom*. School of American Research Advanced Seminar Series. Santa Fe, NM: School of American Research, 2005.

Fash, William L. "Religion and Human Agency in Ancient Maya History: Tales from the Hieroglyphic Stairway." *Cambridge Archaeological Journal* 12, no. 1: 5–19, 2002.

Pezzati, Alessandro. "The Excavation of the Hieroglyphic Stairway at Copan." *Expedition* 54, no. 1: 4–6, 2012.

■ WALTER R. T. WITSCHEY

HIEROGLYPHS

See DECIPHERMENT; LANGUAGE AND WRITING OVERVIEW; SYLLABARY; WRITING SYSTEMS OF MESOAMERICA

HIGHLAND MAYA LANGUAGES

Linguists posit the Proto-Maya homeland amid the peaks of the Cuchumatán Mountains of western **Guatemala** in the departments of Huehuetenango and El Quiché (see also **Map 1**). Most of the groups that would form three branches of the Maya language family—Ch'olan, Wastekan, and Yucatecan—moved out to the Maya lowlands. The remaining groups spread through the highlands of **Guatemala** and Chiapas. These highland Maya branches are Tzeltalan, Q'anjob'alan, Mamean, and K'iche'an (see also **Map 4**).

The Tzeltalan group, composed of Tzeltal (400,000 speakers) and Tzotzil (330,000 speakers), have their home communities in Chiapas. The Ch'ol (130,000 speakers), members of the Ch'olan branch, did not follow their sisters, Chontal and Ch'orti', to lowland areas, but rather settled in Chiapas. Also in Chiapas are the Tojolab'al (35,000 speakers) and Mocho' (75 speakers), members of the Q'anjob'alan group.

The other Q'anjob'alan languages—Chuj (45,000), Q'anjob'al (99,000), Akateko (60,000), and Popti' (alternate name Jakalteko, (15,000 speakers)—are primarily spoken in Guatemala, with some adjoining communities in Chiapas and immigrant communities in the United States, chiefly in California and Florida.

The Mamean group consists of Mam (550,000), Awakateko (17,000), Chalchiteko (35,000), Tektiteko (1,300), and Ixil (175,000). These languages are spoken in the northern Guatemalan highlands. Chalchiteko was not officially deemed an independent language until 2003. An 1881 administrative consolidation merged the townships of Aguacatán and Chalchitán. The speech of these communities was considered to vary only slightly and was simply labeled "Awakateko" until Chalchiteko activists appealed directly to the Guatemalan Congress for recognition.

The last and most diversified of the Mayan language branches is the K'iche'an group. These languages are located in the Central Highlands, with Q'eqchi' having spread rapidly in the last 70 years through the Petén and **Belize**. The most divergent of the K'iche'an languages are Uspantek (1,300 speakers) and Q'eqchi' (730,000 speakers).

Uspantek has developed a phonemic tonal contrast, distinguishing between long vowels with high tones (realized as a rise) and long vowels with low tones (heard as a fall); Uspantek is also the only language of this group to have nonfinal word stress.

Q'eqchi' has two major dialects, one centered around Cobán and an eastern dialect spoken in Cahabón, Senahu, and Lanquín. Two closely related languages, Poqomam (10,000) and Poqomchi' (70,000), occupy areas of the south-central highlands, near Guatemala City. The Poqomchi' and Ixil territories overlap. Many Poqomchi' are also fluent in Ixil, and there is frequent lexical borrowing. Some Mayan linguists proposed that Poqomam and Poqomchi' should be treated as variants of one language, Poqom. A unique feature of Poqom is the use of a glottalized bilabial nasal as an allophone of /b'/. In initial and medial position this phoneme is realized as [w'], a voiced glottalized labio-velar glide. In final position, it becomes a glottalized voiced nasal occlusive [m']: e.g., [**q'aw**is] "hand, unpossessed"; [ni**q'am'**] "my hand."

Sipakapense (6,500) and Sakapulteko (4,100) form another sub-branch of K'iche'an. These languages have lost the Proto-K'iche'an negative marker *ma(n)*, replacing it with *mi* in commands; Sakapulteko has reinterpreted the irrealis *taj* as a generic negation for verbs. Lexical and morphological borrowings in both languages indicate extensive contact with Ixil.

The core K'iche'an languages are Kaqchikel (500,000), Tz'utujiil (50,000), Achi' (52,000), and K'iche' (1,000,000). Some linguists consider the latter two to be so closely related that they might better be treated as a single language; however, the politico-social histories of the groups define them as separate.

In 2003 Guatemala passed the National Language Law, guaranteeing the right to education, police and judicial protection, and health services in indigenous languages. In 2010 the Ministry of Education decreed that every national school, kindergarten through university, would teach a national (i.e. "indigenous") language. Four highland Mayan Guatemalan communities founded their own universities in 2013 and 2014. In Chiapas, both the national and Zapatista governments support teaching indigenous languages and promote Mayan language literacy and literature. While Mocho' is in danger of extinction, the other highland Mayan language communities are adopting new technologies, neologisms, and resources to thrive in the thirteenth *b'ak'tun*.

See also BAJOS; BELIZE; COTZUMALHUAPA; DECIPHERMENT; GUATEMALA; HONDURAS; LANGUAGE AND WRITING OVERVIEW; MAYA AREA; MESOAMERICA; MEXICO; *POPOL VUH*; SOUTHERN PERIPHERY; SYLLABARY; UTATLÁN/Q'UM'ARKAJ; WRITING SYSTEMS OF MESOAMERICA; YUCATECAN MAYA LANGUAGES

Further Reading

England, Nora C., ed. *Papers in Mayan Linguistics*. Miscellaneous Publications in Anthropology, No 6. Columbia: Museum of Anthropology, University of Missouri-Columbia, 1978.

———. *La autonomía de los idiomas mayas: Historia e identidad*. Guatemala City, Guatemala: Editorial Cholsamaj, 1992.

Garzon, Susan, R. McKenna Brown, Julia Becker Richards, and Wuqu' Ajpub' (Arnulfo Simón). *The Life of Our Language: Kaqchikel Maya Maintenance, Shift, and Revitalization*. Austin: University of Texas Press, 1998.

Laughlin, Robert M. *The Great Tzotzil Dictionary of Santo Domingo Zinacantan: With Grammatical Analysis and Historical Commentary*. With commentary by John B. Haviland. Washington, DC: Smithsonian Institution Press, 1988.

Sexton, James Dean, and Ignacio Bizarro Ujpán. *Heart of Heaven, Heart of Earth and Other Mayan Folktales*. Washington, DC: Smithsonian Institution Press, 1999.

■ JUDITH M. MAXWELL

HIGHLANDS

See NORTHERN HIGHLANDS; SOUTHERN HIGHLANDS

HOCHOB

The small site of Hochob (19.4° N, 89.8° W), located on an artificially flattened hilltop in the state of Campeche, had a Late Classic occupation ca. AD 800. The site was visited by

Figure 18. Hochob Str. II. Replica at the Mexican National Museum of Anthropology, Mexico City. Str. II is considered a prototypical example of *Chenes*-style architecture. Courtesy of Walter Witschey.

Teobert Maler in 1887 and published the following decade. It is most remarkable for an exemplary *Chenes*-**style** temple (Str. II), with a well-preserved monster-mouth doorway, as well as a **Río Bec**–style false-façade temple-**pyramid** (Str. III). Structure II has been replicated at the Museum of Anthropology in Mexico City. See figure 18.

Further Reading

Zona Arqueológica Hochob. Instituto Nacional de Antropología e Historia (CONACULTA), 2014. http://www.inah.gob.mx/index.php?option=com_content&view=article&id=5464.

■ WALTER R. T. WITSCHEY

HOLMUL

The ancient site of Holmul (17.3° N, 89.3° W) was first reported by Raymond E. Merwin of Harvard based on his 1909–1911 work, which also reported an early **stela** from nearby **Cival**. He documented elite burials from the Late Formative, Late Classic, and Terminal Classic (see also **Royal Tombs**). Regrettably, no map of the site was prepared at this time. **Ceramic** studies identified a Late Formative (AD 150–250) phase, as well as a distinctive Late Classic polychrome ceramic style portraying the "Holmul Dancer." Holmul is situated 32 km east-southeast of **San Bartolo**, and 41 km east-northeast of **Tikal**, on a peninsula of higher ground within a C-shaped *bajo*. The *bajo* varies from about 160 m asl at its northeast to 180 m asl in the southwest. The peninsula on which Holmul is built has higher elevations, about 230 m asl.

Since 2000, Francisco Estrada-Belli has led an ongoing program of research at Holmul and nearby sites, including Cival, Riverona, T'ot, Hahakab, Hamontun, K'o, La Sufricaya, and Dos Aguadas. During several field seasons, the ceremonial centers of Holmul and of the sites in the region were mapped, as well as residential areas within 4 km around Holmul, Cival, Hamontun, and K'o. Work at the sites has included numerous restoration and consolidation projects, especially the recording of exposed construction episodes and then backfilling of looters' trenches to prevent structural collapse, and the posting of guards to protect the sites.

The site center of Holmul consists of several large hilltop architectural groups, including numerous temples atop flat-topped platforms. A Group-E configuration occupies the East Plaza of Group I (see also **Astronomical Observatories**). A **ball court** occupies the plaza south of Group II. Building B of Group II was the site of important **burials** first recorded by Merwin. In deeper excavations, Estrada-Belli recovered fine ceramics dated to ca.1000 BC, some 200 years earlier than expected for settlement of the lowlands.

Work in 2013 focused on explorations in Holmul and Cival plus the region north of Cival. Goals of the project included definition of the beginnings of monumental **architecture** in the Preclassic, the abandonment of the sites in both the Late Preclassic and the Late Classic, the impressive construction program at Holmul in the Late Classic, and the effects of climate and natural resource use in the region (see also **Classic Maya Collapse**; **Drought**; **Subsistence**).

Incomplete wall **fortifications** from the Terminal Classic surround the centers of Holmul and Cival, testifying to both unrest and the rapid collapse of the sites.

Dos Aguadas (17.3° N, 89.4° W) was a medium-sized site whose ceremonial center held a Group E plaza (350 BC), a **pyramid** with large stucco 2.5 m by 3 m *Chak* masks (80–20 BC) to the north, and a palace to the south (see also **Deities**). There is no Middle Formative occupation. Dos Aguadas likely began as the elites of Cival (or another nearby site) expanded their territory in the Late Preclassic. There is an extensive residential area around the site center.

The collection of sites near Cival and Holmul provides new and intriguing insights into the precociously early developments of the earliest Maya, as well as the military challenges they faced at the end of the Late Preclassic. Estrada-Belli points to the possible succession of power at these nearby sites, beginning with Cival in the Preclassic, a possible power shift involving Tikal and **Teotihuacán** documented at La Sufricaya, and a Late Classic presence at Holmul.

See also CLIMATE; EL MIRADOR; MIRADOR BASIN; NAKBÉ

Further Reading

Estrada Belli, Francisco. *The First Maya Civilization: Ritual and Power before the Classic Period.* London; New York: Routledge, 2011.

———. *Investigaciónes arqueológicas en la región de Holmul, Petén: Holmul, Cival, La Sufricaya y K'o; Informe preliminar de la temporada 2007.* Vanderbilt University, 2007. http://www.bu.edu/holmul/.

———. *Investigaciónes arqueológicas en la región de Holmul, Petén: Cival, y K'o.* Boston University, 2008. http://www.bu.edu/holmul/.

———. *Investigaciones arqueológicas en la región de Holmul, Petén: Holmul, Cival, La Sufricaya y K'o.* Foundation for the Advancement of Mesoamerican Studies Inc. (FAMSI), 2008. http://www.famsi.org/reports/07028es/07028esEstradaBelli01.pdf.

———. *Investigaciónes arqueológicas en la región de Holmul, Petén: Holmul y Hamontun; Informe preliminar de la temporada 2009.* Boston University, 2009. http://www.bu.edu/holmul/.

———. *Investigaciónes arqueológicas en la región de Holmul, Petén: Holmul y Dos Aguadas; Informe preliminar de la temporada 2012.* Boston University, 2012. http://www.bu.edu/holmul/.

———. *Investigaciónes arqueológicas en la región de Holmul, Petén: Holmul y Cival; Informe preliminar de la temporada 2013.* Boston University, 2013. http://www.bu.edu/holmul/.

Merwin, R. E., and G. Vaillant. *The Ruins of Holmul.* Memoirs of the Peabody Museum of American Archaeology and Ethnology III, no. 2. Cambridge, MA: Harvard University, 1932.

Reents-Budet, Dorie. "The 'Holmul Dancer' Theme in Maya Art." In *Sixth Palenque Round Table, 1986*, edited by Virginia M. Fields, 217–22. Norman: University of Oklahoma Press, 1991.

■ WALTER R. T. WITSCHEY

HONDURAS

The modern nation of Honduras is located on the Caribbean coast (the Mosquito Coast) of Central America, bounded by **Guatemala** to the west, **El Salvador** to the south, and Nicaragua to the southeast. A portion of Honduras abuts the Bay of Fonseca on the Pacific coast, between El Salvador and Nicaragua. Today the population is 90 percent mestizo (mixed Amerindian and European). Spanish is the official and primary language, with small pockets of native languages remaining.

The western part of Honduras participated in the Maya culture area and includes the large and important Classic Maya site **Copán**, today a national park. Hundreds of (non-Maya) archaeological sites are reported for Honduras, especially along the river valleys, and date early occupation to at least 1600 BC.

See also ARCHITECTURE OVERVIEW; BELIZE; CACAO; EL SALVADOR; GUATEMALA; IXTEPEQUE; MAYA AREA; MESOAMERICA; OLMEC; QUIRIGUÁ; SOUTHERN ARCHITECTURAL STYLE; SOUTHERN PERIPHERY; TIKAL; TRADE ROUTES; YUCATECAN MAYA LANGUAGES

Further Reading

Andrews, E. Wyllys, V., and William Leonard Fash, eds. *Copán: The History of an Ancient Maya Kingdom.* School of American Research Advanced Seminar Series. Santa Fe, NM: School of American Research, 2005.

The Copan National Park: Copan Ruinas—Honduras. Ecotourism and Adventure Specialists, 2013. http://www.copanpark.com/.

Rejas, J. G., M. C. Pineda, S. V. Veliz, D. Euraque, E. Martinez, J. R. Rodriguez, and M. Farjas. *Archaeological Remote Sensing Approach in Honduras. A Project for Cultural Heritage and Human Habitats Protection.* B.A.R. International Series, no. 2118. Oxford: Archaeopress, 2010.

Robinson, Eugenia J., ed. *Interaction on the Southeast Mesoamerican Frontier: Prehistoric and Historic Honduras and El Salvador.* Oxford: British Archaeological Reports, 1987.

Stone, Doris. *The Archaeology of Central and Southern Honduras.* Papers of the Peabody Museum of Archaeology and Ethnology, no. 3 Cambridge, MA: Harvard University, 1957.

U.S. Central Intelligence Agency. *The World Factbook, Central America and Caribbean: Honduras.* 2014. https://www.cia.gov/library/publications/the-world-factbook/geos/ho.html.

■ WALTER R. T. WITSCHEY

HOUSEHOLD PRODUCTION

In the Maya economy, researchers distinguish between household production, household industry (production for **trade**), and workshop production. The nuclear family household was the basic unit of production. Each household fulfilled its own basic needs for food, clothing, and shelter. For **subsistence**, each household had access to land for farming, which it cleared, burned, sowed, weeded, and harvested. Households may have participated in efforts to increase the intensity of agriculture by the construction of raised fields in lowlands or **terraces** on hill slopes.

Agricultural fields, *milpas*, remote from the house, were tended chiefly by the man of the house and focused on the raising of corn, intercropped with beans, squashes, and chilies. Each household also had a garden adjacent to its dwelling, a kitchen garden, which was mostly tended by the woman of the house. The kitchen gardens included orchard trees, food plants, medicinal plants, and flowers, and might have upwards of 400 species of plants. To this, the Maya added hunting, by men, and the raising of animals close to the house (deer, turkeys) by women. All corn-grinding and cooking was done at the house, most indoors on a three-stone hearth, which is well-documented in both ancient and modern times. Discovery of a *mano-y-metate* corn grinder set archaeologically is taken as strong evidence for a domestic location.

The one-room Maya hut served as the primary dwelling for the family, as it was easily crafted and maintained by the man. Materials for its construction and repair, poles up to about 10 cm in diameter, and thatch were readily available in the forest on land available to the family. The family hut was often rebuilt generation to generation on the same site to venerate the ancestors buried beneath the floor. The family provided its own water, from natural wells, **cenotes**, in the **Northern Lowlands**; from **caves** in higher karstic terrain; and from rivers, streams, and springs elsewhere.

Clothing was provided at home by the spinning and weaving of natural fibers, such as cotton and agave (see also **Textiles and Clothing**). Archaeologically, **ceramic** spindle whorls (without their center wooden pin) also represent domestic contexts. The household could produce its own tools, chiefly stone axes and knives, and ceramics. In addition to household production, however, the Maya produced surplus items for trade outside the home and traded for workshop-produced items, including stone tools, ceramics, cloth, and foodstuffs.

See also Chert; Craft Specialization; Diet; Fauna; Portable Objects; Vegetation

Further Reading

Lohse, Jon C., and Fred Valdez, eds. *Ancient Maya Commoners*. Austin: University of Texas Press, 2004.

McKillop, Heather. *The Ancient Maya: New Perspectives*. New York: W. W. Norton & Company, Inc., 2004.

Sharer, Robert J., and Loa P. Traxler. *The Ancient Maya*. 6th ed. Stanford, CA: Stanford University Press, 2006.

■ WALTER R. T. WITSCHEY

HOUSES

Maya houses throughout the ages are highly varied in size and design to reflect the potential number of occupants and the labor invested in their construction. These contrasts reflect the social organization of the builders and users.

The lower ranks of Maya society lived in one-room thatched cottages walled with wattle and daub or dry masonry. This is the typical Maya house seen all over contemporary Yucatan today and in only slightly different form served Maya farmers through the centuries. Inexpensive in construction cost, these dwellings could easily be abandoned and new ones built by the migratory sector of society.

A variety of long structures with multiple rooms and thatched roofs served a social group intermediate between those occupying the highest levels of society and those that lived in the basic thatched cottage. These buildings indicate larger domestic units.

Smaller vaulted buildings with one to five rooms or more constitute the majority of all-masonry houses. These were the domiciles of the lower echelons of the Maya elite. The great majority of vaulted dwellings were small, with one to five rooms; most of these buildings have collapsed to form small mounds. A few single-roomed vaulted buildings still stand on low platforms in settings similar to that of thatched structures. The map of **Dzibilchaltun** shows the locations of 240 vaulted structures containing approximately 540 rooms; most of these served as domiciles for the elite.

The highest levels of the Maya society concentrated their relatives in large, all-masonry "**palaces**" or in large architectural complexes with multiple buildings. Some famous palaces contain 50 or more rooms that were characteristically divided into mostly one-roomed apartments. The palaces of **Tikal**, **Yaxchilan**, **Sayil**, **Labna**, **Kabah**, and **Uxmal** serve as examples. See Figure 39.

Most contemporary dwellings in northern Maya villages are single-roomed cottages with thatched hip roofs made with A-frames holding a ridge pole. The roof structure is supported by four forked main posts surmounted by crossbeams and pole plates. Walls, whether of horizontal wickerwork, upright poles tied together, or dry wall stonework, stand about 75 cm away from the main posts and are not usually attached in a firm way to the roof structure. The walls usually do not carry any of the weight of the building. While some houses are quadrilateral, the most conservative plan is apsidal with the wall corners rounded rather than forced into a right angle. Both the hip roof and the curved corners are vortex shedding features that add to structural stability in high winds and storms. See Figure 19.

Figure 19. Typical Maya house with upright poles woven together. Kiwic, 1978. Courtesy of Edward Kurjack.

Archaeological survey has proved the presence of thatched structures with apsidal ground plans at **Dzibilchaltun**, **Cobá**, and many other sites. Evidence for numerous small houses should be found at all Maya sites, but the mostly perishable material used to build common Maya houses has disappeared. The ceremonial arch of **Labna**, dated to the ninth century, clearly portrays ancient Maya thatched houses.

One clear contrast between Colonial house styles imported from Europe and traditional Maya housing past and present is that many Maya dwellings are too small to accommodate cooking, bathing, and dressing within the house; these functions are carried out in auxiliary structures or the large area surrounding the main house. Evidence of pre-Columbian housing compounds on large platforms or within house plots delineated by stone boundary walls shows that they are all large enough for these purposes.

Since Colonial authorities began to carry out royal town planning policies, Maya village dwellings have been aligned along rectilinear streets, so back doors were added to orient household activities behind the homes. Some isolated cottages in the forest have only front doors; these structures, arranged on the sides of small plazas, preserve an older organization with domestic labor at the front.

See also ARCHITECTURE OVERVIEW; BURIALS; CEREN; CLASS STRUCTURE; COMALCALCO; COTZUMALHUAPA; COUNCIL HOUSE; CRAFT SPECIALIZATION; DIET; DZIBILCHALTUN; EK BALAM; EL MIRADOR; EL PILAR; HOUSEHOLD PRODUCTION; JAINA; KIUIC; KOMCHEN; MARKETS AND MARKETPLACES; MAYAPÁN; RITES AND RITUALS; RITES OF PASSAGE; SAN BARTOLO; SAYIL; SETTLEMENT PATTERNS (CENTRAL LOWLANDS); SETTLEMENT PATTERNS (NORTHERN LOWLANDS); SIN CABEZAS; TERRACING; TEXTILES AND CLOTHING; TIKAL; TULUM; WATER MANAGEMENT; WOMEN, MEN, AND GENDER ROLES; YAXHOM; YUCATECAN MAYA LANGUAGES

Further Reading

Ashmore, Wendy, ed. *Lowland Maya Settlement Patterns*. School of American Research Advanced Seminar Series. Albuquerque: University of New Mexico Press, 1981.

Folan, William J., Ellen R. Kintz, and Laraine A. Fletcher. *Coba: A Classic Maya Metropolis*. Edited by Stuart Struever. Studies in Archaeology. New York: Academic Press, 1983.

Manzanilla, Linda, ed. *Coba, Quintana Roo: Análisis de dos unidades habitacionales mayas*. México, D.F.: Instituto de Investigaciones Antropológicas, Universidad Nacional Autónoma de México, 1987.

Sabloff, Jeremy A. "Settlement Patterns and Community Organization in the Maya Lowlands." *Expedition* 38, no. 1: 3–13, 1996. http://www.penn.museum/documents/publications/expedition/PDFs/38-1/settlement1.pdf.

■ EDWARD B. KURJACK

ICHKABAL

The ancient site of Ichkabal (18.6° N 88.6° W) is located within the communal lands of the Bacalar *ejido* in the southern portion of the state of Quintana Roo, in **Mexico's** southern Yucatan peninsula. At present it is not open to visitors, but it will be accessible in the near future. The site's name means "in-between *bajos*" in Yucatec Maya, a name that describes the landscape where the site lies: a flat area with small hills, which alternate with seasonally flooded lowlands called *bajos*. Although not all of the site has been surveyed, the first investigations suggest that it could extend more than 30 km².

Ichkabal was first reported by Javier López Camacho and Luz Evelia Campaña in 1995, but archaeological explorations were not started until 2009, when they began under the direction of Enrique Nalda and Sandra Balanzario, both researchers from the INAH Center for Quintana Roo.

The site is composed of six major groups, but the largest architecture is concentrated in the Grupo Principal. Examples include Strs. 1 and 4, which are two massive pyramidal buildings that surpass 40 m in height. Other notable features at the site are the Str. 5 and a complex of buildings called the Cinco Hermanos (Five Brothers), as well as a large rectangular *aguada* (water reservoir) created in ancient times.

The **architectural** style that dominates at the site is the **Petén style**. Its occupational history spans from Late Preclassic (250 BC) through the Late Postclassic, although its climax was during the Preclassic, when it might have been the regional capital of the southern portion of Quintana Roo.

Its proximity to **Dzibanché** (9 km to the southwest), the largest settlement in this region during Classic times, is noteworthy. Although there is still much to discover about the local history of this site and its role within this region, judging by the size and antiquity of its constructions, archaeologists hypothesize that Ichkabal could be related to the origins of the Kaan dynasty of Dzibanché, and **Calakmul**.

Without a doubt, with further investigations, this site will provide a critical part of the Maya history for this region, as well as informing us about the relationship between the Petén region and the **Northern Lowlands** of the Yucatan during the Preclassic.

Further Reading

Espinoza, Jezel. *Ichkabal no puede abrir al público este año*. La Verdad Quintana Roo, 2014. http://laverdad
noticias.com/ichkabal-podra-abrir-al-publico-en-2014/360422/.

Exploran Ichkabal. Instituto Nacional de Antropología e Historia, 2009. http://www.inah.gob.mx/bole
tines/7–zonas-arqueologicas/3052-exploran-ichkabal.

Horta, Carlos. *Anuncian apertura de la zona arqueológica de Ichkabal*. Novedades Quintana Roo, 2013.
http://sipse.com/novedades/anuncian-apertura-de-ichkabal-en-bacalar-39457.html.

Ichkabal Zona Arqueológica / 2010. INAH TV, April 29, 2010. https://www.youtube.com/watch?v=
YwXLQIqjgKg.

Zona Arqueológico Ichkabal. Instituto Nacional de Antropología e Historia, 2013. http://www.inah.gob
.mx/component/content/article/265-red-zonas-arqueologicas/5499-zona-arqueologica-de-ich
kabal.

■ ALBERTO G. FLORES COLIN AND JUSTINE M. SHAW

ICHMUL

See COCHUAH REGION

ICONOGRAPHY

Maya **art** and **architecture** is filled with images that carry meaning important to the culture and society in which they were created. In addition, items with ancient script, such as **stelae**, usually show interplay between the visual images and the script in creative ways. The imagery, such as headdresses, may have hieroglyphs embedded within it, while the script itself may carry images.

At **Palenque**, the picture of a war shield (*pacal*) may be used as a rebus for the glyphs pa-ca-l(a) that spell out the king's name, "Pacal," phonetically. This intertwining of script and image make Maya iconography both exciting and challenging to study.

As **decipherment** has produced more readings in the last half century, it has become clearer, for example, that many once-static images on **stelae**, such as of a Maya ruler with one heel lifted in a fixed pose (the Xibalba shuffle), are, as described in the accompanying text, meant to be read as active scenes, with the king performing ritual dances in an elaborate socio-religious ritual (see also **Deities**; **Music and Dance**; **Religion**; **Theater**). The effect is as if we must now reconsider photographs carved in stone to be videos represented in stone.

The imagery portrayed by the Maya dealt with their gods, their rulers, their ritual activities, the natural world, and their cosmos. Gods are portrayed in the **codices**, on **pyramids** as stucco masks, and on Classic polychrome **ceramics**. Rulers are portrayed on their thrones, or taking captives, or playing the ritual **ball game**. Ritual activities include dancing and bloodletting self-sacrifice. Nature is represented by realistic portraits of plants and animals, as well as powerful cosmic imagery, such as using a corn plant to represent the birth, growth, and death of humans. The cosmos is portrayed with images of the sun and moon, of planetary symbols, of the Milky Way and Orion's sword, and of the sky (as a band of constellations like a zodiac) and the earth (as a large turtle with a chasm opened in its back.)

Much of this rich collection of images, as it appears in architecture, on stelae, on **royal tomb** walls, and in the codices, unfolds and retells the story of the Maya creation myth as found in the *Popol Vuh*.

See also ASTRONOMICAL OBSERVATORIES; CACAO; CHICHEN ITZA; CAHAL PECH; CHAC II; DECIPHERMENT; DIET; ECCENTRIC LITHICS; FAUNA; KOHUNLICH; PRIESTS; PUSILHA; RELIGION; RITES AND RITUALS; SAN BARTOLO; SCHELE, LINDA; SCULPTURE; SOUTHERN PERIPHERY; TEOTIHUACÁN (MAYA INTERACTIONS WITH); TEXTILES AND CLOTHING; UXMAL; WARFARE, WARRIORS, AND WEAPONS; WATER MANAGEMENT; WOMEN, MEN, AND GENDER ROLES

Further Reading

Joralemon, P. D. *A Study of Olmec Iconography*. Washington, DC: Dumbarton Oaks, 1971.

Kerr, Justin. *Maya Vase Database*. Kerr Associates, 2014. http://www.mayavase.com/.

Miller, Mary Ellen, and Megan Eileen O'Neil. *Maya Art and Architecture*. 2nd ed. London: Thames & Hudson, 2014.

Miller, Mary Ellen, and Karl Taube. *The Gods and Symbols of Ancient Mexico and the Maya: An Illustrated Dictionary of Mesoamerican Religion*. London: Thames & Hudson, 1993.

Stone, Andrea Joyce. *Images from the Underworld: Naj Tunich and the Tradition of Maya Cave Painting*. Austin: University of Texas Press, 1995.

Stuart, David, and George E. Stuart. *Palenque: Eternal City of the Maya*. New York: Thames & Hudson, 2008.

■ WALTER R. T. WITSCHEY

ITZIMTE

Itzimte (20° N, 89.7° W) is a major Maya archaeological site located in the Bolonchen Hills portion of the Puuc region in the modern Mexican state of Campeche (see also **Maps 1** and **3**). The site is located on the outskirts of the town of Bolonchén de Rejón, a situation that has led to centuries of stone robbing that has played havoc with the site. Nevertheless, substantial architecture remains at the site, which is best known for its 11 carved stelae and other monuments.

Itzimte was first brought to the attention of the outside world by American explorer John Lloyd Stephens, who visited the site in 1841 (transcribing its name as Ytsimpte). Even then, the site had suffered from substantial depredation, and Stephens and his party spent little time there. Teoberto Maler visited the site in 1897 and photographed the façade of Structure 58 ("Serpent's Head **Palace**"), which was then still standing, as well as the vaulted archway into a palace quadrangle (see also **Corbel Vault**). Harry Pollock spent one day at the site in 1938 and made notes on several buildings.

In 1973, as part of the Corpus of Maya Hieroglyphic Inscriptions project, Eric von Euw spent 18 days at the site, mapping much of the site center and recording 11 carved **stelae**, one carved lintel, and miscellaneous glyphic architectural stones. George Andrews visited the site in 1974, 1978, 1985, and 1987 (the last visit in the company of Hanns Prem) and recorded additional **architectural** details. Nicholas Dunning also visited the site in 1987 and recorded additional information about the site features, dimensions, and setting. Stephen Merk further documented Itzimte and neighboring sites between 2010 and 2013.

No archaeological excavations have been undertaken at the site. Although very little standing architecture remains, Itzimte was clearly a major regional center. Several large architectural complexes are clustered on the floor of a small valley, including two acropolis features and courtyards surrounded by **pyramids** and multilevel palace structures. The valley floor complexes also include a **ball court** and intra-site *sacbe* (**causeway**), and a platform on which were located 12 stelae (11 sculpted, 1 plain); several of the stelae have been moved to the Campeche Museum. Major architectural complexes also adorn the sides and tops of several hills overlooking the valley, with extensive **terracing** used to create level building surfaces. Architecture includes both **Puuc** and Puuc-*Chenes* transitional **styles**, suggesting that its primary occupation dates to around AD 600–900.

Nikolai Grube and Daniel Graña-Behrens have worked extensively on Itzimte's inscriptions. Dates on the sculpted monuments range from Long Count 9.15.0.0.0 to 10.4.1.0.0 (AD 731–910) and mention six or seven Itzimte rulers. These rulers are sometimes mentioned in conjunction with an Emblem Glyph, indicating that they regarded themselves as sacred lords or **divine kings**, further confirming Itzimte's importance.

See also EDZNA

Further Reading

Andrews, George F. *Architectural Survey Puuc Archaeological Region: 1984 Field Season.* Vol. 3. Austin: University of Texas Library, 1990. http://repositories.lib.utexas.edu/handle/2152/14260.

Dunning, Nicholas P. *Lords of the Hills: Ancient Maya Settlement in the Puuc Region, Yucatán, Mexico.* Madison, WI: Prehistory Press, 1992.

Graña-Behrens, Daniel. "Emblem Glyphs and Political Organization in Northwestern Yucatan in the Classic Period (A.D. 300–1000)." *Ancient Mesoamerica* 17, no. 1: 105–23, 2006.

———. "The Ruins and Hieroglyphic Inscriptions of Itzimte-Bolonchen, Campeche: Rulers and Political Affairs from Burned Stones." In *The Long Silence 2: Itzimte and Its Neighbors*, edited by Stephan Merk. Markt Schwaben, Germany: Verlag Anton Saurwein, 2014.

Grube, Nikolai K. "Hieroglyphic Inscriptions from Northwest Yucatan: An Update of Recent Research." In *Escondido en la Selva*, edited by Hanns J. Prem. México, D.F., and Bonn, Germany: Instituto Nacional de Antropología e Historía and the University of Bonn, 2003.

Maler, Teobert. *Península Yucatán.* Annotated by Hanns J. Prem. With contributions by Ian Graham. Monumenta Americana, no. 5. Berlin, Germany: Ibero-Amerikanischen Institut, Gebr. Mann, 1997.

Pollock, Harry E. D. *The Puuc: An Architectural Survey of the Hill Country of Yucatan and Northern Campeche, Mexico.* Memoirs of the Peabody Museum, vol. 19. Cambridge, MA: Peabody Museum of Archaeology and Ethnology, Harvard University, 1980.

Stephens, John Lloyd. *Incidents of Travel in Yucatan.* New York: Harper & Brothers, 1843. Reprinted, New York: Dover, 1963.

Von Euw, Eric. *Corpus of Maya Hieroglyphic Inscriptions.* Vol. 4, pt. 1, *Itzimte, Pixoy, Tzum.* Cambridge, MA: Peabody Museum of Archaeology & Ethnology, Harvard University, 1977.

■ NICHOLAS DUNNING

IXIMCHÉ

Iximché ("Corn Tree") (14.7° N, 91.1° W) is a Kaq'chik'el Maya Protohistoric (AD 1470–1526) capital in the Department of Chimaltenango in the **Southern Highlands** of **Guatemala**. It is located 2.5 km south of the town of Tecpan at an altitude of 2,260 m asl on the Ratz'am Ut mountain (see also **Map 3**).

Iximché is situated on a defensible narrow projection of land surrounded by steep ravines, with the Tzaragmajya River to the northeast and an unnamed tributary to the southwest. It has over 160 buildings arranged around five contiguous plazas that extend across the narrow finger of land. Plazas A–D are reconstructed; Plaza E at the far end of the site has not been explored archaeologically and is used for ritual by Maya religious practitioners. Although Preclassic pottery has been reported at the site, the structures that have been explored so far date to Protohistoric period (see also **Ceramics**; **Fortifications**; **Rites and Rituals**).

George Guillemin excavated Iximché from 1958 to 1972. The restored site has two complexes, probably one for each of two Kaq'chik'el kings, separated by a ditch. Plaza A is located near the entrance and has opposing Temples 2 and 3, facing respectively east and west; a **ball court** on the south side; and altars; Plaza B has Grand **Palace** I and Temple 1 (see figure 20). Plazas C and D have almost identical buildings and spatial arrangements, but Plaza D has been turned 90 degrees to the south. The temples are the tallest buildings, reaching 7 m in height, and are built in a *talud-tablero* architectural style with a central staircase in most cases. The construction is of faced stone blocks set in mortar with a thick layer of plaster, and superstructures were made of adobe block. There were murals on Temple 2 and remnants of red, blue, and ochre paint on Temple 1. Guillemin recognized two and three phases of construction in some places; for example, the earliest construction phase of Great Palace 1 was four **house** units around a square court with an altar at its center.

Guillemin summarized the ethnohistory and excavations and gold and jade objects found in **burials** in numerous articles, but his untimely death after working at **Copán** prohibited his completion of a final publication of the excavations. Roger Nance and Stephen Whittington published the ceramics and human skeletal burial and sacrificial remains (see also **Physical/Biological Anthropology**).

In 2011 the Proyecto Arqueológico del Área Kaq'chik'el (PAAK) surveyed the hills and plains around Iximché. One goal of the survey was to corroborate the data shown in

Figure 20. Iximche Temple 1. Courtesy of Eugenia Robinson.

the 1690 map of Fuentes and Guzman that showed watchtowers and grand administrative buildings surrounding Iximché. Robert Hill first located the "tribunal" drawn by Fuentes and Guzman; the PAAK mapped it and found it most resembled Temple 1 of Iximché, although 5/7 of the size. The survey found several plaza groups from the Protohistoric period; there were only some sites remaining with single mounds that looked most like the watchtowers drawn by Fuentes and Guzmán. Domestic ceramics at many sites indicated that one function was residential at sites that could have had a "lookout" function; many sites had Classic and Preclassic diagnostic pottery.

The *Annals of the Cakchiquel*, an indigenous history, explains that the site was a center for two leaders who were forced out of the K'iche' court at **Utatlán/Q'um'arkaj**. It was conquered by Pedro de Alvarado in AD 1524 and became the first Spanish capital (Santiago) in the Kingdom of Guatemala. Today the site is restored and managed by the Guatemalan government. It is a sacred center for the Kaq'chik'el Maya people.

See also COTZUMALHUAPA; PORTABLE OBJECTS; WARFARE, WARRIORS, AND WEAPONS

Further Reading

Guillemin, George F. "Urbanism and Hierarchy at Iximche." In *Social Process in Maya Prehistory*, edited by Norman Hammond, 227–64. New York: Academic Press, 1977.

Nance, Charles Roger, Stephen L. Whittington, and Barbara E. Jones-Borg. *Archaeology and Ethnohistory of Iximche*. Gainesville: University Press of Florida, 2003.

Robinson, Eugenia J., Marlen Garnica, and Juan Pablo Herrera. "El Postclásico Tardio: Asentamientos alrededor de Iximché en el Altiplano de Guatemala." In *XXVI Simposio de Investigactiones Arqueológicas en Guatemala*, edited by Bárbara Arroyo and Médez Salinas. Guatemala City, Guatemala: Museo de Arqueología y Ethnología, 2013.

■ EUGENIA J. ROBINSON

IXTEPEQUE

Volcán Ixtepeque (14.4° N, 89.7° W) is an extinct volcano located in the department of Jutiapa, in southeastern **Guatemala**. The volcano's 1,292-m-high lava dome may constitute the largest single deposit of volcanic glass on the North American continent. Ixtepeque was a major source of **obsidian** for the pre-Columbian cultures of eastern **Mesoamerica** and lower Central America, especially during the Terminal Classic and Postclassic periods. Its name means "Obsidian Mountain" in Nahua.

The Ixtepeque source area includes the volcano itself and smaller flows and domes to the northeast. Two additional outcrops, located about 20 km to the southeast in **El Salvador**, might also be part of the source area. Ixtepeque obsidian is translucent or transparent, with a lustrous surface and very fine texture. The most common color is brown or dark amber, but the range also includes jet black, pale gray, and mahogany red. Opaque bands and mottling are sometimes present. The cortex can be thin and smooth or frothy and perlitic.

At least seven pre-Columbian quarries and workshops have been identified at Ixtepeque. A geological study of the region was conducted by Howel Williams and colleagues in 1961–1962. The first archaeological reconnaissance of the source and the nearby work-shop of Papalhuapa was carried out in 1965 by Robert Heizer and John Graham, accom-panied by Williams. Raymond Sidrys, John Andresen, and Derek Marcucci sampled the source area in 1974, and Payson Sheets conducted further studies at Ixtepeque in 1977.

Exploitation of the Ixtepeque source probably began during Paleo-Indian and Archaic times. Obsidian from Ixtepeque appeared throughout southeastern Guatemala, western and central **Honduras**, and El Salvador beginning in the late Early Formative, and was traded as far west as the Gulf Coast region. It is possible that distribution of Ixtepeque obsidian during the Formative period was controlled by the nearby site of Chalchuapa.

Ixtepeque obsidian was traded widely throughout the Maya **highlands** and **lowlands** during the Classic period, especially in western Honduras and all of El Salvador. None-theless, material from **El Chayal** or San Martín Jilotepeque was generally more common at most Maya sites until the end of the Late Classic. Kazuo Aoyama's work at **Copán** has demonstrated that its rulers controlled the distribution of Ixtepeque obsidian blade cores to much of the Maya region during the Classic. It appears that **Quiriguá** served as a major node in this **trade** network.

The Terminal Classic and Postclassic periods witnessed the expansion of what Geof-frey Braswell terms the southeast Maya obsidian exchange sphere. Ixtepeque became the dominant source of obsidian for Maya sites along the Caribbean coast, reaching inland settlements along major rivers. Throughout the **northern** Maya **lowlands**, the prevalence of Ixtepeque obsidian serves as a temporal marker of the Middle and Late Postclassic. In lower Central America, small quantities of prismatic blades were traded to Late Bagaces–period Gran Nicoya. Local production using Ixtepeque obsidian began in the following Sapoá and Ometepe periods. Extraction and production at Ixtepeque during the Post-classic were likely carried out by local inhabitants of the region.

See also Copan; El Chayal; Obsidian; Sin Cabezas; Trade Routes; Tulum

Further Reading

Aoyama, Kazuo. "Classic Maya State, Urbanism, and Exchange: Chipped Stone Evidence of the Copán Valley and Its Hinterland." *American Anthropologist* 103, no. 2: 346–60, 2001.

Braswell, Geoffrey E. "Obsidian Exchange Spheres." In *The Postclassic Mesoamerican World*, edited by Michael E. Smith and Frances Berdan. Salt Lake City: University of Utah Press, 2003.

Sidrys, Raymond V., John Andresen, and Derek Marcucci. "Obsidian Sources in the Maya Area." *Journal of New World Archaeology* 1, no. 5: 1–13, 1976.

■ BENIAMINO VOLTA

IZAMAL

The ancient city of Izamal (20.9° N, 89.0° W) was located on the northern plains of the Yucatan Peninsula about midway between Mérida (ancient **Tiho** or Ichcaansiho') and **Chichen Itza**, 48 km south of the Gulf of Mexico in the state of Yucatan, **Mexico** (see also **Map 3**). Although seriously affected by stone-robbing, Izamal was once one of the largest of all Maya sites, graced with gigantic **pyramids** and platforms. First occupied in the Middle Formative, much of the monumental **architecture** was built in the Late Formative and Early Classic periods. Some of this early architecture was built with the megalithic masonry characteristic of the period. The site retained its outstanding importance throughout the Classic period but declined sharply in the Terminal Classic period with the rise of Chichen Itza, 53 km to the southeast. At the time of the conquest, Izamal was a pilgrimage destination, dedicated to the god Itzamná, head of the Maya pantheon (see also **Deities**). At its peak, Izamal boasted five enormous temple-pyramids, including the K'inich K'ak' Mo', covering 8,000 m², with a 10-stepped pyramid rising 35 m above the plain (see figure 21). Its importance as a regional capital was attested by large intersite *sacbes* connecting it with Ake, 29 km west, and Kantunil, 18 km south (see also **Causeways**). One of the original structures was partially destroyed during the construction of the large Franciscan monastery San Antonio de Padua over the ancient acropolis. Today the larger buildings have been partly excavated and restored and are easy to visit within the confines of the modern town of Izamal.

See also Architecture Overview; Landa, Bishop Diego de; Mexico; Northern Lowlands; Portable Objects; Territorial Entities; Trade Routes

Figure 21.   The K'inich K'ak' Mo' of Izamal. It covers 8,000 m², with a 10-stepped pyramid rising 35 m above the plain. The structure has greater volume than all the mounds at nearby Ake, to which it is connected by a *sacbe*. Sheer volume of architecture puts Izamal at the top of the settlement hierarchy in northwest Yucatan. Photo courtesy of Edward Kurjack.

Further Reading

Andrews, George F. *Architectural Survey in the Northern Plains Area 1994/1995*. University of Oregon, 1995. http://repositories.lib.utexas.edu/bitstream/handle/2152/13951/txu-aaa-gfa00326.pdf.

Hundewadt, Mette Hald. *Izamal: History, Archeology and Mythology*. Copenhagen, Denmark: Indianske Sprog og Kulturer, 2003.

Lincoln, Charles E. "A Preliminary Assessment of Izamal, Yucatán, Mexico." BA thesis, Tulane University, 1980.

Maldonado C., Rubén. *Izamal, Yucatán*. México, D.F., México: Instituto Nacional de Antropología e Historia, 1991.

Stephens, John Lloyd. *Incidents of Travel in Yucatan*. New York: Harper & Brothers, 1843. Reprinted, New York: Dover, 1963.

Tozzer, Alfred M. *Landa's "Relación de las cosas de Yucatán": A Translation*. Papers of the Peabody Museum of American Archaeology and Ethnology, vol. 18. Cambridge, MA: Harvard University, 1941.

■ CLIFFORD T. BROWN AND WALTER R. T. WITSCHEY

IZAPA

Two km west of the **Guatemala** border with Chiapas, **Mexico**, and 33 km northwest of the Pacific Ocean, the Formative period city of Izapa (14.9° N, 92.2° W) sits at an elevation of 250 m above sea level (see also **Map 3**; **Pacific Coastal Plain**). The site core covered 2 km² and included 160 earthen mounds, mainly constructed of clay and faced with river cobbles. The site has temples, **ball courts**, and plazas. Izapa is famed for its carved monuments; over 100 **stelae**, altars, and **sculptures**, most carved in the Late Formative period, ca. 300–50 BC, carry no inscriptions. Monumental **architecture** at the site began in the Middle Formative period. Izapa displays a unique **art** style, one that seems descended from the earlier **Olmec** style and ancestral to that of the Maya. As seen on some late Olmec monuments, the Izapans preferred bas-relief carving to in-the-round carving, a trait carried on in the Maya Late Formative and Classic periods.

In contrast to much more restrained and "classic" Olmec art, Izapan art is both baroque and narrative. The baroque quality comes from the busy scenes filled with people, animals, plants, and objects (see also **Fauna**; **Vegetation**). Add to that the plentiful use of scrolls and volutes to frame scenes and fill in empty space, and one senses the baroque qualities of the style. The narrative structure of the art derives from the composition of scenes that tell a story. The actors, whether people, animals, or **deities**, are usually shown in the process of doing something specific. This contrasts with the monumental stillness of Olmec art, in which the focus is usually on a single, motionless figure pregnant with power.

Much Maya art, however, is narrative, like Izapa's. A number of other characteristics also link Izapan culture with the Maya: the use of sky bands to separate the earth from the heavens in the bas-reliefs (see also **Astronomy**); the stela-altar complex, which first appears there; and an early version of Chac as a long-lipped god (see also **Deities**). The Izapan art style is not restricted to the type site of the same name. It is also found at the large site of **Takalik Abaj** across the border in Guatemala, and it occurs at a number of sites in **El Salvador**. Its easternmost known expression is the megalithic jaguar altar from Quelepa, excavated by E. Wyllys Andrews V.

Further Reading

Guernsey, Julia. *Ritual & Power in Stone: The Performance of Rulership in Mesoamerican Izapan Style Art.* Austin: University of Texas Press, 2006.

Lowe, Gareth W., Thomas A. Lee, and E. Eduardo Martínez. *Izapa: An Introduction to the Ruins and Monuments.* Provo, UT: New World Archaeological Foundation, Brigham Young University, 1982.

Norman, V. Garth. *Izapa Sculpture.* 2 vols. Provo, UT: New World Archaeological Foundation, Brigham Young University, 1973.

Smith, Virginia G. *Izapa Relief Carving: Form, Content, Rules for Design, and Role in Mesoamerican Art History and Archaeology.* Washington, DC: Dumbarton Oaks, 1984.

■ CLIFFORD T. BROWN AND WALTER R. T. WITSCHEY

J

JADE

See ECCENTRIC LITHICS; PORTABLE OBJECTS

JAINA

During 10 centuries Maya men and women gave life and sense to the landscape, to the flora and **fauna** of this little island on the western shore of the Yucatan peninsula 40 km north of Campeche City, Mexico (see also **Map 3**).

Hieroglyphic inscriptions indicate that during the Classic period (AD 250–900) the island and its surrounding territory were known as the Caan (Sky) kingdom with its own Emblem Glyph. After the disintegration of that society its vestiges were known as Hina, a Maya term that could mean "seed of the generation" or could also be translated as "that, that was the house." In later times the name was transformed and became Jaina (20.2° N, 90.5° W), more commonly known as "the house in the water." Architectonic and **ceramic** analyses give us a temporal sequence beginning around AD 100: **Petén style** structures in the Early Classic, **Puuc style** buildings during the Late and Terminal Classic (AD 600–900/1000), and modest structures during Postclassic times.

Jaina's extent is less than a half km² (42 hectares), and archaeological excavations have found that it was built during the Early Classic (ca. AD 250–400) by carrying thousands of *sascab* cargoes from inland. Jaina has public buildings forming three monumental groups: Zayosal, Zacpool, and Central. The cores of the structures were made of *sascab*, but exterior walls were covered with veneer stones. High-ranking leaders and governors lived in masonry structures; the other people lived in perishable **houses** in domestic clusters built on platforms around the principal groups. On the eastern section of the island they built a 400-m-long dock, an important element for the shipment of goods and also a useful bad weather protection for many vessels (see also **Trade Routes**).

Excavations confirmed that Jaina was a small political unit (probably around 70 km²) but a powerful one due to its trade relationships. The settlement was part of two complementary worlds. As a seaport, Jaina was in communication with faraway **Mesoamerican** regions; as a coastal site on the Yucatan peninsula, Jaina had deep Mayan roots. A population estimate for the Late Classic period is 5,000 inhabitants.

For many years Jaina was mistakenly seen as a regional cemetery, but today we know that the necropolis hypothesis was wrong. Human **burials** from the island have been found under the spaces that in ancient times were used as domestic units. As occurred in many other Maya settlements, Jaina dwellers used to bury their dead under their houses. This fact was ignored because during the second part of the nineteenth century all the stones found on surface were collected to sell as construction material in Campeche; other stones were burned and converted into lime, also a lucrative commodity. So the first explorers of Jaina did not know they were digging holes within spaces previously used as houses.

Besides Jaina's role as a port, a **market**, and a living place, it also served as a regional sanctuary. This religious function was related with very special features. It was placed just on the frontier between the land and the sea, on the western side of the peninsula. For the ancient Maya, the sea and the west direction were related with the underworld and its supernatural inhabitants (see also **Deities**; **Iconography**; **Religion**).

Burials at Jaina frequently include offerings of jade, shell, or semiprecious stone necklaces, rings, and pectorals and ceramic dishes, pots, and figurines (see also **Portable Objects**). Sometimes there are also earrings, bone needles, and spindle-whorls. Adults were buried in simple graves, while little children were placed in big pots.

Jaina's fame in modern times is based on the abundant and exquisitely made ceramic figurines found there (see figure 22). Figurines were either molded or modeled. Molded pieces are always hollow, sometimes also useful as rattles, sometimes as whistles or as flutes. Females and males were commonly represented, but there are also images of many animals and some flowers. Articulated figurines have also been registered. As an artificial island, Jaina had no clays, and neutron–activation analysis has demonstrated a dynamic movement of figurines and many other products on a regional exchange network from the northern coast of Yucatan to southern and central Veracruz.

Figure 22. Figurine from a Jaina burial excavated in 2001 by the Campeche Regional Center of the National Institute of Anthropology and History, Mexico. Scale is 10 cm long. Courtesy of Antonio Benavides C., INAH.

See also AGUATECA; ART; BALL GAME/BALL COURT; CERAMIC ANALYSIS; CEREN; CRAFT SPECIALIZATION; FAUNA; PORTABLE OBJECTS; ROYAL TOMBS; TEXTILES AND CLOTHING; UNDERWATER ARCHAEOLOGY; WOMEN, MEN, AND GENDER ROLES

Further Reading

Benavides C., Antonio. *Jaina: Ciudad, puerto y mercado.* Colección Justo Sierra, no. 1. Campeche, Mexico: Gobierno del Estado de Campeche, 2012.

Piña Chán, Román. *Jaina: La casa en el agua.* México D.F., México: Instituto Nacional de Antropología y Historia, 1968.

■ ANTONIO BENAVIDES C.

K

KABAH AND NOHPAT

The sites of Kabah and Nohpat (20.4° N, 89.8° W and 20.3° N, 89.7° W) are located in the northwestern area of the Puuc region of the modern state of Yucatan (see also **Map 3**). This zone, Santa Elena Valley, is known for its broad expanse of deep soils. Kabah is one of the largest sites in the Puuc and directly linked to the site of **Uxmal**, the probable capital of the Late/Terminal Classic Maya living in the Puuc, via an ancient Maya road or *sacbe* (see also **Causeways**). The *sacbe* is 18 km long and 4.5 m wide, and numerous other sites have been identified between Kabah and Uxmal. The most important is Nohpat, located 8.5 km east of Uxmal or roughly halfway between the two major sites.

The earliest descriptions and illustrations of the ruins of Kabah and Nohpat were made by John Lloyd Stephens and Frederick Catherwood (1843), who visited the sites during the time they were working at Uxmal. Other early visitors include Charnay (1887) and Maler. Pollock studied the **architecture** of Kabah in the 1930s, and early salvage work was undertaken by Ruz in the late 1940s. George Andrews carried out architectural investigations at Kabah from 1960 until the mid-1990s. Excavations and consolidation of major structures at Kabah were performed in the 1950s by INAH, but it wasn't until the 1990s that Ramón Carrasco and a team of INAH archaeologists began a series of major excavations. Since the turn of the twenty-first century Lourdes Toscano and colleagues have carried out detailed excavations at Kabah, providing important new data on the Puuc Maya.

Kabah was founded at least by the Middle Formative (700–300 BC), but most of what is known about the site relates to its apogee in the Late and Terminal Classic Periods (AD 700–1000). Archaeologists estimate the settlement area of Kabah might have been as large as 10 km² and consisted of hundreds of structures ranging from monumental elite complexes to medium-sized architectural compounds and numerous small residential groups. The central core of the site is composed of three main architectural groups aligned east-west (a western group, a central group, and an eastern group). Overall, the site is centered on a **pyramid** compound and a series of civic and ceremonial buildings forming a set of virtually contiguous courtyards. It is likely the eastern and western zones were elite residential **palaces**, and the central zone was the site's civic-ceremonial center.

Little is known of the central group except for the famous Maya freestanding vaulted arch that marks the Kabah end of the Uxmal-Kabah *sacbe* (see also **Corbel Arch**). The largest pyramid at Kabah (Str. 1B2) is also found in this group. Unexcavated, the pyramid stands over 20 m in height and supported a four-room vaulted temple. The western zone is also poorly known, although it consists of numerous vaulted buildings forming several quadrangles and terrace groups.

The best known area of Kabah is the east group, also called the palace group. It has seen the greatest amount of architectural restoration and provides some of the finest examples of Maya architecture in the Northern Lowlands, many in the distinctive **Puuc** mosaic **style**. The palace group is composed of at least three large palace complexes and a wide assortment of associated structures, including several with important architectural façades and carved jambs. Undoubtedly the most famous building in the east group and one of the most distinctive in the Maya world is the Codz Poop. This structure's façade is decorated with some 250 stone mosaic masks representing the god Chac (see also **Deities**). The building has been named the Codz Poop (or rolling mat) for as long as is known historically, apparently in reference to repeated use of masks. See figures 23 and 24.

Well-preserved carved jambs with hieroglyphic inscriptions have been found in the back of the Codz Poop (sometimes considered a separate building) and the Building of the Red Hands in the west group. The themes of the jambs, dated to AD 859 and 873, include Kabah kings receiving supplicants (Building of the Red Hands) and militaristic dancing and warfare on the back of the Codz Poop (see also **Music and Dancing**; **Theater**; **Warfare, Warriors, and Weapons**).

Figure 23.   The importance of rain to the ancient Maya in the Puuc hills is dramatically emphasized in the architecture of the Codz Poop (or rolling mat). The entire building façade is covered with 250 repetitive mosaic masks of the rain god Chac.

Figure 24. Detail of the Codz Poop masks of the rain god with eyes and snouts clearly visible. Note adjacent masks are sharing a single ear flare. Each mask is made of several carved stones, set into the façade mosaic style.

Recent efforts by Lourdes Toscano have focused on better understanding the life of the royal court of Kabah. She has identified and excavated an ancient kitchen area associated with the Codz Poop palace area. The kitchen area is 40 m by 14 m and includes the remains of perishable buildings and cooking areas. Large numbers of artifacts have been recovered in situ, helping to identify how food preparation was carried out during the Terminal Classic period in royal quarters (see also **Diet**; **Subsistence**).

Nohpat, despite its accessible location and long history of visitors, remains poorly known. Situated on the *sacbe* between Uxmal and Kabah, it was clearly a major ancient Maya city. Its location aligns with the heliacal rising of Venus as seen from the Governor's Palace at Uxmal. It consists of a number of vaulted architectural structures that are dated to the Late and Terminal Classic periods and form three distinct complexes. There is a large pyramid in the site center (Str. 1), whose megalithic stairway suggests the building's origins might be in the Formative or Early Classic, and there is a **ball court**. A number of glyph panels and carved monuments have also been recovered at Nohpat.

The sites of Kabah and Nohpat, linked by a *sacbe* to Uxmal, were undoubtedly part of a Puuc polity whose center was at Uxmal. Between these cities would have been numerous towns and villages, so that during their apogee in the Terminal Classic we can infer they formed a huge multi-urban capital that controlled either the Santa Elena Valley or perhaps the entire Puuc region.

See also ALLIANCES; ARCHITECTURE OVERVIEW; CLASSIC MAYA COLLAPSE; HOUSES; KIUIC; NORTHERN LOWLANDS; PORTABLE OBJECTS; PROSKOURIAKOFF, TATIANA AVENIROVNA; PUUC ARCHITECTURAL STYLE; SAYIL; TERRITORIAL ENTITIES; TRADE ROUTES

Further Reading

Carrasco Vargas, Ramón. "Formación sociopolítica en el Puuc: El sacbe Uxmal-Nohpat-Kabah." In *Perspectivas antropológicas en el mundo Maya*, edited by María Josefa Iglesias Ponce de León and Francesc Ligorred Perramon. Publicaciones de la S.E.E.M., núm. 2. Madrid: Sociedad Española de Estudios Mayas, Instituto de Cooperación Iberoamericana, 1993.

Dunning, Nicholas P., and Jeff K. Kowalski. "Lords of the Hills: Classic Maya Settlement Patterns and Political Iconography in the Puuc Region, Mexico." *Ancient Mesoamerica* 5: 63–95, 1994.

Mayer, Karl Herbert. "Maya Hieroglyphic Inscriptions from Nohpat, Yucatan, Mexico." *Mexicon* 32, no. 1: 9–13, 2010.

■ GEORGE J. BEY III

KAMINALJUYÚ

A major Maya site occupied from the Middle Formative period to the Terminal Classic period, today Kaminaljuyú (14.6° N, 90.5° W) is located within modern **Guatemala** City, where a city park preserves some larger Classic structures (see also **Map 3**). The site is quite possibly the most important archaeological settlement in highland Guatemala, primarily for what it says about regional contact during the development of Maya culture.

The site originally had at least 200 mounds and structures, but urban encroachment of the modern capital has destroyed most of the site, except for the small section preserved in the public park. Archaeological remains or deposits are sometimes fortuitously uncovered in surrounding neighborhoods, too. The site has been investigated by archaeologists a number of times since the first half of the twentieth century, and ongoing research there continues to contribute to our understanding of the region.

The site was originally founded at the end of the Early Formative period or the beginning of the Middle Formative period (ca. 1000–900 BC) along the margin of an extinct **lake** named Lake Miraflores. In the Middle Formative the local people built extensive public works, including a sophisticated irrigation system to bring water from Lake Miraflores for maize fields to the south of the city. The largest of their canals was 1 km long, with a cross-section 4 m wide by almost 6 m deep. Another possible irrigation structure, an earthwork named "La Culebra," is 4 km long and in places 9 m high, but it has barely been investigated (see also **Subsistence**; **Water Management**).

In the Late Formative period Kaminaljuyú may have reached its apogee. Many large structures, both residential and ceremonial, were constructed, including a 20-m-tall **pyramid**. Little stone is available in the Valley of Guatemala, and therefore the buildings were built of adobe and *talpetate*, a kind of soft, welded volcanic ash. In this period, the site shared cultural traits with **Izapa** and **Takalik Abaj** on the **Pacific Coast**, as well as **El Mirador** in northern Guatemala. **Stelae** carved in the Izapan style have been found from this period, as well as others that display a more obviously Maya style. One stela bears an early hieroglyphic inscription, as yet undeciphered, that shares some characteristics with other early **Mesoamerican** texts from the Isthmian region. Rich and elaborate tombs from the Late Formative illustrate the existence of extreme social stratification in Kaminaljuyú society. The scenes on the stelae also depict themes of rulership (see also **Class Structure**; **Divine Kings and Queens**; **Royal Tombs**; **Writing Systems of Mesoamerica**).

The irrigation system expanded in this period, suggesting the political organization of large numbers of people in public projects. In sum, the evidence from Late Formative Kaminaljuyú points to the evolution of a powerful early state. The state's fortunes may have been closely linked to its irrigation system, since, as Lake Miraflores dried up at the end of the Formative and the canals clogged with silt, the city went into decline (see also **Climate**; **Drought**).

In the Early Classic period, Kaminaljuyú developed close links with **Teotihuacán**, the dominant city of Central **Mexico**, which was then also interacting with other Maya cities, such as **Tikal**, **Uaxactún**, **Piedras Negras**, and **Copán**. In addition to distinctive Teotihuacán-style *talud-tablero* platforms, Kaminaljuyú also had green **obsidian**, Thin Orange ceramics, and painted **ceramics** with images of Tlaloc, the Central Mexican Rain God—all objects associated with Teotihuacán. The nature of the relationship between Kaminaljuyú and Teotihuacán remains a matter of debate. Some scholars see outright military conquest by Teotihuacán, while others interpret the evidence as indicating a mainly commercial relationship. In its location, Kaminaljuyú was ideally situated to serve as a port of trade, and its eclectic sculpture and architecture attest to the multicultural nature of its connections. In the Late Classic period, Kaminaljuyú experienced a significant resurgence in population and power, but eventually succumbed to the forces driving the **Classic Maya collapse**.

See also CRAFT SPECIALIZATION; DEITIES; EL CHAYAL; TRADE ROUTES

Further Reading

Braswell, Geoffrey E. *The Maya and Teotihuacan: Reinterpreting Early Classic Interaction.* Austin: University of Texas Press, 2004.

Kidder, A. V., J. D. Jennings, and E. M. Shook. *Excavations at Kaminaljuyu, Guatemala.* Washington, DC: Carnegie Institution of Washington, 1946.

Michels, Joseph W. *The Kaminaljuyu Chiefdom.* University Park: Pennsylvania State University Press, 1979.

Parsons, Lee Allen. *The Origins of Maya Art: Monumental Stone Sculpture of Kaminaljuyu, Guatemala, and the Southern Pacific Coast.* Studies in Pre-Columbian Art and Archaeology, no. 28. Washington, DC: Dumbarton Oaks Research Library and Collection, 1986.

Popenoe de Hatch, Marion. *Kaminaljuyú/San Jorge: Evidencia arqueológica de la actividad económica en la Valle de Guatemala, 300 a.C. a 300 d.C.* Guatemala City: Universidad del Valle de Guatemala, 1997.

———. "New Perspectives on Kaminaljuyú, Guatemala: Regional Interaction during the Preclassic and Classic Periods." In *Incidents of Archaeology in Central America and Yucatán: Studies in Honor of Edwin M. Shook*, edited by Michael Love, Marion Popenoe de Hatch, and Héctor L. Escobedo, 277–96. Lanham, MD: University Press of America, 2002.

■ CLIFFORD T. BROWN AND WALTER R. T. WITSCHEY

KARST
See GEOLOGY

KINSHIP

Among the ancient Maya, rules of descent, marriage, and residence played a major role in organizing society, providing the structural principles underlying political organization, **settlement patterns**, economic patterns such as inheritance, and religious institutions. Based on **Diego de Landa**'s *Relacion* reporting on the late Postclassic Maya, as well as on ethnographic studies of the modern Maya, we may estimate how to reconstruct kinship and family ties for ancient times.

The mileposts of a Maya life are birth, naming ceremonies, childhood, marriage, and death. A Maya **highlands** child may be named for a day in the sacred *tzolk'in* 260-day calendar, or in the **lowlands**, be named during a divination ceremony. A modern Maya, for example, would carry a given name, "Pedro," and both the mother's surname, "Cobá," and the father's surname, "Ka'amal."

Marriage links families both socially and economically. Landa reports that weddings were held at the bride's father's home, officiated by a priest, and then followed by feasting. The young couple lived with her parents for six or seven years while the groom worked for his father-in-law. Afterward, the couple established a new home close to the home of his parents.

Archaeologists see the effects of this form of residence in the patio groups and *plazuelas*, where several Maya dwellings surround one open-air space. There is still debate over whether such nearby houses were strictly occupied by kin groups, or whether the residences might be more properly termed households, whose membership was more open than defined by strict kinship ties.

See also CLASS STRUCTURE; HOUSES; RITES AND RITUALS

Further Reading

Gillespie, Susan D. "Rethinking Ancient Maya Social Organization: Replacing 'Lineage' with 'House'." *American Anthropologist* 102, no. 3: 467–84, 2000.

McAnany, Patricia A. *Living with the Ancestors: Kinship and Kingship in Ancient Maya Society*. rev. ed. Austin: University of Texas Press, 2014.

Tozzer, Alfred M. *Landa's "Relación de las cosas de Yucatán": A Translation*. Papers of the Peabody Museum of American Archaeology and Ethnology, vol. 18. Cambridge, MA: Harvard University, 1941.

■ WALTER R. T. WITSCHEY

KIUIC

Kiuic (20.1° N, 89.5° W) is a medium-sized Maya archaeological site located in the southern hills of the Puuc region of the modern state of Yucatan, known as the Bolonchen (see also **Map 3**). It is one of numerous Maya centers located in the southern

Puuc and is only 4 km from the site of Huntichmul and 12 km from the site of **Labna**. This region is known in the **northern** Maya **lowlands** for both its rich **soils** and almost total lack of surface water. The Maya of Kiuic built their society based on the successful management of rainwater. (see also **Groundwater/Water Table**; **Water Management**).

Kiuic was visited by the famous explorers John Lloyd Stephens and Fredrick Catherwood as part of their Yucatan expedition in the early 1840s and later briefly studied by Teobert Maler (1881) and Harry E. D. Pollock (1930s). It has been the focus of intensive study since 2000 as part of the Bolonchen Regional Archaeological Project under the direction of Tomás Gallareta Negrón, George J. Bey III, and William M. Ringle.

Nestled in one of the small valleys formed by low hills, which characterize the Bolonchen, Kiuic, based on radiocarbon-14 dates and associated **ceramics**, was founded between 900 and 800 BC (see also **Dating**). By the late Middle Formative (700–300 BC) a small community had developed, centered around a low plaza supporting a number of ceremonial structures, including N1015E1015-sub, a modest cut stone platform with a central staircase and a presumed perishable temple.

Although there is evidence for continued occupation through the Late Formative (300 BC–AD 250) and Early Classic (AD 250–600), it was not until the second half of the sixth century AD that the site began to grow dramatically. At this time the plaza was expanded and the earlier platform covered by a long stone building with a simple slab vaulted roof. This building is thought to have served as a **council house**, known in Maya as a *popol nah*, suggestive of greater social complexity and wealth in the community. Northern Maya *popol nahs* are characterized by a single long chamber, multiple entryways, and a stairway composed of several broad risers.

By the beginning of the Late Classic around AD 700, the center of Kiuic was transformed into a complex of structures named by archaeologists the Yaxche Group. The Yaxche Group served as the first **palace** of the city of Kiuic. It was composed of at least 20 vaulted buildings and a number of perishable ones centered around three adjoining plazas. The vaulted buildings are in the Early **Puuc architectural style**, defined by small rooms, the use of columns, and an emphasis on complex modeled stucco decoration.

The heyday of the Yaxche palace, based on C14 dates, **architectural** style, detailed stratigraphic analysis, and ceramics was AD 700–800. At some point in the early ninth century, the main central vaulted buildings, believed to be the royal quarters within the palace, were buried by at least two phases of pyramidal construction. The second one was at least 10 m high and crowned by a single vaulted room temple. Concurrently, several areas of the Yaxche palace were allowed to fill up with debris, and the *popol nah*, in use since AD 550, had all but two of its many doorways sealed, indicating it no longer functioned as a council house.

These changes in the Yaxche Group at AD 800 were associated with the construction of a grouping to the west of it, which is believed to be a new larger palace with structures in the Late Puuc "Colonnette" style, characterized by the use of either sets or continuous friezes of colonnettes. There is very little evidence for the use of the more baroque Puuc mosaic style found in other Puuc sites such as **Uxmal**, **Kabah**, and Labna. The new palace, started in the ninth century was still under construction when the site was abandoned in the tenth century. It consists of two main plaza groups, with numerous Late Puuc vaulted structures located along the west side of the plazas, including the famous House of the Diamonds, first illustrated by Catherwood in the nineteenth century. The east sides of the plazas were largely left open. The new palace was several times larger in scale than the Yaxche Group and compares favorably in size to the better known Late Puuc palaces at Sayil and Labna. It is connected to the nearby earlier palace by a *sacbe* (see also **Causeways**; **Classic Maya Collapse**).

The existence of similar arrangements at other nearby sites such as Huntichmul and Labna suggests that the historic events that led to the construction of enormous new palaces connected by *sacbes* to earlier palace groups that had *popol nahs* were a regional phenomenon heralding an unprecedented period of wealth and growth in the Puuc region, somehow related to the success of Uxmal, the largest Late/Terminal Classic Puuc center. The building of the pyramid, *sacbe*, and other associated changes suggest the original palaces were transformed into monuments legitimizing the authority of the rulers occupying the new palace complexes.

Although evidence for earlier occupation is found throughout Kiuic, it is during the seventh to tenth centuries that the site reaches its greatest size. Hundreds of buildings, many forming architectural groups, have been mapped or identified through remote sensing techniques, with a very high percentage of vaulted structures. The site center covers several square kilometers. In addition, there are a number of elite "suburban" complexes on the hills surrounding the site center.

One of these complexes, located 1.4 km from the palaces of Kiuic, is known as Stairway to Heaven and was the subject of intensive excavation from 2008 to 2014. Dating primarily to the Terminal Classic period (AD 800–1000), it consists of a multiroom vaulted "palace" as well as a residential area with four multiroom vaulted structures and numerous support structures composed of perishable materials. Excavations have revealed that Stairway to Heaven underwent a process of rapid abandonment, and as a result many of the objects used by the ancient Maya of Puuc were left on the floors or in activity areas around the buildings. Evidence suggests that the Maya abandoned Kiuic with the intention of returning; however, except for Post-Classic offerings scattered on the main Yaxche pyramid, there is no evidence of occupation after the Terminal Classic.

See also AGUATECA; HOUSES; PORTABLE OBJECTS

Further Reading

Bey, George J., III, and Rosanna May Ciau. "The Role and Realities of Popol Nahs in Northern Maya Archaeology." In *The Maya and Their Central American Neighbors: Settlement Patterns, Architecture, Hieroglyphic Texts and Ceramics*, edited by Geoffrey E. Braswell. New York: Routledge, 2014.

Simms, Stephanie R., Evan Parker, George J. Bey III, and Tomás Gallareta Negrón. "Evidence from Escalera al Cielo: Abandonment of a Terminal Classic Puuc Maya Hill Complex in Yucatán, Mexico." *Journal of Field Archaeology* 37, no. 4: 270–88, 2012.

■ GEORGE J. BEY III

KNOROSOV, YURI VALENTINOVICH (1922–1999)

The Russian epigrapher Yuri Knorosov made a critical contribution to the **decipherment** of the ancient Maya script in his 1952 paper "Ancient Writing of Mesoamerica." He used the "alphabet" from **Diego de Landa**'s *Relación*, images of the pages in the Dresden codex, and a Maya–Spanish dictionary to make several correct assertions about the Maya script (see also **Codices [Maya]**). He agreed with earlier scholars that the Landa alphabet contains glyphs for sounds, the sounds of the Latin letters as pronounced in Spanish. From this he concluded that many, but not all, Maya hieroglyphs referred to sounds—phoneticism. Second, he showed that Maya phonetic symbols were syllabic and represented a consonant-vowel pair. Third, he showed that for many Maya words without a final vowel, such as P'op', the word was written phonetically, P'o-p'o to choose, for the second and silent vowel, the same vowel as used in the first syllable, a principle he called synharmony.

His paper, in Russian, coming as it did during the Cold War, was not quickly noticed in the West. When it was translated and understood, several Mayanists grasped its import for reading the script, while others rejected it outright as wrong. Knorosov's work has stood the test of time and is today recognized as seminal in decipherment, whose principles are applied by all modern linguistics and epigraphers studying the Maya hieroglyphs.

See also WRITING SYSTEMS OF MESOAMERICA

Further Reading

Coe, Michael D. *Breaking the Maya Code*. 3rd ed. London: Thames & Hudson, 2012.

Coe, Michael D., and Mark Van Stone. *Reading the Maya Glyphs*. 2nd ed. London: Thames & Hudson, 2005.

Houston, Stephen, Oswaldo Fernando Chinchilla Mazariegos, and David Stuart, eds. *The Decipherment of Ancient Maya Writing*. Norman: University of Oklahoma Press, 2001.

Johnson, Scott A. J. *Translating Maya Hieroglyphs: Recovering Languages and Literacies of the Americas*. Norman: University of Oklahoma Press, 2013.

■ CLIFFORD T. BROWN AND WALTER R. T. WITSCHEY

KOHUNLICH

The site of Kohunlich (18.4° N 88.8° W) is located in the southern portion of the state of Quintana Roo, **Mexico**, about 40 km north of the border with **Belize** (see also **Map 3**). It can be accessed by Federal Highway 186, which runs between the cities of Chetumal and Escarcega. From this road, 70 km from Chetumal at the small village of Francisco Villa, there is a 10-km secondary road that leads directly to the site.

Contrary to what might supposed, the site's name does not have a Mayan origin, but is derived from the English words "Cohune Ridge," a name that describes the geographical area in which the settlement lies, consisting of plains alternating with small hills. The settlement is a secondary site in comparison to other cities of the region, such as **Calakmul** and **Dzibanché**. Vestiges of Kohunlich are scattered across an area of roughly 9 km^2, with the site being comprised of several major **architectural** groups including the Complejo Norte, Yaxná, Complejo 27 Escalones, and the Complejo Pixa'an.

This site was first reported between 1905 and 1912 by Raymond Merwin, of the Harvard Peabody Museum. In the late 1960s and early 1970s Victor Segovia, from INAH, conducted a series of investigations focused on exploration and preservation of several areas of the settlement. From 1993 to the late 2000s the site was investigated and restored by the Projecto Sur de Quintana Roo, directed by Enrique Nalda and Adriana Velázquez, joined by other archaeologists, including Sandra Balanzario, Alan Maciel, and other researchers from INAH's Quintana Roo center.

The architectural style of the site is variable. While some buildings have features similar to the **Petén style**, others display elements of the **Río Bec** or **Puuc styles**, although these include several local variations that can be observed in the Pixa'an and 27 Escalones groups. Among the most prominent architectural features of this site is the Edificio de los Mascarones (building of the masks), an 11-m-tall **pyramid** that has six stucco masks flanking the central stairway, as well as the Edificio de las Estelas (building of the stelae), which had a stucco crest with six personages sitting over the sacred mountain or *witz*. Both buildings date from the Early Classic period (see also **Art**; **Deities**; **Iconography**).

Ceramic dates have revealed that the site was occupied from the Middle Preclassic (800–300 BC) through the Early Postclassic (AD 1000–1200), with a population climax around AD 900–1000, when it had close to 10,000 inhabitants. Throughout this time, it had three major occupations, followed by demographic depressions shown in changes in the style of the construction. The site was definitely abandoned around AD 1100–1200, after a period in which several immigrants from other regions of the Maya area arrived at the site. The reasons the site was abandoned are not clear, since there is no evidence of overpopulation or a climate crisis. It was hypothesized that the abandonment was caused by a balkanization of its political power.

Politically, Kohunlich could have been ruled by a council or confederated government, as has been suggested based on the iconography of the Edificio de las Estelas and the Edificio de los Mascarones. Both constructions had stucco sculptures that depict six royal individuals, perhaps members of the council that ruled the settlement.

See also CLASSIC MAYA COLLAPSE; COUNCIL HOUSE; SCULPTURE

Further Reading

Franco Torrijos, Enrique, Arturo Romano Pacheco, Carlos Navarrete, and Victor Segovia Pinto. *Kohunlich: Una ciudad Maya del Clásico Temprano*. México, D.F., México: San Angel Ediciones, 1981.

Nalda, Enrique. "Dinámica ocupacional, estilos arquitectónicos y desarrollo histórico en Kohunlich." In *Escondido en la Selva*, edited by Hanns J. Prem. México, D.F., and Bonn, Germany: Instituto Nacional de Antropología e Historia and the University of Bonn, 2003.

———. *Kohunlich: Emplazamiento y desarrollo histórico*. México D.F., México: Instituto Nacional de Antropología e Historia, 2004.

———. "Kohunlich and Dzibanché. Parallel histories." In *Quintana Roo Archaeology*, edited by Justine M. Shaw and Jennifer P. Mathews, 228–44. Tucson: University of Arizona Press, 2005.

Nalda, Enrique, and Adriana Velázquez Morlet. "Kohunlich: Mitos y reflexiones sobre su historia prehispánica." In *Guardianes del tiempo*, edited by Adriana Velázquez Morlet, 15–35. Chetumal, Quintana Roo, México: Universidad de Quintana Roo, Instituto Nacional de Antropología e Historia, 2000.

■ALBERTO G. FLORES COLIN AND JUSTINE M. SHAW

KOMCHEN

Komchen (21.1° N, 89.6° W) is a Formative Maya site in northwest Yucatan, about 16 km due north of Merida and 19 km south of the Gulf of Mexico (see also **Map 3**). The center of the vast Classic-period city of **Dzibilchaltun** lies 6 km to the southeast. Komchen is the largest known Formative settlement in the far northwest corner of the peninsula and was also likely the earliest large village in this region. The site was investigated by the Middle American Research Institute of Tulane University during the 1957–1962 Dzibilchaltun project and again in 1980.

Although this is the driest part of the Yucatan Peninsula, with only about 650–700 mm of rain a year, and with shallow and poor **soils**, farming and probably rich marine resources were able to support large populations. The present and probably past **vegetation** is a low, dense, thorn forest. The water table lies only 3–3.5 m below the surface, and many ancient man-made wells and a few small **cenotes** are scattered across the site (see also **Map 5**; **Groundwater/Water Table**).

Komchen was a roughly circular town with densely packed platforms covering 2 km². The Central Plaza, 80 by 150 m, is flanked by four platforms (now gutted for construction material) that were many times larger than other buildings at Komchen. A *sacbe* (stone **causeway**) runs 250 m northeast to a fifth large platform. Surrounding the core are about 1,000 stone-faced and gravel platforms ranging from > 1,000 m² to < 10 m². Most were dwellings, although some small ones were outbuildings for storage, cooking, or other household tasks. Hundreds of boulder metates lay on or beside the platforms. The large flat-topped platforms, enlarged from time to time, supported perishable **houses** for extended families. Large structures tend to be closer to the center, with smaller ones toward the periphery. At its peak, about 400 BC to AD 1, Komchen was home to at least 2,500 to 3,000 people. Other Formative sites of varying sizes lie within a few hours' walk of Komchen, indicating a settlement hierarchy of at least three levels. (See figure 25.)

The earliest Cunil-related pottery at Komchen, dating to about 900 BC, was found at the base of two of the large platforms on the Central Plaza (23F1 and 24G1), suggesting that this public space with its administrative and elite structures was laid out at the beginning of the site's occupation in the early Middle Formative. Late Middle Formative (Mamom-related) **ceramics** (700–400 BC) are abundant at Komchen, and most of the base for the pyramidal platform at the north end of the plaza (21J1) was constructed during these years. The heaviest occupation, most construction, and greatest extent of the community date to the Late Formative (400 BC–AD 150 or 250). Toward the end of this long span the population declined, and by the end of the Formative Komchen was abandoned for about half a millennium. Small groups moved back in and built a few stone houses on old platforms in the Late Classic period, perhaps expanding from Dzibilchaltun.

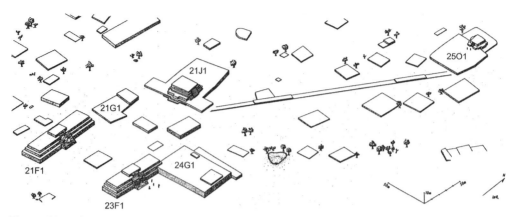

Figure 25. The Central Plaza at Komchen, Yucatan, as it appeared toward the end of the Late Formative period. Isometric reconstruction by Linda Roundhill, courtesy of E. Wyllys Andrews.

Although Komchen imported almost no imperishable **trade** goods, such as jade, **obsidian**, and **chert**, ceramic vessels show close ties to the **southern** Maya **lowlands**, especially from about 700 to 300 BC. The rise of Komchen may have been stimulated by coastal salt production, but archaeological evidence for this is lacking. The linear north-south arrangement of the Central Plaza, with a **pyramid** at the north and an elite or royal residential platform (24G1) on the east, is similar to that of La Venta and several early Middle Formative Chiapas sites. The presence of this formal plaza surrounded by masonry structures before 800 BC shows that powerful chiefdoms developed in the far northern Maya lowlands as early as anywhere else in the Maya area.

See also OLMEC-MAYA INTERACTIONS; PORTABLE OBJECTS

Further Reading

Andrews, E. Wyllys, V, George J. Bey III, and Christopher Gunn. "The Earliest Ceramics of the Northern Maya Lowlands." In *Pathways to Complexity: A View from the Maya Lowlands*, edited by Kathryn Brown and George J. Bey III. Gainesville: University of Florida Press, 2015.

Ringle, William M. "The Settlement Patterns of Komchen, Yucatan, Mexico." PhD diss., Tulane University, 1985.

Ringle, William M., and E. Wyllys Andrews V. "Formative Residences at Komchen, Yucatan, Mexico." In *Household and Community in the Mesoamerican Past*, edited by Richard R. Wilk and Wendy Ashmore, 171–97. Albuquerque: University of New Mexico Press, 1988.

———. "The Demography of Komchen, an Early Maya Town in Northern Yucatan." In *Precolumbian Population History in the Maya Lowlands*, edited by T. Patrick Culbert and Don Stephen Rice. Albuquerque: University of New Mexico Press, 1990.

■ E. WYLLYS ANDREWS

L

LA CORONA

The modern history of La Corona (17.5° N, 90.4° W) is that of unraveling an archaeological enigma. More than two dozen beautifully carved limestone stair risers appeared in the American art world in the 1960s, looted from **Guatemala**. Their texts referred to a then-unknown Maya site that Peter Mathews called Site Q (for *Que?*, "what"). In 1997 Ian Graham and David **Stuart** learned of, investigated, and named La Corona. While in the field, they noted inscriptions matching those of the Site Q carvings: the place-name (*sak nikte'*), a ruler's name (Chak Ak'aach Yuk), unique titles for the local rulers (*sak wayis*), and references to the Snake Kingdom of **Calakmul**. Stuart believed they had found the lost Site Q (see also **Map 3**).

In 2005 Marcello Canuto spent five days at the site (as part of the project at **El Perú-Waka'** of David Freidel and Héctor Escobedo). While exploring a looter's trench, he found well-preserved in situ panels that matched those of Site Q; the confirmation of La Corona as Site Q was complete.

Canuto and Tomás Barrientos Q. have led a multiseason program of research at La Corona and the region: Proyecto Regional Arqueológico La Corona (PRALC). They offer a five-phase chronology of the site. The history of the site opens in AD 314 with the founding lineage. At AD 520 La Corona celebrates the first marriage alliance with a Snake princess. The third interval, with active production of inscriptions beginning in AD 625, marks the reign of Sak Maas. A new phase begins in AD 700, shortly after **Tikal** defeats **Calakmul**. El Perú-Waka' and **Naranjo** fall, opening the final phase at AD 750, a time perhaps of dramatic political change for La Corona, leading ultimately to its abandonment as part of the general **Classic Maya collapse**.

Canuto points out the unusual nature of this small site with elaborate carved panels and **hieroglyphic stairways**. Its connections over a long period of time included several marriage **alliances** with Calakmul, repeated documented **ball games**, and on-site visits by Snake Kingdom royalty. It had no Emblem Glyphs; its rulers carried a unique title.

From the evidence, he proposes that La Corona was a key point and loyal ally along a **trade route** leading southward from **Dzibanché** (in the Early Classic) and Calakmul (in the Late Classic) through Uxul, La Corona, Waka', and Polol to **Dos Pilas**, **Ceibal**, and Cancuen. La Corona was so important to protecting a key trade route for the Snake Kingdom that the investment in it, by marriage alliance, royal visits, and elite trappings, was sustained over many centuries.

See also APOCALYPSE; ART; MUSIC AND DANCE; PORTABLE OBJECTS

Further Reading

Barrientos Q., Tomás, Marcello A. Canuto, and Jocelyne Ponce. *Proyecto Arqueológio La Corona: Informe final temporada 2012.* Middle American Research Institute, Tulane University, 2013. http://mari .tulane.edu/PRALC/Files/PRALC%20–%20Informe%20final%202012.pdf.

Canuto, Marcello A. *La Corona Archaeological Project: Investigating an Extraordinary Classic Maya Center.* Middle American Research Institute, Tulane University, 2013. http://mari.tulane.edu/PRALC/ index.html.

Canuto, Marcello A., and Tomás Barrientos Q. *The Importance of La Corona.* Mesoweb, 2013. http:// www.mesoweb.com/LaCorona/LaCoronaNotes01.pdf.

Guenter, Stanley. *La Corona Find Sheds Light on Site Q Mystery.* Mesoweb, 2005. http://www.mesoweb .com/reports/SiteQ.html.

■ WALTER R. T. WITSCHEY

LA LAGUNITA

During reconnaissance in Campeche, **Mexico**, in April 2014, Ivan Šprajc relocated the ruins of La Lagunita (18.6° N, 89.5° W), which had been lost since their first discovery in the 1970s by Eric von Euw of the Corpus of Maya Hieroglyphic Inscriptions project (see also **Map 3**). Von Euw recorded numerous **stelae** and altars from the site. Stela 2, which carries a Long Count date of 9.14.0.0.0 6 Ahau 13 Muan (December 5, AD 711), is called out by David **Stuart**, who noted that not only is the glyph reading order unusual (row-by-row), but it also carries a name-tagging phrase that labels the stela "his carved Six Ajaw stone (*wak ajaw tuun*)." Such expressions are most often found on Classic polychrome **ceramics** and other **portable objects**. The ruler, whose name is eroded away, is called a four-*k'atun* lord, indicating he was over 60 and then in his fourth 20-year *k'atun*.

See also CALENDAR

Further Reading

Lorenzi, Rossella. *Ancient Maya Cities Found in Jungle.* Discovery Communications, Inc., 2014. http:// news.discovery.com/history/archaeology/three-ancient-maya-cities-found-in-jungle-140815.htm.

Stuart, David. "Lagunita's Unusual 'Six Ajaw Stone.'" *Maya Decipherment: Ideas on Ancient Maya Writing and Iconography* (blog), August 25, 2014. http://decipherment.wordpress.com/2014/08/25/laguni tas-unusual-six-ajaw-stone/.

■ WALTER R. T. WITSCHEY

LABNA

The ruins of Labna (20.2° W, 89.6° N) are located in the southern portion of the Mexican state of Yucatan, in the Puuc region of the **northern** Maya **lowlands** (see also **Map 3**). During the Terminal Classic Period (AD 800–950/1000), the settlement reached its maximum development and extension. Most of the standing **architecture** dates from this time period. However, a number of collapsed buildings were built in the previous century (AD 700–800), although they continued in use during the Terminal Classic. Remains of structures dating from the last centuries BC, buried inside later buildings, attest that the site was settled for over a thousand years, from about 350 BC to AD 950.

Labna was reported by John Stephens in 1843. His book, *Incidents of Travel in Yucatan*, included accurate engravings of the **palace**, the arch, and the mirador by Frederick Catherwood. In the last years of the ninetenth and the turn of the twentieth centuries, Edward Thompson mapped and conducted excavations, and Teobert Maler photographed the main standing buildings. The architectural studies of Harry Pollock (published in 1980) and George Andrews constitute the major sources of data available. In several seasons from 1991 to 2002 the Centro INAH Yucatan, Mexico, funded a program of research and preservation of the site, under the direction of Tomás Gallareta Negrón.

The layout and architectural forms of the main buildings are representative of scores of archaeological communities in the region. The site center consists of two architectural complexes linked by a **causeway**. One such complex is the palace, a two-story building that was under expansion when Labna was abandoned. A central kitchen and several throne rooms have been identified in the lower story. The buildings of the other complex date mostly from earlier times. The central spaces were bordered by a *popol nah* or **Council House** and several single-chambered buildings with **corbel vaults** of true masonry manufacture, open at the front with two columns. The causeway, built in Terminal Classic times, symbolizes an **alliance** between the two most powerful groups of elites of the city represented by the two complexes. The north end includes the headquarters of the ruler of the community in a court-like complex, with built spaces for social and political activities that included banquets and ceremonies. The buildings on the south end represent local noble families and their land holdings, as well as other undefined institutions.

Foundations of domestic residences, most with roofs and walls of palms and poles, respectively, are found surrounding the site center. Variations in size and composition support the existence of a complex social organization. Las Gemelas, a secondary group built with expensive stone architecture, is located near the southwest edge of the urban settlement on hilltops and their slopes. Such buildings housed members of the elite involved in the management of economic resources such as arable land, quarries for extracting building materials, lands for agro-forestry, and gaming activities. The inhabitants of such outlying complexes formed social units based on economic interests, coresidence, and affinity, rather than consanguinity.

The economy of Labna relied on seasonal agricultural practices for the production of corn and on the procurement and transformation of limestone for building purposes. Deep local **soils**, combined with intrinsic qualities of the local limestone, produced a boom in the construction of public architecture from AD 800 to 900, sponsored by at least three generations of consecutive rulers. The palace and the archway, with expensive mosaic decoration, were built during the second half of the ninth century. A mask in the central patio of the Palace carries a date of AD 862, supporting this assumption.

See also CLASS STRUCTURE; DIET; DIVINE KINGS AND QUEENS; GEOLOGY; HOUSES; KINSHIP; AND SUBSISTENCE

Further Reading

Andrews, George F. *Pyramids and Palaces, Monsters and Masks: The Golden Age of Maya Architecture; The Collected Works of George F. Andrews.* Vol. 1. Lancaster, CA: Labyrinthos, 1995.

Gallareta Negrón, Tomás. "The Social Organization of Labna, a Classic Maya Community in the Puuc Region of Yucatan." PhD diss., Tulane University, 2013.

Pollock, Harry E. D. *The Puuc: An Architectural Survey of the Hill Country of Yucatan and Northern Campeche, Mexico.* Memoirs of the Peabody Museum, vol. 19. Cambridge, MA: Peabody Museum of Archaeology and Ethnology, Harvard University, 1980.

Stephens, John Lloyd, and Frederick Catherwood. *Incidents of Travel in Yucatan.* New York: Dover, 1843, 1962.

■ TOMÁS GALLARETA NEGRÓN

LAKAMHÁ

See PALENQUE

LAKES

Lakes are critical resources for humans because they provide multiple ecosystem services (see **Map 5** for lake locations). They are also important habitats for wildlife. The ancient Maya relied on lakes for (1) drinking water; (2) places to bathe and wash household items; (3) transportation, (4) sources of protein, including fish, frogs, turtles, snails, and crocodiles; and (5) rituals and ceremonies. Not surprisingly, many Maya archaeological sites are found close to lakes (e.g., **Cobá**, **Yaxhá**). In the limestone terrain of the Maya **lowlands**, most water bodies owe their origin to dissolution and/or tectonic (earth movement) processes. Over millions of years, slightly acidic rainfall dissolved the regional bedrock, creating fissures and voids that gave rise to **caves**, surface depressions, and sinkholes (**cenotes**), some of which filled with water. In Central Petén, **Guatemala**, "faulting" produced a string of east-west-aligned lakes that have steep north shores and gently sloping south shores. On the northern Yucatan Peninsula, rainfall quickly infiltrates the karst bedrock, travels underground, and discharges to the sea at the coastal margins. Thus, most large lakes and rivers are found in the **southern** Maya **lowlands** and the highlands of Guatemala.

Lakes in the Maya region have been subject to human influences for millennia. Lake sediments in the region preserve a detailed record of past environmental conditions, which can be inferred from stratigraphic study of the geochemistry and microfossils (such as pollen, ostracodes, and gastropods) of sediment cores. Radiocarbon dates on lake sediment cores show that most shallow water bodies on the Yucatan Peninsula began to fill with water about 10,000–8,000 years ago (see also **Dating**). Sea level rose as high-latitude glaciers melted, thereby raising the height of the freshwater aquifer. **Climate** also became warmer and wetter at the onset of the Holocene, about 11,700 years ago, promoting lake filling. Some deep lakes in the lowlands held water even during the dry, cold period of the last ice age. Large, deep Lake Petén-Itza, Guatemala (area = ~100 km^2, maximum depth = ~165 m), has held water continuously for more than 200,000 years.

Lakes of the Maya lowlands show diverse chemical and biological characteristics. Central Petén lakes display a broad range of total dissolved ion concentrations and can differ with respect to their major cation (calcium or magnesium) and anion (bicarbonate or sulfate). Some coastal lakes have high concentrations of sodium and chloride, reflecting their proximity to the sea. Lakes of the region also display differences with respect to productivity. Some have low nutrient concentrations, low algal biomass, and high water transparency, whereas others display higher nutrient values and have abundant algae and green, turbid waters. Lowland Lake Izabal is the largest lake in Guatemala (area = ~590 km^2, maximum depth = 18 m) and drains to the sea (Gulf of Honduras) via the Rio Dulce.

Highland lakes of the Maya region owe their origin to volcanic activity, including eruptions, collapse of subterranean magma chambers, and lava damming. The basin of Lake Atitlan (Guatemala) formed about 84,000 years ago as a result of the Los Chocoyos eruption. The lake lies some 1,560 m asl and is famous for its large size (130 km^2); great depth (~340 m); and spectacular lake-level views of extinct volcanoes Atitlan, Toliman, and San Pedro. The watershed is home to three modern Maya groups, the K´iche´e, Kaqchikel, and Tz´utujil. Submerged ruins and pottery from the Maya city Samabaj were discovered and dated to between ca. 300 BC and AD 300. Lake Ayarza (area = 14 km^2, maximum depth = 230 m) lies at 1,409 m asl and is younger, having formed approximately. 20,000 years ago. The watershed of Lake Amatitlan (1,188 m asl, area = 15.2 km^2, maximum depth = 33 m) boasts a long history of human occupation, and divers have recovered numerous **ceramic**, stone, and bone artifacts from the lake. In the past century the lake became a weekend getaway destination for residents of Guatemala City. Unfortunately, recent excessive nutrient runoff and sewage input to the lake caused severe cultural eutrophication, and today the lake experiences persistent cyanobacteria blooms. Other volcanic lakes of note include Güija (430 m asl, area = 45 km^2, maximum depth = ~25 m), on the border of Guatemala and El Salvador, and Ilopango, in central El Salvador (440 m asl, area = 72 km^2, maximum depth = ~25 m).

Ancient Maya settlements were often situated near water sources, including rivers, cenotes, and lakes. Drinking water availability was a concern, especially during the long dry season. Surface waters could also be used for bathing and washing household wares, and for ceramic production. People navigated by boat between lakeside villages and extracted animal protein from the aquatic ecosystems. Thus, lakes played a critical role in ancient Maya cultural development.

See also FAUNA; GROUNDWATER/WATER TABLE; PORTABLE OBJECTS; REJOLLADAS; SUBSISTENCE; VEGETATION; WATER MANAGEMENT

Further Reading

Alcocer, Javier, and Fernando W. Bernal-Brooks. "Limnology in Mexico." *Hydrobiologia* 644, no. 1: 15–68, 2010.

Deevey, Edward S. "Limnological Studies in Middle America: With a Chapter on Aztec Limnology." *Transactions of the Connecticut Academy of Arts and Sciences* 39: 213–328, 1957.

Pérez, Liseth, Rita Bugja, Julia Lorenschat, Mark Brenner, Jason Curtis, Philipp Hoelzmann, Gerald A. Islebe, Burkhard Scharf, and Antje Schwalb. "Aquatic Ecosystems of the Yucatán Peninsula (Mexico), Belize, and Guatemala." *Hydrobiologia* 661, no. 1: 407–33, 2011.

■ MARK BRENNER AND LISETH PÉREZ

LAMANAI

The Maya site of Lamanai (17.8° N, 88.7° W) is located on the New River Lagoon at the headwaters of the river in northern **Belize** (see also **Map 3**). David Pendergast chose the name when he began excavations in 1974; until then it had long been known as "Indian Church," a name now claimed by the modern local community. The Spanish authorities recorded the community as "Lamanay" in the sixteenth century, probably a Hispanicization of the Mayan "Lama'an/ayin," "submerged crocodile."

Lamanai has a long history, extending from about 1500 BC until Spanish involvement ceased ca. AD 1700. Sugar extraction, evidenced through the construction of a sugar mill, was attempted in the late nineteenth century, but recent research suggests that the site may well have been occupied, if intermittently, throughout the eighteenth and early nineteenth centuries. Pendergast's Royal Ontario Museum excavations ran from 1974 to 1986; new excavations involving a wide range of researchers under the aegis of University College London began in 1999 and are ongoing. Periodic conservation, excavation, and restoration also continue to be carried out by the Belize Institute of Archaeology.

The date of 1500 BC comes from carbon associated with a high concentration of corn pollen from a core taken in "The Harbour," an area of waterlogged sediments not far from the lagoon in the northern part of the site that became a hub of Late Preclassic (ca. 400 BC–AD 100) activity. The earliest solid **ceramic** evidence, from residential and communal structures, dates to the Middle Preclassic, ca. 600–400 BC. Late Preclassic habitation is widespread, from the site's limits in the north for at least 3.5 km southward. At around 100 BC the site saw a southward shift in its central ceremonial precinct; Pendergast dubs this an "urban renewal," in which small residential structures were supplanted by Str. N10-43 (The High Temple), a tall, terraced ceremonial platform supporting three small structures at its summit, which almost certainly served as the focal point of the community at the time. It underwent a number of modifications in the Early (AD 250 to 600) and Late (AD 600 to 800) Classic, but at its Late Preclassic height of 33 m, it remained the tallest and most massive structure throughout the site's history.

Construction activity continued into the Late Classic, with a number of plaza groups supporting civic and ceremonial buildings, but the only two tombs from this period are associated with Str. N9-56, The Mask Temple, and both individuals—a man in one tomb and a woman in the other—had been interred in "cocoons" of hoopwork covered in textiles soaked in red pigment. Surrounding the individuals were wooden objects, vessels dating to the early sixth century AD, jade and shell mosaic ear ornaments, and pendants. The sixth and seventh centuries saw a flurry of activity at the site; Lamanai's best known monument, **Stela** 9, celebrating the dead king Tzik'in Xook, was erected in AD 625 by the *elk'in kaloomte'* (high ruler of the eastern quarter) Chan Yopaat, probably Tzik'in Xook's son.

The site is distinguished from a number of others by its continued occupation into the Postclassic and the Spanish and British Colonial periods. Construction in Plaza Group N10-[3], just south of The High Temple complex, continued through the Terminal Classic into the Postclassic. Most of the Terminal Classic buildings, although they stood on masonry platforms, were of wood daubed with clay and lime plaster, construction that continued in the Postclassic. Polychromes from Terminal Classic deposits demonstrate

continuity from Classic times, but by the Early Postclassic, ca. AD 1000, polychrome production gave way to incised and gouged decoration on orange-red monochrome pottery.
Late Postclassic pottery resembles ceramics found throughout northern Yucatan, and
there is evidence of lively coastal **trade**. In the Spanish Colonial period two Franciscan
churches were built at Lamanai, but Spanish interest in the area waned, owing partly to
Maya resistance but also to diminishing Colonial resources. By 1700, British logwood
cutters were filling the Spanish vacuum.

See also BURIALS; CERAMIC ANALYSIS; DATING; HOUSES; PORTABLE OBJECTS; ROYAL TOMBS

Further Reading

Belanger, Louise, David M Pendergast, Elizabeth Graham, Scott E. Simmons, and Jaime Awe. *Lamanai
    Guide Book*. 2014. http://www.louisebelanger.com/lamanai_guidebook.html.
Graham, Elizabeth. *Maya Christians and Their Churches in Sixteenth-century Belize*. Gainesville: University
    Press of Florida, 2011.
Howie, Linda. *Ceramic Change and the Maya Collapse: A Study of Pottery Technology, Manufacture and Con-
    sumption at Lamanai, Belize*. B.A.R. International Series. Oxford: Archaeopress, 2012.
Pendergast, David M. "Lamanai, Belize: Summary of Excavation Results, 1974–1980." *Journal of Field
    Archaeology* 8, no. 1: 29–53, 1981.
Pendergast, David M, and Elizabeth Graham. Lamanai Archaeology Project. 2014. http://www.lamanai
    .org.uk/.

■ ELIZABETH GRAHAM

LANDA, BISHOP DIEGO DE (1524–1579), AND *RELACIÓN DE LAS COSAS DE YUCATÁN*

Diego de Landa was a sixteenth-century Spanish friar of the Franciscan order.
He led Spanish efforts to convert the indigenous Maya of the Yucatan peninsula
to Christianity.

He achieved lasting fame (and infamy) for two reasons. First, in the summer of
1562, frustrated by his lack of progress in evangelizing Maya villagers, he initiated
a brutal campaign to destroy their traditional religious practices; thousands were
arrested and tortured under interrogation. In the course of that investigation he also
destroyed thousands of Maya sacred objects and dozens of books (**codices**). Second,
he wrote a vast compendium that recorded Maya culture and history, the earliest
such account from Yucatan, **Mexico**. Although the manuscript was lost, a selection
of excerpts from it has survived. Titled *Relación de las cosas de Yucatan*, or *Account of
the Things of Yucatan*, it is a unique and much-used source of information on the
pre-Colonial and early Colonial-era Maya. (See figure 26.)

Diego de Landa was born in 1524 in Cifuentes, an old Moorish town in Spain's
Alcarría region. At age 16 he entered the Franciscan monastery in Toledo. He was
about 25 when he committed himself to the missionary challenge of Spain's new

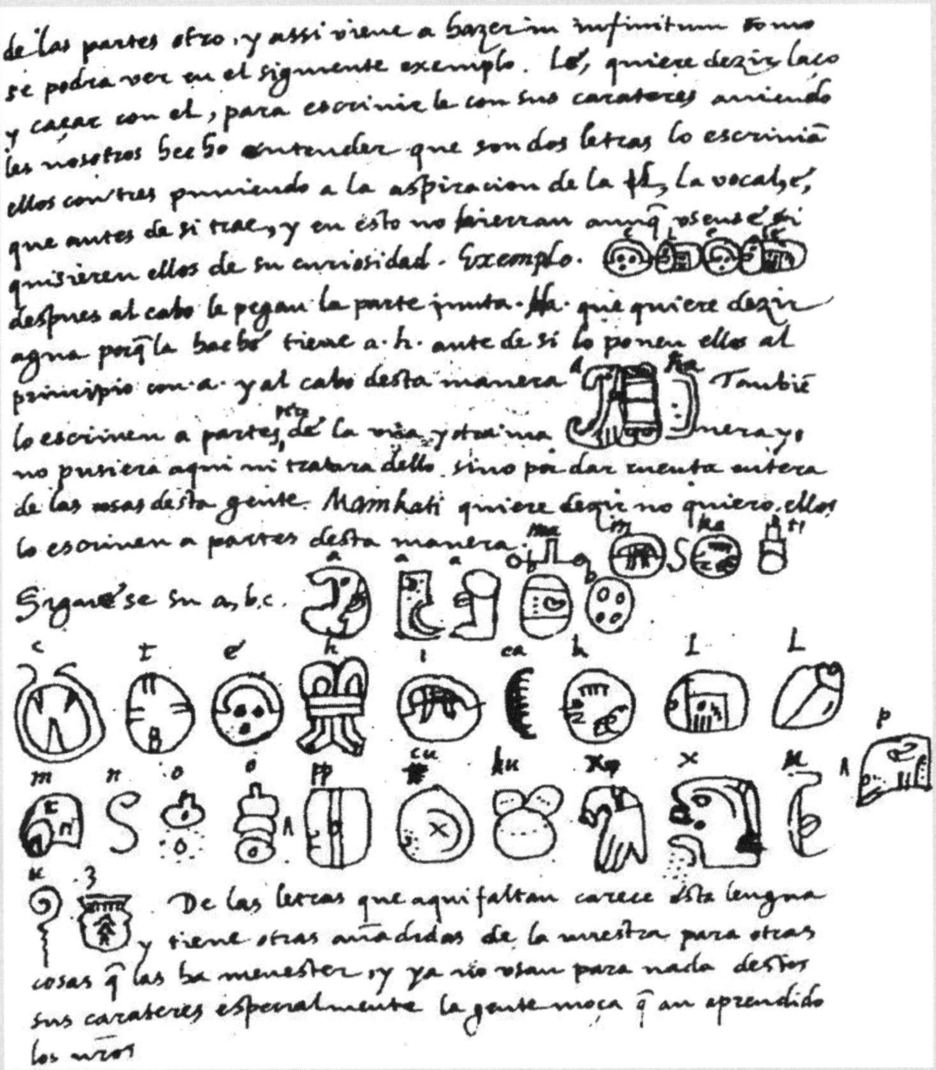

de las partes otro, y assi viene a hazer in infinitum como
se podra ver en el siguiente exemplo. Le, quiere dezir laço
y caçar con el, para escrivirle con sus caracteres aviendo-
les nosotros hecho entender que son dos letras lo escrivian
ellos con tres poniendo a la aspiracion de la l, la vocal e,
que antes de si trae, y en esto no hierran aunque usen della si
quisieren ellos de su curiosidad. Exemplo.
despues al cabo le pegan la parte junta. Ha. que quiere dezir
agua porque la hache tiene a. h. ante de si lo ponen ellos al
principio con a. y al cabo desta manera. Tambie
lo escriven a partes de la una y otra manera. yo
no pusiera aqui ni tratara dello sino por dar cuenta entera
de las cosas desta gente. Mamhati quiere dezir no quiero. ellos
lo escriven a partes desta manera.
Siguese su a, b, c.
De las letras que aqui faltan carece esta lengua
y tiene otras añadidas de la nuestra para otras
cosas que las ha menester, y ya no usan para nada destos
sus caracteres especialmente la gente moça que an aprendido
los nuestros

Figure 26. A page from the surviving manuscript of Bishop Landa's *Relación de las cosas de Yucatán*. Photographed ca. 1882 by Juan de Dios de la Rada y Delgado, reproduced by George Stuart in *Glyph Drawings from Landa's Relación: A Caveat to the Investigator*, Center for Maya Research, Research Report no. 19 (December 1988), www.mesoweb.com/bearc/cmr/19.html. Courtesy David Stuart and the Boundary End Archaeological Research Center BEARC).

Mexican colonies, arriving in Yucatan seven years after the 1542 founding of the provincial capital of Mérida. He was first charged with starting a mission outpost at Itzmal (today **Izamal**) with the more experienced Lorenzo de Bienvenida. Landa soon revealed his ambitions, not only learning Mayan but translating Catholic texts into it, as well as traveling extensively in the peninsula, preaching to Maya communities and destroying their traditional religious statues or "idols."

In 1558 Landa was elected custodian of the Franciscan order in the colony, and three years later became provincial or regional head of the order. As custodian, he became involved in a legal dispute between the church and one of the colony's founding conquistadors, Francisco Hernández; Landa harried Hernández mercilessly for years, until on his deathbed Hernández confessed his "crimes" against the ecclesiastical authorities. The conquistador families would not forget Landa's role in this affair, which symbolized the difficult relationship between colonists and clerics that persisted throughout Yucatan's Colonial period. Yet ironically, Landa's fall from power and exile in Spain in the 1560s was caused not by the colonists but his persecution of the Maya and by another Franciscan, Bishop Francisco de Toral.

Fray Toral became the province's first resident bishop in 1560, but did not arrive until August 1562, by which time Landa had already begun investigating the alleged "return to their ancient and evil customs" by dozens of Maya communities. Their leaders and others, mostly nobles, were arrested under accusation of "worshipping idols and sacrificing to them publicly and in secret," thereby "destroying Christianity among the simple people" (as Spanish officials put it). Some 4,500 Mayas, including women, were tortured (nearly 200 to death). In July, Landa held autos-da-fé (confessions of faith) in the Maya towns of Maní, Sotuta, and Hocaba-Homun—public hearings at which Maya "heretics" who had survived torture were whipped and chastised, and over 5,000 "idols" and 27 hieroglyphic books were burned. This "great persecution" (as one Maya noble, Don Francisco de Montejo Xiu, termed it) caused the Maya "much grief" (as Landa himself noted). Toral immediately began to dispute the legality of Landa's use of violence and the veracity of the confessions thereby extracted. Many of the colonists agreed. "There is in this province a friar called fray Diego de Landa who . . . enjoys broils and having a finger in every pie, and he expects to rule in both spiritual and temporal matters," wrote one senior government official in Yucatan to the king of Spain in 1562.

In 1563, in the wake of a condemnatory report sent by Toral, Landa returned to Spain to defend himself. There he assembled a great compilation of writings by himself and others on Yucatan—a pioneering ethnographic study of the land, its people, and its history before and after the conquest. The only surviving portion of this work is the *Relación de las cosas de Yucatán*, an excerpt made in the eighteenth century. Drawn from the friar's own observations and from his conversations with two Maya informants, Nachi Cocom and Gaspar Antonio Chi, the *Relación* is unique to Yucatan and one of the most important such manuscripts to have survived from Colonial Mexico. Perhaps by trying to view Landa's inquisition as conducted in the spirit of care and concern for the Maya, we can begin to reconcile their suffering at his hands with the book's veritable celebration of the Yucatec people.

In exile, Landa worked for his political rehabilitation with typical fervor and tenacity. When Toral died in 1571, Landa himself was appointed Yucatan's bishop. He returned in 1573, older but vindicated and no less determined to uproot Maya "idolatry." Despite the opposition of both colonists and Maya leaders, Landa promoted the authority of the church with an iron hand until his death in 1579; he was buried in the

Franciscan monastery at Mérida, site of **Tiho**. As a defender of the Franciscan order and ecclesiastical authority, Landa was no doubt "a great friar," as his colleagues wrote in 1570. But he was also a missionary friar who compiled knowledge about the Mayas while burning books that were sources for the same subjects, and he was a colonizer who strove to protect indigenous people from Spanish settlers, yet campaigned for the brutal torture of their leaders. As such, Landa offers a fascinating and tantalizing window onto the Maya past and the complex Maya-Spanish experience.

See also APOCALYPSE; CACAO; CALENDAR; DECIPHERMENT; DROUGHT; Förstemann, Ernst Wilhelm; KINSHIP; KNOROSOV, YURI VALENTINOVICH; MATHEMATICS; MUSIC AND DANCE; PRIESTS; RELIGION; RITES OF PASSAGE; SETTLEMENT PATTERNS (NORTHERN LOWLANDS); SUBSISTENCE; THEATER; TIHO; WOMEN, MEN, AND GENDER ROLES; WRITING SYSTEMS OF MESOAMERICA

Further Reading

Clendinnen, Inga. *Ambivalent Conquests: Maya and Spaniard in Yucatan, 1517–1570*. Cambridge [Cambridgeshire], UK, and New York: Cambridge University Press, 1987.

Landa, Diego de. *Relación de las cosas de Yucatán* [1566]. Mexico City, D.F.: Porrua [1959]. Translated and edited by William Gates, *Yucatan before and after the Conquest, by Friar Diego de Landa* (Baltimore, MD: The Maya Society, 1937 [Reprinted by Dover, 1978]); Alfred M. Tozzer, *Landa's "Relación de las cosas de Yucatán": A Translation* (Cambridge, MA: Peabody Museum, 1941 [Reprinted by Kraus, 1966 and 1978]); Anthony R. Pagden, *The Maya: Diego de Landa's Account of the Affairs of Yucatan* (Chicago: O'Hara, 1975)

Restall, Matthew. *Maya Conquistador*. Boston: Beacon Press, 1998.

Restall, Matthew, and John F. Chuchiak. "A Re-evaluation of the Authenticity of Fray Diego de Landa's Relación de las cosas de Yucatán." *Ethnohistory* 49, no. 3: 651–69, 2002.

Scholes, France V., and Ralph Loveland Roys. "Fray Diego de Landa and the Problem of Idolatry in Yucatan." In *Cooperation in Research*, 585–620. Washington, DC: Carnegie Institution of Washington, 1938.

Tedlock, Dennis. "Torture in the Archives: Mayans Meet Europeans." *American Anthropologist* 91, no. 1: 139–52, 1993.

■ MATTHEW RESTALL AND AMARA SOLARI

LANGUAGE AND WRITING OVERVIEW

The Maya people speak 28 different languages today. Two that had been in recent use are now extinct. Linguists trace the family tree of these languages back to a common proto-Mayan tongue that has a time-depth of about 4,000 years, well before visible signs of a Maya culture in archaeology (see also **Map 4**). With the exception of 66,000 Huastec (Wastek) speakers along the Pánuco River and Gulf Coast, Mayan languages are found adjacent to each other within the Maya region. (Generally, articles about the Maya use "Mayan" as an adjective for languages only, and "Maya" in all other cases.)

Language comparisons show that Huastec split from the other language families first, after which Yucatec Maya diverged from a group that subsequently split into the Greater

K'ichean, Mamean, Greater Q'anjob'alan, and Tzeltalan-Ch'olan groups by the beginning of the Early Formative. Subsequent splits within these families, chiefly in the highlands, gave rise to the 28 languages spoken today. (See also **Yucatecan Maya Languages**; **Highland Maya Languages.**)

Modern Mayan languages are written with Latin letters and have been since the arrival of the Spaniards. In ancient times, the script was written in a visually dynamic script that employed hieroglyphs grouped into blocks, often written in double vertical columns read left-right, top-to-bottom. The ancient script is now known to be syllabic, with individual glyphs representing a vowel-consonant pair, combined to write out the sounds of words. Other glyphs are pictorial or numerical. The ancient script is called "fully productive" because the Maya could use it to write anything they could voice out loud (see also **Decipherment**).

New inscriptions, found on carved stone monuments (**stelae**), stairway risers, **ceramic** vessels, **wall paintings**, and **portable objects**, provide a steady source of fresh information to epigraphers who study the script. A new text not only provides new information in the intrinsic sense, but also aids in the proper translation of scripts that have been known for some time. The ancient script frequently deals with royal elites, their activities (coronations, bloodletting ceremonies, captive-taking, defeat of enemies in battle), and their family genealogies. They also show that the scribes were members of the elite class or royal family members.

See also Ball Game/Ball Court; Dynastic Sequences; Hieroglyphic Stairways; Knorosov, Yuri V.; Rites and Rituals; Stuart, George E., and David Stuart; Syllabary; Warfare, Warriors, and Weapons

Further Reading

Coe, Michael D. *Breaking the Maya Code*. 3rd ed. London: Thames & Hudson, 2012.

Coe, Michael D., and Mark Van Stone. *Reading the Maya Glyphs*. 2nd ed. London: Thames & Hudson, 2005.

Longacre, Robert. "Systemic Comparison and Reconstruction." In *Handbook of Middle American Indians*. Vol. 5, *Linguistics*, edited by Norman McQuown, 117–59. Austin: University of Texas Press, 1967.

"Mayan Languages." In *Wikipedia*, 2014. http://en.wikipedia.org/wiki/Mayan_languages#Geography_and_demographics.

Sharer, Robert J., and Loa P. Traxler. *The Ancient Maya*. 6th ed. Stanford, CA: Stanford University Press, 2006.

U.S. Central Intelligence Agency. *The World Factbook*. 2014. https://www.cia.gov/library/publications/the-world-factbook/.

■ WALTER R. T. WITSCHEY

LIDAR

LiDAR is an acronym for "Light Detection and Ranging." It is an active laser scanning technology that has come into prominence in archaeology because of its ability to provide detailed renderings of archaeological features and sites and particularly for its ease

Figure 27. A LiDAR 2.5D "bare-earth" rendering of the Ceiba Terminus at Caracol, Belize. Shown are monumental architecture, a reservoir, roadways, and agricultural terracing constructed on the landscape. Courtesy of Arlen Chase.

in penetrating tree and vegetative cover over a landscape, resulting in a comprehensive record of the ground surface. (See figure 27.)

The platform supporting the technology can be ground-based or air-based, and with future technological advances, may eventually also be satellite-based. LiDAR uses lasers to perform its scanning operations. The technology produces point clouds—a series of point measurements recorded with the x, y, and z axes—that can be further manipulated for interpretation and imagery by researchers. A greater density of the points produces a more detailed rendering. Point-LiDAR uses a single laser in short, rapid pulses that return multiple points per pulse; flash-LiDAR uses a series of lasers in a single concentrated burst to return multiple points simultaneously; waveform-LiDAR yields a vertical summation of the returns from the pulse; and Geiger-LiDAR uses multiple lasers to produce even more sensitivity. While each of the points has unique spatial and elevation coordinates, images created from the points are usually shown on a flat screen or piece of paper; this has resulted in this technology being referred to as either 2D and 2.5D (but not 3D).

In archaeology, LiDAR scanning operations can be applied on a variety of scales, ranging from artifacts to buildings to entire sites. Terrestrial LiDAR has been used to record monuments and buildings. This extremely detailed surface scanning not only provides a full record of ancient remains, but the results can also be used for multi-dimensional rotation and virtual manipulation. Perhaps the most revolutionary use of this technology in archaeology, however, has been its aerial application, which provides spatial information that is largely unavailable in any other format. LiDAR has been used to record sites and landscapes that are obscured beneath vegetative canopies. Ground resolution is usually on the order of 5–30 cm, but can be better depending on the point density. To accomplish this, an airborne platform is usually employed. Helicopters, drones, and planes are all used to deploy lasers, and the parameters change for each kind of aerial platform. No matter the platform used, lasers are deployed toward the ground. Using a plane as a platform means that it is flown at an elevation that is generally 600 to 1,000 m above the surface in an established pattern that forms either a grid or parallel lines. Onboard GPS units triangulate with ground GPS units in conjunction with an onboard computer that measures and corrects for flight variations. The laser sensors are capable of penetrating gaps in the tree cover to record the ground surface and also provide returns for the covering trees and vegetation. The last return provides points that can be assembled into a "bare-earth" model (also called a DTM, digital terrain model, or a DEM, digital elevation model). This model permits archaeologists to make interpretations about ground-surface cultural features that are normally obscured from sight by tree foliage. Before striking the ground, the initial returns from the canopy are useful in terms of the biological analysis of forest structure and carbon storage. The point clouds derived from this exercise can be quite substantial and usually require a relatively high-capacity computer for processing.

Introduced in Mesoamerica through a 2009 aerial survey of **Caracol**, **Belize**, covering 200 km², airborne LiDAR has now been used by archaeologists to record a wide variety of sites and landscapes. Other areas and sites that have been surveyed include western Belize (1,050 km²), **Mayapan** (40 km²), **Izapa** (43 km²), Angamuco (12 km²), and El Tajin. Outside of Mesoamerica, LiDAR has been used for interpreting archaeological remains in Europe and in Southeast Asia. LiDAR is having a profound effect on archaeology because it provides a spatial control for the discipline that finally complements the temporal control provided by 14C dating in the 1950s.

One ethical concern about LiDAR usage is how public these data should be made. Formal data management plans at federal agencies often call for the public dissemination of all archaeological data. However, the full release of geo-referenced LiDAR data could have a detrimental effect on archaeological sites worldwide, especially as the technology provides a virtual road map that could be used for looting. Thus, policies need to be promulgated so that the release of LiDAR data does not exacerbate the problems associated with the unauthorized excavation or destruction of archaeological sites.

See also GROUND SURVEY TECHNIQUES; SUBSISTENCE

Further Reading

Chase, Arlen F., Diane Z. Chase, Christopher T. Fisher, Stephen J. Leisz, and John F. Weishampel. "Geospatial Revolution and Remote Sensing LiDAR in Mesoamerican Archaeology." *Proceedings of the National Academy of Sciences* 109, no. 32: 12916–921. 2012.

Chase, Arlen F., Diane Z. Chase, and John F. Weishampel. "Lasers in the Jungle: Airborne Sensors Reveal a Vast Maya Landscape." *Archaeology* 63, no. 4: 27–29, 2010.

Chase, Arlen F., Diane Z. Chase, John F. Weishampel, Jason B. Drake, Ramesh L. Shrestha, K. Clint Slatton, Jaime J. Awe, and William E. Carter. "Airborne LiDAR, Archaeology, and the Ancient Maya Landscape at Caracol, Belize." *Journal of Archaeological Science* 38: 387–98, 2011.

Chase, Diane Z., Arlen F. Chase, Jaime J. Awe, John H. Walker, and John F. Weishampel. "Airborne Li-DAR at Caracol, Belize and the Interpretation of Ancient Maya Society and Landscapes." *Research Reports in Belizean Archaeology* 8: 61–73, 2011.

Corns, Anthony, and Robert Shaw. "High Resolution 3-dimensional Documentation of Archaeological Monuments & Landscapes Using Airborne LiDAR." *Journal of Cultural Heritage* 108: e72–e77, 2009.

Glennie, C. L., W. E. Carter, R. L. Shrestha, and W. E. Dietrich. "Geodetic Imaging with Airborne Li-DAR: The Earth's Surface Revealed." *Reports on Progress in Physics* 76: 2013.

Opitz, Rachel S. and David C. Cowley, eds. *Interpreting Archaeological Topography: 3D Data, Visualisation, and Observation.* Oxford: Oxbow Books, 2013.

Weishampel, J. F., J. N. Hightower, A. F. Chase, and D. Z. Chase. "Use of Airborne LiDAR to Delineate Canopy Degradation and Encroachment along the Guatemala-Belize Border." *Tropical Conservation Science* 5, no. 1: 12–24, 2012.

■ ARLEN F. CHASE AND DIANE Z. CHASE

LIMESTONE
See GEOLOGY

LOLTUN CAVE

The cave of Loltun (20.3° N, 89.5° W) lies in the Puuc hills of Yucatan, Mexico, 7 km southwest of the modern village of Oxcutzcab. The first reports of the site were from Edward H. Thompson, who also dredged artifacts from the sacred **cenote** at **Chichen Itza**. The cave takes its name from the Maya *Lol-tun* "Flower Stone," from the pecked petroglyph designs found on the walls. Painted hands and other cave wall designs and ceramic offerings are found within. Controlled excavations in the late 1970s by Norberto Gonzáles Crespo revealed the bones of Pleistocene animals, including mammoth, horse, bison, cats, and deer, associated with unifacial points beneath a long preceramic sequence. Occupation in the cave extends from the Archaic to recent times—the Caste War.

Near the Nahkab entrance to the cave, as reported by Thompson, is a bas-relief of a personage in Maya regalia. In 1996 Nikolai Grube and Linda Schele provided a translation of the associated glyphs, which to them indicated a likely date of 8.3.0.0.0 3 Ahaw 3 Xul (October 29, AD 100) in the Late Preclassic. This would place the date among the earliest in the Maya region and demonstrate the early arrival of kingship governance in the Northern Lowlands.

Further Reading

Freidel, David A., and Anthony P. Andrews. "The Loltun Bas Relief and the Origins of Maya Kingship" Unpublished manuscript, 1984. (MS courtesy A. P. Andrews.)

Grube, Nikolai, and Linda Schele. "New Observations on the Loltun Relief" *Mexicon* 18, no. 1: 11–14, 1996.

Hixson, David. *Mesoamerican Photo Archives: Loltun.* Mesoweb, 1997–2010. http://www.mesoweb.com/mpa/loltun/loltun.html.

Schubert, Blaine W., Jim I. Mead, and Russell W. Graham. *Ice Age Cave Faunas of North America.* Bloomington, IN, and Denver, CO: Indiana University Press and Denver Museum of Nature & Science Press, 2003.

Thompson, Edward Herbert. *Cave of Loltun, Yucatan.* Memoirs of the Peabody Museum of American Archaeology and Ethnology, vol. 1, no. 2. Cambridge, MA: Peabody Museum of American Archaeology and Ethnology, Harvard University, 1897.

Velázquez Valadez, Ricardo. *Loltún, Yucatán.* Mexico: Instituto Nacional de Antropología e Historia, 1991.

Zavala Ruiz, Roberto, Luis Millet Cámara, Ricardo Velázquez Valadez, and Roberto MacSwiney. *Guía de las grutas de Loltún, Oxkutzcab, Yucatán.* México, D.F., México: SEP, Instituto Nacional de Antropología e Historia, 1978.

■ WALTER R. T. WITSCHEY

LOWLANDS

See CENTRAL LOWLANDS; NORTHERN LOWLANDS; SOUTHERN LOWLANDS

M

MAIZE

See DIET; SUBSISTENCE

MARKETS AND MARKETPLACES

At archaeological sites across **Mesoamerica** (southern **Mexico** and northern Central America) the distribution of stone, sea shell, and pottery artifacts from distant places of origin provides evidence of trade, but that is only one aspect of the ancient Maya economic system. Trade of **obsidian** from distant volcanoes demonstrates the interconnection between populations. Exotic goods found in **house** groups of commoners indicate possible trade for all levels of Maya society. Pottery trade is documented along many explicit routes, such as the 100-km-long **causeway** between **Cobá** and **Yaxuná**. Were high-value trade items distributed to the people by the king in a system of tribute and redistribution, or was there a market-based system of exchange between buyers and sellers at designated marketplaces?

Europeans reported elaborate marketplaces and merchant activities in the open plazas of population centers at the time of conquest (sixteenth and seventeenth centuries). Throughout Mesoamerica today there are designated market days on which vendors display and sell products in designated portions of open-air marketplaces. At the end of each market day, both unsold merchandise and the tables and awnings are packed up and removed from the marketplace.

Archaeological evidence of ancient Maya marketplaces has been difficult to discover. Artifacts would not have been left behind at open marketplaces, and most of the merchandise was perishable and did not survive to become part of the archaeological record. In recent studies, the configuration of some plazas and open spaces within ancient Maya sites has supported the hypothesis that marketplaces existed. The configurational approach is based on similar attributes that are found at both ancient and contemporary marketplaces. These attributes include proximity to population centers at the largest communities; high traffic areas at the termini and intersections of causeways (*sacbeob*) and major pathways; adjacent public structures such as temples and **ball courts**, where crowds would gather for public events; and proximity to public amenities such as water wells and reservoirs.

Another important source of evidence for marketplace activity in plazas has been found in the geochemical traces of food items and manufactured goods that were traded on the soils and floors of these open marketplaces over many years.

Phosphorus and trace elements contained in perishable food items that were spilled and pressed into the floor are relatively insoluble and remain fixed on the surfaces of soil particles following decomposition. Geochemical distribution of element concentrations is spatially analyzed and graphically plotted to outline areas within the plaza that were the site of long-term marketing of specific items. Elevated levels of phosphorus and zinc have been discovered in portions of plaza floors, and in some cases, linear patterns of phosphorus and zinc concentrations were discovered in parallel lines across the plaza. These patterns suggest a linear arrangement of vendors across the plaza, selling vegetables and other foods. In other portions of plaza floors, elevated levels of copper, iron, and manganese have been discovered that likely originated with the display and sale of mineral substances or items that were painted with mineral pigments.

Both configurational and geochemical evidence of Maya marketplaces have been reported at plazas and open spaces within the ancient sites of Motul de San Jose and Trinidad de Nosotros, in the Department of Petén, **Guatemala**, and at the satellite center of Conchita near **Caracol**, Belize. Positive evidence of marketplaces has also been reported at **Chunchucmil** and **Cobá** on the Yucatan Peninsula. Similar configurational and geochemical patterns of marketplace activities have been reported for the contemporary open-air market at Antigua, Guatemala.

See also CALAKMUL; CAVES; DIET; EL CHAYAL; FAUNA; GROUND SURVEY TECHNIQUES; IXTEPEQUE; JAINA; MAYAPÁN; PORTABLE OBJECTS; SETTLEMENT PATTERNS; SOILS; SUBSISTENCE; TIHO; TRIBUTE; VEGETATION

Further Reading

Chase, Diane Z., and Arlen F. Chase. "Ancient Maya Markets and the Economic Integration of Caracol, Belize." *Ancient Mesoamerica* 25, no. 1: 239–50, 2014.

Coronel, E. G., Scott R. Hutson, Aline Magnoni, Austin Ulmer, and Richard E. Terry. "Geochemical Analysis of Late Classic and Post Classic Maya Marketplace Activities at the Plazas of Cobá, Mexico." *Journal of Field Archaeology* 40(1): 89–109, 2015.

Dahlin, Bruce H., Daniel Bair, Timothy Beach, Matthew Moriarty, and Richard Terry. "The Dirt on Food: Ancient Feasts and Markets among the Lowland Maya." In *Pre-Columbian Foodways: Interdisciplinary Approaches to Food, Culture, and Markets in Ancient Mesoamerica; University of Calgary Archaeological Association Conference*, edited by John E. Staller and Michael D. Carrasco. New York: Springer, 2009.

Dahlin, Bruce H., Christopher T. Jensen, Richard E. Terry, David R. Wright, and Timothy Beach. "In Search of an Ancient Maya Market." *Latin American Antiquity* 18, no. 4: 363–84, 2007.

Masson, Marilyn A., and David A. Freidel. "An Argument of Classic Era Maya Market Exchange." *Journal of Anthropological Archaeology* 31: 455–84, 2012.

Shaw, Leslie C. "The Elusive Maya Marketplace: An Archaeological Consideration of the Evidence." *Journal of Archaeological Research* 20, no. 2: 117–55, 2012.

■ AUSTIN ULMER AND RICHARD E. TERRY

MARRIAGE

See KINSHIP; RITES AND RITUALS

MATHEMATICS

The ancient Maya **calendar** system used a modified base-20 (vigesimal) counting system of strictly integers, including place values, and the concept of zero. Maya numerals were most typically written with three symbols. A shell stood for zero, and bar-and-dot combinations stood for the values from one to nineteen. For example, one was written as one dot; two as two dots. Five was written with a bar. Six used a bar and a dot. Ten was two bars; seventeen required three bars and two dots. When the count reached 19 (17 in the second place in the Long Count) the count carried into the next position. Thus, when the count in the units position reached 19, the next number consisted of a one in the 20s position, and a zero in the units position.

The Maya Long Count consisted of five places, named and with appropriate glyphs in the writing system. Starting in the low order position, the units position was called *k'in* (the word for day or sun). The second position, which counted 20s, was called *uinal*. The third, fourth, and fifth positions were called *tun* (groups of 360), *k'atun* (groups of 7,200 days, about 20 years), and *b'ak'tun* (groups of 144,000 days, about 400 years).

In the inscriptions, Maya dates are typically written as a vertical column, *b'ak'tuns* on top, *k'in* on the bottom, or in a two-column stack, alternating left-right and downward, again with *b'ak'tuns* first and *k'in* last. When written in Latin letters, modern usage writes Maya numbers with each place separated by a period. Thus 9.17.15.3.12 stands for 9 *b'ak'tuns*, 17 *k'atuns*, 15 *tuns*, 3 *uinals*, and 12 *k'in*. Mathematically this is $(9 \times 144,000$ days$)$ + $(17 \times 7,200$ days$)$ + $(15 \times 360$ days$)$ + $(3 \times 20$ days$)$ + 12 = 1,423,872 days since the start of the Long Count calendar on August 11, 3114 BC.

It is common in the inscriptions to find short numbers (*tun*, *uinal*, *k'in* combinations) that count forward or backward by adding to or subtracting from a larger Long Count date. Thus, a dated monument often shows economy of carving by presenting one Long Count date, and short counts to refer to other dates near it.

Maya scribes had great freedom of expression in how they wrote the ancient script. In some cases, numerals were represented by faces, or even full figures, rather than bars and dots. Dates written in the modified base-20 system appear at least as early as the Late Formative. There are some inscriptions that carry numerals in the sixth, seventh, and eighth positions. Clearly the ancient royal scribes were enthralled by timekeeping and used their sophisticated number system to count days and relate the counts to the sun and moon cycles, and to the orbits of the planets Venus and Mars.

Diego de Landa said that the number system was used for counting, as in the trade of **cacao** beans. There are no known instances of the use of the place value system with zeroes, as found in the calendar, for doing math about objects. As David Stuart points out, when counts are mentioned, they refer to a specific large quantity, such as tribute of $5 \times 8,000 = 40,000$ cacao beans, using a specific glyph for 8,000 with a multiplier of 5. There are no lower-order positions shown in the tally smaller than 8,000. These references are our only clues to uses of higher order unmodified base-20 values for noncalendric counting.

In sum, the Maya devised an elaborate counting system. When counting objects, it appears to use an unmodified set of base-20 counts, but not place values and zeroes. When used for the Long Count calendar with zeroes and positional place values, it was modified in the second position to count to 360, not 400, and could extend to the furthest reaches of time, including mythological dates in the ancient past and in the far-distant future.

See also CODICES (MAYA); DECIPHERMENT; STELA

Further Reading

Stuart, David. *The Misunderstanding of Maya Math*. Austin, TX: Wordpress, 2012. http://decipherment .wordpress.com/2012/05/02/the-misunderstanding-of-maya-math/.

Tozzer, Alfred M. *Landa's "Relación de las cosas de Yucatán": A Translation*. Papers of the Peabody Museum of American Archaeology and Ethnology, vol. 18. Cambridge, MA: Harvard University, 1941.

■ WALTER R. T. WITSCHEY

MAYA AREA

The Maya region is a unified geographic area in which the archaeological remains of the cities and settlements of the ancient Maya culture are found (see also **Map 2**). It is also the area in which the modern descendants of the ancient Maya are found living today. It includes the Yucatan Peninsula and the land south of it stretching to the **Pacific coast**. In terms of modern nations, this region includes the eastern portion of **Mexico** (east of the Isthmus of Tehuantepec), all of **Belize** and **Guatemala**, and the western portions of **Honduras** and **El Salvador**.

Although the coastal perimeter (Pacific Ocean, Gulf of Mexico, and Caribbean Sea) forms clear boundaries to the north and south of the Maya area, the land-based eastern and western borders are uncertain and somewhat fluid over time. Chiapas and Guatemala coasts on the Pacific were settled by speakers of non-Maya languages and formed a rich ethnic mix with unclear boundaries there. Western sites along the perimeter of the area include **Comalcalco** on the Gulf Coast, **Toniná**, and **Palenque**, and sites in Chiapas west of Tuxtla Gutiérrez. On the eastern border, running from the Bay of Honduras to the south-southwest, the Maya area is generally bordered by the ancient cities **Quiriguá**, **Copán**, and Chalchuapa, and portions of western Honduras and western El Salvador.

Further Reading

Coe, Michael D. *The Maya*. 8th ed. London: Thames & Hudson, 2011.

Evans, Susan Toby. *Ancient Mesoamerica & Central America: Archaeology and Culture History*. 2nd ed. London: Thames & Hudson, 2008.

Sharer, Robert J., and Loa P. Traxler. *The Ancient Maya*. 6th ed. Stanford, CA: Stanford University Press, 2006.

■ WALTER R. T. WITSCHEY

MAYA QUEENS

Royal women are well represented in the archaeological, epigraphic, and iconographic record in the Maya lowlands. They were first identified in mortuary contexts during the Late Preclassic period (400 BC–AD 150). **Tikal** Burial 166, dated to 50 BC, is the earliest formal vaulted tomb at Tikal (see also **Royal Tombs**). The tomb is located in Structure 5D-sub 11 and contained the remains of two women and 20 **ceramic** vessels. The incorporation of Burial 166 into the **architecture** of the newly formed North Acropolis established this place as the principal **burial** ground for Tikal's rulers.

During the Early Classic (AD 150–550), Ix (Lady) Yok'in of Tikal was one of the few queens portrayed on public monuments. She was an enigmatic figure who ruled from AD 511 to 527(?), although it is doubtful that she ever ruled independently. Nonetheless, Ix Yok'in is mentioned on three **stelae** (Tikal Stelae 6, 12, and 23) during her reign and may be depicted on a fourth (Tikal Stela 25), which was commissioned by her husband and coregent, Kaloomte B'alam.

More Early Classic queens were afforded entombment in religious structures and royal **palaces**. At least nine tombs or cysts containing royal women have been discovered to date, including Tikal Burial 162, **El Perú–Waka'** Burial 25, **Copán** Motmot tomb, and **Rio Azul** Tomb 25. One of the richest interments from the Early Classic was found in the Copán Margarita tomb. Dated to the early fifth century, the tomb contained the remains of a local woman aged 50–60 years. The tomb itself consisted of two chambers, an upper offering chamber and a lower burial chamber. The queen's body was placed in an extended position on stone slab with her head facing south. The body may have been defleshed prior to burial, as the bones were embedded in and covered with cinnabar. The queen wore a massive jade, shell, and pearl necklace; jade ear flares; and double-stranded jade armbands. She also wore an elaborate belt of jade beads, shells, and bird heads. Sixteen ceramic vessels and two pyrite mirrors were placed on the floor surrounding the slab. Additional burial offerings included stuccoed baskets, jade and mother of pearl ear flares, bone needles, and more ceramic vessels, as well as many other elaborately crafted objects. Clearly this queen, who may have been the wife of Kinich Yax K'uk Mo', the founder of the dynasty, was highly respected and admired during her lifetime.

During the Late Classic (AD 550–900), the presence of royal women in public art and public mortuary contexts grew. Also, the manner in which they were portrayed, conducting rituals, dedicating stelae, and capturing prisoners, signifies the new level of power and authority commanded by royal women.

Many queens appear to have ruled without male consorts. Perhaps the best-known example is Ix Wak Chan Ajaw of **Naranjo**, who ruled from AD 682 to 741, both independently and as coregent with her son. She is depicted as a warrior standing on the back of her captive, K'inichil Kab of Ucanal, on Stela 24, which was dedicated in AD 699 (see also **Warfare, Warriors, and Weapons**).

Another warrior queen, Ix K'awiil Ek of **Cobá**, also appears to have ruled independently of a male consort. On Stela 1 (AD 682), Ix K'awiil Ek appears on both front and back panels, a unique occurrence for a queen. She holds an elaborate ceremonial bar across her chest on both sides and stands atop two diminutive bound captives.

Queens are also depicted as powerful rulers in partnership with their husbands. Ruling couples were very prominent at **Calakmul**, seat of the powerful Kaan kings during the Late Classic period, and at sites affiliated with Calakmul. For example, Ix K'abel of El Perú-Waka' ruled from AD 672 to 692 with her husband, K'inich B'alam II. She is portrayed carrying a shield and wearing a war headdress on Stela 34, the companion to Stela 33, which depicts her husband. As the sister of Yich'aak K'ahk', the king of Kaan, Ix K'abel's marriage to K'inich B'alam II solidified the **alliance** between these two kingdoms in the late seventh century. Because of her powerful family connections, Ix K'abel appears to have outranked her husband, as she is named in the accompanying inscriptions as an Ix Kaloomte, the most high-ranking title in Maya politics.

Recently, in Ix K'abel's tomb was discovered an important temple that was the focus of ritual activity for generations after the abandonment of El Perú-Waka'. A carved alabaster jar with her name inscribed on the surface was recovered next to the body of a mature woman. Other funerary offerings included roughly 21 ceramic vessels, a large Spondylus shell, and many carved jade and shell artifacts.

During the Postclassic (AD 900–1521) period, queens all but disappear from the archaeological record. This is likely due to the changes in the roles of kings and queens during this period.

See also DECIPHERMENT; PORTABLE OBJECTS

Further Reading

Ardren, Traci, ed. *Ancient Maya Women.* Walnut Creek, CA: AltaMira Press, 2002.

Joyce, Rosemary A. *Gender and Power in Prehispanic Mesoamerica.* Austin: University of Texas Press, 2000.

Martin, Simon. "The Queen of Middle Classic Tikal." *Pre-Columbian Art Research Institute Journal* 27: 4–5, 1999.

Martin, Simon, and Nikolai Grube. *Chronicle of the Maya Kings and Queens: Deciphering the Dynasties of the Ancient Maya.* 2nd ed. London: Thames & Hudson, 2008.

Reese-Taylor, Kathryn, Peter Mathews, Julia Guernsey, and Marlene Fritzler. "Warrior Queens Among the Classic Maya." In *Blood and Beauty: Organized Violence in the Art and Archaeology of Mesoamerica and Central America*, edited by Heather S. Orr and Rex Koontz. Los Angeles, CA: Cotsen Institute of Archaeology Press, 2009.

■ KATHRYN REESE-TAYLOR

MAYAPÁN

Mayapán (20.6° N, 89.5° W) was the largest political capital of the Late Postclassic Maya realm. It is located in the west-central portion of the modern **Mexico** state of Yucatan, about 40 km south of the city of Mérida, adjacent to the Mérida-Chetumal highway and 1 km south of the village of Telchaquillo (see also **Map 3**).

Mayapán represents one of the most densely populated urban sites in pre-Columbian Maya history. The principal residential zone encompassed a 4.2 km² area, enclosed by a tall stone wall 9.1 km in circumference that was entered through 12 formal gates (see also **Fortifications**). Residential density is as high as 77–126 people per ha in the downtown

Figure 28. Aerial view of the center of Mayapán, Yucatan, Mexico, in 2013. The cleared area of restorations is about 200 m wide by 150 m long. Beneath the trees and fields, the portion of the site within the city wall extends 3.5 km by 2 km. Photo courtesy of Marilyn Masson.

zone. Today, the urban settlement zone is under forest cover, but the monumental center is open for tourism. The city's largest edifice is the Temple of Kukulcan, 15 m tall. Far eastern Gate H is marked by the second largest **pyramid** in the Itzmal Ch'en ceremonial group. Dispersed agrarian **houses** are found around the city wall to a distance of 500 m. Mayapán was home to 15,000–17,000 persons. (See figure 28.)

This site is situated within the sprawling **Chicxulub** crater that affected this part of Yucatan and created an especially high density of **caves** and **cenotes** that provide access to underground water sources (see also **Groundwater/Water Table**; **Water Management**). The city's topography is characterized by numerous small hillocks that were often modified into rectangular house platforms.

Research at Mayapán was performed by the Carnegie Institution of Washington in the 1950s, followed by Clifford Brown, who wrote a dissertation in 1999 at Tulane University on the city's social organization (see also **Class Structure**). More recently, Carlos Peraza Lope of INAH has directed the restoration of the monumental center (1996 to present). The Economic Foundations of Mayapán Project (2001 to present), overseen by Marilyn Masson, Carlos Peraza Lope, and Timothy Hare, has reconstructed the complex nature of urban life and household economy at the city. In 2013 this team conducted a **LiDAR** remote-sensing survey of 40 km² surrounding the site and discovered hundreds of houses, cenotes, and public buildings that reflect a 2,000-year history of local human occupation and landscape transformation.

Mayapán dates to the Postclassic period, AD 1150–1461. The city was rapidly founded by a confederacy government that united the influential polities of Yucatan. These governors constructed monumental buildings and resettled subject peoples to the city in order to support a robust urban economy. Prior to the rise of this capital, the area was heavily occupied by dispersed yet relatively continuous agrarian households of Late Preclassic through Terminal Classic date. Before Mayapán, this location was a rural backwater that was at least 30 km distant from Yaxcopoil, the nearest Rank II political center.

The Postclassic era urban zone was administered by elites who held myriad political and religious offices. Outlying monumental groups such as Itzmal Ch'en replicated functions of the site center and integrated residential activities with the initiatives of the central government. Stone lanes encircled most of Mayapán's dwelling groups, and they formed major and minor thoroughfares that guided pedestrians through neighborhoods and from gates to key interior features such as a **market** plaza, the principal *sacbe* (see also **Causeway/Sacbe**), and the site center. Commoners living at Mayapán engaged in a variety of occupations, working out of their homes on pursuits that included surplus **craft** and food production, military service, farming, deer and turkey husbandry (see also **Subsistence**), making lime plaster, and working in construction. Households were heavily dependent on one another and on regional market trade for the essentials of daily life.

One extraordinary fact about Mayapán is that it collapsed (~AD 1458) less than one century before the Spanish conquest (AD 1542). The recollections of descendants of this city's population were written down by chroniclers in the Colonial period. Rich documentary accounts, along with archaeological research, make Mayapán an ideal place for interdisciplinary research. Mayapán collapsed due to **warfare** among members of the confederacy's ruling council, aggravated by many decades of **drought** and crop shortages.

See also ARCHITECTURAL OVERVIEW; COUNCIL HOUSE; CRAFT SPECIALIZATION; MARKETS AND MARKETPLACES; RITES AND RITUALS; TULUM; UXMAL; ZACPETÉN

Further Reading

Brown, Clifford T. "Mayapán Society and Ancient Maya Social Organization." PhD diss., Tulane University, 1999.

Masson, Marilyn A. *The Economic Foundations of Mayapán, Yucatan* (and documentary film links). Institute for Mesoamerican Studies, University of Albany, State University of New York, 2014. http://www.albany.edu/ims/mayapan.html.

Masson, Marilyn A., and Carlos Peraza Lope. *Kukulcan's Realm: Urban Life at Ancient Mayapán*. Boulder: University Press of Colorado, 2014.

Pollock, Harry E. D., Ralph L. Roys, Tatiana Proskouriakoff, and A. Ledyard Smith. *Mayapán, Yucatan, Mexico*. Carnegie Institution of Washington, Publication 619. Washington, DC: Carnegie Institution of Washington, 1962.

Russell, Bradley W. "Postclassic Settlement on the Rural-Urban Fringe of Mayapán, Yucatán." PhD diss., University at Albany, State University of New York, 2008.

Tozzer, Alfred M. *Landa's "Relación de las cosas de Yucatán": A Translation*. Papers of the Peabody Museum of American Archaeology and Ethnology, vol. 18. Cambridge, MA: Harvard University, 1941.

■ MARILYN MASSON

MEDICINAL PLANTS

See MEDICINE; VEGETATION

MEDICINE

The Maya notion of good health is based on completeness, wholeness. Disease then is an absence or missing element in one's spirit or soul. Curing is a mixture of science and **religion** to restore what is missing. Our knowledge of ancient medicines and medical practice today is a combination of archaeologically derived information and modern ethnography and ethno-botanical studies (see also **Vegetation**).

Curers (*h-men* = a man, or *x-men* = a woman) used their understanding of the sick person, based on interview and observation, to establish a course of action. Spiritual action meant to intervene with the gods, to conduct ritual ceremonies with prayers, offerings, and blood sacrifice to cleanse the disease, sometimes by transference to an animal, which was then sacrificed. Direct action meant to apply physical medical intervention such as suturing, bone-setting, trephining (trepanning), and administration of plant- and animal-based medicines by herbal tea infusions, poultices, direct eating, smoking, inhaling, or enema.

See also DEITIES; FAUNA; PHYSICAL/BIOLOGICAL ANTHROPOLOGY; RELIGION; RITES AND RITUALS

Further Reading

Ankli, Anita, Otto Sticher, and Michael Heinrich. "Yucatec Maya Medicinal Plants Versus Nonmedicinal Plants: Indigenous Characterization and Selection." *Human Ecology* 27, no. 4: 557–80, 1999.

Bolles, David, and Alejandra Bolles. *A Grammar of the Yucatecan Mayan Language: Ritual of the Bacabs.* Foundation for the Advancement of Mesoamerican Studies, Inc. (FAMSI), 2003. http://www.famsi.org/reports/96072/grammar/section32.htm.

Kunow, Marienna Appel. *Maya Medicine: Traditional Healing in Yucatan.* Albuquerque: University of New Mexico Press, 2003.

Schuster, Angela M. H. "On the Healer's Path." *Archaeology* 54, no. 4: 34–38, 2001.

Stuart, David. *On the Paired Variants of TZ'AK.* Mesoweb, 2003. http://www.mesoweb.com/stuart/notes/tzak.pdf.

■ WALTER R. T. WITSCHEY

MESOAMERICA

The Maya region is totally encompassed by the larger culture area of Mesoamerica, a region within which the inhabitants share many or most elements of a cultural tradition. Though it corresponds to no single modern nation-state, Mesoamerica as a concept finds universal use among social scientists because it describes an area with a common pattern of life and heritage, where people share languages, foods, religions, and technologies, and where they have engaged socially, politically, militarily, and economically for thousands of years. Although scholars sometimes debate the definition of Mesoamerica and the details of its boundaries, they agree that it encompasses central, southern, and eastern **Mexico**; all of **Guatemala** and **Belize**; and at least western **Honduras** and **El Salvador**.

Coherency of culture, that is, shared "culture traits," was used first by Paul Kirchhoff in the 1940s to describe a region he called "Mesoamerica" ("between the Americas," formerly called, less precisely, "Middle America"). The region was an obviously important study area filled with archaeological remains and lingering traces of great ancient civilizations, but one that was not well defined by modern political boundaries. He identified numerous cultural features, such as the unique **calendar** and the ubiquitous ritual **ball game**, that were shared across a wide region of southern Mexico and northern Central America. He used the appearance of these shared culture traits to establish boundaries for Mesoamerica.

The region he defined is clearly bounded on the south and west by the Pacific Ocean and to the north and east by the Gulf of Mexico and the Caribbean Sea. The boundaries on land are less well defined. To the north, Mesoamerica includes the Basin of Mexico (modern Mexico City, D.F., and the eastern part of the state of Mexico, and coastal areas along the Pacific and the Gulf stretching farther north in a broad "U"). The northern boundary separates the more complex agricultural peoples of Mesoamerica from the desert cultures of northern Mexico and the American Southwest. Kirchhoff's southern boundary of Mesoamerica runs from the Caribbean near Puerto Cortes in western Honduras southward to include El Salvador and then southeast, encompassing the Pacific region of Nicaragua and the Nicoya region of Costa Rica. While data developed in the 70 years subsequent to Kirchhoff's paper suggest variations in the north and southeast land boundaries, the basic suite of traits and the major area he called Mesoamerica remain little changed.

Mesoamerica is an unusually interesting area. Its landscape is varied and picturesque. It runs the gamut from deserts to tropical jungles and alpine forests, from **caves** to volcanoes. Its diverse languages and cultures often seem exotic to outsiders. It includes the land of the ancient **Maya** to the east and south; the land of the **Olmec** on the southern coast of the Gulf of Mexico; and the areas controlled by the Aztecs, Toltecs, and Teotihuacanos in central Mexico. The ancient Maya were a part of this rich cultural heritage that extended beyond their own lands.

Millions of foreigners visit the countries of Mesoamerica each year, often with the goal of enjoying those cultures and admiring their archaeological and historical heritage. The archaeological sites alone attract millions of visits per year. Mexico currently has 32 properties inscribed on UNESCO's World Heritage Site list.

Mesoamerica excites not only popular interest but also scholarly attention, particularly to its history, heritage, and archaeology. The idea of Mesoamerica evokes images of **pyramids**, **palaces**, and hieroglyphic inscriptions. Thousands of archaeologists, epigraphers, architects, and historians, local and domestic, have dedicated their careers to the study of ancient Mesoamerica.

See also Ball Game/Ball Court; Calendar; Caves; Ceibal; Champotón; Classic Maya Collapse; Climate; Copán; Cotzumalhuapa; Deities; Diet; Eccentric Lithics; El Chayal; Fauna; Groundwater/Water Table; Ixtepeque; Jaina; Kaminaljuyú; Knorosov, Yuri Valentinovich; LiDAR; Markets and Marketplaces; Mexico; Obsidian; Olmec-Maya Interactions; Palace; Puuc Architectural Style; Rejollada; San Bartolo;

SOUTHERN PERIPHERY; TEOTIHUACÁN (MAYA INTERACTIONS WITH); TIKAL; TRIBUTE; TULUM; UAXACTUN; UTATLÁN/Q'UM'ARKAJ; WRITING SYSTEMS OF MESOAMERICA

Further Reading

Evans, Susan Toby. *Ancient Mesoamerica & Central America: Archaeology and Culture History*. 2nd ed. London: Thames & Hudson, 2008.

Kirchhoff, Paul. "Mesoamérica, sus límites geográficos, composición étnica y caracteres culturales." *Acta Americana* 1, no. 1: 92–107, 1943.

Sharer, Robert J., and Loa P. Traxler. *The Ancient Maya*. 6th ed. Stanford, CA: Stanford University Press, 2006.

Witschey, Walter R. T., and Clifford T. Brown. *Historical Dictionary of Mesoamerica*. Edited by Jon Woronoff. Historical Dictionaries of Ancient Civilizations and Historical Eras. Lanham, MD: Scarecrow Press, 2012.

■ CLIFFORD T. BROWN AND WALTER R. T. WITSCHEY

MEXICO

The modern nation of Mexico, bordered by the United States to the north and **Guatemala** and **Belize** to the south, includes the northern region of Mesoamerica and was home to several important pre-Hispanic cultures.

Mexican **cave** sites document the continent's earliest settlers. By Early Formative times sophisticated culture and major cities began to blossom. At the southernmost shore of the Gulf of Mexico, the Isthmus of Tehuantepec, the **Olmec** culture flourished from 1500 BC onward. The first major Olmec city, San Lorenzo Tenochtitlan, dominated the region for 600 years. By 900 BC, La Venta was the foremost Olmec city. As La Venta declined around 400 BC, the contemporaneous site of Tres Zapotes grew in size and evolved into an epi-Olmec culture during the Late Formative.

The largest pre-Hispanic city in the new world, indeed, possibly in the entire world at the time, **Teotihuacán**, is situated about 45 km northeast of Mexico City, in an area rapidly becoming modern suburbs of that great metropolis. Teotihuacanos began constructing monumental architecture at the site around 150–100 BC. Much of the major construction at the site, such as the **Pyramid** of the Sun, the Pyramid of the Moon, the channelized San Juan River, and the Street of the Dead and its residences, was completed by AD 400. Teotihuacán was destroyed by fire and abandoned by AD 550. The far-reaching influence of Teotihuacán affected numerous Maya cities, among them **Tikal** and **Kaminaljuyú**.

In the Maya territory of eastern Mexico, early cities appear along the **Pacific coast** of Chiapas and in northwest Yucatan. Indeed, as archaeological work continues, later major Mexican sites in the Classic and Postclassic include **Comalcalco**, **Yaxchilan**, **Uxmal**, **Izamal**, **Chichen Itza**, and **Cobá**, among many others.

In central Mexico, the Zapotec culture built Monte Alban and Mitla in the Oaxaca valley. Monte Alban was occupied by 500 BC and flourished for 1,000 years thereafter. Tula, in the state of Hidalgo, home to the Toltec culture, was settled at the end of the Middle Formative and grew in a settlement called Tula Chico, ultimately abandoned in favor of Tula Grande about AD 850. Tula Grande expanded vigorously until about AD 1100, in part filling the power vacuum in the Basin of Mexico left by the fall of Teotihuacán. Tula Grande shared numerous architectural and **iconographic** features with Chichen Itza, its distant Maya neighbor on the Yucatan peninsula.

By AD 1300, people from north of Mexico City moved south into the basin, establishing their principal settlement, Tenochtitlan, on an island in Lake Texcoco. These warriors were the heart of the growing Aztec Empire, which ultimately ruled the basin and many areas around it. The empire was expanding when the Spaniards arrived in 1519. Cortés and his small army, sailing from Cuba, landed at Veracruz ("true cross"), allied themselves with Aztec enemies such as the Tlaxcalans, and conquered Tenochtitlan between 1519 and 1521. From there, the Spanish conquerors moved to conquer Guatemala, Yucatan, and ultimately much of the New World.

Among its population of 120 million persons, Mexico counts 60 percent mestizo and about 30 percent Amerindian. Spanish is spoken by 93 percent of the people, and native languages plus Spanish are spoken by about 6.5 percent, including especially Maya in eastern Mexico and Nahuatl (the language of the Aztecs) in central Mexico.

Further Reading

Braswell, Geoffrey E. *The Maya and Teotihuacan: Reinterpreting Early Classic Interaction.* Austin: University of Texas Press, 2004.

Coe, Michael D., and Rex Koontz. *Mexico: From the Olmecs to the Aztecs.* 6th ed. London: Thames & Hudson, 2008.

Evans, Susan Toby. *Ancient Mesoamerica & Central America: Archaeology and Culture History.* 2nd ed. London: Thames & Hudson, 2008.

Millon, René. "Teotihuacan: City, State, and Civilization." In *Supplement to the Handbook of Middle American Indians*, no. 1, edited by Victoria R. Bricker and Jeremy A. Sabloff, 198–243. Austin: University of Texas Press, 1981.

U.S. Central Intelligence Agency. *The World Factbook, North America: Mexico.* 2014. https://www.cia.gov/library/publications/the-world-factbook/geos/mx.html.

■ WALTER R. T. WITSCHEY

MIDDLE CLASSIC HIATUS

The Middle Classic Hiatus refers to the years AD 537 to 672, when a pause occurred in monumental construction and **stelae** carving at the ancient Maya city of **Tikal**, Guatemala. More broadly, it was once thought to represent a temporary cultural decline across the southern Maya lowlands. Nonetheless, the phenomenon was limited to Tikal and its close allies and related to a surge in the importance of the Kaan (Snake) Kingdom, eventually located at **Calakmul** (see also **Alliances**).

Sylvanus G. Morley was among the first to write about the Hiatus, which he dated to AD 534–593 across the **Maya region** and until AD 692 at Tikal. Later scholars also noted significant changes to **burial** offerings at Tikal during this interval. Impoverished elite tombs dating to the Hiatus were interpreted as the result of economic crisis (see also **Royal Tombs**). The loss of **trade routes** and the decline of wealth at Tikal was once seen a consequence of the fall of **Teotihuacán** in central Mexico. Gordon Willey noted that the gap in recorded history and the impoverishment of material culture affected only the **Southern Lowlands** and speculated that the same factors that caused the hiatus eventually led to the **Classic Maya collapse** and abandonment of much of the Maya area.

More recent excavations, together with better understanding of hieroglyphic texts, provide a new perspective. The temporary downturn of Tikal is now interpreted in terms of relations with other Maya centers rather than with Teotihuacán. Moreover, paleoclimate research by James Webster demonstrates that **drought** was not a cause of the hiatus, as some have argued. Before and during the hiatus, rainfall was within the normal range (see also **Map 5**; **Climate**). A refined chronology based on new epigraphic data also has been proposed (see also **Decipherment**).

One of the oldest and most powerful Classic Maya states, Tikal entered a period of political instability with the death of the ruler Chak Tok Ich'aak II in AD 508. Ix Kaloo'mte' Ix Yok'in ("Lady of Tikal") became the new ruler in AD 510. The accession of a six-year-old girl marked the end of the male dynastic line founded by Yax Nuun Ahyiin I in AD 379 and may have spurred a political crisis. The Lady of Tikal probably had a male coruler, an older consort, or a guardian, named Kaloomte' B'ahlam. In AD 527 the Lady of Tikal appeared on **Stela** 8, attributed to the lord "Bird Claw," thought to be the twentieth Tikal ruler. Under his supervision, the huge East Acropolis and the first twin **pyramid** complex of Tikal were built.

After this, there is a gap in the record until the celebration of the twentieth anniversary of the accession of Wak Chan K'awiil ("Double Bird") in AD 557 on Stela 17. This king may have been a son of Chak Tok Ich'aak II who managed to return from exile and gain the throne in AD 537. That year is often considered to mark the beginning of the Middle Classic Hiatus.

Nonetheless, records of Tikal's fortunes are preserved at other sites. A very important source for following events is **Caracol** Altar 21 (see figure 29). In AD 553, Wak Chan K'awiil of Tikal installed Yajaw Te' K'inich II as ruler of Caracol. But just three years later, Tikal's influence on Caracol ended when the ruler of that site switched his allegiance to the Kaan (Snake) Lords (later based at Calakmul). Caracol Altar 21 mentions how Tikal suffered a major defeat in AD 562 orchestrated by the Snake Lords. Wak Chan K'awiil was captured and presumably sacrificed. This defeat is often assumed to be a cause of the Tikal hiatus, but it is equally possible that it was merely a symptom of the greatly reduced power of the kingdom after the end of the dynastic line 54 years earlier.

The death of Wak Chan K'awiil ushered in a long "dark age." The next dated monument was erected at Tikal in AD 672. The twenty-second ruler of Tikal, K'ihnich Waaw ("Animal Skull"), is known only from pottery and a painted board found within his tomb, Burial 195. It is doubtful that he was from the previous royal lineage, because texts emphasize his mother's line, and his father had no royal title. Animal Skull is thought to have built Temple V, the tallest pyramid at Tikal constructed since the Late Preclassic period. He died in AD 593 in middle age. Both the twenty-third and twenty-fourth Tikal rulers are missing from the dynastic sequence.

Nuun Ujol Chaak, the twenty-fifth ruler, has no surviving monuments but is first mentioned in AD 657 when he fled from Tikal during an attack orchestrated by Yuknoom Ch'een the Great of Calakmul and carried out by B'alaj Chan K'awiil of **Dos**

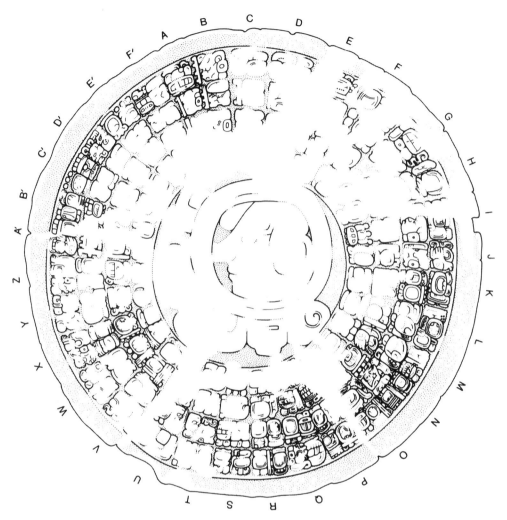

Figure 29. Caracol Altar 21. Glyphs R2b–Q3 describe the defeat of Tikal and the highly eroded glyphs Q4–R4 name the perpetrator of that act, possibly "Sky Witness," Divine Snake Lord. Inked by Karen Kievit from a drawing by Stephen Houston for the Caracol Archaeological Project. Courtesy of the Caracol Archaeological Project.

Pilas. It has long been argued that in AD 659, the exiled Nuun Ujol Chaak visited the famous king K'inich Janaab' **Pakal** at Palenque. Nonetheless, newer readings imply that the Nuun Ujol Chaak mentioned in Palenque inscriptions was a namesake of the Tikal king from the "Wa-Bird" polity of Santa Elena Balancan.

The end of the hiatus at Tikal dates to AD 672, when that site waged an effective military campaign against **Dos Pilas**. Even though it was followed by defeats in AD 677 and 679, the lineage of Nuun Ujol Chaak was not overthrown. The complete resurrection of Tikal dates to the reign of his son Jasaw Chan K'awiil I, whose victory over Calakmul in AD 695 is recorded on two carved wooden lintels inside Tikal Temple I.

Although monuments were not erected at Tikal during the hiatus, epigraphic evidence from other Maya sites proves that local and regional processes—rather than the decline of **Teotihuacán** or climatic deterioration—played central roles in Tikal's hiatus. The Middle Classic Hiatus was not a stagnant or static era, but one of great change and reorganization. Emerging from the hiatus, Tikal experienced a great revival during the eighth century and once again was a great power.

See also CALAKMUL; CEIBAL; CLASSIC MAYA COLLAPSE; CLIMATE; DOS PILAS; DROUGHT; EL PERÚ-WAKA'; RIO AZUL; WARFARE, WARRIORS, AND WEAPONS

Further Reading

Guenter, Stanley P. "Under a Falling Star: The Hiatus at Tikal." MA thesis, La Trobe University, 2002.

Martin, Simon. "Caracol Altar 21 Revisited: More Data on Double Bird and Tikal's Wars of the Mid-Sixth Century." *The PARI Journal* 6, no. 1: 1–9, 2005.

Martin, Simon, and Nikolai Grube. *Chronicle of the Maya Kings and Queens: Deciphering the Dynasties of the Ancient Maya.* 2nd ed. London: Thames & Hudson, 2008.

Webster, James W. "Speleothem Evidence of Late Holocene Climate Variation in the Maya Lowlands of Belize Central America and Archaeological Implications." PhD diss., University of Georgia, 2000.

Willey, Gordon. "The Classic Maya Hiatus: A 'Rehearsal' for the Collapse?" In *Mesoamerican Archaeology: New Approaches*, edited by Norman Hammond, 417–44. Austin: University of Texas Press, 1974.

■ MAYA AZAROVA

MIRADOR BASIN

The Mirador Basin is an area of seasonally flooded lowlands, *bajos*, in the northern portion of **Guatemala** in the Department of Petén and into southern Campeche to **Calakmul, Mexico**. The basin tends to trap water in low-lying areas, from which it gently flows toward the San Pedro or Candelaria Rivers. Karstic limestone hills form the eastern and southern boundaries of the basin. The basin is home to several of the largest Maya sites, with impressively large architectural complexes, and both Group-E configurations and triadic group pyramids.

Numerous archaeological research projects generally dealing with large Middle (1000–350 BC) and Late (350 BC–AD 150) Formative sites are being pursued in the basin, including those of Richard Hansen, Marcello Canuto, and Kathryn Reese-Taylor, collectively investigating the large Preclassic sites of **El Mirador**, **Nakbé**, Tintal, Wakna, **Naachtun**, and Xulnal. There are many other smaller Classic period settlements, such as La Florida, Maaxte, Zacatal, Chan Kan, Tsab Kan, Pedernal, Isla, La Muerta, and La Muralla. Since most of the large Formative sites were abandoned in the Late Formative about AD 150, the question of what happened and why is the focus of much of the research.

Further Reading

Hansen, Richard D. *Publications and Papers of the Mirador Basin Project* (bibliography). Foundation for Anthropological Research and Environmental Studies (FARES) in collaboration with the Instituto de Antropología e Historia de Guatemala, Ministry of Culture and Sports, 2007. http://www.miradorbasin.com/about/bibliography02-07.pdf.

———. *Mirador Basin Project: The Cradle of Maya civilization*. 2010. http://www.miradorbasin.com/index.php.

Hansen, Richard D., and Renaldo Acevedo. *Investigaciones arqueológicas en Nakbé, Petén: El resumen de la temporada de campo de 1993; Proyecto Regional de Investigaciones Arqueológicas en al Norte del Petén, Guatemala (PREIANPEG) = Regional Archaeological Investigation of the North Petén, Guatemala (RAINPEG): Un proyecto de University of California, Los Angeles, Instituto de Antropología e Historia de Guatemala, National Geographic Society*. Los Angeles: University of California, Los Angeles, 1993.

■ WALTER R. T. WITSCHEY

MONTEREY
See YAXNOHCAH

MUSIC AND DANCE

In a stunning display of power, family relationships, political solidarity, and control of the cosmos, Maya rulers danced in public spectacle. The evidence for music and dance comes from archaeological contexts, including building façades, murals, and **stelae**, as well as **portable objects** such as carved jades and painted ceramics. Since the **decipherment** of the glyph for "to dance," *ahk'ot*, by Nikolai Grube in 1992, many inscriptions from the Late Classic era have been identified with dance ceremonies and associated with the portraits of the principles. Grube's work was preceded by that of Peter Mathews, who identified glyphs for objects or paraphernalia being carried by royal dancers. Stephen Houston also identified glyphs for the elaborate backrack costumes in rulers' portraits.

The murals of **Bonampak** (AD 791) provide an elaborate repertoire of music and dance in two of the three rooms of Str. 1. The entire scene plays out as presentation of a new heir to the throne and preparation for the battle and captive-taking portrayed in Room 2. Music and dancing are part of the preparations, and both a band, with musical instruments, and dancers in elaborate costumes are active participants in front of the royal family and local governors.

The all-male band of twelve includes five men playing gourd rattles, three men playing large turtle shells using deer antlers, two men playing large wooden or paper trumpets, a man standing at a large drum, and one band member carrying a small ceramic drum and a rattle. **Diego de Landa** describes seeing similar instruments shortly after the conquest: small drums played with the hand; large, hollow wood drums; long, thin wooden trumpets with gourd ends; large tortoise shells struck by hand; conch shells (trumpets); and whistles and flutes of deer leg bones and reeds. Room 3 of Bonampak Str. 1 shows the celebration following the battle: dancing, with music provided by the band. There is no evidence of any stringed instruments among the ancient Maya.

In addition to murals of musical instruments in performance, painted **ceramics** provide a view of conch-shell trumpets and friction drums. Occasionally, remains of instruments are found in **burials**, implying music and dance at funerals, and in the excavation of structures near dance platforms. Tikal Burial 10, the tomb of Yax Nuun Ayiin, contained a marimba-like instrument assembled of turtle shells.

In Maya **iconography**, there is a particular pose long called the "Xibalba shuffle." In it, a Maya lord or functionary is shown with feet turned outward and one heel raised off the ground. Today, thanks to the accompanying inscriptions, we know many of these scenes are portrayals of rulers giving a dance performance (see also **Rites and Rituals**; **Theater**). Dances were a critical element of many Maya ceremonies.

Mathew Looper has identified a variety of circumstances in which dances were held and deemed worthy of permanent documentation on stelae or building decorations. He notes that the first mention of dance in the script falls in the Late Classic (AD 653) on Altar L of **Quiriguá**. Most early mentions of dance using glyph T516, from AD 668 to 733, occur at a very few sites: **Dos Pilas**, **Piedras Negras**, **La Corona**, and other sites in the same region. During the years AD 752 to 780, a large number of dance inscriptions occur at **Yaxchilan**, and the murals of nearby Bonampak date to AD 791. A few other instances appear before AD 820.

Looper also observes that, when mentioned in the hieroglyphs, the dancers are male (but occasionally dance with females); they are ruling elites, but occasionally include subordinate governors; and they are always human dancers, not supernaturals. Many of the dances are in a context of sacrificial or offering ceremonies in which the ruler plays a key role. Sacrifices may include human captives or personal bloodletting. There are examples of dances performed for *tun-* and *k'atun*-ending date ceremonies and summer solstice events (see also **Calendar**). In the political realm, dances were given to celebrate birthdays, accession to the throne, building dedication, bloodletting, reception of **tributes**, and military victories. There are signs that many of the dance ceremonies in the **Dos Pilas-Naranjo-Piedras Negras-La Corona** area related to the political organization of this bloc in **alliance** under the **Calakmul** superpower. The inscriptions from Piedras Negras illustrate the combined power of dance as a part of drinking and feasting with royal visitors and celebration of local dynastic historical events.

Dance costumes are elaborately detailed, often with animal or god-figure headdresses and a backrack with an array of long quetzal feathers, and frequently include masking in order to impersonate a particular god (see also **Deities**). Dressed as a god impersonator, a ruler could presume to become the god and speak for it to the audience. Costumes include noise-making elements to add to the music, such as tinklers (shells drilled and suspended together as a belt), and jade celts, also drilled as pendants. Other rich elite goods, such as jaguar pelts, make up the ensemble.

Elites are shown with a variety of handheld devices, beyond drums and rattles. One finds God K manikin-scepters with one foot as a snake, basket-staffs, flapstaffs, and bird staffs, cross-shaped with a descending bird at the top. Dancers are portrayed carrying snakes, or large fans, or war symbols such as shields and axes.

Dance and music played a supremely important ritual function for Maya elites, who in the Late Classic were documenting their importance on building façades, ceramic vessels, and murals.

See also ARCHITECTURE OVERVIEW; ART; COPÁN; COTZUMALHUAPA; DIVINE KINGS AND QUEENS; DOS PILAS; HOLMUL; ICONOGRAPHY; LA CORONA; PORTABLE OBJECTS; PRIESTS; QUIRIGUÁ; THEATER; WALL PAINTING; WARFARE, WARRIORS, AND WEAPONS

Further Reading

Brill, Mark. "Music of the Ancient Maya: New Avenues of Research." In *AMS-SW Conference, "Revisioning the Maya World: New Directions in Scholarship and Teaching"*. Mexico and Belize: American Musicological Society-Southwest Chapter, 2012. http://ams-sw.org/Proceedings/AMS-SW_V1Fall2012Brill.pdf.

Kerr, Justin, and Barbara Kerr. *The Kerr Collections*. Foundation for the Advancement of Mesoamerican Studies, Inc., 2014. Electronic data set. http://www.famsi.org/research/kerr/index.html.

Looper, Matthew George. *To Be Like Gods: Dance in Ancient Maya Civilization*. Austin: University of Texas Press, 2009.

Miller, Mary Ellen. *The Murals of Bonampak*. Princeton, NJ: Princeton University Press, 1986.

Miller, Mary Ellen, and Simon Martin. *Courtly Art of the Ancient Maya*. New York: Thames & Hudson, 2004.

Schele, Linda, and Mary Ellen Miller. *The Blood of Kings: Dynasty and Ritual in Maya Art*. New York and Fort Worth, TX: G. Braziller and the Kimbell Art Museum, 1986.

Tozzer, Alfred M. *Landa's "Relación de las cosas de Yucatán": A Translation*. Papers of the Peabody Museum of American Archaeology and Ethnology, vol. 18. Cambridge, MA: Harvard University, 1941.

■ WALTER R. T. WITSCHEY

MUYIL

Muyil (20.1° N, 87.6° W) is a small Maya archaeological site in the modern state of Quintana Roo, México, 15 minutes south of its better-known neighbor, **Tulum** (see also **Map 3**). The site is centered on a 2-m-deep collapse zone with access to **caves** in the karst.

Muyil was briefly surveyed by the Mason-Spinden Expedition of 1926, then by the amateur explorer Michel Peissel in 1963. The family of E. Wyllys Andrews IV visited several times from 1956 onward, reporting that Muyil looked like a Classic site architecturally, with a Postclassic overlay. Subsequent excavations documented the fact. Walter Witschey and Elia del Carmen Trejo conducted a project of mapping and excavation there between 1987 and 1991. Restoration of Str. 8I-13 (the Castillo) by INAH in 2002 revealed an earlier interior temple; offerings of jadeite, shell, and conch; and molded stucco waterfowl similar to one on the painted interior of a Late Classic bowl found in a cache in front of Str. 9K-1.

Muyil is an inland port city, located on the edge of a freshwater lagoon on an 8-m-high karstic shelf, beyond which is a 10-km-wide sea-level region of mangrove swamp and grasslands. Access from the sea is through a natural route that crosses two freshwater lagoons joined by a natural outflow channel and finally through a meandering creek that leads to the Caribbean. The channel between the two lagoons is popularly believed to have been dug by the Maya in ancient times, but **underwater** archaeological investigations showed its fully natural origins as part of the drainage of freshwater from the Muyil lagoon. A small Postclassic temple, called Vigía del Lago or Xlahpak, sits at the eastern edge of the Chunyaxche lagoon at the entrance to the channel leading to the sea, perhaps controlling access.

A few **ceramics** indicate that Muyil was settled in the Middle Formative period before 400 BC and was then continuously occupied until the arrival of the Spaniards. It was then abandoned, and there are no archaeological finds, either Maya or Spanish, until the area was reoccupied in the 1800s, when it was developed for chicle (chewing gum) trade. Significant quantities of Sierra Red **ceramics** from the Late Formative period document occupation then, but no known Late Formative structures have been revealed thus far. Classic period ceramics are found with Classic style architecture somewhat similar to that of the Petén to the south. In the Postclassic period, many new structures were added in the East Coast architectural style, overlaying earlier buildings or occupying earlier plazas.

From the Late Formative until the end of the Classic, Muyil shows ties with **Belize** and the Petén. Belizean ceramics disappear about AD 900, concurrent with the **Classic Maya collapse**, and are replaced by Muna Slate ceramics associated with the Puuc region. Late in the terminal Classic small numbers of Dzitas Slate sherds show the widening influence of **Chichen Itza** at Muyil.

The most significant structures at the site include the Castillo (Str. 8I-13), a 17-m-tall truncated stepped **pyramid** with small rooms and an unusual round masonry turret atop. Other structures of note include Temple 8 (Str. 9K-1), built above extensive **caves** on a platform that fully encloses a similar earlier temple. The inner temple is still accessible by a Maya-built passageway in the new platform, all within a walled sacred precinct. Major other structures include those of the Entrance Plaza group, a set of pyramids similar to the Castillo, surrounding a plaza, and the Great Platform, a large multidwelling residential platform.

Muyil has a multipart *sacbe* (**causeway**) system punctuated by structures along its length, leading eastward from the site center to the Chunyaxche lagoon. The *sacbe* is interrupted approximately every 120 m by a temple structure, the largest being the Castillo itself. The *sacbe* appears to function to support foot traffic to a likely docking area for canoes arriving via the protected channel from the Caribbean. Muyil probably served as a port on **trade routes** for its nearby neighbor, **Cobá**.

See also DIET; GROUNDWATER/WATER TABLE; PETÉN ARCHITECTURAL STYLE; WATER MANAGEMENT

Further Reading

Muyil, entre el misterio maya. INAH, April 15, 2013. http://www.inah.gob.mx/boletines/7-zonas-arque-ologicas/3066-muyil-entre-el-misterio-maya.

Shaw, Justine M., and Jennifer P. Mathews, eds. *Quintana Roo Archaeology.* Tucson: University of Arizona Press, 2005.

Witschey, Walter R. T. "The Archaeology of Muyil, Quintana Roo, Mexico: A Maya Site on the East Coast of the Yucatan Peninsula." PhD diss., Tulane University, 1993.

———. "Muyil: An Early Start and Late Finish in East Coast Settlement." In *Quintana Roo Archaeology,* edited by Justine M. Shaw and Jennifer P. Mathews, 127–43. Tucson: University of Arizona Press, 2005.

———. *Muyil, Quintana Roo, Mexico.* 2008. http://muyil.smv.org/.

■ WALTER R. T. WITSCHEY

NAACHTUN

Discovered in 1922 by Sylvanus Morley, remote Naachtun remains one of the least known large cities in the Maya region. The site is in the geographic center of the Yucatan peninsula; it lies just over 1 km south of the Mexico-Guatemala border and is approximately 20 km east of El Mirador (see also **Map 3**). Prior to the early twenty-first century, only a handful of archaeologists had investigated the site. Scientific investigations began by the Naachtun Archaeological Project, University of Calgary, commenced in 2002 (2002–2009), followed by the investigations of the Proyecto Petén-Norte Naachtun (2010–2014), sponsored by the Archaeology of the Americas Unit, CNRS, the University of Paris, and CEMCA-Guatemala.

Although presently considered a very remote place, during the Classic Maya period (AD 150–850) Naachtun was very much in the thick of things. The site lies directly between **Tikal** and **Calakmul**, the two greatest cities in the ancient Maya world. As the two "superpowers" of the Classic Maya world, Calakmul and Tikal formed large confederacies and fought several major wars, both directly against each other and "by proxy" (see also **Warfare, Warriors, and Weapons**). Lying between these two sites, Naachtun held not only a strategic position but also a vulnerable one in the Classic Maya world of endemic warfare. The control of Naachtun must have been seen as a necessary prologue to any concerted attempt by either Tikal or Calakmul to attack the other.

Naachtun consisted of a civic/ceremonial epicenter that included three major complexes, Group C in the west, Group A in the center, and Group B to the east. Interestingly, each architectural group corresponds to a major construction episode in Naachtun's history, so one can literally see the expansion of the site over time. Group C was the focus of civic/ceremonial activity from AD 150 to 250. Subsequently, Naachtun expanded to the east and Group A supplanted Group C as the primary civic/ceremonial precinct from AD 250 to 550. Finally, Group B, the furthest eastern complex, dominated the urban landscape from AD 550 to 850. The epicenter is surrounded by a dispersed settlement to the east, south, and west. A large *bajo*, a seasonally inundated wetland, flanks the epicenter on the north.

Although scholars expected to find a robust Late Preclassic (1000 BC–AD 150) occupation, as documented at numerous other sites within the region, in fact Naachtun appears to have been only a small village during this period. Further, in contrast to many nearby sites, Naachtun flourished immediately following the collapse of **El Mirador**, a large Preclassic city to the west, in ca. AD 150.

The Early Classic (AD 150–550) period at Naachtun was one of explosive growth, as well as recurrent warfare. During the planning and construction of their expansive city, the people of Naachtun incorporated substantial defensive **fortifications**, as exemplified in the walled compound that guarded the entrance to Group A. At this time the North Plaza, which included a large E-Group **astronomical observatory**, was remarkably similar to the Lost World complex at Tikal in style and scale. In addition, **ceramic**, epigraphic, and **iconographic** data suggest strong affiliations with Tikal during the later part of the fifth through the early sixth centuries (see also **Alliances**).

Naachtun's Late Classic (AD 550–850) settlement was the most extensive in the site's history. Beginning in the mid-sixth century, ceramics show a shift to the sphere dominated by types found at Calakmul. This suggests that Naachtun developed a stronger affiliation with sites to the north and decreased interactions with sites to the south, such as Tikal. This shift correlates with the defeat of Tikal at the hands of the Snake Kingdom Kaan kings and their allies from **Caracol**.

However, by AD 700–750, Calakmul's influence on Naachtun had disappeared. **Stela 18**, located in Group B, clearly demonstrates this downturn in Calakmul's fortunes. The monument depicts a Naachtun queen standing on a captive, who is identified by a single glyph, which reads "Ox te' tun," a well-known place-name from Calakmul.

Naachtun was abandoned by AD 850, like most sites in the **Southern** and **Central Lowlands** during the **Classic Maya collapse**. The causes remain unclear, but both warfare and **drought** have been proposed as central to its demise.

See also ARCHITECTURE OVERVIEW; CLIMATE; MIRADOR BASIN; PORTABLE OBJECTS; RÍO BEC

Further Reading

Nondédéo, Philippe, Alejandro Patiño, Julien Sion, Dominique Michelet, and Carlos Morales-Aguilar. *Crisis múltiples en Naachtun: Aprovechadas, superadas e irreversibles.* Mesoweb, 2013. http://www.me soweb.com/publications/MMS/9_Nondedeo_etal.pdf.

Rangel, Martin, and Kathryn Reese-Taylor, eds. *Proyecto Arqueológico Naachtun 2004–2009, informe no. 2, segunda temporada de campo en el sitio arqueológico Naachtun.* Mesoweb, 2013. http://www.mesoweb .com/resources/informes/Naachtun2005.html.

Rangel Guillermo, Martin, and Kathryn Reese-Taylor. *Resultados de Investigaciones Arqueologicos en Naachtun, Temporada 2004.* Mesoweb, 2005. http://www.mesoweb.com/resources/informes/ Naachtun2004.pdf.

Walker, Debra S., and Kathryn Reese-Taylor. *Naachtún, Petén, Guatemala: First Analyses, Guatemala.* Foundation for the Advancement of Mesoamerican Studies, Inc. (FAMSI), 2012. http://www.famsi .org/reports/06035/index.html.

■ KATHRYN REESE-TAYLOR

NAJ TUNICH

Located about 17 km east-southeast of Poptun, Guatemala, in the foothills of the Maya Mountains, the **cave** of Naj Tunich (16.3° N, 89.3° W) offers an unusual and provocative view of the Maya relationship to the sacred Earth (see also **Map 3**). The cave interior contains a rich corpus of incense bowls for copal, carved jades, human sacrifices, stone altars, elite masonry tombs (until recently, the only such tombs known from the Maya area until one was found in 2007 in Quen Santo), hieroglyphic inscriptions, and drawings that document its long use as a pilgrimage site by elites of several major Maya cities. The balcony structure is the largest and most extensive modification ever reported from a Maya cave.

The cave was discovered in 1979, reported in *National Geographic* in 1981, and ultimately photographed in detail by Andrea Stone and James Brady. During the photography project in 1988, an extensive, previously unknown branch of the cave was discovered, with artifact contexts that had not been recently disturbed or looted.

Naj Tunich shows evidence of Maya use from the Late Formative (100 BC) that continued into the Late Classic, with heaviest use in the Protoclassic (AD 0–250). Two low platforms, at a distance of 50 m from the cave mouth, guard its entrance and highlight the sacredness of the cave precinct. The cave interior reveals more than 500 drawings, including rare examples of erotica. (See figure 30.) This is still the largest corpus of elite inscriptions known from a cave. Multispectral imaging has shown that some of the drawings were retouched in antiquity. Twenty skeletons have been recovered, including one well-preserved small child with three unhealed holes in the skull, a clear sign of human sacrifice.

Bone needles and **obsidian** blades attest to bloodletting rituals within the cave, while nearby drawings are explicit in portraying penis perforation and bloodletting by three

Figure 30.   Drawing 21 from the cave of Naj Tunich. Depicted is a ballplayer in heavy hip and knee padding hitting a ball off the side of a stepped ball court. The number 9 has been painted just above the ball. Such drawings at Naj Tunich constitute the largest known body of Maya elite inscriptions from a cave. Photograph courtesy James E. Brady.

individuals. **Calendar** round dates, clustering near the summer and winter solstices, fall in the range AD 692 to 771.

Andrea Stone pointed out, based on epigraphic work by David Stuart, Barbara MacLeod, Stephen Houston, Nikolai Grube, and others, that the cave documents a number of visits by Maya elites, borne to the site on litters. Verbs in the texts that refer to "seeing" and "arriving" occur in other contexts at other sites to describe elite visits. Visits may have been by elites in person or by their emissaries. The paintings identify several rulers from **Caracol**, **Calakmul**, and **Dos Pilas**. Portraits of scribes with brushes and paint pots document their pilgrimage to the cave for rendering the **wall paintings**. Together, these texts tell, in a standardized way, who visited the cave and for what purpose.

In this remarkable place, evidence is clear of long-distance pilgrimages for ritual sacrifice, ceremonial bloodletting, offerings of food, and burial. Left unknown is the mind-set of the Maya royalty, their view of this sacred place, and what caused them to make such arduous journeys here.

See also ART; BURIALS; DECIPHERMENT; DYNASTIC SEQUENCES; RITES AND RITUALS; ROYAL TOMBS

Further Reading

Brady, James E. *Summary of Naj Tunich Cave Archaeology*. California State University, Los Angeles, 2000. http://web.calstatela.edu/academic/anthro/jbrady/najtunich/Naj%20Tunich%201.htm.

Brady, James E., George Veni, Andrea Stone, and Allan Cobb. "Explorations in the New Branch of Naj Tunich: Implications for Interpretation." *Mexicon* 14, no. 4: , 1992.

Brady, James Edward. "An Investigation of Maya Ritual Cave Use with Special Reference to Naj Tunich, Petén, Guatemala." PhD diss., University of California, Los Angeles, 1989.

Clark, Chip, Jennifer Clark, and Andrea Joyce Stone. *Portraits of a Sacred Maya Cave: Photographs of Naj Tunich, Guatemala*. Milwaukee: University of Wisconsin-Milwaukee Art History Gallery, 1990.

Stone, Andrea Joyce. *Images from the Underworld: Naj Tunich and the Tradition of Maya Cave Painting*. Austin: University of Texas Press, 1995.

———. "Spiritual Journeys, Secular Guises: Rock Art and Elite Pilgrimage at Naj Tunich Cave." *Mexicon* 36: 49–64, 2014.

Stuart, George E. "Maya Art Treasures Discovered in Cave." *National Geographic* 160, no. 2: 220–35, 1981.

■ WALTER R. T. WITSCHEY

NAKBÉ

Nakbé (17.7° N, 89.8° W) is a very large Middle Formative period Maya city in the **Mirador Basin**, Department of Petén, **Guatemala** (see also **Map 3**). It was connected to its contemporary and successor city, **El Mirador**, 12 km to the northwest by a *sacbe* (see also **Causeway/Sacbe**). The Nakbé-El Mirador region documents the precociously early formation of complex city-states in the Maya area, contemporaneous with similar sites in the **Olmec** heartland. Nakbé was settled early in the Middle Formative ca. 1000–800 BC. Its rapid development resulted in masonry architecture in the late Middle Formative, 800–400 BC. The city plan includes a large ceremonial group with three radiating *sacbes*, one to a large eastern group. This east-west plan is similar to the city plan at El Mirador, but contrasts with that of the large Olmec sites, which had north-south alignments. Nakbé had monumental masonry **pyramids** up to 45 m tall, which presumably once held perishable temples atop. An early **stela**, ca. 500–200 BC, shows facing figures with elaborate headdresses and jade ear flares, but otherwise has no written inscription or dates.

Nakbé was discovered in 1930 by aerial photo and first excavated by Ian Graham. Since the late 1980s Richard D. Hansen and colleagues from the Guatemalan Institute of Anthropology and History have led work at Nakbé, most recently as part of the larger Mirador Basin Project.

See also ARCHITECTURAL OVERVIEW; ASTRONOMICAL OBSERVATORIES; *BAJOS*; CALAKMUL; CENTRAL LOWLANDS; CIVAL; CODEX-STYLE VASES; GUATEMALA; OLMEC-MAYA INTERACTIONS; PORTABLE OBJECTS; SETTLEMENT PATTERNS (CENTRAL LOWLANDS); TERRITORIAL ENTITIES; TIKAL

Further Reading

Hansen, Richard D. *Proyecto Arqueológico Cuenca Mirador: Investigación, conservación y desarrollo en El Mirador, Petén, Guatemala, informe final temporada de Campo 2003*, 2004.

———. *Publications and Papers of the Mirador Basin Project* (bibliography). Foundation for Anthropological Research and Environmental Studies (FARES) in collaboration with the Instituto de Antropología e Historia de Guatemala, Ministry of Culture and Sports, 2007. http://www.miradorbasin.com/about/bibliography02-07.pdf.

———. *Mirador Basin Project: The Cradle of Maya Civilization.* 2010. http://www.miradorbasin.com/index.php.

Hansen, Richard D., and Renaldo Acevedo. *Investigaciones arqueológicas en Nakbé, Petén: El resumen de la temporada de campo de 1993: Proyecto Regional de Investigaciones Arqueológicas en al Norte del Petén, Guatemala (PREIANPEG) = Regional Archaeological Investigation of the North Petén, Guatemala (RAINPEG): Un proyecto de University of California, Los Angeles, Instituto de Antropología e Historia de Guatemala, National Geographic Society.* Los Angeles: University of California, Los Angeles, 1993.

Šprajc, Ivan, and Carlos Morales-Aguilar. "Alineamientos astronómicos en el sitios arqueológicos de Tintal, el Mirador y Nakbe, Petén, Guatemala." In *Investigación y conservación en los sitios arqueológicos de la zona cultural y natural Mirador*, 123–58, 2007.

■ CLIFFORD T. BROWN AND WALTER R. T. WITSCHEY

NARANJO

The large ancient Classic Maya city of Naranjo (17.1° N, 89.2° W), in the Department of the Petén, **Guatemala**, was unfortunately situated in a power nexus among **Tikal**, **Caracol**, and **Calakmul**, between **Yaxhá** and **Xunantunich**, and astride Tikal's connections to the Caribbean (see also **Map 3**). This placed its rulers in an often precarious position, as **alliances** changed, losers recovered to become winners, and vengeful enemies exacted a toll. Nakum is 16 km northwest, and Tikal 24 km further. The large site of Yaxhá is located 16 km southwest, and Caracol is 45 km south-southeast. The neighborhood was crowded with large sites.

First explorations at the site were by Teobert Maler, who lived on site three months and photographed **stelae** and the **hieroglyphic stairway**. Sylvanus Morley made three trips to the site in the 1930s. R. E. W. Adams made several castings of carvings in 1962, under very trying conditions. Looting of carvings from the site began early and picked up in earnest in the 1960s. From 1969 to 1975 Ian Graham made trips to Naranjo to record inscriptions for the Corpus Project. In the past decade, Vilma Fialko has led a project at the site.

The site center of ceremonial and royal buildings occupies about 1 km², with 112 buildings, triadic arrangements, **palaces**, two **ball courts**, reservoirs, a short *sacbe* (**cause-way**), and a Group-E configuration. An unusual hieroglyphic stairway originally carved and situated at Caracol as a victory monument recording the conquest of Naranjo was looted in Classic times by a then-victorious Naranjo and reinstalled in the center of Naranjo on a radial pyramid.

Martin and Grube have detailed the dynastic history of the site, summarized here. Tzik'in Bahlam, the first ruler in historical times (ca. AD 450), was mentioned on Stela 45 at Naranjo, with Naatz Chan Ahk, a successor. At Tikal, he was named as the maternal grandfather of Chak Tok Ich'aak II, who was ruling ca. AD 488–508. This Early Classic reference links the two sites by marriage and thus allies them politically.

Naatz Chan Ahk (ca. AD 475) and K'inich Tajal Chaak (ca. AD 510) preceded Aj Wosal Chan K'inich ('Double Comb,' 'Ruler I'), who came to power on May 5, AD 546, and ruled until his death ca. AD 615. He demonstrated military prowess at an early age in an attack on "Ko-Bent-Cauac." He was inaugurated as Naranjo's thirty-fifth dynastic ruler under the aegis of K'altuun Hix of Calakmul, a sign of Calakmul's emerging power and of the power of its kings to dominate rulers of smaller polities. The stability of his long reign was subsequently shattered during the reigns of his successors.

K'uxaj ("Ruler 36") came to power ca. AD 615 and ruled until ca. 644. During his rule, Naranjo was twice attacked in AD 626 by K'an II of Caracol and soundly defeated. This was followed by another loss—a successful Star War against Naranjo by Yuknoom Head of Calakmul in December AD 631. K'an II documented his victories over Naranjo on a hieroglyphic stairway commissioned for the half-*k'atun* ending 9.10.10.0.0, December 6, AD 642. As Naranjo's fortunes later recovered, it sacked the stairway from Caracol and rebuilt it at Naranjo.

K'ak' Skull Chan Chaak came to power by AD 644, ruling until ca. AD 680. Under his rule, Naranjo made a successful Star War attack on Caracol in AD 680. He may be the victor who took Caracol's hieroglyphic stairway in triumph.

Lady Six Sky ("Lady Wac Chanil Ahau," "Lady of Dos Pilas," "Lady of Tikal") was installed on August 27, AD 682, and died on February 10 or 11, AD 741. The daughter of Dos Pilas king Bajlaj Chan K'awiil and an outsider at Naranjo, she was installed on the Naranjo throne, but continued to carry the Mutal Emblem Glyph of Tikal rather than take up a position in the Naranjo dynastic sequence. As the likely mother of K'ak' Tiliw' Chan Chaak, the next king, Lady Six Sky began a new dynasty with close ties to **Dos Pilas**. She was portrayed on stelae like many Maya warrior kings: standing on the backs of bound captives.

K'ak' Tiliw' Chan Chaak ("Rain-God who fire-burns the sky," "Smoking Squirrel," "Scroll Squirrel") was born January 3, AD 688, and ascended to the throne on May 28, AD 693, ruling until at least AD 728. The five-year-old boy-king ruled with his mother,

Lady Six Sky, as his regent. Following his inauguration, she mounted a successful series of mostly small wars on neighboring towns, including K'inichil Kab, Tuubal, and Bital in AD 693; Tikal in AD 695; Dotted Ko in AD 696; Eared Skull in AD 697; and K'inchil Kab (again) and Ucanal (capturing its king) in AD 698. A maturing K'ak' Tiliw' Chan Chaak successfully attacked Yootz in AD 706; Yaxhá, capturing its king in AD 710; and Sakha' in AD 714. In AD 712 he supervised the inauguration of kings at Ucanal and Yootz. In a not-uncommon political move, he married a member of the royal family of the defeated Tuubal, Lady Baby Jaguar. The history of Naranjo then goes silent for nearly 30 years, most likely because Naranjo was conquered and subjugated. There were brief mentions of two kings during that era.

Yax Mayuy Chan Chaak came to power after AD 741, was ruling in AD 744, and died ca. AD 744. This probable son of K'ak' Tiliw' Chan Chaak was defeated by Tikal in February AD 744. Six months later, he was portrayed as a bound captive on a Tikal monument, undoubtedly in preparation for his sacrifice.

K'ak' Yipiiy Chan Chaak ("Smoking New Squirrel," "Smoking B'ak'tun") was inaugurated on August 15, AD 746. The only surviving mention of him is his inaugural stela. The long subsequent silence may reflect his capture by Tikal in AD 748, whose ruler recorded capturing a high-ranking royal from the Naranjo region.

K'ak' Ukalaw Chan Chaak ("Smoking Batab," "He-of-flint," "Smoking Axe," "Axe Blade") came to power on November 8, AD 755, and ruled beyond AD 780. He claimed that his parents were K'ak' Tiliw' Chan Chaak and Lady Baby Jaguar of Tuubal. Due perhaps to foreign control, there are no monuments that record the first 25 years of his reign. He erected five monuments for the half-*k'atun* ending of 9.17.10.0.0, December 2, AD 780. He also recorded two military victories, one over Bital in AD 775, and the other place, unknown, in AD 778. Inscriptions record that he married Lady Shell Star from the royal family of **Yaxhá**. They had two sons, both of whom ruled Naranjo.

Bat K'awiil ruled ca. AD 781–784. A single painted plate mentions his royal status. Itzamnaaj K'awiil ("Shield God K") was born March 13, AD 771, and inaugurated on February 4, AD 784. His last dated inscription falls in AD 810. Coming to power at age 13 as the second son of K'ak' Ukalaw Chan Chaak and Lady Star Shell of Yaxhá, he erected six stelae over the course of 26 years. In February AD 799 he began to attack Yaxhá, notwithstanding his mother's origins there. His assault was successful in AD 800, and inscriptions record his capture of the Yaxhá king. His reign was marked by a calm and prosperous Naranjo, successful in battle.

Waxaklajuun Ubaah K'awiil ("18-images-of-K'awiil," "18 Rabbit," "18 JOG") came to power on June 24, AD 814. Brief records show that he participated in a tribute-giving ceremony of quetzals and jaguars in AD 815 and celebrated a significant event at Ucanal, not Naranjo, in AD 820. The records for Naranjo end here, as the **Classic Maya collapse** rolls across the cities and crushes fortunes of the region. At **Xunantunich**, 13 km southeast, there is some evidence of activity by the Naranjo rulers for another decade, then complete silence.

See also Alliances; Architecture Overview; Astronomical Observatories; Central Lowlands; Cobá; Craft Specialization; Dynastic Sequences; Hieroglyphic Stairways;

La Corona; Maya Queens; Music and Dance; Petén Architectural Style; Portable Objects; Pyramid;Warfare,Warriors, and Weapons

Further Reading

Fialko,Vilma. *Archaeological Research and Rescue Project at Naranjo: Emerging Documentation in Naranjo's Palacio de la Realeza, Petén, Guatemala* (2005 Season). Foundation for the Advancement of Meso-american Studies, Inc. (FAMSI), 2009. http://www.famsi.org/reports/05005/.

———. *The map of the southwest periphery of Naranjo, Petén, Guatemala* (2006 Season). Foundation for the Advancement of Mesoamerican Studies, Inc. (FAMSI), 2009.http://www.famsi.org/reports/06098/06098Fialko01.pdf.

Fialko,Vilma, and Angela M. H. Schuster. *Naranjo-Sa'al, Petén, Guatemala: Preserving an Ancient Maya City—Plan for Documentation, Conservation, and Presentation.* New York: World Monuments Fund, 2012.

Graham, Ian, and Eric Von Euw. *Naranjo.* Corpus of Maya Hieroglyphic Inscriptions, Peabody Museum of Archaeology and Ethnology, Harvard University, 1975–1978. https://www.peabody.harvard.edu/cmhi/site.php?site=Naranjo#loc.

Martin, Simon, and Nikolai Grube. *Chronicle of the Maya Kings and Queens: Deciphering the Dynasties of the Ancient Maya.* 2nd ed. London:Thames & Hudson, 2008.

■ WALTER R. T. WITSCHEY

NIXTUN-CH'ICH'

Nixtun-Ch'ich' (17.0° N, 89.9° W) is one of the largest (> 4 km²) Maya sites in the Petén **Lakes** region of central Petén, **Guatemala** (see also **Map 3**). The site rests on private land and can only be accessed with special permission. It stands on a peninsula on the western edge of Lake Petén Itzá. Most of the site rests around 14 m above the lake level and is bordered by the lake to the northeast, east, and south and karstic hills to the north-northwest.

Nixtun-Ch'ich' was noted but not mapped by Sylvanus Morley and surface collected by George Cowgill. Arlen Chase visited the site and recorded some **ceramic** data from looters' pits, which indicated a substantial Middle Preclassic occupation of the area. In 1995 the site was surveyed and mapped by Proyecto Maya Colonial, directed by Don and Prudence Rice. Prudence Rice returned to the site to conduct excavations in 2006–2007, as did Timothy Pugh in 2013–2014.

Nixtun-Ch'ich' has pre-Mamom ceramics associated with cultural deposits dated to the late Early Preclassic period (beginning ca. 1100 BC). Its Mamon (600–300 BC) and Chicanel (300 BC–AD 200) occupations cover the entire site area. Most of the site also includes Late Classic (AD 600–800) to Terminal Classic (AD 800–930) and Postclassic (AD 930–1525) period deposits. Some contact (AD 1525–1697) and Colonial (AD 1697–1821) period occupations are found in the eastern part of the site.

This site has more than 450 buildings, including two **ball courts**, a triadic group, a number of high substructural **pyramids**, and a large wall and ditch complex (see also **Fortifications**). A large platform in the easternmost portion of Nixtun-Ch'ich' has substantial late Early Preclassic deposits. A newer survey conducted in 2013 suggests that most of the architecture of Nixtun-Ch'ich' was guided by an orthogonal grid.

While these data are preliminary, the detection of such a grid would be the first in the Maya world and parallel Nixtun-Ch'ich' with **Teotihuacán** and Tenochtitlan in Central Mexico. One of the ball court complexes at the site, dated to the Late to Terminal Classic period, is I-shaped and 135 m long, making it the second largest in the Maya region after **Chichen Itza**. This finding is remarkable given that the contact and Colonial period occupants claimed to have been Itza, who migrated from Chichen Itza. Contact period deposits located at the point at which the peninsula meets the mainland may be the historically known site of Ch'ich'. Dated glass beads and other Spanish artifacts suggest that the Colonial mission of San Jerónimo (AD 1702–1734) once stood on the large platform at the eastern end of the site, though the mission church seems to have been destroyed by modern construction.

See also CRAFT SPECIALIZATION; GROUND SURVEY TECHNIQUES; WARFARE, WARRIORS, AND WEAPONS

Further Reading

Chase, Arlen F. "A Contextual Consideration of the Tayasal-Paxcaman Zone, El Petén, Guatemala." PhD diss., University of Pennsylvania, 1983.

Cowgill, George Lewis. "Postclassic Period Culture in the Vicinity of Flores, Petén, Guatemala." PhD diss., Harvard University, 1963.

Jones, Grant D. *The Conquest of the Last Maya Kingdom.* Stanford, CA: Stanford University Press, 1998.

Morley, Sylvanus Griswold. *Inscriptions of Petén.* Vols. 1–4. Carnegie Institution of Washington, Publication 437. Washington, DC: Carnegie Institution of Washington, 1938.

Rice, Prudence M. "Mound ZZ1, Nixtun-Ch'ich', Petén, Guatemala: Rescue Operations at a Long-lived Structure in the Maya Lowlands." *Journal of Field Archaeology* 34, no. 4: 403–22, 2009.

■ TIMOTHY W. PUGH

NOH KAH

The National Institute of Anthropology and History (INAH)–**Mexico**, Quintana Roo Center, and researchers from the National School of Anthropology (ENAH) have recently undertaken mapping of an unexplored site in southern Quintana Roo called Noh Kah ("Great City") (18.3° N, 88.6° W; see also **Map 3**). Surveys in the 2013 and 2014 seasons revealed six major **architectural** groups on rough terrain along the Hondo River and Belize border—El Corozal, El Pich, El Paredón, El Pocito, Hop Na, and El Veinte—with a somewhat open spacing between them ranging from 500 m to 3,000 m.

At the El Corozal area, adjacent to a large *aguada* and primary water source for the site, there are two large architectural groupings around plazas. Nearby, the El Pich group reveals through its architecture, on a platform base more than 100 m long, that it may have been the primary seat of power. There are three plazas at different levels, residential architecture, and terracing.

Preliminary work to understand the site chronology has begun, indicating that Noh Kah was occupied throughout the Classic. The site is expected to cast additional light on the extent to which the immediate region was under the sway of the Snake

Kingdom at **Dzibanché** in the Early Classic, and **Calakmul** in the Late Classic after the Kaan dynasty relocated there.

See also CRAFT SPECIALIZATION; DZIBANCHÉ; GROUNDWATER/WATER TABLE; PYRAMID; WATER MANAGEMENT

Further Reading

Mapean Noh Kah, una "gran ciudad" maya en Quintana Roo. May 12, 2014. http://www.inah.gob.mx/boletin/17-arqueologia/7180-mapean-noh-kah-una-gran-ciudad-maya-en-quintana-roo.

López Camacho, Javier, Araceli Vázquez Villegas, and Luis Antonio Torres Díaz. *Noh Kah: Pobladores de la montaña; Nuevos hallazgos.* Arqueología Mexicana, Editorial Raíces, S. A. de C.V. and Mexican National Council for Culture and the Arts, 2014. http://www.arqueomex.com/S2N3nQuintana Roo120.html.

Rodriguez, Edgardo *Noh-Kah, registrada en la arqueología nacional.* Noverdades Quintana Roo, SIPSE.com, 2013. http://sipse.com/novedades/bautiza-ruinas-noh-kah-por-habitantes-de-rovi rosa-20052.html.

■ WALTER R. T. WITSCHEY

NOHPAT
See KABAH AND NOHPAT

NORTHERN HIGHLANDS

North of the drainage of the Grijalva River westward and the Motagua River eastward, the mountains of the Chiapas highlands rise over 3,000 m. Rainfall in most of the area exceeds 1,500 mm annually and in places is more than 4,000 mm, most during the May–December rainy season. Most of the region is based on older sedimentary limestone, with large caverns and disappearing rivers. A broad upland interior plateau in Chiapas separates the Northern and **Southern Highlands**, and today there is a modern reservoir there (Presa de la Angostura) whose construction inundated a number of ancient sites. Three mountain ranges are part of the Northern Highlands—Sierra los Chuchumatanes, Sierra de Chuacas, and Sierra las Minas—from which, since ancient times, jadeite and serpentine have been quarried. The region includes highland rainforest and cloud forest. The terrain has leant itself to fragmentation of the modest populace into small mountain valley communities and into the isolation of languages.

See also MAPS 2, 4, 5, 7; CERAMICS; GEOLOGY; LAKES; LANGUAGE AND WRITING OVERVIEW; TONINÁ; ZACULEU

Further Reading

Coe, Michael D. *The Maya.* 8th ed. London: Thames & Hudson, 2011.

Evans, Susan Toby. *Ancient Mesoamerica & Central America: Archaeology and Culture History.* 2nd ed. London: Thames & Hudson, 2008.

Sharer, Robert J., and Loa P. Traxler. *The Ancient Maya*. 6th ed. Stanford, CA: Stanford University Press, 2006.

■ WALTER R. T. WITSCHEY

NORTHERN LOWLANDS

From the top of any **pyramid** in the Northern Lowlands one is struck by the tabletop flatness of the terrain, stretching toward the Caribbean or the Gulf of Mexico. Although the land is mostly near sea level in elevation, the flatness disappears at ground level, where the eroded limestone karst forms an uneven terrain that varies locally several meters in elevation. South of Mérida, the Puuc region pops up in elevation, but seldom more than 100 m asl (see also **Maps 2, 5, 6, 7**, and **8**).

The porous karst quickly drains water to the level of the water table (see also **Groundwater/Water Table**), and there are few **lakes** or streams. The combinations of humic and carbonic acids in the water have eroded solution caverns in the karst. Some of these have collapsed, forming **cenotes** with the water table visible; others have formed *rejolladas*, in which the surface terrain has dropped and forms a depressed cone in the landscape. The Northern Lowlands are the site of the **Chicxulub** impact crater, and fracture zones near the rim of the crater have been susceptible to the formation of a zone of cenotes. Without lakes or streams, the ancient Maya accessed water via cenotes, **caves**, and wells, and in the slightly higher elevations of the Puuc, resorted to creating *chultunes* (cisterns) to capture and store rainwater runoff from plazas. The site of **Cobá** surrounds an unusual group of **lakes** in the eastern part of the Northern Lowlands.

North of Mérida on the Gulf Coast the annual rainfall is essentially zero. Moving both southward and eastward from the coast, rainfall increases, although the annual precipitation is below 1,000 mm in most of the region. In this somewhat arid terrain, **vegetation** is low, with an abundance of thorny bushes. **Soil** is quite thin on the karst, and Maya farmers looked for small pockets of fertile soil for planting corn and other crops (see also **Subsistence**). Heat can be oppressive here, and the climate has distinct wet and dry seasons (wet from June to December; dry from January through May).

To the south, the Northern Lowlands grade slowly into the **Central Lowlands** along a variable and imprecise boundary that roughly parallels Mexico Highway 186, running east-west 60–80 km north of the **Guatemala** border between the Laguna de Terminos and the Bay of Chetumal.

The Northern Lowlands encompass the ancient cities of **Chichen Itza**, Cobá, **Izamal**, **Tiho**, **Ek Balam**, **Uxmal**, **Kabah**, **Komchen**; **Labna**, and **Sayil**, among many others, plus **Loltun cave** and the **Puuc** and *Chenes* **architectural styles**.

Further Reading

Marshall, Jeffrey S. "Geomorphology and Physiographic Provinces of Central America." In *Central America: Geology, Resources, and Natural Hazards*, edited by Jochen Bundschuh and Guillermo E. Alvarado Induni, 75–122. London and New York: Taylor and Francis, 2007.

Sharer, Robert J., and Loa P. Traxler. *The Ancient Maya*. 6th ed. Stanford, CA: Stanford University Press, 2006.

■ WALTER R. T. WITSCHEY

O

OBSIDIAN

Obsidian is an extrusive igneous rock that is produced when high-silica felsic lava is expelled from a volcano and rapidly cools with minimal crystal growth. Intrusions or trace elements within the obsidian affect its color, which is typically brown, black, or green, although on rare occasions other colors have been noted. Obsidian is a hard and brittle vitreous rock that breaks in a predictable and controlled manner through conchoidal fracturing. As a result of this predictability, it can be chipped into very complex tools with extremely sharp edges.

From the early Paleo-Indian to the Colonial era, obsidian was considered a highly valuable resource. Obsidian artifacts appear in a variety of ritual and domestic contexts as well as in elite residences and large civic-ceremonial centers, suggesting it served a variety of utilitarian and religious functions. Due to its sharpness, the Maya preferred obsidian, often in the form of prismatic blades, for sacrificial bloodletting (see also **Religion**; **Rites and Rituals**). It was also manufactured into knives, scrapers, bifacially flaked projectile points, and the more rare "**eccentrics**."When found in caches and other special contexts, eccentrics with little to no use wear may have served a ritual function.

Elites at major political and economic centers were responsible for the acquisition and redistribution of obsidian through reciprocal exchanges. However, they did not maintain a monopoly on the resource. Obsidian is ubiquitous throughout both lowland and highland Maya archaeological sites, from the largest cities to the smallest communities, demonstrating that both commoners and elites had access to it.

Although other sources exist, there are three main outcroppings of black or gray obsidian in the highlands of Guatemala that were utilized by the Maya: the **Ixtepeque** source found in southeastern Guatemala; the San Martín Jilotepeque or Río Pixcaya source in the Southern Highlands; and **El Chayal**, located 24 km north of present-day Guatemala City in the Motagua Valley.

In addition, the Maya also utilized obsidian known as Green Pachuca from the Cerro de las Navajas source located in the Valley of Mexico. The name is derived from its translucent shade of bottle-glass green. It appears in Maya caches, **burials**, and other contexts throughout the Maya highlands and lowlands and was considered a prized possession because of its association with the large Classic period site of **Teotihuacán** in the Valley of Mexico.

The Maya obtained obsidian from the aforementioned outcrops through surface collection and mining from shafts and tunnels within the outcrops. Typically obsidian was prepared at specialized workshops near the source material into conical cores for transport and then traded throughout **Mesoamerica**. Once the cores reached their final destination, they were worked into finished products at local workshops. However, unlike black or gray obsidian, Green Pachuca obsidian was typically traded in finished form.

Due to the chemical uniformity and uniqueness of individual obsidian deposits, obsidian can be chemically matched to specific outcrops in the volcanic ranges of highland Mesoamerica. Archaeologists have utilized this information to identify the specific sources of the obsidian artifacts they encounter. The ability to source obsidian has had broad impacts in Maya archaeology, including the reconstruction of various **trade routes**.

Obsidian can also be used to provide relative **dating**. Obsidian hydration analysis dating measures the rind on an obsidian edge. Since the rind forms at a known rate on a freshly exposed surface, archaeologists can estimate the time that has passed since the surface was exposed. However, factors such as chemical composition, temperature, and water vapor can impact rind growth.

Obsidian was a highly valued Maya trade good, utilized by both elite and commoners for a variety of utilitarian and religious purposes.

See also BURIALS; CAHAL PECH; CEREN; CHAC II; CHERT; CLASS STRUCTURE; COTZUMAL-HUAPA; CRAFT SPECIALIZATION; ECCENTRIC LITHICS; EDZNA; EL CHAYAL; EL PILAR; GEOLOGY; IXTEPEQUE; KAMINALJUYÚ; MARKETS AND MARKETPLACES; NAJ TUNICH; OLMEC; PORTABLE OBJECTS; RITES AND RITUALS; ROYAL TOMBS; SAYIL; SOUTHERN HIGHLANDS; SOUTHERN PERIPHERY; TEOTIHUACÁN (MAYA INTERACTIONS WITH); TRADE ROUTES; TULUM; WARFARE, WARRIORS, AND WEAPONS

Further Reading

Golitko, Mark, James Meierhoff, Gary M. Feinman, and Patrick Ryan Williams. "Complexities of Collapse: The Evidence of Maya Obsidian as Revealed by Social Network Graphical Analysis." *Antiquity* 86, no. 332: 507–23, 2012.

McKillop, Heather. *The Ancient Maya: New Perspectives*. New York: W. W. Norton, 2004.

Moholy-Nagy, Hattula. "Source Attribution and the Utilization of Obsidian in the Maya Area." *Latin American Antiquity* 14, no. 3: 301–10, 2003.

■ ALEXANDRIA HALMBACHER AND RACHEL EGAN

OLMEC

The name Olmec, from the Spanish *olmeca*, derives from the Nahuatl word *olli*, meaning "rubber." Emergent social complexity in early **Mesoamerica** is tied to the term, which at once denotes an archaeological culture; an **art** style expressed in stone, clay, and murals; and a particular set of visual motifs associated with pottery. The multiple meanings of "Olmec" lie at the root of a debate concerning the role the archaeological Olmec played in the origin and spread of this art style and the rise of early Mesoamerican kingdoms.

Olmeca means "people of the rubber country," referring to the tropical lowlands of the southern coastal plain of the Gulf of Mexico. Archaeological interest in the region developed with the discovery of megalithic monuments: portrait heads, "thrones" with **cave** imagery, seated figures, and **stelae**. Research at sites where these monuments were encountered—notably, San Lorenzo, La Venta, and Tres Zapotes—began in the mid-twentieth century, driven by the identification of portable art recognizably similar in style from sites across Mesoamerica. Objects stylistically "Olmec" were initially deemed to fall within the compass of Mesoamerica's Classic period (AD 250–950); however, it became apparent with excavation that the style developed during the Early and Middle Formative. Radiocarbon **dating** placed the earliest expression of the Olmec style horizon found at a wide range of geographically distant points, from the Basin of Mexico to western Honduras and the Maya Lowlands, to 1250 to 950 BC. These regions differentially shared elements of the style horizon; however, a set of motifs often executed on the exterior of pottery vessels was almost universally present (see also **Ceramics**; **Ceramic Analysis**). Crucially, these motifs are present in regionally distinctive patterns indicative of culturally specific uses.

Early Formative San Lorenzo (1400–950 BC) saw the construction of large earthen platforms, planned placement of monumental heads, "thrones," large seated depictions of humans and fantastical creatures, deployment of sinuous stone channels that mimic a landscape of rivers, and architectonic use of natural basalt columns. Excavation at earlier El Manatí, a spring site with anaerobically well-preserved wooden bust offerings from 1600 BC, showed that earlier generations had already mastered the art of fine woodworking, production of greenstone axes, and manufacture of rubber balls. La Venta and Tres Zapotes developed during the Middle Formative (950–400 BC), when greater emphasis was placed on the production of portable greenstone objects and cultural innovations, including incipient writing, developed. Tres Zapotes became an important epi-Olmec center with Mesoamerica's first dated historical monument of 32 BC.

While the nature of the San Lorenzo polity is contested, these later Olmec sites reflect the continuing evolution of Mesoamerican political systems toward the institution of kingship and social stratification. San Lorenzo is striking for its size, monuments, and implied social complexity. As a consequence of the dating of San Lorenzo, some scholars advocated a "mother culture" model with the archaeological Olmec as prime movers in the development of Mesoamerica. As research in other regions progressed, it became apparent that Early Formative developments in Mesoamerica were more complex and nuanced than a donor-recipient model allowed. Polities were developing in other regions, and trade in a variety of materials, notably ceramic vessels, obsidian, and valued stone, was well-established. While the Olmec developed great proficiency in sculpture, societies in the Basin of Mexico and adjoining regions, for instance, employed a larger repertoire of Early Formative ceramic motifs. Various scholars have proposed models of interregional sharing and interaction that better fit contemporary archaeological knowledge. These models posit a landscape of sociopolitical change in which the different regions of Mesoamerica contributed, shared, reinterpreted, and differentially deployed elements of a common culture that together constituted the "Olmec" horizon.

See also BALL GAME/BALL COURT; CAHAL PECH; CALENDAR; CEIBAL; CIVAL; COPÁN; EL MIRADOR; ICONOGRAPHY; IZAPA; MESOAMERICA; NAKBÉ; OBSIDIAN; OLMEC–MAYA INTERACTIONS; PACIFIC COASTAL PLAIN; PALENQUE; SAN BARTOLO; SCULPTURE; SIN CABEZAS; SOUTHERN PERIPHERY; STELA; TAKALIK ABAJ; WALL PAINTING; WRITING SYSTEMS OF MESOAMERICA

Further Reading

Diehl, Richard A. *The Olmecs: America's First Civilization*. New York: Thames & Hudson, 2004.

Pool, Christopher A. *Olmec Archaeology and Early Mesoamerica*. Cambridge, UK: Cambridge University Press, 2007.

Sharer, Robert J., and David C. Grove, eds. *Regional Perspectives on the Olmec*. Cambridge, UK: Cambridge University Press, 1989.

■ CHRISTOPHER L. VON NAGY

OLMEC-MAYA INTERACTIONS

Scholarly perception of the relationship of the Maya to their **Olmec** neighbors has evolved in rough measure to the degree to which the Early to Late Formative archaeology of both regions and of greater **Mesoamerica** developed. Historical interrelationships between the two regions are multiplex, involving interaction across the geographically complex space of the Tabasco coastal plain, Chiapas interior, and southern **Pacific coastal plain** between differentiating Maya and Mixe-Zoquean groups, including the archaeological Olmec, and their southern Mokaya neighbors. Shared Formative cultural elements contrast these eastern Mesoamerican societies against those farther to the west, while other cultural features signal coparticipation in Formative Mesoamerican cultural horizons. Notable commonalities in eastern Mesoamerica include early **ceramic** cross-ties; ritual practice; a shared tradition of narrative and commemorative **stelae**; canons of design; linguistic borrowings; the parallel development of logosyllabic writing; and an evolving, shared approach to public representations of history employing text and the Mesoamerican Long Count (see also **Calendar**; **Deities**; **Iconography**; **Language and Writing**; **and Rites and Rituals**).

However, this interaction was not limited strictly to the Maya and the archaeological Olmec, and it remains a project for future research to further elucidate these interactions. Little evidence exists to allow an argument to be built that Early Formative San Lorenzo had any direct relationship with Maya settlements, a suggestive presence of northern Isthmus style cultural materials at the site of Canton Corralito on the Pacific Coast aside. Later, Olmec La Venta had a documented pottery exchange relationship with some lowland Maya communities, but other sites, including Tres Zapotes, **Izapa**, San Isidro, and Chiapa de Corzo, also participated in regional interaction.

A late population expansion of ceramic-using agriculturalists into the Maya lowlands as much as a thousand years after the earliest ceramic-using populations occupied the northern Isthmus area, combined with an early florescence of the San Lorenzo Olmec some two to three centuries before the Maya expansion and development of certain perceived key Maya cultural traits in the Olmec region, such as the use of stelae, provided a reasonable basis for some scholars to posit a progenitor role for the Olmec in the earliest development of lowland Maya civilization. The excavation of a limited number of examples of "Olmec" ritual caches in the Maya lowlands gave further credence to the "mother culture" model in vogue during the middle decades of the twentieth century. A more nuanced view had to await the development of a robust understanding of the Early and Middle Formative in the Maya highlands and lowlands. Perhaps a majority of Mesoamerican scholars now favor models that posit a decentralized, multiregional view of the development of Maya civilization and their relationships with their Mixe-Zoquean neighbors. Recent research in the lowland Maya region has demonstrated both an early ceramic horizon, the Cunil, coeval with the earliest pan-Mesoamerican style horizon, and the rapid, vibrant development of early Maya polities centered on sites with monumental **architecture**, such as **El Mirador** and **Nakbé** in the **Southern Lowlands** and **Komchen** and Xtobo in the **Northern Lowlands**.

Geographically, the Tabasco coastal plain most directly linked Gulf Olmec polities, especially La Venta, to incipient lowland Maya polities. While the Early Formative is incompletely delineated on this coastal plain, research, including archaeological salvage, shows an important distribution of Middle Formative and later sites with pottery traditions first related to the Olmec, later to the Maya. Both Early Olmec and Cunil horizon Maya potters employed elements of a complex of motifs commonly found on Mesoamerican pottery during the Early and Middle Formative. Decorative patterns on Early to Middle Formative Olmec dishes and plates is distinct from that of the Maya, as it is equally distinct from the pottery of various regions of central Mesoamerica. Nonetheless, Cunil horizon pottery in the Southern Lowlands shared specific commonalities with early Middle Formative pottery of the western Tabasco Coastal Plain. Seemingly peculiar and Cunil-specific wide-everted rim plates and dishes have direct counterparts in Olmec pottery assemblages from western Tabasco. Plain, red, and black bolstered rim dishes, bowls, and *tecomates* are common to both traditions. These commonalities suggest interaction between the Cunil horizon Maya and their contemporaries on the Tabasco coastal plain. Pottery design commonalities are supplemented by a pattern of ceramic exchange linking Tabasco sites to Maya communities during the Middle Formative. Waxy-slipped Dzudzuquil Cream-to-buff, Joventud Red, and waxy bi-chromes are present at La Venta, surrounding sites, and elsewhere within the western Tabasco coastal plain. Ceramic vessels may have circulated within a gifting economy, as would have fine jade or greenstone adornments and **sculptures**, but any of the latter cannot be securely attributed to the archaeological Olmec (see also **Ceramic Analysis**).

Linguistic borrowings and specific elements of both the Late Formative Maya and epi-Olmec writing systems, both of which evolved during the Late Formative from Middle Formative antecedents, suggest another form of close interaction between specific Mixe-Zoquean and Mayan groups, perhaps along the same northern coastal corridor. Maya *ahau*, lord or king, derives from proto-Mixe-Zoquean or proto-Zoquean "he who proclaims"; Maya *pom*, incense, is another borrowing, as is *kakaw*, "**cacao**," from which chocolate is made. The word *pom* may occur in the Maya murals at **San Bartolo** (ca. 100 BC) as an early example of a loan word. Comparisons between epi-Olmec textual conventions, developed during the Late Formative, and early examples of Maya textual conventions provide further instances of specific borrowings: for instance, so-called reed-based title glyphs used in Early Classic Maya texts invariably surmounting text blocks may have epi-Olmec headdress title correlates. Borrowing appears bidirectional. The Maya sign *na-* may derive from an epi-Olmec prototype; the epi-Olmec sign year/drum may derive from a Maya prototype.

See also BALL GAME/BALL COURT; CAHAL PECH; CALENDAR; CEIBAL; CIVAL; COPÁN; DECIPHERMENT; EL MIRADOR; ICONOGRAPHY; IZAPA; MESOAMERICA; NAKBÉ; OBSIDIAN; OLMEC-MAYA INTERACTIONS; PACIFIC COASTAL PLAIN; PALENQUE; SAN BARTOLO; SCULPTURE; SIN CABEZAS; SOUTHERN PERIPHERY; STELA; TAKALIK ABAJ; WALL PAINTING; WRITING SYSTEMS OF MESOAMERICA

Further Reading

Boot, Erik. "Loan Words, 'Foreign Words,' and Foreign Signs in Maya Writing." In *The Idea of Writing: Play and Complexity*, edited by Alexander J. de Voogt and Irving L. Finkel.

Hansen, Richard D. "Perspectives on Olmec-Maya Interaction in the Middle Formative Period." In *New Perspectives on Formative Mesoamerican Cultures*, edited by Terry G. Powis, 51–72. B.A.R. International Series, no. 1377. Oxford: Archaeopress, 2006.

Lowe, Gareth W. "The Mixe-Zoque as Competing Neighbors of the Early Lowland Maya." In *The Origins of Maya Civilization*, edited by Richard E. W. Adams. Albuquerque: University of New Mexico Press, 1977.

Robinson, Eugenia J., Marlen Garnica, and Juan Pablo Herrera. "El Postclásico Tardío: Asentamientos alrededor de Iximché en el Altiplano de Guatemala." In *XXVI Simposio de Investigactiones Arqueológicas en Guatemala*, edited by Bárbara Arroyo and Médez Salinas. Guatemala City, Guatemala: Museo de Arqueología y Ethnología, 2013. Leiden: Brill, 2010.

■ CHRISTOPHER L. VON NAGY

OXKINTOK

Oxkintok (20.5° N, 89.9° W) is a large site in the Puuc region of Yucatan, **Mexico** (see also **Map 3**). Located 30 km northwest of **Uxmal**, Oxkintok was a major center throughout the Classic period. It is known for the earliest recorded Long Count **calendar** date in the **Northern Lowlands** (9.2.0.0.0 or AD 475) as well as for its importance in the development of the **Puuc architectural style**. The modern site name means "Three Sun/Day Chert."

The central portion of Oxkintok, covering about 2 km², sits in a broad valley at the southern foot of the Sierrita de Ticul, an escarpment separating the hilly Puuc region from the flat northern plains of Yucatan. This strategic location gave Oxkintok access to an important trade route connecting the northern Maya lowlands to the Gulf Coast and Central Highland regions. The site center is comprised of six large **architectural** groups arranged along a north-south axis and connected by **causeways**. As throughout the Puuc region, rainwater was collected in numerous *chultunes* (cisterns) for daily use (see also **Water Management**). The nearby Calcehtók **caves** were likely used to collect water for ritual purposes (see also **Rites and Rituals**).

Oxkintok was first visited in 1588 by Franciscan friars Alonso Ponce and Antonio de Ciudad Real, who described the labyrinthine Satunsat, an unusual building featuring narrow vaulted passageways on three connected levels. John Lloyd Stephens and Frederick

Catherwood explored the site in 1842, and University of Pennsylvania excavations under Henry Mercer followed in 1895. Edwin Shook, H. E. D. Pollock, and George Brainerd of the Carnegie Institution of Washington conducted research at Oxkintok between 1932 and 1940. Large-scale excavations in the site center were led by Miguel Rivera Dorado of the Spanish Archaeological Mission in Mexico between 1986 and 1991. Since 1996, Ricardo Velázquez Valadéz and other archaeologists of Mexico's National Institute of Anthropology and History (INAH) have continued research at Oxkintok.

Oxkintok was occupied from the Middle Preclassic until the Terminal Classic, with occasional use up to conquest times. The site became a major regional center at the beginning of the Early Classic. The **ceramics** of the Ichpa phase (AD 300 to 500/550) include polychromes and other types similar to those of the **southern Maya lowlands**. They are associated with buildings in the Early Oxkintok style, with walls of rough block masonry and stepped vaults.

The sixth century AD saw a marked increase in social complexity, as evidenced by monumental architecture in the Proto-Puuc style, inscriptions on stone lintels, a **stela**, and a **hieroglyphic stairway**. In this period, which Carmen Varela Torrecilla calls the Oxkintok Regional Phase of the Middle Classic, the site's pottery diverged significantly from Southern Lowland ceramic traditions. Tomb 1 from this time, excavated in the Satunsat and containing a jade mosaic mask, is the richest **burial** at the site (see also **Royal Tombs**). Although some Proto-Puuc style **pyramids** in three of the main groups feature *talud-tablero* forms reminiscent of the architecture of **Teotihuacán**, there is no evidence for a direct connection between the two sites.

Oxkintok flourished in the Late Classic period. Many buildings in the center were built in the Early Puuc style, which is associated with Ukmul-phase ceramics of the Cehpech sphere. An eighth-century ruler named Walas is mentioned in hieroglyphic inscriptions on the **ball court** ring (AD 713/714), Stela 23, and various carved lintels.

The Terminal Classic saw the construction of Classic Puuc buildings in the Colonnette and Mosaic styles. Most of Oxkintok's 27 stelae were erected during this period. Stela 3 carries a date of 10.1.0.0.0 (AD 849), and Stelae 9 and 21 were erected about 10 years later. Stylistic differences from Late Classic monuments, together with a 29-year hiatus in inscriptions, point to a possible change in rulership during this period. Oxkintok and other Puuc sites were abandoned at the end of the Terminal Classic. Oxkintok remained a pilgrimage location well into the Colonial period.

See also Astronomical Observatories; Burials; Craft Specialization; Hieroglyphic Stairways; Teotihuacán (Maya Interactions With)

Further Reading

Andrews, George F. "The Puuc Regions and Architectural Styles: A Reassessment." In *Pyramids, Palaces, Monsters and Masks: The Golden Age of Maya Architecture*, 3–131. Lancaster, CA: Labyrinthos Press, 1995.

Rivera Dorado, Miguel. "La emergencia del estado maya en Oxkintok." *Mayab* 12: 71–78, 1999.

Varela Torrecilla, Carmen, and Geoffrey E. Braswell. "Teotihuacan and Oxkintok: New Perspectives from Yucatán." In *The Maya and Teotihuacan: Reinterpreting Early Classic Interaction*, edited by Geoffrey E. Braswell. Austin: University of Texas Press, 1995.

■ BENIAMINO VOLTA

P

PACIFIC COASTAL PLAIN

Extending along the Pacific coast of Chiapas and Guatemala is a rich and fertile sloping plain of **soils** produced by the weathering of volcanoes just to the north (see also **Maps 2, 5**, and **8**). Rivers from the volcanic region drain through the coastal plain to the ocean, forming a region of meander channels, brackish lagoons, and mangrove swamps behind the shoreline teeming with aquatic **fauna**. Along the Chiapas coast rainfall is 2,000–3,000 mm per year, while along the coast of **Guatemala** it is 1,500 mm per year or less.

The region has been a transit route for people moving southeast-northwest since ancient times. Several early sites show both unique developments and mixes of Maya and **Olmec** traits ca. 400 BC. Of note in the area are the sites of **Izapa**, **Takalik Abaj**, **Cotzumalhuapa**, and **Sin Cabezas**. The climate is hot and humid, and in pre-Hispanic times was known for cotton and **cacao** crops. Modern agriculturists now produce coffee on the higher-elevation slopes and cotton, cardamom, bananas, and sugarcane at lower altitudes. Areas of cattle ranching alternate with the cropped areas on large estates (*fincas*).

See also Astronomical Observatories; Ball Game/Ball Court; Burials; Cacao; Ceramics; Classic Maya Collapse; Craft Specialization; El Chayal; El Mirador; El Salvador; Guatemala; Hieroglyphic Stairways; Honduras; Kaminaljuyú; Mesoamerica; Mexico; Olmec-Maya Interactions; Sculpture; Southern Highlands; Southern Periphery; Stela; Teotihuacán (Maya Interactions With)

Further Reading

Coe, Michael D. *The Maya*. 8th ed. London: Thames & Hudson, 2011.

Evans, Susan Toby. *Ancient Mesoamerica & Central America: Archaeology and Culture History*. 2nd ed. London: Thames & Hudson, 2008.

Sharer, Robert J., and Loa P. Traxler. *The Ancient Maya*. 6th ed. Stanford, CA: Stanford University Press, 2006.

■ WALTER R. T. WITSCHEY

PAINTING

See Wall Painting

PALACE

The earliest examples of civic ceremonial **architecture**, from Paso de la Amada during the early Middle Formative, on the Pacific coast of Chiapas, **Mexico**, are the remains of a **ball court** and of a perishable but outsized dwelling for the chief. From these humble beginnings, Mesoamerican communities have typically had at least one elite-status residence: a palace.

The label "palace" usually refers to a masonry building with a long range of adjacent rooms on an elevated platform near the ceremonial center of a city or town, and used, based on remains found within, as the residence of a ruler, his extended family including elite scribes, and his retainers and the artisans whose output he controlled. Palaces vary in form considerably, from single long structures with multiple rooms and doorways along one or both long sides, to similar such buildings grouped in fours or more around courtyards and patios, forming large enclosed open spaces between them. Palace rooms often contained masonry benches for sitting and sleeping.

Examples of palace structures from the Maya area include the rectangular, multistory palaces at **Palenque** and **Sayil**, and the multilevel Nunnery Quadrangle and Governor's Palace at **Uxmal**, the Central Acropolis of **Tikal**, palace A-V at **Uaxactun**, and **Dos Pilas**. The enormous palace at **Cancuen** contained 200 rooms and covered 23,000 m^2 (2.3 ha, about 5.7 acres). (See figures 23, 24, 39, and 49.)

See also AGUATECA; ALLIANCES; ARCHITECTURE OVERVIEW; ASTRONOMY; BONAMPAK; CALAKMUL; CARACOL; CEIBAL; CERAMICS; CHAC II; *CHENES* ARCHITECTURAL STYLE; COCHUAH REGION; COMALCALCO; COPÁN; CORBEL ARCH; COTZUMALHUAPA; DOS PILAS; EK BALAM; EL MIRADOR; EL PERÚ-WAKA'; EL PILAR; HOLMUL; HOUSES; IZIMTE; IXIMCHÉ; KABAH AND NOHPAT; KIUIC; LABNA; MAYA QUEENS; NARANJO; OXKINTOK; PALENQUE; PIEDRAS NEGRAS; PUUC ARCHITECTURAL STYLE; SAN BARTOLO; SAYIL; SETTLEMENT PATTERNS (NORTHERN LOWLANDS); SOUTHERN PERIPHERY; TEXTILES AND CLOTHING; THEATER; TIKAL; UXMAL; WARFARE, WARRIORS, AND WEAPONS

Further Reading

Andrews, George F. *Pyramids and Palaces, Monsters and Masks: The Golden Age of Maya Architecture*. Vol. 1 of *The Collected Works of George F. Andrews*. Lancaster, CA: Labyrinthos, 1995.

Cancuen Palace Reported. Mesoweb, 2001. http://www.mesoweb.com/reports/cancuen.html.

Christie, Jessica Joyce. *Maya Palaces and Elite Residences: An Interdisciplinary Approach*. Austin: University of Texas Press, 2003.

Demarest, Arthur A. *The Petexbatun Regional Archaeological Project: A Multidisciplinary Study of the Maya Collapse*. Vanderbilt Institute of Mesoamerican Archaeology. Nashville, TN: Vanderbilt University Press, 2006.

Kowalski, Jeff Karl. *The House of the Governor: A Maya Palace at Uxmal, Yucatan, Mexico*. Norman: University of Oklahoma Press, 1987.

Stuart, David, and George E. Stuart. *Palenque: Eternal City of the Maya*. New York: Thames & Hudson, 2008.

■ WALTER R. T. WITSCHEY AND CLIFFORD T. BROWN

PALENQUE

The ancient Classic period Maya city of Palenque (17.5° N, 92.0° W), located in northern Chiapas, **Mexico**, holds myriad delights for tourists and archaeologists alike (see also *Map 3*). Tucked into the north-facing hillside, looking across the plain to the southern Gulf of Mexico, its unique buildings, extensive inscriptions, and the **royal tomb** of Pakal, the first found in a Maya temple-pyramid, give it a compelling character unlike any other.

Palenque is named for the small colonial town 8 km away, but recent **decipherments** reveal its Maya name to be Lakamhá, "Big Water," surely an allusion to the several creeks cascading down the hillside through the site. There are 1,500 documented structures clustered in groups, and among them clear evidence of aqueducts and channeling creeks for **water management**. Field **terracing** testifies to intensive agriculture to feed the local populace.

Palenque was occupied from the Late Formative period until it succumbed to the **Classic Maya collapse** around AD 800. The site core was dominated by a magnificent multiroom **palace** with a four-story tower unique in Maya architecture. Adjacent to the palace are a **ball court**, and numerous temple-**pyramids**, including the astonishing Temple of the Inscriptions, in which Mexican archaeologist Alberto Ruz Lhuillier discovered the tomb of K'inich Janaab' Pakal I, who reigned AD 615–683. After three years of excavations within the pyramid, Ruz opened the tomb in June 1952 to reveal an intricately carved stone sarcophagus, within which were the remains of Janaab' Pakal.

Archaeological explorations at Palenque began in 1784 with a visit by José Antonio Calderón, followed in 1787 by Antonio del Río, and in 1805–1809 by Guillermo Dupaix and José Luciano Casteñeda. "Count" Jean-Frédéric Maximillien de Waldeck, who had previously redrawn images from Palenque, visited for a year in 1832. Visits by John Lloyd Stephens and Frederick Catherwood, Désiré Charnay, and Alfred P. Maudslay brought the nineteenth-century visits to a close. Important excavations occupied the first half of the twentieth century, reaching a peak with Ruz's discovery of Pakal's tomb. (See figure 31.) During the latter half of the twentieth century, both excavation and restoration continued under the Instituto Nacional de Antropología e Historia (INAH), and as the twenty-first century began, epigraphic work and translation of extensive scripts from Palenque became a major focus in understanding the site. Those translations form the basis of understanding Palenque's history, as they describe the **dynastic sequence** for the city.

Figure 31. Palenque Temple of the Inscriptions. In 1952 Alberto Ruz discovered a below-ground royal tomb, that of Lord Pacal, accessible by a hidden stairway from the floor of the upper temple. This was the first of many royal tombs to be discovered in the Maya region. Courtesy of Walter Witschey.

Palenque is known for the graceful proportions of its architecture and the refinement of its artwork. The city's buildings form the archetype of the western Maya architectural style, which not only characterizes the Palenque area, but extends as far west as **Comalcalco**. This style places less emphasis on height and massed volumes than the **Petén style** and instead strives for a lighter feeling and more delicately balanced proportions. The lighter feeling is achieved, for example, through the use of mansard roofs, unique in the Maya area, that reduce the heavy, blocky shape of most vaulted Maya buildings. Similarly, the roof-combs are narrower and taller than in some other styles of Maya architecture. Palenque is also famous for the elegance of its relief carvings and stucco panels. The naturalistic proportions of the figures and their dynamic movements confer exceptional power and grace.

The king list and dynastic history of Lakamhá (Palenque) comes chiefly from inscriptions on the Temple of the Cross and the Temple of the Inscriptions (Pakal's tomb). Lakamhá texts mention two early rulers. U-K'ix-Chan, "Snake Spine," born in 993 BC, ascended to the throne in 967 BC. These dates in the Middle Formative period make his rule contemporary with the flourishing Olmec civilization, and perhaps this is a reference to an early Olmec ruler. Ch'a Ruler I, "Casper" ascended to power in 252 BC.

The following, summarizing Martin and Grube, are the known rulers for the balance of Lakamhá's history.

K'uk' B'alam I ("Quetzal Jaguar") was born March 31, AD 397, and ruled March 10, AD 431–435). He took office four years before the important Long Count *b'ak'tun* ending date 9.0.0.0.0, December 11, AD 435. David Stuart suggests that the founding of several Maya dynasties about this time was likely intentional, if not coordinated. Lakamhá changed in his reign, with relations to distant Maya sites reflected by imported polychrome ceramics. K'uk' B'alam is called "Holy Lord of Toktahn'" in the inscriptions, as are his two successors, referring either to the nearby Early Classic settlement at Lakamhá, or to a more distant site, where this lineage had its origins a century before the founding of Lakamhá in AD 490.

Casper was born August 10, AD 422, and ruled August 11, 435–87. He came to power at age 13 and immediately participated in the *b'ak'tun*-ending celebrations of Toktahn'. He takes his name from Ch'a Ruler I (the first Casper).

B'utz'aj Sak Chiik was born November 14, AD 459, and ruled July 29, AD 487–501. His coronation is one calendar round (52 years) and a day after his father's coronation—a deliberate calendric choice. During his reign Lakamhá was first mentioned in inscriptions, and perhaps he was the "founder" of Lakamhá at the location we know as Palenque, moving the lineage here from Toktahn in concert with his younger brother, who succeeded him as Holy Lord.

Ahkal Mo' Naab' I ruled from June 3, AD 501, until his death on November 20, AD 524. While in office, he celebrated the *k'atun* ending of 9.4.0.0.0, October 18, AD 514, as did the other nearby sites **Yaxchilan**, **Piedras Negras**, and **Toniná**. He reappears in later inscriptions, highlighting his position in the direct lineage of the great K'inich Janaab' Pakal I.

K'an Joy Chitam I was born May 3, AD 490, and ruled from AD 529 until his death on February 6, AD 565. Perhaps political unrest consumed Lakamhá during its four-year hiatus before the next coronation. Little is known of his 36-year reign.

Ahkal Mo' Naab' II was born September 3, AD 523, and ruled from May 2, AD 565, until his death on July 21, AD 570. As grandson of the first Ahkal Mo' Naab', he assumed the throne 85 days after the death of his predecessor.

K'inich Kan B'alam I ("Snake Jaguar," "Chan Bahlum") was born September 18, AD 524, and ruled from April 6, AD 572, until his death on February 1, AD 583. Kan B'alam I was the younger brother by a year of Ahkal Mo' Naab' II. He is the first to use the title K'inich, "radiant," like the Sun God. The title was subsequently adopted by Pakal I and all rulers thereafter.

(Lady) Ix Yohl Ik'nal ruled from December 21, AD 583, until her death on November 4, AD 604. Following the death of Kan B'alam I she, as his sister, or more likely, daughter, assumed the throne and reigned for 20 years. During her reign, the first military defeat of Lakamhá was recorded as a conquest by **Calakmul**, the Kaan (Snake) Kingdom, on April 23, AD 599, with the participation of their ally Lakam Chaak of Santa Elena, a contemporary Maya site with a modern name. Whether this was a full-scale war or a smaller raid for the taking of elite captives is not known, but in either case it reflects Lakamhá's growing power and prestige in the Maya world.

Ajen Ohl Mat ruled from January 1, AD 605, until his death on August 8, AD 612. Son of Lady Yohl Ik'nal, Ajen Ohl Mat was subject to a second defeat of Lakamhá by Calakmul, on April 4, AD 611, under the leadership of its ruler Uk'aychan (Scroll Serpent). Although he survived the defeat, Ajen Ohl Mat was dead 16 months later.

Muwaan Mat ruled from October 19, AD 612, to AD 615. Following its second defeat, Lakamhá was in disarray, and in the short reign of Muwaan Mat, the *k'atun* ending 9.9.0.0.0 occurred, but deserves attention as an occasion when Muwaan Mat did *not* perform the usual rituals and make the required offerings, as had been done by his predecessors. Into this leadership vacuum came a heroic new ruler.

K'inich Janaab' Pakal I ("Lord Radiant War Shield") was born March 23, AD 603, and ruled from July 26, AD 615, until his death on August 28, AD 683. Pakal stands as Lakamhá's greatest and best-known ruler. With his father K'an Hix Mo' alive, and his mother Ix Sak K'uk, "Lady Beastie," politically active, Pakal ascended the throne at age 12. Six years later his mother supervised the important *k'atun*-ending rituals of 9.10.0.0.0, January 27, AD 633. For the celebration of 9.11.0.0.0, October 14, AD 652, however, he was clearly in a leadership position. Of this 20-year span little is known. Afterward, Pakal engaged in significant civic enterprises, of which the greatest was the construction of the palace and its tower in AD 650–660. The East Court of the palace carried descriptions of subsequent feats, on relief panels built into the platform bases, including the capture of several important prisoners in AD 662. In sum, inscriptions in this part of the palace attest to Lakamhá regaining its regional power. Pakal was buried in the Temple of the Inscriptions, likely completed by his son and heir, Kan B'alam II. The heavily inscribed sarcophagus was placed and Pakal interred before the temple was completed around it.

K'inich Kan B'alam II was born May 20, AD 635, and ruled from January 7, AD 684, until death and burial on February 16, AD 702. The architectural achievements of Kan B'alam exceed even those of his father. He completed and dedicated the tomb of his father Janaab' Pakal, the Temple of the Inscriptions, on July 6, AD 690. His crowning achievement was construction of the Cross group, three temples with complex texts and iconography celebrating three ancient Maya gods known as the "Palenque Triad." In AD 692, Kan B'alam II dedicated the Temple of the Cross, the Temple of the Sun, and the Temple of the Foliated Cross, all situated to overlook the tomb of his father, the Temple of Inscriptions. Major events celebrated there included a successful attack on Toniná in September AD 687; the conjunction of Jupiter, Mars, Saturn, and the moon in July AD 690; and the erection of a stela to commemorate the 9.13.0.0.0 *k'atun* ending of March 18, AD 692.

K'inich K'an Joy Chitam II was born November 2, AD 644 and ruled from May 30, AD 702 to AD 711. Upon the death of his older brother, K'an Joy Chitam II assumed the throne at age 57. In AD 711, Lakamhá was defeated by Toniná. A Toniná stela showed him as a bound captive. He apparently survived this defeat and capture to become active again, possibly as an agent of Toniná, at both Piedras Negras (AD 714) and Lakamhá (AD 718), finally dropping from the stage before AD 722.

Neither K'an B'alam II nor K'an Joy Chitam II left an heir, and the throne passed to their nephew, Ahkal Mo' Naab' III, son of their brother Tiwol Chan Mat. K'inich Ahkal Mo' Naab' III was born September 13, AD 678, and ruled from December 30, AD 721 to AD 741. Effects of the earlier defeat by Toniná lingered, but by AD 730 the king began a series of raids led by his general, Chak Sutz' ("Red Bat").

Upakal K'inich Janaab' Pakal II ruled ca. AD 742. Upakal, likely the brother of Ahkal Mo' Naab' III, held the title "Holy Lord of Lakamhá" in parallel with his sibling for several years before his brother died. During the interval from AD 741 to AD 764 the inscriptions were meager. There was no mention at Lakamhá of celebrating the 9.16.0.0.0 *k'atun* ending, May 9, AD 751.

K'inich Kan B'alam III ruled ca. AD 751. We know of Kan B'alam III from a stela recording the 9.16.0.0.0 *k'atun*-ending rites at Pomoná, where he assisted the ruler there, K'inich Hix Mo' B'alam.

K'inich K'uk' B'alam II ruled from March 4, AD 764 to AD 783. K'uk' B'alam was the last securely documented ruler from Lakamhá.

The rule of Six Death Janaab' Pakal III began on November 17, 799. A vase from Lakamhá bearing his inauguration date, 9.18.9.4.4, hinted at the end of dynastic rule at Palenque. The adoption of a calendar date name, Six Death, is common in Central Mexico, but not in the Maya area. The recorded history of Lakamhá then fell silent as the Classic Maya collapse swept across the Maya region.

See also AGUADAS; AGUATECA; ALLIANCES; ARCHITECTURE OVERVIEW; ASTRONOMY; BONAMPAK; CALAKMUL; CARACOL; CEIBAL; CERAMICS; CHAC II; *CHENES* ARCHITECTURAL STYLE; CLASSIC MAYA COLLAPSE; COCHUAH REGION; COMALCALCO; COPÁN; CORBEL ARCH; COTZUMALHUAPA; DECIPHERMENT; DIVINE KINGS AND QUEENS; DOS PILAS; DYNASTIC SEQUENCES; EK BALAM; EL MIRADOR; EL PERÚ-WAKA'; EL PILAR; HOLMUL; HOUSES; ICONOGRAPHY; IZIMTE; IXIMCHÉ; KABAH AND NOHPAT; KIUIC; LABNA; MAYA AREA; MAYA QUEENS; MIDDLE CLASSIC HIATUS; NARANJO; OLMEC-MAYA INTERACTIONS; OXKINTOK; PALENQUE; PIEDRAS NEGRAS; PUUC ARCHITECTURAL STYLE; SAN BARTOLO; SAYIL; SCHELE, LINDA; SETTLEMENT PATTERNS (NORTHERN LOWLANDS); SOUTHERN PERIPHERY; TEXTILES AND CLOTHING; THEATER; TIKAL; UXMAL; WARFARE, WARRIORS, AND WEAPONS

Further Reading

Guenter, Stanley. *The Tomb of K'inich Janaab Pakal: The Temple of the Inscriptions at Palenque.* Mesoweb, 2007. http://www.mesoweb.com/articles/guenter/TI.html.

Liendo Stuardo, Rodrigo "Palenque y su área de sustentación: Patrón de Asentamiento y organización política en un centro Maya del Clásico." *Mexicon* 23, no. 2: 36–42, 2001.

Marken, Damien B. *Palenque: Recent Investigations at the Classic Maya Center.* Lanham, MD: AltaMira Press, 2006.

Martin, Simon, and Nikolai Grube. *Chronicle of the Maya Kings and Queens: Deciphering the Dynasties of the Ancient Maya.* 2nd ed. London: Thames & Hudson, 2008.

Schele, Linda, and Mary Ellen Miller. *The Blood of Kings: Dynasty and Ritual in Maya Art.* New York and Fort Worth, TX: G. Braziller and the Kimbell Art Museum, 1986.

Stuart, David, and George E. Stuart. *Palenque: Eternal City of the Maya.* New York: Thames & Hudson, 2008.

■ CLIFFORD T. BROWN AND WALTER R. T. WITSCHEY

PETÉN ARCHITECTURAL STYLE

The Petén style appears throughout the **Central Lowlands** of **Guatemala**, **Belize**, and southern Campeche and Quintana Roo. Cities with such architecture include **Tikal**, **Uaxactún**, **Naranjo**, **Yaxhá**, **Calakmul**, **Xunantunich**, and numerous others. Peter Harrison suggested that there is a "Petén Corridor" of sites stretching northward from the Petén sites to **Cobá** in the Late Classic. Sites in that corridor include Chachoben, Limones, Kantunilkin, **Muyil**, Chamax, and the powerful city of **Cobá**. The architectural affinities imply political affinities as well, perhaps linking Calakmul and Cobá.

A hallmark of the Central or Petén style of architecture is the building of extraordinarily tall, steep-sided temple-**pyramids**. (See figure 32.) They begin with a square or

Figure 32. Tikal Temple I. An example of Petén-style architecture. Courtesy of Walter Witschey.

rectangular base, from which rises a tall truncated pyramid. The pyramidal sides are usually terraced, with a single front stairway from ground to top. Temples I and II at **Tikal** provide a clear example. Corners may be inset; terraces may have aprons or moldings. The whole effect provides a stimulating and changing mix of light and shadow throughout the day. At the top and toward the rear sits a small temple, which frequently bears a tall roof-comb, not only for added height, but also to bear large stucco masks of **deities**. Buildings in the Petén style utilize rubble fill with an exterior of very well dressed, well-laid, and tightly cemented blocks of limestone.

See also ARCHITECTURE OVERVIEW

Further Reading

Andrews, George F. *Pyramids and Palaces, Monsters and Masks: The Golden Age of Maya Architecture.* Vol. 1 of *The Collected Works of George F. Andrews.* Lancaster, CA: Labyrinthos, 1995.

Harrison, Peter D. "Some Aspects of Preconquest Settlement in Southern Quintana Roo, Mexico." In *Lowland Maya Settlement Patterns,* edited by Wendy Ashmore. Santa Fe, NM: School of American Research, 1981.

———. *The Lords of Tikal: Rulers of an Ancient Maya City.* New Aspects of Antiquity. New York: Thames & Hudson, 1999.

Miller, Mary Ellen. *Maya Art and Architecture.* London: Thames & Hudson, 1999.

Proskouriakoff, Tatiana. *An Album of Maya Architecture.* Carnegie Institution of Washington, Publication 558. Washington, DC: Carnegie Institution of Washington, 1962.

■ WALTER R. T. WITSCHEY

PHYSICAL/BIOLOGICAL ANTHROPOLOGY

Physical/biological anthropology is the study of human biology that includes adaptation, variability, and evolution. Specific to the ancient Maya, physical anthropologists seek to understand the human record by examining human remains to answer questions regarding identity, disease, occupation, social status, **diet**, and population dynamics. They address research questions regarding human biology such as health and stature, but also social questions with evidence such as cranial modification and **burial** practices as markers of status and regional typologies. The entire representation of the human body and how it was treated during life and after death is significant to physical anthropologists. To get at these particular research areas, several specialties have been developed: osteology, skeletal biology, bioarchaeology, and paleopathology.

Osteologists and skeletal biologists examine and interpret human remains by analyzing the physical and molecular makeup of bone. Once skeletal remains are removed from an archaeological context, the osteologist macroscopically assesses the bones and takes measurements to determine age, sex, stature, disease, and cultural changes to the body such as cranial or dental modifications. Microscopic analysis provides for more specific research in pathology and bone density studies. Still further, genetics, diet, and health information can be extracted through DNA studies and isotopic and trace element analysis, as well as tooth enamel phosphate analysis to determine region of origin. Demography, the study of populations, analyzes life expectancy, birth and death rates, growth, and size of a population. Paleodemography, the study of ancient population demography, is applied to ancient Maya groups to reconstruct relationships and trends over time in various regions for population comparisons. Unavoidable problems that affect these studies are differential rates of preservation of the skeletal material and small sample sizes. Natural conditions such as weather, water, and acidic **soils** distress remains, and so too do intentional changes such as cremation, fragmentation, and dismemberment.

Bioarchaeologists combine the skill sets of physical/biological anthropology and archaeology to study skeletal material in archaeological contexts to comprehensively understand the interaction between biology and culture. For example, bioarchaeologists study both the physical manifestations of cranial and dental modification and how the practice relates to culture and identity. Bioarchaeological studies also focus on Maya diet, health, and disease and how these reflect culture. Paleopathologists specifically examine disease in human remains. This includes the identification of infectious diseases, disorders, lesions, joint pathology, dental disease, and other diseases that leave evidence on bone. In addition, trauma is assessed, such as evidence of trepanation or brain surgery, bones broken and healed during the individual's lifetime, and bones injured at time of death. These approaches allow investigation into behavior, **warfare**, sacrifice, and politics (see also **Rites and Rituals**).

Together, osteologists, human biologists, and bioarchaeologists address who the ancient Maya were in terms of cultural and physical persons. These specialists contribute explicit pieces of information to fully understand the significance of Maya adaptation and variability and allow for inference and comparison with other Maya through time and with contemporary populations. Analyses of physical and cultural aspects, disease, trauma, and diet in combination with work from other anthropological disciplines provides answers about what it meant to be Maya throughout life and afterlife.

See also BONAMPAK; CACAO; CALAKMUL; CARACOL; CERRO MAYA/CERROS; CHAC II; CLASS STRUCTURE; COPÁN; DZIBILCHALTUN; ECCENTRIC LITHICS; FAUNA; GEOLOGY; HOLMUL; IXIMCHÉ; JAINA; MAYA QUEENS; MIDDLE CLASSIC HIATUS; MUSIC AND DANCE; NAJ TUNICH; OBSIDIAN; OXKINTOK; PALENQUE; PHYSICAL/BIOLOGICAL ANTHROPOLOGY; PIEDRAS NEGRAS–DYNASTIC SEQUENCE; PUSILHA; RIO AZUL; RITES OF PASSAGE; ROYAL TOMBS; SIN CABEZAS; TEOTIHUACÁN (MAYA INTERACTION WITH); TEXTILES AND CLOTHING; TRADE ROUTES; TULUM; WALL PAINTING; WARFARE, WARRIORS, AND WEAPONS; ZACUALPA; ZACULEU

Further Reading

Larsen, Clark Spencer. *Bioarchaeology: Interpreting Behavior from the Human Skeleton.* Cambridge, UK: Cambridge University Press, 1999.

Mays, Simon. *The Archaeology of Human Bones.* 2nd ed. London; New York: Routledge, 2010.

Ortner, Donald J. *Identification of Pathological Conditions in Human Skeletal Remains.* San Diego, CA: Academic Press, 2003.

Tiesler, Vera, and Andrea Cucina. "New Perspectives on Human Sacrifice and Ritual Body Treatment in Ancient Maya Society." In *Society for American Archaeology Annual Meeting.* New York: Springer, 2007.

White, Tim D., Michael Timothy Black, and Pieter A. Folkens. *Human Osteology.* 3rd ed. Boston: Elsevier Academic Press, 2012.

Whittington, Stephen L., and David M. Reed. *Bones of the Maya: Studies of Ancient Skeletons.* Tuscaloosa: University of Alabama Press, 2006.

■ KENDRA L. PHILMON

PIEDRAS NEGRAS

Piedras Negras (17.2° N, 91.2° W) was a major ancient Maya city situated on the Guatemalan side of the Usumacinta River, which now divides the modern countries of **Mexico** and **Guatemala** (see also **Map 3**). Today there is no easy access to the site, for it is in a remote area of Guatemala's Department of the Petén.

Piedras Negras was a small village around 600 BC, attracting people for its location on the river and also for the abundant amount of local **chert** for tool making. Because of the many **caves** in the immediate vicinity, known to have been holy places, there may also have been more esoteric reasons for settlement. Recent excavations have shown that by the Early Classic period (AD 250–600) Piedras Negras had grown into a fairly large and important city that was able to take some control of both riverine and overland traffic, especially goods being brought from the west bound for areas to the east.

Most structures seen in the city today are of Late Classic date (AD 600–800). Three major plaza groups in the city have been archaeologically examined: the South Group is the earliest, with **architecture** and relief-carved monuments dating from the Early Classic, and where there is also some evidence of civic architecture from the Preclassic period. The next is the West Group, which primarily dates to the Late Classic period. Its architecture is defined by an acropolis consisting of **pyramids**, **palaces**, and civic structures with courtyards. The East Group was the last large ceremonial area to be constructed and has a major pyramid rising on the north side of its plaza. Sweat baths, associated with Late Classic palaces, have been archaeologically studied, and Piedras Negras is unusual for its concentration of such distinctive and carefully built structures.

Anciently, Piedras Negras was probably known as Yokib, or the Entrance, and was a regal center ruled by the Turtle dynasty throughout the Early and Late Classic periods. Eleven dynasts, known to us through hieroglyphs carved on the stone monuments, ruled Yokib from AD 460 to circa 808. All but one of the rulers' names include the glyph *ahk*, or turtle. The carved monuments can be attributed to the reign and patronage of specific rulers.

Relief-carved **stelae**, upright slabs of stone, were generally placed on terraces that fronted the major plazas and were devoted to hieroglyphs and images. The hieroglyphs are formulaic, telling of the important events in a ruler's life, such as birth, marriage, military successes, performing traditional royal rituals, and ultimately death. The images illustrate the ruler, and often his wife as well, performing royal ceremonies. Because actual dates were attached to the hieroglyphs describing these events, Tatiana **Proskouriakoff** was able in 1960 to demonstrate that Maya glyphs and images were essentially historical in nature rather than devoted to the esoterica of the cosmic time as had previously been thought. Carved thrones or pedestals were placed directly in the plazas. They are also carved with hieroglyphs relating the lives of the rulers. Relief-carved panels were probably originally placed on the exterior, upright walls of temples high atop the pyramids. They were carved and erected to honor a deceased ancestor. One relief-carved throne was located in a temple atop a memorial pyramid in the acropolis. It was found broken into many small pieces but is now beautifully restored and in the Museo Nacional de Arqueología y Ethnología in Guatemala City (see figure 33).

The throne, telling of the important events in the last known ruler's life, was carved early in the ninth century. Known as K'inich Yat Ahk II, he is thought to have lost his life

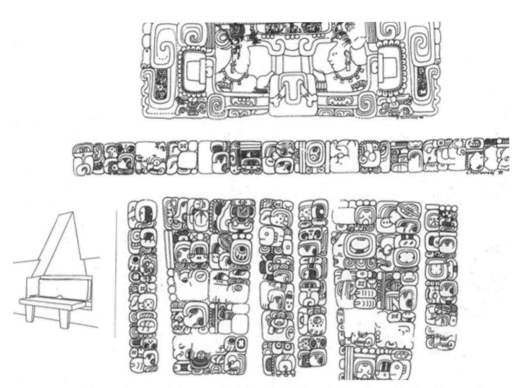

Figure 33. Elaborately carved throne with hieroglyphic inscriptions from Piedras Negras. The throne, which dates to the ninth century AD, tells of important events in the life of ruler K'inich Yat Ahk II, the last known ruler at the site. Drawn by John Montgomery, whose permission is published in the same volume of drawings, courtesy of Flora Clancy.

and a war with the city of **Yaxchilan**, located approximately 50 km upriver. The broken throne is taken as a sign of the devastation visited upon Piedras Negras at the end of its long and remarkable existence.

See also BURIALS; CALAKMUL; CLASSIC MAYA COLLAPSE; CRAFT SPECIALIZATION; DECIPHERMENT; DIVINE KINGS AND QUEENS; DYNASTIC SEQUENCES; ECCENTRIC LITHICS; EDZNA; GUATEMALA; KAMINALJUYÚ; MUSIC AND DANCE; PALACE; PALENQUE; PHYSICAL/ BIOLOGICAL ANTHROPOLOGY; PROSKOURIAKOFF, TATIANA AVENIROVNA; RELIGION; RITES AND RITUALS; SOUTHERN LOWLANDS; SYLLABARY; WARFARE, WARRIORS, AND WEAPONS; WESTERN ARCHITECTURAL STYLE

Further Reading

Clancy, Flora S. *The Monuments of Piedras Negras, an Ancient Maya City*. Albuquerque: University of New Mexico Press, 2009.

Houston, Stephen, Héctor L. Escobedo, Mark Child, Charles W. Golden, Richard Terry, and David Webster. "In the Land of the Turtle Lords: Archaeological Investigations at Piedras Negras, 2000." *Mexicon* 22, no. 5: 97–110, 2000.

O'Neil, Megan Eileen. *Engaging Ancient Maya Sculpture at Piedras Negras, Guatemala*. Norman: University of Oklahoma Press, 2012.

Proskouriakoff, Tatiana. "Historical Implications of a Pattern of Dates at Piedras Negras, Guatemala." *American Antiquity* 25, 4: 454–75, 1960.

■ FLORA S. CLANCY

PIEDRAS NEGRAS-DYNASTIC SEQUENCE

Separating fact from fancy is difficult in Maya inscriptions that reflect back into mythological times. At Piedras Negras, a Late Classic period altar reported kings who ruled in 4691 BC and in 3114 BC, clearly long before the existence of Maya culture. The same altar also records a more reasonable *k'atun*-ending date of 8.13.0.0.0, December 14, AD 297, the beginning of the Maya Classic period, and perhaps reflects a real king of that era. The following summary is based on the detailed work of Martin and Grube.

Ruler A ("Itzam K'ahnak," "Turtleshell," "Precious or Yellow Turtle") ruled ca. AD 460. Rulers given letter designations were identified after the remarkable work of **Tatiana Proskouriakoff** on a later dynastic sequence. The inscriptions of **Yaxchilan** reported the capture of a Piedras Negras king by Yaxchilan king Moon Skull ca. 460. This early reference testifies to the beginnings of a long and contentious rivalry between the two neighboring Usumacinta cities.

Ruler B ("Itzam K'ahnak," "Turtleshell," "Precious or Yellow Turtle") ruled ca. AD 478. The name Itzam K'ahnak was used repeatedly by Piedras Negras rulers. In the Late Postclassic Dresden codex, Itzam K'ahnak was portrayed as the aged earth **deity**, God N, with both a turtle carapace and a k'an sign for yellow/precious. Yaxchilan's king Bird Jaguar II captured a noble from Piedras Negras ca. AD 478.

Turtle Tooth ("Ah Cauac Ah K'in") ruled ca. AD 508–510. Yaxchilan's king Knot-eye Jaguar I captured a Piedras Negras noble from Turtle Tooth's reign ca. AD 508. In AD 510, Turtle Tooth was portrayed as receiving **Teotihuacán**-style helmets, which he presented to lords of **Bonampak**, Yaxchilan, and Lacanha, all under the aegis of the importantly titled foreigner Tajoom Uk'ab Tuun, possibly of Teotihuacán.

Ruler C came to power on June 30, AD 514 and was ruling in AD 518. The dedication of a temple at Piedras Negras began the local recorded history. In addition to the king's accession date, it honored the *k'atun*-ending date 9.4.0.0.0, October 18, AD 514. Ruler C was portrayed with four captives, one from Santa Elena, and another the king of Yaxchilan, Knot-eye Jaguar I.

Two other royal texts at Piedras Negras commemorate the 9.5.0.0.0 *k'atun*-ending date of July 5, AD 534, and the subsequent quarter-*k'atun*-ending date of 9.5.5.0.0, June 9, AD 539. There is a serious gap, a hiatus, in the recorded history at the site, however, from AD 539 until the crowning of Ruler 1.

K'inich Yo'nal Ahk I ("Ruler 1," "Radiant Turtle") came to power on November 14, AD 603, and ruled until his death on February 3, AD 639. He began a remarkable sequence of monuments to his own exploits, a practice followed by his successors. His inauguration monument established a "niche-style" presentation of the seated ruler, and other monuments presented him as a warrior king, wearing a Teotihuacán headdress and displaying bound captives. In AD 628 he reported taking captives from **Palenque** and Sak Tz'i'.

Ruler 2 was born May 22, AD 626, came to power on April 12, AD 639, and ruled until his death on November 15, AD 686. Possibly using the name "Rain God Precious Turtle," Ruler 2 made battle conquests in AD 662 against Santa Elena, and in AD 669 against an unknown enemy. He is also shown receiving a Teotihuacán-style war helmet on the twentieth anniversary of his father's death. By ca. AD 677, Ruler 2 had mounted an aggressive construction program. He participated in a ritual supervised by lord Yuknoom the Great of **Calakmul**, signaling perhaps a shift from Teotihuacán relations toward connections with Calakmul. Ruler 2 supervised the marriage arrangements for his son in November 686, but passed away on November 15, a few days before the marriage took place.

K'inich Yo'nal Ahk II ("Ruler 3") was born December 29, AD 664, married on November 20, AD 686, took the throne on January 2, AD 687, and ruled until his death in AD 729. Ruler 3 took his grandfather's name, "Radiant Turtle," and ruled for 42 years. His marriage during his father's funeral period drew attention to his 12-year-old princess-bride Lady K'atun Ajaw, and she subsequently appeared on monuments during his reign. He erected a dated monument celebrating the quarter-*k'atun*-ending date of 9.12.15.0.0, April 14, AD 687, and every quarter *k'atun* (about five years) thereafter until 9.14.15.0.0, September 17, AD 726. His military exploits reflected seesaw efforts: controlling La Mar, losing a noble to Palenque, and capturing a noble from Yaxchilan.

Ruler 4 was born November 18, AD 701, came to power on November 9, AD 729, and ruled until his death on November 26, AD 757. Because he likely was not a descendant of K'inich Yo'nal Ahk II, Ruler 4 used one large stela to emphasize his link to Teotihuacán, perhaps his mother's home. Evidence indicates he began a new royal line at Piedras Negras. During his reign, he too erected a monument for each quarter-*k'atun*-ending date. Continuing warfare in the region was amply confirmed on a pyrite disk in his tomb, bearing the image of the decapitated head of a noble from Hix Witz.

Ik Na' Yo'nal Ahk III ("Ruler 5," "Black House Great Turtle") came to power March 10, AD 758, and ruled until his death ca. AD 767. During the reign of Ruler 5, political relations in the region continued to be important to the king. He recorded the inauguration of the king for La Mar. He supervised the burial of the ruler of Yax Niil (El Cayo), although the inauguration of Yax Niil's successor was supervised by the ruler of Sak Tz'i', Aj Sak Maax. Yaxchilan was able to seize prince T'ul Chik of Piedras Negras in AD 759.

Ha' K'in Xook ("Water Sun Shark") came to power on February 14, AD 767, and ruled until his death on March 28, AD 780. Water Sun Shark may have been the son of Ruler 4 and brother to Ruler 5. He erected quarter-*k'atun* monuments in AD 771 and 775. He was reported at a ritual (burial) at El Cayo in AD 772.

K'inich ? Ahk ("Ruler 7," "Radiant Turtle Tooth") was born April 7, AD 750, came to power on May 31, AD 781, and ruled until he was captured in AD 808. Ruler 7 was an aggressive warrior, and in addition to erecting quarter-*k'atun* monuments, he also wrote that he took a captive from Santa Elena in AD 787 and twice mounted successful Star Wars against Pomona, defeating its king, Kuch Bahlam, in AD 792 and 795, in concert with his war ally Parrot Chaak of La Mar. Ultimately Ruler 7 was taken captive himself, by K'inich Tatbu Skull IV of Yaxchilan, as both cities were succumbing to the forces of the **Classic Maya collapse**.

Although an altar was carved at Piedras Negras in AD 810, the city itself was soon overrun and burned.

See also PIEDRAS NEGRAS

Further Reading

Clancy, Flora S. *The Monuments of Piedras Negras, an Ancient Maya City.* Albuquerque: University of New Mexico Press, 2009.

Houston, Stephen, Héctor L. Escobedo, Mark Child, Charles W. Golden, Richard Terry, and David Webster. "In the Land of the Turtle Lords: Archaeological Investigations at Piedras Negras, 2000." *Mexicon* 22, no. 5: 97–110, 2000.

Martin, Simon, and Nikolai Grube. *Chronicle of the Maya Kings and Queens: Deciphering the Dynasties of the Ancient Maya.* 2nd ed. London: Thames & Hudson, 2008.

Proskouriakoff, Tatiana. "Historical Implications of a Pattern of Dates at Piedras Negras, Guatemala." *American Antiquity* 25, no. 4: 454–75, 1960.

■ WALTER R. T. WITSCHEY

POPOL VUH

The *Popol Vuh*, the most significant aboriginal text that survived from the preconquest Americas, opens a window onto the landscape of ancient Maya history, **religion**, and worldview. Written in the highlands in Quiché Maya, the existing manuscript is a copy transcribed in the Roman alphabet by Francisco Ximénez, a Spanish friar, in the early eighteenth century in Chichicastenango, in highland **Guatemala**. The original alphabetic manuscript that Ximénez copied was evidently written by Quiché nobles in the 1550s, facts inferred from internal evidence. The Quiché, in turn, appear to have transcribed the text into the Roman alphabet from a hieroglyphic original (see also **Codices [Maya]**). Ximénez's manuscript was rediscovered and published in the mid-nineteenth century, attracting intense scholarly interest.

Popol Vuh means "Council Book," and the title describes the book's function literally. It was consulted by the governing council of lineage elders of the Quiché kingdom when they assembled to make decisions. They believed the book granted them a divine power to see afar and know the past and future. The text achieved this by combining scripture (what today we call myth), history, and implied prognostication.

The story begins in darkness, when only the sea, the sky, and the primordial gods existed. The gods of sky and sea then create the land, the mountains, the plants, and the animals (see also **Deities**; **Fauna**; **Vegetation**). The creation of humans, however, fails three times before succeeding. The first attempt created the birds and animals, which were unsatisfactory because they could not speak and therefore could not pray to their creators. Then they tried to create humans out of clay, but these dissolved into mud. Then the gods tried to fashion people of wood, but these beings were disorderly, incorrigible, and senseless. They had to be destroyed, and their remains transformed into monkeys. Finally, much later in the text success is achieved when the gods mold the first humans out of corn dough.

Interwoven with the creation story is another mythic narrative that describes the heroic exploits of two pairs of hero twins. The first pair, named One Hunahpu and Seven Hunahpu, are the twin sons of the god Xpiyacoc and the goddess Xmucane, the oldest gods and the primordial couple. The twins are players of the **ball game**. The noise of their playing disturbs the gods of the Underworld, who summon the twins to their domain, Xibalba, ostensibly to play ball. But the overlords of Xibalba, One Death and Seven Death, trick the twins and sacrifice them, hanging the severed head of One Hunahpu in a calabash tree. A maiden named Blood Moon, unmarried daughter of one of the lords of Xibalba, visits the calabash tree, and the skull of One Hunahpu spits in her hand and impregnates her.

When her father discovers her pregnancy, although she truthfully denies sleeping with anyone, he sends her away to be sacrificed. She, however, persuades her executioners to spare her, and she goes to the home of the twins' mother, Xmucane. She initially rejects her daughter-in-law, setting her an impossible task, but when Blood Moon miraculously accomplishes it, she is accepted. She gives birth to the second pair of Hero Twins, Hunahpu and Xbalanque. Despite conflicts with their half brothers, the twins grow up to be hunters, magicians, and ballplayers, like their fathers. Using clever tricks, they slay several monsters, such as Seven Macaw, before their ballplaying earns them their own summons to Xibalba. They, however, astutely avoid the traps set for them by the lords of Xibalba, and eventually Hunahpu and Xbalanque triumph over the gods and sacrifice One Death and Seven Death. The twins finally undergo apotheosis and rise as the Sun and the Moon.

After the creation of the first four true men from corn dough, the story shifts slowly from myth to history, and specifically to the history of the Quiché state. The formation and propagation of the lineages is described. The four lineage heads then make an epochal journey to a great eastern city, a kind of primordial city conceptually related to Tollan, city of kingmakers, where they are endowed with the divine right of lordship. Evidence in the *Popol Vuh* and other documents suggests that the city was Late Classic **Copán**. For example, a related version says that the insignia of the city was the bat, and the Emblem Glyph of Copán was a bat. There the first Quiché lords acquire their three principal tutelary gods: Tohil, Auilix, and Hacauitz. After returning, the Quiché ancestors begin to establish their dominance over surrounding territories. Later their lords make a second pilgrimage, this time to a city, probably in Yucatan, where they receive emblems of lordship from a king called Nacxit, one name for Quetzalcoatl. The narrative continues by recounting the glories of succeeding generations of Quiché rulers, up to the 1550s.

The complicated blending of myth and history in the *Popol Vuh* is similar to that found in other scriptures, including the Judeo-Christian bible. In the Maya case, however, we see signs of a cyclic view of past and future. As history repeated itself, the past was the guide to the future, through the omens and prognostications derived from the sacred 260-day (*tzolk'in*) **calendar**. Events never repeated exactly, but there were patterns that could be divined by priests and seers skilled in the art of foretelling. The surviving Maya hieroglyphic **codices** were composed mostly of almanacs designed for determining the omens and portents forecast by the sacred calendar. The *Popol Vuh* played a related role, alluding to the calendrics that marked Quiché myth and history. The narrative also embodies a subtext related to the cycles of Venus, which for the Maya were pregnant with meaning.

We find a similar mytho-historical narrative in inscriptions of some Classic Maya sites, especially at **Palenque**, where the texts begin in a legendary past of totemic ancestor **deities** and end in the historical present with contemporary rulers and their deeds.

Perhaps the most fascinating aspects of the *Popol Vuh* are its connections to Classic Maya **religion**. In the 1970s Michael Coe discovered that beautifully painted Classic Period funerary vases from the Maya lowlands often depicted scenes from the *Popol Vuh*. (See figures 34 and 35.) In these masterful works of art, we can see Hunahpu and Xbalanque come alive as the Maya envisaged them over a thousand years ago, slaying Seven Macaw with a blowgun, playing ball, and overcoming the gods of death. We can now link many of the gods and personages from the *Popol Vuh* with their Classic period names and images. Hunahpu is named "Hun Ahau," or "One Lord," and he is recognized by patterns of spots on his body. Xbalanque is called "Yax Balam" and carries patches of jaguar pelt to identify him. Tohil is the Classic period K'awiil, the Manikin Scepter, also called God GII at Palenque and God K in the Maya codices. One Hunahpu from the *Popol Vuh* is known to iconographers as the "Foliated Maize God" or the "Tonsured Maize God," and he appears in the codices as God E. These iconographic and epigraphic discoveries reveal that much of the *Popol Vuh* is not uniquely Quiché, but rather is a pan-Maya scripture.

The *Popol Vuh* is also a major source of information about Maya literature and poetics. Some passages are written in verse. The most common poetical structure is the couplet, sometimes rhyming, that expressed pairs of related ideas in similar words. This kind of couplet is also found elsewhere in Maya literature, such as in the Books of Chilam Balam. Various kinds of discourse are found in the *Popol Vuh*. Some passages address the reader directly, and even suggest that parts may have been performed as dramatic readings or plays. Other sections can be interpreted as describing painted illustrations that were in the hieroglyphic original but not copied with the transcription into Latin letters.

The *Popol Vuh* has been translated many times into various languages. Ximénez provided the first translation, in parallel columns accompanying his transcription of the Quiché text. Ongoing research in Maya literature, linguistics, and archaeology has helped create ever-improved translations. The outstanding English translation is currently Dennis Tedlock's, which reflects and benefits from his lifelong study of the Quiché and his intimate collaboration with Quiché experts, such as Andrés Xiloj Peruch of Momostenango.

The *Popol Vuh* has influenced modern art and literature. For example, Miguel Ángel Asturias, the Nobel prize–winning Guatemalan author, wove elements of the *Popol Vuh* into his writing, most notably in his masterpiece, *Men of Maize*. The *Popol Vuh* itself remains the closest thing to a Maya "Bible" that survived the ravages of Spanish conquest and evangelization, and therefore is the best source of information about Maya religion.

See also ART; BALL GAME/BALL COURT; CACAO; CERAMICS; CODEX-STYLE VASES; COPÁN; COUNCIL HOUSE; DECIPHERMENT; DEITIES; DIET; FAUNA; HIGHLAND MAYA LANGUAGES; ICONOGRAPHY; TRIBUTE; UNDERWATER ARCHAEOLOGY; UTATLÁN/Q'UM'ARKAJ; UXMAL; WRITING SYSTEMS OF MESOAMERICA

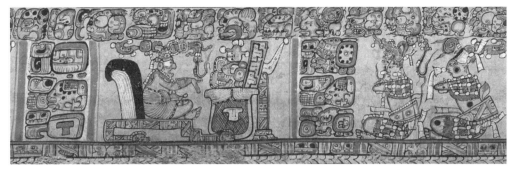

Figure 34. Hunahpú and Xbalanqué, Hero Twins from the *Popol Vuh*, in jade bead costumes. They are looking at their father's head in a cache vessel in front of Itzamná (God D). Roll-out photo of a cylindrical vase captured by a custom camera and turntable. Courtesy of and copyright by Justin Kerr. Maya Vase Database No. K1183.

Figure 35. Hunahpú and Xbalanqué, Hero Twins from the *Popol Vuh*, in jade bead costumes. Profile view of a cylindrical vase. Courtesy of and copyright by Justin Kerr. Maya Vase Database No. K1183.

Further Reading

Amlin, Patricia. *Popol Vuh: The Creation Myth of the Maya*. Film. Berkeley, CA: Berkeley Media LLC, 1989.

Christenson, Allen J. *Popol Vuh: The Sacred Book of the Maya*. Norman: University of Oklahoma Press, 2007.

Danien, Elin C., and Robert J. Sharer, eds. *New Theories on the Ancient Maya*. University Museum Monograph, vol. 77. Philadelphia: University of Pennsylvania Museum, 1992.

Tedlock, Dennis. "The Popol Vuh as a Hieroglyphic Book." In *New Theories on the Ancient Maya*, edited by Elin C. Danien and Robert J. Sharer. University Museum Monograph, vol. 77. Philadelphia: University of Pennsylvania Museum, 1992.

———. *Popol Vuh: The Mayan Book of the Dawn of Life*. rev. ed. New York: Simon & Schuster, 1996.

———. *2000 Years of Mayan Literature*. Berkeley: University of California Press, 2010.

■ CLIFFORD T. BROWN AND WALTER R. T. WITSCHEY

PORTABLE OBJECTS

Portable objects within the archaeological record are defined as moveable objects created, shaped, and distributed by people. For the Maya these objects consisted mainly of **ceramics** and **lithics**, in addition to a variety of small shell- or metal-crafts. These portable objects function as a proxy to understanding Maya polities, influential boundaries, and the intensification of the Maya political/social economy. In addition, portable objects help to understand trading networks and power dynamics of the region.

Portable objects can be further classified as either utilitarian or prestige objects. Utilitarian objects were used for everyday subsistence and were typically less time-consuming to make. Prestige objects were used as tribute, as funerary/ritual offerings, or as gift exchange among the rulers and elite (see also **Rites and Rituals**; **Trade Routes**).

Ceramics: Utilitarian ceramics were distributed within local economies and were generally produced in-house. While the ceramic traditions fluctuated through time and region, Maya ceramics can generally be characterized as highly polished wares with a black or brown surface. Varying techniques applied to these ceramics include incising, carving, slipping, punctuation, applique, and painting (see also **Ceramic Analysis**).

Preclassic Maya vessels used for storage or cooking were unslipped. Polychrome vessels in black, white, red, and yellow, along with Usulutan fired-resist techniques, first appear during the Middle Preclassic. Some forms, such as necked jars, a variety of bowls, and cylindrical incense burners, flourished. Handmade clay anthropomorphic effigies were also prevalent along with cylindrical or flat clay seals and whistles (see also **Jaina**).

Classic Maya pottery is defined by the prevalence of polychrome wares, typically red and black with orange or cream base. Mold-made figurines replaced handmade effigies and were restricted to elite-ritual contexts. These figurines also functioned as ocarinas and were used for ritual and entertainment purposes. New ceramic forms of cylindrical vessels and small pitchers appeared that were similar in shape to those of Central Mexico, showcasing increased influence from that area.

Postclassic wares showed a decline in intricacy and breadth of style, with the pottery becoming more standardized and mass produced. Jars, bowls, and tortilla griddles, among other forms, were still used.

Lithics: The Maya used percussion and pressure-flaking techniques to shape flint (see also **Chert**) and **obsidian** into cutting tools and scrapers, while basalt and igneous rocks were ground into chisels for cutting stone, bark beaters, and/or manos and metates. These cutting stones and manos/metates were used for utilitarian **subsistence** purposes, while bark beaters were used to make paper for binding into **codices**. Other lithic items include large oval bifaces; tranchet bit tools, adzes, and stemmed macroblades. Obsidian blades are most common since they served both utilitarian and ritual purposes.

Carefully worked sacrificial knives, scepters, and decapitators made of obsidian and jade were used as prestige markers. In addition, obsidian bloodletting tools and **eccentrics** were used in ritual capacities. Eccentrics account for some of the most elaborate stonework within the Maya area and first appeared during the Late Preclassic. Figurines made of flint or obsidian complete with ornaments of office and headdresses representing humans or gods functioned as symbols of elite status (see also **Deities**; **Divine Kings and Queens**). These objects have been found ritually buried beneath Maya monuments and buildings.

Other Portable Objects: The Maya adorned themselves with mosaic jade-and-shell masks, metal disks, bead jewelry, ear plugs, and metal bells. They also used mirrors made of polished obsidian or pyrite; while typically found in high-status households, these mirrors were not restricted to elite use. Ear plugs, pendants, and beads made of jade, feathers, or worked Spondylus shells were worn by rulers and upper-class citizens. Some objects, like small copper bells, were used both for adornment and as currency.

Overall, certain portable objects set the elite apart due to their rarity or the specialization needed to craft them. Both prestige and utilitarian portable objects have defined Maya culture and have been essential to understanding past Maya trade and life.

See also AGUATECA; ALTUN HA; BURIALS; CAHAL PECH; CALAKMUL; CARACOL; CARACOL-DYNASTIC HISTORY; CEIBAL; CERAMIC ANALYSIS; CEREN; CERRO MAYA/CERROS; CHAC II; CRAFT SPECIALIZATION; DECIPHERMENT; DOS PILAS; DZIBANCHÉ; EDZNA; EL CHAYAL; EL PILAR; FAUNA; GEOLOGY; HOUSEHOLD PRODUCTION; IXIMCHÉ; IXTEPEQUE; IZAMAL; KABAH AND NOHPAT; KAMINALJUYÚ; KIUIC; KOMCHEN; LA CORONA; LA LAGUNITA; LABNA; LAKES; LAMANAI; LANGUAGE AND WRITING OVERVIEW; MARKETS AND MARKETPLACES; MAYA QUEENS; MUSIC AND DANCE; MUYIL; NAACHTUN; NAJ TUNICH; NAKBÉ; NARANJO; NORTHERN HIGHLANDS; OBSIDIAN; OLMEC; OLMEC-MAYA INTERACTIONS; OXKINTOK; RITES AND RITUALS; ROYAL TOMBS; SAYIL; SOUTHERN HIGHLANDS; SOUTHERN PERIPHERY; SYLLABARY; TEOTIHUACÁN (MAYA INTERACTIONS WITH); TIKAL; TRADE ROUTES; TRIBUTE; TULUM; UNDERWATER ARCHAEOLOGY; WARFARE, WARRIORS, AND WEAPONS; WRITING SYSTEMS OF MESOAMERICA; ZACULEU

Further Reading

Foster, Lynn V. *Handbook to Life in the Ancient Maya World*. New York: Facts on File, 2002.

Halperin, Christina T. "Circulation as Placemaking: Late Classic Maya Polities and Portable Objects." *American Anthropologist* 116, no. 1: 110–29, 2014.

Sharer, Robert J., and Loa P. Traxler. *The Ancient Maya*. 6th ed. Stanford, CA: Stanford University Press, 2006.

■ ASHLEY HAMPTON

POTTERY
See CERAMICS

PRIESTS

The extent to which **religion** was hierarchically organized not only varied over time, but also is obscured from detailed view prior to the arrival of Spanish friars in the New World. **Diego de Landa** reported that the Late Postclassic Maya had priests, *chilan*, whose duties were to discuss and teach their sciences and proclaim the festival days, implying knowledge of the details of the ancient **calendar**; to conduct **rites and rituals**; and to make sacrifices of animals, people, and personal bloodletting. They also served as seers of the future and curers. There are hints of a hierarchy from major centers to smaller ones. As keepers of the calendars and the almanacs written in **codices**, the *chilan* were among the few literate members of society. By the time Landa arrived in Yucatan, even the Postclassic city-states had collapsed, and he had no examples of what the priesthood must have been like in Classic times.

From the **iconography** and inscriptions left behind at the great Classic Maya city-states, we can draw a rather different picture. The **divine king**, legitimately ruling from a power base that included his dynastic ancestors and city founders, was clearly the high priest of his city (see also **Dynastic Sequences**). The additional staffing of religious positions for the city came from his family, the elite class of nobles, and clearly drew on just those people who were skilled in divination, literate in the ancient hieroglyphs, literate in the workings of the ancient calendar and its multiple cycles, and capable of serving as scribes for the books as well as the less-perishable stone monuments (**stelae**) of the city. Illustrations of Classic performances, found on ceramics and murals, led by the king and an array of elites from the court, suggest that the elite ruling class and the religious functionaries were virtually the same (see also **Music and Dance**; and **Theater**).

In addition to the state-level function of the king serving as high priest, there was another religious leader operating at the neighborhood and village level. This was the shaman and curer, whose duties were similar, but whose duties were more personal, divining the future for a single person, rather than the city, and providing personal intercession with the gods for an individual rather than corporate intercession on behalf of the society.

The Maya priesthood evolved over time, from shamans and wise elderly persons, to vesting in the royal courts of the Classic period, to a modest priestly class in the Postclassic following the **Classic Maya collapse**.

See also CLASS STRUCTURE; DECIPHERMENT; DROUGHT; KINSHIP; *POPOL VUH*; RITES OF PASSAGE; WRITING SYSTEMS OF MESOAMERICA

Further Reading

Looper, Matthew George. *To Be Like Gods: Dance in Ancient Maya Civilization*. Austin: University of Texas Press, 2009.

Martin, Simon, and Nikolai Grube. *Chronicle of the Maya Kings and Queens: Deciphering the Dynasties of the Ancient Maya*. 2nd ed. London: Thames & Hudson, 2008.

Milbrath, Susan. *Star Gods of the Maya: Astronomy in Art, Folklore, and Calendars*. Austin: University of Texas Press, 2000.

Miller, Mary Ellen, and Karl A. Taube. *The Gods and Symbols of Ancient Mexico and the Maya: An Illustrated Dictionary of Mesoamerican Religion*. New York: Thames and Hudson, 1993.

Sharer, Robert J., and Loa P. Traxler. *The Ancient Maya*. 6th ed. Stanford, CA: Stanford University Press, 2006.

Zender, Marc Uwe. "A Study of Classic Maya Priesthood." PhD diss., University of Calgary, 2004.

■ WALTER R. T. WITSCHEY

PRIMARY STANDARD SEQUENCE

In 1973 Michael Coe wrote *The Maya Scribe and His World*, which contained a number of exquisite roll-out photographs of Classic Maya polychrome vases with heiroglyphic inscriptions around the rims. Coe called these texts the Primary Standard Sequence (PSS), noting their formulaic similarity from vase to vase. He offered that they probably contained a ritual funeral incantation. Since Coe's publication, more vessels with texts have been found, and **decipherments** by David **Stuart**, Stephen Houston, and Karl Taube have advanced considerably from Coe's book, when none of the glyphs could be read.

David Stuart**,** after decipherment, called these texts the "Dedicatory Formula." As Mark Van Stone says, they are essentially an elaborate form of name-tagging, stating that the vase was painted or carved, was made sacred by painting and writing, was meant to hold a specific food or beverage, and was created for the owner (often listing titles and lineage). Some carry the artist's name and genealogy as well. The widespread use and composition of the Dedicatory Formula suggest that this formula goes back to the very beginnings of Maya civilization.

See also CERAMICS; WRITING SYSTEMS OF MESOAMERICA

Further Reading

Coe, Michael D. *The Maya Scribe and His World*. New York: The Grolier Club, 1973.

Houston, Stephen, and Karl Taube. "'Name Tagging' in Classic Mayan Script: Implications for Native Classifications of Ceramics and Jade Ornaments." *Mexicon* 9: 38–41, 1987.

Stuart, David. "Hieroglyphs on Maya Vessels." In *The Maya Vase Book: A Corpus of Rollout Photographs of Maya Vases*, edited by Justin Kerr and Michael D. Coe, 1:v. New York: Kerr Associates, 1989.

———. "ARCHIVES: Glyphs on Pots." *Maya Decipherment: Ideas on Ancient Maya Writing and Iconography* (blog), September 9, 2013. https://decipherment.wordpress.com/2013/09/09/archives -glyphs-on-pots/.

■ WALTER R. T. WITSCHEY

PUSILHA

Located in the modern Q'eqchi' village of San Benito Poite, Pusilha (16.1° N, 89.2° W) is the largest Classic Maya site in southern **Belize**. Pusilha is best known for its unique Maya bridge crossing the Machaca River and numerous monumental inscriptions, including the only **hieroglyphic stairway** known in Belize (see also **Decipherment**). Despite its clear importance on a regional level, relations between Pusilha and more distant centers such as **Caracol**, **Quiriguá**, and **Copán** are unclear. Moreover, the nature of political interaction between Pusilha and its nearest neighbors is also unknown. Pusilha's Emblem Glyph is read as *Un*, meaning avocado.

Pusilha was rediscovered in 1926 and investigated by the British Museum from 1928 until 1930. Their work consisted of limited excavations, sketch mapping, and removing well-preserved monuments to Great Britain. Limited excavations were conducted in 1970 by Norman Hammond, in 1979–1980 by Richard Leventhal, and in 1992 by Gary Rex Walters. From 2001 until 2008 Geoffrey Braswell directed survey and excavations at the site. During the course of this research, eight structures were excavated and numerous **burials** were discovered. Among these is a **royal tomb** dating to the eighth century—the first such royal tomb of a ruler known from hieroglyphic inscriptions found in Belize. The inscriptions of Pusilha were analyzed by Sylvanus G. Morley, Berthold Riese, Dorie Reents, and most recently and thoroughly by Christian Prager.

Pusilha is approximately 6 km^2 in area, of which only 2 km^2 have been surveyed. The population of the city during the Late Classic is estimated to have been about 7,000, and the population density was equal to that of the urban core of **Tikal** and other cities. The most important **architectural** groups include the Gateway Hill Acropolis (which rises in a series of terraces and platforms 70 m above the Maya Bridge), the **Stela** Plaza, the Ball Court Group, Moho Plaza, and Machaca Plaza.

Hieroglyphic texts describe the inauguration of the first king of Pusilha, K'awiil Chan K'inich, in AD 571. As a dynastic founder, he employed the title *ochk'in kalomte'*. A founding date at the very end of the Early Classic period agrees with the **ceramic** chronology of the site. Six more rulers—including a woman and a second *ochk'in kalomte'*—have been identified up to AD 731 (see also **Maya Queens**). A few more potential rulers are depicted in iconography or are discussed in texts. Stela F, dating to AD 751, mentions a man in what seems to be a royal context but does not use the Pusilha Emblem Glyph. The hieroglyphic stairway probably dates to AD 798 and refers to another ruler whose name is illegible. After this date the hieroglyphic record falls silent. Archaeological evidence from the Gateway Hill Acropolis, however, demonstrates continued occupation well into the Terminal Classic period. The "Bulldozed Mound," a partially destroyed structure in Poite Village, shows evidence of limited Postclassic settlement. Thus Pusilha was inhabited from the late sixth until at least the tenth centuries.

Some scholars argue that the hieroglyphic inscriptions and sculpted monuments of Pusilha show affiliation with Quiriguá and more distant Copán. Nonetheless, actual evidence for such connections is very tenuous. The Pusilha corpus does not contain a single Emblem Glyph of another identified site. Moreover, the inscriptions of other sites seem to ignore Pusilha. This observation is true not only for distant polities but also for others in the southern Belize region. The hieroglyphic texts of Uxbenka, Lubaantun, and Nim li Punit contain no unambiguous references to Pusilha, nor is there a clear reference to these royal capitals at Pusilha. The political and economic relationships among the four kingdoms in this small region, therefore, are a subject of important current inquiry.

Further Reading

Prager, Christian M., Beniamino Volta, and Geoffrey E. Braswell. "The Dynastic History and Archaeology of Pusilha, Belize." In *The Maya and Their Central American Neighbors: Settlement Patterns, Architecture, Hieroglyphic Texts, and Ceramics*, edited by Geoffrey E. Braswell. New York: Routledge, 2014.

■ GEOFFREY E. BRASWELL

PROSKOURIAKOFF, TATIANA AVENIROVNA (1909–1985)

Tania Proskouriakoff was born in Russia of well-educated parents. Her mother was a physician and her father an engineer and chemist. Her father, commissioned by the tsar to make munitions inspections in America, took the family to Philadelphia in 1916. After the Russian Revolution in 1917, the family settled permanently in Philadelphia. Proskouriakoff received a degree in architecture from Pennsylvania State University in 1930 and immediately faced the realities of the Great Depression.

Unable to find a job in **architecture**, she began illustrating artifacts for the University of Pennsylvania Museum. From 1934 to 1938 she worked at **Piedras Negras, Guatemala**, making architectural renderings of the buildings excavated there. The skill and quality of the drawings resulted in a full-time job with the Carnegie Institution of Washington, where Sylvanus Morley launched her on a program of making architectural drawings of major Maya sites, beginning with **Copán**. She followed up with drawings at **Chichen Itza** and several Puuc sites, including Xpuhil, **Sayil**, **Labna**, **Kabah**, and **Uxmal**. The entire collection appears in *An Album of Maya Architecture*.

Proskouriakoff's most important work, "Historical Implications of a Pattern of Dates at Piedras Negras, Guatemala," was published in *American Antiquity* in 1960. In it, she asserted that the monumental inscriptions on Maya **stelae** contained the history of Maya rulers and were illustrated with the likenesses of Maya rulers, men and women. Since the prevailing views of the time, led by the foremost Maya archaeologist of the day, J. Eric S. **Thompson**, held that the inscriptions contained nothing historical, but strictly auguries and astronomically important dates, the Proskouriakoff findings shocked the Maya world (see also **Decipherment**).

Her assertions were based on a careful tabulation of stelae erected in front of a set of temples at Piedras Negras. She noted that in each monument set, the first monument showed an individual (ruler) seated within a niche. The date closest to the date of erecting the stela was marked with a "toothache" glyph, which looked like a bird's head with a jaw bandage. This date was frequently commemorated on subsequent monuments in the same group. The earliest date in each monument group was earlier by 12 to 31 years and accompanied by a glyph that looked like a frog's head, tilted skyward. She postulated that the later date marked the accession to the throne of the individual in the niche, and that the earlier date marked his birthday.

She found three sets of monuments with complete date sets, and the span of dates was 60, 64, and 56 years—reasonable lengths for a human lifespan. She further noted that the monuments also contained female figures, with their birth-dates, and she identified the glyph prefix *na*, which is translated today as "Lady," to indicate a female.

While Proskouriakoff's work did not contain translations of glyphs into any spoken Maya tongue, her brilliant work on the content of the inscriptions changed Mayanists' views of the script. Combined with the work of **Yuri Knorosov** and Heinrich Berlin, her views led inevitably to the decipherment of the Maya **dynastic sequence** histories that provide a critical part of Maya studies today. Proskouriakoff received both the Alfred V. Kidder Medal for Eminence in the Field of American Archaeology in 1962 from the American Anthropological Association and the Order of the Quetzal, Guatemala's highest award, in 1980.

Further Reading

Coe, Michael D. *Breaking the Maya Code: The 200-Year Quest to Decipher the Hieroglyphs of the Ancient Maya.* New York: First Run Features, 2008.

———. *The Maya.* 8th ed. London: Thames & Hudson, 2011.

Proskouriakoff, Tatiana. "Historical Implications of a Pattern of Dates at Piedras Negras, Guatemala." *American Antiquity* 25, no. 4: 454–75, 1960.

———. *An Album of Maya Architecture.* Carnegie Institution of Washington, Publication 558. Washington, DC: Carnegie Institution of Washington, 1962.

Sharer, Robert J., and Loa P. Traxler. *The Ancient Maya.* 6th ed. Stanford, CA: Stanford University Press, 2006.

■ WALTER R. T. WITSCHEY

PUUC ARCHITECTURAL STYLE

The Puuc **architectural** style probably originated in the Yucatecan hill district of the same name, but soon spread across the western half of the northern plains, most notably to **Chichen Itza**. Sometimes referred to as the Florescent style (Modified Florescent at Chichen Itza), it dates to the Late and Terminal Classic periods, with most construction between AD 800 and 950. Classic examples can be found at **Sayil**, **Kabah**, **Labna**, and **Uxmal**, among many others. Puuc structures are characterized by walls and vaults built of concrete and rubble covered by finely cut veneer stones. As a result, Puuc vaults were able to span somewhat wider rooms, even though true arching was unknown (see also **Corbel Vault**). Although sometimes characterized as elite construction, vaulted masonry buildings comprise 25–40 percent of the structures at some Puuc sites.

Veneer decoration tended to become ever more elaborate, though some structures remained simple. Initially characterized by stepped vaults and plain façades framed by simple moldings at sites such as **Oxkintok**, friezes of colonnettes and multipart beveled moldings later became popular. Modeled stucco may also have been widely employed.

Another characteristic was the frequent use of columns in some doorways, though not within rooms, as at Chichen Itza. Stone mosaic decoration also became popular, most spectacularly zoomorphic masks, but also stepped-frets and other geometric patterns. The final stage of the Puuc style, most prominent at Uxmal, features stonework rivaling any in **Mesoamerica**. Common architectural forms include expansive multiroom **palaces**, sometimes multistoried, and range structures. The few Puuc pyramids often enclose earlier palaces, suggesting their commemorative role.

Puuc architectural sculpture tends to be relatively crude in comparison to the south. Most notable are the zoomorphic masks. Sometimes identified as masks of the **deity** Chac or personified mountains, they in fact exhibit considerable variation. Some buildings, such as the Codz Pop of Kabah, had façades composed entirely of these masks; other sites had few or no masks, reinforcing the notion that their symbolism had both political and religious dimensions (see also **Iconography**; **Religion**).

Similarities to the Puuc style can be seen in earlier and later architecture from many regions of **Mesoamerica**, but the fact that the earliest Puuc buildings are extremely simple suggests local development, rather than importation from elsewhere. (See figure 36.)

See also ARCHITECTURE OVERVIEW; EDZNA; EK BALAM; FORTIFICATIONS; ITZIMTE; JAINA; KIUIC; KOHUNLICH; NORTHERN LOWLANDS; PROSKOURIAKOFF, TATIANA AVENIROVNA; RÍO BEC; TIHO; WALL PAINTING; XCOCH; YAXHOM

Further Reading

Andrews, George F. *Pyramids and Palaces, Monsters and Masks: The Golden Age of Maya Architecture.* Vol. 1 of *The Collected Works of George F. Andrews.* Lancaster, CA: Labyrinthos, 1995.

Pollock, Harry E. D. *The Puuc: An Architectural Survey of the Hill Country of Yucatan and Northern Campeche, Mexico.* Memoirs of the Peabody Museum, vol. 19. Cambridge, MA: Peabody Museum of Archaeology and Ethnology, Harvard University, 1980.

■ WILLIAM M. RINGLE

Figure 36. At Chacmultun, Yucatan, Mexico, this building façade exemplifies Puuc-style architecture with a plain lower façade, colonnettes in the upper wall, and medial and upper moldings. Photo courtesy of William Ringle.

PYRAMID

A common architectural form in the ceremonial center of Maya cities and towns is a truncated (flat-topped) pyramid made of earth or masonry, with a simple structure atop, made of perishable materials such as pole and thatch, or more permanent masonry. Since in most cases flat-topped pyramids had temples on the uppermost surface, the term "temple-pyramid" is frequently used to refer to them. Pyramids had a square or rectangular base and four sides.

Maya pyramids are quite different from Egyptian pyramids in their construction. In the Maya area, most pyramids are built with an earthen-fill or rock-rubble core, instead of the Egyptian practice of using cut stones throughout. The exterior is then faced, sometimes with very large stones (megalithic **architecture**), sometimes with smaller cut stones, and sometimes with masonry veneer. The upper temples were accessed by either a single stair up the front, or in the case of radial pyramids, by stairways on all four sides. Stairways might be steep, with risers taller than the tread depth.

Pyramid exteriors might have square, inset, or rounded corners. They often rose in multiple terraces, rather than with smoothly rising sides. Sides might have apron-like recesses in the lower terrace faces or be finished Teotihuacán style with a *talud-tablero* terrace face, often an indicator of association with **Teotihuacán**.

Upper temples, where absent, were likely build of wood and thatch. Surviving masonry temples sometimes carried roof-combs, tall walls fitted to carry molded stucco masks of **deities** or **divine kings**.

Temple-pyramids often served as **royal tombs**. The most famous and first example is the Temple of the Inscriptions at **Palenque**, in which Alberto Ruz discovered the richly furnished tomb of Lord Pacal. Four years' excavations within the pyramid revealed the tomb entrance and rock-cut tomb chamber in 1952. Since its discovery, many other royal tombs have been found in the Maya area, and their inscriptions sometimes allow the identification of the ruler interred within.

See also ALLIANCES; ARCHITECTURE OVERVIEW; ART; ASTRONOMICAL OBSERVATORIES; BONAMPAK; CAHAL PECH; CALAKMUL; CAUSEWAY/*SACBE*; CAVES; CEIBAL; CHAC II; *CHENES* ARCHITECTURAL STYLE; CIVAL; COBÁ; COMALCALCO; COPÁN; DZIBANCHÉ; DZIBILCHALTUN; EK BALAM; EL MIRADOR; EL PERÚ-WAKA'; GROUND SURVEY TECHNIQUES; HIEROGLYPHIC STAIRWAYS; HOCHOB; HOLMUL; ICHKABAL; ICONOGRAPHY; ITZIMTE; IZAMAL; KABAH AND NOHPAT; KAMINALJUYÚ; KIUIC; KOHUNLICH; KOMCHEN; LABNA; MAYAPÁN; MESOAMERICA; MIDDLE CLASSIC HIATUS; MIRADOR BASIN; MUYIL; NAKBÉ; NARANJO; NIXTUN-CH'ICH'; NOH KAH; OXKINTOK; PIEDRAS NEGRAS; RIO AZUL; RÍO BEC; RITES OF PASSAGE; SAN BARTOLO; SCULPTURE; SETTLEMENT PATTERNS (NORTHERN LOWLANDS); STELA; TAMCHEN AND CHACTUN; THEATER; TIKAL; UAXACTUN; UXMAL; WARFARE, WARRIORS, AND WEAPONS; WRITING SYSTEMS OF MESOAMERICA; XCOCH; YALAHAU REGION; YAXHÁ; YAXNOHCAH; ZACPETÉN; ZACUALPA; ZACULEU

Further Reading

Andrews, E. Wyllys, V, and William Leonard Fash, eds. *Copán: The History of an Ancient Maya Kingdom.* School of American Research Advanced Seminar Series. Santa Fe, NM: School of American Research, 2005.

Andrews, George F. *Pyramids and Palaces, Monsters and Masks: The Golden Age of Maya Architecture.* Vol. 1 of *The Collected Works of George F. Andrews.* Lancaster, CA: Labyrinthos, 1995.

Kowalski, Jeff K., and Nicholas P. Dunning. "The Architecture of Uxmal: The Symbolics of Statemaking at a Puuc Maya Regional Capital." In *Mesoamerican Architecture as a Cultural Symbol,* edited by Jeff K. Kowalski. Oxford: Oxford University Press, 1999.

Miller, Mary Ellen, and Megan Eileen O'Neil. *Maya Art and Architecture.* 2nd ed. London: Thames & Hudson, 2014.

Proskouriakoff, Tatiana. *An Album of Maya Architecture.* Carnegie Institution of Washington, Publication 558. Washington, DC: Carnegie Institution of Washington, 1962.

Schele, Linda, and Peter Mathews. *The Code of Kings: The Language of Seven Sacred Maya Temples and Tombs.* New York: Scribner/Simon & Schuster, 1998.

Stuart, David, and George E. Stuart. *Palenque: Eternal City of the Maya.* New York: Thames & Hudson, 2008.

■ WALTER R. T. WITSCHEY

Q

Q'UM'ARKAJ
See UTATLÁN

QUETZAL FEATHERS
See TRADE ROUTES

QUIRIGUÁ
Quiriguá (15.3° N, 89.0° W) is a Classic Maya archaeological site on the north side of the Motagua River, in southeastern **Guatemala** about 200 km (120 miles) northeast of Guatemala City. Declared a national park in 1910 and national monument in 1970, the site was named a UNESCO World Heritage Site in 1981. At the entrance are a visitors' center and museum.

Quiriguá is best known for its elaborate, freestanding stone **sculptures—stelae, altars,** zoomorphs—including royal portraits and hieroglyphic inscriptions. (See figures 37 and 38.) Nineteenth-century accounts by John Lloyd Stephens and his artist companion, Frederick Catherwood, brought the sculptures and the site to international recognition. Quiriguá inscriptions also yielded one of the first historical events deciphered for the Classic Maya, an event now understood as when the Quiriguá king in AD 738 captured and beheaded his overlord at **Copán**, about 50 km to the south-southwest (see also **Decipherment**). From the founding of royal dynasties in both political centers in AD 426, Quiriguá served as vassal state to its southern neighbor. The Quiriguá king in AD 738, K'ak' Tiliw' Chan Yopaat, violently cast off Copán's yoke and asserted a newfound independence. The event shook up political, economic, and social relations in the surrounding region of what is now southeastern Guatemala and western Honduras, in which a dozen or so new centers of power arose abruptly to challenge the long-standing Copán-Quiriguá dominance. By the start of the ninth century, diplomatic relations had changed regional dynamics back to the pre-AD 738 order. Hieroglyphs on the bench of Str. 1B-1 describe a visit by Copán's last king, to oversee **rites** at its once-again subordinate, Quiriguá.

Figure 37.   Quiriguá Zoomorph P (north face). Dedicated in AD 795 by Sky Xul, divine king of Quiriguá. This monument, weighing 18 metric tons, is carved on all sides. The fanciful beast has enormous fanged jaws, from which Sky Xul is emerging, seated as befits a king with a K'awiil sceptre. Photo courtesy of Wendy Ashmore.

Visitors to the site see its civic core: a long, open Great Plaza, flanked on the north by the ruins of Str. 1A-3 and on the south by a **ball court** (Str. 1B-7) and the imposing Quiriguá Acropolis (Strs. 1B-1 through 1B-6). Stelae and other stone sculptures occupy multiple positions in the plaza. Smaller but still imposing structures line the east side of the Great Plaza. The East Group lies east of the acropolis, still within the preserve. The west, however, was open to the east-flowing Motagua. The river's course was much closer to the site during Quiriguá's peak than it is today, with a landing dock for ancient visitors west of Str. 1A-11. During the same span, people occupied some 3 km² (1.1 mi²) west, north, and east of the core. Ancient constructions, beyond the modern park boundaries, lie buried under **soils** laid down in centuries of Motagua flooding, now enshrouded as well in banana groves of the Del Monte Fruit Company.

Quiriguá kings commissioned creation and modification of constructions in the civic core. The acropolis was the political administrative heart of the royal court. The Great Plaza and ball court were venues for ritual displays and royal performances (see also **Music and Dance**; **Theater**). Quiriguá lacks the soaring temples of most Classic Maya capitals, and many have commented that the site layout copied that at Copán on a reduced scale. The **architecture** visible today is largely the result of a building program commissioned by K'ak' Tiliw' Chan Yopaat, arguably his attempt at competitive display after defeating

Figure 38. Quiriguá Monument 4 (Stela D). The sculpted image of K'ahk' Tiliw Chan Yopaat, dedicated in AD 766, dwarfs archaeologist Robert Sharer. The stela, standing 6 m tall, is one of the celebratory monuments resulting from the conquest of Copán and the beheading of its king. Photo courtesy of Wendy Ashmore.

his Copán rival. He may have lacked the resources to create buildings as tall as those at newly defeated Copán, but his Quiriguá Great Plaza is notably more expansive. The stelae, zoomorphs, and altars there commemorate particular events, the longevity of the royal dynasty, and the glories of individual rulers; not surprisingly, the tallest stelae celebrate K'ak' Tiliw' Chan Yopaat.

Since Stephens and Catherwood's visit, investigation at Quiriguá has been intermittent, the most prominent of which is listed here. Alfred P. Maudslay's work in the 1890s is best known for his maps, photographs, and artist Annie Hunter's drawings of the carved stone monuments. Edgar Lee Hewett directed work from 1910 to 1914, focusing on a new map and excavations in the acropolis. Initially working with Hewett's project, Sylvanus G. Morley studied the inscriptions and in his search for more texts, documented stelae in Group A, a hilltop across the modern highway (CA9) north of the civic core, and Group B, 1,500 m (0.9 mile) west of the core. Gustav Strømsvik led work in the 1930s, examining the ball court and how the stone monuments had been set in place. His team also discovered **ceramic**-lined wells in residential areas beyond the park. In 1962 David Kelley published Quiriguá's dynastic sequence, or king list, one of the first such to be deciphered from Maya hieroglyphic texts. From 1974 to 1979, William R. Coe and Robert J. Sharer for the University of Pennsylvania Museum, in contract with Guatemala's Instituto de Antropología e História, took on fundamental research previously neglected: detailing Quiriguá's complete occupation history, through ceramic study and construction histories for the architecture; a refined dynastic genealogy to relate to construction; and evidence for where people other than the royal court lived and worked, in the immediate vicinity and in the encompassing 2,100 km² (811 square miles) Lower Motagua Valley. Since 1980 consolidation, site management, and new excavations have continued under supervision by José Crasborn, for Guatemala's Instituto de Antropología e História and Departamento de Monumentos, notably in the East Group, whose northern structure revealed a hieroglyphic bench from AD 808, in the reign of the last Quiriguá king. Damage from earthquakes (1976), as well as hurricanes Mitch (1998), Agatha (2010), and others, underscores the need for continuing protection and repair.

See also ALLIANCES; ARCHITECTURE OVERVIEW; ART; CALAKMUL; CLASSIC MAYA COLLAPSE; COPÁN; COUNCIL HOUSE; DECIPHERMENT; DYNASTIC SEQUENCES; GROUND SURVEY TECHNIQUES; GUATEMALA; IXTEPEQUE; MAYA AREA; MUSIC AND DANCE; PUSILHA; SCULPTURE; SOUTHERN ARCHITECTURAL STYLE; STELA; THEATER; TIKAL

Further Reading

Ashmore, Wendy. *Settlement Archaeology at Quiriguá, Guatemala: Quirigua Reports IV.* University Museum Monograph 126. Philadelphia: University of Pennsylvania Museum of Archaeology and Anthropology, 2007.

Looper, Matthew George. *Lightning Warrior: Maya Art and Kingship at Quirigua.* Linda Schele Series in Maya and pre-Columbian Studies. Austin: University of Texas Press, 2003.

Marroquín, Elizabeth. *Quiriguá: "Patrimonio de la humanidad."* Guatemala City, Guatemala: Gobierno Real de los Países Bajos, Ministerio de Cultura y Deportes, Jade Guatemala: UNESCO, 2010.

Martin, Simon, and Nikolai Grube. *Chronicle of the Maya Kings and Queens: Deciphering the Dynasties of the Ancient Maya.* 2nd ed. London: Thames & Hudson, 2008.

Schortman, Edward M., and Wendy Ashmore. "History, Networks, and the Quest for Power: Ancient Political Competition in the Lower Motagua Valley, Guatemala." *Journal of the Royal Anthropological Institute*, no. 18: 1–21, 2012.

Sharer, Robert J. *Quirigua: A Classic Maya Center & Its Sculptures.* Centers of Civilization Series. Durham, NC: Carolina Academic Press, 1990.

Sharer, Robert J., and Loa P. Traxler. *The Ancient Maya.* 6th ed. Stanford, CA: Stanford University Press, 2006.

■ WENDY ASHMORE

REJOLLADA

The name *rejollada* is used by contemporary Maya in southern **Mexico** and **Guatemala** for at least one type of naturally forming sinkhole. Much of **Mesoamerica** is made up of thick deposits of limestone ($CaCO_3$) bedrock formed by marine organisms millions of years ago (see also **Geology**). Within these limestone deposits there are several types of sinkholes caused by collapsed caverns, and solution depressions. These sinkholes are classified locally by the Maya based on the presence of open water at the bottom. In Mesoamerica *rejolladas* (or *Ko'op* in Yucatec) are defined as sinkholes that are dry year-round and contain deeper **soils** than the surrounding landscape. In contrast, sinkholes that contain open water year-round are called **cenotes**. Although *rejolladas* typically contain deeper soils, there is no consensus by local communities about exactly what a *rejollada* is compared to other similar sinkholes. For example, the bottoms of sinkholes called *dzadz* are close to the water table, and standing water is normally present in a portion of the sinkhole (see also **Groundwater/Water Table**). Many local people, however, interchange the term *dzadz* with *rejollada*. Despite some variation in definition, in general *rejolladas* are sinkholes that remain mostly dry year-round. There is variability in the depth of *rejolladas* and the steepness of their sides. Some have gentle slopes that can easily be walked, while others are nearly vertical and require climbing.

The climate of the northern portion of the Yucatan Peninsula is much dryer than the subtropical forest of the southern Maya lowlands. But the deep, steep-sided *rejolladas* create microclimates similar to the **Southern Lowlands**, suitable for plants that could not otherwise grow in northern Yucatan. One such example is the chocolate-producing **cacao** tree (*Theobroma cacao* L.). Possibly due to these microclimates in conjunction with religious ties to the underworld, *rejolladas* were important geologic features to the ancient Maya. Many Maya settlements such as **Chichen Itza** are clustered near cenotes and *rejolladas*, and in some cases were built specifically around them, such as the ancient site of Xuenkal, Yucatan. In addition to their **religious** and water resource potential, *rejolladas* were important agricultural resources for the ancient Maya. While soils in areas such as northern Guatemala and the Yucatan Peninsula are generally shallow on the hill slopes and karst plains, *rejolladas* act as traps for both soil and moisture resources suitable for cultivating crops. Deeper soils, increased humidity, and proximity to groundwater levels all contribute to an increased agricultural potential within *rejolladas*. Contemporary farmers in the region continue to use *rejolladas* as agricultural land. Modern crops grown in the *rejolladas* include maize, banana, mango, botan, avocado, zapote mamey, nance, caimito, sapodilla, and ramón. The contemporary Maya have also planted fruit trees such as mango in some *rejolladas* to lure deer and large rodents into the steep-walled *rejolladas* for hunting.

While most experts agree that *rejolladas* would logically be the best place to cultivate and produce high-yielding and specialty crops, it is uncertain who owned and operated the *rejolladas*. *Conquistadores* clearly stated that when they arrived in the Americas, *rejolladas* were the property of nobles and leaders. However, it is unclear if *rejolladas* were used to support individual families or small neighborhoods. The ancient Maya and contemporary farmers recognized and capitalized on the agricultural potential of *rejolladas* to produce their sustenance.

See also AGUADAS; BAJOS; WATER MANAGEMENT

Further Reading

Gómez-Pompa, Arturo, José Salvador Flores, and Mario Aliphat Fernandez. "The Sacred Cacao Groves of the Maya." *Latin American Antiquity* 1, no. 3: 247–57, 1990.

Gómez-Pompa, Arturo, José Salvador Flores, and V. Sosa. "The Pet Kot—A Man-made Tropical Forest of the Maya." *Interciencia* 12: 10–15, 1987.

Johnson, Kristofer D., David R. Wright, and Richard E. Terry. "Application of Carbon Isotope Analysis to Ancient Maize Agriculture in the Petexbatún Region of Guatemala." *Geoarchaeology* 22, no. 3: 313–36, 2007.

Munro, P. G, and M. L. M. Zurita. "The Role of Cenotes in the Social History of Mexico's Yucatan Peninsula." *Environment and History* 17, no. 4: 583–612, 2011.

Munro-Stasiuk, Mandy J., and T. Kam Manahan. "Investigating Ancient Maya Agricultural Adaptation through Ground Penetrating Radar (GPR) Analysis of Karst Terrain, Northern Yucatán, Mexico." *Acta Carsologica*, no. 39: 123–35, 2010.

Munro-Stasiuk, Mandy J., T. Kam Manahan, T. Stockton, and T. Ardren. "Spatial and Physical Characteristics of Rejolladas in Northern Yucatán, Mexico: Implications for Ancient Maya Agriculture and Settlement Patterns." *Geoarchaeology* 29, no. 2: 156–72, 2014.

Wright, David R., Richard E. Terry, and Markus Eberl. "Soil Properties and Stable Carbon Isotope Analysis of Landscape Features in the Petexbatún Region of Guatemala." *Geoarchaeology* 24, no. 4: 466–91, 2009.

■ CHRISTOPHER S. BALZOTTI, BRYCE M. BROWN,
AND RICHARD E. TERRY

RELIGION

Religion is a person's way of dealing with the unknown, the incomprehensible, and the invisible. Ancient Maya religion, before becoming syncretized with Catholicism brought by the Spanish, considered everything (stones, trees, sun, wind, animals) in the "real" world to possess a sacred spirit, *k'uh*. The world was also populated by gods, **deities** who took on many forms and appearances.

Part of comprehending the unknown universe, to the Maya, was understanding the obvious regular cycles of the heavens, the motions of the sun and moon, the stars, and the planets. Naked-eye observations and recording of these cycles on a daily basis gave rise, over time, to the **calendars** that formed such a critical part of Maya life (see also **Astronomy**; **Astronomical Observatories**). The gradual development of cyclic day counts (*tzolk'in* and *haab'*) and the Long Count provided a base for more sophisticated insight into lunar and planetary cycles. Days and intervals and cycles had names and patron gods. Added to these were gods for agriculture, such as the corn god; for the weather (rain and thunder); and for fire and death. All were worshiped with specific ceremonies on well-chosen dates, and all were a means to put order into daily living and to explain the unexplainable. They served as a mechanism to reinforce orderliness in a world whose climate, weather, and life events must have seemed all too capricious and random (see also **Rites and Rituals**).

In addition, each person and god had an invisible spirit companion (*way*), and Classic **iconography** sometimes illustrates the *way* of a divine ruler as a real or imagined animal.

At the commoner level of society, a shaman could and did intervene with the gods on behalf of individual human friends and neighbors. At the elite level of Classic Maya society, the rulers, **divine kings**, served as high **priests**, conducting rituals, theatrical performances, and blood sacrifices as dictated by the calendar to propitiate the gods and to assure the safety and continuity of society.

See also BURIALS; CAVES; CLASS STRUCTURE; CODICES (MAYA); DEITIES; DIVINE KINGS AND QUEENS; DZIBILCHATUN; EDZNA; EL PILAR; FAUNA; GROUNDWATER/WATER TABLE; HIEROGLYPHIC STAIRWAYS; ICONOGRAPHY; JAINA; LANDA, BISHOP DIEGO DE; MEDICINE; MESOAMERICA; OBSIDIAN; PIEDRAS NEGRAS; *POPOL VUH*; PUUC ARCHITECTURAL STYLE; SETTLEMENT PATTERNS (NORTHERN LOWLANDS); TEOTIHUACÁN (MAYA INTERACTIONS WITH); THEATER; THOMPSON, J. ERIC S.; UTATLÁN/Q'UM'ARKAJ; WRITING SYSTEMS OF MESOAMERICA

Further Reading

Aveni, Anthony F. *Skywatchers: A Revised and Updated Version of "Skywatchers of Ancient Mexico."* Austin: University of Texas Press, 2001.

Brady, James E. "Offerings to the Rain Gods: The Archaeology of Maya Caves." In *Fiery Pool: The Maya and the Mythic Sea*, edited by Daniel Finamore and Stephen Houston. Salem, MA: Peabody Essex Museum, 2010.

Gonlin, Nancy, and Jon C. Lohse. *Commoner Ritual and Ideology in Ancient Mesoamerica.* Mesoamerican Worlds. Boulder: University Press of Colorado, 2007.

Miller, Mary Ellen, and Karl A. Taube. *The Gods and Symbols of Ancient Mexico and the Maya: An Illustrated Dictionary of Mesoamerican Religion.* New York: Thames & Hudson, 1993.

Sharer, Robert J., and Loa P. Traxler. *The Ancient Maya.* 6th ed. Stanford, CA: Stanford University Press, 2006.

Stuart, David. *The Order of Days: The Maya World and the Truth about 2012.* New York: Harmony Books, 2011.

Thompson, J. Eric S. *Maya History and Religion.* Norman: University of Oklahoma Press, 1970.

■ WALTER R. T. WITSCHEY

RICHMOND HILL

In the late 1970s several sites were reported that appeared to have stratified artifacts from human occupation, but no ceramics. These included the **Loltun cave** in Yucatan, with aceramic layers underlying strata with ceramics, and Richmond Hill (18.0° N, 88.6° W), **Belize**. Fieldwork by Richard S. MacNeish and others on his coastal Belize project to search for the earliest Maya documented 230 new archaeological sites. They proposed that several of these sites documented up to five periods of human occupation during the Archaic period. The earliest phase includes hunters' tools such as Plainview and fishtail projectile points, scrapers, blades, and choppers. The succeeding phase includes retouched chert microblades; scrapers; choppers; projectile points; a grind stone, likely for food processing; and an adze, perhaps for canoe construction. In the third phase, stone bowls and grinders are common. In the fourth phase, scale scrapers and fishnet weights document fishing; coastal sites are larger, suggesting growing sedentism. The final phase includes agricultural village sites. Richmond Hill, Loltun, and other aceramic sites document the earliest peoples in the Maya region.

Further Reading

Hammond, Norman. "The Prehistory of Belize." *Journal of Field Archaeology* 9: 349–62, 1982.

MacNeish, Richard S. *Robert S. Peabody Foundation for Archaeology: Annual Report 1980*. Andover, MA: Philips Academy Andover, 1980.

MacNeish, Richard S., S. Jeffrey K. Wilkerson, and Antoinette Nelken-Terner. *First Annual Report of the Belize Archaic Archaeological Reconnaissance*. Andover, MA: Robert F. Peabody Foundation for Archaeology, 1980.

■ WALTER R. T. WITSCHEY

RIO AZUL

Located in the southeast side of a bend in the Azul River, a tributary of the Hondo River, Rio Azul (17.8° N, 89.3° W) was an ancient Maya city covering about 1.3 km². It is in the northeast Petén, **Guatemala**, 73 km north-northeast of **Tikal**, which figures prominently in its history. Its strategic location on the river route between Tikal and the Caribbean made it an important **trade route** control point for its much larger neighbor.

Rio Azul was reported to Sun Oil geologist John Gatling by local Guatemalan and fellow employee Trinidad Pech in 1962. Richard E.W. Adams visited with Gatling and made a sketch map of 79 structures. From 1976 to 1981 the site was aggressively looted in a well-organized effort, employing up to 80 men excavating more than 125 trenches. Looting was halted by the combined efforts of Ian Graham of Harvard's Peabody Museum and Rafael Morales, director of Prehispanic Monuments of Guatemala. This led to an extensive new research project led by Adams during 1983–1987. The project survey ultimately documented over 700 major structures, most constructed in the early Late Classic period.

Rio Azul was first occupied in the Middle Formative, and an early temple (Str. G103-sub 2) was constructed. Residents built significant monumental **architecture** in the Late Formative between 300 BC and AD 350, including the rebuilding of Str. G103. Inscriptions from AD 393 describe conquest in AD 385 by Siyaj K'ak', the warrior general of

Teotihuacán who conquered Tikal. The rulers of Rio Azul were executed and new rulers established by Siyaj K'ak'. The prior focus on Str. G103 was shifted to a new site center. Rio Azul was firmly established as a defensive outpost and trade control center (see also **Fortifications; Warfare, Warriors, and Weapons**). Stela 1 documents the accession of Zak Balam to rule Rio Azul and includes a reference to Siyaj K'ak', who likely ordered his appointment and supervised the ceremony.

In AD 440 Governor X, son of Siyaj Chan K'awiil II, then ruler of Tikal, was appointed by his father to rule Rio Azul. From AD 450 to 530 the elites of Tikal located at Rio Azul created an extensive array of elaborate **royal tombs** with well-preserved hieroglyphic writing (see also **Decipherment**). Tomb 19 contained an intact burial and rich array of grave goods, including a chocolate pot with locking lid painted with its owner's name and a description of the contents: **cacao**. Vigorous building included temple-**pyramids**, **ball courts**, and water reservoirs with a capacity of 12 million gallons (see also **Water Management**). Since the river was the primary route of transportation, there are no **causeways**.

The region began showing signs of political change and decline with the accession of Wak Chan K'awiil to power at Tikal ca. AD 537. Between AD 530 and 660, Rio Azul was burned and abandoned. This is the period of the **Middle Classic Hiatus** at Tikal, when it was defeated and ruled by **Calakmul**.

Although Rio Azul was reoccupied in AD 680–800, habitants built virtually no monumental architecture. Modest efforts were made to refurbish and remodel existing structures. **Ceramic** evidence shows contact with the Puuc region. Nearby Kinal was established as a fortress site and largely assumed the role that Rio Azul once occupied.

Yucatec raiders, perhaps from the Puuc, burned the site in AD 850, and within a decade Rio Azul was abandoned in the widespread **Classic Maya collapse**.

See also ROYAL TOMBS

Further Reading

Adams, Richard E. W. "Archaeological Research at the Lowland Maya City of Rio Azul." *Latin American Antiquity* 1, no. 1: 23–41, 1990.

———. *Rio Azul: An Ancient Maya City*. Norman: University of Oklahoma Press, 1999.

Hall, Grant D. "Realm of Death: Royal Mortuary Customs and Polity Interaction in the Classic Maya Lowlands." PhD diss., Harvard University, 1989.

Martin, Simon, and Nikolai Grube. *Chronicle of the Maya Kings and Queens: Deciphering the Dynasties of the Ancient Maya*. 2nd ed. London: Thames & Hudson, 2008.

Sharer, Robert J., and Loa P. Traxler. *The Ancient Maya*. 6th ed. Stanford, CA: Stanford University Press, 2006.

■ WALTER R. T. WITSCHEY

RÍO BEC

Archaeological site and architectural style. Río Bec (18.4° N, 89.4° W) is an ancient Classic period Maya site in southern Campeche near the state line shared by Quintana

Roo, **Mexico**, 60 km north of the northern Guatemala border (see also **Map 3**). Its ceremonial **architecture** was spread among widely separated groups across an area 2 by 5 km. After discovery of Río Bec Group A in 1906, there was considerable difficulty relocating the site and the scattered architecture until they began to be definitely located with GPS readings.

Río Bec gives its name to a distinctive architectural style, the defining feature of which is "false towers" that usually occur in pairs. These appear similar to the tall Classic **pyramids** in the Petén to the south, but have none of the depth or functionality. The Río Bec towers were like "false fronts," functionless façades. The front stairway was too steep to climb and led to what looked like a doorway but was in fact a niche, because there was no room inside the narrow slab of masonry forming the apparent "temple" at the top. Geographically, the Petén style to the south overlapped the Río Bec style, for example at **Naachtún**, while stylistically, to the north Río Bec graded into the *Chenes* **architectural style**.

The Río Bec region is also known archaeologically for both its high rural population density and the extensive systems of agricultural **terraces** used to intensify agricultural production.

See also SUBSISTENCE; WATER MANAGEMENT

Further Reading

Adams, Richard E. W. "Preliminary Reports on Archaeological Investigations in the Rio Bec Area, Campeche, Mexico." In *Preliminary Reports on Archaeological Investigations in the Rio Bec Area, Campeche, Mexico*, 103–46. Middle American Research Institute, Publication 31. New Orleans, LA: Tulane University, 1974.

Bueno Cano, Ricardo, ed. *Entre un río de robles: Un acercamiento a la arqueología de la Región Río Bec.* Colección Científica 411. Mexico, D.F., Mexico: Instituto Nacional de Antropología e História, 1999.

Gendrop, Paul, George F. Andrews, and Robert D. Wood. *Rio Bec, Chenes, and Puuc Styles in Maya Architecture*. Lancaster, CA: Labyrinthos, 1998.

Nondédéo, Philippe. "Río Bec: Primeros pasos de una nueva investigación." *Mexicon* 25 (August): 100–105, 2001.

Pollock, Harry E. D. "Architecture of the Maya Lowlands." In *Handbook of Middle American Indians*. Vol. 2, *Archaeology of Southern Mesoamerica*, pt. 1, edited by Gordon R. Willey, 378–440. Austin: University of Texas Press, 1965.

Potter, David F. "Prehispanic Architecture and Sculpture in Central Yucatan." *American Antiquity* 41, no. 4: 430–48, 1976.

———. *Maya Architecture of the Central Yucatan Peninsula*. Middle American Research Institute, Publication 44. New Orleans, LA: Tulane University, 1977.

Ruppert, Karl, and John Hopkins Denison. *Archaeological Reconnaissance in Campeche, Quintana Roo, and Petén*. Carnegie Institution of Washington, Publication 543. Washington, DC: Carnegie Institution of Washington, 1943.

Šprajc, Ivan. "Astronomical Alignments in Río Bec Architecture." *Archaeoastronomy* 18: 98–107, 2004.

Turner, B. L. *Once Beneath the Forest: Prehistoric Terracing in the Rio Bec Region of the Maya Lowlands*. Boulder, CO: Westview Press, 1983.

■ WALTER R. T. WITSCHEY

RITES AND RITUALS

In the context of their animistic and **calendar**-driven **religion**, the ancient Maya had numerous obligations to their **deities** and to each other to keep their world in harmony with the expectations of the gods. These rituals were prescriptive and customary. Many were repeated at fixed intervals determined by the calendar, while others marked special **rites of passage** for an individual.

Actions taken as part of a ritual by **priests**, shamans, elites, and **divine kings** included offerings; preparation of caches for building dedications; sacrifices; preparation and consumption of special foods and drinks; use of hallucinogens; purification of places; self-purification; praying; pilgrimage; and public performance with **music and dancing** and **theater**. A special ritual at Tikal called for the king to construct a twin pyramid complex to celebrate a *k'atun*-ending date (see also **Astronomical Observatories**). To varying degrees, these actions are known from inscriptions, architectural **iconography**, **codices**, ethnohistorical sources, and ethnographic sources.

The purposes behind such ritual activities include appeasement of the gods and invocation of their favorable participation in human activities, such as calling on the rain god Chac to water newly planted fields or to return to fill reservoirs after a long dry season. Gods were invoked for success in **warfare** and for all endeavors of **subsistence**, **house** construction, birth, the transition from puberty to adulthood, marriage, and death. In large city-states, by acts of performing **art**, divine kings impersonated the god they called upon and spoke with the voice of the god to the audience assembled in the great city plazas.

Offerings might be simple, such as a cup of cornmeal gruel, or elaborate, such as the burning of blood-impregnated paper, or copal incense mixed with rubber, or the drinking of a pepper-spiced chocolate drink (see also **Cacao**). Elaborate **ceramic** incense burners survive archaeologically and provide clues to the places where rituals took place and the functions of buildings.

Blood offerings were common in ancient times, as they are today, when turkey blood may be sprinkled during a ritual ceremony. The blood came from a sacrificed animal or from a sacrificed human. Humans, both adults and children, were offered as sacrifice, for adults either by beheading or by having the living heart cut from their chests. Polychrome vases picture humans recumbent on an altar with a bloody open chest cavity.

A major blood-sacrifice ritual conducted by Maya kings was self-sacrifice: bloodletting. Archaeological remains as well as iconography show that **obsidian** blades, stingray spines, and cords with thorns were used to draw blood from earlobes, tongues, and genitals (see also **Yaxchilan**).

Pilgrimages were well-attested immediately after the conquest: abandoned **Chichen Itza** and its sacred well was one such destination. So too, pilgrims traveled offshore to the islands of **Cozumel** for rituals. The cave of **Naj Tunich** was an especially important and often-used destination for pilgrims from **Caracol** and more remote major cities, as documented by its **wall paintings**.

See also ART; ASTRONOMICAL OBSERVATORIES; BALL GAME/BALL COURT; BONAMPAK; CACAO; CAHAL PECH; CARACOL; CAVES; CEIBAL; CENOTE; CERRO MAYA/CERROS; CHICHEN ITZA; CODICES; COPÁN; COTZUMALHUAPA; COZUMEL; DEITIES; DIET; ECCENTRIC LITHICS; FAUNA;

GROUNDWATER/WATER TABLE; ICONOGRAPHY; IXIMCHÉ; KINSHIP; LANDA, BISHOP DIEGO DE; LANGUAGE AND WRITING OVERVIEW; MAYAPÁN; MEDICINE; MUSIC AND DANCE; OBSIDIAN; OLMEC-MAYA INTERACTIONS; OXKINTOK; PALENQUE; PHYSICAL/BIOLOGICAL ANTHROPOLOGY; PIEDRAS NEGRAS; PORTABLE OBJECTS; PYRAMID; QUIRIGUÁ; RITES OF PASSAGE; SAN BARTOLO; TEXTILES AND CLOTHING; TIKAL; UXMAL; WATER MANAGEMENT; WRITING SYSTEMS OF MESOAMERICA; YAXCHILAN; ZACUALPA

Further Reading

Gonlin, Nancy, and Jon C. Lohse. *Commoner Ritual and Ideology in Ancient Mesoamerica*. Mesoamerican Worlds. Boulder: University Press of Colorado, 2007.

Kerr, Justin. *Maya Vase Database*. Kerr Associates, 2014. http://www.mayavase.com/.

Milbrath, Susan. *Mayapán's Effigy Censers: Iconography, Context, and External Connections*. Foundation for the Advancement of Mesoamerican Studies, Inc. (FAMSI), 2007. http://www.famsi.org/reports/05025/.

Miller, Mary Ellen. *The Murals of Bonampak*. Princeton, NJ: Princeton University Press, 1986.

Miller, Mary Ellen, and Karl A. Taube. *The Gods and Symbols of Ancient Mexico and the Maya: An Illustrated Dictionary of Mesoamerican Religion*. New York: Thames and Hudson, 1993.

Thompson, J. Eric S. *Maya History and Religion*. Norman: University of Oklahoma Press, 1970.

Tozzer, Alfred M. *Landa's "Relación de las cosas de Yucatán": A Translation*. Papers of the Peabody Museum of American Archaeology and Ethnology, vol. 18. Cambridge, MA: Harvard University, 1941.

■ WALTER R. T. WITSCHEY

RITES OF PASSAGE

A rite of passage is a ceremony that marks a person's transition from one status in life to another. **Diego de Landa** provides clues to several rites held in immediate postconquest times (see also **Rites and Rituals**). Beyond washing of newborns and cranial deformation (head flattening by binding), young children were taken to a **priest** for the identification of their future profession by divining and for the assignment of their given names.

Among the Yucatec Maya today, the rite of passage known as *hetz-mek* is celebrated for three-month-old girls and four-month-old boys with godparents present. It marks the transition from being carried or swaddled to being carried on the hip by their mother or an older sister.

Landa reported that children becoming eligible for marriage underwent a ceremony known as *caput sihil*, "the descent of the gods." On a propitious day, at a sponsor's house, with five elders assisting the priest, the priest held a purification ceremony for the house, expelling evil spirits. The gods were invoked, and the assembled families then celebrated with a feast. Young men began to live in a special house, paint themselves black, and focus on the skills of hunting and farming. Young women learned cooking, housekeeping, spinning, and weaving from their mothers.

Marriage rituals, with partners and dowries carefully arranged by parents, were conducted by a priest, who held the blessing and solemnization in the bride's home. All attending were treated to a grand feast. Following marriage, the couple lived with the bride's parents, where the groom worked the fields of his father-in-law for six or seven years. Following the period of labor, the family moved to a house near the groom's parents and became a resident part of the groom's patriline. Such actions helped form an alliance between the families of the newlyweds. A number of royal marriages and the wedding dates are recorded in the Classic inscriptions.

Death was marked by elaborate ritual, including grave goods. The body was wrapped in a shroud, and for commoners, buried beneath the dirt floor of the dwelling. Ancestors were kept close in both the spiritual and physical sense. The **burials** of elites in **royal tombs** were far more extensive, involving the creation of a special temple-**pyramid**, burial chamber with painted walls, inscribed sarcophagus, and exotic grave goods.

Except for burials, rites of passage are difficult for archaeologists to recover. David Stuart and Stephen Houston, however, point to evidence on **stelae** and in the inscriptions for ritual bloodletting ("first penance") as a rite of passage for royal princes.

As is true among the modern Maya today (and as is known for the first years after the conquest), the Maya marked important transitional points in their lives with formulaic ceremonies designed to highlight the participants' new roles and obligations within the wider society.

Further Reading

Child, Mark B. "The Symbolic Space of the Ancient Maya Sweatbath." In *Space and Spatial Analysis in Archaeology*, edited by Elizabeth C. Robertson, 157–67. Calgary, AB: University of Calgary Press, 2006.

Houston, Stephen. *A Liquid Passage to Manhood*. Maya Decipherment, 2012. http://decipherment .wordpress.com/2012/05/08/a-liquid-passage-to-manhood/.

Looper, Matthew George. *To Be Like Gods: Dance in Ancient Maya Civilization*. Austin: University of Texas Press, 2009.

Sharer, Robert J., and Loa P. Traxler. *The Ancient Maya*. 6th ed. Stanford, CA: Stanford University Press, 2006.

Stuart, David. *A Childhood Ritual on the Hauberg Stela*. Maya Decipherment, 2008. from http://decipher ment.wordpress.com/2008/03/27/a-childhood-ritual-on-the-hauberg-stela/.

■ WALTER R. T. WITSCHEY

RITUAL

See RITES AND RITUALS

ROYAL TOMBS

Since the discovery of the tomb of Lord Pacal of **Palenque** by Alberto Ruz in 1952, Maya archaeology has turned a significant part of its focus to identifying and excavating royal tombs of **divine kings**. They are typically found under or within temple-**pyramids** or buildings built over temple-pyramids. Since they provide considerable information from both the skeletal material and the accompanying grave goods, these elite interments are helping to fill out **dynastic histories**, family trees, and the relationships between allied or competing city-states (see also **Alliances**). There are dozens of tombs now known with the burials of rulers, elites, family members, and sacrificed companions.

The contents of royal tombs include the widest array of precious objects, including carved sarcophagi, literally fit for a king. Of special import and beauty are Classic polychrome plates, bowls, and vases, with name-tagging (ruler's identification) and offering contents (chocolate, corn gruel). Other funerary objects include plain and carved shell; **codices**; figurines; carved jade and jade mosaic death masks; **eccentrics**; **obsidian**; and necklaces of shell, jade, and other stone beads.

See also ALTUN HA; CACAO; CALAKMUL; CARACOL, CERAMICS; COPÁN; EL PERÚ-WAKA'; LAMANAI; NAJ TUNICH; PUSILHA; RIO AZUL; RITES AND RITUALS; TIKAL; UXMAL; YAXUNÁ

Further Reading

Coe, William R. *Excavations in the Great Plaza, North Terrace, and North Acropolis of Tikal—Tikal Report 14.* Philadelphia: University of Pennsylvania Museum of Archaeology and Anthropology, 1990.

Freidel, David, Michelle Rich, and F. Kent Reilly. "Resurrecting the Maize King: Figurines from a Maya Tomb Bring a Royal Funeral to Life." *Archaeology* 63, no. 5:42–45, 2010.

Pendergast, David M. *Altun Ha, British Honduras (Belize): The Sun God's Tomb.* Toronto: Occasional Paper 19, Royal Ontario Museum, University of Toronto Press, 1969. https://archive.org/details/altunhabritishho00pend.

Roach, John. "Ancient Royal Tomb Discovered in Guatemala." *National Geographic News*, May 4, 2006. http://news.nationalgeographic.com/news/2006/05/0504_060504_maya_tomb.html.

———. "Headless Man's Tomb Found under Maya Torture Mural." *National Geographic News*, March 12, 2010. http://news.nationalgeographic.com/news/2010/03/100312-headless-bonampak-tomb-maya-torture-mural/.

Sharer, Robert J., and Loa P. Traxler. *The Ancient Maya.* 6th ed. Stanford, CA: Stanford University Press, 2006.

■ WALTER R. T. WITSCHEY

S

SACBE
See Causeway / *Sacbe*

SALT
See Trade Routes

SAN BARTOLO

The ancient Maya site of San Bartolo (17.5° N, 89.4° W) was a regional capital located approximately 30 km northeast of **Uaxactun** in the Department of the Petén, **Guatemala** (see also **Map 3**). It is located within the 430 km² San Bartolo-Xultun Territory, which is dominated by *bajos* (seasonally inundated swamps or wetlands), forming a natural boundary around the area. These *bajos* are filled with stunted **vegetation**, including the *palo de tinte* tree, which the Maya harvested and used as a natural dye. The territory also contains many *aguadas* (ponds that have been modified by humans) and **chert** sources, which the Maya mined for making stone tools. Within the territory are the capitals of San Bartolo and Xultun (17.5° N, 89.3° W), as well as a number of regional centers, household groups, and temporary settlements used as agricultural field **houses**. Archaeologists have estimated that at the height of occupation, the territory incorporated approximately 7,700 residents. San Bartolo was dominant during the Late Formative period (ca. 250 BC–AD 250), while Xultun, the largest site in the area, took over as the regional capital starting in the Early Classic (ca. AD 250–400).

San Bartolo is the best-studied site in the region, having been documented since 2001 by the interdisciplinary San Bartolo Project, directed by William Saturno. The earliest occupation of the site appears to have been during the Middle Formative (900–250 BC), when ancient inhabitants quarried stone to build the first public **architecture**. This quarry later became the central *aguada* for the settlement. By the Late Formative there was a population explosion in the territory, and the capital expanded to a total of 240 known buildings, with a large **palace** structure and four **pyramid** complexes, including the Pinturas Pyramid. The site also contains large pot bellied monuments, which were likely used in ancient ancestor rituals, as well as an early writing system that scholars are still working to decipher (see also **Decipherment**; **Rites and Rituals**). Within the Pinturas Pyramid complex, archaeologists recovered a stucco block with 10 painted glyphs, of which the only readable glyph is "*ajaw*" (ruler, noble, or lord). The other glyphs are somewhat abstract and may represent an earlier version of Maya script similar to an epi-**Olmec writing system** known in central Mexico. Besides the painted glyphs, the site is best known for its polychrome murals, also located within the Pinturas Pyramid (see also **Wall Painting**).

Although it was a looter's tunnel that first revealed the murals, they were unknown to the archaeological community until 2001. William Saturno happened upon the murals by accident after his guides had greatly underestimated the length of a trek to some nearby monuments and he stopped in the looter's tunnel to rest in the shade. When he shone his flashlight onto a nearby wall, he saw a mural fragment that would ultimately lead to one of the most important discoveries in the last century of Maya archaeology. Since then the team has uncovered the rest of the mural and made an additional discovery of an even earlier mural. Radiocarbon dating has established the earliest mural dates to 300 BC, with the later murals dating to approximately 100 BC.

The primary mural is found on the north wall of an interior room and shows 14 figures in a mythological scene similar to those known from monuments at sites such as **Tikal** and Uaxactun. The western end of the north wall contains a scene with a male supernatural figure with a serpent face and feathers, likely an early representation of the feathered serpent god (see also **Deities**). He stands in front of a bird figure wearing a jeweled crown and four infants being born in each of the four cardinal directions from a central gourd with a cleft in it. The meaning of this scene is still unclear, as scholars have not found comparable examples from ancient or contemporary Maya imagery or mythology. However, it may be tied to scenes of Flower Mountain known at the central Mexican site of **Teotihuacán**, as just to the right of the birth scene is a zoomorphic mountain. The mountain is marked with bands that in Classic Maya **iconography** signify stone, and it has a fang that probably represents a speleothem (a stalactite or stalagmite formation on the ceiling or floor of a **cave**). The eye of the mountain is marked with a cross symbol, and it is covered with flowers, indicating that it is a precious mountain place from which life and abundance emerge. To the right of the mountain are eight figures standing upon the back of a plumed serpent. A woman sits within the mountain and holds a basket of tamales, surrounded by animals, including lizards, birds, and a jaguar, which may represent supernatural guardians of the mountain. To the right of the mountain entrance, the serpent is marked with footprints, indicating that he symbolizes a supernatural road. Three men and three women flank two central figures representing the Maize God and his wife. The figures present him with offerings of a bottle gourd and tamales, which seem to be sustenance being taken from Flower Mountain. This imagery is commonly depicted in various scenes in Maya art showing the Maize God going through a death journey and then being resurrected. Overall, the scene seems to represent a very early portrayal of the mythological emergence of people from an ancestral cave (or mountain) at the time that the god of corn arrives on the surface of the earth. In part, the significance of this mural demonstrates that there was great continuity in **Mesoamerican** mythology across time and space, and that no one culture seems to have dominated the ideological landscape.

For the territory of San Bartolo–Xultun, evidence suggests that there was extreme environmental degradation during the Late Formative, including major **soil** erosion, deforestation, silting over of the *bajos*, and long periods of **drought**. This seemingly led to the abandonment of San Bartolo during the Late Formative-Early Classic transition (ca. AD 150) and the rise of Xultun. Xultun may have thrived because it was located on a larger and more elevated piece of land and had six large and well-maintained *aguadas*, as compared to only one at San Bartolo. Nonetheless, ritual offerings of **ceramics** during the Early Classic period within the site center indicate that San Bartolo continued to have ritual significance even after its abandonment. During the Late Classic, there is even evidence that people returned to San Bartolo for a minor reoccupation. They cleaned out the *aguada* for use as a water source, modified the Tigrillo structure, and built minor residences throughout the site. By the end of the Late Classic period, however, the entire territory was generally abandoned, although small populations may have persisted into the eleventh century.

See also AGUADAS; ART; CLASSIC MAYA COLLAPSE. CRAFT SPECIALIZATION; DECIPHERMENT; HOLMUL; OLMEC-MAYA INTERACTIONS; STUART, GEORGE E., AND DAVID STUART; WALL PAINTING; WRITING SYSTEMS OF MESOAMERICA

Further Reading

Garrison, Thomas G., and Nicholas P. Dunning. "Settlement, Environment, and Politics in the San Bartolo-Xultun territory, El Petén, Guatemala." *Latin American Antiquity* 20, no. 4: 525–52, 2009.

Saturno, William A., David Stuart, and Boris Beltrán. "Early Maya Writing at San Bartolo, Guatemala." *Science* 311, no. 5765: 1281–83, 2006.

Saturno, William A., Karl Taube, and David Stuart. *The Murals of San Bartolo, El Petén, Guatemala*. Pt. 1, *The North Wall*. Ancient America, no. 7. Barnardsville, NC: Center for Ancient American Studies, 2005.

Taube, Karl A., William A. Saturno, David Stuart, Heather Hurst, and Joel Skidmore. *The Murals of San Bartolo, El Petén, Guatemala*. Pt. 2, *The West Wall*. Ancient America, no. 11. Barnardsville, NC: Boundary End Archaeology Research Center, 2010.

■ JENNIFER P. MATHEWS

SAYIL

The large Terminal Classic site Sayil (29.2° N, 89.7° W) was situated in the Puuc, 23 km southeast of its larger neighbor, **Uxmal**. Settlement began about AD 800 and reached its peak ca. AD 900. Sayil extended over 5 km² and boasted over 10,000 inhabitants. Most **ceramic** evidence shows that the Puuc region and Sayil were occupied sparsely prior to the Late Classic and Terminal Classic periods.

John Lloyd Stephens reported his visit to Sayil in 1841. In the first half of the twentieth century, INAH investigated the site, and Jeremy Sabloff and Gair Tourtellot conducted a major survey and investigation from 1983 to 1988. Surface collections by Michael Smyth and Christopher Dore provided detailed ceramic distributional analysis, confirming the Terminal Classic occupation. Their collection of approximately 30,000 artifacts, mostly ceramic, included only 155 stone tools, mostly **chert**, with a few **obsidian** pieces, mostly from **El Chayal**.

Sayil was built in a valley among the karst hills of the region. The farmland on the valley floors was highly productive, and rainfall was adequate for growing maize, but finding drinking water was a problem because there are no rivers or cenotes. Therefore, at Sayil and many other nearby sites, the Maya constructed *chultunes*, underground cisterns, hewn from the rock and plastered, to store rainwater collected as runoff from roofs and patios.

Like the other major sites in the region, Sayil was built in the **Puuc architectural style**, with finely cut veneer masonry and elaborate stone mosaic **sculpture** on upper façades. The site boasts major buildings, including an elegant three-tiered **palace** (see figure 39). The solid central core, successively smaller at the two upper levels, has rooms around the perimeter. From its south-facing façade, an intrasite *sacbe* (**causeway**) extended southward through several architectural groups, ultimately arriving at the **ball court**. By AD 1000 Sayil had been abandoned, reflecting the similar short occupation of other major Puuc sites: **Uxmal, Labna**, and **Kabáh**.

See also ARCHITECTURAL OVERVIEW; CHAC II; CLASSIC MAYA COLLAPSE; CRAFT SPECIALIZATION; EL CHAYAL; GROUND SURVEY TECHNIQUES; HOUSES; KIUIC; NORTHERN LOWLANDS; OBSIDIAN; PALACE; PORTABLE OBJECTS; PROSKOURIAKOFF, TATIANA AVENIROVNA; PUUC ARCHITECTURAL STYLE; WATER MANAGEMENT

Figure 39. Elite Maya housing. The palace at Sayil, Yucatan, Mexico. Note that upper stories do not rest on lower rooms, but on solid fill. A large *chultun* for water storage is visible at top left. Courtesy of Edward Kurjack.

SCHELE, LINDA (1942–1998)

Linda Schele made substantial contributions to Maya studies and epigraphy, even though her career in Maya studies spanned only 28 years. During that time she became a leading public spokesperson for the study of the Maya culture. Originally from Nashville, Tennessee, she began her career as a trained painter, with both undergraduate and graduate degrees in education and **art** from the University of Cincinnati. She started teaching art in 1968 at the University of South Alabama, the same year that she married David Schele.

In 1970 she experienced a major change in her career focus when she visited the **Palenque** and became obsessed with the art and writing of the ancient Maya (see also **Decipherment**). She became assistant professor in 1972. She returned to Palenque frequently in the early 1970s, mentored in ancient Maya art by Merle Greene Robertson and other Maya scholars. Schele presented her first paper at the *Primera Mesa Redonda de Palenque* in 1973, where she, Peter Mathews, and Floyd Lounsbury were able to recount, for the first time in such detail, an extended dynasty of Maya kings at Palenque by reading Maya script (see also **Dynastic Sequences**). She became a Dumbarton Oaks fellow in 1975 and associate professor of art at the University of South Alabama in 1976.

In 1977 she cofounded the Maya Meetings at the University of Texas at Austin and directed them until her death. These meetings became one of the most influential and largest of any of the Maya hieroglyphic workshops, attracting international scholars as well as laypeople. Her interactive style generated many new ideas and theories about Maya **iconography** and Maya hieroglyphic writing. Through these meetings, her writings, her enthusiasm, television appearances, and guided tours, she became a major force in the popularization of Maya studies. She became a visiting lecturer in art history and Latin American studies at the University of Texas in 1978, enrolled there as a graduate student that same year, and graduated in 1980 with her PhD in Latin American studies. Her dissertation, "Maya Glyphs: The Verbs," was a groundbreaking work.

In 1986 she and Mary Miller coordinated a world-acclaimed exhibition about the ancient Maya at the Kimbell Art Museum of Ft. Worth called "Blood of Kings," with an accompanying book. This was followed in 1990 by *A Forest of Kings* with David Freidel. In 1986 she was presented with the Tatiana **Proskouriakoff** Award for Maya research by Harvard's Peabody Museum. In 1987 she became professor at the University of Texas at Austin. In 1993 she, Freidel, and Joy Parker wrote *Maya Cosmos*, which explored the ancient Maya's conception of human creation and the connection between ancient and modern Maya spiritual thought and practice. In 1997 she and Jorge Pérez de Lara published *Hidden Faces of the Maya*. In addition to books, she published numerous scholarly articles and made many public lectures worldwide. She also produced a large volume of meticulously drawn pen-and-ink reproductions of ancient Maya **stelae** and other stone carvings. She was a warm and gifted teacher with a slow southern drawl. Her endearing generosity of spirit and her mentorship made her an inspiration for many. According to her wishes, her ashes were buried on a mountain that overlooks Lake Atitlan, **Guatemala**.

Further Reading

Freidel, David, Linda Schele, and Joy Parker. *Maya Cosmos: Three Thousand Years on the Shaman's Path*. New York: William Morrow, 1993.

Schele, Linda. *Maya Glyphs: The Verbs*. Austin: University of Texas Press, 1982.

Schele, Linda, and David Freidel. *A Forest of Kings: The Untold Story of the Ancient Maya*. New York: William Morrow, 1990.

Schele, Linda, and Peter Mathews. *The Code of Kings: The Language of Seven Sacred Maya Temples and Tombs*. New York: Scribner/Simon & Schuster, 1998.

Schele, Linda, and Mary Ellen Miller. *The Blood of Kings: Dynasty and Ritual in Maya Art*. New York and Fort Worth, TX: G. Braziller and the Kimbell Art Museum, 1986.

Schele, Linda, and Jorge Pérez de Lara. *Hidden Faces of the Maya*. Poway, CA: ALTI Publishing, 1997.

■ ELAINE DAY SCHELE AND DAVID MARTIN SCHELE

Further Reading

Carmean, Kelli Cummins. "The Ancient Households of Sayil: A Study of Wealth in Terminal Classic Maya Society." PhD diss., University of Pittsburgh, 1990.

Rhyne, Charles S. *Architecture, Restoration, and Imaging of the Maya Cities of Uxmal, Kabah, Sayil, and Labná, the Puuc Region, Yucatán, México*. Reed College, 2008. http://academic.reed.edu/uxmal/.

Sabloff, Jeremy A. *Ancient Maya Settlement Patterns at the Site of Sayil, Puuc Region, Yucatán, Mexico: Initial Reconnaissance (1983)*. Albuquerque: Latin American Institute, University of New Mexico, 1984.

———. *Settlement and Community Patterns at Sayil, Yucatán, Mexico: The 1984 Season*. Albuquerque: Latin American Institute, University of New Mexico, 1985.

Sabloff, Jeremy A., and Gair Tourtellot. *The Ancient Maya City of Sayil: The Mapping of a Puuc Region Center*. New Orleans, LA: Middle American Research Institute, Tulane University, 1991.

Smyth, Michael P., and Christopher D. Dore. "Large-site archaeological methods at Sayil, Yucatan, Mexico: Investigating Community Organization at a Prehispanic Maya Center." *Latin American Antiquity* 3, no. 1: 3–21, 1992.

■ WALTER R. T. WITSCHEY

SCULPTURE

Throughout the Maya region, elegant and symbol-laden **art** dominates city landscapes. Sculpted programs are executed in stone in relief and in three dimensions, and three-dimensional modeled stucco forms decorate monumental structures. Early influences on Classic Maya sculpture appear in the **Olmec** area and at **Izapa** on the Pacific coast of Chiapas. At Izapa, a Formative site at the boundary of Maya speakers and Mixe-Zoque speakers, few sculptures carry hieroglyphs. They do, however, carry a distinctive artistic style with a mixture of Olmec motifs and Maya **iconography**.

Classic Maya elites commissioned sculpture with their portraits and texts of their personal deeds and genealogies. Sculptures took the forms, for example, of carved stone wall panels (**Copan**), lintels (**Yaxchilan**), and **stelae** with full-figure rulers in regalia (**Tikal**), at times fully three-dimensional (Copan, **Quiriguá**). Related commissions included large stone altars, thrones, marker stones for **ball courts**, and carved **hieroglyphic stairways**.

Brightly painted modeled stucco of considerable thickness was used to adorn temple-pyramid roof-combs and the terrace façades of the pyramids (**Cerro Maya**, **Kohunlich**, **Ek Balam**, Balamkú). Illustrations include both **deities** and rulers. **Uaxactun** Str. E-VII-sub, the western structure in an **astronomical observatory** E-Group, has large stucco masks on the façades of the radial pyramid.

Since such a high percentage of Maya sculptures carry hieroglyphs as well as iconography, they are an important source of contemporaneous historical information about Maya elites and their activities.

Further Reading

Fash, William L., and Barbara W. Fash. "Building a World-View: Visual Communication in Classic Maya Architecture." *RES: Anthropology and Aesthetics* 29/30 (Spring–Autumn): 127–47, 1996.

Martin, Simon, and Nikolai Grube. *Chronicle of the Maya Kings and Queens: Deciphering the Dynasties of the Ancient Maya*. 2nd ed. London: Thames & Hudson, 2008.

Miller, Mary Ellen, and Megan Eileen O'Neil. *Maya Art and Architecture*. 2nd ed. London: Thames & Hudson, 2014.

Stone, Andrea, and Marc Zender. *Reading Maya Art: A Hieroglyphic Guide to Ancient Maya Painting and Sculpture*. London: Thames & Hudson, 2011.

■ WALTER R. T. WITSCHEY

SEIBAL

See CEIBAL

SERPENTS

See FAUNA

SETTLEMENT PATTERNS (INTRODUCTION)

Where people choose to live and why is a complex mix of both environmental factors, such as access to water and fertile soil, and social factors, such as access to kin and to markets. In the following articles, we can see that different archaeologists may take different approaches, some stressing environment and some stressing society. In her discussion of the Central Lowlands, Anabel Ford stresses the impact of fertile soil, rainfall, and hydrology. In his Northern Lowlands article, Edward Kurjack stresses more of the social factors: the relationships within kin groups in smaller settlements and between politically powerful kin groups in larger, more complex settlements. Both sets of factors are at work simultaneously in both areas, with resource access and social interaction playing an important role in both areas.

■ WALTER R. T. WITSCHEY

SETTLEMENT PATTERNS (CENTRAL LOWLANDS)

Maya settlement patterns are influenced by the geography of the lowland region characterized by rolling limestone ridges. These verdant Maya forests, threatened today by advancing pasturage and plow, underwrote the Classic Maya civilization and throve on an annual precipitation of 1,000 to 3,000 mm falling mainly from June to January. An annual dry season runs between March and June. Activities today are impacted by this wet/dry deluge and **drought** sequence, as they were in the Maya prehistory. (See **Maps 2, 5, 7**, and **8**.)

The limestone bedrock that underlies the region creates unpredictable access to water. Rarely transported on the surface, water is absorbed through fissures into the bedrock. Two major river systems, along with several smaller ones, flank the east and west sides of the **Central Lowlands**: the Belize/New River on the east and the Usumacinta/ Grijalva on the west. When openings in the limestone are lower than the water level, **lakes**, lagoons, or **cenotes** may form. Water gathers in wetlands, expanding in the rainy season in closed lowland depressions interspersed throughout 40 percent of the region. These variations of karst topography and water access generate the four basic ecosystems in the central Maya lowlands, forming a resource mosaic utilized by both the ancient and modern populations of the region:

- Well-drained ridges and uplands (high to low closed forest)
- Poorly drained lowlands (low, open forests and transitional wetlands)
- Perennial riverine wetlands (riparian forests, aquatic and semi-aquatic vegetation)
- Seasonal closed wetlands (low, open forest tolerant of hydric extremes)

This composite of regional land resources formed the foundation of Maya settlement distribution and density. Settlement appears the earliest (~3000 years ago) and becomes the greatest (1,500–1,000 years ago) in the well-drained ridges. Ridge lands are concentrated in the interior and are characterized by shallow, fertile, **soil** of excellent quality called mollisols, representing only 1 percent of the world's tropics yet up to 50 percent of the Maya forest. These soils are superior for the hand cultivation methods of pre-Hispanic times, in which land management included stone tools and fire. Variably distributed, well-drained slopes comprise less than one-sixth of the area of Northern **Belize**, but nearly half of the interior Petén around the large Classic Maya center of **Tikal**. There is a direct relationship between the presence of well-drained ridges, high settlement density, and the location of elite centers of the Classic Maya kingships. The fertile, well-drained uplands preferred by ancient Maya farming settlements for investment of their skill and labor are inappropriate for contemporary industrial methods, which compound the conservation risks in the region today.

The archaic presence of humans in the central lowland region can be traced back 8,000 years. The material archaeological record of the ancient Maya, however, is firm for the Middle Preclassic. Steady settlement expansion typified the first millennium BC, based essentially on household farming decisions. In the Late Preclassic, around 250 BC, land use diversified and civic-ceremonial centers made a full appearance across the region. Settlements expanded over the area, growing initially along rivers, then **lakes**, and ultimately spread across the entire interior.

There is ample evidence that the interior Petén area around Tikal dominated the region at the height of the civilization in the Late Classic period, AD 600–900. The unevenly distributed well-drained zones created a dispersed settlement pattern that is especially evident in the Late Classic. During this time period, Maya settlement expansion and construction was at its maximum. Yet Maya cities do not fit traditional notions of urbanism, but greatly value "green space" of residential home forest gardens (*solares*).

Urbanization continued through the Classic period until approximately AD 900, when the Maya civilization "collapsed." Major administrative and political centers, such as Tikal in the central Petén, witnessed halts in public projects, but settlements continued through the Terminal Classic period (AD 900–1000), and in some areas, longer. Settlement patterns between Tikal and Yaxhá, in the Belize River area, as well as in northern Belize, attest to persistent occupation. Further, monument building continued at centers such as **El Pilar** and La Milpa through this period, finally ceasing in the Postclassic (see also **Classic Maya Collapse**).

Many scholars focus on the dramatic Classic Maya period, but fail to stress the sustained land use strategies of the ancient Maya that intensified over several millennia. The expansion of settlements and the development of social complexity of the Maya were based on gradual increase in population and concomitant intensity of land use. Early investments in community development endured over time. This centralization process integrated the populations based on the development and management of the assets of the Maya forest. Environmental dimensions constrained **subsistence** strategies, and cultural developments mediated those constraints. The result was clearly agricultural diversity to sustain the steady growth of Maya civilization.

Ancient Maya settlements and, by proxy, the farming populace, were located in proximity to useful resources. The emergence of urban centers depended on the farming populace, and their requirements were integrated into land use strategies. Archaeologists for some time have recognized the geographic distribution of the population as dispersed in well-drained uplands, with little regard for the location of centers.

It is a mistake to view ancient Maya urbanism through the filter of developments in Europe. Patterns of Maya farming settlements developed from extensive to intensive based on skill and labor investment as people began to concentrate and settle in greater numbers in the preferred farming areas. Later, major civic centers grew up in the same places. Control of restricted sources of water may have become a relevant political strategy, particularly in the annual dry season, attracting dispersed farmers into centers as the populations grew. The historical ecology of the Maya lowlands, however, was undeniably connected to their valuable upland farming resources.

The source of the wealth of the Maya lay in their landscape and in their profound understanding of how to utilize and manage it. The success of the ancient Maya farming settlement patterns, the needs of contemporary local populations in the same region, and the conservation demands on the land highlight the value of the ancient Maya success.

See also Class Structure; El Mirador; Fauna; Geology; Nakbé; Settlement Patterns (Northern Lowlands); Vegetation; Water Management

Further Reading

Bullard, William R., Jr. "Maya Settlement Pattern in Northeastern Petén, Guatemala." *American Antiquity* 25, no. 3: 355–72, 1960.

Fedick, Scott L. "The Economics of Agricultural Land Use and Settlement in the Upper Belize River Valley." In *Prehistoric Maya Economies of Belize*, edited by Patricia A. McAnany and Barry L. Isaac, 215–54. Research in Economic Anthropology, Supplement no. 4. Greenwich, CT: JAI Press, 1989.

Fedick, Scott L. "Land Evaluation and Ancient Maya Land Use in the Upper Belize River area, Belize, Central America." *Latin American Antiquity* 6, no. 1: 16–34, 1995.

Ford, Anabel. *Population Growth and Social Complexity: An Examination of Settlement and Environment in the Central Maya lowlands.* Anthropological Research Papers, no. 35. Tempe: Arizona State University, 1986.

Ford, Anabel, Keith C. Clarke, and Gary Raines. "Modeling Settlement Patterns of the Late Classic Maya Civilization with Bayesian Methods and Geographic Information Systems." *Annals of the Association of American Geographers* 99, no. 3: 496–520, 2009.

Johnston, Kevin J. "The Intensification of Pre-industrial Cereal Agriculture in the Tropics: Boserup, Cultivation Lengthening, and the Classic Maya." *Journal of Anthropological Archaeology* 22, no. 2: 126–61, 2003.

Rice, Don Stephen, and Dennis E. Puleston. "Ancient Maya Settlement Patterns in the Petén, Guatemala." In *Lowland Maya Settlement Patterns*, edited by Wendy Ashmore, 125–56. Albuquerque: School of American Research, University of New Mexico Press, 1981.

Sanders, William T. "Classic Maya Settlement Patterns and Ethnographic Analogy." In *Lowland Maya Settlement Patterns*, edited by Wendy Ashmore, 351–69. Albuquerque: School of American Research, University of New Mexico Press, 1981.

Willey, Gordon R., Bullard, William R., Jr., John B. Glass, and James C. Gifford. *Prehistoric Maya Settlements in the Belize Valley*. Papers of the Peabody Museum of American Archaeology and Ethnology, vol. 54. Cambridge, MA: Peabody Museum, Harvard University, 1965.

■ ANABEL FORD

SETTLEMENT PATTERNS (HIGHLANDS AND PACIFIC COASTAL PLAIN)

Along the Pacific coast of Chiapas, **Mexico**, and **Guatemala**, the slope of the terrain from the mountains and volcanoes into the Pacific Trench forms a band of fertile alluvial farmland 30 to 60 km wide, rising from sea level to 600–800 m elevation. Further inland are the highlands, two major ranges of mountains divided by the Grijalva River flowing northwest and the Motagua River flowing east–northeast to the Caribbean.

In the Formative (at least by 1500 BC) impressive settlements began to develop on this coastal plain, including **Izapa**, **Takalik Abaj**, **Sin Cabezas**, and Chalchuapa. Their focus was a **trade route** along the coast and **cacao** production for a valuable trading commodity. This route linked them to the **Olmec** heartland to the northeast, and to the **southern periphery** to the south and west. These cities include some of the earliest evidence of divine rulers, monumental **architecture**, dated **stelae,** and worship of the rain god Chac.

In addition to providing trade links along the coast, several sites were in direct communication with the highlands, the chief source of valuable stone such as jade and **obsidian**. Both Takalik Abaj and Chalchuapa show direct links to the highland sources.

In the highlands, one city rose in size and power to exceed all others. **Kaminaljuyú**, located within modern Guatemala City today, built on both control of obsidian trade and sophisticated irrigation for subsistence to become a dominant force in the highlands, trading with the coast and northward into the **Southern Lowlands.** Recent studies of its chronology suggests that Kaminaljuyú had close interactions with the Olmec prior to 400 BC, and after a hiatus, resumed significant activity, but with Maya contacts to the north as its focus. Current debate concerns whether culture traits were flowing from Kaminaljuyú northward or from the Maya lowlands southward in this era.

During the Early Classic, there was a decline in the power of the coastal cities, as settlement dispersed into smaller villages, although the area continued active trade in cacao. More activity is visible in the highlands, where, in addition to the power of Kaminaljuyú, Maya were settling along the bottom land of streams and rivers in the highlands, likely to control mineral resources. Several such sites are now underwater at the site of the Belisario Dominguez dam on the Grijalva River. Settlement in this era was at open sites without fortification.

Settlement underwent a major change with the eruption of volcano Ilopango in AD 535. The disruption sent immigrants fleeing northward toward Kaminaljuyú and Copán.

Little is heard from this region until the Postclassic, when settlement again changed dramatically. Kaminaljuyú was abandoned. Highland and coastal peoples moved from open valleys to defensible hilltop sites with natural fortifications in the terrain. This was a time of increased warfare and of immigration from Central Mexico and Northern Yucatan. New hilltop sites formed along the Usumacinta and the Motagua Rivers. In the highlands, powerful local kingdoms developed at Atitlan, **Zaculeu**, **Utatlán**, and **Iximché**, among others, with warfare common as states tried to control the coastal cacao trade and the river traffic. The Spaniards arrived during this time of conflict, and their sources plus the locally written *Popol Vuh* document the settlement in the highlands at the start of the Colonial era.

See also OLMEC–MAYA INTERACTIONS

Further Reading

Braswell, Geoffrey E. *The Maya and Teotihuacan: Reinterpreting Early Classic Interaction.* Austin: University of Texas Press, 2004.

Guernsey, Julia. *Ritual & Power in Stone: The Performance of Rulership in Mesoamerican Izapan Style Art.* Austin: University of Texas Press, 2006.

Inomata, Takeshi, Raúl Ortiz, Bárbara Arroyo, and Eugenia J. Robinson. "Chronological Revision of Preclassic Kaminaljuyú, Guatemala: Implications for Social Processes in the Southern Maya Area." *Latin American Antiquity* 25, no. 4: 377–408, 2014.

Nance, Charles Roger, Stephen L. Whittington, and Barbara E. Jones-Borg. *Archaeology and Ethnohistory of Iximche.* Gainesville: University Press of Florida, 2003.

Robinson, Eugenia J., Marlen Garnica, and Juan Pablo Herrera. "El Postclásico Tardio: Asentamientos alrededor de Iximché en el Altiplano de Guatemala." In *XXVI Simposio de Investigactiones Arqueológicas en Guatemala*, edited by Bárbara Arroyo and Médez Salinas. Guatemala City, Guatemala: Museo de Arqueología y Ethnología, 2013.

Woodbury, Richard B., and Aubrey S. Trik. *The Ruins of Zaculeu, Guatemala*. Vol. 1. New York: United Fruit Co., 1953.

■ WALTER R. T. WITSCHEY

SETTLEMENT PATTERNS (NORTHERN LOWLANDS)

Houses, large or small, expensive or inexpensive, were the most important components of northern Maya settlements. These were constructed and controlled by domestic kin groups, some large and powerful, some small and less politically significant. The houses that filled the communities having simple societies are almost identical, reflecting the homogeneity of community. The heterogeneous inhabitants of complex societies, however, occupied different kinds of houses.

Other features found at Maya sites are temple-**pyramids**, family shrines, masonry **causeways** (Maya *sacbeob*, singular *sacbe*), monumental plazas, communal halls such as men's **council houses, ball courts,** and **fortifications**. The identification of which structures were built by the community as a whole and which are dwellings and family shrines remains a basic problem. Nevertheless, the arrangements of such elements in a site plan should provide answers to questions about social organization (see also **Class Structure**).

Some social scientists maintain that early urban centers were dominated by **markets**, fortresses, temples, or **palaces**. Archaeology at Cival and Mirador basin sites suggests that E-Groups may have been among the earliest ceremonial architecture constructed by the Maya. Hints of these features are present at incipient Preclassic Maya urban centers; it is clear that questions about the origins of Maya cities have to be answered by looking at large settlements that predated incipient urbanism.

Diego de Landa reported in the sixteenth century that Maya towns were arranged in a pattern of concentric zoning. Important people lived at the center and poor people on the settlement periphery. Of course the largest concentration of **architecture** is always defined as the nucleus of the settlement, with lesser architecture around it. But Maya settlements seldom exhibit perfect concentric zoning; at most Maya settlements, various large architectural complexes away from site centers break the concentric pattern. If perfect concentric zoning reflects a well-defined stratification system, the presence of large structures away from the center suggests potential countervailing power to political centralization.

Some early researchers believed that larger Maya sites served as religious centers for dispersed rural populations. Archaeological sites were essentially farming hamlets or minor and major ceremonial centers. Today mapping at the major and minor sites reveals too many houses for them to be considered places for ritual only. Ethnohistorical information, together with the presence of shrines in ancient dwelling contexts, suggests Maya **religion** was family oriented. Note that some famous temples such as the Adivino at **Uxmal** seem to have started as houses.

A very different principle may be observed at many northern Maya sites; rather than religion, this interpretation emphasizes social organization. The idea is exemplified in its simplest form by the map of **Labna**. The plan illustrates two large palace complexes connected by a causeway and surrounded by smaller buildings. Other sites repeat this same pattern. The causeways suggest especially frequent contacts between people once living in the palaces. The causeways probably served as material reminders of the permanent **alliance** between two families. In other words, the two largest and most prestigious elite dwelling complexes at **Labna** have a walkway between them that implies especially close interaction. One form of such relationship between families is marriage alliance. An alliance of two elite groups living in palaces, with their numbers and organization, potentially dominated community politics.

More complex settlements such as **Dzibilchaltun** consisted of additional causeways and elite dwelling complexes. The allied elites counted on each other for support as well as on their more distant commoner kin.

The layout of **Cobá**, with at least 50 causeways radiating from the center to numerous outliers in an area of 120 km^2, is the model of a complex settlement. The basic site layout, however, is rooted in the relatively simple Labna plan and implies its essential kin-based character.

Construction of a communal central plaza appears to have accompanied increased centralization of political power in a Maya community. The plazas of Dzibilchaltun and Ake were built by the settlement as a whole. Some of the buildings surrounding those assembly areas, however, are distinct constructions, probably representing different social groups.

Ball courts appear in both elite domestic contexts and in communal areas.

Defensive features, such as walls and moats, at some northern Maya sites are relatively simple features that overlie the earlier settlement plan. Often only the central buildings are situated within the **fortifications**; Tulum is an excellent example.

Further Reading

Ashmore, Wendy, ed. *Lowland Maya Settlement Patterns*. School of American Research Advanced Seminar Series. Albuquerque: University of New Mexico Press, 1981.

Folan, William J., Ellen R. Kintz, and Laraine A. Fletcher. *Coba: A Classic Maya Metropolis*. Edited by Stuart Struever. Studies in Archaeology. New York: Academic Press, 1983.

Kurjack, Edward B., and Silvia Garza Tarazona de González. "Pre-Columbian Community Form and Distribution in the Northern Maya Area." In *Lowland Maya Settlement Patterns*, edited by Wendy Ashmore, 287–309. Albuquerque: University of New Mexico Press, 1981.

Manzanilla, Linda, ed. *Coba, Quintana Roo: Análisis de dos unidades habitacionales mayas*. México, D.F.: Instituto de Investigaciones Antropológicas, Universidad Nacional Autónoma de México, 1987.

Sabloff, Jeremy A. "Settlement Patterns and Community Organization in the Maya Lowlands." *Expedition* 38, no. 1: 3–13, 1996 http://www.penn.museum/documents/publications/expedition/PDFs/38-1/settlement1.pdf.

■ EDWARD B. KURJACK

SHAMAN

See PRIESTS

SIN CABEZAS

Sin Cabezas (14.1° N, 91.5° W) is a Late Preclassic to Terminal Preclassic site traditionally dated ca. 400 BC–AD 200, located on the Pacific Coastal Plain at the western edge of the **Guatemala** Department of Escuintla, 21 km from modern Tiquisate and 10 km from the Pacific Ocean. (See also **Map 3**.)

Sin Cabezas is the only first order site in the zone between the Nahualate and Madre Vieja Rivers. It is located on flat land that is now agricultural.

The **Pacific coast** of Guatemala contains a number of archaeological sites with "Olmecoid" characteristics that show substantial variation in **sculpture** and **architecture** (see also **Olmec**; **Olmec-Maya Interactions**). The ethnicity of the inhabitants of Sin Cabezas is unknown, but their culture has been revealed by archaeological investigations in the 1900s.

In 1947 Edwin Shook found four headless Preclassic "potbelly" sculptures at the site and applied the name "Sin Cabezas" to the site. His sketch map placed the figures in front of one of the largest structures at the site, G2. Later, Lee Parsons described these sculptures as having a naturalistic style related to earlier Olmec monumental in-the-round figures. The Sin Cabezas stone sculptures are seated figures with crossed legs, large bellies, and no heads. They have broad, roughly shaped pedestals and are not too large, averaging about 40 cm tall, with pedestals varying between 30 and 70 cm in height.

A recent map shows the center of the site to be a core area of four earthen mounds forming a *plazuela* group of about 300 m². Shook's sketch map shows the largest earthen structure to have a square base about 50 m long and a height of about 18 m; Beaudry-Corbett's published map shows the same structure as 10 m tall with basal dimensions of 100 m. The difference in shape and size is probably due to earthmoving on the farmland. All the areas of the site were occupied during the Preclassic period. Surveys limited to the west and south have recorded 200 or more earthen mounds, most of them less than 1 m in height and with no particular spatial organization, extending for 1.5 km.

The Tiquisate Archaeological Zone (TAZ) Project, directed by Marilyn Beaudry-Corbett and David Whitley, carried out excavations of the site from 1986 to 1992. The goals of the excavations were to study past societal complexity and elite household economy through the discovery of architecture, **burials**, workshops, middens, and nonutilitarian objects. One elaborate burial was in Structure F4-9, near the western edge of the *plazuela*, where a young person, probably male, was buried with 10 **ceramics**, a dog, beads, some minerals, and some red snake vertebrae. This burial was particularly revealing about the social organization, showing that young people had complex interments and suggesting a ranked, ascribed social order at Sin Cabezas (see also **Class Structure**). Another structure was an elite residence with a workshop of imported alabaster. A smaller mound had a funereal function, revealed by burials of multiple people, some sacrificed. Elevated social status at another structure was demonstrated by finds of nonutilitarian beads and possible dedicatory interments on its west side (see also **Royal Tombs**).

Fred Bove noted there was also a considerable Late Classic population at Sin Cabezas, possibly an extension of the site of **Ixtepeque** to the north. The site's periphery also had Early and Late Classic (AD 300–900) occupations that were more extensive than the Preclassic one; the western half of the site was utilized more during these later occupations.

See also BURIALS; CRAFT SPECIALIZATION; HOUSES; IXTEPEQUE; PACIFIC COASTAL PLAIN; PHYSICAL/BIOLOGICAL ANTHROPOLOGY

Further Reading

Barrientos, Tomás. *Indice ilustrado de la coleccion de fichas de campo de Edwin Shook [texto de Tomás Barrientos]*. Antigua, Guatemala: Centro de Investigaciones Regionales de Mesoamérica (CIRMA), 2010.

Beaudry-Corbett, Marilyn. "The Tiquisate Archaeological Zone: A Case of Delayed Societal Complexity?" In *Incidents of Archaeology in Central America and Yucatán: Essays in Honor of Edwin M. Shook*, edited by Michael Love, Marion Popenoe de Hatch, and Héctor L. Escobedo. Lanham, MD: University Press of America, 2002.

Parsons, Lee Allen. *The Origins of Maya Art: Monumental Stone Sculpture of Kaminaljuyu, Guatemala, and the Southern Pacific Coast*. Studies in Pre-Columbian Art and Archaeology, no. 28. Washington, DC: Dumbarton Oaks Research Library and Collection, 1986.

Whitley, David S., and Marilyn P. Beaudry, eds. *Investigaciones arqueológicas en la costa sur de Guatemala*. Institute of Archaeology, Monograph 31. Los Angeles: Institute of Archaeology, University of California, Los Angeles, 1989.

■ EUGENIA J. ROBINSON

SITE Q
See LA CORONA

SIVAL
See CIVAL

SNAKE KINGDOM
See CALAKMUL; DZIBANCHÉ

SOILS

Production of food depends critically on soils (*lu'um*), which vary widely across the Maya area (see also **Maps 7** and **8**; **Geology**). In the dry Northern Lowlands, soils are thin across the base of limestone karst, and **vegetation** is sparse. They vary considerably between those found on small rises and those that have collected in small, low pockets. Farther south, soils are deeper and more productive.

The Yucatec Maya today distinguish soils on several bases: color, rockiness, depth, texture, and other factors. One may hear mention by Maya of, for example, *box lu'um* (black soil), *chak lu'um* (red soil), and *ek' lu'um* (dark soil), because they are keenly evaluating soil for support of crops. Each soil type has its own characteristics of location, stoniness, and water retention. These are classified in modern research terms by Francisco Bautista and J. Alfred Zinck to permit laboratory comparison with other regions.

Archaeology in the Maya region now devotes considerable time to soil profiling and analysis. New research questions about soil productivity, terrain modification by **terracing** or the construction of raised fields, and loss of soil by erosion have become especially important as they relate to **subsistence**, the **Classic Maya collapse**, and how the Maya dealt with **drought**.

See also AGUADAS; BAJOS; CAUSEWAY/SACBE; CEIBAL; CENTRAL LOWLANDS; COCHUAH REGION; COTZUMALHUAPA; DZIBILCHALTUN; EK BALAM; EL PILAR; GEOLOGY; GROUNDWATER/WATER TABLE; KABAH AND NOHPAT; KIUIC; KOMCHEN; LABNA; MARKETS AND MARKETPLACES; NORTHERN LOWLANDS; PACIFIC COASTAL PLAIN; PHYSICAL/BIOLOGICAL ANTHROPOLOGY; QUIRIGUÁ; REJOLLADA; SAN BARTOLO; SETTLEMENT PATTERNS (INTRODUCTION); SETTLEMENT PATTERNS (CENTRAL LOWLANDS); SOUTHERN HIGHLANDS; TERRACING; VEGETATION; WATER MANAGEMENT; YAXHOM

Further Reading

Bautista, Francisco, and J. Alfred Zinck. "Construction of a Yucatec Maya Soil Classification and Comparison with the WRB Framework." *Journal of Ethnobiology and Ethnomedicine* 6, no. 7: 1–11, 2010.

Dunning, Nicholas P., and Timothy Beach. "Soil Erosion, Slope Management, and Ancient Terracing in the Maya Lowlands." *Latin American Antiquity*, no. 5: 51–69, 1994.

Dunning, Nicholas P., Timothy P. Beach, and Sheryl Luzzadder-Beach. "Kax and Kol: Collapse and Resilience in Lowland Maya Civilization." *Proceedings of the National Academy of Sciences USA* 109, no. 10: 3652–57, 2012.

Fedick, Scott L., ed. *The Managed Mosaic: Ancient Maya Agriculture and Resource Use*. Salt Lake City: University of Utah Press, 1996.

Fedick, Scott L., and Anabel Ford. "The Prehistoric Agricultural Landscape of the Central Maya Lowlands: An Examination of Local Variability in a Regional Context." *World Archaeology* 22, no. 1: 18–33, 1990.

Harrison, Peter D., and B. L. Turner, eds. *Pre-Hispanic Maya agriculture*. Albuquerque: University of New Mexico Press, 1978.

Jacob, John S. "Ancient Maya Wetland Agricultural Fields in Cobweb Swamp, Belize: Construction, Chronology, and Function." *Journal of Field Archaeology* 22, no. 2: 175–90, 1995.

■ WALTER R. T. WITSCHEY

SOUTHERN ARCHITECTURAL STYLE

Copán, **Honduras**, and nearby **Quiriguá**, **Guatemala**, provide the chief examples of the southern architectural style of the Late Classic. Although both sites lie physiographically in the highlands, they were culturally lowland (see also **Map 2**). The style is distinguished by the particularly elegant and well-executed façade sculptures as well as a tendency toward sculpture in the round, which is unusual in the Classic Maya canon. The sculptures at both sites are unusually well preserved because they are carved out of stone that is harder than the limestone that is ubiquitous in the lowlands. In Copán, both buildings and sculptures are made of a volcanic tuff that, though soft and friable, is more durable than limestone. At Quiriguá, the local sandstone has also endured well.

At Copán, fancier buildings boasted elaborate exterior wall carvings as well as mosaic stone sculptures on roofs and upper façades. These were carved out of multiple building blocks that were secured in place before being carved. This produced more perfectly fitted and matched elements than one finds in much other Maya mosaic façade sculpture.

The finer Late Classic buildings at Copán, especially those on the acropolis, were built of well-squared building stones of a consistent size—courses were about 20 cm tall—that were carefully laid to ensure reasonable bonding. The mortar at Copán, however, was not strong. It was a mixture of sticky reddish clay with a little lime. Because of the weak mortar, few vaults survive at Copán. Presumably, the *Copanecos* skimped on use of lime because limestone is rarer in the area than it is in the lowlands. Nevertheless, stucco was heavily used for paving floors, finishing walls and benches, and decorating façades. Much stucco work was painted, although the paint rarely survived the elements.

Further Reading

Andrews, E. Wyllys, V, and William Leonard Fash, eds. *Copán: The History of an Ancient Maya Kingdom*. School of American Research Advanced Seminar Series. Santa Fe, NM: School of American Research, 2005.

Fash, William L. *Scribes, Warriors, and Kings: The City of Copan and the Ancient Maya*. London: Thames & Hudson, 1991.

Sharer, Robert J. *Quirigua: A Classic Maya Center & Its Sculptures*. Centers of Civilization Series. Durham, NC: Carolina Academic Press, 1990.

■ CLIFFORD T. BROWN AND WALTER R. T. WITSCHEY

SOUTHERN HIGHLANDS

The dominant feature of most of the Southern Highlands is a series of active, dormant, and extinct volcanoes forming a line along tectonic plate boundaries parallel to the Pacific coast (Caribbean Plate and North American Plate). This combination creates an area of high volcanic and seismic activity, with frequent serious earthquakes (see also **Map 2**). Rainfall in the region is between 2,000 and 3,000 mm per year (see also **Map 5**). The high rainfall, coupled with fertile **soils** created by the weathering of volcanic deposits, has created an especially productive area of valleys of arable land, which has a congenial climate and high populations (see also **Map 8**). For the early part of its history **Kaminal-juyú** was the dominant highland site, deriving power in part from the nearby **El Chayal** region **obsidian** sources.

See also EL SALVADOR; GUATEMALA; IXIMCHÉ; NORTHERN HIGHLANDS; OBSIDIAN; PACIFIC COASTAL PLAIN; SOILS

Further Reading

Coe, Michael D. *The Maya*. 8th ed. London: Thames & Hudson, 2011.

Evans, Susan Toby. *Ancient Mesoamerica & Central America: Archaeology and Culture History*. 2nd ed. London: Thames & Hudson, 2008.

Global Volcanism Program. Smithsonian Institution, National Museum of Natural History, 2014. http://www.volcano.si.edu/.

Sharer, Robert J., and Loa P. Traxler. *The Ancient Maya*. 6th ed. Stanford, CA: Stanford University Press, 2006.

■ WALTER R. T. WITSCHEY

SOUTHERN LOWLANDS

Ill-defined borders mark the northern edge of the Southern Lowlands as it grades into the **Central Lowlands**—some writers divide the lowlands into only two parts, **northern** and **southern** (see also **Map 2**). To the south, however, the demarcation between lowlands and highlands is better defined, since significant changes take place between the two areas at about 600–800 m asl.

The area encompasses the broad Gulf coastal plain, where rivers are depositing silt and creating meander channels and ox-bows, and land is seasonally or perennially flooded. Many ancient sites are along the southern edge of the Southern Lowlands, including **Palenque**, **Piedras Negras**, and **Yaxchilan**. In ancient times, the rivers of the region provided major thoroughfares for communication and **trade**. The Candelaria, Mamantal, San Pedro Martír, and Usumacinta Rivers all drain toward the Gulf Coast. There is a smaller coastal plain on the Caribbean shore, as well as a portion of the sharply higher Maya Mountains of southern **Belize**. The Motagua River drains the **highlands** through the Southern Lowlands.

Rainfall grades from as high as 4,000 mm annually at the south central edge of the Southern Lowlands to about 1,500 mm along the northern edge (see also **Map 5**). The higher rainfall produces a tropical forest of evergreens and a multistory canopy. **Lakes** and rivers provide more than adequate water. The region participates in the hot zone of the Central and Northern Lowlands.

See also TIKAL

Further Reading

Coe, Michael D. *The Maya*. 8th ed. London: Thames & Hudson, 2011.

Evans, Susan Toby. *Ancient Mesoamerica & Central America: Archaeology and Culture History*. 2nd ed. London: Thames & Hudson, 2008.

Sharer, Robert J., and Loa P. Traxler. *The Ancient Maya*. 6th ed. Stanford, CA: Stanford University Press, 2006.

■ WALTER R. T. WITSCHEY

SOUTHERN PERIPHERY

The ancient Maya interacted in multifarious ways with non-Maya peoples and cultures in the southern periphery of Mesoamerica. Some of those peoples were culturally **Mesoamerican**, while others were non-Mesoamerican peoples more closely affiliated with lower Central American cultures. Thus, the region was a frontier and a borderland. The area has mainly been viewed through the lens of Mesoamerican civilizations and has served as a foil to highlight contrasts with them, but also has long possessed its own indigenous character. It cannot be understood solely by reference to the states and empires to the north and west. Unfortunately, the southern periphery has received less scholarly attention and is therefore less well known than Mesoamerica proper.

The southern boundary, and thus the periphery, of Mesoamerica is poorly defined geographically. It is more accurate to think of the "boundary" as a zone encompassing complicated patterns of interaction, some of which gradually attenuated with distance from Mesoamerica, while others were patchy and discontinuous. Some scholars call this zone of cultural transition an "ethnotone," by analogy to an ecotone, which is a zone of ecological transition. Adding to the complexity, the ethnotone shifted over time, as the type and intensity of ethnic interactions fluctuated over archaeological time. Types of interaction in the southern periphery included **trade**, migration, and colonialism, all which probably operated through a variety of mechanisms that differed over time and historical circumstance.

Despite its vague and impermanent boundaries, the southern periphery is generally understood to include the regions to the east of the Maya border in **Honduras** and **El Salvador**. In Honduras the Maya border is marked by the site of **Copán**, to the east of which historically lived the Jicaque (also called the Tol), the Paya, and other non-Mesoamerican peoples. In El Salvador, the border is sometimes drawn at the Río Lempa, which runs north to south across the country. Historical and archaeological evidence suggests that the Lenca, a Mesoamerican people, occupied large swaths of eastern Honduras and El Salvador. Other scholars consider that the southern Mesoamerican border should encompass all of the Pacific coast of Nicaragua and even the Nicoya Peninsula in Costa Rica. This latter definition, the original one developed by Paul Kirchhoff in the 1940s, still enjoys support today because it was defined by the distribution of cultures and languages at the time of the Spanish conquest. That southeast coast, of Nicaragua and Costa Rica, was then occupied by Mesoamerican immigrants, including the Chorotega, the Maribio, and the Nahua, who migrated there in waves after the end of the Central Mexican Classic period.

The southern periphery is marked by smaller scale and less socially complex societies than those of the Maya or Central Mexico. Major urban centers, huge public monuments, and sprawling palaces are all absent. Platforms and temples are usually built out of unsquared cobbles rather than finely cut stone. Also, the Maya residential **settlement pattern** of patio groups surrounding courtyards is replaced by a grid pattern of mounds in many sites. The area seems to have long been an ethnic mosaic of cultures in which the geographic extent of polities was smaller than in Mesoamerica (see also **Political Entities**). Thus many anthropologists characterize the periphery as having been occupied by chiefdoms, rather than the states or empires found in Mesoamerica.

Social and cultural interactions with the **Maya area** and Mesoamerica started in the southern periphery by the Early Formative period. The **Olmec**-related site of Puerto Escondido in northwest Honduras was first occupied before 1600 BC. It was a small but wealthy village with a trade and interaction network that extended deep into Guatemala and **Mexico**, back toward the Olmec heartland. Farther east, other early sites with cultural and possibly social ties to the Olmec include Yarumela and Los Naranjos in central Honduras. Los Naranjos has remarkable Olmec-style **sculptures** carved in the round, an early Olmec trait rarely seen outside the heartland in Mexico. Farther east, beyond the purported eastern Mesoamerican boundary, the Cuyamel caves and the Río Talgua caves have produced Early to Middle Formative period mortuary assemblages with links to the Olmec and to Mesoamerica more generally.

During the Late Formative period, exchange with Maya groups in western El Salvador spread east and north through the periphery, as can be seen in the distribution of Usulután ware, a technologically advanced pottery decorated in negative with wavy parallel lines. Though Usulután ware evolved in western El Salvador, it reached its highest concentration in eastern El Salvador at the site of Quelepa, sometimes considered the easternmost Mesoamerican site. Usulután and Usulután-like local imitations are also common in western Nicaragua, petering out around Managua. However, Usulután ware appears intrusive in the local **ceramic** assemblages, which otherwise remain distinctively provincial. During the same period, the **Izapa** sculptural style extends at least as far east as Quelepa, linking the periphery to important developments in the Maya area.

Classic period evidence for Mesoamerican and Maya interaction in the periphery is surprisingly weak, even though during this period the population, power, and prestige of Mesoamerican societies reached their zenith. The periphery exhibits little direct cultural influence from the Maya or central Mexico, for example, in the form of ceramic decoration, sculpture, inscriptions, monumental **architecture**, settlement patterns, or urbanism. Exchange may have been lively in commodities such as **obsidian** and jade, but evidence for this is patchy.

During the Central Mexican Epiclassic period (ca. AD 650–850) waves of migration begin heading for the southern periphery, presumably prompted by political instability after the fall of Teotihuacán. The earliest migrants were the Chorotega, driven from Cholula by the Olmeca-Xicalanca, headquartered at nearby Cacaxtla. The Chorotega resettled along the Pacific coast from eastern El Salvador and the Gulf of Fonseca to the Nicoya Peninsula, apparently displacing earlier inhabitants. The Maribio, who, like the Chorotega, spoke an Oto-manguean language, also migrated, from Guerrero or Oaxaca in Mexico to northwestern Nicaragua. During the Postclassic period, waves of people who spoke Nahua and were related to the Aztecs, including the Pipil and Nicarao, migrated to El Salvador and Nicaragua. While the dates of these migrations are uncertain, strong Central Mexican influences appear in that region around AD 900 or 1000. They are visible in the **iconography** of the famous white-slipped Nicoya ceramics, the monolithic columnar statues from Nicaragua, and the ceramics and architecture of El Salvador at sites such as Cihuatán. Similarly, the spread of Tohil Plumbate ware in the region, which extended as far south as Tola in the Department of Rivas, Nicaragua, illustrated the participation of the periphery in Mesoamerican trade networks. Trade also occurred in the other direction. A cache of pottery vessels found at the Toltec capital of Tula, Hidalgo, Mexico, contained both Nicoya Polychrome and Plumbate vessels. When the Spanish arrived in the region, they found a mosaic of cultures in the periphery, including "islands" of Nahua settlement in a sea of Lencas, Chorotegas, Maribios, and other, smaller ethnic groups.

See also OLMEC-MAYA INTERACTIONS

Further Reading

Fowler, William R., Jr. *The Cultural Evolution of Ancient Nahua Civilizations: The Pipil-Nicarao of Central America.* Norman: University of Oklahoma Press, 1989.

Joyce, Rosemary A., and John S. Henderson. "Beginnings of Village Life in Eastern Mesoamerica." *Latin American Antiquity* 12, no. 1: 5–23, 2001.

Lange, Frederick W., Payson Sheets, Anibal Martínez, and Suzanne Abel-Vidor. *The Archaeology of Pacific Nicaragua.* Albuquerque: University of New Mexico Press, 1992.

Schortman, Edward M., and Patricia A. Urban. *Networks of Power: Political Relations in the Late Postclassic Naco Valley, Honduras.* Boulder: University Press of Colorado, 2011.

Sheets, Payson D. *The Ceren Site: An Ancient Village Buried by Volcanic Ash in Central America.* 2nd ed. Belmont, CA: Thomson Wadsworth, 2006.

Urban, Patricia A., and Edward M. Schortman, eds. *The Southeast Maya Periphery.* Austin: University of Texas Press, 1986.

■ CLIFFORD T. BROWN

STELA (PL. STELAE)

A carved or plain tall, upright stone commemorative marker is known as a stela. In the **Maya area**, a stela is an especially important source of information about the reigns of Maya rulers. The value derives from the combination of dates, texts, and visual images combined in a single work of **art**. The origins of stelae in the region lay with the **Olmecs**, from whom the practice spread to the Pacific coast, notably at **Takalik Abaj**, Chiapa de Corzo, and **Izapa**. At Takalik Abaj stelae display ruler portraits. The first dated stela in the Maya **lowlands** is Stela 29 at **Tikal** with a Long Count of 8.12.14.8.15, AD 292, which is considered the beginning of the Classic period. Monument 101 at **Toniná**, which carries the celebratory *k'atun*-ending date 10.4.0.0.0, January 15, AD 909, is the latest known Maya monument with a Long Count, and traditionally marks the end of the Classic period.

Stelae frequently portray a ruler in ceremonial regalia, sometimes standing on a captive from another Maya city. The associated inscriptions describe birthdays, coronations, marriages, wars, and **alliance** links to other cities (superiors and subordinates), and provide other key information, such as royal titles, parentage, and other **kinship** ties. They are high-order propaganda, confirming the ruler's right to the throne and ties to a founding dynastic ancestor. Stelae were often set in front of temple-**pyramids** and behind round carved stone altars, which may have actually served as thrones.

Not all stelae were carved or inscribed. Many were plain, but archaeologists believe that they may have been painted with scenes or hieroglyphic texts similar to those on the carved monuments. The styles of stelae varied geographically and also changed through time. Among the hundreds of stelae known from dozens of sites, Stela E at **Quiriguá** stands out, literally, at a height of 10.6 m.

See also ALTUN HA; ARCHITECTURE OVERVIEW; ART; ASTRONOMICAL OBSERVATORIES; ASTRONOMY; CALAKMUL; CALENDAR; CARACOL; CARACOL-DYNASTIC HISTORY; CAUSEWAY/SACBE; CEIBAL; CLASSIC MAYA COLLAPSE; COBÁ; COCHUAH REGION; COPÁN; COTZUMALHUAPA; CRAFT SPECIALIZATION; DATING; DECIPHERMENT; DYNASTIC SEQUENCES; DZIBILCHALTUN; ECCENTRIC LITHICS; EDZNA; EL MIRADOR; EL PERÚ-WAKA'; FAUNA; GEOLOGY; HOLMUL; ICONOGRAPHY; ITZIMTE; KAMINALJUYÚ; KOHUNLICH; LA LAGUNITA; LAMANAI; LANGUAGE AND WRITING OVERVIEW; MATHEMATICS; MAYA QUEENS; MIDDLE CLASSIC HIATUS; MUSIC AND DANCE; NAACHTUN; NAKBÉ; NARANJO; OLMEC; OLMEC-MAYA INTERACTIONS; OXKINTOK; PALENQUE; PIEDRAS NEGRAS; PRIESTS; PROSKOURIAKOFF, TATIANA

STUART, GEORGE E. (1935–2014), AND DAVID STUART (1965–)

George E. Stuart took an early interest in archaeology, digging at age 17, and became a draftsman and cartographer for National Geographic on projects at **Dzibilchaltun** and **Cobá**. In his 40-year career at National Geographic he rose to become senior archaeologist, then vice president and chair of the Committee for Research and Exploration, the Society's funding arm. He was instrumental in the funding of projects worldwide, but especially in the Maya area, where he would literally fly to the site of a new discovery at the drop of a hat. Among other books, he coauthored *The Mysterious Maya*, as well as *Palenque: Eternal City of the Maya*, the latter with his son, David.

From his youth, when his parents George and Gene worked as archaeologists in Yucatan, David Stuart has been trilingual in English, Spanish, and Maya. This background led to fresh and insightful **decipherments** of Maya script as well as to a MacArthur Foundation grant at age 18. He is the youngest person to be so recognized. In addition to active field archaeology at sites such as **Copán**, **Palenque**, **Dos Pilas**, **La Corona**, and **San Bartolo**, his groundbreaking decipherment research continues at the University of Texas at Austin.

See also CALENDAR; COBÁ; DECIPHERMENT; LA LAGUNITA; MATHEMATICS; MEDICINE; NAJ TUNICH; PRIMARY STANDARD SEQUENCE; RITES OF PASSAGE; SYLLABARY; TERRITORIAL ENTITIES; WRITING SYSTEMS OF MESOAMERICA; YAXHÁ

Further Reading

Stuart, David. "Ten Phonetic Syllables." In *Research Reports on Ancient Maya Writing*, edited by George E. Stuart. Center for Maya Research, no. 14. Barnardsville, NC: Center for Maya Research, 1987.
———. *Maya Decipherment* (blog), 2014. http://decipherment.wordpress.com/.
Stuart, David, and George E. Stuart. *Palenque: Eternal City of the Maya*. New York: Thames and Hudson, 2008.

■ WALTER R. T. WITSCHEY

AVENIROVNA; PUSILHA; RIO AZUL; RITES OF PASSAGE; SCHELE, LINDA; SCULPTURE; SYLLABARY; TAMCHEN AND CHACTUN; TAYASAL; TEOTIHUACÁN (MAYA INTERACTIONS WITH); TERRITORIAL ENTITIES; TEXTILES AND CLOTHING; THEATER; TIKAL; TONINÁ; TULUM; UAXACTUN; UXMAL; WARFARE, WARRIORS, AND WEAPONS; WRITING SYSTEMS OF MESOAMERICA; XUNANTUNICH; YAXCHILAN; YUCATECAN MAYA LANGUAGES

Further Reading

Drew, David. *The Lost Chronicles of the Maya Kings*. Berkeley: University of California, 1999.
Martin, Simon, and Nikolai Grube. *Chronicle of the Maya Kings and Queens: Deciphering the Dynasties of the Ancient Maya*. 2nd ed. London: Thames & Hudson, 2008.

Sharer, Robert J., and Loa P. Traxler. *The Ancient Maya*. 6th ed. Stanford, CA: Stanford University Press, 2006.

Stuart, David. "Kings of Stone: A Consideration of Stelae in Ancient Maya Ritual and Representation." *RES: Anthropology and Aesthetics*, nos. 29/30: 148–71, 1996.

■ WALTER R. T. WITSCHEY

SUBSISTENCE

Since **Diego de Landa** first described the Maya *milpa* or *kol* of the **Northern Lowlands** and farming crops by slash-and-burn or swidden agriculture, this technique has been considered the primary Maya system for food raising. In recent years, however, detailed studies of the population of major Classic Maya sites have called into question whether swidden farming could have provided sufficient food for a large populace. In addition, archaeology and remote-sensing techniques of aerial photography and **LiDAR** have revealed extensive farming areas of irrigated raised fields in low areas and terraced fields on more upland slopes. Pollen and bone analyses have revealed the broad spectrum of foodstuffs the Maya were growing.

The swidden technique slowly evolved as the archaic peoples of the area began to domesticate corn and other cultivars. It is still in widespread use in much of the Maya area. Making *milpa* as an ancient farming system is considered both sustainable in its forest ecosystem and extensive in its rotating use of land. In northern Yucatan it follows a routine schedule timed to the wet and dry seasons. In April (dry season) a patch of jungle is cleared by cutting small **vegetation**. Trees of about forearm size are cut at eye level. Later those tall stumps will be harvested for firewood. Very large trees are not cut.

Within a month the cut vegetation will dry, and the field is set afire. The resulting ash contributes to **soil** fertility. By mid-June the field will be ready for sowing. The Maya farmer uses a dibble stick (walking-cane-like tool) to poke holes into the thin soil as he walks, dropping several corn kernels into the hole. *Chaa-chak* ceremonies are held in the fields to invoke the rain **deity** to deliver essential rain to germinate the seeds. The rainy season in this area typically begins in June and the seeds sprout. After about three weeks, the farmer moves through the field chopping out weeds that have also begun to grow. After a single weeding, the corn grows ahead of the weeds, and further weeding is not required. The corn is harvested at various stages of ripeness for different dishes, and many of the ears will be bent over when ripe, to shed rainwater and be stored on the stalk until needed. The typical *milpa* is intercropped with beans, which climb the corn stalks, squashes, and chilies.

The thin soils of northern Yucatan become depleted quickly, so the second-year productivity of a *milpa* may be only 60 percent of the first year. The third year the crop may be only a quarter of what the first year produced. The farmer must then abandon that field and clear a new field from the jungle. The old field lies fallow, typically for 20 years or more, during which time it regrows and may again be used for farming. The swidden system formed the basis for sound renewable resource management in the Maya area for millennia.

The Maya were more than *milpa* farmers, however, and relied on a number of subsistence techniques beyond the rotating plots. Among these were the household garden (*solar*), closely tended, near the house, fertilized by household and human waste, and producing a variety of edible plants, medicinal plants, ritual-use plants, and decorative flowering plants. The Maya cultivated a variety of fruit trees. Collection of wild plants in the nearby forest was common. The Maya hunted for birds and animals to add meat protein to their diet. Some, such as turkeys, could be tended near the house until consumed. Finally, especially in river and sea coast environments, fishing, shellfish, and turtle collecting provided additional protein-rich resources. There is evidence the Maya also traded foodstuffs. At **Chunchucmil**, for example, production of food on *milpas* was so poor that food was traded in. There was widespread **trade** of salt collected from coastal salt pans, especially on the north coast of Yucatan.

Around major cities, and especially in the Central and Southern Lowlands, the ancient Maya slowly evolved more intensive food production techniques. They learned to modify the landscape and to grow multiple crops per year.

In the past 30 years, evidence for widespread construction of agricultural terraces has emerged from aerial photographs and LiDAR studies and been verified on the ground by survey and excavation. LiDAR use at **Caracol** shows that 80 percent of the 200 km^2 mapped city landscape consists of slopes modified by **terracing**, to control soil erosion, retain water, and permit more intensive farming than swidden agriculture. These terraces still function for water retention and erosion control a thousand years after they were abandoned. Throughout the central spine of the lowlands, for example in the **Río Bec** region and Xpuhil, terraced fields of ancient origin are apparent across broad areas (see also **Map 3**).

The Maya also employed raised field farming, called *chinampas* in central Mexico. Along the Hondo and Candelaria Rivers, among others, evidence for raised field farming is clear in aerial photographs, where the ancient fields still look like a giant waffle iron grid. Ground-truthing of the aerial photo evidence completes the documentation. The Maya utilized the flood-plain areas to cut canals back from the river and build elevated plots for farming. The water level provided irrigation for year-round farming. The canals, cleared of muck from time to time, provided a rich habitat for fish. The muck from the canals, thrown up onto the raised fields, increased soil fertility and raised the field level above the water table. As a result, raised fields were highly productive areas for multiple crops per year.

Construction of canals by the Maya also provided for water collection for drinking and irrigation. They filled reservoirs to provide water during the dry season. At **Calakmul**, canals fill 13 reservoirs with a total water capacity of 200 million liters. The Maya of **Edzna** built a similarly extensive canal system.

The Maya also used a variety of even more special techniques, slowly developed by trial and error over time, to provide food resources. *Aguadas* are low, flat basins that fill with water during the rainy season. As the water evaporated, the Maya used the perimeter of the *aguada* as a well-watered area for planting. As the water receded, additional plantings were made closer to the center of the *aguada*.

In sum, and depending on the soil, terrain, water sources, and rainfall of their particular locale, the Maya used a wide variety of intensive and extensive strategies for food production. This included making *milpas* with multiple species intercropped; tending fruit tree orchards and household gardens; hunting animals and gathering plants in the forest; catching fish and shellfish; and creating labor-intensive infrastructure in the form of canals, raised fields, and terraces to amplify productivity.

See also AGUADAS; BAJOS; CARACOL; CAVES; CENTRAL LOWLANDS; CEREN; CERRO MAYA/ CERROS; CLASS STRUCTURE; CLASSIC MAYA COLLAPSE; CODICES (MAYA); DIET; DIVINE KINGS AND QUEENS; DROUGHT; EK BALAM; EL PILAR; FAUNA; GEOLOGY; GROUND SURVEY TECHNIQUES; HOLMUL; HOUSEHOLD PRODUCTION; KABAH AND NOHPAT; KAMINALJUYÚ; LABNA; LAKES; LANDA, BISHOP DIEGO DE; LiDAR; MARKETS AND MARKETPLACES; MAYAPÁN; NORTHERN LOWLANDS; PORTABLE OBJECTS; RÍO BEC; RITES AND RITUALS; SETTLEMENT PATTERNS (CENTRAL LOWLANDS); SOILS; TERRACING; TIKAL; TRIBUTE; VEGETATION; WOMEN, MEN, AND GENDER ROLES; YALAHAU REGION

Further Reading

Chase, Arlen F., Diane Z. Chase, John F. Weishampel, Jason B. Drake, Ramesh L. Shrestha, K. Clint Slatton, Jaime J. Awe, and William E. Carter. "Airborne LiDAR, Archaeology, and the Ancient Maya Landscape at Caracol, Belize." *Journal of Archaeological Science* 38, no. 2: 387–98, 2011.

Dunning, Nicholas P., and Timothy Beach. "Soil Erosion, Slope Management, and Ancient Terracing in the Maya Lowlands." *Latin American Antiquity*, no. 5: 51–69, 1994.

Dunning, Nicholas P., Timothy P. Beach, and Sheryl Luzzadder-Beach. "Kax and Kol: Collapse and Resilience in Lowland Maya Civilization." *Proceedings of the National Academy of Sciences USA* 109, no. 10: 3652–57, 2012.

Fedick, Scott L., ed. *The Managed Mosaic: Ancient Maya Agriculture and Resource Use*. Salt Lake City: University of Utah Press, 1996.

Harrison, Peter D., and B. L. Turner, eds. *Pre-Hispanic Maya Agriculture*. Albuquerque: University of New Mexico Press, 1978.

Scarborough, Vernon L., Nicholas P. Dunning, Kenneth B. Tankersley, Christopher Carr, Eric Weaver, Liwy Grazioso, Brian Lane, John G. Jones, Palma Buttles, Fred Valdez, and David L. Lentz. "Water and Sustainable Land Use at the Ancient Tropical City of Tikal, Guatemala." *Proceedings of the National Academy of Sciences of the United States of America* 109, no. 31: 12408–413, 2012.

Turner, B. L., and Peter D. Harrison. *Pulltrouser Swamp: Ancient Maya Habitat, Agriculture, and Settlement in Northern Belize*. Texas Pan American Series. Austin: University of Texas Press, 1983.

■ WALTER R. T. WITSCHEY

SYLLABARY

The ancient Maya created the only fully productive writing system in the Western Hemisphere. With it, Maya scribes, usually members of the royal household, could write anything they could speak out loud. The symbols used in the Maya system have long proven to be a challenge for researchers trying to decipher the writing, an effort that now spans more than 150 years. **Decipherment** studies have borne fruit, especially since the mid-1980s. One especially useful tool for epigraphers (those who study the ancient writing) is a table of the signs or hieroglyphs used. See figures 40–43.

For alphabetic writing systems, it is quite simple to provide an overview of graphic marks that represent the individual entries of either a particular alphabet (signs for consonants and vowels) or abjad (signs for consonants only). The number of symbols is usually small, for example, 22 (e.g., Semitic or Phoenician abjad), 26 (e.g., English alphabet or French alphabet without diacritics and ligatures), 30 (e.g., Urgaritic, a cuneiform alphabet that includes 27 basic letters and 3 additional signs), or 36 signs (e.g., original early fifth century AD Armenian alphabet). This number of graphic marks or signs can easily be written in one or several short horizontal or vertical lines, examples of which exist from the late second millennium BC to the present day.

For writing systems that use symbols to represent syllables and complete words (logosyllabic systems) this is more difficult, as the number of graphic marks or signs is much higher. First, there are logographic signs to represent words (i.e., verb roots, nouns, adjectives); second, there are syllabic signs, used for instance for phonetic complementation and/or word disambiguation, the spelling of grammatical affixes, or in specific combinations to substitute for logographic signs. In the case of Maya writing, syllabic signs represent a consonant-vowel (CV) combination; logographic signs are of the shape CVC and, more rarely, CVCVC. Present-day languages within the group of the Maya **lowland languages** provide a total of 21 consonants, which, combined with 5 vowels, minimally would lead to 105 CV syllabic signs. However, certain syllabic signs have not yet been identified in Classic Maya texts. For example, "p" with a glottal stop, followed by any vowel (**p'**V) has not been found, and thus the sound or phoneme /p'/ commonly is not included in a syllabic chart. (/p'/ is an innovation shared by Yucatecan and Tzeltalan languages, perhaps emerging during or after the Late Classic period.) Some syllabic signs are

Figure 40. Maya Syllabary A-H. Courtesy of Erik Boot.

only represented by one or a few graphic variants (e.g., **ko**, **t'u**, **ji**), while other syllables have many graphic variants, especially when they are used frequently (e.g., **'u** [also to be found written **u**, **ʔu**, **ʔu**]).

Researchers of the Maya writing system at different moments in the process of decipherment have devised specific charts to present the syllabic signs that Maya scribes invented. These charts are called syllabaries, syllabograms, or syllabic charts or grids. Early examples of syllabaries were published by John Justeson and Lyle Campbell, David **Stuart**, and Nikolai Grube. A later example is that by Michael Coe and Mark Van Stone. Notebooks or other materials that accompany present-day workshops on Maya writing nearly always contain a syllabary of some kind. The preference for the layout of

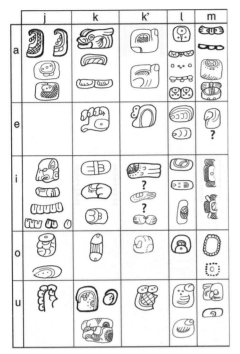

Figure 41. Maya Syllabary J–M. Courtesy of Erik Boot.

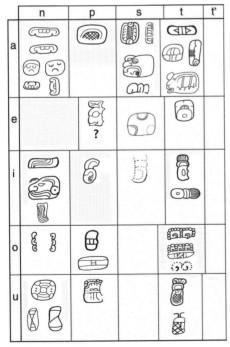

Figure 42. Maya Syllabary N–T'. Courtesy of Erik Boot.

a syllabary in Maya studies follows: consonants in alphabetical order are arranged horizontally from left to right ('/ʔ/7, b, ch, ch', h, j, k, k', l, m, n, p, [p'], s, t, t', tz, tz', w, x, y), vowels in alphabetical order are arranged vertically top to bottom (a, e, i, o, u).

Through a syllabary a researcher or student of Maya writing can obtain insight into a variety of script-related subjects. For instance, one can identify the number of signs per CV syllable structure. A syllabary thus can be used to study the frequency of a certain syllable (commonly, the higher the number of variants, the higher the frequency of the syllable), graphic variation, the rarity of some signs (only used at specific sites and not at others), and sometimes even the nature of graphic variation (i.e., is it a simple or abstract sign, or is it head-shaped/cephalomorphic, or body-shaped/somatomorphic?). However, as the boxes within the syllabaries are normally small, there is a limit to the number of signs that can be contained in any syllabary, and no single syllabary yet devised contains all signs ever invented by Maya scribes.

Most published syllabaries of Maya writing contain a sign inventory, which provides examples of syllabic signs that are either canonical in shape and/or represent rare graphic variants. These common and rare graphic variants can be taken from inscriptions from all over the Maya area, thus from a Maya site which at any one time produced a hieroglyphic text (ca. third century BC to early eighteenth century AD), either on nonportable stone, wooden, or stuccoed and/or painted monumental objects (e.g., **stelae**, lintels, altars, thrones, murals) and **portable objects** (e.g., **ceramic**, bone, wood, stone, shell, screenfold book).

In a 2014 contribution, eight preliminary syllabaries were published by Erik Boot. These syllabaries did not contain examples of the sign inventory of all Maya sites or time periods. Each syllabary contains hieroglyphic signs from one particular site, time period, and/or corpus of texts (**Chichen Itza**, **Caracol**, **Ek' Balam**, Fenton Group [a number of painted ceramic vessels from the Nebaj area], Early **Tikal**, Xcalumkin, Early **Yaxchilan**, Late Yaxchilan). None of these syllabaries contains redrawn idealized signs. The signs are entered as they were found in the original site-specific texts. Thus a particular sign can be reduced to graphic variants used by the Maya scribe that emerged due to sign overlap or graphic reduction. The Maya scribes not only dealt with space limitation, but also with aesthetics (through sign choice, style [outer appearance], mode of composition, and glyph block shape). These particular site-based syllabaries potentially can be useful in both paleographic and calligraphic studies of Maya writing and provide a window into the evolution of part of the script. Preferably a syllabary should be accompanied by a sign-by-sign discussion, some of which are available online in a blog by Erik Boot.

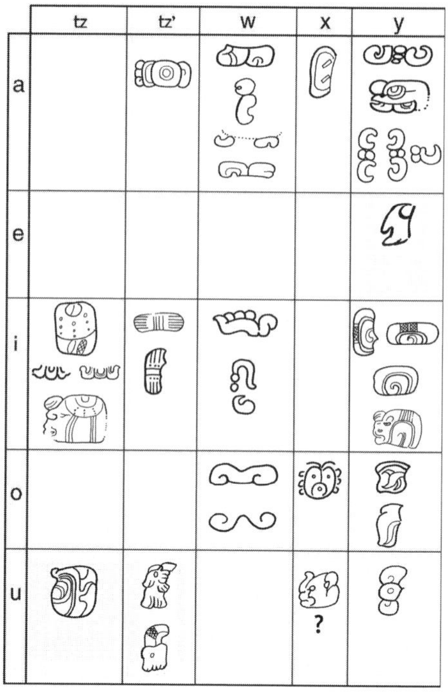

The preliminary syllabary that accompanies this entry is based on the corpus of Late Classic hieroglyphic texts, both portable and nonportable, from the site of **Piedras Negras**. Not all signs survived in good condition (dotted lines indicate erosion). This syllabary does not contain examples of **'e**, **bo**, **hu**, **je**, **ne**, **su**, **t'u**, **tza**, and **xi** (as found in other texts, and in which **su** and **t'u** are rare), as the surviving corpus from

Figure 43. Maya Syllabary TZ–Y. Courtesy of Erik Boot.

Piedras Negras either does not contain spellings or compounds (i.e., words, phrases) that use these syllabic signs, or the identification is anything but secure (i.e., due to erosion). A query mark next to a sign or signs in the syllabary expresses a degree of doubt about the correctness of the proposed decipherment.

See also BALL GAME/BALL COURT; DECIPHERMENT; HIGHLAND MAYA LANGUAGES; KNOROSOV, YURI VALENTINOVICH; LANGUAGE AND WRITING OVERVIEW; OLMEC-MAYA INTERACTIONS; PIEDRAS NEGRAS; STELA; STUART, GEORGE E., AND DAVID STUART; WRITING SYSTEMS OF MESOAMERICA; YUCATECAN MAYA LANGUAGES

Further Reading

Boot, Erik. *Maya Glyph Blog*, 2009. http://maya-glyph-blog.blogspot.com/.

Boot, Erik. "On (Some of) the Principles and Structures of Graphic Sign Substitution in Classic Maya Writing." In *Visualizing Knowledge and Creating Meaning in Ancient Writing Systems*, edited by Shai Gordin. Berliner Beiträge zum Vorderen Orient, vol. 23. Gladbeck, Germany: PeWe-Verlag, 2014.

Coe, Michael D., and Mark Van Stone. *Reading the Maya Glyphs*. London: Thames & Hudson, 2001.

Grube, Nikolai, ed. *Die Entwicklung der Mayaschrift: Grundlagen zur Erforschung des Wandels der Mayaschrift von der Protoklassik bis zur spanischen Eroberung.* Vol. 3, *Acta Mesoamericana.* Markt Schwaben, Germany: Verlag Anton Saurwein, 1990.

Justeson, John S., and Lyle Campbell. *Phoneticism in Mayan Hieroglyphic Writing.* Institute for Mesoamerican Studies, Publication 9. Albany: Institute for Mesoamerican Studies, State University of New York at Albany, 1984.

Stuart, David. "Ten Phonetic Syllables." In *Research Reports on Ancient Maya Writing*, edited by George E. Stuart. Center for Maya Research, no. 14. Barnardsville, NC: Center for Maya Research, 1987.

■ ERIK BOOT

TAKALIK ABAJ

Takalik Abaj (14.6° N, 91.7° W) is a large archaeological site in the Pacific Piedmont of **Guatemala** (see also **Map 3**). Located in the Department of Retalhuleu, the site has a lengthy history of occupation, stretching from at least Middle Preclassic times to the Postclassic era. A portion of the site is now a Guatemalan National Park, with restored constructions and a museum open to visitors.

Takalik Abaj was first identified as an archaeological site by German investigators in the nineteenth century. The site continued to attract attention in the twentieth century, in publications by J. Eric S. **Thompson**, Susan Miles, and Edwin Shook. The first major investigations were conducted by a John Graham and Robert Heizer of the University of California–Berkeley. Since 1985 the Guatemalan government has financed excavations and restoration at the site and established a national park encompassing the central zone.

The archaeological site covers at least 8 km², with major constructions organized on a series of five large terraces. The terraces served to create level spaces on a slope that climbs from 300 m to 800 m elevation in a linear distance of roughly 4 km. The terraces contain over 10 m of fill in many locations, making each a significant construction in its own right.

Takalik Abaj is perhaps best known for its extraordinary **sculptures**, which includes over 200 pieces and includes examples of **Olmec** and early Maya styles. In addition, there are many pieces not easily categorized, including the potbellied sculptures that are widely distributed in the highlands and **Pacific coast** during the Late Preclassic.

The Olmec-style sculptures at Takalik Abaj indicate a major occupation at the site during the early portion of the Middle Preclassic period, contemporary with the apogee of La Blanca, a large Olmec-related site located on the coastal plain 25 km to the southwest. The overall extent of occupation at Takalik Abaj during this time remains uncertain, as pottery contemporary with the Olmec-related sculpture has been found only in limited locations.

During the Late Preclassic, Takalik Abaj reached its maximum size and was one of a number of early city-states in southern Guatemala linked by **trade** and cultural exchanges. The cultural elements shared among these cities include **stelae** with ruler portraits, the use of Long Count dates, glyphic inscriptions, potbellied sculptures, mushroom stones, toad altars, representations of bound captives, and others (see also **Art**;

Calendar; **Decipherment**; **Iconography**). Although often described as representing a Late Preclassic "Southern Maya" cultural complex, the interaction zone formed by the cities may in fact have been multiethnic.

Economic and political turmoil characterized the Preclassic to Classic transition in the southern zone, which is often characterized as the "Late Preclassic collapse." Many regions of the Pacific coastal plain were abandoned, possibly due to **drought**. **Kaminaljuyu**, the largest of the Late Preclassic southern city-states, may have seen a significant drop in population and the incursion of new groups from the western Guatemalan **highlands**. Piedmont sites such as Takalik Abaj and **Izapa** seemed to have fared better, although they shrank in size and wealth in the Early Classic. The cultural florescence of the Late Preclassic came to a decided halt, and ruler stelae with their texts were no longer erected; the Long Count ceased to be used in the region.

Monumental construction at Takalik Abaj continued in the Early Classic, and a new florescence took place in the Late Classic, when many of the terraces were modified and/or resurfaced. In the Late Classic many sculptures and sculpture fragments of earlier periods were repositioned in the major plazas. A small number of **Cotzumalhuapan** style monuments and possibly some crudely worked pieces were dedicated at this time.

The Postclassic period at Takalik Abaj remains poorly known, but the major occupation concentrated at the northern portion of the site. Excavations in that portion of the site have recovered caches of Tohil Plumbate vessels. The ethnic identity of the latter occupants is uncertain. The site lies near the modern boundary between speakers of Kiche and speakers of Mam (see also **Map 4**). The Postclassic inhabitants may have been mostly speakers of Kiche, although in recent times the Mayan people living around the site were speakers of Mam.

Further Reading

Love, Michael. "City States and City-State Culture in the Southern Maya Region." In *The Southern Maya in the Late Preclassic: The Rise and Fall of an Early Mesoamerican Civilization*, edited by Michael Love and Jonathan Kaplan, 47–76. Boulder: University Press of Colorado, 2011.

Love, Michael, and Julia Guernsey. "La Blanca and the Soconusco Formative." In *Early Mesoamerican Social Transformations: Archaic and Formative Lifeways in the Soconusco Region*, edited by Richard G. Lesure, 170–89. Berkeley: University of California Press, 2011.

Miles, Suzanne W. "Sculpture of the Guatemala-Chiapas Highlands and Pacific Slopes, and Associated Hieroglyphs." In *Handbook of Middle American Indians*. Vol. 2, *Archaeology of Southern Mesoamerica*, pt. 1, edited by Gordon R. Willey, 237–75. Austin: University of Texas Press, 1965.

Popenoe de Hatch, Marion. "New Perspectives on Kaminaljuyú, Guatemala: Regional Interaction during the Preclassic and Classic Periods." In *Incidents of Archaeology in Central America and Yucatán: Studies in Honor of Edwin M. Shook*, edited by Michael Love, Marion Popenoe de Hatch, and Héctor L. Escobedo, 277–96. Lanham, MD: University Press of America, 2002.

Popenoe de Hatch, Marion, Christa Schieber de Lavarreda, and Miguel Orrego. "Late Preclassic Developments at Takalik Abaj." In *The Southern Maya in the Late Preclassic: The Rise and Fall of an Early Mesoamerican Civilization*, edited by Michael Love and Jonathan Kaplan, 203–36. Boulder: University Press of Colorado, 2011.

Schieber de Lavarreda, Christa, and Miguel Orrego Corzo. "Preclassic Olmec and Maya Monuments and Architecture at Takalik Abaj." In *The Place of Stone Monuments in Mesoamerica's Preclassic Transition: Context, Use and Meaning*, edited by Julia Guernsey, John E. Clark, and Bárbara Arroyo, 177–205. Washington, DC: Dumbarton Oaks Research Library and Collection, 2010.

Shook, Edwin M. "Archaeological Survey of the Pacific Coast of Guatemala." In *Handbook of Middle American Indians*. Vol. 2, *Archaeology of Southern Mesoamerica*, pt. 1, edited by Gordon R. Willey, 180–94. Austin: University of Texas Press, 1965.

Thompson, J. Eric S. "Some Sculptures from Southeastern Quetzaltenango, Guatemala." *Notes on Middle American Archaeology and Ethnography* 17: 100–102, 1943.

■ MICHAEL LOVE

TAMCHEN AND CHACTUN

Ivan Šprajc, associate professor at the Research Center of the Slovenian Academy of Sciences and Arts, has been conducting reconnaissance and research in southern Campeche, **Mexico**, in the vicinity and to the north of **Calakmul** since 1998. During that period he has reported a number of sites. Most recently, in August 2014, Šprajc reported the discovery of Tamchen (18.7° N, 89.5° W) and rediscovery of **La Lagunita** after reporting Chactun the previous year. The sites are approximately 20 km north of **Becan**, and 80 km north–northeast of Calakmul. The Šprajc team mapped 10–12 ha at Tamchen, but reported the site likely has a larger extent. They discovered large monuments and more inscriptions than is typical for **Río Bec** region sites, which document in part that indicated settlement extended from the Late Formative (300 BC–AD 250) through a peak in the Late Classic to abandonment in the Terminal Classic AD 1000. Tamchen has a Triadic architectural group, typical of the Formative, as well as a **pyramid**, with well-preserved temple atop, and a **stela**-altar combination at the base. (See figure 44.)

Further Reading

Šprajc, Ivan. *Archaeological Reconnaissance in Southeastern Campeche, Mexico*. ZRC SAZU–Research Centre for the Slovenian Academy of Sciences and Arts, 2014. http://gis.zrc-sazu.si/campeche/.

"Two Ancient Maya Cities Discovered in the Jungle of Southeastern Mexico." *MISLI*, August 13, 2014. http://ms.sta.si/2014/08/two-ancient-maya-cities-discovered-in-the-jungle-of-southeastern-mexico/.

■ WALTER R. T. WITSCHEY

Figure 44. Entrance to a *chultun*, a man-made underground storage reservoir, with carefully dressed stones forming the entrance. From Tamchen, Campeche, Mexico. Courtesy of Ivan Šprajc, ZRC SAZU.

TAYASAL

The archaeological site of Tayasal (16.9° N, 89.9° W) rests on a peninsula less than 300 m north of Flores, Petén, **Guatemala**. Tayasal is partially covered by the modern town of San Miguel, which was established as a mission settlement on May 12, 1702. The name "Tayasal," a variant of *TajItza*, means "place of the Itza," recorded by Bernal Diaz del Castillo, who visited the area in AD 1525. This name properly refers to the capital and the entire territory controlled by the group of the Itza, while the Itza capital known as *Nojpetén* was actually located on the modern Flores Island.

Previous research at Tayasal was conducted by the Carnegie Institution of Washington in the 1920s and the University of Pennsylvania in the 1970s. Although various researchers attempted to define the Postclassic occupation at Tayasal, they encountered Early Classic remains dating to AD 200–600. Recent investigations by the Proyecto Arqueológico Tayasal (PAT) have revealed a large Late Postclassic population at Tayasal, including additional residences and ceremonial buildings and some Postclassic **deity** effigy censers (see also **Ceramics**).

The site was initially occupied in the Middle Preclassic, with periodic occupations through the present, having a hiatus in the Early Classic period. Structures in the center of the site stand on a massive Preclassic period raised platform. During the transition from the Late Preclassic to the Early Classic, a major cultural shift occurred in the main group at Tayasal. This cultural shift included the construction of an E-Group and the erection of **stelae** (see also **Astronomical Observatories**). Four carved stelae have been reported in the main group. The construction of temples during the Late Classic period included a large raised acropolis and various plaza groups accompanied with crypt **burials**. The so-called **Classic Maya collapse** around AD 900 in the lowland Maya region did not occur at Tayasal; instead, Tayasal appeared to have served as a refuge center during the Postclassic period. The largest Postclassic ceremonial group was built upon the Late Preclassic E-Group.

After the Spaniards conquered the Itza capital in 1697, they established San Miguel and a second mission, San Bernabé, within the Tayasal site boundaries. In 2010 PAT uncovered the San Bernabé mission on the northwestern tip of the peninsula, recovering 32 burials beneath the church floor. All of the interments were extended supine, with their heads to the west and feet to the east. A mixture of Maya and Spanish objects as offerings in the burials and the mixed construction style of mission residences suggest that San Bernabé was part Maya and part Spanish.

See also CHICHEN ITZA

Further Reading

Chase, Arlen F. "A Contextual Consideration of the Tayasal-Paxcaman Zone, El Petén, Guatemala." PhD diss., University of Pennsylvania, 1983.

Jones, Grant D. *The Conquest of the Last Maya Kingdom.* Stanford, CA: Stanford University Press, 1998.

Pugh, Timothy W., José Rómulo Sánchez, and Yuko Shiratori. "Contact and Missionization at Tayasal, Petén, Guatemala." *Journal of Field Archaeology* 37, no. 1: 3–19, 2012.

■ YUKO SHIRATORI

TEOTIHUACÁN (MAYA INTERACTIONS WITH)

Teotihuacán, located in the northeast suburbs of modern Mexico City, was the largest and most powerful city of Classic **Mesoamerica**. For decades scholars have debated the impact of Teotihuacán on its Early Classic Maya neighbors. Researchers once argued that the first Maya states were inspired by Teotihuacán. Others contend that sites such as **Tikal** and **Kaminaljuyú** contained Colonial enclaves and that a Teotihuacán empire extended more than 1,000 km into the Maya region. In great contrast, many scholars have suggested that Teotihuacán "influence" in the Maya area is better understood as elite emulation of a foreign culture or the adoption of a pan-Mesoamerican religious cult. Material evidence used to support this wide range of perspectives on Maya-Teotihuacán interaction include hieroglyphic texts, foreign style pottery, monuments containing Teotihuacán **iconography**, central Mexican *talud-tablero* architecture, green **obsidian** from north of Teotihuacán, and even isotope data derived from human teeth (see also **Ceramics**; **Stela**; **Writing Systems of Mesoamerica**).

Teotihuacán grew during the Late Formative period. Interaction with the Maya at the beginning of the current era is demonstrated by the presence of imported ceramics in the fill of the **Pyramid** of the Sun, one of the largest structures ever built in ancient America. Unlike **El Mirador** and many other contemporary Maya cities, Teotihuacán did not collapse at about AD 150. Instead, it entered a period of tremendous growth and reached its maximum population of ca. 125,000 by about AD 250. During the third century AD, the first pulse of interaction with Teotihuacán was seen in the Maya area. Evidence includes a **burial** at **Altun Ha** containing a Teotihuacán-style offering, the presence of green obsidian at sites in Pacific Guatemala, and buildings in the *talud-tablero* style at Tikal. These Tikal structures are contemporary with or even predate the earliest examples at Teotihuacán itself. Contextual data imply that early interaction was at the level of ruler-to-ruler and consisted of gift-giving or other sorts of elite exchange (see also **Alliances**).

The late fouth and early fifth centuries—especially after AD 378—saw a dramatic change in interaction. At Tikal, **Uaxactun**, and **Yaxhá**, carved stelae in the Maya style depict individuals dressed as Teotihuacán warriors (see also **Warfare, Warriors, and Weapons**). The two most prominent figures have Mayan names: Siyaj K'ahk' ("Fire is Born"), an enigmatic warrior and kingmaker, and Yax Nuun Ahyiin I, his protégé and a young king of Tikal (see also **Divine Kings and Queens**; **Dynastic Sequences**). A third individual, nicknamed "Spear Thrower Owl," has a name glyph borrowed from Teotihuacán. Nonetheless, this father of the young Tikal king is said to be the ruler of a yet unidentified place with a Mayan name.

Royal tombs of this period at Tikal contain a small number of ceramic vessels from Teotihuacán and many more copies, as do a rich series of tombs at Kaminaljuyú. The dynastic founder of **Copán**, K'inich Yaax K'uk' Mo', and his wife were laid to rest in rich tombs containing Teotihuacán-style pottery. Most dramatic of all, locally made but obviously Teotihuacán-inspired incense burners have been found in Escuintla, Guatemala. These are tied to Teotihuacán state-sponsored **religion**. Also appearing at this time are more *talud-tablero* structures (especially at Tikal, Kaminaljuyú, and Copán) and green obsidian from the Pachuca, Hidalgo, volcanic source 85 km northeast of Teotihuacán. The last is found in small quantities in the royal precincts of most Early Classic Maya centers.

In contrast, isotope analyses of teeth—particularly of the burials of Yax Nuun Ahyiin, K'inich Yaax K'uk' Mo', and a large sample from Kaminaljuyú—have not revealed a single person of Teotihuacán origin in the Maya region. The two famous kings of Tikal and Copán came from the **southern Maya lowlands**. Foreigners have been identified at Southern Lowland sites, but they likely came from the **northern Maya lowlands**, the **highlands**, or the **Pacific coast**. A single locally born individual from Kaminaljuyú might have spent part of his childhood at Teotihuacán, but the data are insufficient to prove this.

Ample evidence also exists for interaction with the Maya at Teotihuacán itself, particularly during the Xolalpan phase. The Merchants' Barrio at that city was settled by Maya or their close neighbors from the Gulf Coast. Just as Teotihuacán-inspired pottery is found in the Maya region, so too is Maya pottery found at Teotihuacán. Isotope analyses suggest that several sacrificed individuals buried in the heart of the Moon Pyramid came from the Maya area. Finally, mural paintings containing Mayan hieroglyphs are known at Teotihuacán (see also **Wall Painting**).

After just a few generations, this second wave of interaction passed. A third pulse, seen for the first time in the Northern Lowlands of Yucatan, dates to the late sixth and early seventh centuries. At that time—when Teotihuacán was no longer a major international power—hybrid Maya *talud-tablero* architecture was built at sites including **Oxkintok** and **Dzibilchaltun**, and again at Tikal. Small numbers of Teotihuacán-inspired vessels have been found at a few sites, and an eclectic mural at Xelha suggests knowledge of central Mexico. Nonetheless, interaction at this time was indirect and indicative more of participation in the greater Mesoamerican world than of political intervention or colonization by Teotihuacán.

The second wave of interaction has generated the most controversy. "Internalists" stress local events and political relations within the Maya area. Teotihuacán "influence" is seen most clearly during times of dynastic upheaval, such as at Tikal and Copán. The formation or establishment of a new dynasty might have required appeal to a powerful, exotic, and distant civilization. The need for legitimization, therefore, could account for elite emulation. "Externalists," in contrast, argue for direct Teotihuacán intervention in the form of colonialism or conquest. The data individual scholars study often drive their perspective on interaction. Many epigraphers are externalists and argue for a Teotihuacán *entrada*. In contrast, bioarchaeologists are skeptical of invasion or colonization because they have not identified a single Teotihuacano in the Maya region. Finally, the debate is made more complex by modern politics—many influential externalists are from or work near Mexico City, while many internalists are from the Maya region.

See also ARCHITECTURE OVERVIEW; ASTRONOMY; BECAN; CAVES; CERAMICS; CHAC II; COPÁN; COTZUMALHUAPA; ECCENTRIC LITHICS; EL MIRADOR; EL PERÚ-WAKA'; GUATEMALA; ICONOGRAPHY; KAMINALJUYÚ; MESOAMERICA; MEXICO; MIDDLE CLASSIC HIATUS; NIXTUN-CH'ICH'; OBSIDIAN; OXKINTOK; PIEDRAS NEGRAS; PYRAMID; RIO AZUL; SAN BARTOLO; SOUTHERN PERIPHERY; TIKAL; UAXACTUN; WARFARE, WARRIORS, AND WEAPONS; WRITING SYSTEMS OF MESOAMERICA

Further Reading

Braswell, Geoffrey E., ed. *The Maya and Teotihuacan: Reinterpreting Early Classic Interaction*. The Linda Schele Series in Maya and Pre-Columbian Studies. Austin: University of Texas Press, 2003.

Stuart, David. "'The Arrival of Strangers': Teotihuacan and Tollan in Classic Maya History." In *Mesoamerica's Classic Heritage: From Teotihuacan to the Aztecs*, edited by David Carrasco, Lindsay Jones, and Scott Sessions, 465–513. Boulder: University Press of Colorado, 2000.

Wright, Lori E. "In Search of Yax Nuun Ayiin I: Revisiting the Tikal Project's Burial 10." *Ancient Mesoamerica* 16, no. 1: 89–100, 2005.

■ GEOFFREY E. BRASWELL

TERRACING

As archaeological studies have expanded from site centers and monumental **architecture** to settlement studies of the total population, so too has research begun to focus on agricultural intensification techniques to support expanding Classic period populations. Research in several areas has revealed that terracing as a means of increasing agricultural productivity has an import that rivals wetland management techniques, such as raised field agriculture (see also **Subsistence**; **Water Management**). Terracing was also used extensively by the Maya to modify city centers.

Agricultural terracing has been well documented in both the **Río Bec** region (estimated to cover 10,000 km²) and the Vaca Plateau-**Caracol** region (over 400 km²). Terraces are known in the Petexbatún region, the Three Rivers area of **Belize**, the Puuc, the Maya Mountains, the Petén fracture zone east of Lake Petén Itzá, and along the Río Pasión, among others. Further exploration will undoubtedly reveal more areas of landscape modification by the ancient Maya.

Nick Dunning and Tim Beach classify terraces in five categories, all using rubble rock walls of various designs for **soil** retention. A check dam crosses a water channel, slowing runoff and providing water for side-channel irrigation. Dry-slope contour terraces create wide concave slopes for planting. Box terraces are small three-sided terraces, often near dwellings, to support household gardens. Foot-slope terraces are long terraces, constructed at the base of steep slopes to accumulate naturally eroding soils from the slope. *Chich* (gravel) berms 50–70 cm high and 2 m wide, without a bedrock foundation, were laid in parallel rows to stop downslope erosion.

The time during which terracing was used by the Maya for agricultural intensification is not yet well known. Clearly modifications to the terrain, such as for water reservoirs as at **Tikal** and **El Mirador**, date to the Late Formative. Most known terracing begins on a small scale in the Early Classic, and then shows vigorous expansion in the Late Classic. Further research is needed to determine dates of the earliest terraces, as well as the extent to which terracing formed a significant part of city planning supervised by the elites.

See also ARCHITECTURE OVERVIEW; CARACOL; CHICHEN ITZA; EL CHAYAL; HOUSEHOLD PRODUCTION; ITZIMTE; KABAH AND NOHPAT; LAMANAI; NOH KAH; PALENQUE; RÍO BEC; SOILS; SUBSISTENCE; TAKALIK ABAJ; VEGETATION; YAXCHILAN; YAXHOM; ZACUALPA.

Further Reading

Beach, Timothy, Sheryl Luzzadder-Beach, Nicholas P. Dunning, Jon Hageman, and Jon C. Lohse. "Upland Agriculture in the Maya Lowlands: Ancient Maya Soil Conservation in Northwestern Belize." *Geographical Review* 92, no. 3: 372–97, 2002.

Dunning, Nicholas P., and Timothy Beach. "Soil Erosion, Slope Management, and Ancient Terracing in the Maya Lowlands." *Latin American Antiquity*, no. 5: 51–69, 1994.

Fischbeck, Shelly L. "Agricultural Terrace Productivity in the Maya Lowlands of Belize." BS thesis, University of Wisconsin, 2001.

Turner, B. L. *Once Beneath the Forest: Prehistoric Terracing in the Rio Bec Region of the Maya Lowlands.* Boulder, CO: Westview Press, 1983.

Turner, B. L., II, and Jeremy A. Sabloff. "Classic Period Collapse of the Central Maya Lowlands: Insights about Human-Environment Relationships for Sustainability." *Proceedings of the National Academy of Sciences of the United States of America* 109, no. 35: 13908–914, 2012.

■ WALTER R. T. WITSCHEY

TERRITORIAL ENTITIES

The territory controlled by a site is documented in three ways: settlement size, inscriptions that refer to larger dominant sites, and *sacbes* that link sites together (see also **Decipherment**; **Causeway/Sacbe**). Settlement hierarchy is evidence for the existence of pre-Columbian Maya states; this means that political leaders at sites with many big buildings had the potential to dominate nearby settlements with fewer, smaller structures. Instead of population parameters to rank settlements, the volume of architecture at a site is used as an approximation of community size. (See figure 45.) Although architecture at any

Figure 45. The Adivino at Uxmal and its companion buildings at the ceremonial center of the site. By sheer volume of construction and the causeway connecting it to Nohpat and Kabah, Uxmal is at the top of the settlement hierarchy in its region. Courtesy of Walter Witschey.

place accumulates through time, the energy fossilized in construction constitutes a permanent form of wealth; in other words, rich settlements controlled less wealthy neighbors.

Causeways linking settlements are another sign of territorial organization. The Maya used causeways to join together the key settlements in a political entity. If the linked settlements form a settlement hierarchy, it is clear that the populations were interacting, and larger settlements had the means to control smaller ones.

The 5,000 km² area surrounding **Izamal** contains major settlements at Uci, Dzilam, Ake, and Kantunil, together with 213 other sites. Two causeway complexes, one beginning at Uci and the other radiating from Izamal, delineate settlement hierarchies. (See figure 46.) Dzilam, another large settlement contains stelae that mark a seat of centralized political power. However, if settlement hierarchy were the only consideration, the massive mounds at Izamal dwarf the buildings at all of the other sites in the region, so at one time the entire area may have been ruled from Izamal.

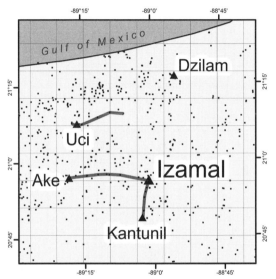

Figure 46. Map of the area surrounding Izamal. Shown are the two causeway complexes and Dzilam, a third seat of a territorial entity. Each grid square is 10 by 10 km. Courtesy of Edward Kurjack.

The causeway from **Cobá** to **Yaxuná** joins sites 100 km apart, and the star-shaped pattern of Maya roads emanating from the center of Cobá spreads over another 120 km². This network suggests a huge pre-Columbian territorial entity. Alfonso Villa Rojas first explored the Cobá-Yaxuná *sacbe* in 1933, but with the exception of David Freidel's work at Yaxuná, the settlements along the causeway have yet to be properly studied.

Further evidence of territorial extent is documented at **Uxmal**, where a *sacbe* with entrance archways extends southward to Nohpat and **Kabah**. The *sacbes* constructed at El Mirador total over 100 km, and coupled with their great width, up to 40 m, exude royal power and conspicuous consumption to linked sites and neighbors.

The presence of inscriptions with Emblem Glyphs and the names of rulers are also evidence of a government seat. Inscriptions commissioned by kings at smaller sites may refer to their larger neighbors and the elite rulers who rank above them. Although such links are far more commonly found in the Central and Southern Lowlands, such as at **Yaxchilan, Calakmul**, **Dos Pilas, Caracol**, and **Naranjo**, Alexander Voss has identified Emblem Glyphs for Acanceh, **Dzibilchaltun**, **Tiho**, and **Ek Balam**; all of these major settlements are just outside the proposed area of Izamal's suzerainty. At Yo'okop, elite rulers documented their ties to the Snake Kingdom, perhaps by a marriage **alliance** (see also **Cochuah Region**). Such inscriptions at medium-sized settlements in the south often contain the name and power relationship of the ruler at the nearest large neighboring site.

Current research continues to uncover new evidence of political ties between polities and territorial entities across moderately long distances.

See also CARACOL; CIVAL; DZIBILCHALTUN; EL MIRADOR; IZAMAL; JAINA; NAKBÉ; SAN BARTOLO; STELA; TAYASAL; WARFARE, WARRIORS, AND WEAPONS

Further Reading

Ashmore, Wendy, ed. *Lowland Maya Settlement Patterns.* School of American Research Advanced Seminar Series. Albuquerque: University of New Mexico Press, 1981.

Folan, William J., Ellen R. Kintz, and Laraine A. Fletcher. *Coba: A Classic Maya Metropolis.* Edited by Stuart Struever. Studies in Archaeology. New York: Academic Press, 1983.

Garza Tarazona de González, Silvia, and Edward B. Kurjack Bacso. *Atlas arqueológico del estado de Yucatán.* México, D.F.: Instituto Nacional de Antropología e Historia, 1980.

Graña-Behrens, Daniel. "Emblem Glyphs and Political Organization in Northwestern Yucatan in the Classic Period (A.D. 300–1000)." *Ancient Mesoamerica* 17, no. 1: 105–23, 2006.

Manzanilla, Linda, ed. *Coba, Quintana Roo: Análisis de dos unidades habitacionales mayas.* México, D.F.: Instituto de Investigaciones Antropológicas, Universidad Nacional Autónoma de México, 1987.

Stuart, David. *The Inscribed Markers of the Coba-Yaxuna Causeway and the Glyph for Sakbih.* Mesoweb, 2006. http://www.mesoweb.com/stuart/notes/sacbe.pdf.

Voss, Alexander W., and H. Juergen Kremer. *K'ak'-u-pakal, Hun-pik-tok' and the Kokom: The Political Organization of Chichén Itzá.* Edited by Pierre Robert Colas. (The Sacred and the Profane: Architecture and Identity in the Maya Lowlands: 3rd European Maya Conference, University of Hamburg, November 1998). Acta Mesoamericana, vol. 10. Markt Schwaben, Germany: A. Saurwein, 2000.

■ EDWARD B. KURJACK

TEXTILES AND CLOTHING

Weaving and the making of cloth have deep roots in the Maya area; however, ancient textiles rarely survive because the region is so humid. Some special environments—such as that of the Sacred Cenote at **Chichen Itza**—do, nevertheless, allow for preservation. Several thousand cloth fragments were recovered from the cenote in a variety of weaves (plain, supplementary weft brocading, warp float, gauze, and twill), with plain being the most common. The Sacred Cenote was one of the principal pilgrimage sites in the Maya area, so the date when the textiles were deposited, likely as part of other offerings, remains uncertain.

Weaving technology has changed little since Classic times (ca. AD 250–900). The process begins with gathering and processing the fibers. Cotton and maguey were used in pre-Hispanic times. After being spun into thread, they were optionally dyed, using various plants and mineral substances (see figure 47). Before weaving could begin, the warp threads were measured on a warping frame to determine the length and width of the textile. They were wound in a figure-eight pattern, which served to establish their sequential position when transferred to the loom and created the alternating openings through which the weft threads would pass. They were then soaked in corn gruel to strengthen them for weaving (see figure 48).

The backstrap loom used by pre-Hispanic and contemporary Maya women consists of a number of sticks and a strap, only becoming a true loom once the warp threads have

Figure 47. Contemporary Maya woman using a spindle to spin fibers into thread. Photograph by Nicholas Manting-Brewer. Courtesy of Gabrielle Vail.

been transferred. One end is attached to a tree or post and the other to the strap worn by the weaver to control the tension when weaving (figure 48, lower image).

Decorative techniques included brocading, embroidery, and painting. Painting has been documented in the Classic period, whereas brocading and embroidery were likely Late Postclassic innovations (ca. AD 1250–1500). Archaeologists learn a great deal about the production of cloth and the types of clothing worn by studying specialized weaving tools and depictions of elite personages and deities from stone monuments and painted murals, **ceramic** vessels, and screenfold books (see also **Codices [Maya]**; **Stela**; **Wall Painting**). These depictions indicate that weaving was associated exclusively with women. To underscore this connection, creator goddesses often wear a figure-eight headdress (symbolizing warped threads) and spindles in their hair.

Textiles are a prominent theme in Classic period **iconography**, appearing as clothing worn by the elite, as **tribute** payments, as curtains and room dividers in **palaces**; and as gifts cementing elite relationships (see also **Alliances**). Cloth also played a significant role in rituals, since it was used to wrap sacred objects and **deity** effigies to contain their power when not in use (see also **Rites and Rituals**). In addition, tombs sometimes contain cloth, likely used to wrap the body prior to **burial**.

Classic period **art** provides important information about elite clothing. Of particular interest to archaeologists studying textiles are a series of lintels from the site of **Yaxchilan** carved in exquisite detail, panels from **Palenque** showing dynastic accession rituals, and figurines from the burial site of **Jaina** that portray elite individuals engaged in various activities, including spinning and weaving. They show that headdresses, typically made of cloth and/or feathers, appear in various forms and were used to indicate one's role and status and that ceremonial garments differed from those in everyday use. In certain regions, women wore an ankle-length garment or *huipil* when performing ceremonial functions; in others, a netted skirt and top linked the wearer with the moon goddess and the maize cycle. Elite men and women are both depicted wearing capes. Men of all classes wore loincloths, and women wore skirts or wraparound (sarong-like) garments. The production of fine cotton cloth was the prerogative of Maya elites during the pre-Hispanic period, and its use may have been reserved for them as well.

Figure 48.   Madrid codex. Upper image: Use of a warping board, or chuch, to warp the threads in a figure-eight pattern prior to transferring them to the loom (Madrid 102c). Lower image: Weaving on a backstrap loom tied to a wooden post on Madrid 102d. After Charles E. Brasseur de Bourbourg, *Manuscrit Troano: Etudes sur le système graphique et la langue des Mayas* (Paris: Imprimerie Impériale, 1869–1870). Courtesy of Gabrielle Vail.

At the time of the Spanish conquest, cloth was being produced for **trade** and tribute, as well as household consumption. Its manufacture was one of the principal activities of Maya women, a pattern that appears to have roots far back in time. The focus on textiles and elaborate clothing in Classic period art highlights both women's status and their economic power.

See also ALTUN HA; ARCHITECTURE OVERVIEW; ART; BURIALS; COUNCIL HOUSE; CRAFT SPECIALIZATION; TIKAL; TRADE ROUTES; WOMEN, MEN, AND GENDER ROLES; WRITING SYSTEMS OF MESOAMERICA

Further Reading

Anawalt, Patricia R. "Textile Research from the Mesoamerican Perspective." In *Beyond Cloth and Cordage: Archaeological Textile Research in the Americas*, edited by Penelope B. Drooker and Laurie D. Webster, 205–28. Salt Lake City: University of Utah Press, 2000.

Looper, Matthew George, and Thomas G. Tolles. *Gifts of the Moon: Huipil Designs of the Ancient Maya*. San Diego Museum Papers, no. 38. San Diego, CA: San Diego Museum of Man, 2000.

Reents-Budet, Dorie. "Power Material in Ancient Mesoamerica: The Role of Cloth among the Classic Maya." In *Sacred Bundles: Ritual Acts of Wrapping and Binding in Mesoamerica*, edited by Julia Guernsey and F. Kent Reilly III, 105–26. Barnardsville, NC: Boundary End Archaeology Research Center, 2006.

■ GABRIELLE VAIL

THEATER

The combination of post-Conquest sources, such as **Diego de Landa**; the archaeology of ancient sites; and hieroglyphic **decipherments** provides a complex picture of rich theater in the Maya area. Although Maya dances were elaborate (one reported by Landa had 800 dancers), of recent interest is the performance **art**, including god-impersonators, masks of **deities** and spirits, large backrack-borne costumes, and lengthy story-telling conducted by Maya rulers and their courts, likely with large audiences in the expansive plazas ubiquitous in Maya central cities (see also **Divine Kings and Queens**; **Music and Dancing**). One pre-Classic Maya drama survives: the Rabinal-Achi, which tells the story of the warrior Man-of-Rabinal in a recounting of local history (see also **Warfare, Warriors, and Weapons**).

Plaza areas, central to sites from **Copán** to **Palenque** to **Chichen Itza**, provided audience space. On the dance platforms, **palace** steps, and **pyramid** tops, rulers were able to perform in front of an audience that fully participated in the continuity of their own culture by seeing and hearing stories of the gods, feats of the rulers, replay of history, and reconnection with the spiritual forces around them. The appearance of E-Groups and their solar hierophanies may be an early sign of the development of theater.

The murals of **Bonampak**, and likely many **stelae** and their inscriptions, such as those of Copán and **Quiriguá**, point to performances, not only sponsored by but actually performed by costumed ruling elites of society, divine rulers repeating for all to see the actions and interests of the gods by "becoming" those gods in a spectacle often loaded with religious significance. Accompanying texts on the stelae refer to *cha'nil*, "something being watched"—a performance.

There are difficulties with comparing ancient Maya theater with modern views of Western theater, yet the spaces, inscriptions, murals, and stelae of the Maya all point to the major significance of ritual activities, publicly performed by rulers, as a powerful means of imprinting and reinforcing cultural continuity, **calendar**, and **religion** on their audiences of commoners.

Further Reading

Grube, Nikolai. "Classic Maya Dance." *Ancient Mesoamerica* 3, no. 2: 201–18, 1992.

Inomata, Takeshi. "Plazas, Performers, and Spectators: Political Theaters of the Classic Maya." *Current Anthropology* 47, no. 5: 805–42, 2006.

Inomata, Takeshi, and Lawrence S. Coben, eds. *Archaeology of Performance: Theaters of Power, Community, and Politics*. Lanham, MD: AltaMira Press, 2006.

Klein, Maxine. "Theatre of the Ancient Maya." *Educational Theatre Journal* 23, 3: 269–76, 1971.

Tedlock, Dennis. *Rabinal Achi: A Maya Drama of War and Sacrifice*. New York: Oxford University Press, 2005.

Tozzer, Alfred M. *Landa's "Relación de las cosas de Yucatán": A Translation*. Papers of the Peabody Museum of American Archaeology and Ethnology, vol. 18. Cambridge, MA: Harvard University, 1941.

■ WALTER R. T. WITSCHEY

THOMPSON, J. ERIC S. (1898–1975)

For more than a third of a century the fertile brain and keen understanding of Eric Thompson dominated Maya studies. After work at **Chichen Itza**, **Cobá**, Lubaantun, and **Pusilha** early in his career, Thompson moved to the Carnegie Institution of Washington. Following the Second World War, he shifted his focus from field archaeology and **ceramic** sequences for relative **dating** to **decipherment**. He published several important contributions, including *Maya Hieroglyphic Writing: An Introduction*; *A Catalog of Maya Hieroglyphs*; *The Rise and Fall of Maya Civilization*; *Maya History and Religion*; *Maya Hieroglyphs without Tears*; and an autobiography, *Maya Archaeologist*. The *Catalog of Maya Hieroglyphs*, which illustrated and categorized hundreds of Maya glyphs, is in active use today by epigraphers, and decipherment literature is filled with glyph references (T numbers) to the Thompson Catalog, such as T533 (*Ahau*). The catalog contains drawings of 862 affixes, main signs, and suffixes.

Following the publication of Yuri **Knorosov's** 1952 paper about phoneticism in the hieroglyphs, Thompson stood in strong and critical opposition to those findings. Most Maya scholars, carefully guarding their own careers, feared to challenge the preeminent Thompson on the issue of phoneticism. Yet the ideas slowly gained traction, including with David H. Kelley and Michael Coe. A few months after Thompson's death in 1975, Kelley published *Deciphering the Maya Script*, and with it, the modern wave of decipherments relying on phonetic values in the glyphs began in earnest.

Thompson's body of work gained him a reputation for being the outstanding Maya scholar of his era, and he was knighted by Queen Elizabeth II for his work.

See also Cobá; Cotzumalhuapa; Proskouriakoff, Tatiana Avenirovna; Religion; Rites and Rituals; Takalik Abaj

Further Reading

Coe, Michael D. *The Maya*. 8th ed. London: Thames and Hudson, 2011.

———. *Breaking the Maya Code*. 3rd ed. London: Thames & Hudson, 2012.

Hammond, Norman. "Sir Eric Thompson, 1898–1975." *American Antiquity* 42, no. 2: 180–90, 1977.

Sharer, Robert J., and Loa P. Traxler. *The Ancient Maya*. 6th ed. Stanford, CA: Stanford University Press, 2006.

Thompson, John Eric Sidney. *Maya Archaeologist*. Norman: University of Oklahoma Press, 1994.

■ WALTER R. T. WITSCHEY

TIHO (T'HO, HO', ICHCAANSIHO')

Tiho (21.0° N, 89.6° W) is the name usually applied by archaeologists to the large Maya archaeological site anciently located where the modern city of Mérida, Yucatan, now lies (see also **Map 3**). Tiho is a Hispanicized version of the Yucatec Maya name *Ho'*, that is, in modern Maya speech, Mérida is called "Ho'," while the *ti* is a locative, which can be translated roughly as "place of." The ancient name of the site appears to have been Ichcaansiho', which is sometimes translated as "in Heaven born."

When the Spanish, led by Francisco de Montejo, arrived at the spot in 1541, they found huge ruined buildings. This prompted them to name the place Mérida, because the Spanish city of that name was famous for its Roman ruins. Almost nothing remains of the ancient ruins today because they were quarried for building stone by the Spaniards.

Though reused stones from the Maya buildings can be seen in the older Spanish buildings of Mérida, most of what we know about the Maya site comes from early Spanish accounts, such as **Diego de Landa**'s *Relación* and López de Cogolludo's *Historia de Yucatán*. These sources indicate that Ichcaansiho was one of the largest Maya sites in the state of Yucatan, probably similar in scale to **Izamal** or **Uxmal**. Landa describes and provides a sketch of a Tiho building much like the Nunnery Quadrangle of Uxmal and describes other features that connect Tiho architecture with the **Puuc style**. Chiefly by **ceramic** evidence, archaeologists know Tiho was occupied first in the Late Formative, continuing through the Early Classic. In the Late Classic and Terminal Classic, major building programs demonstrate Tiho's rise to become a major center. Tiho has Postclassic ceramics that link it to nearby northern sites such as Acanceh, **Dzibilchaltun**, **Mayapan**, Chichen Itza, and Isla Cerritos.

The early Franciscan friars built a large fortress monastery atop one of the largest Maya platforms, located southeast of the modern main plaza of the city, approximately where the marketplace is today. In the 1830s John Lloyd Stephens toured the crumbling remains of the monastery and saw Maya **corbelled vaults**. Fragments of this huge Maya platform survived into the twentieth century, when they were definitively razed for modern construction.

Occasionally archaeological excavations in downtown Mérida reveal small deposits of artifacts related to the ancient occupation, but these say little about the overall character of the site. They do suggest, however, that it had a long occupation, stretching from the Formative period to modern times.

See also MARKETS AND MARKETPLACES; NORTHERN LOWLANDS; PUUC ARCHITECTURAL STYLE; TERRITORIAL ENTITIES

Further Reading

Barrera Rubio, Alfredo. "La conquista de Yucatán y la fundación de Mérida." *Boletín de la Escuela de Ciencias Antropológicas de la Universidad de Yucatán* 10, no. 58: 9–21, 1983.

Gallareta Negrón, Tomás, and James Callaghan. "Proyecto arqueológico de conservación de la ciudad de Mérida, Yucatán." In *Memoría del congreso interno 1979*, 145–52. México, D.F., México: Instituto Nacional de Antropología e Historia, Centro Regional del Sureste, 1981.

Garza Tarazona de González, Silvia, and Edward B. Kurjack Bacso. *Atlas arqueológico del estado de Yucatán.* México, D.F.: Instituto Nacional de Antropología e Historia, 1980.

Tozzer, Alfred M. *Landa's "Relación de las cosas de Yucatán": A Translation.* Papers of the Peabody Museum of American Archaeology and Ethnology, vol. 18. Cambridge, MA: Harvard University, 1941.

■ CLIFFORD T. BROWN AND WALTER R. T. WITSCHEY

TIKAL

Tikal (17.2° N, 89.6° W) (*Mutal*) is often regarded as the most important of all Classic period **lowland** Maya cities. The immense volume of public **architecture**, the large size of the population, and the long reach of the power of its rulers combined to make it the leading kingdom of its epoch. Classic Tikal is located in the northeast part of the Department of the Petén, **Guatemala**, on the Central Karstic Mesa, strategically situated along ridges at a drainage divide—to the northeast, swamps and *bajos* ultimately empty to the Caribbean via the rivers of Belize; to the west, they flow to the Gulf of Mexico (see also **Maps 2** and **3**). Some archaeologists believe that this strategic position favored the growth of Tikal because it enabled the inhabitants to profit from **trade routes** crossing the base of the Yucatan Peninsula. While this tempting hypothesis remains unproven, it does seem clear that the precise location of the site was influenced by the presence of the large *bajos*, which supplied important agricultural resources to the inhabitants (see also **Subsistence**).

Tikal has, not surprisingly given its charisma, been investigated repeatedly by several teams of archaeologists. The site was visited by explorers and government officials in the nineteenth century, of whom the most significant were Gustav Bernoulli, Alfred Maudslay, and Teobert Maler. Bernoulli had elaborately carved wooden lintels removed from Temples I and IV and shipped them to Switzerland, where they remain today in the Museum für Völkerkunde. By modern standards, this was a stunning act of vandalism, but such activities were common in the nineteenth century. Fortunately, the lintels in Switzerland are now in better condition than those that remained in situ in the rain forest.

The most famous investigations at Tikal were the excavations of the University of Pennsylvania, directed mainly by Edwin Shook and William Coe, that lasted from 1955 to 1969. Under the influence of the "New Archaeology" of the time, the Pennsylvania archaeologists succeeded in answering many important questions about history, demography, urbanism, social stratification, and subsistence at the site through extensive mapping and carefully designed excavations. Because Tikal was the archetype of the lowland Maya site, in many cases it served as a test case to address broad questions about the nature of Maya society. There was a concerted search for "invisible" **house** mounds that showed that every *chultun* had at least one undiscovered dwelling nearby. The project changed thinking about the population of Maya centers—it had been much larger than expected.

Detailed attention was paid to ancient **water management** and the array of plaza drains and reservoirs that held water for the inhabitants. Overall, the project was outstandingly successful, but unfortunately the full publication of the results has been slow and uneven, and it continues today.

After the end of the project, research and excavation by international teams has continued to the present day under the leadership of the federal agency Instituto de Antropología e Historia de Guatemala (IDAEH). These intensive studies have produced detailed knowledge of **settlement** (3,000 structures across 16 km²), population (estimated at 50,000 or more), history (ruling **dynasties** including 33 rulers spanning 800 years), politics, and **warfare** (involving other Maya city-states, such as **Calakmul**, **Uaxactún**, **Caracol**, and **Toniná**). Archaeologists have also cleared and consolidated many of the most outstanding buildings in the site core, creating a major cultural attraction.

Tikal's occupation began late, by about 800 BC, during the Middle Formative period. In the Middle and Late Formative periods, the region was probably dominated by other sites, first by **Nakbé** and then by **El Mirador**. With the collapse of El Mirador near the end of the Formative about AD 150, Tikal ascended to become a dominant power in the Classic period, from AD 200 to ca. 900. Inscriptions throughout the Southern Lowlands suggest that Tikal played a key role in the Byzantine **alliances**, rivalries, and wars that marked the Classic. Nearby city-states interrupted Tikal's reign of power several times, as they jockeyed for domination of the area. A small population of squatters occupied the site through the Early Postclassic, after which the city lay abandoned until its rediscovery in the eighteenth century. As the Conquistador Hernán Cortés marched to Honduras, he passed near Tikal without hearing of it.

Tikal's inner ceremonial core is the Great Plaza. The North Acropolis, studded with royal funerary **pyramids**, looms above the Great Plaza. Its east and west sides are marked by Temples I and II respectively, towering temple-pyramids dedicated to Jasaw Chan K'awiil, one of the greatest of Tikal's kings, and his wife. To the south of the Great Plaza lies the labyrinthine royal **palace**, drily named the South Acropolis by archaeologists. About the plaza is an array of carved monuments, **stelae**, and stelae-altar pairs, recording Tikal's **dynastic sequence** and the feats of its rulers.

From the Great Plaza, short *sacbes* (**causeways**) lead to other large temples, including the stunning 70-m-tall Temple IV, pyramids, **ball courts**, and ceremonial structures. Astronomical alignments of the largest pyramids, which protrude above the jungle canopy, demonstrate that the elite of Tikal were concerned with **astronomy** and heavenly events. The sightline from Temple I across Temple III marks the equinoctial sunsets; the sightline from Temple IV across Temple III marks the winter solstice sunrise.

In addition to its extraordinary temple-tombs, Tikal is noted for multiple twin pyramid groups, architectural complexes with a courtyard, two radial pyramids, a small sacred precinct, and a small nine-doorway elite structure. Each twin pyramid complex is dedicated to the celebration of a *k'atun*-ending date, such as 9.17.0.0.0, January 24, 771 (see also **Calendar**).

An area near the site center, called the Mundo Perdido ("Lost World") complex, was constructed during the Formative and Early Classic periods. Excavations in the Lost World complex have revealed important information about the early history of Tikal.

Other important buildings and tombs at Tikal have provided evidence of **Teotihuacán's** influence at the site, in the form of *talud-tablero* façades on structures Additional evidence of Teotihuacán's relationship to the site has come from inscriptions at both Tikal and **Uaxactun**. Although difficult to interpret, they may suggest that Tikal was conquered by Teotihuacán in AD 378 (8.17.1.4.12). It seems that a personage named Siyaj K'ak' arrived at that time and helped install a new dynasty, after which Teotihuacán traits swelled in number and significance.

The modern name Tikal, apparently from the Yucatec Maya, has been interpreted in various ways. It may or may not be the ancient name of the site. Most epigraphers read the famous Emblem Glyph of the site as Mutal, and the city proper as Yax-Mutal, "first Mutal." Tikal has a rich corpus of inscriptions and is mentioned in the inscriptions of other sites, well described by Martin and Grube and summarized here.

Yax Ehb Xook ("First Step Shark"), who ruled ca. AD 90, was the nominal founder of Tikal but actually ruled long after Tikal's initial settlement in the Middle Formative period. No contemporaneous dates place his rule precisely, yet later numbered king lists tied to Long Count dates place the approximate date of his rule near the end of the Formative period.

? Balam ("Foliated Jaguar," "Scroll Ahau Jaguar"), for whom dates are unknown, is named as second dynastic ruler. Rulers 2–9 are not known; there is a 200-year span from the designated founding of Tikal until the first dated monument was inscribed. Stela 29, dated 8.12.14.13.15, October 16, AD 292, carries the earliest Long Count date in the Maya lowlands and traditionally marks the beginning of the Maya Classic period.

Ruler K'inich Ehb' ("Animal Headdress") is recorded as the father of Siyaj Chan K'awiil on a stela at El Encanto, together with his wife Lady Skull. Siyaj Chan K'awiil I ("Sky-born K'awiil") ruled ca. AD 307 as the eleventh ruler of Tikal. Other rulers are frequently shown with a specific glyph giving their numbered place in the Tikal dynastic sequence. Siyaj Chan K'awiil as well as Rulers 13 and 14 are identified this way on a painted vase commissioned by Ruler 22, Animal Skull II.

Unen B'alam ("Baby Jaguar") was Tikal's twelfth ruler. He conducted a *k'atun*-ending ceremony for 8.14.0.0.0, September 1, AD 317.

K'inich Muwaan Jol ("Radiant Hawk Skull," "Mahk'ina Bird Skull," "Feather Skull") ruled until death on May 23, AD 359 and was the father of Chak Tok Ich'aak.

Chak Tok Ich'aak I ("Great Misty Claw," "Jaguar Paw," "Great Jaguar Paw") ascended to power on August 7, AD 360 and ruled until his death on January 15, AD 378. As Tikal's fourteenth dynastic ruler, he presided over an already great Tikal. He celebrated the *k'atun*-ending of 8.17.0.0.0, October 21, AD 376, by commissioning Stela 39, which shows him in full regalia, standing on the back of a bound captive. During his reign, Central Mexican influences increased at Tikal and in the region, as evidenced by trade objects and *talud-tablero* architecture, and perhaps including intermarriage between distant ruling families. His death in AD 378, however, coincided with an arrival of Central Mexicans led by Sihyaj K'ak', thought by some to be a conquering general from the huge and flourishing city-state **Teotihuacán**, 1,000 km west of Tikal. Coincident with his death, Chak Tok Ich'aak's lineage also ended, replaced by royalty perhaps from Teotihuacán, and all the extant carved monuments of Tikal were ritually destroyed, their fragments relocated and buried.

Sihyaj K'ak' (also spelled Siyaj K'ak', "Fire Born"), according to the inscriptions, arrived in **El Perú-Waka'**, 8 km west, eight days before appearing in Tikal, likely traveling up the San Pedro Martír River route from Central Mexico. In the Petén, he presided over the installation of new rulers at Tikal in AD 379, at Bejucal about AD 381, at Rio Azul in AD 393, and at once-powerful Uaxactún, which thereafter became a dependent city of Tikal.

Sihyaj K'ak' is thought to have acted as general for a powerful Teotihuacán ruler, called Spearthrower Owl by archaeologists, who figured prominently in Teotihuacán and Tikal imagery as an owl with an *atlatl* dart-throwing stick. Spearthrower Owl was later described as the father of the next Tikal ruler, Yax Nuun Ayiin I, possibly by a wife from Tikal. Some believe the monuments are claiming that Teotihuacán, in a sweeping military march, came to dominate Tikal and the region and installed its rulers in place of the local dynasty.

Yax Nuun Ayiin I ("Curl Snout"), fifteenth ruler, was placed on the throne on September 12, AD 379, and ruled until ca. AD 404/406. He was put in office by Sihyaj K'ak', who continued to act as his overlord for a number of years. For his portraits of the *k'atun*-ending celebration of 8.18.0.0.0, July 8, AD 396, Yax Nuun Ayiin was shown seated, in contrast to the prior Tikal custom of showing standing rulers, wearing complete Teotihuacán regalia, including helmet, *atlatl*, and shield with a goggle-eyed Central Mexican god. On the monument "Hombre of Tikal," his death falls in AD 406, yet Stela 31 indicates he died two years earlier. Whatever was the case, he did not preside at the mid-*k'atun* celebration of 8.18.10.0.0, May 17, AD 406. The celebrant, Sihyaj Chan K'inich, may have ruled in the few years before Yax Nuun Ayiin's son came to power.

Siyaj Chan K'awiil II ("Stormy Sky") came to power on November 26, AD 411, and ruled until his death February 3, AD 456. As Tikal's sixteenth ruler, he may have embarked on a sophisticated program to rewrite history. In the revised version, Teotihuacán's conquest revitalized the Tikal dynasty, rather than conquering it. On Stela 31, recovered from his tomb in the North Acropolis, he was pictured in royal Maya finery and traced his lineage back to Yax Ehb Xook, yet showed symbols of Spearthrower Owl, his grandfather, of Teotihuacán, and pictures of his father dressed as a Teotihuacán soldier.

K'an Chitam ("Precious, or Yellow, Peccary," "Kan Boar," "Kan Ak") was born November 26, AD 415, ascended to power on August 8, AD 458, and possibly died in AD 486. As Ruler 17, the son of Siyaj Chan K'awiil II, he continued the earlier practice of using Teotihuacán imagery in stela portraits, but later in his reign, he began to portray himself as a Fire God. He celebrated the *k'atun*-ending of 9.2.0.0.0, May 15, AD 475, and he may still have been alive when Tikal attacked Maasal in August 486.

Chak Tok Ich'aak II ("Jaguar Paw Skull," "Jaguar Paw II," "Great Misty Claw") was mentioned in AD 486, was ruling by AD 488, and ruled until his death on July 24, AD 508. As eighteenth ruler of Tikal, son of K'an Chitam, he celebrated the *k'atun*-ending of 9.3.0.0.0, January 30, AD 495, by erecting three monuments to himself. The complexities and hazards of the political landscape began to emerge during his reign. He wrote that Tzik'in Bahlam of **Naranjo** was his maternal grandfather, documenting a key political tie to a city 40 km to the east. His death was mentioned in inscriptions at Toniná, 250 km west of Tikal, and two weeks after his death, one of his underlords was captured by then-weak Yaxchilan, 145 km west.

Ix Kaloomte' Ix Yok'in ("Lady of Tikal") was born September 1, AD 404, came to power on April 19, AD 511, and ruled until at least AD 527. During this increasingly troubled time for Tikal, the daughter of Chac Tok Ich'aak II emerged as queen, yet she was not numbered in the dynastic sequence of the inscriptions. Neither did she serve alone, but governed with at least one male coruler, consort, or guardian, Kaloomte' B'alam, and likely later with Bird Claw. She celebrated the *k'atun*-ending rites of 9.4.0.0.0, October 18, AD 514.

Kaloomte' B'alam ("Curl Head") dates to ca. AD 511–527 as Ruler 19. He was much older than his queen. He was perhaps a general of Chak Tok Ich'aak II, for inscriptions say that he led the attack on Maasal in August 486 and took captives.

Bird Claw ("Animal Skull I," "Ete I") ruled ca. AD 527–537. Apparently this twentieth ruler at Tikal left but one monument, Stela 8. Its dates have not been deciphered, nor do we understand clearly how Bird Claw and Lady of Tikal related to each other. During the reign of Bird Claw, amid other constructions in the center of Tikal, the first twin pyramid group was constructed, and then used for multiple *k'atun*-ending celebrations. Later in Tikal's history, a new twin pyramid group was constructed for each *k'atun* ending.

New research suggests that an eruption of the volcano Ilopango in El Salvador in AD 536 was substantially more disruptive worldwide than previously believed, resulting in both local catastrophes due to ash fall, which affected cities such as **Copán**, **Quiriguá**, and **Kaminaljuyú**, and more widespread global climate change caused by the pall of dust that enveloped the earth. The lengthy global cooling from AD 536 to 550 also cast a pall on the politics of Mesoamerica that seriously affected Bird Claw's successors.

Wak Chan K'awiil ("Double Bird") was born ca. January AD 508, ascended to power possibly on December 29, AD 537, and ruled until ca. AD 562. As Tikal's Ruler 21 and son of Chak Tok Ich'aak II, he left but one monument, Stela 17, which was carved in AD 557 but refers to events one *k'atun* (two decades) earlier. Monuments in other cities say that on April 16, AD 553, Wak Chan K'awiil participated in the crowning of Yajaw Te' K'inich II of Caracol, an ally 75 km southeast. This Tikal-Caracol **alliance** was threatened by new ties formed between Calakmul and Naranjo, once also a Tikal ally through the bloodlines of Chak Tok Ich'aak himself. Double Bird celebrated the *k'atun*-ending of 9.6.0.0.0, March 22, AD 554, and refers in retrospect to the celebration three *k'atuns* earlier by his father Chac Tok Ich'aak II. Wak Chan K'awiil brought his Caracol alliance to an end when he attacked Caracol in April AD 556.

Calakmul, 100 km north of Tikal, deployed its growing power and used alliances forged with Naranjo and Caracol to attack and conquer Tikal in April AD 562. This was an event that coincided with a special orbital position of Venus, the War Star in Maya cosmology. The inscriptions of Caracol seem to record the ritual killing of Wak Chan K'awiil, who then vanished from the record.

No stelae have been found at Tikal that were carved and erected during the next 130 years, the **Middle Classic Hiatus**. During this time, Rulers 22–25 may have been puppets of Caracol, but in any case, Tikal experienced a dark age, with no inscriptions and little civic construction.

K'inich? ("Animal Skull II") ruled ca. AD 593. As Tikal's twenty-second ruler, he did not claim to be of the Tikal dynastic bloodlines, but claimed his legitimacy through his mother, Ix Ajaw Bahlam, Lady Lord (of) Jaguar. A contemporary vase, decorated with the woven mat pattern of kings, lists the early rulers of Tikal, up to the arrival of Teotihuacán, and may reflect an attempt by Animal Skull to link himself with the pre-Mexican bloodlines. Objects found in his tomb carry the *k'atun*-ending date of 9.8.0.0.0, August 24, AD 593, and record the fact that he lived between 40 and 60 years (a three-*k'atun* lord). There is no information about the twenty-third ruler.

K'inich Muwaan Jol II dates to ca. AD 640. He was the twenty-fourth ruler and took his royal name from Ruler 13, a king 300 years earlier. He was not only the father of Nuun Ujol Chaak, but also the father of Bajlaj Chan K'awiil, king of **Dos Pilas** and ally of Calakmul. His sons launched an intercity conflict that extended Tikal's dark period.

Nuun Ujol Chaak ("Shield Skull," "Nun Bak Chak") ruled AD 657–679. As twenty-fifth Tikal king, he suffered an early defeat when Calakmul launched another successful Star War against Tikal in AD 657. He was defeated and subjugated by Yuknoom the Great of Calakmul, but soon after attended a ceremony for Yuknoom's son and heir. Shield Skull's brother Bajlaj Chan K'awiil from Dos Pilas also attended, yet in AD 672, Nuun Ujol Chaak attacked him to prevent usurpation of the Tikal throne. Calakmul, likely pushed by the threatened Bajlaj Chan K'awiil, attacked Tikal again in AD 677, forcing Nuun Ujol Chaak off the throne. With the help of Calakmul, Bajlaj Chan K'awiil pressed his advantage during the following two years and ultimately defeated Nuun Ujol Chaak at Tikal.

Jasaw Chan K'awiil I ("Ruler A," "Ah Cacao," "Sky Rain") came to power on May 3, AD 682 and ruled until his death ca. AD 734. This twenty-sixth ruler in the dynastic sequence, a heroic builder and successful warrior-king, brought Tikal out of its dark age, ended the hiatus, and restored Tikal to a place of preeminence among the Maya city-states. He quickly defeated Calakmul, on August 5, AD 695, stripping Calakmul's king Yich'aak K'ak' of his weapons, and recorded the result on his inaugural stela. In a subsequent celebration, held on the 13-*k'atun* anniversary (256 years) of the death of Teotihuacán's Spearthrower Owl, Jasaw Chan K'awiil created a conscious link back to Tikal's glory days. In related images he portrayed himself in both Maya regalia and Central Mexican attire.

Following battles with Naranjo and Dos Pilas, Jasaw Chan K'awiil turned to civic construction. During his long rule, he celebrated three *k'atun*-ending ceremonies by building a twin pyramid group for each, on 9.13.0.0.0, March 18, AD 692; 9.14.0.0.0, December 5, AD 711; and 9.15.0.0.0, August 22, AD 731. Although no tomb has been found in Temple II, which he built, Temple I, its opposing number on the Great Plaza, contained his tomb. Within, the king lay on a stone bench, with a 3.9-kg, 114-bead jade pectoral. Incised bones in the tomb portrayed not only mythological scenes but also king lists and dates of death for non-Tikal rulers, and references to Copán, 265 km south, and Palenque, 260 km west.

Yik'in Chan K'awiil ("Ruler B," "Yaxkin Caan Chaac," "Sun Sky Rain"), twenty-seventh ruler, came to power on December 8, AD 734, and ruled until his death ca. AD 751. He extended his father's gains in both the military arena and civic construction. In a direct assault on the Calakmul alliance, he defeated **Yaxh**á to the west in July AD 743, capturing Jaguar Throne, the ruler of El Perú-Waka', and in AD 744 defeated the city of Wak Kabnal, capturing Mayuy Chan Chaak, the king of Naranjo. As Calakmul lost influence with its subjects and client states, Tikal moved to ascendancy once again. Inscriptions say that Yik'in Chan K'awiil captured Wilan Chak Tok Wayib of the Naranjo/Holmul region on December 8, AD 748. He apparently celebrated the next *k'atun*-ending event, 9.16.0.0.0, May 9, AD 751.

Ruler 28, ca. AD 766, probably the elder son of Yik'in Chan K'awiil, is known from two dates in AD 766, one of which is the three-quarter *k'atun* celebration of 9.16.15.0.0, February 19, AD 766.

Yax Nuun Ayiin II, the twenty-ninth ruler, came to power on December 25, AD 768, and ruled at least until AD 794. He was the younger son of Yik'in Chan K'awiil and adopted the name of the first Teotihuacán ruler to be enthroned at Tikal, likely in an attempt to recapture former glory. During his reign, he built two large twin pyramid groups, to celebrate the *k'atun*-endings of 9.17.0.0.0, January 24, AD 771, and 9.18.0.0.0, October 11, AD 790. Yax Nuun Ayiin II was the last Tikal lord to be numbered in the dynastic sequence—the pressures that led to the **Classic Maya collapse** were building to a crescendo at Tikal.

Nuun Ujol K'inich ruled ca. AD 794 to 810. As Ruler 30, he is known only from mention on Stela 24 of his son Dark Sun.

Dark Sun ruled ca. AD 810. Possibly the thirty-first ruler of Tikal, he was the celebrant of the *k'atun*-ending 9.19.0.0.0, June 28, AD 810, but unlike his predecessors, he failed to erect a twin pyramid group for the occasion. The use of a stela instead speaks to the declining fortunes of the once-great Tikal. No Tikal monuments have been found that report the next critically important calendar celebration, the *b'ak'tun*-ending date of 10.0.0.0.0, March 15, AD 830.

Jewel K'awiil ruled ca. AD 849. Solely from an inscription at **Ceibal**, 90 km to the south, are we made aware of Jewel K'awiil as a Tikal lord. He appeared there as a witness to the local celebration of the *k'atun*-ending 10.1.0.0.0, November 30, AD 849, for which there are no corresponding monuments at Tikal itself. As Tikal's fortunes continued to decline, local client states, such as Ixlu and Jimbal, abandoned the Tikal Emblem Glyph, which linked them with Mutal and the powerful Tikal state, and they adopted Emblem Glyphs of their own.

Jasaw Chan K'awiil II ruled ca. AD 869. As Tikal became a shadow of a once-great city, and the effects of the Classic Maya collapse took their toll, Jasaw Chan K'awiil II held one last *k'atun*-ending celebration, for 10.2.0.0.0, August 17, AD 869. Even taking the name of the great revitalizing Tikal king Jasaw Chan K'awiil I could not stop the uncontrollable forces killing Tikal. Jasaw Chan K'awiil II's celebratory Stela 24 is the final historical document of a dying city.

See also ART; ASTRONOMICAL OBSERVATORIES; BECAN; CARACOL-DYNASTIC HISTORY; CENTRAL LOWLANDS; CIVAL; CLIMATE; COBÁ; CODEX-STYLE VASES; COPÁN; CORBEL ARCH; CRAFT SPECIALIZATION; DECIPHERMENT; DEITIES; DIVINE KINGS AND QUEENS; DROUGHT; DYNASTIC SEQUENCES; ECCENTRIC LITHICS; EL PILAR; FORTIFICATIONS; GROUND SURVEY TECHNIQUES; HOLMUL; HOUSES; KAMINALJUYÚ; LA CORONA; MAYA QUEENS; NAACHTUN; PALACE; PALENQUE; PETÉN STYLE ARCHITECTURE; PORTABLE OBJECTS; PUSILHA; QUIRIGUÁ; RIO AZUL; RITES AND RITUALS; SAN BARTOLO; SCULPTURE; SETTLEMENT PATTERNS (CENTRAL LOWLANDS); SUBSISTENCE; SYLLABARY; TERRACING; TEXTILES AND CLOTHING; TRADE ROUTES; VEGETATION; WARFARE, WARRIORS, AND WEAPONS; WATER MANAGEMENT; WRITING SYSTEMS OF MESOAMERICA; YAXHÁ; YAXNOHCAH

Further Reading

Carr, Robert F., James E. Hazard, and Christopher Carr. *Tikal Report 11: Map of the Ruins of Tikal, El Petén, Guatemala and Georeferenced Versions of the Maps Therein.* Electronic data set. tDAR, The Digital Archaeological Record, 2013. http://core.tdar.org/project/390922.

Lentz, David L., Nicholas P. Dunning, and Vernon L. Scarborough, eds. *Tikal: Paleoecology of an Ancient Maya City.* New York: Cambridge University Press, 2014.

Martin, Simon, and Nikolai Grube. *Chronicle of the Maya Kings and Queens: Deciphering the Dynasties of the Ancient Maya.* 2nd ed. London: Thames & Hudson, 2008.

Puleston, Dennis Edward. *The Settlement Survey of Tikal.* Tikal Reports, no. 13. Philadelphia: University Museum, University of Pennsylvania, 1983.

Sabloff, Jeremy A. *Tikal: Dynasties, Foreigners & Affairs of State: Advancing Maya Archaeology.* School of American Research Advanced Seminar Series. Santa Fe, NM: School of American Research Press, 2003.

Scarborough, Vernon L., Nicholas P. Dunning, Kenneth B. Tankersley, Christopher Carr, Eric Weaver, Liwy Grazioso, Brian Lane, John G. Jones, Palma Buttles, Fred Valdez, and David L. Lentz. "Water and Sustainable Land Use at the Ancient Tropical City of Tikal, Guatemala." *Proceedings of the National Academy of Sciences of the United States of America* 109, no. 31: 12408–413, 2012.

Schele, Linda, and David Freidel. "A War of Conquest: Tikal against Uaxactun." In *A Forest of Kings: The Untold Story of the Ancient Maya*, 130–64. New York: William Morrow, 1990.

Shook, Edwin M., Richard E. W. Adams, and Robert F. Carr, eds. *Tikal Reports: Numbers 1 to 11.* Philadelphia: University of Pennsylvania Museum of Archaeology and Anthropology, 1986.

Tikal Digital Access Project. (430 photographs). University Museum of Archaeology and Anthropology, University of Pennsylvania, 2011. http://research.famsi.org/tikal.html.

■ CLIFFORD T. BROWN AND WALTER R. T. WITSCHEY

TONINÁ

The Classic Maya city of Toniná (16.9° N, 92.0° W) is in highland Chiapas, **Mexico**, 13 km from the town of Ocosingo, on a hillside of the Ocosingo Valley (see also **Map 3**). It is on the western edge of the Maya region. Early visitors included Fray Jacinto Garrido, Guillermo Dupaix, John Lloyd Stephens and Frederick Catherwood, Eduard Seler, Karl Sapper, Frans Blom, and Oliver La Farge. Pierre Becquelin and Claude Baudez directed the French Toniná Project 1972–1975 and 1979–1980. INAH began investigations in 1981 under the direction of Juan Yadeun Angulo.

The largest structure is a terraced hillside acropolis, facing southward over an extensive ceremonial plaza with a sunken **ball court** and many other structures. Identifiable captives represented in the AD 699 ball court are from **Palenque**. The ball court was renovated in AD 766.

Survey of the valley shows extensive residential **architecture**. Most dated monuments refer to events in the Late Classic period, but excavations in the acropolis revealed Early Classic remains. Toniná is 64 km south of Palenque, and inscriptions cross-reference **warfare** and captive-taking between the two cities. They shared a similar artistic flair for three-dimensional molded stucco portraits of kings. Toniná has numerous royal **stelae** carved in the round, although Palenque has but one. A retrospective date of AD 217 refers to an early Toniná king, but the known dynastic sequence begins in AD 514, summarized here from Martin and Grube.

Ruler 1 ("Cabeza de Reptil," "Reptile Head") appears on two monuments, where his career is linked with other Maya sites and rulers. Then Bahlam Yaxuun Tihl ("Jaguar Bird Peccary or Tapir") came to power on January 16, AD 563.

Chak B'olon Chaak's dates of rule are unknown, but several events likely occurred in his reign. In AD 573, the site of Chinikiha recorded capture of a Toniná subject; the tomb of Chak B'olon Chaak was visited, according to an unprovenienced panel, in AD 579. Local nobles were installed in office in AD 612, and the *k'atun*-ending of 9.9.0.0.0, May 12, AD 613, was celebrated.

K'inich Bahlam Chapaat ("Radiant Jaguar Centipede") was born April 13, AD 606, and ruled from January 30, AD 615 until ca. AD 665–668. From age 8 to 58 or more, Bahlam Chapaat ruled Toniná, and contemporary monuments recorded the installation of nobles and a calendar celebration in AD 665.

Ruler 2 ("Jaguar Casper") took the throne on August 20, AD 668 and ruled until September AD 687. Numerous monuments, including Giant Ahaw altars, celebrated the 19-year reign of Ruler 2 and displayed many illustrations of rope-bound captives, one of them a woman. (See figure 29 for an illustration of a Giant Ahaw altar.) Ruler 2, according to victory inscriptions at Palenque, was captured by Palenque's king K'inich Kan B'alam II. The immediate succession of the next ruler implies that Ruler 2's capture had fatal consequences.

K'inich B'aaknal Chaak ("Serpent Head," "Radiant Bone-place Rain God," "Ruler 3") was born December 23, AD 652, and ruled from June 16, AD 688 until his death ca. AD 704–708. Serpent Head led the restoration of Toniná to its former glory and beyond. In AD 692/693 his war against Palenque and Kan B'alam achieved the capture of Lord K'awiil Mo'. In AD 699 he celebrated capture of several regional lords under Palenque's aegis by dedicating the sunken ball court (Ball Court I) with bas-relief illustrations of the captives.

Ruler 4 ("Radiant Jaguar-God Fire") was born September 12, AD 706, came to power as an infant on November 24, AD 708, and ruled until ca. AD 723. He initially served at the mercy of two important nobles, perhaps regents, K'elen Hix and Aj Ch'anaah. These leaders captured Palenque's king K'an Joy Chitam and commemorated the event with a bas-relief panel. K'elen Hix held the rituals for the calendar observance of 9.14.5.0.0, November 8, AD 716, and died the following year.

K'inich Ich'aak Chapat ("Radiant Claw Centipede," "Ruler 5") was born January 11, AD 709, acceded to power on November 15, AD 723, and ruled past AD 739. He appears on numerous monuments, but without proclaiming captive-taking. He opened the tomb of B'aaknal Chaak and "entered his tomb with fire" in AD 730, to conduct a Maya ritual that is not well understood.

K'inich Tuun Chapat ("Radiant Stone Centipede," "Ruler 6"), who died ca. February 9, AD 762, is the one king mentioned in a half-century notable for few records and missing rulers.

K'inich Chapat ("Radiant Centipede," "Ruler 8") was born July 6, AD 756, acceded to power by AD 787, and ruled until AD 806 or later. He led Toniná into battle and captive-taking, again with considerable success, claiming the title "He of many captives." His conquests included Sak Tz'i and Pomoy, regional sites whose locations are unknown.

Uh Chapat ("Ruler 9"), who ruled ca. 830–837, was mentioned on a single stela pedestal. Ruler 10, who ruled ca. AD 904, was mentioned on a single poorly crafted stela. A subsequent king, whose name is eroded, erected Monument 158 at Toniná, the last of the known Maya Classic-era Long-Count-dated monuments. It marks the *k'atun*-ending celebration of 10.4.0.0.0, January 15, AD 909.

See also ALLIANCES; CALAKMUL; CALENDAR; DIVINE KINGS AND QUEENS; DYNASTIC SEQUENCES; MAYA AREA; TIKAL

Further Reading

Becquelin, Pierre, and Claude Baudez. *Tonina: Une cité maya du Chiapas (Mexique)* (poster with map of the ruins). Service des archives scientifiques, Maison René-Ginouvès, Archéologie et Ethnologie, Archives de Missions Archéologiques Françaises À L'Étranger, 1990. http://www.mae.u-paris10.fr/site-expo/images/images-posters/posters-archives%20PDF/tonina.pdf.

Graham, Ian, Peter Mathews, and Lucia Henderson. *Tonina*. Corpus of Maya Hieroglyphic Inscriptions, Peabody Museum of Archaeology and Ethnology, Harvard University, 1983–2006. https://peabody.harvard.edu/cmhi/site.php?site=Tonina.

Itzel Mateos González, Frida. *Toniná, la pintura mural y los relieves: Técnica de manufactura*. Mexico City: Instituto Nacional de Antropología e Historia, Centro de Investigaciones Humanísticas de Mesoamérica y del Estado de Chiapas-UNAM, 1997.

Martin, Simon, and Nikolai Grube. *Chronicle of the Maya Kings and Queens: Deciphering the Dynasties of the Ancient Maya*. 2nd ed. London: Thames & Hudson, 2008.

Miller, Mary Ellen, and Megan Eileen O'Neil. *Maya Art and Architecture*. 2nd ed. London: Thames & Hudson, 2014.

■ WALTER R. T. WITSCHEY

TRADE ROUTES

The ancient Maya used land and water to transport trade goods from nearby and more distant lands. Several factors affected the selection of trade routes, including geography, politics, and the type of trade good. When the Spaniards encountered the Maya in the sixteenth century, they were engaged in active sea trade around the Yucatan peninsula of **Mexico** and **Belize**. Columbus encountered a trading canoe near the Bay Islands off the north coast of Honduras during his fourth voyage to the Americas in 1502. The canoe was laden with cotton cloth, honey, copper objects, chocolate, and other goods (see also **Cacao**; **Portable Objects**; **Textiles and Clothing**).

Archaeological research indicates sea trade extended back in time to the Preclassic period at **Cerros**, Belize (300 BC–AD 300). Trading ports are identified by exotic trade goods, harbors, strategic location, and often, location at the juncture of an inland transportation route, either by land or river. The mercantile Maya at the trading ports had an unusual amount of wealth relative to other communities, including highly crafted pottery and exotic **obsidian**, gold, and copper as offerings in graves of the deceased (see also **Burial**s; **Ceramics**). Trading ports along the Yucatan coast of Mexico include Isla **Jaina**, Isla Piedras, Isla Cerritos, **Muyil**, and **Cozumel**, with San Juan and Marco Gonzalez on Ambergris Cay, Moho Cay (by the Belize River), False Cay, and Wild Cane Cay in Belize. Isla Cerritos was the port for the nearby inland city of **Chichen Itza**, bringing coastal products such as shells for ornaments to the city, as well as exotic obsidian from volcanic regions north of Mexico City (Pachuca) and the **southern** Maya **highlands** of **Guatemala** (**El Chayal**, **Ixtepeque**, Rio Pixcaya). At the southern end of the coastal route off the coast of Belize, the trading port of Wild Cane Cay served a similar function. Obsidian from Pachuca and Ucareo (also north of Mexico City), **Honduras** (La Esperanza), and Guatemala was abundant at the port. Gold from lower Central America, copper from Honduras, Las Vegas Polychrome from Honduras, and pottery from various locations were recovered from burials.

Coastal ports also served to facilitate inland trade of marine resources to the dynastic Maya of the Classic period (AD 300–900). Salt, a basic biological necessity that was limited to some upland salt springs in the interior of the Yucatan, was a major commodity, traded inland by rivers and overland trails from solar evaporation ponds on the north coast of the Yucatan. Along the rainier coast of Belize, brine was evaporated in pots over fires to make salt, with wooden buildings preserved at the Paynes Creek salt works in southern Belize. Xcambo off the north coast of the Yucatan also was a trading port that included salt from the Celestun salt flats.

Trade routes were defined by available technology. The lack of suitable draft animals meant that overland trade used porters, who may have carried an estimated 15 kg per day per person. Ancient roadways called *sacbeob,* well-suited for use by porters, connected many cities, such as **Cobá-Yaxuná**; **Uxmal-Kabah**; and **Izamal**-Ake (see also **Causeway/Sacbe**). River and oceangoing travel was by paddlers in dugout canoes, as shown on incised bones from Burial 116, Temple 1 at **Tikal**, from a painted mural on the Temple of the Warriors at **Chichen Itza**, and from an actual wooden canoe paddle and canoe from the Paynes Creek salt works.

Although sea trade endured throughout Maya prehistory, overland trails and inland rivers were heavily used in the **southern** Maya **lowlands** during the Classic period (A.D. 300–900), when the dynastic Maya rulers at inland cities imported both foodstuffs and exotic and highly crafted goods used as gifts in marriage and political **alliances**, and in their **royal tombs**.

See also ALLIANCES; ALTUN HA; BURIALS; CACAO; CAHAL PECH; CARACOL; CEIBAL; CERAMIC ANALYSIS; CERRO MAYA/CERROS; CHAMPOTÓN; CLASS STRUCTURE; CLASSIC MAYA COLLAPSE;

Cochuah Region; Cozumel; Craft Specialization; Diet; Divine Kings and Queens; Drought; Eccentric Lithics; Edzna; El Chayal; El Perú-Waka'; Geology; Household Production; Ixtepeque; Izamal; Jaina; Kabah and Nohpat; Kaminaljuyú; Komchen; La Corona; Lamanai; Markets and Marketplaces; Mathematics; Mayapán; Middle Classic Hiatus; Muyil; Obsidian; Olmec; Oxkintok; Physical/Biological Anthropology; Portable Objects; Rio Azul; Southern Lowlands; Southern Periphery; Subsistence; Takalik Abaj; Textiles and Clothing; Tikal; Tribute; Tulum; Underwater Archaeology

Further Reading

McKillop, Heather. "Finds in Belize Document Late Classic Maya Salt Making and Canoe Transport." *Proceedings of the National Academy of Sciences of the United States of America* 102, no. 15: 5630–34, 2005.

McKillop, Heather. *In Search of Maya Sea Traders.* Texas A&M University Anthropology Series, no. 11. College Station: Texas A&M University Press, 2005.

■ HEATHER MCKILLOP

TRIBUTE

In **Mesoamerica**, tribute operated at two levels: obligations by commoners to their ruler, and payments by a locality to a larger state that controlled it. Local rulers and their elite families were supported by an imposed obligation on their subjects to make payments of food, corvée labor, craft goods, and raw materials. The construction of the monumental **architecture** in Maya city-states was the direct result of labor under direction of their ruler.

In the larger sense, towns under the control of another city-state paid tribute that increased the wealth and power of the more powerful polity. Tribute was exacted through both **warfare** and peaceful **alliance**, sometimes coercive, sometimes peaceable. The inscriptions and **ceramics** found archaeologically document tribute giving and receiving of well-crafted ceramics; quetzal feathers; bundles of cloth; perishables such as seafood; small artifacts of jade; and commodities such as pelts, salt, and **cacao** beans (see also **Portable Objects**; **Subsistence**).

A ceremonial office mentioned in the *Popol Vuh*, Keeper of the Reception House Mat, is perhaps a holdover from preconquest times, when it would have served as the collection point for tribute. Through this flow of wealth, great Maya city-states became more powerful, and smaller localities acquired both protection and exotic goods.

Further Reading

Dacus, Chelsea. "Weaving the Past: An Examination of Bones Buried with an Elite Maya Woman." Master's thesis, Southern Methodist University, 2005.

Demarest, Arthur A. *Ancient Maya: The Rise and Fall of a Rainforest Civilization.* New York: Cambridge University Press, 2004.

Masson, Marilyn A., and David A. Freidel, eds. *Ancient Maya Political Economies.* Walnut Creek, CA: AltaMira Press, 2002.

McKillop, Heather. *The Ancient Maya: New Perspectives.* New York: W. W. Norton, 2004.

Tokovinine, Alexandre, and Dmitri Beliaev. "People of the Road: Traders and Travelers in Ancient Maya Words and Images." In *Merchants, Markets and Exchange in the Pre-Columbian World,* edited by

Kenneth G. Hirth and Joanne Pillsbury. Washington, DC: Dumbarton Oaks Research Library and Collection, Trustees for Harvard University, 2013.

■ WALTER R. T. WITSCHEY

TULUM

Tulum (87.4° W, 20.2° N) is a Late Postclassic Maya archaeological site on the east coast of the Yucatan Peninsula in Quintana Roo, **Mexico** (see also **Map 3**). It is approximately 125 km south-southwest of Cancun and is a popular tourist destination today. Founded late, about AD 1200, Tulum was occupied when the Spanish arrived. It was seen from passing Spanish ships, as when Juan de Grijalva reported in 1518, "We have seen a town more grand than Seville." Tulum likely drew populace from Tancah, a Classic period site 5 km north.

Central Tulum is a walled city, protected from land attack by 6-m-thick masonry walls that rise 3 to 5 m (see also **Fortifications**; **Warfare, Warriors, and Weapons**). The city wall measures 385 m north-south by 165 m east-west. In modern Yucatec Maya, *tulum* means "wall." The prehistoric name of the site was evidently Tzama or Zama.

There are five **corbel-arch** entrances through the city wall. A **cave** under the northern wall leads to a freshwater **cenote**. Small temples on the cliff served as lighthouses to guide Maya trading canoes through a break in the barrier reef beyond the beach. As coastal **trade** around the Yucatan Peninsula was extensive in the Postclassic period, Tulum must have been a major port city.

The main temple of Tulum (Str. 1, the Castillo) is dramatically poised with its rear near the edge of a 12-m-high natural coastal cliff. The Castillo, by its size, location, and orientation, is clearly the central ceremonial structure. Its single axial stairway faces north of west and leads up a 7.5-m-high platform. Feathered-serpent columns flank the temple doorway. The Castillo is built over an earlier masonry building with a colonnade and beam-and-mortar roof.

John Lloyd Stephen and Frederick Catherwood published a description of Tulum in 1843. At the Temple of the Initial Series they found remnants of an Early Classic **stela** from Tancah dated AD 564. The Temple of the Descending God or Diving God (Str. 5) borders the front plaza of the Castillo on the north. Together these buildings and their plaza are the main ceremonial precinct.

The Temple of the Frescoes (Str. 16), which has mural paintings inside and an unusual exterior corner stucco mask, sits west of the Castillo (see also **Wall Painting**). The lower level fronts the broad north-south avenue line with elite residences, while the upper level faces the Castillo. The murals are executed in the pan-Mesoamerican "Mixteca-Puebla" style of the period. The **architecture** was built in the East Coast style, with upright slab masonry and flat beam-and-mortar roofs.

Beyond the city wall are networks of field walls, enclosing 1- to 3-ha plots and isolated **house** mounds. The population living within the city wall perhaps numbered in the low hundreds, with that outside the walls rising to 1,000 to 3,000 individuals.

Tulum **ceramics** begin in the Early Postclassic period and, during the Late Postclassic, include types like those of **Mayapán**. Effigy censers are common. **Obsidian** at Tulum is from the **Ixtepeque** source in Guatemala. Fishing-net weights are plentiful at the site.

Carved from potsherds, they are roughly rectangular, measuring 3 by 6 cm, with notches cut in the short sides. Conch shells (*Strombus gigas*) were placed in **burials** (Str. 20). Tools and ornaments of shell include fishhooks, scoops, and scrapers, as well as drilled beads, pendants, and tinklers.

While close to its grand neighbor Cobá, Tulum was settled well afterward and did not participate in its activities. Its role instead was active coastal trade during the Late Postclassic.

See also DIET; HOUSES; MUYIL; PORTABLE OBJECTS; SETTLEMENT PATTERNS (NORTHERN LOWLANDS); UNDERWATER ARCHAEOLOGY

Further Reading

Andrews, Anthony P. "Reconocimiento Arqueológico de Tulum a Punta Allen, Quintana Roo." *Boletín de la Escuela de Ciencias Antropológicas de la Universidad de Yucatán*: 15–31, 1983.

Barrera Rubio, Alfredo. "Littoral-marine Economy at Tulum, Quintana Roo, Mexico." In *The Lowland Maya Postclassic*, edited by Arlen F. Chase and Prudence M. Rice. Austin: University of Texas Press, 1985.

Lothrop, Samuel Kirkland. *Tulum: An Archaeological Study of the East Coast of Yucatan*. Carnegie Institution of Washington, Publication 335. Washington, DC: Carnegie Institution of Washington, 1924.

Miller, Arthur G. "The Maya and the Sea: Trade and Cult at Tancah and Tulum." In *The Sea in the Pre-Columbian world: A Conference at Dumbarton Oaks, October 26th and 27th, 1974*, edited by Elizabeth P. Benson and Dumbarton Oaks. Washington, DC: Dumbarton Oaks Research Library and Collections, Trustees for Harvard University, 1974.

———. "The Postclassic Sequence of Tancah and Tulum, Quintana Roo, Mexico." In *The Lowland Maya Postclassic*, edited by Arlen F. Chase and Prudence M. Rice. Austin: University of Texas Press, 1985.

Taube, Karl. *At Dawn's Edge: Tulum, Santa Rita, and Floral Symbolism in the International Style of Late Postclassic Mesoamerica*. Washington, DC: Dumbarton Oaks, 2010.

Vargas Pacheco, Ernesto. *Tulum: Organización político-territorial de la costa oriental de Quintana Roo*. México D.F.: Universidad Nacional Autónoma de México, Instituto de Investigaciones Antropológicas, 1997.

■ WALTER R. T. WITSCHEY AND CLIFFORD T. BROWN

TZIBANCHÉ

See DZIBANCHÉ

U

UAXACTUN

Sylvanus Morley of the Carnegie Institution of Washington discovered the ancient Maya site of Uaxactun (17.4° N, 89.6° W) in 1916 (see also **Map 3**). He soon encountered a **stela** (upright stone monument) with the Long Count date 8.14.10.13.15, April 11, AD 328 (see also **Calendar**). Since this was the first monument with a cycle 8 glyph ever found, he named the site "Uaxactun" from the Maya *uaxac*, meaning "eight," and *tun*, meaning "stone." In addition to Morley, a number of notable Carnegie Institution archaeologists worked at the site, including Frans Blom, Oliver Ricketson, A. Ledyard Smith, and Edwin Shook. They led projects at Uaxactun in 1916 (Morley), 1924 (Blom), from 1926 to 1937 (Ricketson), in 1940 (Smith and Shook), and finally in 1974 (Shook). It was the first large-scale **architectural** excavation in the Maya region that combined artifact and **ceramic analysis** with **dating** and detailed interpretation of architectural chronology and site layout. Edith Bayles Ricketson was the first project ceramic analyst and produced a sequence that was later expanded upon by Robert Smith. The type-chronology that they developed influenced all subsequent Mesoamerican ceramic classifications for several decades.

Uaxactun is located within the Department of Petén, **Guatemala** approximately 19 km north of **Tikal**, amid a series of *bajos* (seasonally inundated swamps or wetlands) and *aguadas* (ponds that have been modified by humans). The site was first settled by 300 BC around a centrally located *aguada* and upon an artificially flattened hilltop. The architecture includes *sacbeob* (**causeways**), temples, plazas, sunken courts, a large number of carved stelae, and altars. Archaeologists also uncovered a number of caches of two flared ceramic vessels placed lip to lip, containing severed human skulls.

The site is best known for its E-Group, which was the first example found and has subsequently emerged as the prime example of an ancient Maya solar observatory; similar examples have been found at many sites (see also **Astronomy**; **Astronomical Observatories**). A large radial **pyramid**, known as E-VII sub, sits 50 m due west of an elongated terraced mound upon which sit three west-facing structures (E-1, E-II, and E-III). In the 1920s, Blom first noted that when viewing the three structures from E-VII sub during the annual solstices and equinoxes, the sun rose directly over the northernmost point of E-1, central point of E-II, or southernmost point of E-III, depending on the time of year. Additional research by Anthony Aveni and his colleagues has shown that during the Late

Formative and Early Classic transition (~200 BC–AD 400) this complex was likely used to mark significant events in the Maya solar calendar.

The most noteworthy historic event at Uaxactun was its defeat by neighboring **Tikal** in AD 378. The war was led by Siyaj K'ak', a king or general who is believed to have come from **Teotihuacán** in central Mexico and whose feats are recorded at several sites in the Petén. Upon the defeat of Uaxactun, a new king may have been installed, who introduced rituals and imagery from Teotihuacán into local Maya traditions. For the next two centuries, Tikal and Uaxactun dominated the region and continued their tradition of the erection of stela and the construction of temples and pyramids. Around AD 600, when Tikal and Teotihuacán went into decline, Uaxactun experienced a hiatus in which no new monuments or buildings were dedicated. However, by the Late Classic there appears to have been a population increase, and residents engaged in new construction and remodeling of older structures. This site was abandoned after AD 889, when the last monument was dedicated, coinciding with a general abandonment of the region (see also **Classic Maya Collapse**). Today, the ruins of Uaxactun lie within the protected nature preserve of Tikal National Park.

See also Classic Maya Collapse; Guatemala; Palace; Pyramid; San Bartolo; Sculpture; Wall Painting

Further Reading

Aveni, Anthony F., Anne S. Dowd, and Benjamin Vining. "Maya Calendar Reform? Evidence from Orientations of Specialized Architectural Assemblages." *Latin American Antiquity* 14, no. 2: 159–78, 2003.

Schele, Linda, and David Freidel. "A War of Conquest: Tikal against Uaxactun." In *A Forest of Kings: The Untold Story of the Ancient Maya*, 130–64. New York: William Morrow, 1990.

Smith, A. Ledyard. *Uaxactun, Guatemala: Excavations of 1931–1937.* Carnegie Institution of Washington, Publication 588. Washington, DC: Carnegie Institution of Washington, 1950.

■ JENNIFER P. MATHEWS

UNDERWATER ARCHAEOLOGY

Underwater Maya sites include land sites submerged by sea-level rise, as well as archaeological remains placed or lost in **cenotes** (sinkholes), **lakes**, or rivers. Submerged sites often have excellent preservation of organic material, including bone and wood, which normally decay in the tropical landscape. According to the story of Maya creation in the *Popol Vuh* and depicted in scenes on painted pottery and stone carvings from the Classic period (AD 300–900), water bodies were sacred (see also **Ceramics**; **Sculpture**). The sea was equated with the underworld. A wide variety of offerings have been recovered from the Cenote of Sacrifice at **Chichen Itza**, as well as from other cenotes in the Yucatan Peninsula of **Mexico** and **Belize**. Some **caves** with archaeological material also contain underwater sections, underscoring the ideological correspondence of caves, cenotes, and the underworld to the ancient Maya.

The sacred Cenote of Sacrifice at Chichen Itza was dredged in the early part of the twentieth century by Edward Thompson. The material found included wooden scepters (figurines), gold and copper artifacts, jadeite, and other exotic and highly crafted objects, now stored at Harvard University (see also **Portable Objects**). In addition, Thompson's dredging recovered skeletal remains. The human skeletal remains as well as the objects were interpreted as offerings. Mexican government archaeologists, led by Pilar Luna of the Instituto Nacional de Antropología e Historia (INAH), have investigated cenotes throughout the Yucatan Peninsula. Underwater archaeologist Guillermo de Anda from the University of Yucatan has led teams diving in cenotes in the Yucatan with support from National Geographic. Sac Actun near the Maya site of **Tulum** is the longest recorded underwater cave system in the world (measuring 230 km), where divers have recovered a human skull and mastodon bone, providing tantalizing clues to early settlement. The Cara Blanca cenote in **Belize** was investigated by Lisa Lucero of the University of Illinois. The team of scuba divers found carved stone, bone, and wood in the main cenote beside a Maya settlement.

Ancient Maya sites in low-lying coastal areas were subject to sea-level rise up to 2 m since the end of the Classic period. Submerged archaeological deposits at coastal sites around the Yucatan Peninsula are found at Isla Cerritos, **Cerros**, Moho Cay (near Belize River), Wild Cane Cay, Frenchman's Cay, Pork and Doughboy Point, and other sites in southern Belize. In cases where the archaeological deposits are below the water table on land sites, regular excavation techniques are used, as at Wild Cane Cay. A series of 172 shovel test excavations (using a shovel to remove sediment in 20-cm levels and sieve through screens) were carried out in the water offshore of Wild Cane Cay, yielding submerged archaeological deposits below the seafloor.

Underwater sites discovered in a shallow coastal lagoon in Paynes Creek National Park in southern Belize are a good example of underwater archaeological techniques as well as the exceptional preservation of organic remains. The sites were submerged by sea-level rise after they were abandoned about AD 900. Snorkeling side by side on research flotation devices, archaeologists traversed the lagoon to locate and mark artifacts on the seafloor. The seafloor was composed of red mangrove (*Rhizophora mangle*) peat (organic debris) accumulated during sea-level rise that buried the sites. The peat also provided an oxygen-free sediment for preservation of thousands of wooden posts of buildings—the only well-preserved remains of ancient Maya wooden buildings. Underwater sites present problems for preserving waterlogged material, which begins to decay when exposed to air. The Paynes Creek material was desalinated, with selected wooden artifacts preserved by Wayne Smith at Texas A & M University using a polymer process.

The site of Samabaj in Lake Atitlan was an island that was rapidly submerged under 15 m of water by volcanic or tectonic activity. The Classic period site has stone architecture and other materials that are only accessible by experienced divers. Archaeologist Sonia Medrano led the diving teams on the project.

Underwater archaeology holds promise for recovering more intact, well-preserved organic material to extend interpretations of the ancient Maya, better known by stone temples, pottery, and stone tools.

See also ART; BURIALS; CHAC II; COCHUAH REGION; DEITIES; DROUGHT; GEOLOGY; HOUSE-HOLD PRODUCTION; LAKES; MAYAPÁN; MUYIL; OXKINTOK; RELIGION; XCOCH

Further Reading

Esteban Amador, Fabio. *Skulls in Underwater Cave May Be Earliest Trace of First Americans*. National Geographic Society, 2011. http://newswatch.nationalgeographic.com/2011/02/18/skull_in_mex ico_cave_may_be_oldest_american_found/.

McKillop, Heather. "Underwater Archaeology, Salt Production, and Coastal Maya Trade at Stingray Lagoon, Belize." *Latin American Antiquity* 6, no. 3: 214–28, 1995.

———. *Salt, White Gold of the Ancient Maya*. Gainesville: University Press of Florida, 2002.

———. "Mapping Ancient Maya Wooden Architecture on the Sea Floor, Belize." *Underwater Archaeology Proceedings*, 277–86, 2009.

■ H E A T H E R   M C K I L L O P

UTATLÁN/Q'UM'ARKAJ

The archaeological site of Utatlán (15.0° N, 91.2° W) was the Quiché Maya capital in the Late Postclassic (see also **Map 3**). Its proper name in the Quiché language, Q'um'arkaj, translates literally as "Rotten Cane." It is 2 km from Santa Cruz. The Quiché ruled one of the most powerful states in highland **Guatemala** at the time of the Spanish conquest. Their capital embodied their power and replicated their cosmology, **religion**, and social structure in the architecture there. The site was occupied during the Late Postclassic period until it was abandoned after the Spanish conquest.

The ***Popol Vuh***, with its oft-told Maya creation story, and other Colonial documents supply extensive information about the site and the social and political organization of the Quiché who lived there. Those ethnohistorical accounts have permitted more detailed interpretations of the site, its **architecture**, and layout than are normally possible for **Mesoamerican** archaeological sites. Furthermore, because of the nature of the historical sources, the interpretations can often incorporate much of the original native worldview. The site has been investigated several times by archaeologists, beginning in the 1940s by Robert Wauchope of the Middle American Research Institute at Tulane University. The most intensive investigations were conducted in the 1970s by the State University of New York at Albany under the direction of Robert Carmack. Raquel Macario and the team from the Q'um'arkaj Ethnoarchaeological Project conducted additional important investigations at the site from 2003 to 2006.

Further Reading

Brown, Kenneth L. "Postclassic Relationships between the Highland and Lowland Maya." In *The Lowland Maya Postclassic*, edited by Arlen F. Chase and Prudence M. Rice, 270–81. Austin: University of Texas Press, 1985.

Carmack, Robert M. *The Quiché Mayas of Utatlán: The Evolution of a Highland Guatemala Kingdom*. Norman: University of Oklahoma Press, 1981.

Fox, John W. *Quiche Conquest: Centralism and Regionalism in Highland Guatemalan State Development*. Albuquerque: University of New Mexico Press, 1978.

———. "The Lords of the Night versus the Lords of Dark: The Postclassic Highland Maya ballgame." In *The Mesoamerican Ballgame: International Ballgame Symposium: Selected Papers*, edited by Vernon L. Scarborough and David R. Wilcox, 213–38. Tucson: University of Arizona Press, 1991.

Laporte, Juan Pedro, Bárbara Arroyo, and Héctor E. Mejía, eds. *XX Simposio de Investigaciones Arqueológicas en Guatemala, 2006.* Guatemala City: Museo Nacional de Arqueología y Etnología, Guatemala, 2007.

Macario, Raquel, Yvonne Putzeys, Marie Fulbert, Edgar Telón, Edgar Ortega, Jorge Cáceres, Juan Manuel Palomo, Sandra Carrillo, Luis I. Pérez, Manuel Colón, Rafael Cambranes, and Karla Cardona. *Proyecto Etnoarqueológico Q'um'arkaj, Quiché, Guatemala.* Museo Nacional de Arqueología y Etnología, Guatemala, 2007. http://www.asociaciontikal.com/pdf/57_-_Macario.pdf.

■ CLIFFORD T. BROWN AND WALTER R. T. WITSCHEY

UXMAL

Uxmal (20.4° N, 89.8° W), possibly from Maya *oxmal*, meaning "thrice built," is one of the largest pre-Columbian sites in the Puuc region of the northwestern Yucatan peninsula (see also **Map 3**). It is located some 80 km south-southwest of Mérida, **Mexico**, the current capital of Yucatan State. Uxmal's principal occupation and major **architectural** expansion corresponds to the Terminal to Early Postclassic periods (ca. AD 800–950/1000), with evidence for minor earlier habitations.

According to Maya ethnohistorical sources (i.e., the books of Chilam Balam of Chumayel, Mani, and Tizimin), Uxmal was founded by the ruler Aj Kuy Tok' ("He of the owl flint"; perhaps also known as Hun Witzil Chahk, "First Raingod of the hill country" of the Xiu lineage in a *k'atun* 2 Ajaw; see also **Calendar**). In these sources, historic events, blended with myth or legend, and perhaps manipulated for prophetic and political purposes, were presented within a framework of successive 20-year *k'atuns*, each named for the numbered day *Ajaw* on which it ended. Sylvanus G. Morley and Alfredo Barrera Vásquez earlier placed this *k'atun* date for the city's "foundation" between AD 987 and 1007, but more recent interpretations by Linda Schele and Peter Mathews put it between AD 731 and 751, a timing in better accord with archaeological evidence.

The Puuc region, an area of isolated limestone hills south of the long ridge of hills known as the Puuc (or *serranía de Ticul*), is known for its distinctive, expertly constructed, and visually striking Late to Terminal Classic **architecture**. Elite "**Puuc architectural style**" buildings feature lime concrete and rubble cores, sheathed in sharply cut and relatively thin facing stones. The latest Puuc structures, such as the House of the Governor and the Nunnery Quadrangle **palaces** at Uxmal, have specialized "boot-shaped" vault stones with sloping soffit faces and "toes" anchored into the vaulted roof core. Puuc upper façades (and occasionally lower walls) often bear complex sculptural programs, composed of hundreds of precut and carved stone elements arranged to form geometric-symbolic patterns, including angular step-frets, simple "mat-weave," and complex textile-based "lattice" designs, and colonnettes, as well as long-snouted mask panels (representing either the Yucatec rain god *Chahk* or personified mountain *Witz* monsters) and human figures.

Settlement studies conducted by Nicholas Dunning have identified a regional site hierarchy in the Eastern (Santa Elena) Puuc region. These data suggest that during the late ninth- to early tenth-century reign of the ruler Chan Chahk K'ak'nal Ajaw ("Lord Chahk"), Uxmal emerged as this area's largest city, surpassing other regional centers in population and political power. Kowalski and Dunning identify it as the capital of a regional state, perhaps confederated with **Kabah and Nohpat**, nearby large centers linked to Uxmal via a *sacbe* (raised road, **causeway**). This king's name glyph and titles appear on hieroglyphic rings of Uxmal's Main **Ball Court** (AD 905), a painted capstone from the Nunnery Quadrangle (AD 907), Altar 10 (on which he bears a *K'uhul Ajaw* or "sacred lineage lord" title), and **Stela** 14, which originally stood with other stelae on a separate platform.

At its peak around AD 850–925, Uxmal covered about 8 km², with a walled precinct containing ample plazas and monumental architecture occupying massive platforms forming its civic-ceremonial core. There is evidence for significant occupation prior to Chan Chahk K'ak'nal Ajaw's reign, indicated by several eighth-century **Chenes-style** buildings underlying the platform of the House of the Governor, and by the Pigeons Group, an earlier ninth-century acropolis-like courtyard complex named for the open-work roof-comb of the palace range known as The House of the Pigeons. An imposing **pyramid**-temple, the Adivino or Pyramid of the Magician, was built in stages. Two inner pyramid-temples (ca. AD 750–850), perhaps coeval with an adjacent courtyard including the House of the Birds, were later covered by a massive pyramidal platform with rounded ends. This pyramid's western stairway conducts to a temple with a dragon mouth doorway flanked by stacked *Witz* masks, marking this as a cave portal to a sacred creation mountain. The uppermost temple, bearing a complex geometric façade, was reached by narrow stairs flanking the western dragon mouth temple and a majestic eastern stairway.

Several of Uxmal's most imposing architectural projects, including the Nunnery Quadrangle and the House of the Governor, to use the names given them by early Spanish chroniclers, were built during Chan Chahk K'ak'nal Ajaw's reign. The Nunnery Quadrangle (ca. AD 895 to 907) consists of four imposing vaulted palace ranges framing a broad courtyard, entered through a tall southern portal vault. According to William Ringle, the Nunnery's monumental scale, formality, and iconography mark it as an administrative/ritual complex, whose vaulted ranges housed various royal councils (see also **Council House**; **Rites and Rituals**). Such sociopolitical functions were embedded in sacred space, with the Nunnery's quadrangular layout mirroring the quadripartite horizontal organization of the Maya cosmos. Important aspects of its sculptural **iconography** (e.g., feathered serpents, Pawahtuns, a jaguar throne) are associated with creation mythology that sanctioned divinely ordained political authority (see also ***Popol Vuh***).

The House of the Governor (ca. AD 900) is a grandiose, 100-m-long vaulted palace that perhaps combined royal residential and administrative functions (see figure 49). A complex array of architectural sculpture, including "mat weave" latticework, step frets, and long-snouted *Chahk* (rain god) or *Witz* masks, and a series of seated human figures adorns its eastern upper façade. The largest figure, seated above the central doorway and wearing an immense feather headdress, was likely a portrait of Chan Chahk K'aknal Ajaw. Flanking him are smaller subsidiary lords, implying that the building's long central rooms housed council meetings or royal receptions.

Sometime in the tenth century, after Chan Chahk K'ak'nal's rule, Uxmal's political organization disintegrated, perhaps due to intensifying **drought** and/or competition with **Chichen Itza**. Pieces of its monumental Puuc buildings were reused in shoddily constructed structures occupied by Postclassic period inhabitants, and the Xiu lineage of the Late Postclassic city of **Mayapán** claimed the ancient city of Uxmal as their ancestral home long after its abandonment.

Figure 49. Uxmal. The House of the Governor is a 100-m-long palace with a stunning façade in the Puuc architectural style. It was likely commissioned by Chan Chahk K'aknal Ajaw, ruling ca. AD 900. Courtesy of Jeff Kowalski.

See also ALLIANCES; ASTRONOMICAL OBSERVATORIES; FORTIFICATIONS; HOUSES; ICONOGRAPHY; KIUIC; NORTHERN LOWLANDS; OXKINTOK; PROSKOURIAKOFF, TATIANA AVENIROVNA; RITES AND RITUALS; SAYIL; SETTLEMENT PATTERNS (NORTHERN LOWLANDS); TERRITORIAL ENTITIES; TIHO; TRADE ROUTES; WARFARE, WARRIORS, AND WEAPONS; WATER MANAGEMENT; XCOCH

Further Reading

Foncerrada Molina, Marta. *La escultura arquitectónica de Uxmal*. México, D.F.: Universidad Nacional Autónoma de México, 1965.

Kowalski, Jeff Karl. *The House of the Governor: A Maya Palace at Uxmal, Yucatan, Mexico*. Norman: University of Oklahoma Press, 1987.

Kowalski, Jeff K., and Nicholas P. Dunning. "The Architecture of Uxmal: The Symbolics of Statemaking at a Puuc Maya Regional Capital." In *Mesoamerican Architecture as a Cultural Symbol*, edited by Jeff K. Kowalski. Oxford: Oxford University Press, 1999.

Ringle, William M. "The Nunnery Quadrangle of Uxmal." In *The Ancient Maya of Mexico: Reinterpreting the Past of the Northern Maya*, edited by Geoffrey E. Braswell, 189–226. Bristol, CT: Equinox Publishing Ltd., 2012.

Schele, Linda, and Peter Mathews. *The Code of Kings: The Language of Seven Sacred Maya Temples and Tombs*. New York: Scribner/Simon & Schuster, 1998.

■ JEFF KOWALSKI

V

VEGETATION

The ancient Maya lived in a mosaic of forest, savanna, wetland, and managed vegetation. This vegetation mosaic reflected differences in rainfall, **soil**, topography, and ancient Maya land use (see also **Maps 2, 5, 6, 7, and 8; Geology**). Understanding the mosaic is crucial to understanding the Maya; how the Maya used the mosaic may explain their success— and their failure. This article describes the present vegetation mosaic, the possible ancient Maya mosaic, and the link between ancient and present.

Lowland forest (~0–600 m asl) dominated the mosaic when the Maya entered the region. This pre-Maya forest was likely similar to the old-growth forest in the area today, except that the abundances of certain tree species in today's forest reflect ancient Maya land use. From north to south in the lowlands today, rainfall increases (~500 to 3,000 mm per year, but wetter in the west, e.g., **Palenque**), dry season length decreases, and soil depth increases. These gradients support increasingly tall, increasingly evergreen, and increasingly species-rich forests (e.g., from ca. 48 to 91 tree species $\geq$ 10 cm diameter per ha, north to south in **Belize**).

The dry forests of the **Northern Lowlands** have a high density of mainly small trees (5–15 m high) with small or compound leaves (leaf composed of small leaflets), or succulent leaves or stems (e.g., Cactaceae). Many species are deciduous in the dry season. As in most forests, a few tree species are common, and many species are rare, and the common and rare species may change from place to place. (Table 2 lists tree species for vegetation types.)

Table 2.   Vegetation in the Maya Area

Vegetation Type	Scientific Name	Common Name
Northern dry forest		
	Acacia spp.	—
	Bursera simaruba	gumbo limbo
	Coccoloba spp.	—
	Drypetes lateriflora	—
	Gymnopodium floribundum	bastard logwood
	Lsysiloma latislaquum	salóm
	Manilkara zapota	chicle
	Metopium brownei	chechem
	Piscidia piscipula	jabín
	Thouinia paucidentata	dzol
	Vitex gaumeri	yashnik
	Caesalpinia gaumeri	bastard logwood
Midlatitude moist forest[1]		
	Alseis yucatanensis	manzanillo
	Aspidosperma cruentum	milady
	Attalea cohune (palm)	cohune
	Brosimum alicastrum[2]	ramón, breadnut
	Cryosophila stauracantha (palm)	escoba
	Drypetes brownii	bullhoof
	Manilkara zapota	chicle, sapote, zapotillo
	Melicoccus oliviformis[b]	guaya
	Pouteria campechiana	mammee ciruela
	Pouteria reticulata[3]	zapotillo
	Protium copal	copal
	Pseudolmedia spuria	cherry
	Sabal mauritiiformis (palm)	botán
	Swietenia macrophylla	caoba, mahogany
Southern wet forest[4]		
	Astrocaryum mexicanum (palm)	lancetillo
	Dialium guianense	ironwood
	Guarea glabra	cramante
	Nectandra lundellii	timbersweet
	Poulsenia armata	chi-chi-costé
	Protium schippii	copal
	Quararibea funebris	bastidos
	Virola koschnyi	banak
Riparian forest		
	Schzolobium parahybum	quamwood
	Bucida buceras	pucte
	Cassia grandis	bookut
	Enterolobium cyclocarpum	guanacaste
	Roystonea oleracea	palma real
Swamp (*bajo*)		
	Byrsonima bucidaefolia	crabboo
	Coccoloba reflexiflora	wild grape
	Croton spp.	—
	Eugenia rhombea	—
	Gymnopodium floribundum	bastard logwood
	Haematoxylon campechianum	tintal

Vegetation Type	Scientific Name	Common Name
Secondary forest, gaps, edges		
	Cecropia peltata	yagrumo
	Cedrela odorata	Spanish cedar
	Ceiba pentandra	ceiba
	Dendropanax arboreus	mano de león
	Gliricidia sepium	madre cacao
	Guazuma ulmifolia	guacimo
	Spondias mombin	jobo
	Trichospermum grewiifolium	moho
Montane forest		
	Abies spp.	fir
	Alnus sp.	alder
	Cupressus spp.	cypress
	Liquidambar styraciflua	—
	Pinus spp.	pino
	Quercus spp.	roble
Savanna		
	Acoelorraphe wrightii	palmetto
	Byrsonima crassifolia	nance
	Crescentia cujete	calabash
	Curatella americana	craboo
	Pinus caribea	pino
	Quercus oleoides	roble, oak

Note: Some abundant, characteristic, or noteworthy tree species in the Maya region. Note that there are many more tree species in the Maya region than are listed here, that species abundances vary site-to-site, and that multiple common names exist for most species.

1. Plus many species also found in dry forest.
2. Common on Maya ruins.
3. The most abundant tree species (stems ≥ 10 cm diameter) at Tikal and at La Milpa, Belize.
4. Plus most species found in moist forest.

Farther south in the **Central Lowlands** (e.g., **Tikal**), the moist, taller (15–25 m) forests exhibit more complex structure. In addition to numerous tree species, there are many species of shrubs, lianas (woody vines), and epiphytes (plants growing on other plants), such as Orchidaceae (orchids), Bromeliaceae (bromeliads), and bryophytes (mosses). Stranglers (trees that germinate on and grow around other trees) are present. In these moist forests about 5–25 percent of the species and individuals are deciduous in the dry season. The southernmost lowland forests are wetter and taller (25–35 m) than the moist forests, with some trees reaching 50 m. The wet forests are more "luxuriant," with more epiphytes and tall, perennial herbs, including Heliconiaceae (heliconias), Marantaceae (arrowroots), and Zingiberaceae (gingers). Wet forests may be almost completely evergreen. Hurricanes alter forest structure and open the canopy, allowing colonization by light-demanding species. Hurricanes, however, tend to stabilize species composition, as common tree species generally survive best.

The highland forests (> ~600 m asl) of **Guatemala** and southern **Mexico** vary according to elevation, soil, slope, and slope aspect. A mix of broadleaf tree species and conifers gives way to pure conifers at the highest elevations. Many highland plant genera are shared with the temperate zone.

Other vegetation types include savannas and wetlands. Savannas are grasslands with trees, scattered or in patches. Savannas typically occur in areas of sandy, nutrient-poor soils and may flood in the wet season and burn in the dry season. Wetlands are areas with standing water part of the year. Swamps are wetlands dominated by woody plants. Mangrove swamps occur along coasts and river mouths. Here trees can reach 30 m, and the understory may be bare mud or have stands of tall ferns. Inland, swamps are found along rivers or in poorly drained depressions. The depressions include *tintales*, or **bajos**, with short trees and dense stems. *Bajos* may be flooded in the wet season. Their dry season soils are damp, but the clayey soil holds the water so tightly that it is hardly available to plants. This stressful environment supports a distinctive flora. High light penetration in *bajos* supports a Cyperaceae (sedge) ground layer in places. Marshes are wetlands dominated by herbaceous plants, including Poaceae (grasses), Cyperaceae (sedges), and Juncaceae (rushes), with occasional woody plants.

The vegetation mosaic is less discrete than the above description suggests. There are gradual transitions, blending vegetation types. Forest types change locally, reflecting soil variation and the strong, valley-to-ridge soil and moisture gradient. In forest valleys there are riparian (riverside) forests on rich alluvial soils, with a distinctive flora of large trees; in savannas there are species-rich "gallery" forests bordering streams. The mosaic is intricate in places, mingling forest, savanna, and wetland.

The ancient Maya changed the natural vegetation to what some say was a deftly managed and productive "managed mosaic" that fueled the Maya civilization. The intricate mosaic of soil types, slope, and moisture could have supported an intricate variety of land uses. Former forest areas could have supported fields for various crops, terraced slopes, and areas in early stages of regrowth after clearing (secondary forest) (see also **Subsistence**; **Terracing**). The regrowth was probably managed for useful, colonizing tree species, as found on forest edges, in gaps in old forest, and in the large areas of secondary forest today. There may have been orchards (plantations of one or a few tree species). There were surely kitchen gardens, rich in useful species of herbs, shrubs, lianas, and trees. These probably resembled the species-rich Maya household gardens (*solares*) of today. Patches of old-growth forest likely persisted in the mosaic. The ancient Maya also farmed wetlands, by controlling soil and water levels (see also **Water Management**).

Maya land use would have had strong effects on the vegetation that regrew after the collapse and in places has matured and persisted undisturbed to the present (see also **Classic Maya Collapse**). The Maya changed soil and topography, built lasting structures, and cultivated certain tree species, giving those species a lasting advantage through the centuries of regrowth. Geo-archaeology reveals substantial erosion of soil from hills to valley bottoms during the Maya zenith, which may have decreased farming output and is why some argue that environmental degradation contributed to the Maya collapse. In any case, given the species-specific requirements of trees for particular soil characteristics, this soil erosion suggests that pre- and post-Maya spatial distributions of many tree species would be different. Likewise, the effects of ancient alteration of wetlands should be seen in today's wetland flora. It is also clear that Maya buildings, terraces, **causeways**, canals, and reservoirs created distinctive substrates that now support distinctive sets of tree species after natural regrowth of forest. Less clear is how ancient cultivation of certain plant species has shaped today's forest composition. At some forest sites today certain tree species probably dominate because the ancient Maya cultivated them. At other sites, most of the dominant species are not especially useful.

Sophisticated use of the vegetation mosaic supported ancient Maya civilization. Overuse may explain its decline. The vegetation post-Maya is resource rich, but whether it is richer or poorer than it was pre-Maya is unknown. In our era of global change, ancient Maya land use and its legacy are lessons for the modern world.

See also AGUADAS; BAJOS; CAUSEWAY/SACBE; EL PILAR; GROUND SURVEY TECHNIQUES; KOMCHEN; LiDAR; NORTHERN LOWLANDS; SAN BARTOLO; SETTLEMENT PATTERNS (CENTRAL LOWLANDS); SOILS; SUBSISTENCE

Further Reading

Fedick, Scott L., ed. *The Managed Mosaic: Ancient Maya Agriculture and Resource Use*. Salt Lake City: University of Utah Press, 1996.

Gómez-Pompa, Arturo, Michael F. Allen, Scott L. Fedick, and Juan J. Jiménez-Osornio, eds. *The Lowland Maya Area: Three Millennia at the Human-Wildland Interface*. Binghamton, NY: Food Products Press, 2003.

Hayashida, Frances M. "Archaeology, Ecological History, and Conservation." *Annual Review of Anthropology* 34: 43–65, 2005.

Ross, Nanci J. "Modern Tree Species Composition Reflects Ancient Maya 'Forest gardens' in northwest Belize." *Ecological Applications* 21, no. 1: 75–84, 2011.

Schulze, Mark D., and David F. Whitacre. "A Classification and Ordination of the Tree Community of Tikal National Park, Petén, Guatemala." *Bulletin of the Florida Museum of Natural History* 41: 169–297, 1999.

White, D. A., and C. S. Hood. "Vegetation Patterns and Environmental Gradients in Tropical Dry Forests of the Northern Yucatan Peninsula." *Journal of Vegetation Science* 15, no. 2: 151–60, 2004.

■ NICHOLAS BROKAW AND SHEILA E. WARD

W

WAKA'

See EL PERÚ-WAKA'

WALL PAINTING

For the Maya, painting was a critical medium: they painted books (**codices**), **ceramics**, and walls; they coated **sculpture**, both three-dimensional and low relief, with paint; and they painted their buildings. Maya artists wrote; they sketched; they took up pens and brushes to master calligraphy and paint; they were skilled at paper and pigment-making. Painting was for the living and the dead, to be viewed both at a distance and in the quiet privacy of the tomb.

The earliest wall paintings to survive reveal a painting tradition confident in both style and subject at **San Bartolo**, **Guatemala**, securely dated to 100 BC. There, within a building known as Pinturas, narrative scenes wrap around the upper interior walls. First discovered (2001) was the north wall, which depicts the Maize God honored by four maize maidens; three male attendants offer him thrones and a calabash, all atop a double-headed serpent marked with footprints. At left four bloody babies erupt from an enormous calabash, while a clothed youth emerges last. The face of the Maize God—who reappears in various scenes across the walls--bears marked **Olmec** influence. An enthroned lord is crowned as ruler on the west wall, just at the join with north. On the west wall, five standing lords draw blood from the penis in front of sequential trees, bird **deities**, and sacrificial offerings, further evidence of complex sacred narratives that would be familiar to indigenous culture 1,600 years later, at the time of the Spanish invasion (see also **Religion**).

Fragments at **Tikal** and **Uaxactun** suggest a continuing wall painting tradition, but little is known until tomb paintings appear at Tikal and **Rio Azul** in the fifth century, where dated inscriptions note deaths and **burials** in beautiful monochromatic schemes. An elaborate polychrome mural with a 260-day count running underneath it was discovered at **Uaxactun** as the excavation season closed in 1937, just long enough for a copy to be made; it was gone the following year (see also **Calendar**). In the painting, women gather around an empty throne within a house; processions and musicians form tight lines; two important men at larger scale greet one another (see also **Music and Dance**). The artist's work demonstrates an ease of representing crowded bodies in space that would not appear in carved stone for 150 years.

The Maya murals at **Calakmul** offer the rare example of a building whose exterior setbacks were fully articulated with colorful murals meant to be seen at a distance, with figures larger than life against a white ground and oversized, brief inscriptions. Probably painted in the seventh century, when the lords of Calakmul were at the height of their power and wealth, the murals depict purveyors of humble goods—tamales, *atole*, and gruel—alongside the luxuries of snuff, tobacco, and salt. Brilliant pigments, including the transparent blue dress of a powerful female figure, bring the figures to life (see also **Divine Kings and Queens**; **Maya Queens**; **Women, Men, and Gender Roles**). All this wealth on display vanished; within a few years, the paintings were covered up.

Traces of paint remain in evidence in vaults and on walls across the **Yaxchilan** region, along with thick application of paint on wall panels and lintels. Structure 1 at **Bonampak** of the late eighth century houses the most complete and complex program to survive from the first millennium, and traces even survive of the external stucco program, which included painted seated figures and victorious warriors with captives (see also **Warfare, Warriors, and Weapons**); below the molding and the lintels a long text of at least 125 glyphs ran across the entire front façade. Ties for curtains, to protect the interior paintings, were built into both the inside and outside of the building.

Other paintings of the first millennium that have come to light since 1990 include painted tombs at **Palenque** and **Caracol**, and murals at **Cival**, **Ek Balam** (including many painted vault capstones), and Xultun, where a small building discovered in 2012 was found to include inscriptions noting the lunar calendar and calculations using ring numbers, otherwise known only from painted books made centuries later. Kneeling attendants in black body paint address a seated ruler depicted in bright colors.

Ninth- and tenth-century painters worked in the Puuc region, with well-preserved examples at Mul-Chic and Chacmultun, sustaining earlier traditions to the south; tenth- and eleventh-century painters worked at **Chichen Itza**, establishing new subject matter and style.

The best-preserved and most complete Chichen Itza paintings are known from the Temple of the Warriors, now destroyed, and its "fossil" temple buried within, the Temple of the Chacmool, along with the Upper Temple of the Jaguars, extant, although in poor condition. (See figure 50.) Two extensive scenes record conquering warriors at the water's edge; victors set houses on fire while green feathered serpents rise up. In the Upper Temple of the Jaguars, painted panels of two larger-than-life warriors, one wrapped within a feathered serpent and one with emanating solar rays, face the doorway. Detailed battle scenes with distinctive settings include hundreds of warriors, all on a diminutive scale.

In the last decades before the Spanish invasion, Maya painters worked at **Mayapan**, **Iximché**, Tancah, Santa Rita, and **Tulum**, where painting style adhered to the restricted body conventions known in Central Mexico in the same era. Although usually characterized by rich use of Maya blue pigments, the palette was highly limited overall. Against a stunning blue background, one Tulum painting in black, white, and blue features four dancing *Chahks*, or rain gods, who prepare to sacrifice a young Maize God. Set inside a small structure at the site, this didactic narrative harkens back to the sacred story that

Figure 50. Illustration of a wall painting from the Temple of the Warriors, Chichen Itza, by Ann Axtell Morris. A raided village and procession of victors and captives. Photo courtesy Mary Miller after Plate 130 in Earl Halstead Morris, Jean Charlot, and Ann Axtell Morris, *The Temple of the Warriors at Chichen Itzá, Yucatan* (2 vols., Washington, DC: Carnegie Institution of Washington, 1931). Photo by Mary Miller of an illustration in a book that is deliberately not copyrighted: CIW 1931.

early Maya painters had painted on the walls of San Bartolo at least 1,500 years earlier. For Maya painters, innovation of style and subject matter was simultaneously grounded in continuity of belief.

See also ART; BALL GAME/BALL COURT; CODEX-STYLE VASES; CRAFT SPECIALIZATION; WRITING SYSTEMS OF MESOAMERICA

Further Reading

de la Fuente, Beatriz, and Leticia Staines Cicero. *La pintura mural prehispánica en México II: Área Maya.* Tomo III, *Estudios.* México, D.F.: Universidad Nacional Autónoma de México, Instituto de Investigaciones Estéticas, 2001.

Miller, Mary Ellen, and Megan Eileen O'Neil. *Maya Art and Architecture.* 2nd ed. London: Thames & Hudson, 2014.

Saturno, William A., Karl Taube, and David Stuart. *The Murals of San Bartolo, El Petén, Guatemala.* Pt. 1, *The North Wall.* Ancient America, no. 7. Barnardsville, NC: Center for Ancient American Studies, 2005.

Taube, Karl A., William A. Saturno, David Stuart, Heather Hurst, and Joel Skidmore. *The Murals of San Bartolo, El Petén, Guatemala.* Pt. 2, *The West Wall.* Ancient America, no. 11. Barnardsville, NC: Boundary End Archaeology Research Center, 2010.

■ MARY MILLER

WARFARE, WARRIORS, AND WEAPONS

Large-scale archaeological investigations, epigraphic **decipherments**, and **iconographic** studies since the 1960s have shattered the older notions of the Classic Maya as a basically peaceful people. Classic Maya warfare was fought mainly by elites; that is, the rulers and elite scribes/artists were also warriors. Classic Maya elites were involved in hand-to-hand combat mainly with handheld spear points and, to a smaller degree, *atlatl* darts. Classic Maya warfare was aimed at political and economic profit, but critically, not expansion of distant territory per se. Direct (as opposed to hegemonic) territorial control was possible for some large Maya polities within a 60-km marching radius. The main goal of Classic Maya warfare was to take captives for expanding access to **tribute** and wealth as well as for seeking power and prestige. Once the rival was captured, he lost honor and became a "captive." Epigraphic records indicate that military achievements of Classic Maya warriors were measured mainly in terms of being the captors of prominent enemies and the number of captives they had taken. Marriage **alliances** were another alternative to expand access to wealth and prestige.

Both epigraphic and archaeological records clearly show that fortunes of Classic Maya dynasties were associated with influential warfare (see also **Dynastic Sequences**). **Tikal**'s twenty-sixth ruler Jasaw Chan K'awiil defeated the **Calakmul** ruler Yich'aak K'ahk' in AD 695. Calakmul's golden age came to an end. In contrast, the Tikal dynasty regained the upper hand over Calakmul dynasty. **Copán**'s thirteenth ruler Waxaklajuun Ubaah K'awiil was captured in battle and killed by a subordinate lord of neighboring **Quiriguá**, K'ahk' Chan Yopaat, in AD 738. K'ahk' Chan Yopaat won Quirigua's political independence; sponsored the construction of several new buildings; and created an impressive public space for stone monuments, including several of the largest carved **stelae** ever erected by the Maya. The Copán dynasty weathered this critical period and was to prosper for nearly a century after the disastrous defeat of Waxaklajuun Ubaah K'awiil. Iconographic evidence, such as wall murals at **Bonampak**, shows the capture of Classic Maya scribes and the custom of breaking their fingers during warfare of destruction. Thus, both the rulers and elite scribe/warriors who produced texts, through which the rulers asserted and displayed power, were targeted by the enemies.

In addition to inscriptions and iconography, potentially useful evidence for warfare in the archaeological record includes **fortifications** (walls and moats), weapons, human skeletal remains with signs of war-related trauma, incidents of violent destruction, settlement shifts to higher locations, and sudden disruption of cultural patterns (such as changes in **ceramic** styles). Although fortifications remained rare until the end of the Late Classic period, defensive features were present at some cities such as **Becan**, **El Mirador**, **Edzna**, and **Cerros** during the Late Preclassic period. The burning and destruction of public architecture about 650 BC at Blackman Eddy (which was strategically located on a hilltop) is similar to patterns of desecratory termination rituals related to warfare as seen at **Aguateca**, **Yaxuná**, Colha, and **Cerros**. Late Preclassic mass burials at Cuello appear to be those of sacrificed male captives of military age. Most Classic cities were located in easily accessible terrain without fortifications and generally lack clear evidence of destruction resulting from battles. While most combat probably took place in areas outside of major settlements, the epicenters of some cities such as Aguateca and Yaxna were attacked and burned. Limited wars were socially and politically disruptive.

The archaeological investigations in the Petexbatún region of Guatemala have provided the best evidence for intensive warfare, which was certainly the direct cause of the fall of the Petexbatún kingdoms in the late eight and early ninth centuries, although this process is not necessarily applicable to other parts of the Maya lowlands. Aguateca probably served as the primary center of the **Dos Pilas**/Aguateca dynasty after the fall of its twin capital, Dos Pilas, at a time of endemic regional warfare in the late eighth century. This warfare was not caused by malnutrition or ecological catastrophe. Aguateca occupied a highly defensible location on the top of a steep, 90-m escarpment. Defensive walls over 4 km long were constructed in a hasty manner in the Aguateca center toward the end of the Late Classic period. Its epicenter was burned down during an attack by its enemy around AD 810. Concentrations of small **chert** bifacial thinning flakes were found in some elite residences in the epicenter of Aguateca, suggesting that some elite household members manufactured chert spear and dart points in or near their residences. Some 30 to 40 broken chert spear or dart points were found in each of the residences of elite scribes/artists and the royal **palace**, indicating that elite residents of the central part did engage fiercely in battle but then finally fled or were taken as captives, leaving most of their belongings behind. The enemy conducted the desecratory termination rituals of the Palace Group, but did not stay long at Aguateca. The areas outside the epicenter were abandoned shortly after the destruction of the epicenter, and the commoners were probably forced to leave. Thus, the aim of the enemy was not to conquer or subjugate this city, but to terminate it as a political and economic power.

In the **northern** Maya **lowlands**, cities such as **Uxmal**, **Chunchucmil**, Yaxna, and **Ek Balam** were fortified during the Late and Terminal Classic periods, while a substantial number of cities did not show any defensive features. Warfare was associated with the development of **Chichen Itza**. Excavations at **Yaxuná** provided evidence that forces allied with or from nearby Chichen Itza attacked and burned the epicenter of Yaxuná during the tenth century, including a defensive tower, stone wall foundations suitable for wooden palisades comparable to the fortifications at Dos Pilas and Aguateca, ritually destroyed buildings, and the appearance of distinctive ceramics of the Sotuta sphere associated with Chichen Itza. During the Postclassic period, fortifications became more common, as seen at the walled cities of **Mayapan** and **Tulum** in northern Yucatan, **Zacpetén** and **Nixtun-Ch'ich'** in central Petén, and the hilltop cities of **Iximché** and **Q'um'arkaj** in the Guatemalan highlands. There were 16 or more variably sized, independent polities in northern Yucatan during the early sixteenth century. Warfare between and even within polities was frequent.

Major weapons included spears, *atlatl* darts, as well as bows and arrows. Other implements such as clubs, axes, and slings are less common in the archaeological and iconographic records. Judging by the presence of microscopic traces in association with projectile-impact damage, many **obsidian** and chert bifacial points were used as spears or darts. Some of them were also used as knives for the artistic and craft production of shell and bone ornaments, wood carving, and other domestic activities. If one's objective was to kill or severely injure, projectile weapons were far outclassed by handheld shock weapons such as axes, maces, and bladed wooden swords. Because of their sharper cutting edges, obsidian spear points should have caused heavier bleeding than those made from chert. Chert spear points, although less effective to kill or wound than those of obsidian, were prevalent in most Maya lowland areas. At **Copán**, however, inhabitants took advantage of its unusual location near one of the primary obsidian sources for the Maya lowlands and used mainly obsidian points.

Some women from the Classic Maya elite may have played a more important role in warfare than previously thought. Although portraits of Maya warrior queens are rare in Classic Maya art, two **stelae** of **Naranjo** show Lady Six Sky (AD 682–741) trampling captives in the manner of a warrior-king. Similar depictions are also known from Calakmul, **Naachtun**, and **Cobá**. The epigraphic and iconographic records indicate that warrior queens ruled autonomously, participated in battles, and captured enemies during the seventh and eighth centuries. Household archaeology at Aguateca suggests that some elite women may have engaged in the production of chert bifacial points and used them for defense of the city or other purposes. At least some elite women acted as warriors.

The spear points were major chipped stone weapons among the Preclassic Maya. The chert spear points and a shell ornament representing a decapitated human head, both recovered from the Central Plaza of **Ceibal** and dated to the early Middle Preclassic period (1000–700 BC), might be the earliest evidence of warfare in the Maya lowlands. The scarcity of Preclassic chert points suggests that more perishable weapons, such as those of hard wood, may have been used during the Preclassic period than in later periods.

The adaption of the *atlatl* darts from highland Central Mexico in the fourth century AD did not replace handheld spears as a predominant weapon in the Maya lowlands. Bifacial *atlatl* dart points made of green obsidian from the Pachuca source and other Mexican sources have been found in Early Classic deposits of several major Maya sites. Their material, form, and workmanship, especially overlapping, fine transverse, parallel pressure flaking along the edges and faces, leave no doubt that they were manufactured at **Teotihuacán**, Central Mexico. The appearance of Mexican obsidian artifacts in the archaeological record may reflect the presence of foreigners, developing long-distance exchange networks, or marriage alliances that entailed some tribute coming from Central Mexico.

Spear points were more important than the bow and arrow in Classic Maya warfare. Some scholars once contended that the bow and arrow was introduced into the Maya lowlands, either by Mexican mercenaries during the Postclassic period or by the Chontal Maya during the Terminal Classic period. Nevertheless, both notched and unnotched obsidian prismatic blade points were present at Copán during the Early and Late Classic periods as well as at Aguateca during the Late Classic period. The results of high-power-magnification microwear analysis indicate that both obsidian prismatic blade points and small chert unifacial points were mainly used as arrowheads. The bow and arrow was present in the Maya lowlands earlier than has been previously suggested.

The increase in the production and use of *atlatl* darts as well as bows and arrows during the Terminal Classic period may indicate a change in the practice of warfare. Several lines of evidence suggest that warfare may have been among the several causes that led to the demise of centralized dynastic authority at several Classic Maya cities. Large concentrations of obsidian spear and dart points as well as arrow points in the final phase occupation layers in the central part of Copán in the early ninth century, along with other lines of evidence for warfare, such as stone sculptures of warriors and violent destruction of several buildings of central Copán, indicate that warfare was critical in the downfall of centralized dynastic rule. The fall of the Ceibal dynasty was marked by the destruction of its temple-**pyramid** and **royal palace** during the tenth century. Stucco **sculptures** of human figures that decorated the royal palace were intentionally beheaded. There is increasing evidence of the production and use of chert and obsidian spear and dart points, as well as arrow points, in the central part of Ceibal during the Late and Terminal Classic periods, as there is compelling epigraphic and archaeological evidence for warfare in the Petexbatún and Pasion regions. In summary, warfare played an important role in the development and decline of some Maya cities.

See also ARCHITECTURE OVERVIEW; ASTRONOMY; BURIALS; CARACOL; CLASS STRUCTURE; CLASSIC MAYA COLLAPSE; DIVINE KINGS AND QUEENS; DROUGHT; ICONOGRAPHY; KABAH AND NOHPAT; MAYA QUEENS; MAYAPÁN; MEXICO; MUSIC AND DANCE; PALENQUE; PHYSICAL/BIOLOGICAL ANTHROPOLOGY; PIEDRAS NEGRAS; PIEDRAS NEGRAS–DYNASTIC SEQUENCE; RIO AZUL; RITES AND RITUALS; STELA; THEATER; TONINÁ; TULUM; UAXACTUN; WALL PAINTING; WATER MANAGEMENT; WOMEN, MEN, AND GENDER ROLES; YALAHAU REGION; YAXCHILAN

Further Reading

Aoyama, Kazuo. *Ancient Maya State, Urbanism, Exchange, and Craft Specialization: Chipped Stone Evidence from the Copán Valley and the La Entrada Region, Honduras*. University of Pittsburgh Memoirs in Latin American Archaeology, no. 12. Pittsburgh, PA: University of Pittsburgh Department of Anthropology, 1999.

———. *Elite Craft Producers, Artists, and Warriors at Aguateca: Lithic Analysis*. Monographs of the Aguateca Archaeological Project First Phase, vol. 2. Salt Lake City: University of Utah Press, 2009.

Brown, M. Kathryn, and Travis W. Stanton. *Ancient Mesoamerican Warfare*. Walnut Creek, CA: AltaMira Press, 2003.

Graham, Elizabeth A., Scott E. Simmons, and Christine D. White. "The Spanish Conquest and the Maya Collapse: How 'Religious' Is Change?" *World Archaeology* 45: 161–85, 2013.

Inomata, Takeshi, and Daniela Triadan, eds. *Burned Palaces and Elite Residences of Aguateca: Excavations and Ceramics*. Monographs of the Aguateca Archaeological Project First Phase, vol. 1. Salt Lake City: University of Utah Press, 2010.

■ KAZUO AOYAMA

WATER MANAGEMENT

Ancient Maya water management systems were developed to meet the needs of farmers as well as city dwellers in a tropical climate that had distinct wet and dry seasons (see also **Climate; Groundwater/Water Table; Map 5**). Prehispanic Maya water management practices transformed seasonally available natural water bodies into year-round water supplies capable of supporting dense urban populations in areas with no naturally occurring permanent water bodies such as rivers and **lakes**. As farmers living in a tropical environment with distinct wet and dry seasons, the pre-Hispanic Maya were concerned not only with channeling rainfall to provide potable water throughout the dry season, but also with predicting the start of the rainy season in order to ensure that crops were planted in time to thrive. Most Maya water management systems were built to address the problem of dry-season scarcity. Early Maya settlement focused around *aguadas* (natural rain-fed depressions), *bajos* (seasonal wetlands), and swamps. In order to maximize the abundance of water, the Maya transformed these natural features by enlarging their capacity and lining the reservoirs with lime plaster to create an impermeable surface. Maya water management systems also addressed the overabundance of water. The perennial wetlands of Northern **Belize** were enhanced with ditches and platforms, which allowed farmers to cultivate raised beds irrigated by the canals. The canals also provided additional resources, including aquatic animals such as fish and shellfish, and rich sediment that was dredged and used in replenishing agricultural land.

Tikal has the best-known Classic Maya reservoir system. The central precinct of Tikal has four reservoirs, while the site margin houses an additional six reservoirs. As with most Maya cities, the ground surface of the site core was covered with a layer of lime plaster, which prevents runoff from seeping into the soil and escaping. Tikal's reservoirs are fed by runoff, which flows across the plaster-covered ground into the catchment tanks, where the water is stored. Reservoir construction began by the Late Preclassic and was greatly expanded throughout the Classic Period to support an urban population numbering in the tens of thousands. Even today, the reservoirs are year-round sources of water.

Maya rulers gained power through controlling and administering water management systems at large centers. Maya kings acted as intermediaries between commoners and the supernatural, conducting water rituals to ensure rainfall and abundant water supply as well as controlling access to water reservoirs (see also **Divine Kings and Queens**; **Rites and Rituals**). Moreover, Maya rulers were responsible for maintaining the quality of reservoir water. The reservoirs at Tikal, for example, were rich with plant and microbial organisms that balanced nutrients and ensured that standing water remained potable throughout the year. Symbols of abundant and pure water, particularly water lilies, were central to elite power and are common elements of royal **iconography** in Classic period sites such as Tikal and **Copán**.

In the northern Yucatan Peninsula, where the lack of seasonal water bodies creates conditions of greater scarcity, the ancient Maya constructed small storage tanks, or *chultunes*, by digging into the limestone bedrock. *Chultunes* were constructed both at large urban centers such as **Uxmal** and **Sayil**, as well as at hinterland households. These water storage systems complemented reservoirs at northern lowland cities, providing an additional source of water during the dry season. Unlike the larger reservoirs that supplied entire cities, *chultunes* provided water for several households and were not associated with royal control. In addition, the higher water table of the Northern Lowlands allowed people living in the Yucatan Peninsula to tap into natural wells.

Despite the elaborate and carefully maintained water management systems the Maya created, urban populations remained susceptible to climatic fluctuations. A series of **droughts**, documented in sediment cores and speleothems, **cave** formations such as stalagmites and stalactites, struck the Maya area at the end of the Late Classic. Between AD 750 and 1050, several prolonged droughts caused reservoir water supplies to dwindle and fail, leaving urban populations without adequate water. These droughts have been implicated in the ultimate failure of Classic period sociopolitical systems and the end of royal power, as major centers throughout the lowlands experienced **warfare**, political fragmentation, and abandonment (see also **Classic Maya Collapse**). In response to the droughts and changing political and environmental conditions, the Maya moved away from their cities and back to small farming communities centered near more reliable water sources.

See also ALTUN HA; ARCHITECTURE OVERVIEW; BECAN; BURIALS; CACAO; CALAKMUL; CAUSEWAY/*SACBE*; CENOTE; CENTRAL LOWLANDS; CEREN; CERRO MAYA/CERROS; CHAC II; CHICXULUB CRATER (AND THE CENOTE ZONE); CLASS STRUCTURE; COBÁ; COCHUAH REGION; COMALCALCO; DIET; DZIBILCHALTUN; EDZNA; FAUNA; GEOLOGY; GROUNDWATER/WATER TABLE; HOUSEHOLD PRODUCTION; ICHKABAL; JAINA; KAMINALJUYÚ; KIUIC; KOMCHEN; LAMANAI; MARKETS AND MARKETPLACES; MAYAPÁN; MIRADOR BASIN; MUYIL; NOH KAH; NORTHERN LOWLANDS; OXKINTOK; PALENQUE; PHYSICAL/BIOLOGICAL ANTHROPOLOGY; REJOLLADA; RIO AZUL; RITES AND RITUALS; SAN BARTOLO; SETTLEMENT PATTERNS (INTRODUCTION); SETTLEMENT PATTERNS (CENTRAL LOWLANDS); SOILS; SOUTHERN LOWLANDS; SUBSISTENCE; TERRACING; TIKAL; TULUM; UNDERWATER ARCHAEOLOGY; VEGETATION; WALL PAINTING; WOMEN, MEN, AND GENDER ROLES; XCOCH; YALAHAU REGION; YAXHÁ; YAXHOM

Further Reading

Fedick, Scott L., ed. *The Managed Mosaic: Ancient Maya Agriculture and Resource Use*. Salt Lake City: University of Utah Press, 1996.

Isendahl, Christian. "The Weight of Water: A New Look at Pre-Hispanic Puuc Maya Water Reservoirs." *Ancient Mesoamerica* 22, no. 1: 185–97, 2011.

Lucero, Lisa J., Joel D. Gunn, and Vernon L. Scarborough. "Climate Change and Classic Maya Water Management." *Water* 3, no. 4: 479–94, 2011.

Lucero, Lisa Joyce, and Barbara W. Fash, eds. *Precolumbian Water Management: Ideology, Ritual, and Power*. Tucson: University of Arizona Press, 2006.

Medina-Elizalde, Martin, Stephen J. Burns, David W. Lea, Yemane Asmerom, Lucien von Gunten, Victor Polyak, Mathias Vuille, and Ambarish Karmalkar. "High Resolution Stalagmite Climate Record from the Yucatán Peninsula Spanning the Maya Terminal Classic Period." *Earth and Planetary Science Letters* 298, nos. 1–2: 255–62, 2010.

Scarborough, Vernon L. *The Flow of Power: Ancient Water Systems and Landscapes*. Santa Fe, NM: SAR Press, 2003.

Scarborough, Vernon L., Nicholas P. Dunning, Kenneth B. Tankersley, Christopher Carr, Eric Weaver, Liwy Grazioso, Brian Lane, John G. Jones, Palma Buttles, Fred Valdez, and David L. Lentz. "Water and Sustainable Land Use at the Ancient Tropical City of Tikal, Guatemala." *Proceedings of the National Academy of Sciences of the United States of America* 109, no. 31: 12408–413, 2012.

■ JESSICA HARRISON

WATER
See AGUADAS; BAJOS; CAVES; CLIMATE; DROUGHT; WATER MANAGEMENT

WEAPONS
See WARFARE, WARRIORS, AND WEAPONS

WESTERN ARCHITECTURAL STYLE

The Western architectural style includes sites such **Palenque**, in northern Chiapas, and Comalcalco, in Tabasco; some archaeologists would also include the major sites of the Usumacinta River valley, such as **Piedras Negras** and **Yaxchilán**, in the Western style, while others consider the Usumacinta sites as possessing their own distinctive character.

The Western style is most easily recognizable by the use of mansard roofs and pierced roof-combs that convey a lightness and grace not often achieved elsewhere in the Maya area. **Comalcalco** is the westernmost major Maya site. Located on the alluvial plains of Tabasco where stone is not available, Comalcalco's buildings were constructed of fired brick. Both sites are also justly famous for their beautiful stucco work.

See also ARCHITECTURE OVERVIEW

Further Reading

Andrews, George F., and Donald L. Hardesty. *Comalcalco, Tabasco, Mexico: Maya Art and Architecture*. Culver City, CA: Labyrinthos, 1989.

Guenter, Stanley. *The Tomb of K'inich Janaab Pakal: The Temple of the Inscriptions at Palenque*. Mesoweb, 2007. http://www.mesoweb.com/articles/guenter/TI.html.

Schele, Linda, and Mary Ellen Miller. *The Blood of Kings: Dynasty and Ritual in Maya Art*. New York and Fort Worth, TX: G. Braziller and the Kimbell Art Museum, 1986.

Stuart, David, and George E. Stuart. *Palenque: Eternal City of the Maya*. New York: Thames & Hudson, 2008.

■ CLIFFORD T. BROWN AND WALTER R. T. WITSCHEY

WOMEN, MEN, AND GENDER ROLES

Early views of men and women's roles in ancient Maya society (beyond obvious biological roles) have been shaped by the observations of **Diego de Landa** and others in the **Northern Lowlands** and **ethnographic** reports since John Lloyd Stephens's travels. A consistent view shows men as caretakers of the cornfield, clearing, planting, and harvesting; hunting; bringing firewood; and building houses. Women are cast as caretakers of the home, preparers of food by grinding maize and cooking; buyers and sellers of items of household need; fetchers of water; and makers of thread, cloth, and clothing. These consistently reported roles are now being reexamined in the light of new ethnographic studies and archaeological research; findings indicate that the roles of men and women substantially overlapped, especially in the weeding and harvesting of crops (see also **Maya Queens**; **Subsistence**).

A constant across elites and commoners alike is the association of cloth production with women. Figurines and Classic polychrome vases consistently link spinning and weaving with women (see also **Ceramics**; **Textiles and Clothing**). The goddess Chak Chel is noted as the goddess of weaving as well as of birth and healing (see also **Deities**). **Royal tombs** of women sometimes carry the symbolic tools of spinning and weaving, such as spindle whorls and pins.

At the elite level, it is clear that the majority of inscriptions and **iconography** of the Classic have men as protagonists. We hear of their birth, accession, captive-taking, successes in **warfare**, dynastic history, and death. Yet the minority of monuments and inscriptions that do deal with women are now receiving a more nuanced analysis. In a significant way, new readings and translations of the scripts are providing information about the critical roles played by women in ruling; acting as regents; and marrying outside their place of birth to forge new dynastic **alliance** links, commercial ties, and defense pacts. For example, when lack of a male heir involves a dynastic shift, women become key actors in the adoption of a new ruler from the matrilineal family (see also **Divine Kings and Queens**; **Maya Queens**; **Dynastic Sequences**).

At **Copán**, a **royal tomb**, the Margarita structure, dated to AD 465, likely contains the wife of the dynastic founder K'inich Yax K'uk' Mo', whose tomb was kept open for subsequent years for ritual offerings during the life of her son, K'inich Popol Hol, the second ruler of Copán. Her bone chemistry matches the locals, and her high status and lengthy veneration at the accessible tomb may be the result of newcomers to the Copán valley establishing a new dynastic line by intermarriage with a local royal family.

See also CACAO; CARACOL; CAVES; CEREN; HOUSEHOLD PRODUCTION; JAINA; LAMANAI; LANDA, BISHOP DIEGO DE; MEDICINE; PROSKOURIAKOFF, TATIANA AVENIROVNA; PUSILHA; RITES OF PASSAGE; SAN BARTOLO; TEXTILES AND CLOTHING; TONINÁ; WALL PAINTING; WARFARE, WARRIORS, AND WEAPONS; YAXCHILAN

Further Reading

Ardren, Traci, ed. *Ancient Maya Women*. Walnut Creek, CA: AltaMira Press, 2002.

Claassen, Cheryl, and Rosemary A. Joyce, eds. *Women in Prehistory: North America and Mesoamerica*. Philadelphia: University of Pennsylvania Press, 1997.

Dacus, Chelsea. "Weaving the Past: An Examination of Bones Buried with an elite Maya Woman." Master's thesis, Southern Methodist University, 2005.

Josserand, J. Kathryn. "The Missing Heir at Yaxchilán: Literary Analysis of a Maya Historical Puzzle." *Latin American Antiquity* 18, no. 3: 295–312, 2007.

Martin, Simon, and Nikolai Grube. *Chronicle of the Maya Kings and Queens: Deciphering the Dynasties of the Ancient Maya*. 2nd ed. London: Thames & Hudson, 2008.

■ WALTER R. T. WITSCHEY

WRITING SYSTEMS OF MESOAMERICA

Introduction: What is Mesoamerican writing? The writing systems of Mesoamerica have long refused to fit into our long-established Old World categories. David Diringer defines "writing" in its simplest sense as "graphic representation of speech." Indeed all writing systems depend to some extent on their "home" language, though each also has signs—sometimes many—that transcend linguistic boundaries. (The writing subsystem with the greatest trans-linguistic transparency is our own [Hindu-Arabic] numerals. Of course numbers, and mathematical notation in general, no matter how useful and universal, in no way constitute a complete writing system.) This definition-based-on-speech was articulated to define Old World writing systems, before the decipherment of Maya hieroglyphs in the 1970s and 1980s. As it became obvious that Maya worked very much like Babylonian or Japanese, scholars classed it among "full" or "true" writing systems, but continued to argue about the status of Aztec, Mixtec, and other New World scripts. These are unique in their operation and are often described as "incomplete" or "not fully developed" writing systems. Since they satisfy the most central functions of a writing system, however, these others ought to be considered on a par with Old World systems, although uniquely different.

Most discussions of written forms have been composed by westerners. Saturated since birth in alphabetic writing, we are inclined to consider it the summit of communicative efficiency. Without much reflection, most of us would claim that alphabetic writing is indeed supremely efficient in its task.

Greco-Roman civilization did reach a state of almost-pure alphabetic writing, during the millennium between classic Greece and the fall of Rome about AD 500. A set of 24 letters sufficed to encode all necessary information. In the 1,500 years since, however, we have added several characters and features to this once purely alphabetic writing system, which have improved its efficiency. These improvements have added two whole rows of keys to our typewriters and keyboards. All the added characters, including the inter-word "space," have a "logographic" function, and their presence greatly improves the efficiency of reading and writing beyond that of fourth-century Latin. Apple Inc.'s introduction of gesture into our interaction with computer screens added another significant improvement.

The writing systems of the Americas are the only ones we can say with certainty developed in total isolation from those of the Old World. As happens with isolated species, these scripts exhibit qualities and features found nowhere else, which makes them difficult for many scholars to fit into the Old World paradigm of "written forms." This is especially true of Late Postclassic books.

With the possible exception of Sumerian cuneiform on clay tablets, early and developmental stages in the evolution of writing systems are always missing. Writing everywhere was developed on the most cheap and abundant media (clay, swamp grass, bamboo, palm leaves, bark), which have inevitably perished. Only when someone decided to commit an announcement or record to a permanent material such as stone or metal was early writing preserved. We simply have no firm evidence of how writing systems were invented.

This situation is exacerbated in Mesoamerica, whose jungles provide a moist, acidic environment, whose deserts are not as dry as in Egypt or Peru, and whose later conquerors were fanatical about destroying books filled with "superstitions and lies of the devil" (see also **Codices [Maya]**; **Landa, Bishop Diego de**). Few Mesoamerican peoples chose to display writing on stone; the Maya were the exception (see also **Hieroglyphic Stairways**; **Stela**). Maya inscriptions, therefore, number in the tens of thousands, but short Zapotec texts amount to only a few hundred, and the remaining corpus of Mesoamerican writing is pitifully small. However, it is obvious from the well-developed examples that do survive that their scribes and script were sophisticated and artistic.

In general, their characters were written top-to-bottom, in *orthograde* columns (columns arranged left to right), though considerable variation is found; Mayan **ceramic** inscriptions (particularly the very ancient formula found around the rims of vases) are most often written horizontally, just as the text you are reading here. The mysterious *Cascajal Block* is an anomaly in this regard, its passages written consistently in orthograde rows.

Michael Coe called rim texts on Maya ceramics the "Primary Standard Sequence." David **Stuart** called them the "Dedicatory Formula." They are essentially an elaborate form of name-tagging, stating that the vase is painted or carved, is made sacred by painting and writing, is meant to hold a specific food or beverage, and was created for the owner (often listing titles and lineage). The widespread use and composition suggest that this formula goes back to the very beginnings of Mayan civilization.

Surviving Mesoamerican writing (and its matrix of iconic and pictorial art), especially that carved on stone, deals primarily with religious ceremonies and rituals (see also **Religion**; **Rites and Rituals**). These are usually tied to sacred cycles of time, often laden with **calendric** specificity. One might say that the purpose of more permanent Mesoamerican writing was to communicate with the gods (see also **Deities**). Second, it records and creates a public display of **dynastic sequence** history. Many Late and Colonial documents survive in the form of historical pictographic accounts, made and preserved for legal purposes.

Though surviving examples are often meager, it is apparent that the many ethnic groups in Mesoamerica developed a substantial number of distinct scripts. It is in this broad context of multiple writing systems, widely distributed across Mesoamerica, that the distinctive Maya writing system developed.

Early Preclassic (San Lorenzo era, ca. 1500–900 BC): The earliest text we have, discovered in the late 1990s in the Veracruz lowlands in the "**Olmec** heartland" near the large Olmec site San Lorenzo Tenochtitlan, is the *Cascajal Block,* lightly but carefully engraved on a stone tablet (serpentinite, 36 cm by 21 cm by 13cm thick). We have no other example of writing from the Early Preclassic, which is problematic. Formally, it resembles an inscription, but a couple of features give one pause. The characters appear in rows, not columns, unlike in all its likely descendant scripts. Few of the signs seem to appear in later scripts, although Karl Taube has identified examples of nearly every symbol, appearing (perhaps as labels) in Early Preclassic Olmec artworks. Most troubling, the rows are just irregular enough to appear as about 15 separate short texts, unrelated to one another except by proximity. They might be separate entries in some sort of list or inventory, like early Sumerian account-tablets. Unfortunately, no other inscription of this type, or this age, has come to light.

Middle Preclassic (La Venta era, ca. 900–300 BC): The *Humboldt Celt* (lost in 1945) is a typical Middle Preclassic ceremonial greenstone "axe," polished and engraved with several symbols. Its upper section appears text-like, signs arranged in a linear column, but the lower section is dominated by a diagram, it components arranged in a quincunx. The *El Sitio Celt* is also engraved with a column of signs, which may have been carved in the Late Preclassic or later. Neither of these comes from a controlled context, so we can identify them only by comparison with other similar artifacts.

Archaeologist Mary Pohl has found a few tantalizing fragments of jade mosaic near the Olmec capital of La Venta, Tabasco, carrying three engraved fragmentary hieroglyphs. At La Venta itself we find *LV Monument 13* (nicknamed "The Ambassador"), a cylindrical monument about 2 m in diameter and height, containing the image of a walking, bearded man carrying a pennant, along with four glyphs arranged in a column. Three of these are in a column under his banner (suggesting the pennant itself might be part of the inscription), and a fourth is behind him: a footprint, which in later documents universally appears as a sign for "travel" or "road." Details of the characters have eroded away; outlines include a tri-lobed glyph and a bird head. The figure itself is a striding, bearded man wearing a turban similar to ones appearing on some other Middle Preclassic Olmec monuments. Its many unusual features make its age uncertain; it might date from, say, the Late Preclassic, after the fall of La Venta. At the Middle Preclassic Olmec (or "Olmecoid") site of Chalcatzingo, on the border between Morelos and Puebla, one of the monuments bears four dates in the 260-day system, but no other text or image. This might constitute the earliest recorded use of this calendar, vying with San José Mogoté.

The Zapotec people in Oaxaca first consolidated power in Monte Albán around the end of the Middle Preclassic, labeling the figures on their *Danzante* monuments with short inscriptions carved in relief. Kent Flannery and Joyce Marcus discovered a similar monument in the pre-Monte-Albán site of San Jose Mogoté. This monument apparently portrays a disemboweled sacrificed man, labeled with a calendrical name "1 Earthquake." Naming a child with the sacred 260-day-cycle date of his or her birth was a common practice in Nahuatl, Mixtec, and Zapotec culture. Later "Danzantes" (see below) are similarly labeled. Its excavators dated it to 600 BC, but other scholars doubt that it is so early, preferring a date about 400–300 BC.

Late Preclassic (300 BC–AD 200): In the Late Preclassic era there is solid evidence for widespread use of writing. Here we find complete texts, not just labels. In addition to the sacred 260-day calendar, used by all Mesoamerican civilizations right up to and beyond the conquest, evidence appears in the Late Preclassic for the use of a 365-day calendar and the Long Count. The Zapotecs of the great capital of Monte Albán emulated their immediate predecessors in San José Mogoté, erecting over 200 "*Danzantes*," portraits of apparently sacrificed captives, engraved in outline, and nearly life-sized, on expensive slabs of imported stone. Many of these carry labels, two or more glyphs long, by their heads or on their chests. These captives were likely nobles of some importance, to have earned this kind of memorial even after their execution. They are accompanied by a couple of reliefs with fuller texts, including some of the earliest indications of a "year sign," naming a specific year using a 365-day calendar.

The similarly large slabs mounted on the anomalous Monte Alban Building J might be victory monuments and may date from a century or two later. These consist of a generic "city" glyph, labeled above with a specific name-sign, all balanced upon the neck of an inverted generic head (indicating "conquest"?). The Monte Alban script appears on stones right up to the end of the Classic period (ca. AD 800).

The civilizations living in the Isthmus of Tehuantepec, who occupied the former Olmec heartland and Chiapas to its south, have left a dozen or two inscriptions on stone. They date from about 450 BC (just before the fall of the Olmec) to about AD 450, the apogee of **Teotihuacán**. Four of these bear precise dates in the Long Count: 36 and 32 BC (7.16.3.2.13 on the fragmentary Chiapa de Corzo St. 2 and 7.16.6.16.18 on Tres Zapotes St. C) respectively, and AD 156 and 162 on La Mojarra St. 1 and the Tuxtla Statuette. As paltry as this sample is, it includes the extraordinary La Mojarra St. 1, dated AD 156 (8.5.16.9.7), with approximately 535 glyphs. The Tuxtla Statuette, dated AD 162 (8.6.2.4.17), has 75 glyphs. In private collections, an undated Teotihuacán mask also has about 75 glyphs, while the glyphs on the O'Boyle Mask number about 23. A fragmentary text on a sherd from Chiapa de Corzo has only 11 glyphs. Longer texts in the script appear on some Cerro de las Mesas stelae, but eroded illegibly.

Isthmian script remains a challenge, but apparently its users invented the Long Count calendar, soon borrowed by their eastern neighbors, the Maya (and no other peoples). The Maya used writing on monuments in much the same way, but took it to its most copious and prolix level, on a par with the inscriptions of Assyria or Rome. The earliest Mayan Long Count dates appear on late Late Preclassic stelae from El Baúl and Takalik' Abaj.

A few Late Preclassic stela inscriptions appear in the southern Maya sites of **Kaminaljuyú**, **Cotzumalhuapa**, and **Takalik Abaj**, and the remarkably well-preserved paintings at **San Bartolo** contain a few short, enigmatic inscriptions from about 300 BC and 100 BC. These, like other inscriptions we have seen (excepting of course the *Cascajal Block*), arrange the glyphs in single columns. However, Kaminaljuyú *"Stela" 10* (actually an altar) has a text in double columns, which became the unique hallmark of Mayan writing. Ears of maize grow in double columns, and single Mayan glyphs are (uniquely among writing systems) *shaped* like grains of corn. Maya inscriptions consciously emulated maize. Some early Classic monuments such as Tikal St. 31 are even tapered to resemble an ear of corn. Maya Creation myths tell us humanity was created from cornmeal (see also *Popol Vuh*). This overarching metaphor extended to their cosmology: the five directional colors (red, white, yellow, black, and green) are the colors of maize.

To the west, Teotihuacán, the greatest city in ancient Mesoamerica (ca. 100 BC–AD 600) had a sophisticated writing system, but very rarely chose to use it on their murals, ceramics, or monuments. Karl Taube has collected the scarce and difficult-to-recognize examples of these—there are a few dates, name-tags, titles, and toponyms, but no long texts.

Classic (AD 200–900): The Classic period is so called—echoing the classical Greek era—because early writers loved the **art** of the Maya. Their culture was a little less alien, their art more humanistic (to our eyes).

To the greatest extent of any Mesoamerican culture, the Maya employed writing as a political tool. Despite having a largely illiterate public, they displayed hieroglyphic inscriptions on stelae in their public plazas; on their **architecture**; on personal items such as jewelry, dishes, and clothing; and probably on articles such as banners, furniture, and other items that have completely perished (see also **Portable Objects**). Tens of thousands of Mayan inscriptions survive on stone and ceramic objects, and many hundreds in stucco, wood, shell, and other media. Their books were written on beaten-fig-bark paper (*hu'un* in Mayan, *amate* in Nahuatl, *tapa* in Polynesian), smoothed with lime stucco, in long horizontal strips about 9 inches high, folded accordion-style into codices about 4 inches wide. The material had a wide range of uses, just as *tapa* does to this day: the word *hu'un* also means "Headdress," for example. Like Chinese ink, their ink was made largely from soot, and their pens were cut from both reed and quill, as we see from surviving hieroglyphs and paintings of scribes at work.

Though no Maya books (**codices**) survive from the Classic, we have images and archeological vestiges of them. Archaeologists have identified the remains of perhaps eight or ten codices buried in tombs. They now consist merely of organic stains peppered with tiny fragments of paper-thin stucco, hopelessly jumbled by rot and devouring insects. One of these at **Copán** was a very large luxury-book, nearly a foot square. Painted vases show scribes and readers reading or writing in books, which are often bound in sacred jaguar-skin. No doubt the long genealogies and complex calendrical calculations that we find inscribed on stelae were copied from codices. Four codices survive. Though all four date from the Postclassic (see below), they probably largely replicate the form of Classic Maya books.

Mesoamerican artistic conventions blur the distinctions among icon, glyph, design, and illustration. Perfectly readable glyphs appear as icons in many Mayan images, from the Late Preclassic Cerros architectural masks onward. Some of these are clearly labels, particularly when worn on a lord's head, but often their "readings" do not make sense to us . . . yet. For example, the elements of a commonly depicted Mayan ear flare seem composed of the syllabic signs *mu*, *bi*, and *la*, but words like *mubiil* do not appear in any Mayan glossary. "Sky-bands," "earth-bands," and "water-bands" incorporate appropriate glyphic signs (such as "star," "sun," "night," and "moon" in "skybands"), but these are clearly not texts.

The abundance of Mayan hieroglyphic examples overshadows its rivals. As noted above, Epi-Olmec Isthmians and Zapotecs both employed writing in the Late Preclassic. Both these cultures continued to write into the Classic period, though we do not yet know of any Isthmian inscriptions later than about AD 450. (Considering the paucity of known Isthmian inscriptions, this certainly does not prove that the script was extinct. We also have no *Maya* inscriptions from the half-millennium between ca. AD 900 and AD 1400, yet certainly scribes had continued to write.)

At Monte Albán and other centers, Zapotec artisans continued to inscribe stelae and the like right through the Classic era. Related writing systems were practiced in Cacaxtla and Xochicalco, and there is evidence of yet another species of writing, perhaps descended from Teotihuacán, in the Mixtec area, known as Nuiñe. Perhaps most civilized Mesoamerican cities had their own writing systems. Certainly the later dominant cultures in the Oaxaca-Cholula-Valley of México axis wrote books and histories, though they developed them into a unique kind of literature, as we shall see.

Postclassic and Early Colonial (AD 900–1600): The Late **Classic Maya collapse** brought profound changes to the cultural landscape. All over eastern and southern Mesoamerica, royal houses were overthrown and their considerable artistic manifestations brought to an end. Stela carving and the construction of monumental architecture— **pyramids**, **palaces**, and virtually all constructions of stone—ceased, along with the production and exchange of luxury ceramics, jades, etc. Opulent art production in wood, textile, and other perishable media also doubtless ended. The great cities were emptied out, some rapidly, some over a century or two.

Sparks of what we esteem as civilization, however, survived in Central Mexico, particularly in Oaxaca, Puebla, and the Valley of México, eventually to create new artistic production centers in the Postclassic. This land is polyglot, comprising over a dozen languages even today, and the intellectuals of the ruling culture developed a unique kind of book to communicate as broadly as possible. Their codices remove text as much as possible, telling their stories in pictures. These books identify participants and dates with hieroglyphic labels and convey the rest of the information by conventional gestures and icons.

Fortunately several of these books and documents are well preserved. Some Europeans collected books from México as curiosities, such as the Borgia codex. The Spanish friars and law courts of the region accepted indigenous documents as legal evidence of land claims, and the tax collectors of New Spain co-opted the Aztec tribute system. Books such as the Mendoza codex and the *Libro de Tributos* were painted completely in traditional style, by indigenous scribes, to be used by their new Spanish lords. Most of these books also contain added Spanish or Nahuatl glosses, in alphabetic script. Pohl points out that some of them are so faithful to the old style that it is irrelevant whether they were made before or after the conquest. Some, such as the Bodley codex, were clearly produced under Colonial rule (ca. 1540–1550), but were done totally in preconquest style, even portraying then-living noble persons in traditional costume, as if they were still living in the fifteenth century. This, even though these local nobility were by that time converted Christians, dressing in Spanish style, christened with Spanish names.

The Mendoza codex has a little more "real" writing in it: place-names are rendered with rebuses and other vestiges of "true" writing.

Other Postclassic Writing Systems: Though they only rarely inscribed in stone after the collapse, the Maya continued to write on native-paper screenfold books. There are only four preconquest Maya books known, three collected probably in Yucatan and sent to Europe around 1520–1560, the fourth discovered by *huaqueros* ("grave robbers") and sold to collector Josue Saenz in the 1960s, known today as the Grolier codex. The other three, known for their present homes, are the Dresden codes, Paris codex, and Madrid codex.

Mayan codices exhibit a later form of the Classical writing system. While the form of hieroglyphs is relatively conservative—the fifteenth-century versions of most glyphs are recognizably the same as their sixth- to eighth-century cognates—they show considerable simplification, as one expects when comparing a book in script with a carved monumental-display style. The literary style, as well as the glyphic, seems less poetic or flowery and puts more emphasis on phonetic spelling. For example, when writing "**cacao**" they use the simplest forms of the glyphs of *ka-ka-wa*, versus the Classic habit of spelling the word with the "full-fish" variant of *ka* (T738) rather than the simpler "fin" form (T25). Though the writing system was apparently developed by Cholan speakers, the Dresden codex contains many phonetic complements and full spellings in Yucatec.

All four deal with ritual, with **astronomical** cycles of Venus and eclipses, and complex horoscopes based on the 260-day *tzolk'in* ritual calendar. It is possible that this narrow range of subjects reflects the state of Maya literacy on the eve of the conquest; perhaps by that time the scribal tradition had become the exclusive domain of astronomers and calendar-priests. However, informants told **Diego de Landa** and others that books contained the usual range of literature, including history, poetry, the arts, and science.

See also ALTUN HA; ART; ASTRONOMICAL OBSERVATORIES; ASTRONOMY; BALL GAME/BALL COURT; CACAO; CALAKMUL; CALENDAR; CARACOL; CARACOL-DYNASTIC HISTORY; CAUSEWAY/ *SACBE*; CEIBAL; CLASSIC MAYA COLLAPSE; COBÁ; COCHUAH REGION; CODEX-STYLE VASES; CODICES (MAYA); COPÁN; COTZUMALHUAPA; CRAFT SPECIALIZATION; DATING; DECIPHERMENT; DEITIES; DIET; DROUGHT; DYNASTIC SEQUENCES; DZIBILCHALTUN; ECCENTRIC LITHICS; EDZNA; EL MIRADOR; EL PERÚ-WAKA'; FAUNA; FÖRSTEMANN, ERNST WILHELM; HOLMUL; ICONOGRAPHY; ITZIMTE; KAMINALJUYÚ; KOHUNLICH; LA LAGUNITA; LAMANAI; LANDA, BISHOP DIEGO DE; MATHEMATICS; MAYA QUEENS; MIDDLE CLASSIC HIATUS; MUSIC AND DANCE; NAACHTUN; NAKBÉ; NARANJO; OLMEC; OLMEC-MAYA INTERACTIONS; OXKINTOK; PALENQUE; PIEDRAS NEGRAS; *POPOL VUH*; PORTABLE OBJECTS; PRIESTS; PROSKOURIAKOFF, TATIANA AVENIROVNA; PUSILHA; RIO AZUL; RITES OF PASSAGE; RITES AND RITUALS; ROYAL TOMBS; SCHELE, LINDA; SCULPTURE; SYLLABARY; TAMCHEN AND CHACTUN; TAYASAL; TEOTIHUACÁN (MAYA INTERACTIONS WITH); TERRITORIAL ENTITIES; TEXTILES AND CLOTHING; THEATER; TIKAL; TONINÁ; TULUM; UAXACTUN; UXMAL; WALL PAINTING; WARFARE, WARRIORS, AND WEAPONS; XUNANTUNICH; YAXCHILAN; YUCATECAN MAYA LANGUAGES

Further Reading

Boone, Elizabeth Hill, and Walter Mignolo, eds. *Writing without Words: Alternative Literacies in Mesoamerica and the Andes*. Durham, NC: Duke University Press, 1994.

Boone, Elizabeth Hill, and Gary Urton, eds. *Their Way of Writing: Scripts, Signs, and Pictographies in Pre-Columbian America*. Washington, DC: Dumbarton Oaks Research Library and Collection, 2011.

Bricker, Victoria Reifler, ed. *Epigraphy*. Vol. 5 of *Supplement to the Handbook of Middle American Indians*. Austin: University of Texas Press, 1991.

Coe, Michael D. *Breaking the Maya Code*. London: Thames & Hudson, 1992.

Coe, Michael D., and Mark Van Stone. *Reading the Maya Glyphs*. 2nd ed. London: Thames & Hudson, 2005.

Dibble, Charles E. "The Aztec Writing System." In *Readings in Anthropology*, edited by E. Adamson Hoebel, Jesse D. Jennings, and Elmer R. Smith. New York: McGraw-Hill, 1955.

———. "Writing in Central Mexico." In *Handbook of Middle American Indians*. Vol. 10, *The Archaeology of North America*, pt. 1, edited by Gordon F. Ekholm and Ignacio Bernal. Austin: University of Texas Press, 1971.

Harris, John F., and Stephen K. Stearns. *Understanding Maya Inscriptions: A Hieroglyphic Handbook*. 2nd ed. Philadelphia: University of Pennsylvania Museum, 1997.

Johnson, Scott A. J. *Translating Maya Hieroglyphs*. Recovering Languages and Literacies of the Americas. Norman: University of Oklahoma Press, 2013.

Macri, Martha J., and Matthew G. Looper. *The New Catalog of Maya Hieroglyphs*. Vol. 1, *The Classic Period Inscriptions*. Civilization of the American Indian Series, vol. 247. Norman: University of Oklahoma Press, 2003.

Macri, Martha J., and Gabrielle Vail. *The New Catalog of Maya Hieroglyphs*. Vol. 2, *The Codical Texts*. Civilization of the American Indian series, vol. 264. Norman: University of Oklahoma Press, 2009.

Montgomery, John. *How to Read Maya Hieroglyphs*. New York: Hippocrene Books, 2002.

■ MARK VAN STONE

X

XCOCH

Located between the town of Santa Elena and the site of **Uxmal**, Yucatan, **Mexico**, Xcoch (20.4° N, 89.7° W) was first visited by John Stephens in 1841 (see also **Map 3**). He describes a giant **pyramid** but fails to mention its massive 1 ha building platform, though he did journey deep into a water **cave** near the site center. The first scientific work at Xcoch began in 2006 and remains ongoing. A large settlement with huge monumental architecture in the Middle Preclassic period (before 400 BC), Xcoch grew to its maximum size at the end of the Late Classic (~AD 800) before abandonment. Mapping survey and surface collections have covered more than 2 km² of a site that extends more than 10 km². Roughly centered near the Great Pyramid, a colossal multilevel acropolis supporting 10 architectural groups covering 10 ha is one of the largest constructions in the Puuc region. At least 25 platform groups have pyramids, and some are over 1 km from the site center. The Great Pyramid, Grand Platform, and other early groups are constructed in the early megalithic style, an indicator of Preclassic to Early Classic occupation. Test excavations from megalithic contexts across the site produced rich Formative diagnostics (**ceramics**, greenstone, and stucco floors) and Middle Preclassic radiocarbon assays (see also **Dating**).

A study of past **climate** change and human response was initiated at Xcoch and the vicinity in 2009, emphasizing the phenomena associated with the **Classic Maya collapse** (AD 800–900). As part of this work, water features such as *aguadas* (water ponds), small reservoirs, canals, and *chultuns* (underground water cisterns) were located and tested. Also, the Xcoch **cave** and La Vaca Perdida cave, 11 km to the east, were explored, mapped, and sampled. The contents of the Xcoch cave, especially its permanent water source, suggest that it served a vital ritual component in an elaborate system of **water management**. The Vaca Perdida cave produced speleothems and pollen core evidence for repeated **drought** cycles near the ends of both the Preclassic and Late Classic periods. These data correspond to contemporaneous construction activity at Xcoch, its water features, and comparable patterns of cyclical drought in the Yucatan and elsewhere. Stratigraphic evidence at Xcoch revealed a hiatus in Preclassic occupation followed by a reoccupation near the end of the Early Classic period (before AD 500). Indeed, the site reaches a maximum in the Late Classic, when a series of severe drought cycles forced Xcoch populations to intensify water storage by resurrecting and/or expanding old water control systems or by constructing new ones for rainwater capture. Evidently these efforts were insufficient, because the site was abandoned, perhaps abruptly, by the outset of the Terminal Classic period, though the cave continued to be visited during the Postclassic period and after.

Further Reading

Dunning, Nicholas P., Eric M. Weaver, Michael P. Smyth, and David Ortegón Zapata. "Home of the Maya Rain Gods: Ancient Maya Water Management at Xcoch, Yucatán." In *The Archaeology of Yucatan: New Directions and Data*, edited by Travis W. Stanton. B.A.R. International Series. Oxford: Oxford University, Archaeopress Pre-Columbian Archaeology, 2014.

Smyth, Michael P., and David Ortegón Zapata. "A Preclassic Center in the Puuc Region: A Report on Xcoch, Yucatán, Mexico." *Mexicon* 30, no. 3: 63–68, 2008.

Smyth, Michael P., David Ortegón Zapata, Nicholas P. Dunning, and Eric M. Weaver. "Settlement Dynamics, Climate Change, and Human Response at Xcoch in the Puuc Region of Yucatán, México." In *The Archaeology of Yucatán: New Directions and Data*, edited by Travis W. Stanton. B.A.R. International Series. Oxford: Oxford University, Archaeopress Pre-Columbian Archaeology, 2014.

Smyth, Michael P., Ezra Zubrow, David Ortegón Zapata, Nicholas P. Dunning, Eric M. Weaver, and Philip van Beynen. *Exploratory Research into Arctic Climate Change and Ancient Maya Response: Paleoclimate Reconstruction and Archaeological Investigation at the Puuc Region of Yucatán, México.* Washington, DC: Report to the National Science Foundation, 2012. www.FARINCO.org.

■ MICHAEL P. SMYTH

XULTUN

See SAN BARTOLO

XUNANTUNICH

Xunantunich (17.1° N, 89.1° W) is an archaeological site in **Belize**, midway in the north-south extent of the country, near the western border with **Guatemala** (see also **Map 3**). Visitors arrive most often via the Western Highway, where a hand-cranked ferry at San José Succotz crosses the Mopan River to the base of the mountaintop site. The tall ancient buildings on the summit offer panoramic views, and location was doubtless important for establishing the place in antiquity. In 2014 a new visitors' center opened on the site grounds.

More than a century of investigation informs what we know of Xunantunich today. From the first excavations, by British physician Thomas Gann in the 1890s, and especially since the 1930s, multiple programs have documented the founding and growth of Xunantunich, through studies of **ceramics**, **architecture**, hieroglyphic inscriptions, and nearby ancient farming villages. Major recent work includes the Xunantunich Archaeological Project (1991–1997); Belize's Tourism Development Project (2000–2004); the Mopan Valley Preclassic Project (2008–present); and continuing research, consolidation, and site development directed by Belize Archaeological Commissioner Jaime J. Awe.

The earliest traces of activities on the summit date to the Middle Formative period (ca. 1000–300 BC) but included no remains of architecture. In or before that period, however, two smaller, ceremonial sites downhill to the east acknowledged the sacredness of this mountain. On the summit, the buildings visible today are the result of construction and growth spanning less than 200 years, from ca. AD 600 to 780, in the Late Classic period, with modifications extending to perhaps AD 900, in the Terminal Classic period. The most visually prominent building is the Castillo (Str. A-6), now rising 40 m (130 feet) above the plaza. North and west of that building are two **ball courts**, where the ritual ball game was played. Extending north from the Castillo, on the east flank of the site, are three temple buildings; they likely formed the eastern side of an **E-Group**, for public ritual tracking the apparent seasonal movement of the sun's rising point (see also **Astronomical Observatories**). A high-ranking official, perhaps a king, was buried in the southernmost of those temples, Str. A-4. At the far northern end of the civic center is Plaza III and Str. A-11, the royal residence after AD 670. *Sacbe* (**causeway**) construction at that time formalized site access and entries and transformed the site's linear arrangement of buildings to a cross-shaped plan. Dividing the civic plaza space in half is the imposing Str. A-1, built in the late eighth century, the western edge of which partly overlies the site's early ball court. Xunantunich has 12 known stone monuments—**stelae**, altars, and panels—6 of which bear hieroglyphic texts that hint at scattered events and people between ca. AD 670 and 849. Discovered on the Castillo in 2003, Panel 2 bears hieroglyphs of the likely original name of this Maya city, Kat Witz (Clay Mountain).

The archaeological record clearly indicates the emergence of Xunantunich as a political and religious center in the seventh century AD. It was then that the first stages of the Castillo (Str. A-6) began. Initially the residence of the king, the building became a royal ancestor shrine after AD 670, when a new palace was established at the north end of the civic center. The Castillo replaced the E-Group as primary ritual focus. At its peak in the eighth century AD, Xunantunich was a locally powerful political and religious center, and ceremonial visits and offerings continued long after its dissolution a century later.

See also DECIPHERMENT; RELIGION; ROYAL TOMBS; SUBSISTENCE

Further Reading

Awe, Jaime J. *Maya Cities and Sacred Cenotes: A Guide to the Maya Sites of Belize*. Benque Viejo del Carmen, Belize: Cubola Productions, 2006.

———. "Architectural Manifestations of Power and Prestige: Examples from the Monumental Architecture at Baking Pot, Cahal Pech, and Xunantunich." In *Research Reports in Belizean Archaeology*, 159–73. National Institute of Culture and History, vol. 5. Belmopan, Belize: The Institute of Archaeology, 2008.

Brown, M. Kathryn, Jennifer Cochran, Leah McCurdy, and David Mixter. *Preceramic to Postclassic: A Brief Synthesis of the Occupation History of Group E, Xunantunich*. National Institute of Culture and History, vol. 8. Belmopan, Belize: The Institute of Archaeology, 2011.

LeCount, Lisa J., and Jason Yaeger. *Classic Maya Provincial Politics: Xunantunich and Its Hinterlands*. Tucson: University of Arizona Press, 2010.

■ WENDY ASHMORE

Y

YALAHAU REGION

This 3,000-km² region is located in northern Quintana Roo, **Mexico**, in the northeastern corner of the Yucatan Peninsula. The boundary of this region runs from the north coast 75 km southward, is 40 km wide, and is defined primarily by its unique water resources. It is characterized by a karstic limestone platform that contains only a few small **lakes** and no surface rivers. Despite this, it has the most abundant water sources of the entire peninsula. First, it receives the greatest annual rainfall of the **northern Maya lowlands** (up to 2,000 mm), which recharges an underground aquifer and contributes to widening a series of north-south fractures within the porous limestone shelf, known as the Holbox fracture zone. These fractures contain freshwater wetlands, which the ancient Maya exploited for fish, periphyton (a nutrient-rich algae used as fertilizer), and propagating food plants (see also **Subsistence**). The region is dotted with thousands of cenotes (karstic sinkholes) that provided direct access to the water table, and **caves** are common, which the ancient Maya believed represented entrances to the underworld (see also **Groundwater/Water Table**). Due to their symbolic importance, some regional caves contain architecture (i.e., altars, small **pyramids**), petroglyphs (symbolic designs incised into the cave walls; see also **Iconography**), and remnants of **ceramic** vessels that would have been used to collect sacred water from pools found deep within the caverns.

Although the water-rich region is strewn with hundreds of ancient Maya sites, archaeological research in this region was scant until Scott Fedick and Karl Taube formed the Yalahau Regional Human Ecology Project in 1993. Since 1998, Jennifer P. Mathews has codirected with Fedick. The Yalahau Project has documented over 100 sites, with settlement starting in the Middle Formative (before 400 BC) period, reaching its height during the Late Formative period (~250 BC–AD 250). The most monumental site of this period was El Naranjal, although the nonelite site of T'isil is one of the most densely settled sites known in the Maya lowlands, with a settlement density of 731 structures per km². A total of 1,270 structures have been systematically mapped at the site, and an estimated 466 structures remain in the 27 percent of the site that remains unmapped (64 ha). Population is estimated as 6,200.

The Early Classic (~AD 250–400) was struck by **drought**, which likely contributed to a general depopulation of the region for hundreds of years. There was a small reoccupation during the Late Postclassic (~AD 1100–1250), in which Maya pilgrims added small shrines and altars to the previously abandoned Late Formative **architecture**, perhaps as tribute to ancient ancestors (see also **Rites and Rituals**). After Spanish contact, the regional populations dropped by over 90 percent, due to the spread of disease and **warfare**. In the years following the Caste War (1847–1901), the remaining populations signed a treaty in 1855 calling for cessation of hostilities in the area. The Mexican government gave two land grants in an attempt to regain political and economic control of the area, and starting in the 1870s encouraged the harvesting of *chicle* (the latex used in chewing gum), hardwoods, and the development of several sugar and rum processing sites. Today, although located outside of the boundaries of the "Maya Riviera," the region is being heavily impacted by tourism, particularly drawing those interested in birding, fishing, SCUBA, and snorkeling.

See also WATER MANAGEMENT

Further Reading

Fedick, Scott L., and Jennifer P. Mathews. "The Yalahau Regional Human Ecology Project: An Introduction and Summary of Recent Research." In *Quintana Roo Archaeology*, edited by Justine M. Shaw and Jennifer P. Mathews, 35–50. Tucson: University of Arizona Press, 2005.

Glover, Jeffrey B., Dominique Rissolo, and Jennifer P. Mathews. "The Hidden World of the Maritime Maya: Lost Landscapes along the North Coast of Quintana Roo." In *The Archaeology of Maritime Landscapes*, edited by Benjamin Ford, 195–216. New York: Springer Press, 2011.

Rissolo, Dominique. *Ancient Maya Cave Use in the Yalahau Region, Northern Quintana Roo, Mexico.* Association for Mexican Cave Studies, Bulletin 12. Austin, TX: Association for Mexican Cave Studies, 2003.

◼ JENNIFER P. MATHEWS

YAXCHILAN

From a strategic location on a hilly horseshoe bend on the west (**Mexico**) bank of the Usumacinta River, Yaxchilan's (16.9° N, 91.0° W) rulers were important players in the political struggles of the region (see also **Map 3**). Founded in the fourth century, much of the city was built, or rebuilt, by two Late Classic rulers, Itzamnaaj Balam (also called Shield Jaguar) III and his son, Bird Jaguar IV. Fortunately the Yaxchilan rulers' commitment to creating an impressive city extended to the commissioning of around 60 carved lintels, 6 **hieroglyphic staircases**, and over 30 **stelae**. These have provided scholars with a trove of historical and ritual information about Yaxchilan, its allies, its rivals, its rituals, and notably, its women (see also **Alliances**; **Rites and Rituals**; **Women, Men, and Gender Roles**).

Around 120 stone buildings have been located at Yaxchilan. The builders took advantage of a series of hills as bases for small acropoli and important temples. Tall open-framed stone roof-combs increased the height of the elevated temples. Although little of them remains, life-sized stucco figures of rulers surrounded by politico-cosmic symbols, all colorfully painted, once decorated the roof-combs and façades of numerous structures (see also **Art**; **Wall Painting**).

There are three major groups of buildings. Thirty structures, including two **ball courts**, border an artificially leveled terrace that parallels the river bank. This area, known as the Great Plaza, is about 400 m long. On the south side of the plaza rises the first range of hills that serve as platforms for a series of buildings.

One of these is Str. 23. Texts on its inscribed and figural lintels refer to it as the house of Lady K'abal Xook, principal wife of Itzamnaaj Balam III. Three of its stone lintels depict the couple engaging in ritual activities. (See figure 51.) The central one (Lintel 25) shows her conjuring a part–centipede, part–serpent creature that seems to traverse time to bring forth a warrior whose garb includes **Teotihuacán**-style symbols (see also **Warfare, Warriors, and Weapons**). Because the date on the lintel is that of Itzamnaaj Balam's accession to the throne (in 9.12.9.8.1, or AD 681), the warrior that the creature manifests might be the city's founder reborn as the new king. On Lintel 24, she draws blood from her tongue while the king brandishes a flaming spear. A wholly hieroglyphic lintel in this

Figure 51. Lintels over the doorways of structures at Yaxchilan. They tell many of the stories of the exploits of rulers. Courtesy of Walter Witschey.

building details Lady K'abal Xook's lineage and commemorates 25 years of her husband's reign (see also **Divine Kings and Queens**; **Dynastic Sequences**; **Maya Queens**). No other ancient Maya woman is featured this prominently in a building. Analyses show that several artists collaborated on the design of these innovative compositions and the detailed treatment of the fine **textiles** worn.

Most wives of Itzamnaaj Balam III and Bird Jaguar IV were elites from other sites. While K'abal Xook was from Yaxchilan, the mother of Bird Jaguar IV was a royal woman of **Calakmul**. Bird Jaguar married one local woman, Lady Great Skull, and other women from Motul de San José and Hix Witz. Many of these women are depicted on lintels and stelae at the site, participating in royal ceremonies and performing bloodletting sacrifices.

Victorious conquest is another theme commonly shown at Yaxchilan. Itzamnaaj Balam III commissioned a war memorial (Str. 44) on the West Acropolis, a second group of buildings. Texts on the lintels and hieroglyphic steps detail his captures from AD 681 to 732. Scholars have determined that the victims were not great rulers but men from local sites, and that the captures were part of the king's efforts to expand his influence in the region.

Frequent battles disrupted the political situation, and when Itzamnaaj Balam died, in his nineties, a period of instability known as the interregnum occurred. The venerable Lady K'abal Xooc lived six more years, and after four more, a son of Itzamnaaj Balam, called Bird Jaguar IV, took the throne. Most scholars think that Bird Jaguar destroyed some records of another ruler, perhaps Yopaat Balaam II, a Yaxchilan noble recorded at **Piedras Negras** as having paid a visit during this time, but this is inconclusive. Once Bird Jaguar became king (he acceded to the throne in 9.16.1.0.0., or AD 752, and ruled about 20 years), he embarked on an unprecedented campaign of building and artistic production. Scholars have explored the many innovative strategies he used to create a sense of continuity of tradition, to show favor to important allies, and, most say, to deploy a propagandistic campaign to establish his own legitimacy.

His grandest building was Str. 33, built atop a hill that towers over the Great Plaza. Its high roof-comb was adorned with a figure of a seated ruler that would have been visible from the floor of the Great Plaza. This building faced the rising sun on summer solstice. The first rays illuminated a large statue of a seated king, probably Itzamnaaj Balam III, as well as a series of 13 carved stair risers that portrayed the ancestral rulers of Yaxchilan engaged in cosmic ball games and some women engaged in rituals involving supernatural serpents. The carved lintels of this building documented Bird Jaguar IV's own accession to the throne, accompanied by his local wife, his appointment of their son as heir to the throne, and an alliance with an important ally.

The third group of buildings is the South Acropolis, on the highest hill. Its three structures overlook the river. Str. 41 dates from an early reign and was reused by several later rulers, who erected at least six stelae in front of it, each commemorating a capture, the history of a ruler within a *k'atun*, or both. Remnants of paint within Str. 40 reveal the elegant calligraphic painting style that characterized Yaxchilan's florescence (see also **Wall Painting**).

Only two more kings ruled after Bird Jaguar IV, his son and grandson. Bird Jaguar's son, Itzamnaaj Balam IV, continued the tradition of erecting east-facing accession shrines before which the *k'atun*-marking stelae were installed. He had the loyalty of the lords of several dependent or allied sites, including La Pasadita, Laxtunich, and **Bonampak**. These sites included Itzamnaaj Balaam IV in their visual and textual records. A royal woman of Yaxchilan married King Yajaw Chan Muwaan of Bonampak and appears in that site's well-known murals. Despite Itzamnaaj Balaam IV's efforts to expand and decorate the city, and to strengthen alliances with other sites, the environmental, population, and cultural stresses that precipitated the collapse of the **Central Lowlands** affected Yaxchilan and Bonampak around AD 800 (see also **Classic Maya Collapse**). The last ruler, K'inich Tatbu Skull IV, commissioned one small lintel, packed with a now-familiar—but ineffective—litany of conquest and dynastic ritual. After the erection of Lintel 10 in AD 808, Yaxchilan fell silent.

See also CLIMATE; CORBEL ARCH; CRAFT SPECIALIZATION; PALACE; PALENQUE; SCULPTURE; SOUTHERN LOWLANDS; SYLLABARY; TERRACING; TERRITORIAL ENTITIES; TIKAL; WRITING SYSTEMS OF MESOAMERICA

Further Reading

Martin, Simon, and Nikolai Grube. *Chronicle of the Maya Kings and Queens: Deciphering the Dynasties of the Ancient Maya.* 2nd ed. London: Thames & Hudson, 2008.

Mathews, Peter. *La escultura de Yaxchilán.* México, D.F., México: Instituto Nacional de Antropología e Historia, 1997.

Nahm, Werner. "Hieroglyphic Stairway I at Yaxchilan." *Mexicon* 19, no. 4: 65–69, 1997.

O'Neil, Megan Eileen, and Marc G. Blainey. "Object, Memory, and Materiality at Yaxchilan: The Reset Lintels of Structures 12 and 22." *Ancient Mesoamerica* 22, no. 2: 245–69, 2011.

Tate, Carolyn Elaine. *Yaxchilan: The Design of a Maya Ceremonial City.* Austin: University of Texas Press, 1992.

■ CAROLYN E. TATE

YAXHÁ

Yaxhá (17.1° N, 89.4° W) was a large lowland Maya site on the northeast shore of **Lake Yaxhá**, east northeast of Lake Petén Itzá in the Department of the Petén (see also **Map 3**). David **Stuart** suggested that the Emblem Glyph in the Yaxhá inscriptions was readable in Maya as *Yax* "green" *Ha* "waters" and therefore that the modern name had its roots in the Classic period, making it a rare case of the survival of the original name of the site. Located 30 km southeast of Tikal, it displays a similar **Petén architectural style**. The presence of a twin-pyramid group, an architectural arrangement known mainly from **Tikal**, to celebrate a *k'atun* ending, testified to its close relations with this near neighbor (see also **Calendar**).

The ceremonial core of the site, which is about 500 m across, consists of a several plazas and buildings organized around the largest (Plaza E) to place an E-Group on the west side, a triadic group to the north (North Acropolis) and east (Northeast Acropolis), and a palace structure to the south. From the south palace, accessible by a rather narrow walkway along the palace, a 10-m-wide *sacbe* runs 350 m south-southwest downhill to the edge of Yaxhá Lake. From the west side of the north acropolis, the Blom *sacbe* runs 300 m north to the Maler Group, on a platform about 150 m by 150 m. From the plaza between the Northeast Acropolis and the South Acropolis (Palace) two **causeways** extend to the east 200 m to the East Acropolis (east *sacbe*), and 200 m southeast (Lincoln *sacbe*) to a southern section of the East Acropolis. Plaza E has two ball courts, one adjacent to the South Acropolis and one adjacent to the North Acropolis.

During the past decade, research and excavation by Paulino Morales and Erwin Valiente in the East Acropolis (a twin pyramid group and a triadic group) have produced several interesting findings. Leveling of the site for first construction took place in the Formative (600 BC–AD 350). Additional *sascab* was added to complete the leveling. One intrusive **burial** contained a bone pendant and Joventud Red vase; another had eight vases of the Achiotes Unslipped type. The main structures in the East Acropolis date to the Early Classic (AD 150–350) when Yaxhá prospered. Stela 5 carries an Early Classic date of AD 357, although in general the monuments at the site are badly weathered. One of the buildings was fractured by seismic activity, it is thought, at the end of the Early Classic, perhaps the result of activity in the east-west Yaxhá fault. Other Yaxhá buildings and structures at Nakum show the same earthquake damage. This event may have resulted in the abandonment of this part of Yaxhá and corresponding growth at Pozo Maya. Alternatively, its general decline at the end of the Early Classic may be due to disruption by **Naranjo**, whose monuments record **warfare** with Yaxhá, acting in concert with its then ally **Calakmul**.

Construction resumed in this area in the Late Classic (AD 700–800), raising the height of the pyramid to over 23 m, crowned by a three-doorway building with two vaulted rooms. This palace in the East Acropolis contains mural paintings and a likely elite burial with skull deformation and inlaid teeth. Accompanying offerings included eccentric flints, obsidian, and shell. Another burial contained jade mosaics, shell, bone, lithics, a Spondylus shell, cinnabar, animal teeth, a tetrapod jar, and a miniature beetle vessel. Stelae 11 and 41 are associated with this acropolis; stela 11 compares closely to Tikal Stela 32 and carries many central Mexican attributes of **Teotihuacán** (butterfly mouth ornament, goggle eyes, spear and shield) and is related to the arrival events at Tikal. In the twin pyramid group, Stela 13 shows a ruler of Yaxhá with a commemorative equinox date. The palace of the East Acropolis survived until the Terminal Classic (AD 800–900), and Yaxhá succumbed to the pressures of the Classic Maya collapse.

See also ALLIANCES; ARCHITECTURE OVERVIEW; CENTRAL LOWLANDS; CERAMICS; CORBEL ARCH; CIVAL; CLASSIC MAYA COLLAPSE; CRAFT SPECIALIZATION; ECCENTRIC LITHICS; GEOLOGY; PORTABLE OBJECTS; PYRAMID; SETTLEMENT PATTERNS (CENTRAL LOWLANDS)

Further Reading

Maler, Teobert. *Explorations in the Department of Petén, Guatemala and Adjacent Region: Topoxte; Yaxha; Benque Viejo; Naranjo: Reports of Explorations for the Museum.* Memoirs of the Peabody Museum of American Archaeology and Ethnology. Cambridge, MA: Peabody Museum of American Archaeology and Ethnology, Harvard University,., 1908.

Martin, Simon, and Nikolai Grube. *Chronicle of the Maya Kings and Queens: Deciphering the Dynasties of the Ancient Maya.* 2nd ed. London: Thames & Hudson, 2008.

Morales, Paulino I., and Erwin Franciné Valiente. "Secuencia de construcción y presentación del Edificio 218 en la Acrópolis Este de Yaxha " In *XIX Simposio de Investigaciones Arqueológicas en Guatemala, 2005*, edited by Juan Pedro Laporte, Bárbara Arroyo, and Héctor E. Mejía, 1010–17. Guatemala City, Guatemala: Museo Nacional de Arqueología y Etnología, 2006.

Sharer, Robert J., and Loa P. Traxler. *The Ancient Maya*. 6th ed. Stanford, CA: Stanford University Press, 2006.

Stuart, David. *The Yaxha Emblem Glyph as Yax-ha*. Center for Maya Research, 1985. http://www.mesoweb.com/bearc/cmr/01.html.

■ WALTER R. T. WITSCHEY

YAXHOM

Yaxhom (20.2° N, 89.5° W) is an archaeological site in the eastern Puuc district of Yucatan, **Mexico**, located in the subregion known as the Valle de Sta. Elena near its juncture with the hill zone to the south, the Distrito Bolonchen (see also **Map 3**). Yaxhom has as yet been studied only in preliminary form, but is noteworthy for its size and early monumental **architecture**. First reported under the name of Xpotoit by Teobert Maler in 1888, the next report was that of Nicholas Dunning, who, noting the density of sites surrounding Yaxhom, suggested the area was a great urban sprawl.

In 2011–2012, William Ringle initiated mapping and limited excavations in the region, with the goal of determining its extent and occupation history. The focus of Yaxhom is an extensive low terrace supporting numerous civic structures. The largest of these is an acropolis measuring 145 m on a side and rising 6–8 m, with other mounds on its surface rising to a total of over 20 m. Megalithic blocks were used in its construction. Excavations indicate it is certainly Formative in date, most likely during the latter Middle Formative, as is another acropolis about 1.5 km to the east. These bear resemblances to the Xocnaceh acropolis excavated by Gallareta. **Causeways** connect several outlying architectural complexes of varying time periods, some with megalithic construction. Preliminary results suggest the site covered 8–12 km² at its peak.

Yaxhom was probably settled to take advantage of a shallow basin of extremely rich **soils** (the Valle de Yaxhom), which, however, possess no natural water sources. Like most Puuc residents, Late Terminal Classic period inhabitants made use of underground cisterns (*chultunes*) built into their house platforms. In contrast, earlier inhabitants relied on the *aguada* Xpotoit, a large pond that could have held water for thousands. Preliminary excavations indicate that it was almost certainly man-made during the Formative period.

See also NORTHERN LOWLANDS; WATER MANAGEMENT

Further Reading

Dunning, Nicholas P. *Lords of the Hills: Ancient Maya Settlement in the Puuc Region, Yucatán, Mexico*. Madison, WI: Prehistory Press, 1992.

Ringle, William M., and Gabriel Tun Ayora. *The Yaxhom Valley Survey: Pioneers of the Puuc Hills, Yucatan; Second Field Season, 2012*. Report prepared for the Waitt Foundation and the National Geographic Society, 2013.

■ WILLIAM M. RINGLE

YAXNOHCAH (MONTEREY)

Monterey (17.9° N, 89.7° W) was discovered by Ruppert and Denison of the Carnegie Institution of Washington in 1933 and reported in their 1943 volume. Unaware of its prior discovery, Ivan Šprajc reached and investigated the site in 2004 and published a detailed report and site map in 2008. He used the name "Yaxnohcah," Yucatec Maya for "first great city," in his report. In 2011 Kathryn Reese-Taylor and Armando Anaya Hernández conducted additional research at the site. Yaxnohcah is located just north of the **Guatemala** border in southeast Campeche, **Mexico**, in the middle of the north-south central elevation in the Maya area called the Karstic Central Plateau (see also **Map 3** and **6**). The plateau spans roughly the region from **Tikal** to **Becan**, running a length of 175 km at elevations of ~350 m amsl.

Based on **ceramic** evidence, Yaxnohcah was first occupied between 600 BC and AD 400, and later from AD 750 to 900. The architectural evidence of triadic groups shows most of the structures at the site date to the Middle and Late Formative. The additional presence of a Group E configuration for tracking solar alignments makes the Middle Formative Yaxnohcah similar to **Nakbé** 33 km to the south-southwest (see also **Astronomical Observatories**). There is considerable population growth during the Late Formative, as is also found at **El Mirador**, just 30 km away, the largest Late Formative site in the region. **Calakmul**, 20 km to the north-northwest, erects Str. II in the same era.

The site has six large groupings of civic-ceremonial **architecture** (A–F). The central area of Groups A–C overlooks **Bajo** El Tomatal. Groups D–F lie at distances of 500–1,000 m away. All have massive platforms larger than 50 m by 50 m in area topped by large temple-**pyramids**, many in the triadic group configuration. Str. A-1 is the largest structure at the site, with a 38-m-tall pyramid situated on a platform 75 m by 85 m. An intrasite *sacbe* (**causeway**) joins Groups A and B.

Yaxnohcah presents and will help answer many interesting questions about the development of Maya society, including, "Why are so many of the very large, very early Formative Maya sites located near *bajos* in the central plateau?"

Further Reading

Reese-Taylor, Kathryn. *Yaxnohcah*. 2013. http://people.ucalgary.ca/~kreeseta/research/yaxnohcah.html.

Reese-Taylor, Kathryn, and Armando Anaya Hernández, eds. *Proyecto Arqueológico Yaxnohcah, 2011 Informe de la Primera Temporada de Investigaciones*. Calgary, AB: Universidad de Calgary, 2013.

Ruppert, Karl, and John Hopkins Denison. *Archaeological Reconnaissance in Campeche, Quintana Roo, and Petén*. Carnegie Institution of Washington, Publication 543. Washington, DC: Carnegie Institution of Washington, 1943.

Šprajc, Ivan. *Reconocimiento arqueológico en el sureste del estado de Campeche, México: 1996–2005*. B.A.R. International Series, no. 1742. Paris Monographs in American Archaeology. Oxford, UK: Archaeopress, 2008.

◼ WALTER R. T. WITSCHEY

YAXUNA

The ancient site of Yaxuna (20.5° N, 88.7° W) is situated in the center of the **Northern Lowlands** just 18 km south-southwest of **Chichen Itza**, yet is connected by the longest known Maya *sacbe* (**causeway**) to **Cobá**, 100 km to the east. Uxmal **lies** about 125km to the west (see also **Map 3**).

Early explorers to the site include Sylvanus Morley, **J. Eric S. Thompson**, Alfonso Villa Rojas, and George Brainerd, who sampled for **ceramics** with test pits. David Freidel began an intensive research project in 1996 that continued for a decade.

Yaxuna was settled in the Middle Formative ca. 500 BC. Although no clearly Middle Formative **architecture** is known, an abundance of ceramics from the period was recovered from a Late Formative triadic group. In the Late Formative, Yaxuna elites launched a major building program producing triadic configurations in the North and East Acropoli and the site's largest structure, Str. 5F-3. A cache within a Sierra Red "bucket" contained symbolic hearthstones and a jade axe and mirror, strongly linked to **Olmec** iconography. Residential architecture documents an extensive settlement in the Late Formative.

In the Early Classic, in additional to widespread residential and ceremonial construction, **royal tomb** B.-23 documents Yaxuna's links to the central Petén sites via **Becan**, and **iconographic**, if not direct physical links, to **Teotihuacán**. B.-24's containing a sacrificed family appears to document a hostile takeover of Yaxuna and termination of the existing rulers. A young female, never pregnant but perhaps in line to bear a ruling heir, bore a royal crown (*sak hunal*) and cradled a unique ceramic figurine "Las Muñecas." A cylindrical tripod vase documents the connections to Teotihuacán. Elites of Yaxuna also constructed copies of Teotihuacán patio-quad architecture. Toward the end of the Early Classic, ritual destruction of buildings, plus further change in ceramics, shows Yaxuna political fortunes were aligned less with the Petén sites and more with northern Yucatan sites such as Cobá and Ek Balam.

During the Late Classic, population was lower and construction diminished. In this somewhat weakened state, Cobá rulers pushed the 100-km-long *sacbe* from east to west, making Yaxuna Cobá's westernmost outpost. This physical statement of political power was perhaps aimed at Chichen Itza, which grew in strength to threaten Cobá. Significant ceramic changes suggest that Cobá was both conquering and colonizing.

The Terminal Classic was a troubled time for Yaxuna, which met threats from Chichen Itza in part by hastily constructing **fortifications**. The Xkanha Group was sealed with a 10-m-long wall and a defensive tower with a dedicatory cache with a bowl holding a human head. The North Acropolis was fitted with a 330-m-long wall. Ceramics at the site began to reflect western connections, suggesting that Cobá was trading with the Puuc region and Uxmal through Yaxuna via the *sacbe*.

Late in the Terminal Classic, or in the Early Postclassic, Yaxuna was overcome by Chichen Itza, but occupation seems not to have been lengthy. There is little occupation evidence for the Postclassic, but ceramics indicate Yaxuna fell to western control when Chichen Itza fell, and that the mostly abandoned ruins were used for rituals, as documented by small shrines and Chen Mul censers.

See also BURIALS; PHYSICAL/BIOLOGICAL ANTHROPOLOGY; PORTABLE OBJECTS; RITES AND RITUALS; TERRITORIAL ENTITIES; WARFARE, WARRIORS, AND WEAPONS

Further Reading

Freidel, David, Charles Suhler, and Rafael Cobos P. *The Selz Foundation Yaxuna Project: Final Report of the 1991 Field Season.* Foundation for the Advancement of Mesoamerican Research, Inc (FAMSI), 1991. http://www.famsi.org/research/freidel/1991Freidel.pdf.

Hofstetter, Phillip. *Map of the Ruins of Yaxuna.* 1996. http://maya.csueastbay.edu/yaxuna/yaxmapframes.html.

McKillop, Heather. *The Ancient Maya: New Perspectives.* New York: W. W. Norton, 2004.

Stanton, Travis W., and David A. Freidel. "Placing the Centre, Centring the Place: The Influence of Formative Sacbeob in Classic Site Design at Yaxuná, Yucatán." *Cambridge Archaeological Journal* 15, no. 2: 225–49, 2005.

Suhler, Charles, Traci Ardren, David Freidel, and Dave Johnstone. "The Rise and Fall of Terminal Classic Yaxuna, Yucatan, Mexico." In *The Terminal Classic in the Maya Lowlands: Collapse, Transition, and Transformation,* edited by Arthur A. Demarest, Prudence M. Rice, and Don Stephen Rice, 551–87. Boulder: University Press of Colorado, 2004.

Suhler, Charles, Traci Ardren, and Dave Johnstone. "The Chronology of Yaxuna: Evidence from Excavation and Ceramics." *Ancient Mesoamerica* 9: 167–82, 1998.

■ W A L T E R   R .   T .   W I T S C H E Y

YO'OKOP

See CΟCHUAH REGION

YUCATECAN MAYA LANGUAGES

Around 1000 BC, the peoples who would become speakers of the Yucatecan Mayan languages left the Proto-Mayan homelands, postulated to be in the heights of the Cuchumatan Mountains of **Guatemala**, migrating to the lowlands of the Yucatan Peninsula, Guatemala's Petén and **Belize**. Those who would become speakers of Ch'olan languages left around the same time, situating themselves at the base of the highlands and throughout the lowlands as far south as modern-day **Honduras**. The Yucatecan speakers occupied a wide territory and maintained a high degree of linguistic uniformity. In the following 3,000 years, the branch diversified into only four languages: Yucatec Maya, spoken today by nearly 800,000 people in Campeche, Quintana Roo, and Yucatan; Lakantun (alternate spelling Lacandón), with about 1,000 speakers living in the upper reaches of the Usumacinta River and in Chiapas; Mopán, having some 16,000 speakers in Guatemala and Belize; and Itzaj (alternate spelling Itza'), spoken in San José Petén. Itzaj today is in grave danger of extinction despite efforts by the Academy of Mayan Languages of Guatemala to revive it. Though around 2,000 people claim Itzaj heritage, fewer than 100 can speak the language.

As Yucatecan developed and differentiated from Proto-Maya, the languages of this branch underwent a series of sound changes. Proto-Mayan post-velars //q// and //q'// became velars //k// and //k'//. The velar nasal of the mother language became a dental nasal: //ŋ// > //n//.

Thus, the original word for "sun, day" ⋆//q'iŋ// became //k'in// in Yucatecan languages. Proto-Maya //t// and //tʸ// both went to //č// in Yucatecan: ⋆ tʸe ʔ > če ʔ "tree". The //r// of Proto-Maya turned into //y// in Yucatecan: ⋆kar > kay "fish". During most of the Classic Period (250–900 CE) royal Yucatecan scribes recorded events on **stelae**,

architecture, pots, and amate-paper books in standardized Ch'olan (see also **Ceramics**; **Codices [Maya]**). But by the end of the period, features of Yucatecan speech began to appear in writing instead of, or alongside, their Ch'olan counterparts: *kaan* rather than *chaan* "sky," *keeh* rather than *chij* "deer," and *yotoch* for *yotot* "his/her house." The surviving manuscripts we have from the early Colonial period in Yucatan, the Madrid, Dresden, and Paris codices, are written in Yucatec Maya, though they conserve some of the Ch'olan elements.

Yucatec Maya is distinguished from its sister Yucatecan languages by having developed phonemic tone contrasts. Two other Mayan languages, Uspantek and one variant of Tzotzil, have independently developed tone. Proto-Maya is postulated to have had four kinds of syllabic nuclei: V, VV, Vh, and VɁ. In Yucatec Maya, the long vowel (VV) developed a low tone; the two V + glottal sequences, Vh and VɁ yielded high tones. The short vowel (V) now carries a mid or neutral tone. The words *míis* "broom" and *mìis* "cat" differ only in that "broom" carries a high tone and "cat" is realized with a low level tone. Similarly Ɂáak "turtle" and Ɂàak "reed" are distinguished by their high and low tones respectively. The near minimal pair *b'ak* "meat" carries the short vowel's neutral or mid tone.

Today Yucatec Maya remains a robust language. The Secretaría de Educación Pública (SEP) de México promotes the teaching of Yucatec Maya in public schools throughout the Yucatan Peninsula. In 2012 SEP approved a university *bachillerato* (baccalaureate) in intercultural studies, which mandatorily includes study of Yucatec language and culture and offers a certificate program in "High Maya Culture." The Academy of the Maya Language of Yucatan (U Molay Ah Maya Than Yucalpetén Yucatán) has worked since 1937 to sponsor linguistic investigation, to stimulate Yucatec literary and academic writing, and to promote language instruction. Three government radio stations and a number of community radios broadcast in Yucatec. In 2013 the first Maya language soap opera premiered on public television in the state of Quintana Roo. Yucatec's sister languages have not fared so well. Concerted revitalization efforts are needed to ensure their survival.

See also Decipherment; Highland Maya Languages; Writing Systems of Mesoamerica

Further Reading

Academia de las Lenguas Mayas de Guatemala, and Comunidad Lingüística Maya Mopan. *Muuch't'an Mopan: Vocabulario Mopan*. Guatemala City, Guatemala: K'ulb'il Yol Twitz Paxil, 2003.

Bricker, Victoria Reifler, Eleuterio Po'ot Yah, and Ofelia Dzul de Po'ot. *A Dictionary of the Maya Language: As Spoken in Hocabá, Yucatán*. With a botanical index by Anne S. Bradburn. Salt Lake City: University of Utah Press, 1998.

Burns, Allan F. *An Epoch of Miracles: Oral Literature of the Yucatec Maya*. Translated with commentaries by Allan F. Burns. Foreword by Dennis Tedlock. Austin: University of Texas Press, 1983.

Hofling, Charles Andrew, and Félix Fernando Tesucún. *Itzaj Maya Grammar*. Salt Lake City: University of Utah Press, 2000.

Po'ot Yah, Eleuterio. *Yucatec Maya Verbs (Hocaba Dialect)*. Grammatical introduction by Victoria R. Bricker. Translated by James Ward. New Orleans, LA: Center for Latin American Studies, Tulane University, 1981.

Pryor, Hilary, and Shendra Hanney. *The Lacandon Maya*. DVD. May Street Group Film Video & Animation Ltd. in association with History Television and Delphis Films. New York: Filmakers Library, 2007.

■ JUDITH M. MAXWELL

Z

ZACPETÉN

Sitting on a peninsula at the northeast corner of Lake Salpetén, a small lake to the immediate east of Lake Petén Itza, **Guatemala**, Zacpetén (16.0° N, 89.7° W) is a Maya archaeological site most notable for its Late Postclassic and Contact period occupation by the Kowoj (see also **Map 3**). The Kowoj controlled the region to the north and northeast of Lake Petén-Itza at this time, with centers at Zacpetén as well as the nearby sites of Muralla de Leon and Topoxté.

Initial occupation and construction at the site dates to the Middle Preclassic, although evidence shows abandonment by the Early Classic. A large-scale reoccupation began in the Late/Terminal Classic, a period that also witnessed a rebuilding effort that included erection of a defensive wall. Spanning the neck of land at the north of the site where the peninsula joins the mainland, the **fortifications** controlled access into the site and were renovated throughout the ensuing Postclassic period, reflecting continuity of occupation at the site from the Terminal Classic onward to the Colonial era.

Two Late Postclassic ceremonial groups (Groups A and C), two elite household groups (Groups D and E), and a twin pyramid group (Group B) from the Terminal Classic, in addition to 137 visible patio groups and 23 other structures, constitute the known **architecture** at the site. A "tandem" form, with an open front room and a private back room, describes the residences at Zacpetén. Meanwhile, Kowoj claims of migration from **Mayapán** are supported by the conformity of Groups A and C to the "temple assemblage" arrangement characteristic of that site. The examples present here contain the same architectural elements but differ slightly from the Mayapán archetype in their directionality, the presence of extra structures, and the buildings themselves lacking bilateral symmetry, a variation also observed at the two other Kowoj centers mentioned above.

Further Reading

Pugh, Timothy W. "Activity Areas, Form, and Social Inequality in Residences at Late Postclassic Zacpetén, Petén, Guatemala." *Journal of Field Archaeology* 29, nos. 3/4: 351–67, 2002–2004.

Rice, Don Stephen, Prudence M. Rice, and Timothy W. Pugh. "Settlement Continuity and Change in the Central Petén Lakes Region: The Case of Zacpetén." In *Anatomía de una civilización: Aproximaciones interdisciplinarias a la cultura maya*, edited by Andrés Ciudad Ruíz, 207–52. Madrid: Sociedad Española de Estudios Mayas, 1998.

■ JUSTIN BRACKEN

ZACUALPA

Zacualpa (15.0° N, 90.9° W) is a Maya archaeological site in the modern department of El Quiché, in the **Northern Highlands** of **Guatemala** (see also **Map 3**). Zacualpa was a Mam (Maya) provincial center. Its occupation spans the Protoclassic through the Late Postclassic periods. During the latter period site activity displays cremation **burials**, and ethnohistoric sources suggest that the expansionistic K'iche Maya conquered the site from their base at Q'um'arkaj (**Utatlán**).

Zacualpa is located on the northeast side of the La Vega River Valley, situated on a plateau at the edge of the ravine overlooking the river. On the north side of the river are tuff cliffs, with the higher Sierra Chuacas to the north.

Archaeological exploration of the site was first undertaken in 1935 by Robert Wauchope, working with the Carnegie Institution of Washington. His explorations uncovered stratigraphy and artifacts permitting the definition of the first prehistoric sequence for the region.

The occupation of the site started in the Protoclassic period. Cist graves (stone-lined **burials**) with green stone figurine caches from a ravine at the edge of the settlement date to this time period. The practice of caching greenstone figures continued in the Early Classic but declined in the Late Classic period. Censers are other ritual objects found during the Classic period that became increasingly more elaborate with time (see also **Ceramics**; **Rites and Rituals**).

There are three architectural groups at Zacualpa. Group A, dating primarily to the Early Classic period, is the earliest and largest of the three. It has two areas: on the west side are nine structures. The largest, Str. A-IV is located in the center of the group and is a 15-m-tall **pyramid** with basal dimensions of 75 m. On the east side of Group A is an impressive acropolis with eight or nine structures assembled around three plazas, one of which is a **ball court**. Research avoided excavating buildings but did find fine clay facings on the building's exteriors and earthen floors, retaining walls, and stone slab pavements beneath the building.

In the Late Classic, Group A was abandoned and building activities and occupation moved to the residential Group B, on the other side of the La Vega Valley. Construction started at the beginning of the Late Classic; two cist **burials** date to this period. Later additions were carried out around the cardinal points of the plaza of Group B and created a rectilinear arrangement. Some of the additions had stone terraces and steps, arranged around two plazas, but no elite burials have been found in the group.

The Early Postclassic Tohil period was culturally innovative at Zacualpa and elsewhere in the highlands. During this period there was a change from the centuries of Classic traditions and lifeways. New pottery types included Plumbate pottery, vessels in pyriform (hourglass) shape, and mold-made vessels with animal-effigy legs. The last use of Group B was during the Tohil period; ceramics and burials were discovered in the upper layers of the excavations that overlay the architectural expansion that took place during the Late Classic to Early Postclassic transition.

In the Late Postclassic period, Zacualpa was conquered by the K'iche' ruler Quicab, according to ethnohistoric sources. Robert Wauchope postulated that the takeover took place in AD 1460. Little Late Postclassic period archaeological remains were found at the

site: only some cremations, cremation jars, and a few other ceramic pieces. The cremations were intrusive into the Early Postclassic structures at Zacualpa, suggesting that it was
abandoned before or soon after the conquest by the K'iche'.

See also CRAFT SPECIALIZATION; FAUNA; PHYSICAL/BIOLOGICAL ANTHROPOLOGY; *POPOL VUH*;
PYRAMID; TERRACING

Further Reading

Borgstede, Greg, and Eugenia J. Robinson. "The Archaeology of the Late Postclassic Maya Highlands."
    In *The Oxford Handbook of Mesoamerican Archaeology*, edited by Deborah L. Nichols and Christopher
    A. Pool, 405–18. New York: Oxford University Press, 2012.
Wauchope, Robert. *Excavations at Zacualpa, Guatemala.* Middle American Research Institute, Publication
    14. New Orleans, LA: Tulane University, 1948.
———. *Zacualpa, El Quiche, Guatemala: An Ancient Provincial Center of the Highland Maya.* Middle Amer-
    ican Research Institute, Publication 39. New Orleans, LA: Tulane University, 1975.

■ EUGENIA J. ROBINSON

ZACULEU

Zaculeu (15.3° N, 91.5° W) is a Maya archaeological site in the northwestern Huehuetenango Valley at the base of the Cuchumatanes in western highland **Guatemala**, located
4 km northwest of the modern city of Huehuetenango at an altitude of 1,940 m (see
also **Map 3**).

Zaculeu is situated on a defensible plateau surrounded by steep ravines, with the Sele-
guá River to the north and the Minerva River to the south. The 43 buildings at the site
include **pyramids** and **palaces** arranged around plazas. The structures date to the Classic
and Postclassic periods. The Postclassic buildings remain visible and were constructed in the
talud-tablero style with double staircases. The entrance to Zaculeu was protected by a narrow
land bridge to the north and a **fortified** structure. The site is enigmatic in that its highly
defensive nature would suggest a Postclassic date, when internecine **warfare** was common
in the region, yet some of the largest structures at the site date to the Classic period.

Excavations at Zaculeu were carried out by the United Fruit Company and directed
by Richard Woodbury, Aubrey Trik, and John Dimick between 1946 and 1949. At the
time of their work, there was an intense interest in garnering archaeological information in this unknown area of the highlands and in preparing sites for tourists. Zaculeu
offered the opportunity to excavate and reconstruct a site near an urban center and the
Pan-American Highway. The United Fruit Company project also reconstructed the site
for tourism.

During the Classic period, architecture was constructed with stone and adobe mortar.
A tomb from under Str. 1, the main pyramid, dates to this period and had the remains of
at least seven children and adults and more than 100 painted, carved, stuccoed **ceramic**
vessels; pyrite mirrors; a sizable quantity of jade beads and jade mosaics; a stuccoed conch
shell; rabbit head; jaws of a leopard; and grinding stones (see also **Burials**; **Fauna**; **Portable Objects**).

Building continued in the Early Postclassic period, but in the Late Postclassic period the site took its final form, with cut-stone buildings covered with stucco and architectural features characteristic of the "Mexicanization" of the Maya highlands, showing features of Central Mexico, perhaps derived from the archaeological site of Tula. During this period, Str. 1 was modified; it was built in *talud-tablero* form with vertical risers and a divided staircase ascending to the top of the structure. A one-room structure with three entrances delimited by two cylindrical columns was located on top of Str. 1. Str. 4 was built with a semicircular section on its south side, similar to round structures erected in honor of the Wind God Ehecatl, in Central Mexico. Str. 4 also has colonnaded chambers on each of its two sides, with round columns defining the multiple entrances. The Postclassic site also has an I-shaped **ball court** with sloping walls.

Archaeologists uncovered fine orange tripod vases, effigy head tripod bowls, perforated tripod vessels, and painted red-on-white pottery; all ceramic types common to the Postclassic. About 30 metal artifacts were found; they were crafted of gold, copper, and their alloys. Two of these pieces could have been influenced or imported from Mexico and southern Central America.

According to ethnohistoric sources, Zaculeu (which means "white" [*zac*] and "Earth" [*uleu*] in Mam Maya) was the capital of the Mam Maya in the Late Postclassic or Proto-historic period (AD 1250–1524). Zaculeu was conquered by the K'iche' Maya based in Q'um'arkaj (**Utatlán**) in the mid-fifteenth century. The K'iche' control of the site continued until AD 1525, when Spanish forces under Gonzalo de Alvarado conquered the capital after a long siege; it is recorded that the Maya forces were led by the legendary Maya ruler Kayb'il B'alam.

See also CAVES; CRAFT SPECIALIZATION; NORTHERN HIGHLANDS; PHYSICAL/BIOLOGICAL ANTHROPOLOGY

Further Reading

Borgstede, Greg, and Eugenia J. Robinson. "The Archaeology of the Late Postclassic Maya Highlands." In *The Oxford Handbook of Mesoamerican Archaeology*, edited by Deborah L. Nichols and Christopher A. Pool, 405–18. New York: Oxford University Press, 2012.

Woodbury, Richard B., and Aubrey S. Trik. *The Ruins of Zaculeu, Guatemala.* Vol. 1. New York: United Fruit Co., 1953.

■ EUGENIA J. ROBINSON

GLOSSARY

achiote	(*Bixa orellana* L) annatto, a spice with bright red seeds
Ahaw	also *Ahau* and *Ajaw*; title for king, ruler, holy lord
albarradas	stone walls
apsidal	adjective to describe a hut with rounded ends, not rectangular ends
atlatl	spear-thrower
b'ak'tun	twenty k'atuns; approximately 400 years
basalt	dark dense gray-black volcanic rock
bolide	large meteorite
burnish	polish the surface of a ceramic vessel before firing
C14	radiocarbon dating of organic remains using the ^{14}C isotope
cache	a buried offering, often on the centerline or corners of a pyramid
calcite	calcium carbonate grains or crystals, used as temper in ceramics
cenote	a natural well formed by collapsed karst; from '*d'zonot*' 'well'
Chaac	(*Chac, Chahk, Chaahk*) rain god
Chacmool	carved stone altar shaped as a recumbent person holding an offering plate
chen	*ch'ee'n*; water well, natural or manmade
chert	naturally occurring nodules of fine-grained quartz found in cavities in limestone karst; common in the Maya lowlands; used for stone tools
chicle	latex tree sap used in chewing gum
chiclero	a chicle worker who harvests tree sap for chewing gum
chinampas	artificial raised agricultural fields in swampy areas
ch'ok	Young man
chultun	large lined bottle-shaped reservoir, usually for water, excavated into karst terrain
chiefdom	village(s) permanently ruled by a single powerful individual, and with social status differences, but without a central government
cinnabar	red mercury sulfide (HgS) ore; used as pigment or heated for mercury
codex	a Maya fan-fold fig-bark paper book; four known: Dresden, Paris, Madrid, Grolier
colonnettes	grouped adjacent short columns as decorative panels on Puuc-style buildings *See* http://mayaruinscom/background/bkg_m1_083html

conchoidal | shell-like; the arced pattern formed by breaking off a piece of ceramic or crystalline stone

copal | also *pom*; tree resin for ceremonial incense

debitage | waste flakes and debris from the production of stone tools

dibble | dibber; a slightly pointed stick to make holes in the ground to plant seeds

ear flare | ear spool; disks of jade, obsidian, or ceramic worn by Maya elites

eccentric flint | elaborately flaked stone profiles of rulers and gods that may have served as the upper end of a ceremonial staff; often found in royal burials

ejido | agricultural land belonging to a community, and assigned to village members for farming

Emblem Glyph | Identified by Heinrich Berlin; usually read as "Holy Lord of (place)"

entrepôt | a port or city for intermediate trans-shipment (import/export) of goods

epi-Olmec | post-Olmec culture in the Olmec region of the Veracruz gulf coast

epigrapher | one who studies ancient inscriptions

eutrophication | enriching waters with nutrients, especially nitrogen and phosphorus, stimulating algae growth

E-group; Group-E | configuration of buildings arranged to observe the equinoxes and solstices at sunrise

flint | a type of chert found only in deposits of chalk

haab' | the Maya secular calendar cycle of 365 days, consisting of 18 twenty-day months, and a five-day month

hematite | red ore of iron oxide (Fe_2O_3) used as a pigment

hierophany | a revelation of the sacred, as the serpent revealed by patterns of light on the Castillo of Chichen Itza at the equinoctial sunsets

house | a small domestic dwelling structure

household | the people who live in one house, whether related or not

karst | natural terrain of porous soluble limestone, with a rough surface, cavities, sinkholes (cenotes), and caves

k'atun | twenty *tuns*; approximately 20 years; the fourth position in the Maya Long Count

K'awiil | god of lightning

k'in | sun, day, the low-order (ones) position in the Maya Long Count

K'inich Ajaw | Sun-eyed Lord or *Ahau K'in*, Lord Sun

lintel | supporting beam over a doorway or window

Long Count | five-place day-counting calendar system

mansard roof | a two-part roof with a steeply sloped lower portion

mestizo | a mixed-race person, particularly of Spanish and American Indian descent

metate | corn-grinding stone, used with a hand-held mano

midden | archaeological remains of an ancient waste or garbage area

milpa | also *kol*; cornfield

mosaic style | the use of individually carved stones, fitted onto a building façade

name-tagging | inscribing or painting the name of an object's owner on it

obsidian	naturally occurring volcanic glass; prized for making sharp-edged tools
Olmecoid	sites or artifacts that show Olmec traits, but are not Olmec
petén	natural raised islands of vegetation in inundated terrain; the largest department of Guatemala
phytolith	hard silica remains of plant fibers useful for identification in archaeology
plazuela group	set of platform structures, usually two to six, formally organized around a small, shared open patio
popol nah	a Maya council house; typically Late Classic and later (after the era of divine kings)
port of trade	elite-administered area to control long-distance trade
resist	a decorative pattern of wax applied to the surface of a ceramic vessel before applying slip, to create areas where slip does not adhere
rind	the outer layer of a piece of obsidian which grows in thickness over time
ring number	a method for counting date distance numbers in the Dresden **Codex**
roof comb	a vertical masonry superstructure above the roof of a Maya temple to add height and a decorative façade
sacbe	a raised causeway; literally 'white road' from *sac* 'white' and *be* 'road'
sajal	Regional Governor
sascab	also *sahcab*; white powdery limestone marl, quarried for making mortar
shaman	a person believed to be able to communicate with the spirits or gods while in a state of altered consciousness using meditation, alcohol, and hallucinogens
slip	a thin wash of clay in water applied to a ceramic vessel before firing; both decorative and utilitarian
state	a socially stratified society with an organized central government
stela/stelae	carved upright stone commemorative marker(s)
swidden	low intensity slash-and-burn agriculture
talpetate (*tepetate*)	hardened soil from pyroclastic flows, unsuitable for farming
talud-tablero	iconic architectural feature of Teotihuacán in which a pyramid terrace has a lower sloped part (*talud*) and upper vertical portion (*tablero*) with a rectangular inset panel
tecomate	a restricted-neck vessel, in form like a gourd with the neck cut off
temper	fine grit added to ceramic paste to prevent shrinkage and cracking
triadic group	a cluster of three temple pyramids one large, two small, in a "C" shape atop a platform; distinctive of Formative Period ceremonial architecture
tun	stone; drum; the third position in the Maya Long Count; 360 days
tzolk'in	sacred calendar cycle of 260 days, using 13 numbers with 20 day-names
uinal	twenty days; the second position in the Maya Long Count
vigesimal	base-20 counting system; a modified version is used in the Long Count

wayeb	in the Maya calendar *haab'* cycle, a short month of five unlucky days
witz	first mountain in Maya creation; temples as representations of mountains
Xibalba	the underworld
zenith passage	for areas between the Tropics and the Equator, the two days each year when the sun passes directly overhead

INTRODUCTION TO RESOURCES AND BIBLIOGRAPHY

In 1962 Ignacio Bernal, one of Mexico's most eminent archaeologists, published a monumental bibliography of Mesoamerican archaeology and ethnography. Printed in folio format between light blue cloth covers, the tome weighed in at 634 pages, in which 13,990 entries were listed. Fifty years later, we can only guess at the number of books and articles published on ancient Mesoamerica, but we can say with confidence that the pace of publication has increased. Perhaps the best estimate comes from the *Bibliografía Mesoamericana*, an online, searchable bibliography produced by the Foundation for the Advancement of Mesoamerican Studies and the Museum Library of the University of Pennsylvania (www.famsi.org/research/bibliography.htm). It contains nearly 74,000 records and was substantially updated in 2015. A library of fair size would be required to shelve all those publications. The ocean of information has spread far beyond the ability of any single scholar to comprehend it, and we cannot hope to summarize it effectively in this brief note. In this essay, while discussing some foundational references, we focus on newer books in English. Our bibliography still includes many of the most important citations regardless of their age, but we have highlighted newer contributions to the field.

The single most comprehensive source on Mesoamerican culture, prehistory, and ethnohistory remains the *Handbook of Middle American Indians*, an encyclopedic, 16-volume work prepared under the general editorship of Robert Wauchope, then director of the Middle American Research Institute of Tulane University. Prepared in the 1960s and 1970s, it still contains much valuable information, but some of the entries have now been superseded. Starting in the 1980s, supplementary volumes have been issued on various topics (e.g., archaeology, ethnohistory, literature, epigraphy) under the general editorship of Victoria R. Bricker of Tulane. Those works have served to update the handbook and keep it current.

Because of its scope and quality, the most important single journal in this field is *Ancient Mesoamerica* (Cambridge), currently edited by William Fowler (Vanderbilt). The only other journal with the same scope is *Mexicon*, which, though published in Germany, is mostly written in English and Spanish. *Latin American Antiquity*, published by the Society for American Archaeology, routinely publishes pieces on Mesoamerican archaeology, although its scope includes all of Latin America. Both *Ancient Mesoamerica* and *Latin American Antiquity* are relatively young. Many other journals publish occasional articles relevant to the themes in this volume: *Antiquity*, the preeminent British archaeological journal; the *Journal of Archaeological Science*, the leading (and highest impact) periodical in its field, published by the Society for Archaeological Science; *American Anthropologist*, the flagship journal of the American Anthropological Society; and general scientific journals, such as *Science, Nature*, and the *Proceedings of the National Academy of Sciences*. Finally, a number of regional journals are published that focus on parts or aspects of Mesoamerica. *Mesoamérica* probably falls into this category. Published in Guatemala mainly in Spanish, its coverage extends beyond archaeology and prehistory to include history, ethnography, and some other topics, with a focus on southern Mesoamerica, mainly the Maya. *Estudios de Cultura Maya* is a Mexican journal that publishes mainly in Spanish on the anthropology of the Maya.

In the last few years, numerous works on Mesoamerica have appeared in print. The best is Oxford University Press's *The Oxford Encyclopedia of Mesoamerican Cultures* (2001), compiled under the general editorial direction of Davíd Carrasco, who was assisted by a cohort of other distinguished editors. This three-volume work is a uniquely modern and authoritative contribution to the field, with a plethora of articles written by renowned scholars. In 2000, Cambridge issued volume 2, *Mesoamerica*, of *The Cambridge History of the Native Peoples of the Americas*, which is actually two quarto tomes. It has fewer (only 21) but longer entries than the Oxford encyclopedia. *Archaeology of Ancient Mexico and Central America: An Encyclopedia* (2010), edited by Susan Toby Evans and David L. Webster, is similar in scale to the Cambridge volume, but focuses more tightly on the archaeology as opposed to history or ethnography.

In addition to encyclopedias, new or revised general works, including textbooks, have emerged. Works by Sharer and Coe continue to be the most outstanding and useful narratives about the Maya. Robert Sharer and Loa Traxler have produced the sixth edition of *The Ancient Maya* (2006), and Michael Coe's *The Maya* has also been updated in an eighth edition (2011). The third edition of Susan Toby Evans's important *Ancient Mexico & Central America: Archaeology and Culture History* (Thames & Hudson, 2013) has also come out.

That the Maya continue to fascinate is shown by many new books. Stephen Houston and Takeshi Inomata published *The Classic Maya* in the Cambridge World Archaeology Series in 2009, while Arthur Demarest's *Ancient Maya: The Rise and Fall of a Rainforest Civilization*, also published by Cambridge, came out in 2005. *The Memory of Bones: Body, Being, and Experience among the Classic Maya* by Stephen Houston, David Stuart, and Karl Taube (University of Texas Press, 2006) is an intellectually innovative examination of a topic of current interest to scholars. David Stuart's *The Inscriptions from Temple XIX at Palenque: A Commentary* (Pre-Columbian Art Research Institute, 2005) is an outstanding work on an even more beautiful monument, the magnificent bas-reliefs recently uncovered at Palenque. Also recently published is another visually compelling book, *Reading Maya Art* by Andrea Stone and Marc Zender (Thames & Hudson, 2011), which offers a lavishly illustrated catalog of 100 hieroglyphic elements that were incorporated by the ancient Maya into the iconography of their art. A new edition of *The Chronicle of the Maya Kings and Queens* by Simon Martin and Nikolai Grube also came out (Thames & Hudson, 2008). This book is an essential reference by two eminent scholars. Regarding our views of when and where Maya civilization arose, watch for the 2015 publication of *The Earliest Ceramics of the Northern Maya Lowlands* by E. Wyllys Andrews V, George J.

Bey III, and Christopher Gunn. Geoffrey Braswell has compiled two new volumes: *The Ancient Maya of Mexico: Reinterpreting the Past of the Northern Maya* and *The Maya and Their Central American Neighbors: Settlement Patterns, Architecture, Hieroglyphic Texts and Ceramics*.

Numerous books were published about the end of the current Long Count great cycle at 13.0.0.0.0 in December 2012. Standing above the many works that predicted global or cosmic disasters, three scholarly books are notable: David Stuart's *The Order of Days: The Maya World and the Truth about 2012* (Random House, 2011), Anthony Aveni's *The End of Time: The Maya Mystery of 2012* (University of Colorado, 2009), and Mark Van Stone's *2012: Science & Prophecy of the Ancient Maya* (Tlacaélel, 2011). As experts in epigraphy, calendrics, and astronomy, these authors are particularly well-suited to avoid the sensationalism surrounding this topic and focus on the facts.

As higher resolution photographs are posted to Google Earth, new aerial views of archaeological sites become widely available. Official reports and documents from federal agencies in Mesoamerica are becoming available electronically, such as from the website of the Mexican Instituto Nacional de Antropología e Historia (http://www.inah.gob .mx/). A search for artifacts, images, reports, and journal articles via open sources such as Google (www.Google.com) and WorldCat (www.WorldCat.org), as well as membership sources through libraries, such as JSTOR (www.JSTOR.org), provides an extensive array of helpful postings.

Internet resources have become a particularly valuable asset to researchers in recent years. It is more common now to find complete websites for individual archaeological sites in Mesoamerica. Among many examples are http://www.caracol.org/, http://www.kiuic.org/, and governmental sites, such as http://www.inah.gob.mx/zonas-arqueologicas. Libraries are posting photos of artifacts and structures to the web. An outstanding example of a photographic research collection is that of Justin Kerr's rollout photographs of Maya vases, found at http://research.mayavase.com/kerrmaya.html. There is a KML database for use with Google Earth available from the Electronic Atlas of Ancient Maya Sites project by Clifford Brown and Walter Witschey at http://MayaGIS.SMV. org. It provides site locations for more than 5,000 Maya sites on a Google Earth display.

SELECTED INTERNET RESOURCES

Academia de Lenguas Mayas de Guatemala. Academia de Lenguas Mayas de Guatemala K'ulb'il Yol Twitz Paxil, 2014. http://www.almg.org.gt/.

Archaeology of Altun Ha. Belize National Institute of Culture and History, Institute of Archaeology. http://nichbelize.org/ia-maya-sites/archaeology-of-altun-ha.html.

Belize Institute of Archaeology. National Institute of Culture and History, Institute of Archaeology, 2014. http://www.nichbelize.org/ia-general/welcome-to-the-institute-of-archaeology.html.

Boot, Erik. *Maya Glyph Blog*. 2009. http://maya-glyph-blog.blogspot.com/.

Brown, Clifford T., and Walter R. T. Witschey. *Electronic Atlas of Ancient Maya Sites*. 2014. http://MayaGIS.smv.org.

Carr, Robert F., James E. Hazard, and Christopher Carr. *Tikal Report 11: Map of the Ruins of Tikal, El Petén, Guatemala and Georeferenced Versions of the Maps Therein* [electronic data set]. tDAR, The Digital Archaeological Record, 2013. http://core.tdar.org/project/390922.

Cerros (Cerro Maya) Research Online Catalogue. Florida Museum of Natural History, University of Florida, 2014. http://www.flmnh.ufl.edu/cerros/.

Corpus of Maya Hieroglyphic Inscriptions Project. Peabody Museum of Archaeology and Ethnology, 2014. https://www.peabody.harvard.edu/CMHI/.

FAMSI Research Reports, Maps, and a Searchable Bibliographic Database. Foundation for the Advancement of Mesoamerican Studies, Inc., 2014. http://www.famsi.org/index.html.

Google Earth [overhead visualization of sites]. http://www.google.com/earth/.

Instituto Hondureño de Antropología e Historia (IHAH). http://www.ihah.hn/.

Instituto Nacional de Antropología e Historia (INAH-Mexico). CONACULTA, 2014. http://www.inah.gob.mx/.

International Phonetic Association. *International Phonetic Alphabet* (2005 version). Division of Psychology and Language Sciences, University College London, 2013. https://www.langsci.ucl.ac.uk/ipa/index.html.

Kerr, Justin. *Maya Vase Database*. Kerr Associates, 2014. http://www.mayavase.com/.

"Mayan Languages." In *Wikipedia*, 2014. http://en.wikipedia.org/wiki/Mayan_languages#Geography_and_demographics.

MesoAmerican Research Center. *2014 Articles and Events*. http://www.marc.ucsb.edu/news.

Middle American Research Institute, Tulane University, 2014. http://www.tulane.edu/~mari/.

Ministerio de Cultura y Deportes de Guatemala (Archaeology). http://mcd.gob.gt/tag/arqueologia/.

Reese-Taylor, Kathryn. *Yaxnohcah*. 2013. http://people.ucalgary.ca/~kreeseta/research/yaxnohcah.html.

Skidmore, Joel, and Marc Zender. Mesoweb, 2014. http://www.mesoweb.com/.

Stuart, David. *Maya Decipherment* (blog). 2014. http://decipherment.wordpress.com/.

Tikal Digital Access Project (430 photographs). University Museum of Archaeology and Anthropology, University of Pennsylvania, 2011. http://research.famsi.org/tikal.html.

University of Pennsylvania Museum of Archaeology and Anthropology. http://www.penn.museum/.

U.S. Central Intelligence Agency. *The World Factbook*. 2014. https://www.cia.gov/library/publications/the-world-factbook/.

Vail, Gabrielle, and Christine Hernández. *Maya Hieroglyphic Codices*, Version 5.0, March 2, 2014 [electronic data set]. www.mayacodices.org.

Van Laningham, Ivan. *Mayan Calendar Tools*. 2013. http://www.pauahtun.org/Calendar/tools.html.

WorldCat—Library Catalog. OCLC Online Computer Library Center, Inc., 2014. http://www.worldcat.org/.

RESEARCH INSTITUTIONS

There are numerous institutions with staff qualified to address issues related to the ancient Maya. This brief list should be considered a starting point for additional research.

**American Museum
of Natural History**
Central Park West at 79th Street
New York, NY 10024
http://www.amnh.org/

Arizona State University
School of Human Evolution & Social
   Change
SHESC 233
P.O. Box 872402
Tempe, AZ 85287-2402
https://shesc.asu.edu/

Art Institute of Chicago
Michigan Avenue at Adams Street
Chicago, IL 60603
http://www.artic.edu/

Boston University
Archaeology Department
675 Commonwealth Avenue, Suite 347
Boston, MA 02215
http://www.bu.edu/archaeology/

Brigham Young University
Department of Anthropology
800 SWKT
Provo, UT 84602- 5522
https://anthropology.byu.edu/Pages/
   home.aspx

The British Museum
Great Russell Street
London, England WC1 3DG
http://www.britishmuseum.org/

Brown University
Department of Anthropology
Giddings House, 128 Hope Street
Box 1921
Providence, RI 02912
http://www.brown.edu/academics/
   anthropology/

**Centro de Investigaciones Regionales
de Mesoamerica (CIRMA)**
5a. Calle Oriente No. 5
La Antigua Guatemala, Sacatepéquez
Guatemala 03001 http://cirma.org.gt/
   glifos/index.php/P%C3%A1gina
   _principal

Cotsen Institute of Archaeology
University of California, Los Angeles
308 Charles E. Young Drive North
A210 Fowler Building, Box 951510
Los Angeles, CA 90095-1510
http://www.ioa.ucla.edu/

Dumbarton Oaks
Research Library and Collection
1703 32nd Street NW
Washington, DC 20007
http://www.doaks.org/

Field Museum of Chicago
Roosevelt Road at
   1400 S. Lake Shore Drive
Chicago, IL 60605-2496
http://www.fieldmuseum.org/

Florida Museum of Natural History
University of Florida Cultural Plaza
SW 34th Street at 3215 Hull Road
PO Box 112710
Gainesville, FL 32611-2710
http://www.flmnh.ufl.edu/

**Foundation for Advancement of
Mesoamerican Studies (FAMSI)**
268 South Suncoast Boulevard
Crystal River, FL 34429
http://www.famsi.org/

The George Gustav Heye Center
The National Museum of the American
   Indian–New York
Alexander Hamilton U.S. Custom House
One Bowling Green at the south side
   of Bowling Green, adjacent to the
   northeast corner of Battery Park
New York, NY 10004
http://www.nmai.si.edu/visit/newyork/

Idaho State University
Department of Anthropology
921 S. 8th Avenue, Stop 8005
Pocatello, ID 83209-8005
http://www.isu.edu/anthro/

Institute of Archaeology
National Institute of Culture and History
Archaeology Museum and Research
   Centre
Culvert Road
Belmopan, Belize
http://www.nichbelize.org/ia-general/
   welcome-to-the-institute-of-
   archaeology.html

Instituto de Antropología e Historia
Dirección de Patrimonio Cultural y
   Natural
Ministerio de Cultura y Deportes
Avenida 12, 11-11 Zona 1
Antiguo Convento Sto. Domingo
Ciudad de Guatemala, Guatemala
http://mcd.gob.gt/direccion-de
   -patrimonio-cultural-y-natural/

**Instituto Nacional de Antropología
e Historia de México**
Insurgentes Sur No. 421
Colonia Hipódromo
México D.F. CP 06100 México
http://www.inah.gob.mx/

**Instituto Hondureño de
Antropología e Historia**
Barrio Buenos Aires,
Apartado Postal 1518 Tegucigalpa,
   Honduras
http://www.ihah.hn/

Louisiana State University
Department of Geography &
 Anthropology
227 Howe-Russell-Kniffen Geoscience
 Complex
Baton Rouge, LA 70803
http://ga.lsu.edu/

Metropolitan Museum of Art
1000 Fifth Avenue at 82nd Street
New York, NY 10028
http://www.metmuseum.org/

Middle American Research Institute
Tulane University
Dinwiddie Hall 3rd Floor
6823 St. Charles Avenue
New Orleans, LA 70118
http://www.tulane.edu/~mari/

Musée du Quai Branly
37, Quai Branly
75007 Paris, France
http://www.quaibranly.fr/en/

Museo de América
Avenida Reyes Católicos, 6
28040 Madrid, Spain
http://www.mecd.gob.es/
 museodeamerica/el-museo.html

Museo de Antropología de Xalapa
Avenida Xalapa s/n
Entre Av. 1° de Mayo y Acueducto
Xalapa, Veracruz, México C.P. 91010
http://www.uv.mx/max/

**Museo de Arqueología Regional de
Comayagua**
Barrio San Francisco
Cuadra al Norte de la Plaza Central
Comayagua, Honduras
http://www.museoscentroamericanos.net/
 museos_honduras/museo_comayagua/
 valle_comayagua.htm

**Museo Nacional de Antropología
"Dr. David J. Guzmán"**
Avenida de la Revolución
Colonia San Benito
San Salvador, El Salvador
http://www.cultura.gob.sv/muna/

Museo Nacional de Antropología
Avenida Paseo de la Reforma y calzada
 Gandhi s/n
Colonia Chapultepec Polanco
Delegación Miguel Hidalgo
México, D.F., México C. P. 11560
http://www.mna.inah.gob.mx/index.html

**Museo Nacional de Arqueología y
Etnología de Guatemala**
Edificio 5, Parque La Aurora
7ta. Avenida, 6a. Calle
Guatemala City, Zona 13; 2475-4399
Guatemala
http://munae.gob.gt/

**Museo Nacional de Nicaragua
"Dioclesiano Chaves"**
Palacio Nacional de la Cultura
Managua, Nicaragua
http://www.inc.gob.ni/
 index.php?option=com_
 content&task=view&id=12&Itemid=27

National Geographic Society
1145 17th Street, N.W.
Washington, DC 20036-4688
http://www.nationalgeographic.com/

National Museum of Natural History
Smithsonian Institution
10th Street & Constitution Avenue NW
Washington, D.C. 20560
http://www.mnh.si.edu/

**National Museum of the
American Indian**
Smithsonian Institution
Fourth Street & Independence Avenue, SW
Washington, DC 20560
http://www.nmai.si.edu/

**Peabody Museum of Archaeology
and Ethnology**
Harvard University
11 Divinity Avenue
Cambridge, MA 02138
https://www.peabody.harvard.edu/

Peabody Museum of Natural History
Yale University
170 Whitney Avenue
P.O. Box 208118
New Haven, CT 06520-8118
http://peabody.yale.edu/

Pennsylvania State University
Department of Anthropology
409 Carpenter Building
University Park, PA 16802
http://anth.la.psu.edu/

**Research Centre of the Slovenian
Academy of Sciences and Arts**
Institute of Anthropological and
    Spatial Studies
Novi trg 2, 1000 Ljubljana
Slovenia
http://iaps.zrc-sazu.si/en#v

Royal Ontario Museum
100 Queen's Park
Toronto, ON M5S 2C6
Canada
http://www.rom.on.ca/en

Santa Fe Institute
1399 Hyde Park Road
Santa Fe, NM 87501
http://www.santafe.edu/

Southern Illinois University
Department of Anthropology
Faner Building, Room 3525
1000 Faner Drive
Carbondale, IL 62901
http://cola.siu.edu/anthro/

**State University of New York
at Albany**
Department of Anthropology
Arts and Sciences 237
1400 Washington Avenue
Albany, NY 12222
http://www.albany.edu/anthro/

**State University of New York
at Albany**
The Institute for Mesoamerican Studies
Arts and Sciences 233
1400 Washington Avenue
Albany, NY 12222
http://www.albany.edu/ims/

Texas Tech University
School of Art
18th Street And Flint Avenue
Lubbock, Texas
http://www.depts.ttu.edu/ART/index
    .php

Tulane University
Department of Anthropology
101 Dinwiddie Hall
6823 St. Charles Avenue
New Orleans, LA 70118
http://anthropology.tulane.edu/

Universidad de San Carlos
Ciudad Universitaria
Zona 12, 01012
Guatemala City, Guatemala
http://www.usac.edu.gt/

Universidad de las Américas Puebla.
Departamento de Antropología
Sta. Catarina Mártir
Cholula, Puebla
C.P. 72820, México
http://www.udlap.mx/ofertaacademica/
    Default.aspx?cvecarrera=LAC

Universidad del Valle de Guatemala
18 Avenida 11-95
Zona 15, 01901
Vista Hermosa III
Apartado Postal No. 82
Guatemala City, Guatemala
http://www.uvg.edu.gt/

Museo Popol Vuh
Universidad Francisco Marroquin
Liberty Plaza
Calle Manuel F. Ayau (6 Calle final)
Zona 10
Guatemala City, Guatemala 01010
http://www.popolvuh.ufm.edu/index
    .php/P%C3%A1gina_Principal

**Universidad Nacional Autónoma
de México**
Ciudad Universitaria
Alvaro Obregon, 04510
México, D.F., México
http://www.unam.mx/

Universidad Autónoma de Yucatán
Facultad de Ciencias Antropológicas
Km. 1 Carretera Mérida-Tizimín
Cholul CP 97305
Mérida, Yucatán, México
http://www.antropologia.uady.mx/

Universidad Veracruzana
Facultad de Antropología
Francisco Moreno y Ezequiel Alatriste
Col. Ferrer Guardia
C.P. 91090 Xalapa
Veracruz, México
http://www.uv.mx/antropologia/

University of Arizona
Arizona State Museum
1013 East University Boulevard
P.O. Box 210026
Tucson, AZ 85721-0026
http://www.statemuseum.arizona.edu/

University of Arizona
School of Anthropology
P.O. Box 210030
1009 East South Campus Drive
Tucson, AZ 85721
http://anthropology.arizona.edu/

University of Calgary
Department of Anthropology
2500 University Drive NW
Calgary, AB T2N 1N4
Canada
https://anth.ucalgary.ca/

University of California, Berkeley
Anthropology Department
232 Kroeber Hall
Bancroft Way
Berkeley, CA 94720-3710
http://anthropology.berkeley.edu/

University of California, Los Angeles
Department of Anthropology
375 Portola Plaza
341 Haines Hall
Box 951553
Los Angeles, CA 90095-1553
http://www.anthro.ucla.edu/

University of California, Riverside
Anthropology Department
1334 Watkins Hall
Riverside, CA 92521
http://anthropology.ucr.edu/

University of California, Santa Barbara
Department of Anthropology
Humanities and Social Sciences Building (HSSB) 2001
Santa Barbara, CA 93106-3210
http://www.anth.ucsb.edu/

University of Central Florida
4000 Central Florida Blvd
Howard Phillips Hall Rm 309
Orlando, FL 32816-1361
http://anthropology.cos.ucf.edu/

University of Colorado
Department of Anthropology
Hale Science 350
1350 Pleasant Street
Campus Box 233
Boulder, CO 80309-0233
http://anthropology.colorado.edu/

University of Illinois
Department of Anthropology
109 Davenport Hall
607 S. Mathews Avenue
Urbana, IL 61801
http://www.anthro.illinois.edu/

University of Kansas
Department of Anthropology
622 Fraser Hall
1415 Jayhawk Boulevard
Lawrence, KS 66045-7556
http://anthropology.ku.edu/

University of Michigan
Department of Anthropology
101 West Hall
1085 S. University Avenue
Ann Arbor, MI 48109-1382
http://www.lsa.umich.edu/anthro/

University of New Mexico
Department of Anthropology
MSC01-1040, Anthropology 1
Albuquerque, NM 87131
http://anthropology.unm.edu/

University of North Carolina at Chapel Hill
Department of Anthropology
301 Alumni Building, CB# 3115
Chapel Hill, NC 27599-3115
http://anthropology.unc.edu/

University of Pennsylvania
Department of Anthropology
University of Pennsylvania Museum of Archaeology and Anthropology
3260 South Street
(33rd and Spruce Streets)
Philadelphia, PA 19104
http://www.sas.upenn.edu/anthropology/

University of Pennsylvania Museum of Archaeology and Anthropology
3260 South Street
(33rd and Spruce Streets)
Philadelphia, PA 19104
http://www.penn.museum/

University of Texas
Department of Anthropology
1 University Station
SAC 4.102 Mail Code C3200
Austin, TX 78712
http://www.utexas.edu/cola/depts/anthropology/

University of Texas
Department of Art and Art History
Art Building
23rd and San Jacinto
Austin, TX 78712
http://www.utexas.edu/finearts/aah/

Vanderbilt University
Department of Anthropology
124 Garland Hall
Box 6050 Station B
Nashville, TN 37235
http://as.vanderbilt.edu/anthropology/

Washington University in St. Louis
Department of Anthropology
Campus Box 1114
One Brookings Drive
St. Louis, MO 63130-4899
https://anthropology.artsci.wustl.edu/

Yale University
Department of Anthropology
10 Sachem Street
New Haven, CT 06511
http://anthropology.yale.edu/

Yale University
Department of the History of Art
The Jeffrey Loria Center for the History
  of Art
190 York Street
P.O. Box 208272
New Haven, CT 06520
http://arthistory.yale.edu/

SERIES AND JOURNALS

Acta Americana. Inter-American Society of Anthropology and Geography, 1943–1948.

American Anthropologist. Journal of the American Anthropological Association. http://www.aaanet.org/publications/ameranthro.cfm.

American Antiquity. Journal of the Society of American Archaeology. http://www.saa.org/AbouttheSociety/Publications/AmericanAntiquity.aspx.

Anales del Instituto Nacional de Antropología e Historia de Mexico. Mexico City. http://www.inah.gob.mx/english.

Ancient Mesoamerica. Cambridge University Press. http://journals.cambridge.org/action/displayJournal?jid=ATM.

Annual Review of Anthropology. Annual Reviews. http://www.annualreviews.org/journal/anthro.

Antiquity. Antiquity Trust. http://antiquity.ac.uk/.

Archaeoastronomy: The Journal of Astronomy in Culture. University of Texas Press. http://utpress.utexas.edu/index.php/journals/archaeoastronomy.

Archaeology. Archaeological Institute of America. http://www.archaeology.org/.

Arqueología Mexicana. Mexico City. http://www.arqueomex.com/.

B.A.R. International Series. Archaeopress. http://www.archaeopress.com/ArchaeopressShop/Public/defaultAll.asp?Series=British+Archaeological+Reports+International+Series.

Boletín de la Escuela de Ciencias Antropológicas de la Universidad de Yucatán. http://www.antropologia.uady.mx/revista/indice.php.

Boletín del Consejo de Arqueología. Instituto Nacional de Antropología e Historia, Mexico City. http://consejoarqueologia.inah.gob.mx/?cat=5.

Boletín informativo la pintura mural prehispánica en México. Instituto de Investigaciones Estéticas, Universidad Nacional Autónoma de México. http://www.pinturamural.esteticas.unam.mx/.

Cambridge Archaeological Journal. Cambridge University Press. http://journals.cambridge.org/action/displayJournal?jid=CAJ.

Contributions to American Archaeology. Washington, DC: Carnegie Institution of Washington.Corpus of Maya Hieroglyphic Inscriptions. Cambridge, MA: Harvard University. https://www.peabody.harvard.edu/cmhi/.

Current Anthropology. University of Chicago Press. http://www.press.uchicago.edu/ ucp/journals/journal/ca.html.

Estudios de Cultura Maya. Centro de Estudios Mayas Instituto de Investigaciones Filológi-cas, UNAM, Mexico City. http://www.revistas.unam.mx/index.php/ecm/index.

Expedition. University of Pennsylvania Museum of Archaeology and Anthropology. http://www.penn.museum/expedition–magazine.html.

FAMSI, Journal of the Ancient Americas. Foundation for the Advancement of Mesoamerican Studies, Inc. http://research.famsi.org/aztlan/papers_index.php.

Foundation for Latin American Anthropological Research. Graz, Austria. http://www .flaar.org/.

Geoarchaeology. Wiley Online Library. http://onlinelibrary.wiley.com/journal/10.1002/% 28ISSN%291520–6548.

Handbook of Middle American Indians. Austin: University of Texas Press. http://www .utexas.edu/utpress/books/wauhan.html.

IMS Explorer. Institute of Maya Studies, Miami, FL. http://www.instituteofmayastudies .org/index.php/publications/newsletter.

International Journal of American Linguistics. Linguistic Society of America. http://www .press.uchicago.edu/ucp/journals/journal/ijal.html.

Journal de la Société des Américanistes. Paris. http://jsa.revues.org/?lang=en.

Journal of Anthropological Archaeology. http://www.sciencedirect.com/science/journal/ 02784165.

Journal of Ethnobiology. Society of Ethnobiology. http://ethnobiology.org/publications/ journal.

Journal of Field Archaeology. Maney Online, Boston, MA. http://www.maneyonline.com/ loi/jfa.

Journal of the Royal Anthropological Institute. Wiley Online Library. http://onlinelibrary .wiley.com/journal/10.1111/%28ISSN%291467–9655.

Journal de la Société des américanistes. http://jsa.revues.org/index.html.

Latin American Antiquity. Journal of the Society of American Archaeology. http://www .saa.org/aboutthesociety/publications/latinamericanantiquity/tabid/127/default.aspx.

Los Investigadores de la Cultura Maya. Campeche, Mexico: Universidad Autónoma de Campeche. http://cihs.uacam.mx/?modulo_micrositio=paginas&acciones_micro sitio=ver&id_pagina=cg.

Maya Decipherment. https://decipherment.wordpress.com/.

Mayab. La Universidad Anáhuac Mayab, Merida, Mexico. http://www.anahuacmayab.mx/.

Memoirs of the Peabody Museum of Archaeology and Ethnology. Cambridge, MA: Har-vard University. https://www.peabody.harvard.edu/node/962.

Mesa Redonda de Palenque/Palenque Round Table. San Francisco: Pre-Columbian Art Research Institute. http://www.precolumbia.org/pari/index.html.

Mesoamérica. Antigua, Guatemala. http://cirma.org.gt/glifos/index.php/P%C3%A1gina _principal.

Mesoweb. http://www.mesoweb.com/.

Mexicon, Journal of Mesoamerican Studies. Verlag Anton Saurwein, Markt Schwaben, Ger-many. http://www.mexicon.de/.

Middle American Research Institute Publications. New Orleans, LA: Tulane University. http://www.tulane.edu/~mari/.

National Geographic Magazine and National Geographic Research and Exploration. National Geographic Society, Washington, DC. http://www.nationalgeographic.com/.

Papers from the Institute of Archaeology. University College London. http://www.ucl.ac.uk/archaeology.

Papers of the New World Archaeological Foundation. Provo, UT: Brigham Young University, http://www.byubookstore.com/ePOS?this_category=238&store=439&listtype=begin&form=shared3/gm/browse.html&design=439.

The PARI Journal. Pre-Columbian Art Institute. http://www.mesoweb.com/pari/journal.html.

Papers of the Peabody Museum of Archaeology and Ethnography. Cambridge, MA: Harvard University. https://www.peabody.harvard.edu/node/304.

Proceedings of the National Academy of Sciences of the United States of America. Washington, DC: National Academy of Sciences. http://www.pnas.org/.

Publications of the Institute for Mesoamerican Studies. Albany: State University of New York. http://www.albany.edu/ims/.

Research Reports in Belizean Archaeology. Gainesville: University of Florida Digital Collections. http://ufdc.ufl.edu/AA00013262/00001.

Research Reports on Ancient Maya Writing. Barnardsville, NC: Center for Maya Research. http://www.precolumbia.org/bearc/CMR/reports.html.

Revista Mexicana de Estudios Antropológicos. Mexico City. http://smamexico.org/publicaciones.htm.

Science. American Association for the Advancement of Science. http://www.sciencemag.org/.

Simposios de investigaciones arqueológicas en Guatemala. Guatemala City: Ministerio de Cultura y Deportes. http://www.asociaciontikal.com/#.

The SAA Archaeological Record (formerly the *SAA Bulletin*). http://www.saa.org/AboutheSociety/Publications/TheSAAArchaeologicalRecord/tabid/64/Default.aspx.

Studies in Ancient Mesoamerica. Berkeley: University of California.

Studies in Precolumbian Art and Archaeology. Washington, DC: Dumbarton Oaks. http://www.hup.harvard.edu/collection.php?recid=139.

Supplement to the Handbook of Middle American Indians. Austin: University of Texas Press. http://www.utexas.edu/utpress/books/wauhan.html.

Tikal Reports. Philadelphia: University Museum, University of Pennsylvania. http://www.upenn.edu/pennpress/series/UPM.html.

Vanderbilt University Publications in Anthropology. Nashville, TN. http://discoverarchive.vanderbilt.edu/handle/1803/5040.

Wayeb Notes. Asociación Europea de Mayistas. http://www.wayeb.org/.

Yaxkin: Revista del Instituto Hondureño de Antropología e Historia. Tegucigalpa, Honduras. http://www.mcu.es/ccbae/en/consulta/registro.cmd?id=4318.

BIBLIOGRAPHY

GENERAL WORKS AND COMPILATIONS, OR WORKS FOR WHICH THE SPECIFIC AUTHOR IS UNKNOWN

Academia de Lenguas Mayas de Guatemala. Academia de Lenguas Mayas de Guatemala K'ulb'il Yol Twitz Paxil, 2014. http://www.almg.org.gt/.

The Archaeological Research Institute. Archaeological Research Institute, Arizona State University, 2014. http://archaeology.asu.edu/.

Archaeology Magazine. Archaeological Institute of America, 2014. http://www.archaeology.org/.

Archaeology of Altun Ha. Belize National Institute of Culture and History, Institute of Archaeology. http://nichbelize.org/ia-maya-sites/archaeology-of-altun-ha.html.

Arqueología Mexicana 20° aniversario: Índice general. Volúmenes I–XIX, *1993–2013.* S1 N4 Supplement. 2014.http://www.arqueomex.com/PDFs/S1N4SUPLEMENTO.pdf.

Belize Institute of Archaeology. National Institute of Culture and History, Institute of Archaeology, 2014. http://www.nichbelize.org/ia-general/welcome-to-the-institute-of-archaeology.html.

Cancuen Palace Reported. Mesoweb, 2001. http://www.mesoweb.com/reports/cancuen.html.

Cerros (Cerro Maya) Research Online Catalogue. Florida Museum of Natural History, University of Florida, 2014. http://www.flmnh.ufl.edu/cerros/.

Champotón: Biografía de un Pueblo. Campeche, Campeche, Mexico: Centro INAH Campeche, 2005.

Codex Dresdensis—Mscr.Dresd.R.310. Saxon State Library, Dresden State and University Library (SLUB), 2013. http://digital.slub-dresden.de/werkansicht/dlf/2967/2/.

The Copan National Park: Copan Ruinas—Honduras. Ecotourism and Adventure Specialists, 2013. http://www.copanpark.com/.

Corpus of Maya Hieroglyphic Inscriptions Project. Peabody Museum of Archaeology and Ethnology, 2014. https://www.peabody.harvard.edu/CMHI/.

Dumbarton Oaks. Dumbarton Oaks, 2014. http://www.doaks.org/. 2014.

Encyclopedia Mesoamericana—Copan, Structure 10L-22A. Mesoweb. http://www.mesoweb.com/encyc/index.asp?passcall=rightframeexact&rightframeexact=http%3A//www.mesoweb.com/encyc/view.asp%3Frecord%3D5404%26act%3Dviewexact%26view%3Dnormal%26word%3D10L-22A%26wordAND%3DCopan%2C+Structure%26redir%3Dno.

Exploran Ichkabal. Instituto Nacional de Antropología e Historia, 2009. http://www.inah.gob.mx/boletines/7-zonas-arqueologicas/3052-exploran-ichkabal.

Explore Mexico's Cenotes [12-image slide show]. Scripps Networks Digital—Travel Channel. http://www.travelchannel.com/destinations/mexico/photos/explore-mexicos-cenotes.

Exploring Solutions Past. 2014. http://exploringsolutionspast.org/what-we-do/archaeology-under-the-canopy/el-pilar-archaeological-reserve/.

FAMSI Research Reports, Maps, and a Searchable Bibliographic Database. Foundation for the Advancement of Mesoamerican Studies, Inc., 2012 and 2014. http://www.famsi.org/index.html.

Global Volcanism Program. Smithsonian Institution, National Museum of Natural History, 2014. http://www.volcano.si.edu/.

Google [search engine]. http://www.google.com/.

Google Earth [overhead visualization of sites]. http://www.google.com/earth/.

Google Scholar [search engine]. Google Inc., 2014.http://scholar.google.com/. 2014.

Harmonized World Soil Database (version 1.2). Electronic data set. FAO and IIASA, 2012. http://webar chive.iiasa.ac.at/Research/LUC/External-World-soil-database/HTML/HWSD_Data.html?sb=4.

Ichkabal Zona Arqueológica/2010. INAH TV, April 29, 2010.https://www.youtube.com/watch?v=YwXLQIqjgKg.

Institute of Archaeology (NICH-Belize). National Institute of Culture and History, 2014. http://www.nichbelize.org/ia-general/welcome-to-the-institute-of-archaeology.html.

Instituto de Antropologia e Historia (IDAEH-Guatemala). Ministerio de Cultura y Deportes, 2014. http://www.mcd.gob.gt/.

Instituto Hondureño de Antropología e Historia (IHAH). http://www.ihah.hn/.

Instituto Nacional de Antropología e Historia (INAH-Mexico). CONACULTA, 2014. http://www.inah.gob.mx/.

Introducción a la arqueología de Copan, Honduras. 2 vols. and map set. Tegucigalpa, DC, Honduras: Proyecto Arqueológico Copán, Instituto Hondureño de Antropología e Historia, Secretaría de Estado en el Despacho de Cultura y Turismo, 1983.

Izamal: Yucatan. Mexico, D.F.: Director General de Cartographía, 1986.

Izamal, Plano de la ciudad de Izamal, Yucatán. Izamal, Yucatán, México: Ayuntamiento, 1976.

JSTOR—A Digital Archive of Over One Thousand Academic Journals. ITHAKA, 2014. http://www.jstor.org/.

"List of Volcanos in El Salvador." In *Wikipedia*, 2014.http://en.wikipedia.org/wiki/List_of_volcanoes_in_El_Salvador.

Mapean Noh Kah, una "gran ciudad" maya en Quintana Roo. May 12, 2014. http://www.inah.gob.mx/boletin/17-arqueologia/7180-mapean-noh-kah-una-gran-ciudad-maya-en-quintana-roo.

The Maya Calendar. Maya World Studies Center/Centro de Estudios del Mundo Maya, 2008. http://mayacalendar.com/mayacalendar.html.

"Mayan Languages." In *Wikipedia*, 2014. http://en.wikipedia.org/wiki/Mayan_languages#Geography_and_demographics.

Mexican National Museum of Anthropology (Museo Nacional de Antropología). Instituto Nacional de Antropología e Historia, 2014. http://www.mna.inah.gob.mx/.

Middle American Research Institute, Tulane University, 2014. http://www.tulane.edu/~mari/.

Ministerio de Cultura y Deportes de Guatemala (Archaeology). http://mcd.gob.gt/tag/arqueologia/.

Muyil, entre el misterio maya. INAH, April 15, 2013. http://www.inah.gob.mx/boletines/7-zonas-arqueo logicas/3066-muyil-entre-el-misterio-maya.

"New Monument Found at El Peru-Waka in Guatemala, Tells Story of Mayan Cleopatra." *Sci-News.com*, July 17, 2013. http://www.sci-news.com/archaeology/science-monument-el-peru-waka-guatemala-mayan-cleopatra-01233.html.

Sitios Arqueologicos México. Edited by Instituto Nacional de Antropologâia e Historia (INAH-Mexico). Mexico City, 2012.

Tikal Digital Access Project (430 photographs). University of Pennsylvania Museum of Archaeology and Anthropology, 2011. http://research.famsi.org/tikal.html.

"Two Ancient Maya Cities Discovered in the Jungle of Southeastern Mexico." *MISLI*, August 13, 2014. http://ms.sta.si/2014/08/two-ancient-maya-cities-discovered-in-the-jungle-of-southeast ern-mexico/.

University of Pennsylvania Museum of Archaeology and Anthropology. University of Pennsylvania, 2014. http://www.penn.museum/.

Waka Research Foundation. 2008. http://www.archaeologywaka.org/faq.html.

WorldCat—Library Catalog. OCLC Online Computer Library Center, Inc., 2014. Available from http://www.worldcat.org/.

Zona Arqueológico Ichkabal. Instituto Nacional de Antropología e Historia, 2013. http://www.inah.gob.mx/component/content/article/265-red-zonas-arqueologicas/5499-zona-arqueologica-de-ichkabal.

————. Instituto Nacional de Antropología e Historia (CONACULTA), 2014. http://www.inah.gob.mx/index.php?option=com_content&view=article&id=5464.

WORKS ALPHABETIZED BY SENIOR AUTHOR

Abramiuk, Marc A., and William P. Meurer. "A Preliminary Geoarchaeological Investigation of Ground Stone Tools in and around the Maya Mountains, Toledo District, Belize." *Latin American Antiquity* 17, no. 3: 335–54, 2006.

Abramiuk, Marc A., Phil Wanyerka, and Todd Pesek. "The Discovery of a Maya Stela at Quebrada de Oro, Toledo District, Belize." *Antiquity* 83, no. 319:, 2009.

Academia de las Lenguas Mayas de Guatemala and Comunidad Lingüística Maya Mopan. *Muuch't'an Mopan: Vocabulario Mopan.* Guatemala City, Guatemala: K'ulb'il Yol Twitz Paxil, 2003.

Acosta, Jorge R. *Teotihuacan: Official Guide.* Mexico City: Instituto Nacional de Antropología e Historia, 1978.

Adams, Richard E. W. *The Ceramics of Altar de Sacrificios.* Papers of the Peabody Museum, vol. 63, no. 1. Cambridge, MA: Harvard University, 1971.

————. "Preliminary Reports on Archaeological Investigations in the Rio Bec Area, Campeche, Mexico." In *Preliminary Reports on Archaeological Investigations in the Rio Bec Area, Campeche, Mexico*, 103–46. Middle American Research Institute, Publication 31. New Orleans, LA: Tulane University, 1974.

————, ed. *The Origins of Maya Civilization.* Albuquerque: University of New Mexico Press, 1977.

————. "Settlement Patterns of the Central Yucatan and Southern Campeche Region." In *Lowland Maya Settlement Patterns*, edited by Wendy Ashmore. Albuquerque: A School of American Research Book, University of New Mexico Press, 1981.

————. "Archaeological Research at the Lowland Maya City of Rio Azul." *Latin American Antiquity* 1, no. 1: 23–41, 1990.

————. *Prehistoric Mesoamerica.* 3rd ed. Norman: University of Oklahoma Press, 1991.

————. *Rio Azul: An Ancient Maya City.* Norman: University of Oklahoma Press, 1999.

Adams, R. E. W., W. E. Brown Jr., and T. Patrick Culbert. "Radar Mapping, Archeology, and Ancient Maya Land Use." *Science* 213: 1457–63, 1981.

Agnew, Neville, and Janet Bridgland. *Of the Past, for the Future: Integrating Archaeology and Conservation; Proceedings of the Conservation Theme at the 5th World Archaeological Congress, Washington, D.C., 22–26 June 2003*, Los Angeles, CA: Getty Conservation Institute, 2006.

Agrinier, P. "The Ballcourts of Southern Chiapas, Mexico." In *The Mesoamerican Ballgame: International Ballgame Symposium; Selected Papers*, edited by Vernon L. Scarborough and David R. Wilcox, 175–94. Tucson: University of Arizona Press, 1991.

Aimers, James J., Terry G. Powis, and Jaime J. Awe. "Preclassic Round Structures of the Upper Belize River Valley." *Latin American Antiquity* 11, no. (1: 71–86, 2000.

Alcocer, Javier, and Fernando W. Bernal-Brooks. "Limnology in Mexico." *Hydrobiologia* 644, no. 1: 15–68, 2010.

Alexander, Rani T. "Architecture, Haciendas, and Economic Change in Yaxcabá, Yucatán, Mexico." *Ethnohistory* 50, no. 1: 191–220, 2003.

Alvarez, W., L. W. Alvarez, F. Asaro, and H. V. Michel. "Anomalous Iridium Levels at the Cretaceous/Tertiary Boundary at Gubbio, Italy: Negative Results of Tests for a Supernova Origin." In *Cretaceous/Tertiary Boundary Events Symposium 2, Proceedings*, edited by Tove Birkelund and W. Kegel Christensen. Copenhagen, Denmark: University of Copenhagen, 1979.

Amlin, Patricia. *Popol Vuh: The Creation Myth of the Maya*. Film. Berkeley, CA: Berkeley Media LLC, 1989.

Anawalt, Patricia. *Indian Clothing before Cortés*. Norman: University of Oklahoma Press, 1981.

Anawalt, Patricia R. "Textile Research from the Mesoamerican Perspective." In *Beyond Cloth and Cordage: Archaeological Textile Research in the Americas*, edited by Penelope B. Drooker and Laurie D. Webster, 205–28. Salt Lake City: University of Utah Press, 2000.

Anderson, E. N. "Managing Maya Landscapes, Quintana Roo, Mexico." In *Landscape Ethnoecology: Concepts of Biotic and Physical Space*, edited by Leslie M. Johnson and Eugene S. Hunn. New York: Berghahn Books, 2010.

Andrefsky, William, Jr. *Lithics: Macroscopic Approaches to Lithic Analysis*. Cambridge, UK: Cambridge University Press, 1998.

Andres, Christopher, Gabriel D. Wrobel, and Shawn Morton. "Tipan Chen Uitz: A Major 'New' Civic-Ceremonial Center in the Cayo District, Belize." *Society for American Archaeology Annual Meeting*. St. Louis, MO, 2010.

Andrews, Anthony P. "Reconocimiento Arqueológico de la Costa Norte del Esatado de Campeche." *Boletín de la Escuela de Ciencias Antropológicas de la Universidad de Yucatán* 4, no. 24: 64–77, 1977.

———. "Reconocimiento Arqueológico de Tulum a Punta Allen, Quintana Roo." *Boletín de la Escuela de Ciencias Antropológicas de la Universidad de Yucatán*, 15–31, 1983.

———. "Travelers in the Night: A Discussion of the Archaeological Visibility of Trade Enclaves, Ethnicity, and Ideology." In *Astronomers, Scribes, and Priests: Intellectual Interchange between the Northern Maya Lowlands and Highland Mexico in the Late Postclassic Period*, edited by Gabrielle Vail, Christine Hernandez, and Dumbarton Oaks. Washington, DC: Dumbarton Oaks, 2010.

Andrews, Anthony P., Tomás Gallareta Negrón, and Rafael Cobos Palma. "Preliminary Report of the Cupul Survey Project: An Archaeological Reconnaissance between Chichén Itzá and the North Coast of Yucatán, Mexico." Report to the Centro Regional de Yucatán, Instituto Nacional de Antropología e Historia, Mexico, 1989.

Andrews, E. Wyllys. *The Archaeology of Southwestern Campeche*, 1943.

———. *Excavations at Dzibilchaltun, Northwestern Yucatan, Mexico*. Lancaster, PA: Lancaster Press, Inc., 1960.

———. *The Archaeological Use and Distribution of Mollusca in the Maya Lowlands*. Middle American Research Institute, Publication 43. New Orleans, LA: Tulane University, 1969.

———. "Excavations at Quelepa, El Salvador." PhD diss., Tulane University, 1971.

———. *Dzibilchaltáun*. Córdoba, Mexico: Instituto Nacional de Antropologâia e Historia, 1978.

Andrews, E. Wyllys, and Anthony P. Andrews. *A Preliminary Study of the Ruins of Xcaret, Quintana Roo, Mexico: With Notes on Other Archaeological Remains on the Central East Coast of the Yucatan Peninsula*. New Orleans, LA: Middle American Research Institute, Tulane University, 1975.

Andrews, E. Wyllys, IV and E. Wyllys Andrews V. *Archaeological Investigations on the Yucatan Peninsula*. New Orleans, LA: Middle American Research Institute, Tulane University, 1975.

Andrews, E. Wyllys, and Instituto Nacional de Antropologâia e Historia (Mexico). *Dzibilchaltun*. Mexico City: Instituto Nacional de Antropología e Historia, 1978.

Andrews, E. Wyllys, Alfredo Barrera Vásquez, Ramón Arzápalo Marín, and Instituto Nacional de Antropologâia e Historia (Mexico). *Balankanche, Throne of the Tiger Priest*. New Orleans, LA: Middle American Research Institute, Tulane University, 1970.

Andrews, E. Wyllys, IV. "Dzibilchaltun, Lost City of the Maya." *National Geographic Magazine* 115, no. 1: 90–109, 1959.

———. "Archaeology and Prehistory in the Northern Maya Lowlands: An Introduction." In *Handbook of Middle American Indians*. Vol. 2, pt. 1, edited by Gordon R. Willey, 288–330. Austin: University of Texas Press, 1980.

Andrews, E. Wyllys, IV, and E. Wyllys Andrews V. *Excavations at Dzibilchaltun, Yucatan, Mexico*. Middle American Research Institute, Publication 48. New Orleans, LA: Tulane University, 1980.

Andrews, E. Wyllys, V. *The Archaeology of Quelepa, El Salvador.* Publications of the Middle American Research Institute, no. 42. New Orleans, LA: Tulane University, 1976.

———. "The Early Ceramic History of the Lowland Maya." In *Vision and Revision in Maya Studies*, edited by Flora S. Clancy and Peter D. Harrison. Albuquerque: University of New Mexico Press, 1990.

Andrews, E. Wyllys, V, George J. Bey III, and Christopher Gunn. "The Earliest Ceramics of the Northern Maya Lowlands." In *Pathways to Complexity: A View from the Maya Lowlands*, edited by Kathryn Brown and George J. Bey III. Gainesville: University of Florida Press, 2015.

Andrews, E. Wyllys, V, and William Leonard Fash, eds. *Copán: The History of an Ancient Maya Kingdom.* School of American Research Advanced Seminar Aeries. Santa Fe, NM: School of American Research, 2005.

Andrews, George F. *Los estilos arquitectónicos del Puuc: Una nueva apreciación.* México, D.F.: Instituto Nacional de Antropología e Historia, 1986.

———. *Architectural Survey Chenes Archaeological Region: 1987 Field Season.* Austin: University of Texas, 1987. http://repositories.lib.utexas.edu/handle/2152/13490.

———. *Architectural Survey Puuc Archaeological Region: 1984 Field Season.* Vol. 3. Austin: University of Texas Library, 1990. http://repositories.lib.utexas.edu/handle/2152/14260.

———. *Architectural Survey in the Northern Plains Area 1994/1995.* University of Oregon, 1995. http://repositories.lib.utexas.edu/bitstream/handle/2152/13951/txu-aaa-gfa00326.pdf.

———. "The Puuc Regions and Architectural Styles: A Reassessment." In *Pyramids, Palaces, Monsters and Masks: The Golden Age of Maya Architecture*, 3–131. Lancaster, CA: Labyrinthos Press, 1995.

———. *Pyramids and Palaces, Monsters and Masks: The Golden Age of Maya Architecture.* Vol. 1 of *The Collected Works of George F. Andrews.* Lancaster, CA: Labyrinthos, 1995.

Andrews, George F., and Donald L. Hardesty. *Comalcalco, Tabasco, Mexico: Maya Art and Architecture.* Culver City, CA: Labyrinthos, 1989.

Ankli, Anita, Otto Sticher, and Michael Heinrich. "Yucatec Maya Medicinal Plants versus Nonmedicinal Plants: Indigenous Characterization and Selection." *Human Ecology* 27, no. 4: 557–80, 1999.

Aoyama, Kazuo. *Ancient Maya State, Urbanism, Exchange, and Craft Specialization: Chipped Stone Evidence from the Copán Valley and the La Entrada Region, Honduras.* University of Pittsburgh Memoirs in Latin American Archaeology, no. 12. Pittsburgh, PA: University of Pittsburgh Department of Anthropology, 1999.

———. "Classic Maya State, Urbanism, and Exchange: Chipped Stone Evidence of the Copán Valley and Its Hinterland." *American Anthropologist* 103, no. 2: 346–60, 2001.

———. "Elite Artists and Craft Producers in Classic Maya Society: Lithic Evidence from Aguateca, Guatemala." *Latin American Antiquity* 18, no. 1: 3–26, 2007.

———. *Elite Craft Producers, Artists, and Warriors at Aguateca: Lithic Analysis.* Monographs of the Aguateca Archaeological Project First Phase, vol. 2. Salt Lake City: University of Utah Press, 2009.

Aoyama, Kazuo, and Jessica Munson. "Ancient Maya Obsidian Exchange and Chipped Stone Production at Caobal, Guatemala." *Mexicon* 34, no. 2: 34–42, 2012.

Ardren, Traci, ed. *Ancient Maya Women.* Walnut Creek, CA: AltaMira Press, 2002.

Armijo Torres, Ricardo. "Comalcalco, la antigua ciudad maya de ladrillo." *Arqueología Mexicana* 9, no. 61 (May–June): 30–37, 2003.

Arnabar Gunam, Tomás. "El Cacicazgo de Champoton en el Siglo XVI." *Los Investigadores de la Cultura Maya* 9, no. 2: 368–80, 2001.

Arnauld, Marie-Charlotte, Véronique Breuil-Martínez, and Erick Ponciano Alvarado. *La Joyanca (La Libertad, Guatemala): Antigua Ciudad Maya del Noroeste del Petén.* Guatemala City, Guatemala: Proyecto Petén Noroccidente La Joyanca, Centro Francés de Estudios Mexicanos y Centroamericanos, Asociación Tikal, Centro de Investigaciones Regionales de Mesoamérica, 2004.

Arnold, Dean E., Hector Neff, Michael D. Glascock, and Robert J. Speakman. "Sourcing the Palygorskite Used in Maya Blue: A Pilot Study Comparing the Results of INAA and LA-ICP-MS." *Latin American Antiquity* 18, no. 1: 44–58, 2007.

Ashmore, Wendy, ed. *Lowland Maya Settlement Patterns*. School of American Research Advanced Seminar Series. Albuquerque: University of New Mexico Press, 1981.

——. *Settlement Archaeology at Quiriguá, Guatemala; Quirigua Reports IV*. University Museum Monograph 126. Philadelphia: University of Pennsylvania Museum of Archaeology and Anthropology, 2007.

Ashmore, Wendy, and Richard M. Leventhal. "Xunantunich (Cayo, Belize)." In *The Archaeology of Ancient Mexico and Central America: An Encyclopedia*, edited by Susan Toby Evans and David L. Webster. New York: Garland Publishing, 2001.

Ashmore, Wendy, Jason Yaeger, and Cynthia Robin. "Commoner Sense: Late and Terminal Classic Social Strategies in the Xunantunich Area." In *The Terminal Classic in the Maya Lowlands: Collapse, Transition, and Transformation*, edited by Arthur A. Demarest, Prudence M. Rice, and Don Stephen Rice, ch. 14. Boulder: University Press of Colorado, 2004.

Atlas Arqueológico de Guatemala (Organization), and Universidad de San Carlos de Guatemala, Escuela de Historia. *Atlas Arqueolâogico de Guatemala: [Revista]*. 3 vols. [Guatemala]: Ministerio de Cultura y Deportes, Universidad de San Carlos de Guatemala, Escuela de Historia, 1993.

Aveni, Anthony F. *Skywatchers: A Revised and Updated Version of "Skywatchers of Ancient Mexico."* Austin: University of Texas Press, 2001.

——. *The End of Time: The Maya Mystery of 2012*. Boulder: University Press of Colorado, 2009.

——. "Cosmology and Cultural Landscape: The Late Postclassic Maya of North Yucatan." In *Astronomers, Scribes, and Priests : Intellectual Interchange between the Northern Maya Lowlands and Highland Mexico in the Late Postclassic Period (Dumbarton Oaks Symposium October 6–7, 2006)*, edited by Gabrielle Vail and Christine Hernandez, 115–32. Washington, DC: Dumbarton Oaks, 2010.

Aveni, Anthony F., Anne S. Dowd, and Benjamin Vining. "Maya Calendar Reform? Evidence from Orientations of Specialized Architectural Assemblages." *Latin American Antiquity* 14, no. 2: 159–78, 2003.

Aveni, Anthony F., Susan Milbrath, and Carlos Peraza Lope. "Chichén Itzá's Legacy in the Astronomically Oriented Architecture of Mayapán." *RES: Anthropology and Aesthetics*, no. 45: 123–43, 2004.

Awe, Jaime. "Cahal Pech." *Archaeology* 2000 (June), 2000.

Awe, Jaime, Cassandra Bill, Mark Campbell, and David Cheetham. "Early Middle Formative occupation in the Central Maya Lowlands: Recent Evidence from Cahal Pech, Belize." *Papers from the Institute of Archaeology* 1: 1–5, 1990.

Awe, Jaime J. *Maya Cities and Sacred Cenotes: A Guide to the Maya Sites of Belize*. Benque Viejo del Carmen, Belize: Cubola Productions, 2006.

——. *Maya Cities and Sacred Caves: A Guide to the Maya Sites of Belize*. Benque Viejo del Carmen, Belize: Cubola Productions, 2007.

——. "Architectural Manifestations of Power and Prestige: Examples from the Monumental Architecture at Baking Pot, Cahal Pech, and Xunantunich." In *Research Reports in Belizean Archaeology*, vol. 5, 159–73. Belmopan, Belize: The Institute of Archaeology, National Institute of Culture and History, 2008.

Ball, Joseph W. *The Archaeological Ceramics of Becan, Campeche, Mexico*. Middle American Research Institute, Publication 43. New Orleans, LA: Tulane University, 1977.

——. *The Archaeological Ceramics of Chinkultic, Chiapas, Mexico*. Provo, UT: New World Archaeological Foundation, Brigham Young University, 1980.

——. *Cahal Pech, the Ancient Maya, and Modern Belize: The Story of an Archaeological Park*. Ninth University Research Lecture. San Diego, CA: San Diego State University Press, 1993.

Ball, Joseph W., and E. Wyllys Andrews. *The Polychrome Pottery of Dzibilchaltun, Yucatan, Mexico: Typology and Archaeological Context*. Middle American Research Institute, vol. 31, no. 8. New Orleans, LA: Tulane University, 1975.

——. *Preclassic Architecture at Becan, Campeche, Mexico*. Middle American Research Institute, Occasional Papers no. 3. New Orleans, LA: Tulane University, 1978.

Ball, Joseph W., and Jennifer T. Taschek. "Late Classic Lowland Maya Political Organization and Central-Place Analysis." *Ancient Mesoamerica* 2, no. 2: 149–65, 1991.

———. "Sometimes a 'Stove' Is 'Just a Stove': A Context-Based Reconsideration of Three-Prong 'Incense Burners' from the Western Belize Valley." *Latin American Antiquity* 18, no. 4: 451–70, 2007.

Barrera, Laura Caso, and Mario Aliphat Fernández. "Organización política de los itzaes desde el posclásico hasta 1702." *Historia Mexicana* 51, no. 4: 713–48, 2002.

Barrera Rubio, Alfredo. "La conquista de Yucatán y la fundación de Mérida." *Boletín de la Escuela de Ciencias Antropológicas de la Universidad de Yucatán* 10, no. 58: 9–21, 1983.

———. "Littoral-marine Economy at Tulum, Quintana Roo, Mexico." In *The Lowland Maya Postclassic*, edited by Arlen F. Chase and Prudence M. Rice. Austin: University of Texas Press, 1985.

Barrera Vásquez, Alfredo [dir.], Juan Ramón Bastarrachea Manzano, and William Brito Sansores. *Diccionario maya Cordemex: Maya-español, español-maya*. Mérida, Yucatán, México: Ediciones Cordemex, 1980.

Barrientos, Tomás. *Indice ilustrado de la coleccion de fichas de campo de Edwin Shook [texto de Tomás Barrientos]*. Antigua, Guatemala: Centro de Investigaciones Regionales de Mesoamérica (CIRMA), 2010.

Barrientos Q., Tomás, Marcello A. Canuto, and Jocelyne Ponce. *Proyecto Arqueológio La Corona: Informe final temporada 2012*. Middle American Research Institute, Tulane University, 2013. http://mari.tulane.edu/PRALC/Files/PRALC%20-%20Informe%20final%202012.pdf.

Baudez, Claude, and Pierre Becquelin. *Archéologie de los Naranjos*. Collection Etudes Mésoamericanistes, no. 11. Mexico City, D.F., Mexico: Mission Archéologique et Ethnologique Française au Mexique, 1973.

Bautista, Francisco, and J. Alfred Zinck. "Construction of an Yucatec Maya Soil Classification and Comparison with the WRB Framework." *Journal of Ethnobiology and Ethnomedicine* 6, no. 7: 1–11, 2010.

Beach, Timothy, Sheryl Luzzadder-Beach, and Nicholas P. Dunning. "Human and Natural Impacts on Fluvial and Karst Systems in the Maya Lowlands." *Geomorphology* 101: 301–31, 2008.

Beach, Timothy, Sheryl Luzzadder-Beach, Nicholas P. Dunning, Jon Hageman, and Jon C. Lohse. "Upland Agriculture in the Maya Lowlands: Ancient Maya Soil Conservation in Northwestern Belize." *Geographical Review* 92, no. 3: 372–97, 2002.

Beaudry-Corbett, Marilyn. "The Tiquisate Archaeological Zone: A Case of Delayed Societal Complexity?" In *Incidents of Archaeology in Central America and Yucatán: Essays in Honor of Edwin M. Shook*, edited by Michael Love, Marion Popenoe de Hatch, and Héctor L. Escobedo. Lanham, MD: University Press of America, 2002.

Becquelin, Pierre, and Claude Baudez. *Tonina: Une cité maya du Chiapas (Mexique)* (Poster with map of the ruins). Service des archives scientifiques, Maison René-Ginouvès, Archéologie et Ethnologie, Archives de Missions Archéologiques Françaises À L'Étranger, 1990. http://www.mae.u-paris10.fr/site-expo/images/images-posters/posters-archives%20PDF/tonina.pdf.

Beetz, Carl P., and Linton Satterthwaite. *The Monuments and Inscriptions of Caracol, Belize*, University Museum Monograph 45. Philadelphia, PA: University of Pennsylvania Museum, 1981.

Belanger, Louise, David M Pendergast, Elizabeth Graham, Scott E. Simmons, and Jaime Awe. *Lamanai Guide Book*. 2014. http://www.louisebelanger.com/lamanai_guidebook.html.

Bell, Ellen E., Marcello A. Canuto, and Robert J. Sharer, eds. *Understanding Early Classic Copan*. Philadelphia: University of Pennsylvania Museum of Archaeology and Anthropology, 2004.

Benavides C, Antonio. "Arquitectura doméstica en Cobá." In *Coba, Quintana Roo: Análisis de dos unidades habitacionales mayas del horizonte clásico*, edited by Linda Manzanilla, 25–67. México, D.F.: Universidad Nacional Autónoma de México, 1987.

———. *Edzná: A Pre-Columbian City in Campeche/Edzná: Una ciudad prehispánica de Campeche*. Mexico City: Arqueología de México, Instituto Nacional de Antropología e Historia; Pittsburgh, PA: University of Pittsburgh, 1997.

———. *Jaina: Ciudad, puerto y mercado*. Colección Justo Sierra, no. 1. Campeche, Mexico: Gobierno del Estado de Campeche, 2012.

Benson, Elizabeth P. *Death and the Afterlife in Pre-Columbian America*. Washington, DC: Dumbarton Oaks, 1975.

———. *Birds and Beasts of Ancient Latin America*. Gainesville: University Press of Florida, 1997.

Benz, Bruce F. *Maize in the Americas*. Walnut Creek, CA: Left Coast Press, 2010.

Benz, Bruce F., Li Cheng, Steven W. Leavitt, and Chris Eastoe. *El Riego and Early Maize Evolution*. Walnut Creek, CA: Left Coast Press, 2010.

Benz, Bruce F., and John E. Staller. *The Antiquity, Biogeography and Culture History of Maize in Mesoamerica*. Walnut Creek, CA: Left Coast Press, 2010.

Berdan, Frances F. *The Aztecs of Central Mexico: An Imperial Society*. Belmont, CA: Thomson Wadsworth, 2005.

Berlin, Heinrich. "El glifo emblema en las inscripciones Mayas." *Journal de la Société des Americanistes* 47: 111–19, 1958.

Bernal, Ignacio. *Teotihuacan [descubrimientos, reconstrucciones]*. Mexico City: Instituto Nacional de Antropología e Historia, 1963.

———. *The Olmec World*. Translated by Doris Heyden and Fernando Horcasitas. Berkeley: University of California Press, 1969.

Bey, George J., III, Tara M. Bond, William M. Ringle, Craig A. Hanson, Charles W. Houck, and Carlos Peraza L. "The Ceramic Chronology of Ek Balam, Yucatan, Mexico." *Ancient Mesoamerica* 9: 101–20, 1998.

Bey, George J., III, and Rosanna May Ciau. "The Role and Realities of Popol Nahs in Northern Maya Archaeology." In *The Maya and Their Central American Neighbors: Settlement Patterns, Architecture, Hieroglyphic Texts and Ceramics*, edited by Geoffrey E. Braswell. New York: Routledge, 2014.

Bey, George J., III, Craig A. Hanson, and William M. Ringle. "Classic to Postclassic at Ek Balam, Yucatan: Architectural and Ceramic Evidence for Defining the Transition." *Latin American Antiquity* 8, no. 3: 237–54, 1997.

Birkelund, Tove, and W. Kegel Christensen, eds. *Cretaceous/Tertiary Boundary Events Symposium 2, Proceedings*. Copenhagen, Denmark: University of Copenhagen, 1979.

Blake, Michael. "Dating the Initial Spread of *Zea mays*." In *Histories of Maize: Multidisciplinary Approaches to the Prehistory, Linguistics, Biogeography, Domestication, and Evolution of Maize*, edited by John E. Staller, Robert H. Tykot, and Bruce F. Benz. Walnut Creek, CA: Left Coast Press, 2010.

Blom, Frans Ferdinand, and Oliver La Farge. *Tribes and Temples: A Record of the Expedition to Middle America Conducted by the Tulane University of Louisiana in 1925*. Vols. 1 and 2. New Orleans, LA: Middle American Research Institute, Tulane University, 1926.

Bolles, David, and Alejandra Bolles. *A Grammar of the Yucatecan Mayan Language: Ritual of the Bacabs*. Foundation for the Advancement of Mesoamerican Studies, Inc. (FAMSI), 2003. http://www.famsi.org/reports/96072/grammar/section32.htm.

Boone, Elizabeth, and Gordon R. Willey, eds. *The Southeast Classic Maya Zone*. Washington, DC: Dumbarton Oaks, 1988.

Boone, Elizabeth Hill. "Topic 71: The Mixtec Writing System." In *The Cloud People: Divergent Evolution of the Zapotec and Mixtec Civilizations*, edited by Kent V. Flannery and Joyce Marcus. New York: Academic Press, 1983.

———. *Stories in Red and Black: Pictorial Histories of the Aztecs and Mixtecs*. Austin: University of Texas Press, 2000.

Boone, Elizabeth Hill, and Walter Mignolo, eds. *Writing without Words: Alternative Literacies in Mesoamerica and the Andes*. Durham, NC: Duke University Press, 1994.

Boone, Elizabeth Hill, and Gary Urton, eds. *Their Way of Writing: Scripts, Signs, and Pictographies in Pre-Columbian America*. Washington, DC: Dumbarton Oaks Research Library and Collection, 2011.

Boone, Elizabeth Hill, and Gordon Randolph Willey, eds. *The Southeast Classic Maya Zone: A Symposium at Dumbarton Oaks, 6th and 7th October, 1984*. Washington, DC: Dumbarton Oaks Research Library and Collection, 1988.

Boot, Erik. *Maya Glyph Blog*. 2009. http://maya-glyph-blog.blogspot.com/.

———. "Loan Words, 'Foreign Words,' and Foreign Signs in Maya Writing." In *The Idea of Writing: Play and Complexity*, edited by Alexander J. de Voogt and Irving L. Finkel. Leiden, The Netherlands: Brill, 2010.

———. "On (Some of) the Principles and Structures of Graphic Sign Substitution in Classic Maya Writing." In *Visualizing Knowledge and Creating Meaning in Ancient Writing Systems*, edited by Shai Gordin. Berliner Beiträge zum Vorderen Orient, vol. 23. Gladbeck, Germany: PeWe-Verlag, 2014.

Borgstede, Greg. *Settlement Patterns and Variation in the Western Highlands, Guatemala*. Foundation for the Advancement of Mesoamerican Studies, Inc., 2002. http://www.famsi.org/reports/00040/index.html.

———. "Ethnicity and Archaeology in the Western Maya Highlands, Guatemala." PhD diss., Department of Anthropology, University of Pennsylvania, 2004.

———. "Exploring the Western Highlands of Guatemala—New Perspectives on the Ancient Maya." *Expedition* 47, no. 1: 10, 2005.

Borgstede, Greg, and James R. Mathieu. "Defensibility and Settlement Patterns in the Guatemalan Maya Highlands." *Latin American Antiquity* 18, no. 2: 191–211, 2007.

Borgstede, Greg, and Eugenia J. Robinson. "The Archaeology of the Late Postclassic Maya Highlands." In *The Oxford Handbook of Mesoamerican Archaeology*, edited by Deborah L. Nichols and Christopher A. Pool, 405–18. New York: Oxford University Press, 2012.

Brady, James E. "Caves and Cosmovision at Utatlán." *California Anthropologist* 18, no. 1: 1–10, 1991.

———. *Summary of Naj Tunich Cave Archaeology*. Los Angeles: California State University, 2000. http://web.calstatela.edu/academic/anthro/jbrady/najtunich/Naj%20Tunich%201.htm.

———, ed. *Exploring Highland Maya Ritual Cave Use: Archaeology & Ethnography in Huehuetenango, Guatemala*. Austin, TX: Association for Mexican Cave Studies, A Project of the National Speleological Society, 2009.

———. "Offerings to the Rain Gods: The Archaeology of Maya Caves." In *Fiery Pool: The Maya and the Mythic Sea*, edited by Daniel Finamore and Stephen D. Houston. Salem, MA: Peabody Essex Museum, 2010.

Brady, James E., George Veni, Andrea Stone, and Allan Cobb. "Explorations in the New Branch of Naj Tunich: Implications for Interpretation." *Mexicon* 14, no. 4, 1992.

Brady, James Edward. "An Investigation of Maya Ritual Cave Use with Special Reference to Naj Tunich, Petén, Guatemala." PhD diss., University of California, Los Angeles, 1989.

———. *Sources for the Study of Mesoamerican Ritual Cave Use*. 2nd ed. Department of Anthropology, Publication 1. Los Angeles: California State University, 1999.

Brady, James Edward, and Keith M. Prufer. *In the Maw of the Earth Monster: Mesoamerican Ritual Cave Use*. Austin: University of Texas Press, 2005.

Braswell, Geoffrey E., ed. *The Maya and Teotihuacan: Reinterpreting Early Classic Interaction*. The Linda Schele Series in Maya and Pre-Columbian Studies. Austin: University of Texas Press, 2003.

———. "Obsidian Exchange Spheres." In *The Postclassic Mesoamerican World*, edited by Michael E. Smith and Frances Berdan. Salt Lake City: University of Utah Press, 2003.

———. *The Maya and Teotihuacan: Reinterpreting Early Classic Interaction*. Austin: University of Texas Press, 2004.

———., ed. *The Ancient Maya of Mexico: Reinterpreting the Past of the Northern Maya*. Edited by Thomas E. Levy. Approaches to Anthropological Archaeology. Bristol, CT: Equinox Publishing Ltd., 2012.

———., ed. *The Maya and Their Central American Neighbors: Settlement Patterns, Architecture, Hieroglyphic Texts and Ceramics*. New York: Routledge, 2014.

Braswell, Geoffrey E., Joel D. Gunn, Maria del Rosario Domínguez Carrasco, William J. Folan, Laraine A. Fletcher, Abel Morales Lopez, and Michael D. Glascock. "Defining the Terminal Classic at Calakmul, Campeche." In *The Terminal Classic in the Maya Lowlands: Collapse, Transition, and Transformation*, edited by Arthur A. Demarest, Prudence M. Rice, and Don Stephen Rice, 162–94. Boulder: University Press of Colorado, 2005.

Brenner, Mark, Michael F. Rosenmeier, David A. Hodell, and Jason H. Curtis. "Paleolimnology of the Maya Lowlands: Long-term Perspectives on Interactions among Climate, Environment, and Humans." *Ancient Mesoamerica* 13, no. 1: 141–57, 2002.

Bricker, Harvey, and Victoria R. Bricker. *Astronomy in the Maya Codices.* Philadelphia, PA: American Philosophical Society, 2010.

Bricker, Victoria R. *A Grammar of Mayan Hieroglyphs.* Middle American Research Institute, Publication no. 56. New Orleans, LA: Tulane University, 1986.

Bricker, Victoria R. "A Comparison of Venus Instruments in the Borgia and Madrid Codices." In *Astronomers, Scribes, and Priests : Intellectual Interchange between the Northern Maya Lowlands and Highland Mexico in the Late Postclassic Period*, edited by Gabrielle Vail and Christine Hernandez. Washington, DC: Dumbarton Oaks, 2010.

Bricker, Victoria Reifler, ed. *Epigraphy.* Vol. 5 of *Supplement to the Handbook of Middle American Indians.* Austin: University Of Texas Press, 1991.

Bricker, Victoria Reifler, Eleuterio Po'ot Yah, and Ofelia Dzul de Po'ot. *A Dictionary of the Maya Language: As Spoken in Hocabá, Yucatán.* With a botanical index by Anne S. Bradburn. Salt Lake City: University of Utah Press, 1998.

Brill, Mark. *Music of the Ancient Maya: New Avenues of Research.* AMS-SW Conference: Revisioning the Maya World: New Directions in Scholarship and Teaching. Mexico and Belize: American Musicological Society-Southwest Chapter, 2012. http://ams-sw.org/Proceedings/AMS-SW_V1Fall 2012Brill.pdf. 2012.

Brown, Cecil H. "Glottochronology and the Chronology of Maize in the Americas." In *Histories of Maize in Mesoamerica: Multidisciplinary Approaches*, edited by John E. Staller, Robert H. Tykot, and Bruce F. Benz. Walnut Creek, CA: Left Coast Press, 2010.

Brown, Clifford T. "Mayapán Society and Ancient Maya Social Organization." PhD diss., Tulane University, 1999.

Brown, Clifford T., and Walter R. T. Witschey. "The Fractal Geometry of Ancient Maya Settlement." *Journal of Archaeological Science* 30, no. 12: 1619–32, 2003.

———. *Electronic Atlas of Ancient Maya Sites.* 2014. http://MayaGIS.smv.org.

Brown, Kenneth L. "A Brief Report on Paleoindian-Archaic Occupation in the Quiche Basin, Guatemala." *American Antiquity* 45, no. 2: 313–24, 1980.

———. "Postclassic Relationships between the Highland and Lowland Maya." In *The Lowland Maya Postclassic*, edited by Arlen F. Chase and Prudence M. Rice, 270–81. Austin: University of Texas Press, 1985.

Brown, M. Kathryn, Jennifer Cochran, Leah McCurdy, and David Mixter. *Preceramic to Postclassic: A Brief Synthesis of the Occupation History of Group E, Xunantunich.* National Institute of Culture and History, vol. 8. Belmopan, Belize: The Institute of Archaeology, 2011.

Brown, M. Kathryn, and Travis W. Stanton. *Ancient Mesoamerican Warfare.* Walnut Creek, CA: AltaMira Press, 2003.

Bueno Cano, Ricardo. "Excavaciones en la región Rio Bec: 1984–1985." Tesís, Escuela Nacional de Antropología e Historia, 1989.

———, ed. *Entre un río de robles: Un acercamiento a la arqueología de la Región Río Bec.* Colección Científica 411. Mexico, D.F., Mexico: Instituto Nacional de Antropología e História, 1999.

Bullard, William R., Jr. "Maya Settlement Pattern in Northeastern Peten, Guatemala." *American Antiquity* 25, no. 3: 355–72, 1960.

Bullard, William Rotch. "Residential Property Walls at Mayapan." In *Current Reports No. 3*, 36–44. Washington, DC: Carnegie Institution of Washington, Department of Archaeology, 1952.

———. "Boundary Walls and House Lots at Mayapan." In *Current Reports No. 13*, 234–353. Washington, DC: Carnegie Institution of Washington, Department of Archaeology, 1954.

Bundschuh, Jochen, and Guillermo E. Alvarado Induni, eds. *Central America: Geology, Resources and Hazards.* London; New York: Taylor & Francis, 2007.

Burham, Melissa, and Jessica MacLellan. "Thinking Outside the Plaza: Ritual Practices in Preclassic Maya Residential Groups at Ceibal, Guatemala." *Antiquity*, no. 340, 2014. http://journal.antiquity .ac.uk/projgall/burham340.

Burke, Heather, Claire Smith, and Larry J. Zimmerman. *The Archaeologist's Field Handbook*. Lanham, MD: AltaMira Press, 2009.

Burns, Allan F. *An Epoch of Miracles: Oral Literature of the Yucatec Maya*. Translated with commentaries by Allan F. Burns. Foreword by Dennis Tedlock. Austin: University of Texas Press, 1983.

Campaña V., Luz Evelia. "Contribuciones a la historia de Becán." *Arqueología Mexicana* 75: 48–53, 2005.

Canuto, Marcello A. *La Corona Archaeological Project: Investigating an Extraordinary Classic Maya Center.* Middle American Research Institute, Tulane University, 2013. http://mari.tulane.edu/PRALC/ index.html.

Canuto, Marcello A., and Tomás Barrientos Q. *The Importance of La Corona*. Mesoweb, 2013. http:// www.mesoweb.com/LaCorona/LaCoronaNotes01.pdf.

Carlson, John B. *Venus-regulated Warfare and Ritual Sacrifice in Mesoamerica: Teotihuacan and the Cacaxtla "Star Wars" Connection.* Center for Archaeoastronomy Technical Publication, no. 7. College Park, MD: Center for Archaeoastronomy, 1991.

———., ed. *The Maya Calendar and 2012 Phenomenon Studies. Archaeoastronomy: The Journal of Astronomy in Culture*, vol. 24. Austin: University of Texas Press, 2011.

Carmack, Robert M. *The Quiché Mayas of Utatlán: The Evolution of a Highland Guatemala Kingdom*. Norman: University of Oklahoma Press, 1981.

Carmean, Kelli Cummins. "The Ancient Households of Sayil: A Study of Wealth in Terminal Classic Maya Society." PhD diss., University of Pittsburgh, 1990.

Carr, Robert F., and James E. Hazard. *Map of the Ruins of Tikal, El Peten, Guatemala*. Tikal Reports 11, Museum Monograph. Philadelphia: University of Pennsylvania Museum, 1961.

Carr, Robert F., James E. Hazard, and Christopher Carr. *Tikal Report 11: Map of the Ruins of Tikal, El Petén, Guatemala and Georeferenced Versions of the Maps Therein*. Electronic data set. tDAR, The Digital Archaeological, 2013. http://core.tdar.org/project/390922.

Carrasco, Davíd, ed. *The Oxford Encyclopedia of Mesoamerican Cultures: The Civilizations of Mexico and Central America*. Oxford: Oxford University Press, 2001.

Carrasco Vargas, Ramón. "Formación sociopolítica en el Puuc: El sacbe Uxmal-Nohpat-Kabah." In *Perspectivas antropológicas en el mundo Maya*, edited by María Josefa Iglesias Ponce de León and Francesc Ligorred Perramon. Publicaciones de la S.E.E.M., núm. 2. Madrid: Sociedad Española de Estudios Mayas, Instituto de Cooperación Iberoamericana, 1993.

Carter, Nicholas P. "Sources and Scales of Classic Maya History." In *Thinking, Recording, and Writing History in the Ancient World*, edited by Kurt A. Raaflaub, 340–71. New York: John Wiley & Sons, Inc., 2013.

Cecil, Leslie G. "Technological Styles of Late Postclassic Slipped Pottery from the Central Petén Lakes Region, El Petén, Guatemala." PhD diss., Southern Illinois University Carbondale, 2001.

Charnay, Désiré. *The Ancient Cities of the New World: Being Travels and Explorations in Mexico and Central America from 1857–1882*. Translated by J. Gonino and Helen S. Conant. London: Chapman and Hall, Ltd., 1887.

Chase, Arlen, and Diane Z. Chase. *Caracol Archaeological Project* [website]. 2014. http://www.caracol.org/.

Chase, Arlen, Diane Z. Chase, Jaime J. Awe, John H. Walker, and John F. Weishampel. "Airborne LiDAR at Caracol, Belize and the Interpretation of Ancient Maya Society and Landscapes." *Research Reports in Belizean Archaeology* 8: 61–73, 2011.

Chase, Arlen, Diane Z. Chase, Christopher T. Fisher, Stephen J. Leisz, and John F. Weishampel. "Geospatial Revolution and Remote Sensing LiDAR in Mesoamerican Archaeology." *Proceedings of the National Academy of Sciences of the United States of America* 109, no. 32: 12916–921, 2012.

Chase, Arlen F. "A Contextual Consideration of the Tayasal-Paxcaman Zone, El Peten, Guatemala." PhD diss., University of Pennsylvania, 1983.

———. "Cycles of Time: Caracol in the Maya Realm, with an Appendix on 'Caracol "Altar 21"'" by Stephen Houston." In *Sixth Palenque Round Table, 1986*, edited by Merle Greene Robertson, VII: 32–44. Norman: University of Oklahoma Press, 1991.

Chase, Arlen F., and Diane Z. Chase. *Investigations at the Classic Maya City of Caracol, Belize: 1985–1987*. Pre-Columbian Art Research Institute, Monograph 3. San Francisco: Pre-Columbian Art Research Institute, 1987.

———, eds. *Studies in the Archaeology of Caracol, Belize*. Pre-Columbian Art Research Institute, Monograph 7. San Francisco, CA: Pre-Columbian Art Research Institute, 1994.

———. "Ancient Maya Causeways and Organization at Caracol, Belize." *Ancient Mesoamerica* 12, no. 2: 273–81, 2001.

———. "Symbolic Egalitarianism and Homogenized Distributions in the Archaeological Record at Caracol, Belize: Method, Theory, and Complexity." *Research Reports in Belizean Archaeology* 6: 15–24, 2009.

———. "Belize Red Ceramics and Their Implications for Trade and Exchange in the Eastern Maya Lowlands." *Research Reports in Belizean Archaeology* 9: 3–14, 2012.

Chase, Arlen F., Diane Z. Chase, and Michael E. Smith. "States and Empires in Ancient Mesoamerica." *Ancient Mesoamerica* 20, no. 2: 175–82, 2009.

Chase, Arlen F., Diane Z. Chase, and John F. Weishampel. "Lasers in the Jungle: Airborne Sensors Reveal a Vast Maya Landscape." *Archaeology* 63, no. 4: 27–29, 2010.

Chase, Arlen F., Diane Z. Chase, John F. Weishampel, Jason B. Drake, Ramesh L. Shrestha, K. Clint Slatton, Jaime J. Awe, and William E. Carter. "Airborne LiDAR, Archaeology, and the Ancient Maya Landscape at Caracol, Belize." *Journal of Archaeological Science* 38, no. 2: 387–98, 2011.

Chase, Arlen F., Nikolai Grube, and Diane Z. Chase. *Three Terminal Classic Monuments from Caracol, Belize*. Research Reports on Ancient Maya Writing. Washington, DC: Center for Maya Research, 1991.

Chase, Arlen F., and Prudence M. Rice, eds. *The Lowland Maya Postclassic*. Austin: University of Texas Press, 1985.

Chase, Diane Z., and Arlen F. Chase. "Texts and Contexts in Classic Maya Warfare: A Brief Consideration of Epigraphy and Archaeology at Caracol, Belize." In *Ancient Mesoamerican Warfare*, edited by M. Kathryn Brown and Travis W. Stanton. Walnut Creek, CA: AltaMira Press, 2003.

———. "Que no nos Cuentan los Jeroglíficos? Arqueología e Historia en Caracol, Belice." *Mayab* 20: 93–108, 2008.

———. "Ancient Maya Markets and the Economic Integration of Caracol, Belize." *Ancient Mesoamerica* 25, no. 1: 239–50, 2014.

———. "Path Dependency in the Rise and Denouement of a Classic Maya City: The Case of Caracol, Belize." In *The Resilience and Vulnerability of Ancient Landscapes: Transforming Maya Archaeology through IHOPE*, edited by Arlen F. Chase and Vernon L. Scarborough, 142–54. Archaeological Papers of the American Anthropological Association, vol. 24, no. 1. Arlington, VA: American Anthropological Association, 2014.

Child, Mark B. "The Symbolic Space of the Ancient Maya Sweatbath." In *Space and Spatial Analysis in Archaeology*, edited by Elizabeth C. Robertson, 157–67. Calgary, AB: University of Calgary Press, 2006.

Chinchilla Mazariegos, Oswaldo. "The Flowering Glyphs: Animation in Cotzumalhuapa Writing." In *Their Way of Writing: Scripts, Signs, and Pictographies in Pre-Columbian America*, edited by Elizabeth Hill Boone and Gary Urton, 43–75. Washington, DC: Dumbarton Oaks Research Library and Collection, 2011.

———. *Cotzumalguapa, la ciudad arqueológica: El Baúl-Bilbao-El Castillo*. Guatemala City, Guatemala: F&G Editores, 2012.

Adams, and Robert F. Carr. Philadelphia: University of Pennsylvania Museum of Archaeology and Anthropology, 1986.

Coggins, Clemency, and Orrin C. Shane. *Cenote of Sacrifice: Maya Treasures from the Sacred Well at Chichén Itzá.* Austin: University of Texas Press, 1984.

Colas, Pierre, and Alexander W. Voss. "A Game of Life and Death—The Maya Ball Game." In *Maya: Divine Kings of the Rainforest,* edited by Nikolai Grube, Eva Eggebrecht, and Matthias Seidel. Cologne, Germany: Könemann, 2006. Distributed by John Wilson.

Comer, Douglas C., and Michael J. Harrower, eds. *Mapping Archaeological Landscapes from Space: In Observance of the 40th Anniversary of the World Heritage Convention.* SpringerBriefs in Archaeology, vol. 5. New York: Springer, 2013.

Con, María José. "Trabajos recientes en Xcaret, Quintana Roo." *Estudios de Cultura Maya* 18: 65–129, 1991.

Conrad, David. *The Ancient Maya: A Commercial Empire.* Mexconnet, 2006. http://www.mexconnect.com/articles/1574-the-ancient-maya-a-commercial-empire.

Corns, Anthony, and Robert Shaw. "High Resolution 3-dimensional Documentation of Archaeological Monuments & Landscapes Using Airborne LiDAR." *Journal of Cultural Heritage Journal of Cultural Heritage* 10, supp. 1: e72–e77, 2009.

Coronel, E. G., Scott R. Hutson, Aline Magnoni, Austin Ulmer, and Richard E. Terry. "Geochemical Analysis of Late Classic and Post Classic Maya Marketplace Activities at the Plazas of Cobá, Mexico." *Journal of Field Archaeology* 40(1): 89–109, 2015.

Cowgill, George L. "The Urban Organization of Teotihuacan, Mexico." In *Settlement and Society: Essays Dedicated to Robert McCormick Adams,* edited by Elizabeth Caecilia Stone, 261–95. Ideas, Debates and Perspectives, vol. 3. Los Angeles and Chicago: Cotsen Institute of Archaeology and the Oriental Institute of the University of Chicago, 2007.

Cowgill, George Lewis. "Postclassic Period Culture in the Vicinity of Flores, Peten, Guatemala." PhD diss., Harvard University, 1963.

Culbert, T. Patrick, ed. *The Classic Maya Collapse.* Albuquerque: University of New Mexico Press, 1973.

———. *Classic Maya Political History: Hieroglyphic and Archaeological Evidence.* Cambridge, UK: Cambridge University Press, 1991.

———. "The Ceramics of Tikal." In *Tikal: Dynasties, Foreigners & Affairs of State; Advancing Maya Archaeology,* edited by Jeremy A. Sabloff. Santa Fe, NM: School of American Research Press, 2003.

Dacus, Chelsea. "Weaving the Past: An Examination of Bones Buried with an Elite Maya Woman." Master's thesis, Southern Methodist University, 2005.

Dahlin, Bruce. "Ahead of Its time?" *Journal of Social Archaeology* 9, no. 3: 341–67, 2009.

———. "A Colossus in Guatemala: The Preclassic Maya City of El Mirador." *Archaeology* 37, no. 5: 18–25, 1984.

———. "The Barricade and Abandonment of Chunchucmil: Implications for Northern Maya Warfare." *Latin American Antiquity* 11, no. 3: 283–98, 2000.

Dahlin, Bruce H., Daniel Bair, Timothy Beach, Matthew Moriarty, and Richard Terry. "The Dirt on Food: Ancient Feasts and Markets among the Lowland Maya." In *Pre-Columbian Foodways: Interdisciplinary Approaches to Food, Culture, and Markets in Ancient Mesoamerica, University of Calgary Archaeological Association Conference,* edited by John E. Staller and Michael D. Carrasco. New York: Springer, 2009.

Dahlin, Bruce H., Christopher T. Jensen, Richard E. Terry, David R. Wright, and Timothy Beach. "In Search of an Ancient Maya Market." *Latin American Antiquity* 18, no. 4: 363–84, 2007.

Danien, Elin C., and Robert J. Sharer, eds. *New Theories on the Ancient Maya.* University Museum Monograph 77, Philadelphia: University of Pennsylvania Museum, 1992.

de la Fuente, Beatriz, and Leticia Staines Cicero, eds. *La pintura mural prehispánica en México II: Área Maya—Bonampak.* 2 vols. México, D.F.: Universidad Nacional Autónoma de México, Instituto de Investigaciones Estéticas, 1998.

———. *La pintura mural prehispánica en México II: Área Maya*. Tomo III, *Estudios*. México, D.F.: Universidad Nacional Autónoma de México, Instituto de Investigaciones Estéticas, 2001.

Deevey, Edward S. "Limnological Studies in Middle America: With a Chapter on Aztec Limnology." *Transactions of the Connecticut Academy of Arts and Sciences* 39: 213–328, 1957.

del Rosario Dominguez, C. M., Rafael Burgos V., Yoly Palomo C., Eric Reyes C., and Efrain Rubio R. "Characterization of Ceramics of the Maya Protoclassic Period in Izamal, Yucatan, Mexico." *Materials Research Society symposia proceedings* 1618: 73–80, 2014.

Demarest, Arthur A. *Ancient Maya: The Rise and Fall of a Rainforest Civilization*. New York: Cambridge University Press, 2004.

———. *The Petexbatun Regional Archaeological Project: A Multidisciplinary Study of the Maya Collapse*. Vanderbilt Institute of Mesoamerican Archaeology. Nashville, TN: Vanderbilt University Press, 2006.

Demarest, Arthur A., Prudence M. Rice, and Don Stephen Rice, eds. *The Terminal Classic in the Maya Lowlands: Collapse, Transition, and Transformation*. Boulder: University Press of Colorado, 2004.

Demarest, Arthur A., and Robert J. Sharer. "The Origins and Evolution of Usulutan Ceramics." *American Antiquity* 47, no. 4: 810–22, 1982.

Departamento de Monumentos Prehispanicos y Coloniales. *Mapa Arqueológico de la República de Guatemala*. Guatemala C.A: Instituto Geographico Militar, Ministerio de la Defensa Nacional y Departamento de Monumentos Prehispanicos y Coloniales, Instituto de Antropología e Historia de Guatemala, 1991.

Díaz del Castillo, Bernal. *The Conquest of New Spain*. Cambridge, MA: Da Capo Press, 1963.

Dibble, Charles E. "The Aztec Writing System." In *Readings in Anthropology*, edited by E. Adamson Hoebel, Jesse D. Jennings, and Elmer R. Smith. New York: McGraw-Hill, 1955.

———. "Writing in Central Mexico." In *Handbook of Middle American Indians*. Vol. 10, *The Archaeology of North America*, pt. 1, edited by Gordon F. Ekholm and Ignacio Bernal. Austin: University of Texas Press, 1971.

Diehl, Richard A. *The Olmecs: America's First Civilization*. New York: Thames and Hudson, 2004.

Diringer, David. *Writing*. Ancient Peoples and Places (Thames & Hudson), vol. 25. New York: Praeger, 1962.

Diringer, David. *The Alphabet*. London: Hutchinson, 1968.

Drew, David. *The Lost Chronicles of the Maya Kings*. Berkeley: University of California, 1999.

Drooker, Penelope B., and Laurie D. Webster. *Beyond Cloth and Cordage: Archaeological Textile Research in the Americas*. Salt Lake City: University of Utah Press, 2000.

Dunning, Nicholas P. *Lords of the Hills: Ancient Maya Settlement in the Puuc Region, Yucatán, Mexico*. Madison, WI: Prehistory Press, 1992.

Dunning, Nicholas P, and Timothy Beach. "Soil Erosion, Slope Management, and Ancient Terracing in the Maya Lowlands." *Latin American Antiquity*, no. 5: 51–69, 1994.

Dunning, Nicholas P., Timothy Beach, and Sheryl Luzzadder-Beach. "Environmental Variability among Bajos in the Southern Maya Lowlands and Its Implications for Ancient Maya Civilization and Archaeology." In *Precolumbian Water Management: Ideology, Ritual, and Power*, edited by Lisa Joyce Lucero and Barbara W. Fash, 111–33. Tucson: University of Arizona Press, 2006.

———. "Kax and Kol: Collapse and Resilience in Lowland Maya Civilization." *Proceedings of the National Academy of Sciences USA* 109, no. 10: 3652–57, 2012.

Dunning, Nicholas P., Robert Griffin, John G. Jones, Richard Terry, Zachary Larsen, and Christopher Carr. "Life on the Edge: Tikal in a Bajo Landscape." In *Tikal: Paleoecology of an Ancient Maya City*, edited by David L. Lentz, Nicholas P. Dunning, and Vernon L. Scarborough. Cambridge, UK: Cambridge University Press, 2015.

Dunning, Nicholas P., John G. Jones, Timothy Beach, and Sheryl Luzzadder-Beach. "Physiography, Habitats, and Landscapes of the Three Rivers Region." In *Heterarchy, Political Economy, and the Ancient Maya: The Three Rivers Region of the East-central Yucatán Peninsula*, edited by Vernon L. Scarborough, Fred Valdez, and Nicholas P. Dunning, 14–24. Tucson: University of Arizona Press, 2003.

Fedick, Scott L. "The Economics of Agricultural Land Use and Settlement in the Upper Belize River Valley." In *Prehistoric Maya Economies of Belize*, edited by Patricia A. McAnany and Barry L. Isaac, 215–54. Research in Economic Anthropology, supp. no. 4. Greenwich, CT: JAI Press, 1989.

———. "Land Evaluation and Ancient Maya Land Use in the Upper Belize River Area, Belize, Central America." *Latin American Antiquity* 6, no. 1: 16–34, 1995.

———, ed. *The Managed Mosaic: Ancient Maya Agriculture and Resource Use*. Salt Lake City: University of Utah Press, 1996.

Fedick, Scott L., and Anabel Ford. "The Prehistoric Agricultural Landscape of the Central Maya Lowlands: An Examination of Local Variability in a Regional Context." *World Archaeology* 22, no. 1: 18–33, 1990.

Fedick, Scott L., and Jennifer P. Mathews. "The Yalahau Regional Human Ecology Project: An Introduction and Summary of Recent Research." In *Quintana Roo Archaeology*, edited by Justine M. Shaw and Jennifer P. Mathews, 35–50. Tucson: University of Arizona Press, 2005.

Ferrand, Ezgi Akpinar, Nicholas P. Dunning, David L. Lentz, and John G. Jones. "Use of Aguadas as Water Management Sources in Two Southern Maya Lowland Sites." *Ancient Mesoamerica* 23, no. 1: 85–101, 2012.

Fialko, Vilma. *Archaeological Research and Rescue Project at Naranjo: Emerging Documentation in Naranjo's Palacio de la Realeza, Petén, Guatemala (2005 Season)*. Foundation for the Advancement of Mesoamerican Studies, Inc. (FAMSI), 2009. http://www.famsi.org/reports/05005/.

———. *The Map of the Southwest Periphery of Naranjo, Petén, Guatemala (2006 season)*. Foundation for the Advancement of Mesoamerican Studies, Inc. (FAMSI), 2009. http://www.famsi.org/reports/06098/06098Fialko01.pdf.

Fialko, Vilma, and Angela M. H. Schuster. *Naranjo-Sa'al, Petén, Guatemala: Preserving an Ancient Maya City—Plan for Documentation, Conservation, and Presentation*. New York: World Monuments Fund, 2012.

Fields, Virginia M., and Dorie Reents-Budet. *Lords of Creation: The Origins of Sacred Maya Kingship*. Los Angeles, CA: Scala, in association with the Los Angeles County Museum of Art, 2005.

Finamore, Daniel. "Navigating the Maya World." In *Fiery Pool: The Maya and the Mythic Sea*, edited by Daniel Finamore and Stephen D. Houston. Salem, MA: Peabody Essex Museum, 2010.

Finamore, Daniel, and Stephen D. Houston, eds. *Fiery Pool: The Maya and the Mythic Sea*. Salem, MA: Peabody Essex Museum, 2010.

Fischbeck, Shelly L. "Agricultural Terrace Productivity in the Maya Lowlands of Belize." BS thesis, University of Wisconsin, La Crosse, 2001.

Fitzsimmons, James L. *Death and the Classic Maya Kings*. Austin: University of Texas Press, 2010.

Fitzsimmons, James L., and Shimada Izumi, eds. *Living with the Dead: Mortuary Ritual in Mesoamerica*. Tucson: University of Arizona Press, 2011.

Flannery, Kent V., and Joyce Marcus, eds. *The Cloud People: Divergent Evolution of the Zapotec and Mixtec Civilizations*. New York: Academic Press, 1983.

Foias, Antonia E., and Kitty F. Emery, eds. *Motul de San José: Politics, History, and Economy in a Classic Maya Polity*. Gainesville: University Press of Florida, 2012.

Folan, William, Abel Morales, Raymundo González, José Hernández, Lynda Florey, Rosario Domínguez, Vera Tiesler Blos, D. Bolles, Roberto Ruiz, and Joel D. Gunn. "Champoton, Campeche: Su Presencia en el Desarrollo Cultural del Golfo de México y su Corredor Eco-Arqueológico." *Los Investigadores de la Cultura Maya* 11, no. 1: 64–71, 2003.

Folan, William J. *The Open Chapel of Dzibilchaltun, Yucatan*, Middle American Research Institute, Publication 26. New Orleans, LA: Tulane University, 1970.

Folan, William J., Joel Gunn, Jack D. Eaton, and Robert W. Patch. "Paleoclimatological Patterning in Southern Mesoamerica." *Journal of Field Archaeology* 10, no. 4: 453–68, 1983.

Folan, William J., Ellen R. Kintz, and Laraine A. Fletcher. *Coba: A Classic Maya Metropolis*. Edited by Stuart Struever. Studies in Archaeology. New York: Academic Press, 1983.

Folan, William J., Joyce Marcus, Sophia Pincemin, Maria del Rosario Dominguez Carrasco, Laraine A. Fletcher, and Abel Morales. "Calakmul: New Data from an Ancient Maya Capital in Campeche, Mexico." *Latin American Antiquity* 6 (December): 310–34, 1995.

Folan, William J., Abel Morales, Rosario Dominguez, Roberto Ruiz, Raymundo González, Joel D. Gunn, Lynda Florey, M. Barredo, Jose Antonio Hernandez, and David Bolles. "La Cuidad y Puerto de Champoton, Campeche: Una Encrucijada del Gulfo de Mexico y su Corredor Eco-Arqueologico." *Los Investigadores de la Cultura Maya* 10, no. 1: 8–16, 2002.

Folan, William J., Abel Morales Lopez, Raymundo González Heredia, José Antonio Hernández Trujeque, Lynda Florey Folan, Donald W. Forsyth, Vera Tiesler, María José Gómez, Aracely Hurtado Cen, Ronals Bishop, David Bolles, Geoffrey E. Braswell, Jerald D. Ek, Joel Gunn, Christopher Götz, Gerardo Vallanueva, Alicia Blanso, Tomás Arnabar Gunam, Maria del Rosario Domínguez Carrasco, and Trenton Noble. "Chakanputun, Campeche: 3,000 Años de Sustentabilidad." In *La Costa de Campeche en los Tiempos Prehispanicos: Una Visión 50 Años Despues*, edited by Rafael Cobos Palma, 257–80. México D.F.: Universidad Nacional Autónoma de México, 2013.

Folan, William J., Abel Morales Lopez, José Antonio Hernández Trujeque, Raymundo González Heredia, Lynda Florey Folan, David Bolles, and Joel D. Gunn. "Recientes Excavaciones en el Barrio de Pozo Monte en las Cuidad y Puerto de Champoton (Chakan Putun) Campeche: Un Lugar Central del Preclassico Medio a Posclasico en la Costa Oeste de la Peninsula de Yucatan." *Los Investigadores de la Cultura Maya* 12, no. 2: 38–53, 2004.

Foncerrada Molina, Marta. *La escultura arquitectónica de Uxmal*. México, D.F.: Universidad Nacional Autónoma de México, 1965.

Ford, Anabel. *Population Growth and Social Complexity: An Examination of Settlement and Environment in the Central Maya Lowlands*. Anthropological Research Papers, No. 35. Tempe: Arizona State University, 1986.

———. "Adaptive Management and the Community of El Pilar: A Philosophy of Resilience for the Maya Forest." In *Of the Past, for the Future: Integrating Archaeology and Conservation*, edited by Neville Agnew and Janet Bridgland, 105–12. Washington, DC: The Getty Institute, 2006.

———. "Action Archaeology and the Community at El Pilar." In *Anthropology: The Human Challenge*, edited by William A. Haviland, Harald E. L. Prins, Dana Walrath, and Bunny McBride, 260–62. Belmont, CA: Wadsworth/Cengage Learning, 2011.

———. "Afterword: El Pilar and Maya Cultural Heritage, Reflections of a Cheerful Pessimist." In *Contested Cultural Heritage: Religion, Nationalism, Erasure, and Exclusion in a Global World*, edited by Helaine Silverman, 261–65. New York: Springer, 2011.

Ford, Anabel, Keith C. Clarke, and Gary Raines. "Modeling Settlement Patterns of the Late Classic Maya Civilization with Bayesian Methods and Geographic Information Systems." *Annals of the Association of American Geographers* 99, no. 3: 496–520, 2009.

Ford, Anabel, and M. Havrda. "Archaeology under the Canopy: Imagining the Maya of El Pilar." In *Tourism Consumption and Representation: Narratives of Place and Self*, edited by K. Meethan, A. Anderson, and S. Miles, 67–93. Wallingford, UK: CAB International, 2006.

Ford, Anabel, and Ronald Nigh. "Origins of the Maya Forest Garden: Maya Resource Management." *Journal of Ethnobiology* 29, no. 2: 213–36, 2009.

Ford, Ben, ed. *The Archaeology of Maritime Landscapes, Society for Historical Archaeology Conference on Historical Underwater Archaeology: When the Land Meets the Sea*. New York: Springer, 2011.

Förstemann, Ernst. *Commentary on the Maya Manuscript in the Royal Public Library of Dresden*. Papers of the Peabody Museum of American Archaeology and Ethnology, Harvard University, vol. 4, no. 2. Cambridge, MA: The Peabody Museum, 1906.

Förstemann, Ernst Wilhelm. *Die Mayahandschrift der Königlichen Öffentlichen Bibliothek zu Dresden*. Leipzig: Verlag der A. Naumann'schen Lichtdruckerei, 1880.

Forsyth, Donald W. *The Ceramics of El Mirador, Petén, Guatemala*. Provo, UT: New World Archaeological Foundation, Brigham Young University, 1989.

Gordin, Shai, ed. *Visualizing Knowledge and Creating Meaning in Ancient Writing Systems*. Berliner Beiträge zum Vorderen Orient, vol. 23. Gladbeck, Germany: PeWe-Verlag, 2014.

Graham, Elizabeth. *Maya Christians and Their Churches in Sixteenth-century Belize*. Gainesville: University Press of Florida, 2011.

Graham, Elizabeth A., Scott E. Simmons, and Christine D. White. "The Spanish Conquest and the Maya Collapse: How 'Religious' Is Change?" *World Archaeology* 45: 161–85, 2013.

Graham, Ian. *Seibal*. Vol. 7, no. 1 of *The Corpus of Maya Hieroglyphic Inscriptions*. Cambridge, MA: Peabody Museum Press, 1996.

———. *The Corpus of Maya Hieroglyphic Inscriptions*. Cambridge, MA: Peabody Museum of Archaeology and Ethnology, Harvard University, 2004–2006.

———. *The Road to Ruins*. Albuquerque, NM: University of New Mexico Press, 2010.

Graham, Ian, Peter Mathews, and Lucia Henderson. *Tonina*. Corpus of Maya Hieroglyphic Inscriptions, Peabody Museum of Archaeology and Ethnology, Harvard University, 1983–2006. https://peabody. harvard.edu/cmhi/site.php?site=Tonina.

Graham, Ian, and Eric Von Euw. *Naranjo*. Corpus of Maya Hieroglyphic Inscriptions, Peabody Museum of Archaeology and Ethnology, Harvard University, 1975–1978. https://www.peabody.harvard.edu/ cmhi/site.php?site=Naranjo#loc.

———. *Uxmal*. Corpus of Maya Hieroglyphic Inscriptions, Peabody Museum of Archaeology and Ethnology, Harvard University, 1992. https://peabody.harvard.edu/cmhi/site.php?site=Uxmal.

Graham, John Allen, ed. *Ancient Mesoamerica: Selected Readings*. 2nd ed. Palo Alto, CA: Peek Publications, 1981.

Graña-Behrens, Daniel. "Emblem Glyphs and Political Organization in Northwestern Yucatan in the Classic Period (A.D. 300–1000)." *Ancient Mesoamerica* 17, no. 1: 105–23, 2006.

———. "The Ruins and Hieroglyphic Inscriptions of Itzimte-Bolonchen, Campeche: Rulers and Political Affairs from Burned Stones." In *The Long Silence 2: Itzimte and Its Neighbors*, edited by Stephan Merk. Markt Schwaben. Germany: Verlag Anton Saurwein, 2014).

Grivetti, Louis Evan, and Howard-Yana Shapiro, eds. *Chocolate: History, Culture, and Heritage*. Hoboken, NJ: Wiley, 2009.

Grofe, Michael J. *The Recipe for Rebirth: Cacao as Fish in the Mythology and Symbolism of the Ancient Maya*. 2007. http://www.famsi.org/research/grofe/GrofeRecipeForRebirth.pdf.

Gronemeyer, Sven, and Barbara MacLeod. "What Could Happen in 2012: A Re-Analysis of the 13-Bak'tun prophecy on Tortuguero Monument 6." *Wayeb Notes*. 2010. http://www.wayeb.org/ notes/wayeb_notes0034.pdf.

Grube, Nikolai, ed. *Die Entwicklung der Mayaschrift: Grundlagen zur Erforschung des Wandels der Mayaschrift von der Protoklassik bis zur spanischen Eroberung*. Vol. 3 of *Acta Mesoamericana*. Markt Schwaben, Germany: Verlag Anton Saurwein, 1990.

———. "Classic Maya Dance." *Ancient Mesoamerica* 3, no. 2: 201–18, 1992.

———. "Epigraphic Research at Caracol, Belize." In *Studies in the Archaeology of Caracol, Belize*, edited by Diane Z. Chase and Arlen Chase, 83–122. Pre-Columbian Research Institute, Monograph 7. San Francisco, CA: Pre-Columbian Research Institute, 1994.

Grube, Nikolai, Eva Eggebrecht, and Matthias Seidel, eds. *Maya: Divine Kings of the Rainforest*. Cologne, Germany: Könemann, 2006. Distributed by John Wilson.

Grube, Nikolai, Eva Eggebrecht, Matthias Seidel, and Mark Van Stone, eds. *Maya: Divine Kings of the Rainforest*. 2nd ed. Potsdam, Germany: H. F. Ullmann, 2012.

Grube, Nikolai, and Linda Schele. "New Observations on the Loltun Relief " *Mexicon* 18, no. 1: 11–14, 1996.

Grube, Nikolai K. "Hieroglyphic Inscriptions from Northwest Yucatan: An Update of Recent Research." In *Escondido en la Selva*, edited by Hanns J. Prem. México, D.F., and Bonn, Germany: Instituto Nacional de Antropología e Historía and the University of Bonn, 2003.

Guenter, Stanley. *La Corona Find Sheds Light on Site Q Mystery*. Mesoweb, 2005. http://www.mesoweb
.com/reports/SiteQ.html.

———. *The Tomb of K'inich Janaab Pakal: The Temple of the Inscriptions at Palenque*. Mesoweb, 2007. http://
www.mesoweb.com/articles/guenter/TI.html.

———. "Under a Falling Star: The Hiatus at Tikal." MA thesis, La Trobe University, 2002.

Guernsey, Julia. *Ritual & Power in Stone: The Performance of Rulership in Mesoamerican Izapan Style Art*.
Austin: University of Texas Press, 2006.

Guernsey, Julia, and F. Kent Reilly III. *Sacred Bundles: Ritual Acts of Wrapping and Binding in Mesoamerica*.
Barnardsville, NC: Boundary End Archaeology Research Center, 2006.

Guillemin, George F. "Urbanism and Hierarchy at Iximche." In *Social Process in Maya Prehistory*, edited
by Norman Hammond, 227–64. New York: Academic Press, 1977.

Gunn, Joel D., William J. Folan, and Hubert R. Robichaux. "A Landscape Analysis of the Candelaria
Watershed in Mexico: Insights into Paleoclimates Affecting Upland Horticulture in the Southern
Yucatan Peninsula Semi-karst." *Geoarchaeology* 10, no. 1: 3–42, 1995.

Gunn, Joel D., John E. Foss, William J. Folan, Maria del Rosario Domínguez Carrasco, and Betty B.
Faust. "Bajo Sediments and the Hydraulic System of Calakmul, Campeche, Mexico." *Ancient Mesoamerica* 13: 297–315, 2002.

Hall, Grant D. "Realm of Death: Royal Mortuary Customs and Polity Interaction in the Classic Maya
Lowlands." PhD diss., Harvard University, 1989.

Halperin, Christina T. "Circulation as Placemaking: Late Classic Maya Polities and Portable Objects."
American Anthropologist 116, no. 1: 110–29, 2014.

Hamblin, Nancy L. *Animal Use by the Cozumel Maya*. Tucson: University of Arizona Press, 1984.

Hammond, Norman. "Obsidian Trade Routes in the Mayan Area." *Science* 178: 1092–93, 1972.

———. "Sir Eric Thompson, 1898–1975." *American Antiquity* 42, no. 2: 180–90, 1977.

———, ed. *Social Process in Maya Prehistory*. New York: Academic Press, 1977.

———. "The Prehistory of Belize." *Journal of Field Archaeology* 9: 349–362, 1982.

———. *Cuello: An Early Maya Community in Belize*. Cambridge, UK: Cambridge University Press, 1991.

Hansen, Richard D. *Excavations in the Tigre Complex, El Mirador, Petén, Guatemala*. Pt. 3. Provo, UT: New
World Archaeological Foundation, Brigham Young University, 1990.

———. *An Early Maya Text from El Mirador, Guatemala*. Boundary End Archaeological Research Center—Mesoweb, 1991. http://www.mesoweb.com/bearc/cmr/37.html.

———. "Continuity and Disjunction: The Pre-Classic Antecedents of Classic Maya Architecture." In
*Function and Meaning in Classic Maya Architecture : A Symposium at Dumbarton Oaks, 7th and 8th Oc-
tober 1994*, edited by Stephen D. Houston. Washington, DC: Dumbarton Oaks Research Library
and Collection, 1998.

———. *Incipient Maya Wetland Agriculture: Definition of Ancient Systems and Sustainable Application in Contemporary Rainforest Populations*. 1998.

———. *Publications and Papers of the Mirador Basin Project: Project Bibliography 01–08*. Foundation for
Anthropological Research and Environmental Studies (FARES), and Idaho State University,
2001–2008. http://www.fares-foundation.org/docs/Bibliography01-08.pdf.

———. *Proyecto Arqueológico Cuenca Mirador: Investigación, conservación y desarrollo en El Mirador, Petén,
Guatemala, informe final temporada de Campo 2003*. 2004.

———. "Perspectives on Olmec-Maya Interaction in the Middle Formative Period." In *New Perspectives
on Formative Mesoamerican Cultures*, edited by Terry G. Powis, 51–72. B.A.R. International Series,
no. 1377 Oxford: Archaeopress, 2006.

———. *Publications and Papers of the Mirador Basin Project*. Foundation for Anthropological Research and
Environmental Studies (FARES) in collaboration with the Instituto de Antropología e Historia de
Guatemala, Ministry of Culture and Sports, 2007. http://www.miradorbasin.com/about/bibliog
raphy02-07.pdf.

———. "The Good Prince: Transition, Texting and Moral Narrative in the Murals of Bonampak, Chiapas, Mexico." *Cambridge Archaeological Journal* 22, no. 2: 153–75, 2012.

Houston, Stephen D., Héctor L. Escobedo, and Juan Carlos Meléndez. *Proyecton arqueologico El Zotz: Informe No. 2, Temporada 2007* Guatemala de la Asunción [accessed October 2015]. Available from http://www.mesoweb.com/2012/El-Zotz-2007.pdf. 2008.

Houston, Stephen D., and Takeshi Inomata. *The Classic Maya.* New York: Cambridge University Press, 2009.

Houston, Stephen D., and Zachary Nelson. *A Thematic Bibliography of Ancient Maya Writing.* Provo, UT: Research Press, Institute for the Study and Preservation of Ancient Religious Texts, Brigham Young University, 2001.

Howie, Linda. *Ceramic Change and the Maya Collapse: A Study of Pottery Technology, Manufacture and Consumption at Lamanai, Belize.* B.A.R. International Series. Oxford: Archaeopress, 2012.

Hruby, Zachary X. "Ritualized Chipped-Stone Production at Piedras Negras, Guatemala." *Archeological Papers of the American Anthropological Association* 17, no. 1: 68–87, 2007.

Hruby, Zachary X., Geoffrey E. Braswell, and Oswaldo Fernando Chinchilla Mazariegos. *The Technology of Maya Civilization: Political Economy and Beyond in Lithic Studies.* Approaches to Anthropological Archaeology. Sheffield, UK, and Oakville, CT: Equinox Publishing, 2011.

Hull, Kerry. "An Epigraphic Analysis of Classic-Period Maya Foodstuffs." In *Pre-Columbian Foodways*, edited by John Staller and Michael Carrasco, 235–56. Springer New York, 2010.

Hundewadt, Mette Hald. *Izamal: History, Archeology and Mythology.* Copenhagen, Denmark: Indianske Sprog og Kulturer, 2003.

Hunt, Will. "Bringing to Light Mysterious Maya Cave Rituals." *Discover*, November 12, 2014. http://discovermagazine.com/2014/dec/15-cave-of-the-crystal-maiden.

Hutson, Scott R., David R. Hixson, Bruce H. Dahlin, Aline Magnoni, and Daniel Mazeau. "Site and Community at Chunchucmil and Ancient Maya Urban Centers." *Journal of Field Archaeology* 33, no. 1: 19–40, 2008.

Hutson, Scott R., Aline Magnoni, Daniel Mazeau, and Travis W. Stanton. "The Archaeology of Urban Houselots at Chunchucmil, Yucatán, Mexico." In *Lifeways in the Northern Maya Lowlands: New Approaches to Archaeology in the Yucatán Peninsula*, edited by Jennifer P. Mathews and Bethany A. Morrison, 72–92. Tucson: University of Arizona Press, 2006.

Iannone, Gyles. *Rural Complexity in the Cahal Pech Microregion.* Monograph Series. Edited by Gyles Iannone and Samuel V. Connell. Los Angeles: The Cotsen Institute of Archaeology at UCLA Perspectives on Ancient Maya Rural Complexity, 2003.

———, ed. *The Great Maya Droughts in Cultural Context: Case Studies in Resilience and Vulnerability.* Boulder: University Press of Colorado, 2013.

Iglesias Ponce de León, María Josefa, and Francesc Ligorred Perramon, eds. *Perspectivas antropológicas en el mundo Maya.* Publicaciones de la Sociedad Española de Estudios Mayas 2. [Madrid]: Sociedad Española de Estudios Mayas, 1993.

Inomata, Takeshi. "Plazas, Performers, and Spectators: Political Theaters of the Classic Maya." *Current Anthropology* 47, no. 5: 805–42, 2006.

Inomata, Takeshi, and Lawrence S. Coben, eds. *Archaeology of Performance: Theaters of Power, Community, and Politics.* Lanham, MD: AltaMira Press, 2006.

Inomata, Takeshi, and Stephen Houston, eds. *Royal Courts of the Ancient Maya.* Boulder: Westview Press, 2001.

Inomata, Takeshi, Raúl Ortiz, Bárbara Arroyo, and Eugenia J. Robinson. "Chronological Revision of Preclassic Kaminaljuyú, Guatemala: Implications for Social Processes in the Southern Maya Area." *Latin American Antiquity* 25, no. 4: 377–408, 2014.

Inomata, Takeshi, and Daniela Triadan, eds. *Burned Palaces and Elite Residences of Aguateca: Excavations and Ceramics.* Monographs of the Aguateca Archaeological Project First Phase, vol. 1. Salt Lake City: The University of Utah Press, 2010.

———, eds. *Life and Politics at the Royal Court of Aguateca: Artifacts, Analytical Data, and Synthesis.* Aguateca Archaeological Project First Phase Monograph Series, vol. 3. Salt Lake City: The University of Utah Press, 2014.

Inomata, Takeshi, Daniela Triadan, Kazuo Aoyama, Victor Castillo, and Hitoshi Yonenobu. "Early Ceremonial Constructions at Ceibal, Guatemala, and the Origins of Lowland Maya Civilization." *Science* 340, 6131: 467–71, 2013.

Instituto Chiapaneco de Cultura. *Cuarto Foro de Arqueología de Chiapas: [21–26 de noviembre de 1993, Comitán, Chiapas].* Tuxtla Gutiérrez, Chiapas, México, 1994.

Instituto de Antropología e Historia. *Monografías Atlas Arqueológico de Guatemala: Registro de sitios Arqueológicos del Sureste y Centro-oeste de Petén 1987–2008.* Guatemala City, Guatemala: Ministerio de Cultura y Deportes, Dirección General de Patrimonio Cultural y Natural, Instituto de Antropología e Historia, 2008. http://www.atlasarqueologico.com/index.php.

Instituto Geográfico Nacional, Ingeniero Pablo Arnoldo Guzmán. *Atlas de el Salvador.* 4th ed. El Salvador, C.A.: Instituto Geográfico Nacional-Centro Nacional de Registros, Ingeniero Pablo Arnoldo Guzmán, Ministerio de Obras Públicas, 2000.

International Phonetic Association. *International Phonetic Alphabet (2005 Version).* Division of Psychology and Language Sciences, University College London, 2013. https://www.langsci.ucl.ac.uk/ipa/index.html.

Isendahl, Christian. "The Weight of Water: A New Look at Pre-Hispanic Puuc Maya Water Reservoirs." *Ancient Mesoamerica* 22, no. 1: 185–97, 2011.

Itzel Mateos González, Frida. *Toniná, la pintura mural y los relieves: Técnica de manufactura.* Mexico City: Instituto Nacional de Antropología e Historia, Centro de Investigaciones Humanísticas de Mesoamérica y del Estado de Chiapas-UNAM, 1997.

Jacob, John S. "Ancient Maya Wetland Agricultural Fields in Cobweb Swamp, Belize: Construction, Chronology, and Function." *Journal of Field Archaeology* 22, no. 2: 175–90, 1995.

Johnson, Kristofer D., David R. Wright, and Richard E. Terry. "Application of Carbon Isotope Analysis to Ancient Maize Agriculture in the Petexbatún Region of Guatemala." *Geoarchaeology* 22, no. 3: 313–36, 2007.

Johnson, Scott A. J. *Translating Maya Hieroglyphs.* Recovering Languages and Literacies of the Americas. Norman: University of Oklahoma Press, 2013.

Johnston, Kevin J. "The Intensification of Pre-industrial Cereal Agriculture in the Tropics: Boserup, Cultivation Lengthening, and the Classic Maya." *Journal of Anthropological Archaeology* 22, no. 2: 126–61, 2003.

Jones, Grant D. *The Conquest of the Last Maya Kingdom.* Stanford, CA: Stanford University Press, 1998.

Joralemon, P. D. *A Study of Olmec Iconography.* Washington, DC: Dumbarton Oaks, 1971.

Josserand, J. Kathryn. "The Missing Heir at Yaxchilán: Literary Analysis of a Maya Historical Puzzle." *Latin American Antiquity* 18, no. 3: 295–312, 2007.

Joyce, Rosemary A. *Gender and Power in Prehispanic Mesoamerica.* Austin: University of Texas Press, 2000.

Joyce, Rosemary A., and John S. Henderson. "Beginnings of Village Life in Eastern Mesoamerica." *Latin American Antiquity* 12, no. 1: 5–23, 2001.

Joyce, Thomas Athol. "The 'Eccentric Flints' of Central America." *Journal of the Royal Anthropological Institute of Great Britain and Ireland* 62: xvii–xxvi, 1932.

Justeson, John S., and Lyle Campbell. *Phoneticism in Mayan Hieroglyphic Writing.* Institute for Mesoamerican Studies, Publication 9. Albany: Institute for Mesoamerican Studies, State University of New York at Albany, 1984.

Kaufman, Terrence, and John S. Justeson. *Epi-Olmec Hieroglyphic Writing and Texts.* Project for the Documentation of the Languages of Mesoamerica (PDLMA), Department of Anthropology, University at Albany, State University of New York, 2001.

Kelly, Joyce. *An Archaeological Guide to Mexico's Yucatan Peninsula.* Norman: University of Oklahoma Press, 1993.

Laughlin, Robert M. *The Great Tzotzil Dictionary of Santo Domingo Zinacantan: With Grammatical Analysis and Historical Commentary*. With commentary by John B. Haviland. Washington, DC: Smithsonian Institution Press, 1988.

Law, Danny. "Mayan Historical Linguistics in a New Age." *Language and Linguistics Compass* 7, no. 3: 141–56, 2013.

LeCount, Lisa J., and Jason Yaeger. *Classic Maya Provincial Politics: Xunantunich and Its Hinterlands.* Tucson: University of Arizona Press, 2010.

Lee, Julian C. *A Field Guide to the Amphibians and Reptiles of the Maya World: The Lowlands of Mexico, Northern Guatemala, and Belize*. Ithaca, NY: Cornell University Press, 2000.

Lentz, David L., Nicholas P. Dunning, and Vernon L. Scarborough, eds. *Tikal: Paleoecology of an Ancient Maya City*. New York: Cambridge University Press, 2014.

Libby, Willard F. *Radiocarbon Dating*. Chicago: University of Chicago Press, 1985.

Liendo Stuardo, Rodrigo "Palenque y su área de sustentación: Patrón de Asentamiento y organización política en un centro Maya del Clásico." *Mexicon* 23, no. 2: 36–42, 2001.

Lincoln, Charles E. "A Preliminary Assessment of Izamal, Yucatán, Mexico." BA thesis, Tulane University, 1980.

Lohse, Jon C., and Fred Valdez, eds. *Ancient Maya Commoners*. Austin: University of Texas Press, 2004.

Longacre, Robert. "Systemic Comparison and Reconstruction." In *Handbook of Middle American Indians*. Vol. 5, *Linguistics*, edited by Norman McQuown, 117–59. Austin: University of Texas Press, 1967.

Looper, Matthew George. *Lightning Warrior: Maya Art and Kingship at Quirigua*. Linda Schele Series in Maya and pre-Columbian Studies. Austin: University of Texas Press, 2003.

———. *To Be Like Gods: Dance in Ancient Maya Civilization*. Austin: University of Texas Press, 2009.

Looper, Matthew George, and Thomas G. Tolles. *Gifts of the Moon: Huipil Designs of the Ancient Maya*. San Diego Museum Papers 38. San Diego, CA: San Diego Museum of Man, 2000.

López Camacho, Javier, Araceli Vázquez Villegas, and Luis Antonio Torres Díaz. *Noh Kah: Pobladores de la montaña; Nuevos hallazgos*. Arqueología Mexicana, Editorial Raíces, S. A. de C.V. and Mexican National Council for Culture and the Arts, 2014. http://www.arqueomex.com/S2N3nQuintana Roo120.html.

Lorenzi, Rossella. *Ancient Maya Cities Found in Jungle*. Discovery Communications, Inc., 2014. http://news.discovery.com/history/archaeology/three-ancient-maya-cities-found-in-jungle-140815.htm.

Lothrop, Samuel Kirkland. *Tulum: An Archaeological Study of the East Coast of Yucatan*. Carnegie Institution of Washington Publication 335. Washington, DC: Carnegie Institution of Washington, 1924.

Lounsbury, Floyd. "Astronomical Knowledge and Its Uses at Bonampak, Mexico." In *Archaeoastronomy in the New World*, edited by Anthony F. Aveni, 143–68. Cambridge, UK: Cambridge University Press, 1982.

Love, Bruce. *The Paris Codex: Handbook for a Maya Priest*. Austin: University of Texas Press, 1994.

Love, Michael. "City States and City-State Culture in the Southern Maya Region." In *The Southern Maya in the Late Preclassic: The Rise and Fall of an Early Mesoamerican Civilization*, edited by Michael Love and Jonathan Kaplan, 47–76. Boulder: University Press of Colorado, 2011.

Love, Michael, and Julia Guernsey. "La Blanca and the Soconusco Formative." In *Early Mesoamerican Social Transformations: Archaic and Formative Lifeways in the Soconusco Region*, edited by Richard G. Lesure, 170–89. Berkeley: University of California Press, 2011.

Love, Michael, and Jonathan H. Kaplan. *The Southern Maya in the Late Preclassic: The Rise and Fall of an Early Mesoamerican Civilization*. Boulder: University Press of Colorado, 2011.

Lowe, Gareth W. "The Mixe-Zoque as Competing Neighbors of the Early Lowland Maya." In *The Origins of Maya Civilization*, edited by Richard E. W. Adams. Albuquerque: University of New Mexico Press, 1977.

Lowe, Gareth W., Thomas A. Lee, and E. Eduardo Martínez. *Izapa: An Introduction to the Ruins and Monuments*. Provo, UT: New World Archaeological Foundation, Brigham Young University, 1982.

Lucero, Lisa Joyce, and Barbara W. Fash, eds. *Precolumbian Water Management: Ideology, Ritual, and Power.* Tucson: University of Arizona Press, 2006.

Lucero, Lisa J., Joel D. Gunn, and Vernon L. Scarborough. "Climate Change and Classic Maya Water Management." *Water* 3, no. 4: 479–94, 2011.

Luzzadder-Beach, Sheryl. "Water Resources of the Chunchucmil Maya." *Geographical Review* 90, no. 4: 493–510, 2000.

Luzzadder-Beach, Sheryl, and Timothy Beach. "Water Chemistry Constraints and Possibilities for the Ancient and Contemporary Maya Wetlands." *Journal of Ethnobiology* 28, no. 2: 211–30, 2008.

———. "Arising from the Wetlands: Mechanisms and Chronology of Landscape Aggradation in the Northern Coastal Plain of Belize." *Annals of the Association of American Geographers* 99, no. 1: 1–26, 2009.

Luzzadder-Beach, Sheryl, Timothy P. Beach, and Nicholas P. Dunning. "Wetland Fields as Mirrors of Drought and the Maya Abandonment." *Proceedings of the National Academy of Sciences USA* 109, no. 10: 3646–51, 2012.

Macario, Raquel, Yvonne Putzeys, Marie Fulbert, Edgar Telón, Edgar Ortega, Jorge Cáceres, Juan Manuel Palomo, Sandra Carrillo, Luis I. Pérez, Manuel Colón, Rafael Cambranes, and Karla Cardona. *Proyecto Etnoarqueológico Q'um'arkaj, Quiché, Guatemala.* Museo Nacional de Arqueología y Etnología, Guatemala, 2007. http://www.asociaciontikal.com/pdf/57_-_Macario.pdf.

MacNeish, Richard S. *Robert S. Peabody Foundation for Archaeology: Annual Report 1980.* Andover, MA: Philips Academy Andover, 1980.

MacNeish, Richard S., and Mary W. Eubanks. "Comparative Analysis of the Río Balsas and Tehuacán Models for the Origin of Maize." *Latin American Antiquity* 11, no. 1: 3–20, 2000.

MacNeish, Richard S., S. Jeffrey, K. Wilkerson, and Antoinette Nelken-Terner. *First Annual Report of the Belize Archaic Archaeological Reconnaissance.* Andover, MA: Robert F. Peabody Foundation for Archaeology, 1980.

Macri, Martha J., and Matthew G. Looper. *The New Catalog of Maya Hieroglyphs.* Vol. 1, *The Classic Period Inscriptions.* Civilization of the American Indian series, vol. 247. Norman: University of Oklahoma Press, 2003.

Macri, Martha J., and Gabrielle Vail. *The New Catalog of Maya Hieroglyphs.* Vol. 2, *The Codical Texts.* Civilization of the American Indian series, vol. 264. Norman: University of Oklahoma Press, 2009.

Makemson, Maud Worcester. *The Book of the Jaguar Priest.* New York: Schuman, 1951.

Maldonado C., Rubén. *Izamal, Yucatán.* México, D.F., México: Instituto Nacional de Antropología e Historia, 1991.

Maldonado Cardenas, Rubén, and Susana Echeverría Castillo. "La Presencia de Chichén Itzá en el Sitio de Dzibilchaltún." *Los Investigadores de la Cultura Maya* 19: 107–22, 2010.

Maler, Teobert. *Researches in the Central Portion of the Usumatsintla Valley: Report of Explorations for the Museum, 1898–1900.* Memoirs of the Peabody Museum of American Archaeology and Ethnology, Harvard University. Cambridge, MA: The Museum, 1901.

———. *Explorations in the Department of Peten, Guatemala and Adjacent Region: Topoxte; Yaxha; Benque Viejo; Naranjo; Reports of Explorations for the Museum.* Memoirs of the Peabody Museum of American Archaeology and Ethnology, Harvard University. Cambridge, MA: The Museum, 1908.

———. *Explorations of the Upper Usumatsintla and Adjacent Region: Altar de sacrificios; Seibal; Itsimte-Sacluk; Cankuen; Reports of Explorations for the Museum.* Memoirs of the Peabody Museum of American Archaeology and Ethnology, Harvard University. Cambridge, MA: The Museum, 1908.

———. *Explorations in the Department of Peten, Guatemala and Adjacent region: Motul de San Jose; Peten-Itza; Reports of Explorations for the Museum.* Memoirs of the Peabody Museum of American Archaeology and Ethnology, Harvard University. Cambridge, MA: The Museum, 1910.

———. *Historia de las ruinas de Chichen-Itza, 1910.* Mérida, Yucatán, México, 1910.

———. *Explorations in the Department of Peten, Guatemala, Tikal; Reports of Explorations for the Museum.* Memoirs of the Peabody Museum of American Archaeology and Ethnology, Harvard University. Cambridge, MA: The Museum, 1911.

Milbrath, Susan. *Star Gods of the Maya: Astronomy in Art, Folklore, and Calendars.* Austin: University of Texas Press, 2000.

———. *Mayapán's Effigy Censers: Iconography, Context, and External Connections.* Foundation for the Advancement of Mesoamerican Studies, Inc. (FAMSI), 2007. http://www.famsi.org/reports/05025/.

Miles, Suzanne W. "Sculpture of the Guatemala-Chiapas Highlands and Pacific Slopes, and Associated Hieroglyphs." In *Handbook of Middle American Indians.* Vol. 2, *The Archaeology of Southern Mesoamerica,* pt 1, edited by Gordon R. Willey, 237–75. Austin: University of Texas Press, 1965.

Miller, Arthur G. "The Maya and the Sea: Trade and Cult at Tancah and Tulum." In *The Sea in the Pre-Columbian World: A Conference at Dumbarton Oaks, October 26th and 27th, 1974,* edited by Elizabeth P. Benson and Dumbarton Oaks. Washington, DC: Dumbarton Oaks Research Library and Collections, Trustees for Harvard University, 1974.

———. "The Postclassic Sequence of Tancah and Tulum, Quintana Roo, Mexico." In *The Lowland Maya Postclassic,* edited by Arlen F. Chase and Prudence M. Rice. Austin: University of Texas Press, 1985.

Miller, Mary Ellen. *The Murals of Bonampak.* Princeton, NJ: Princeton University Press, 1986.

———. *Maya Art and Architecture.* London: Thames & Hudson, 1999.

Miller, Mary Ellen, and Claudia Brittenham. *The Spectacle of the Late Maya Court: Reflections on the Murals of Bonampak.* William & Bettye Nowlin Series in Art, History, and Culture of the Western Hemisphere. Austin: University of Texas Press, 2013.

Miller, Mary Ellen, and Simon Martin. *Courtly Art of the Ancient Maya.* New York: Thames & Hudson, 2004.

Miller, Mary Ellen, and Megan Eileen O'Neil. *Maya Art and Architecture.* 2nd ed. London: Thames & Hudson, 2014.

Miller, Mary Ellen, and Megan O'Neil. "The Worlds of the Ancient Maya and the Worlds They Made." In *Fiery Pool: The Maya and the Mythic Sea,* edited by Daniel Finamore and Stephen Houston. Salem, MA: Peabody Essex Museum, 2010.

Miller, Mary Ellen, and Karl Taube. *The Gods and Symbols of Ancient Mexico and the Maya: An Illustrated Dictionary of Mesoamerican Religion.* London: Thames & Hudson, 1993.

———. *The Gods and Symbols of Ancient Mexico and the Maya: An Illustrated Dictionary of Mesoamerican Religion.* New York: Thames & Hudson, 1993.

Millon, René. "Teotihuacan: City, State, and Civilization." In *Supplement to the Handbook of Middle American Indians No. 1,* edited by Victoria R. Bricker and Jeremy A. Sabloff, 198–243. Austin: University of Texas Press, 1981.

Moholy-Nagy, Hattula. "Source Attribution and the Utilization of Obsidian in the Maya Area." *Latin American Antiquity* 14, no. 3: 301–10, 2003.

Molnar, Peter, and Lynn R. Sykes. "Tectonics of the Caribbean and Middle America regions from focal mechanisms and seismicity." *Geological Society of America Bulletin* 80, no. 9: 1639–84, 1969.

Montgomery, John. *How to Read Maya Hieroglyphs.* New York: Hippocrene Books, 2002.

———. *Dictionary of Maya Hieroglyphs.* New York: Hippocrene Books, 2006.

Morales, Paulino I., and Erwin Franciné Valiente. "Secuencia de construcción y presentación del Edificio 218 en la Acrópolis Este de Yaxha " In *XIX Simposio de Investigaciones Arqueológicas en Guatemala, 2005,* edited by Juan Pedro Laporte, Bárbara Arroyo, and Héctor E. Mejía, 1010–17. Guatemala City, Guatemala: Museo Nacional de Arqueología y Etnología, 2006.

Morley, Sylvanus Griswold. *An Introduction to the Study of the Maya Hieroglyphs.* Smithsonian Institution, Bureau of American Ethnology, Bulletin 57. Washington, DC: Government Printing Office, 1915.

———. *Inscriptions of Peten.* Vols. I–V. Carnegie Institution of Washington, Publication 437. Washington, DC: Carnegie Institution of Washington, 1938.

———. *The Ancient Maya.* Palo Alto, CA: Stanford University Press, 1946.

Müller, Florencia. *Atlas arqueológico de la República Mexicana.* Tomo 1, *Quintana Roo.* Mexico City: Instituto Nacional de Antropología e Historia, 1959.

Munro, P. G, and M. L. M. Zurita. "The Role of Cenotes in the Social History of Mexico's Yucatan Peninsula." *Environment and History* 17, no. 4: 583–612, 2011.

Munro-Stasiuk, Mandy J., and T. Kam Manahan. "Investigating Ancient Maya Agricultural Adaptation through Ground Penetrating Radar (GPR) Analysis of Karst Terrain, Northern Yucatán, Mexico." *Acta Carsologica*, no. 39: 123–35, 2010.

Munro-Stasiuk, Mandy J., T. Kam Manahan, T. Stockton, and T. Ardren. "Spatial and Physical Characteristics of Rejolladas in Northern Yucatán, Mexico: Implications for Ancient Maya Agriculture and Settlement Patterns." *Geoarchaeology* 29, no. 2: 156–72, 2014.

Munson, Jessica, and Takeshi Inomata. "Temples in the Forest: The Discovery of an Early Maya Community at Caobal, Petén, Guatemala." *Antiquity* 85, no. 328, 2011.

Nahm, Werner. "Hieroglyphic Stairway I at Yaxchilan." *Mexicon* 19, no. 4: 65–69, 1997.

Nalda, Enrique. "Dinámica ocupacional, estilos arquitectónicos y desarrollo histórico en Kohunlich." In *Escondido en la Selva*, edited by Hanns J. Prem. México, D.F., and Bonn, Germany: Instituto Nacional de Antropología e Historia and the University of Bonn, 2003.

———. *Kohunlich: Emplazamiento y desarrollo histórico*. México D.F., México: Instituto Nacional de Antropología e Historia, 2004.

———. *Los cautivos de Dzibanché*. México, D.F.: Instituto Nacional de Antropología e Historia, 2004.

———. "Kohunlich and Dzibanché. Parallel histories." In *Quintana Roo archaeology*, edited by Justine M. Shaw and Jennifer P. Mathews, 228–44. Tucson: University of Arizona Press, 2005.

Nalda, Enrique, and Adriana Velázquez Morlet. "Kohunlich: Mitos y reflexiones sobre su historia prehispánica." In *Guardianes del tiempo*, edited by Adriana Velázquez Morlet, 15–35. Chetumal, Quintana Roo, México: Universidad de Quintana Roo, Instituto Nacional de Antropología e Historia, 2000.

Nance, Charles Roger, Stephen L. Whittington, and Barbara E. Jones-Borg. *Archaeology and Ethnohistory of Iximche*. Gainesville: University Press of Florida, 2003.

Nichols, Deborah L., and Christopher A. Pool, eds. *The Oxford Handbook of Mesoamerican Archaeology*. Oxford and New York: Oxford University Press, 2012.

Nondédéo, Philippe. "Río Bec: Primeros pasos de una nueva investigación." *Mexicon* 15 (August 2003): 100–105, 2001.

Nondédéo, Philippe, Alejandro Patiño, Julien Sion, Dominique Michelet, and Carlos Morales-Aguilar. *Crisis múltiples en Naachtun: Aprovechadas, superadas e irreversibles*. Mesoweb, 2013. http://www.mesoweb.com/publications/MMS/9_Nondedeo_etal.pdf.

Norman, V. Garth. *Izapa Sculpture*. 2 vols. Provo, UT: New World Archaeological Foundation, Brigham Young University, 1973.

Normark, Johan. "Involutions of Materiality: Operationalizing a Neo-materialist Perspective through the Causeways at Ichmul and Yo'okop." *Journal of Archaeological Method and Theory* 17, no. 2: 132–73, 2010.

O'Neil, Megan Eileen. *Engaging Ancient Maya Sculpture at Piedras Negras, Guatemala*. Norman: University of Oklahoma Press, 2012.

O'Neil, Megan Eileen, and Marc G. Blainey. "Object, Memory, and Materiality at Yaxchilan: The Reset Lintels of Structures 12 and 22." *Ancient Mesoamerica* 22, no. 2: 245–69, 2011.

Opitz, Rachel S., and David Cowley, eds. *Interpreting Archaeological Topography: Airborne Laser Scanning, 3D Data and Ground Observation*. Oxford: Oxbow Books, 2013.

Orr, Heather S., and Rex Koontz, eds. *Blood and Beauty: Organized Violence in the Art and Archaeology of Mesoamerica and Central America*. Los Angeles, CA: Cotsen Institute of Archaeology Press, 2009.

Ortner, Donald J. *Identification of Pathological Conditions in Human Skeletal Remains*. San Diego, CA: Academic Press, 2003.

Orton, Clive, Paul Tyres, and Alan Vince. *Pottery in Archaeology*. London: Cambridge University Press, 1993.

Pallán Gayol, Carlos. "Secuencia dinástica, glifos emblema y topónimos en las inscripciones jeroglíficas de Edzná, Campeche (600–900 dC): Implicaciones históricas." Tesis de Maestría, Estudios Mesoamericanos, UNAM, México, 2009.

Parsons, Lee Allen. *Bilbao, Guatemala: An Archaeological Study of the Pacific Coast Cotzumalhuapa Region*. 2 vols. Publications in Anthropology. Milwaukee, WI: Milwaukee Public Museum, 1967–1969.

————. *The Settlement Survey of Tikal.* Tikal Reports, no. 13. Philadelphia: University of Pennsylvania Musuem, 1983.

Raaflaub, Kurt A., ed. *Thinking, Recording, and Writing History in the Ancient World.* New York: John Wiley & Sons, 2013.

Rangel, Martin, and Kathryn Reese-Taylor, eds. *Proyecto Arqueológico Naachtun 2004–2009, informe no. 2, segunda temporada de campo en el sitio arqueológico Naachtun.* Mesoweb, 2013. http://www.mesoweb.com/resources/informes/Naachtun2005.html.

Rangel Guillermo, Martin, and Kathryn Reese-Taylor. *Resultados de Investigaciones Arqueologicos en Naachtun, Temporada 2004.* Mesoweb, 2005. http://www.mesoweb.com/resources/informes/Naachtun2004.pdf.

Ratray, Evelyn Childs, ed. *Rutas Intercambio en Mesoamérica, III ColoquioPedro Bosch-Gimpera.* Mexico, D.F.: Universidad Nacional Autónoma de México, Instituto de Investigaciones Antropológicas, 1998.

Redfield, Robert, and Alfonso Villa Rojas. "Chan Kom: A Maya Village." *Carnegie Institution of Washington, Publication* 448: 339–56, 1934.

Reents-Budet, Dorie. "The 'Holmul Dancer' Theme in Maya Art." In *Sixth Palenque Round Table, 1986,* edited by Virginia M. Fields, 217–22. Norman: University of Oklahoma Press, 1991.

————. *Painting the Maya Universe: Royal Ceramics of the Classic Period.* Durham, NC: Duke University Press, 1994.

————. "Power Material in Ancient Mesoamerica: The Role of Cloth among the Classic Maya." In *Sacred Bundles: Ritual Acts of Wrapping and Binding in Mesoamerica,* edited by Julia Guernsey and F. Kent Reilly III, 105–26. Barnardsville, NC: Boundary End Archaeology Research Center, 2006.

Reents-Budet, Dorie, and Ronald L. Bishop. "The Late Classic Maya 'Codex Style' Pottery." In *Primer Coloquio Internacional de Mayistas,* 775–89. MéxicoCity, D.F.: Universidad Nacional Autónoma de México, Centro de Estudios Mayas Coloquio Internacional de Mayistas, 1987.

Reese-Taylor, Kathryn. *Yaxnohcah.* 2013. http://people.ucalgary.ca/~kreeseta/research/yaxnohcah.html.

Reese-Taylor, Kathryn, and Armando Anaya Hernández, eds. *Proyecto Arqueológico Yaxnohcah, 2011 Informe de la Primera Temporada de Investigaciones.* Calgary, AB: Universidad de Calgary, 2013.

Reese-Taylor, Kathryn, Peter Mathews, Julia Guernsey, and Marlene Fritzler. "Warrior Queens Among the Classic Maya." In *Blood and Beauty: Organized Violence in the Art and Archaeology of Mesoamerica and Central America,* edited by Heather S. Orr and Rex Koontz. Los Angeles, CA: Cotsen Institute of Archaeology Press, 2009.

Rejas, J. G., M. C. Pineda, S. V. Veliz, D. Euraque, E. Martinez, J. R. Rodriguez, and M. Farjas. *Archaeological Remote Sensing Approach in Honduras: A Project for Cultural Heritage and Human Habitats Protection.* B.A.R. International Series, no. 2118. Oxford: Archaeopress, 2010.

Restall, Matthew. *Maya Conquistador.* Boston: Beacon Press, 1998.

Restall, Matthew, and John F. Chuchiak. "A Re-evaluation of the Authenticity of Fray Diego de Landa's Relación de las cosas de Yucatán." *Ethnohistory* 49, no. 3: 651–69, 2002.

Restall, Matthew, and Amara Solari. *2012 and the End of the World: The Western Roots of the Maya Apocalypse.* Lanham, MD: Rowman & Littlefield Publishers, 2011.

Rhyne, Charles S. *Architecture, Restoration, and Imaging of the Maya Cities of Uxmal, Kabah, Sayil, and Labná, the Puuc Region, Yucatán, México.* Reed College, 2008. http://academic.reed.edu/uxmal/.

Rice, Don Stephen, and Dennis E. Puleston. "Ancient Maya Settlement Patterns in the Peten, Guatemala." In *Lowland Maya Settlement Patterns,* edited by Wendy Ashmore, 125–56. Albuquerque: School of American Research. University of New Mexico Press, 1981.

Rice, Don Stephen, Prudence M. Rice, and Timothy W. Pugh. "Settlement Continuity and Change in the Central Peten Lakes Region: The Case of Zacpeten." In *Anatomía de una civilización: Aproximaciones interdisciplinarias a la cultura maya,* edited by Andrés Ciudad Ruíz, 207–52. Madrid: Sociedad Española de Estudios Mayas, 1998.

Rice, Prudence M. *Pottery Analysis: A Sourcebook*. Chicago: University of Chicago Press, 1987.

———. "Rethinking Classic Lowland Maya Pottery Censers." *Ancient Mesoamerica* 10: 25–50, 1999.

———. *Maya Calendar Origins: Monuments, Mythistory, and the Materialization of Time*. William & Bettye Nowlin Series in Art, History, and Culture of the Western Hemisphere. Austin: University of Texas Press, 2007.

———. *Maya Political Science*. Austin: University of Texas Press, 2009.

———. "Mound ZZ1, Nixtun-Ch'ich', Peten, Guatemala: Rescue Operations at a Long-lived Structure in the Maya Lowlands." *Journal of Field Archaeology* 34, no. 4: 403–22, 2009.

———. "Texts and the Cities Modeling Maya Political Organization." *Current Anthropology* 54, no. 6: 684–715, 2013.

Richards, Michael. *Atlas Lingüístico de Guatemala*. Guatemala City, Guatemala: SEPAZ, UVG, URL, USAID/G-CAP, Editorial Serviprensa, S.A., 2003. http://pdf.usaid.gov/pdf_docs/pnadd071.pdf.

Ringle, William M. "The Settlement Patterns of Komchen, Yucatan, Mexico." PhD diss., Tulane University, 1985.

———. "The Nunnery Quadrangle of Uxmal." In *The Ancient Maya of Mexico: Reinterpreting the Past of the Northern Maya*, edited by Geoffrey E. Braswell, 189–226. Bristol, CT: Equinox Publishing Ltd., 2012.

Ringle, William M., and E. Wyllys Andrews V. "Formative Residences at Komchen, Yucatan, Mexico." In *Household and Community in the Mesoamerican Past*, edited by Richard R. Wilk and Wendy Ashmore, 171–97. Albuquerque: University of New Mexico Press, 1988.

———. "The Demography of Komchen, an Early Maya Town in Northern Yucatan." In *Precolumbian Population History in the Maya Lowlands*, edited by T. Patrick Culbert, and Don Stephen Rice. Albuquerque: University of New Mexico Press, 1990.

Ringle, William M., George J. Bey III, Tara Bond Freeman, Craig A. Hanson, Charles W. Houck, and J. Gregory Smith. "The Decline of the East: The Classic to Postclassic Transition at Ek Balam, Yucatán." In *The Terminal Classic in the Maya Lowlands: Collapse, Transition, and Transformation*, edited by Arthur A. Demarest, Prudence M. Rice, and Don Stephen Rice, 485–516. Boulder: University Press of Colorado, 2004.

Ringle, William M., and Gabriel Tun Ayora. *The Yaxhom Valley Survey: Pioneers of the Puuc Hills, Yucatan; Second Field Season, 2012*. Report prepared for the Waitt Foundation and the National Geographic Society, 2013.

Rissolo, Dominique. *Ancient Maya Cave Use in the Yalahau Region, Northern Quintana Roo, Mexico*. Association for Mexican Cave Studies, Bulletin 12. Austin, TX: Association for Mexican Cave Studies, 2003.

Rivera Dorado, Miguel. "La emergencia del estado maya en Oxkintok." *Mayab* 12: 71–78, 1999.

Roach, John. "Ancient Royal Tomb Discovered in Guatemala." *National Geographic News*, May 4, 2006. http://news.nationalgeographic.com/news/2006/05/0504_060504_maya_tomb.html.

———. "Headless Man's Tomb Found under Maya Torture Mural." *National Geographic News*, March 12, 2010. http://news.nationalgeographic.com/news/2010/03/100312-headless-bonampak-tomb-maya-torture-mural/.

Robertson, Elizabeth C., ed. *Space and Spatial Analysis in Archaeology*. Calgary, AB: University of Calgary Press,

Robertson, Robin A., and David A. Freidel, eds. *Archaeology at Cerros, Belize, Central America*. Vol. 1, *An Interim Report*. Dallas, TX: Southern Methodist University Press, 1986.

Robicsek, Francis, and Donald M. Hales. *The Maya Book of the Dead: The Ceramic Codex; The Corpus of Codex Style Ceramics of the Late Classic Period*. Charlottesville, VA; University of Virginia Art Museum, 1981. Distributed by University of Oklahoma Press.

Robinson, Eugenia J., ed. *Interaction on the Southeast Mesoamerican Frontier: Prehistoric and Historic Honduras and El Salvador*. Oxford: British Archaeological Reports, 1987.

Schubert, Blaine W., Jim I. Mead, and Russell W. Graham. *Ice Age Cave Faunas of North America*. Bloomington, IN, and Denver, CO: Indiana University Press and Denver Museum of Nature & Science Press, 2003.

Schulze, Mark D., and David F. Whitacre. "A Classification and Ordination of the Tree Community of Tikal National Park, Petén, Guatemala." *Bulletin of the Florida Museum of Natural History* 41: 169–297, 1999.

Schuster, Angela M. H. "On the Healer's Path." *Archaeology* 54, no. 4: 34–38, 2001.

Service, Elman R. *Origins of the State and Civilization: The Process of Cultural Evolution*. New York: , 1975.

Sexton, James Dean, and Ignacio Bizarro Ujpán. *Heart of Heaven, Heart of Earth and Other Mayan Folktales*. Washington, DC: Smithsonian Institution Press, 1999.

Shafer, Harry J., and Thomas R. Hester. "Ancient Maya Chert Workshops in Northern Belize, Central America." *American Antiquity* 48, no. 3: 519–43, 1983.

Sharer, Robert. *The Prehistory of Chalchuapa, El Salvador*. Philadelphia: University of Pennsylvania Press, 1978.

———. *Quirigua: A Classic Maya Center & Its Sculptures*. Centers of Civilization Series. Durham, NC: Carolina Academic Press, 1990.

———. *Daily Life in Maya Civilization*, The Greenwood Press "Daily Life through History" series. Westport, CT: Greenwood Press, 1996.

Sharer, Robert J., and David C. Grove, eds. *Regional Perspectives on the Olmec*. Cambridge, UK: Cambridge University Press, 1989.

Sharer, Robert J., and Loa P. Traxler. *The Ancient Maya*. 6th ed. Stanford, CA: Stanford University Press, 2006.

Shaw, Justine M. "The Late to Terminal Classic Settlement Shifts at Yo'okop." In *Quintana Roo Archaeology*, edited by Justine M. Shaw and Jennifer P. Mathews, 144–57. Tucson: University of Arizona Press, 2005.

———. *White Roads of the Yucatán: Changing Social Landscapes of the Yucatec Maya*. Tucson: University of Arizona Press, 2008.

———. "Roads to Ruins: The Role of Maya Sacbeob in Ancient Maya Society." In *Highways, Byways, and Road Systems in the Pre-modern World*, edited by Susan E. Alcock, John P. Bodel, and Richard J. A. Talbert, 128–46. Chichester, UK: Wiley-Blackwell Press, 2012.

———, ed. *2,500 Years of Occupation in the Cochuah Region: Archaeological and Ethnographic Findings*. Albuquerque: University of New Mexico Press, 2014.

Shaw, Justine M., and Jennifer P. Mathews, eds. *Quintana Roo Archaeology*. Tucson: University of Arizona Press, 2005.

Shaw, Leslie C. "The Elusive Maya Marketplace: An Archaeological Consideration of the Evidence." *Journal of Archaeological Research* 20, no. 2: 117–55, 2012.

Sheets, Payson D. "A Reassessment of the Precolumbian Obsidian Industry of El Chayal, Guatemala." *American Antiquity* 40, no. 1: 98–103, 1975.

———, ed. *Before the Volcano Erupted: The Ancient Cerén Village in Central America*. Austin: University of Texas Press, 2002.

———. *The Ceren Site: An Ancient Village Buried by Volcanic Ash in Central America*. 2nd ed. Belmont, CA: Thomson Wadsworth, 2006.

Shook, Edwin M. "Archaeological Survey of the Pacific Coast of Guatemala." In *Handbook of Middle American Indians*. Vol. 2, *Archaeology of Southern Mesoamerica*, pt. 1, edited by Gordon R. Willey, 180–94. Austin: University of Texas Press, 1965.

Shook, Edwin M., Richard E. W. Adams, and Robert F. Carr, eds. *Tikal Reports: Numbers 1 to 11*. Philadelphia: University of Pennsylvania Museum of Archaeology and Anthropology, 1986.

Sidrys, Raymond V., John Andresen, and Derek Marcucci. "Obsidian Sources in the Maya Area." *Journal of New World Archaeology* 1, no. 5: 1–13, 1976.

Siemens, Alfred H. "Karst and the Pre-Hispanic Maya in the Southern Lowlands." In *Pre-Hispanic Maya Agriculture*, edited by Peter D. Harrison and B. L. Turner. Albuquerque: University of New Mexico Press, 1978.

Silverman, Helaine. *Contested Cultural Heritage: Religion, Nationalism, Erasure, and Exclusion in a Global World*. New York: Springer-Verlag, 2011.

Simms, Stephanie R., Evan Parker, George J. Bey III, and Tomás Gallereta Negrón. "Evidence from Escalera al Cielo: Abandonment of a Terminal Classic Puuc Maya Hill Complex in Yucatán, Mexico." *Journal of Field Archaeology* 37, no. 4: 270–88, 2012.

Sitler, Robert, K. "The 2012 Phenomenon: New Age Appropriation of an Ancient Maya Calendar." *Nova Religio: The Journal of Alternative and Emergent Religions* 9, no. 3: 24–38, 2006.

———. "The 2012 Phenomenon Comes of Age." *Nova Religio: The Journal of Alternative and Emergent Religions* 16, no. 1: 61–87, 2012.

Skibo, James M. *Pottery Function: A Use-Alteration Perspective*. New York: Plenum Press, 1992.

Skidmore, Joel. *Cival: A Preclassic Site in the News*. Mesoweb, 2004 http://www.mesoweb.com/reports/cival.html. 2004.

Skidmore, Joel, and Marc Zender. Mesoweb, 2014. http://www.mesoweb.com/. 2014.

Smith, A. Ledyard. *Uaxactun, Guatemala: Excavations of 1931–1937*. Carnegie Institution of Washington, Publication 588, Washington, DC: Carnegie Institution of Washington, 1950.

Smith, Michael E., and Frances Berdan, eds. *The Postclassic Mesoamerican World*. Salt Lake City: University of Utah Press, 2003.

Smith, Robert Eliot. *Ceramic Sequence at Uaxactun, Guatemala*. New Orleans, LA: Middle American Research Institute, Tulane University, 1955.

Smith, Robert Eliot, Gordon R. Willey, and James C. Gifford. "Type-Variety Concept as a Basis for the Analysis of Maya pottery." *American Antiquity* 25, no. 3: 298–315, 1960.

Smith, Virginia G. *Izapa Relief Carving: Form, Content, Rules for Design, and Role in Mesoamerican Art History and Archaeology*. Washington, DC: Dumbarton Oaks, 1984.

Smyth, Michael P. *A New Study of the Gruta de Chac, Yucatán, México*. Foundation for the Advancement of Mesoamerican Studies, Inc., 1998. http://www.famsi.org/reports/97011/index.html.

———. "The Teotihuacan Factor in the Yucatan: Beyond Economic Imperialism." *Journal of Anthropological Research* 64, no. 3: 395–409, 2008.

Smyth, Michael P., and Christopher D. Dore. "Large-site Archaeological Methods at Sayil, Yucatan, Mexico: Investigating Community Organization at a Prehispanic Maya Center." *Latin American Antiquity* 3, no. 1: 3–21, 1992.

Smyth, Michael P., and David Ortegón Zapata. "Architecture, Caching, and Foreign Ritual at Chac (II), Yucatan." *Latin American Antiquity* 17, no. 2: 123–50, 2006.

———. "Foreign Lords and Early Classic Interaction at Chac, Yucatán." In *Lifeways in the Northern Maya Lowlands: New Approaches to Archaeology in the Yucatan Peninsula*, edited by Jennifer P. Mathews and Bethany A. Morrison, 119–41. Tucson: University of Arizona Press, 2006.

———. "A Preclassic Center in the Puuc Region: A Report on Xcoch, Yucatán, Mexico." *Mexicon* 30, no. 3: 63–68, 2008.

Smyth, Michael P., David Ortegón Zapata, Nicholas P. Dunning, and Eric M. Weaver. "Settlement Dynamics, Climate Change, and Human Response at Xcoch in the Puuc Region of Yucatán, México." In *The Archaeology of Yucatán: New Directions and Data*, edited by Travis W. Stanton. B.A.R. International Series. Oxford: Oxford University. Archaeopress Pre-Columbian Archaeology, 2014.

Smyth, Michael P., Ezra Zubrow, David Ortegón Zapata, Nicholas P. Dunning, Eric M. Weaver, and Philip van Beynen. *Exploratory Research into Arctic Climate Change and Ancient Maya Response: Paleoclimate Reconstruction and Archaeological Investigation at the Puuc Region of Yucatán, México*. Washington, DC: Report to the National Science Foundation, 2012. www.FARINCO.org.

Sotomayor, Arturo. *Dos sepulcros en Bonampak*. Mexico City: Librería del Prado, 1949.

Šprajc, Ivan. "Astronomical Alignments in Río Bec Architecture." *Archaeoastronomy* 18: 98–107, 2004.

———. *A Childhood Ritual on the Hauberg Stela*. Maya Decipherment, 2008. http://decipherment.word press.com/2008/03/27/a-childhood-ritual-on-the-hauberg-stela/.

———. *Notes on Accession Dates in the Inscriptions of Coba*. Mesoweb, 2010. http://www.mesoweb.com/ stuart/notes/Coba.pdf.

———. "The Wide Waters of Palenque." In *Fiery Pool: The Maya and the Mythic Sea*, edited by Daniel Finamore and Stephen Houston. Salem, MA: Peabody Essex Museum, 2010.

———. *The Order of Days: The Maya World and the Truth about 2012*. New York: Harmony Books, 2011.

———. *The Misunderstanding of Maya Math*. Austin, TX: Wordpress, 2012. http://decipherment.word press.com/2012/05/02/the-misunderstanding-of-maya-math/.

———. "Notes on a New Text from La Corona." *Maya Decipherment: Ideas on Ancient Maya Writing and Iconography* (blog), June 30, 2012. http://decipherment.wordpress.com/2012/06/30/notes-on-a -new-text-from-la-corona/.

———. "ARCHIVES: Glyphs on Pots." *Maya Decipherment: Ideas on Ancient Maya Writing and Ico-nography* (blog), September 9, 2013.https://decipherment.wordpress.com/2013/09/09/archives -glyphs-on-pots/.

———. "Lagunita's Unusual 'Six Ajaw Stone'." *Maya Decipherment: Ideas on Ancient Maya Writing and Iconography* (blog), August 25, 2014. http://decipherment.wordpress.com/2014/08/25/lagunitas-un usual-six-ajaw-stone/.

———. *Maya Decipherment: Ideas on Ancient Maya Writing and Iconography* (blog) http://decipherment .wordpress.com/.

Stuart, David, Marcello A. Canuto, and Tomás Barrientos Q. *The Nomenclature of La Corona Sculpture: 2015 La Corona Notes 1(2)*. Mesoweb, 2015. www.mesoweb.com/LaCorona/LaCoronaNotes02.pdf.

Stuart, David, and Meghan Rubenstein. "The Reading of Two Dates from the Codz Pop at Kabah, Yucatan." *Maya Decipherment: Ideas on Ancient Maya Writing and Iconography* (blog), October 30, 2014. https://decipherment.wordpress.com/2014/10/30/the-reading-of-two-dates-from-the-codz-pop -at-kabah-yucatan/.

Stuart, David, and George E. Stuart. *Palenque: Eternal city of the Maya*. New York: Thames and Hudson, 2008.

Stuart, George E. "Maya Art Treasures Discovered in Cave." *National Geographic* 160, no. 2: 220–35, 1981.

Suárez Aguilar, Vicente. "Labores de mantenimiento e impermeabilización en la Estructura I de Becán durante la temporada 1996." *Gaceta Universitaria* 31–32: 41–46, 1996.

———. "Trabajos de restauración llevados a cabo en Becán y Chicanná." *Gaceta Universitaria* 27–28: 50–54, 1996.

Suhler, Charles, Traci Ardren, David Freidel, and Dave Johnstone. "The Rise and Fall of Terminal Clas-sic Yaxuna, Yucatan, Mexico." In *The Terminal Classic in the Maya Lowlands: Collapse, Transition, and Transformation*, edited by Arthur A. Demarest, Prudence M. Rice, and Don Stephen Rice, 551–87. Boulder: University Press of Colorado, 2004.

Suhler, Charles, Traci Ardren, and Dave Johnstone. "The Chronology of Yaxuna: Evidence from Excava-tion and Ceramics." *Ancient Mesoamerica* 9: 167–82, 1998.

Suyuc Ley, Edgar. "The Extraction of Obsidian at El Chayal, Guatemala." In *The Technology of Maya Civilization: Political Economy and Beyond in Lithic Studies*, edited by Zachary X. Hruby, Geoffrey E. Braswell, and Oswaldo Fernando Chinchilla Mazariegos, 130–39. Sheffield, UK, and Oakville, CT: Equinox Publishing, 2011.

Tate, Carolyn Elaine. *Yaxchilan: The Design of a Maya Ceremonial City*. Austin: University of Texas Press, 1992.

Taube, Karl. *At Dawn's Edge: Tulum, Santa Rita, and Floral Symbolism in the International Style of Late Postclassic Mesoamerica*. Washington, DC: Dumbarton Oaks, 2010.

———. "Teotihuacan and the Development of writing in Early Classic Central México." In *Their Way of Writing: Scripts, Signs, and Pictographies in Pre-Columbian America*, edited by Elizabeth Hill Boone and Gary Urton. Washington, DC: Dumbarton Oaks Research Library and Collection, 2011.

————. *The Major Gods of Ancient Yucatan*. Washington, DC: Dumbarton Oaks, 1992.

————. "Where Earth and Sky Meet: The Sea and Sky in Ancient and Contemporary Maya Cosmology." In *Fiery Pool: The Maya and the Mythic Sea*, edited by Daniel Finamore and Stephen Houston. Salem, MA: Peabody Essex Museum, 2010.

Taube, Karl A., William A. Saturno, David Stuart, Heather Hurst, and Joel Skidmore. *The Murals of San Bartolo, El Petén, Guatemala*. Part 2, *The West Wall*. Ancient America, no. 11. Barnardsville, NC: Boundary End Archaeology Research Center, 2010.

Tax, Sol. *Heritage of Conquest: The Ethnology of Middle America*. Wenner-Gren Foundation for Anthropological Research. Glencoe, IL: Free Press, 1952.

Tedlock, Dennis. "The Popol Vuh as a Hieroglyphic Book." In *New Theories on the Ancient Maya*, edited by Elin C. Danien and Robert J. Sharer. University Museum Monograph 77. Philadelphia: University of Pennsylvania Museum, 1992.

Tedlock, Dennis. "Torture in the Archives: Mayans Meet Europeans." *American Anthropologist* 91, no. 1: 139–52, 1993.

————. *Popol Vuh: The Mayan Book of the Dawn of Life*. rev. ed. New York: Simon & Schuster, 1996.

————. *Rabinal Achi: A Maya Drama of War and Sacrifice*. New York: Oxford University Press, 2005.

————. *2000 Years of Mayan Literature*. Berkeley: University of California Press, 2010.

Thomas, Prentice M. *Prehistoric Maya Settlement Patterns at Becan, Campeche, Mexico*. Middle American Research Series, Publication 45. New Orleans, LA: Middle American Research Institute, Tulane University, 1981.

Thompson, Edward Herbert. *Cave of Loltun, Yucatan*. Memoirs of the Peabody Museum of American Archaeology and Ethnology, Harvard University, vol. 1, no. 2. Cambridge, MA: The Museum, 1897.

Thompson, J. E. S. *The Rise and Fall of Maya Civilization*. Norman: University of Oklahoma Press, 1966.

Thompson, J. Eric S. "Some Sculptures from Southeastern Quetzaltenango, Guatemala." *Notes on Middle American Archaeology and Ethnography* 17: 100–102, 1943.

————. *An Archaeological Reconnaissance in the Cotzumalhuapa Region, Escuintla, Guatemala*. Contributions to American Anthropology and History, no. 44. Carnegie Institution of Washington, Publication 574. Washington, DC: Carnegie Institution of Washington, 1948.

————. *Maya History and Religion*. Norman: University of Oklahoma Press, 1970.

Thompson, J. Eric S., Harry E. D. Pollock, and Jean Charlot. *A Preliminary Study of the Ruins of Coba, Quintana Roo, Mexico*. Carnegie Institution of Washington, Publication 424. Washington, DC: Carnegie Institution of Washington, 1932.

Thompson, John Eric Sidney. *Maya Archaeologist*. Norman: University of Oklahoma Press, 1994.

Tiesler, Vera, and Andrea Cucina. "Procedures in Human Heart Extraction and Ritual Meaning: A Taphonomic Assessment of Anthropogenic Marks in Classic Maya Skeletons." *Latin American Antiquity* 17, no. 4: 493–510, 2006.

————. "New Perspectives on Human Sacrifice and Ritual Body Treatment in Ancient Maya Society." In *Society for American Archaeology Annual Meeting*. New York: Springer, 2007.

Tokovinine, Alexandre. *A Classic Maya Term for Public Performance*. Mesoweb, 2003. http://www.mesoweb.com/features/tokovinine/Performance.pdf.

Tokovinine, Alexandre, and Dmitri Beliaev. "People of the Road: Traders and Travelers in Ancient Maya Words and Images." In *Merchants, Markets and Exchange in the Pre-Columbian World*, edited by Kenneth G. Hirth and Joanne Pillsbury. Washington, DC: Dumbarton Oaks Research Library and Collection, Trustees for Harvard University, 2013.

Tokovinine, Alexandre, and Vilma Fialko. "Stela 45 of Naranjo and the Early Classic Lords of Sa'aal." *The PARI Journal* 7, no. 4: 1–14, 2007.

Tozzer, Alfred M. *Landa's "Relación de las cosas de Yucatán": A Translation*. Papers of the Peabody Museum of American Archaeology and Ethnology, vol. 18. Cambridge, MA: Harvard University, 1941.

Turner, B. L. "Prehistoric Intensive Agriculture in the Mayan Lowlands: New Evidence from the Rio Bec Region." PhD diss., University of Wisconsin, Madison, 1976.

———. *Once Beneath the Forest: Prehistoric Terracing in the Rio Bec Region of the Maya Lowlands.* Boulder, CO: Westview Press, 1983.

Turner, B. L., and Peter D. Harrison. *Pulltrouser Swamp: Ancient Maya Habitat, Agriculture, and Settlement in Northern Belize.* Texas Pan American series. Austin: University of Texas Press, 1983.

Turner, B. L., II, and Jeremy A. Sabloff. "Classic Period Collapse of the Central Maya Lowlands: Insights about Human-Environment Relationships for Sustainability." *Proceedings of the National Academy of Sciences of the United States of America* 109, no. 35: 13908–914, 2012.

Tykot, R. H. "Contribution of Stable Isotope Analysis to Understanding Dietary Variation among the Maya." *ACS Symposium Series* 831: 214–30, 2002.

U.S. Central Intelligence Agency. *The World Factbook.* 2014. https://www.cia.gov/library/publications/the-world-factbook/.

———. *The World Factbook, Central America and Caribbean: Belize.* 2014. https://www.cia.gov/library/publications/the-world-factbook/geos/bh.html.

———. *The World Factbook, Central America and Caribbean: El Salvador.* 2014. https://www.cia.gov/library/publications/the-world-factbook/geos/es.html.

———. *The World Factbook, Central America and Caribbean: Guatemala.* https://www.cia.gov/library/publications/the-world-factbook/geos/gt.html.

———. *The World Factbook, Central America and Caribbean: Honduras.* https://www.cia.gov/library/publications/the-world-factbook/geos/ho.html.

———. *The World Factbook, North America: Mexico.* https://www.cia.gov/library/publications/the-world-factbook/geos/mx.html.

Urban, Patricia A., and Edward M. Schortman, eds. *The Southeast Maya Periphery.* Austin: University of Texas Press, 1986.

Vail, Gabrielle, and Anthony F. Aveni. *The Madrid Codex: New Approaches for Understanding a Pre-Hispanic Maya Manuscript.* Boulder: University Press of Colorado, 2004.

Vail, Gabrielle, and Christine Hernandez, eds. *Astronomers, Scribes, and Priests: Intellectual Interchange between the Northern Maya Lowlands and Highland Mexico in the Late Postclassic Period.* Washington, DC: Dumbarton Oaks, 2010.

———. *Re-Creating Primordial Time: Foundation Rituals and Mythology in the Postclassic Maya Codices.* Boulder: University Press of Colorado, 2013.

———. *Maya Hieroglyphic Codices,* Version 5.0, March 2, 2014. Electronic data set. www.mayacodices.org.

Valdés, Juan Antonio, and Jonathan Kaplan. "Ground-Penetrating Radar at the Maya Site of Kaminaljuyu, Guatemala." *Journal of Field Archaeology* 27, no. 3: 329–42, 2000.

Van Laningham, Ivan. *Mayan Calendar Tools.* 2013. http://www.pauahtun.org/Calendar/tools.html.

Van Stone, M. "The Decipherment of Ancient Maya Writing, ed. by Stephen Houston, Oswaldo Chinchilla Mazariegos, and David Stuart." *Studies in American Indian Literatures,* n.s. 15: 189–91, 2003.

Van Stone, Mark. *2012: Science & Prophecy of the Ancient Maya.* Imperial Beach, CA: Tlacaélel Press, 2010.

Varela Torrecilla, Carmen, and Geoffrey E. Braswell. "Teotihuacan and Oxkintok: New Perspectives from Yucatán." In *The Maya and Teotihuacan: Reinterpreting Early Classic Interaction,* edited by Geoffrey E. Braswell. Austin,: University of Texas Press, 1995.

Vargas de la Peña, Leticia, and Víctor R. Castillo Borges. "Ek' Balam: Ciudad que empieza a revelar sus secretos." *Arqueología Mexicana* 7, no. 37: 24–31, 1999.

———. "El mausoleo de Ukit Kan Le'k Tok'." *Investigadores de la Cultura Maya (Campeche, Mex.)* 9, no. 1: 145–50, 2001.

Vargas Pacheco, Ernesto. "Apuntes para el Análisis del Patrón de Asentamiento en Tulum." *Estudios de Cultura Maya* XVI: 55–83, 1986.

———. *Tulum: Organización político-territorial de la costa oriental de Quintana Roo.* México D.F.: Universidad Nacional Autónoma de México, Instituto de Investigaciones Antropológicas, 1997.

Velázquez Morlet, Adriana, ed. *Guardianes del tiempo.* Chetumal, Quintana Roo, México: Universidad de Quintana Roo, Instituto Nacional de Antropología e Historia, 2000.

Velázquez García, Erik. "The Captives of Dzibanche." *The PARI Journal* 6, no. 2: 1–4, 2005.

Velázquez Valadez, Ricardo. *Loltún, Yucatán.* Mexico: Instituto Nacional de Antropología e Historia, 1991.

Veni, George. "Maya Utilization of Karst Groundwater Resources." *Environmental Geology and Water Sciences* 16, no. 1: 63–66, 1990.

Vicek, D. T. "Muros de delimitación de Chunchucmil." *Boletin de la escula de Ciencias Antropológicas de la Universidad de Yucatán* Año 5, no. 28: 55–64, 1978.

Villa Rojas, Alfonso. *The Yaxuna-Cobá Causeway.* Contributions to American Archaeology, no. 9. Carnegie Institution of Washington, Publication 436. Washington, DC: Carnegie Institution of Washington, 1934.

Voit, Claudia Ann. "The Venus 'Shell-over Star' Hieroglyph and Maya Warfare: An Examination of the Interpretation of a Mayan Symbol." MA thesis, Wayne State University, 2013.

Von Euw, Eric. *Corpus of Maya Hieroglyphic Inscriptions.* Vol. 4, Pt. 1, *Itzimte, Pixoy, Tzum.* Cambridge, MA: Peabody Museum of Archaeology & Ethnology, Harvard University, 1977.

Voogt, Alexander J. de, and Irving L. Finkel, eds. *The Idea of Writing: Play and Complexity.* Leiden: Brill, 2010.

Voss, Alexander W., and H. Juergen Kremer. *K'ak'-u-pakal, Hun-pik-tok' and the Kokom: The Political Organization of Chichén Itzá.* Edited by Pierre Robert Colas. (The Sacred and the Profane: Architecture and Identity in the Maya Lowlands: 3rd European Maya Conference, University of Hamburg, November 1998.) Acta Mesoamericana, vol. 10. Markt Schwaben, Germany: A. Saurwein, 2000.

Walker, Debra S. *Sampling Cerros' Demise: A Radiometric Check on the Elusive Protoclassic.* Report to FAMSI on Grant no. 03064. Foundation for the Advancement of Mesoamerican Studies, Inc., 2005. http://www.famsi.org/reports/03064/index.html.

Walker, Debra S., and Kathryn Reese-Taylor. *Naachtún, Petén, Guatemala: First Analyses, Guatemala.* Foundation for the Advancement of Mesoamerican Studies, Inc. (FAMSI), 2012. http://www.famsi.org/reports/06035/index.html.

Wauchope, Robert. *Modern Maya Houses: A Study of Their Archaeological Significance.* Washington, DC: Carnegie Institute of Washington Publication 502, 1938.

———. "Domestic Architecture of the Maya." In *The Maya and Their Neighbors,* edited by C. Hays, 232–41. New York: Dover, Appleton Century, 1940.

———. *Excavations at Zacualpa, Guatemala.* Middle American Research Institute, Publication 14. New Orleans, LA: Tulane University, 1948.

———. *Zacualpa, El Quiche, Guatemala: An Ancient Provincial Center of the Highland Maya.* Middle American Research Institute, Publication 39. New Orleans, LA: Tulane University, 1975.

Weaver, Muriel Porter. *The Aztecs, Maya, and Their Predecessors: Archaeology of Mesoamerica.* 3rd ed. New York: Academic Press, 1995.

Webster, David. "Lowland Maya Fortifications." *Proceedings of the American Philosophical Society* 120, no. 5: 361–71, 1976.

———. "Una Ciudad Maya Fortificada. Becán, Campeche." *Arqueología Mexicana* 18: 32–35, 1996.

Webster, David L. *Defensive Earthworks at Becan, Campeche, Mexico: Implications for Maya Warfare.* Middle American Research Institute, Publication 41. New Orleans, LA: Tulane University, 1976.

Webster, James W. "Speleothem Evidence of Late Holocene Climate Variation in the Maya Lowlands of Belize Central America and Archaeological Implications." PhD diss., University of Georgia, 2000.

Webster, James W., George Brook, L. Bruce Railsback, Hai Cheng, R. Lawrence Edwards, Clark Alexander, and P. P. Reeder. "Stalagmite Evidence from Belize Indicating Significant Droughts at the Time of Preclassic Abandonment, the Maya Hiatus, and the Classic Maya Collapse." *Palaeogeography, Palaeoclimatology, Palaeoecology* 250, nos. 1–4: 1–17, 2007.

Weeks, John M. *Maya Civilization.* New York: Garland Publishing, 1993.

Weishampel, John F., Arlen F. Chase, Diane Z. Chase, Jason B. Drake, Ramesh L. Shrestha, K. Clint Slatton, Jaime J. Awe, Jessica Hightower, and James Angelo. *Remote Sensing of Ancient Maya Land Use*

Features at Caracol, Belize Related to Tropical Rainforest Structure. B.A.R. International Series, no. 2118. Oxford: Archaeopress, 2010.

Weishampel, John F., J. N. Hightower, Arlen F. Chase, and Diane Z. Chase. "Use of Airborne LiDAR to Delineate Canopy Degradation and Encroachment along the Guatemala-Belize Border." *Tropical Conservation Science* 5, no. 1: 12–24, 2012.

Wernecke, D. Clark. "Aspects of Urban Design in an Ancient Maya Center: El Pilar, Belize." MA thesis, Florida Atlantic University, 1994.

Wernecke, Daniel Clark. "A Stone Canvas: Interpreting Maya Building Materials and Construction Technology." PhD diss., University of Texas at Austin, 2005.

Wetherington, Ronald K. *The Ceramics of Kaminaljuyu, Guatemala.* College Station: Pennsylvania State University Press, 1978.

White, Christine D., David M. Pendergast, Fred J. Longstaffe, and Kimberley R. Law. "Social Complexity and Food Systems at Altun Ha, Belize: The Isotopic Evidence." *Latin American Antiquity* 12, no. 4: 371–93, 2001.

White, D. A., and Hood C. S. "Vegetation Patterns and Environmental Gradients in Tropical Dry Forests of the Northern Yucatan Peninsula." *Journal of Vegetation Science* 15, no. 2: 151–60, 2004.

White, Tim D., Michael Timothy Black, and Pieter A. Folkens. *Human Osteology.* 3rd ed. Boston: Elsevier Academic Press, 2012.

Whitley, David S., and Marilyn P. Beaudry, eds. *Investigaciones arqueológicas en la costa sur de Guatemala.* Institute of Archaeology, Monograph 31. Los Angeles: Institute of Archaeology, University of California Los Angeles, 1989.

Whittaker, John C. *Flintknapping: Making and Understanding Stone Tools.* Austin: University of Texas Press, 1994.

Whittaker, John C., Kathryn A. Kamp, Anabel Ford, Rafael Guerra, Peter Brands, Jose Guerra, Kim Mclean, Alex Woods, Melissa Badillo, Jennifer Thornton, and Zerifeh Eiley. "Lithic Industry in a Maya Center: An Axe Workshop at El Pilar, Belize." *Latin American Antiquity* 20, no. 1: 134–56, 2009.

Whittington, Stephen L., and David M. Reed. *Bones of the Maya Studies of Ancient Skeletons.* Tuscaloosa: University of Alabama Press, 2006.

Willey, Gordon. "The Classic Maya Hiatus: A 'Rehearsal' for the Collapse?" In *Mesoamerican Archaeology: New Approaches,* edited by Norman Hammond, 417–44. Austin: University of Texas Press, 1974.

———, ed. *Excavations at Seibal, Department of Peten.* Memoirs of the Peabody Museum of Archaeology and Ethnology, vols. 13–17. Cambridge, MA: Harvard University, 1975–1990.

Willey, Gordon R., William R. Bullard Jr., John B. Glass, and James C. Gifford. *Prehistoric Maya Settlements in the Belize Valley.* Papers of the Peabody Museum of American Archaeology and Ethnology, vol. 54. Cambridge, MA: Peabody Museum, Harvard University, 1965.

Willey, Gordon R., T. Patrick Culbert, and Richard E. W. Adams. "Maya Lowland Ceramics: A Report from the 1965 Guatemala City Conference." *American Antiquity* 32, no. 3: 289–315, 1967.

Willey, Gordon R., and Peter Mathews. *A Consideration of the Early Classic Period in the Maya Lowlands.* Albany: Institute for Mesoamerican Studies, State University of New York at Albany, 1985.

Williams-Beck, Lorraine A. *El dominio de los batabob: El área Puuc occidental campechana.* Campeche, Mexico: Secretaria de Educacion Publica, Universidad Autonoma de Campeche, 1998.

Winter, Marcus. "Monte Alban and Teotihuacan." In *Rutas Intercambio en Mesoamérica, III Coloquio Pedro Bosch-Gimpera,* edited by Evelyn Childs Ratray, 153–84. Mexico, D.F.: Universidad Nacional Autónoma de México, Instituto de Investigaciones Antropológicas, 1998.

Wiseman, Frederick M. "Agricultural and Historical Ecology of the Maya Lowlands." In *Pre-Hispanic Maya Agriculture,* edited by Peter D. Harrison and B. L. Turner, 63–115. Albuquerque: University of New Mexico Press, 1978.

Witschey, Walter R. T. "Muyil: An Early Start and Late Finish in East Coast Settlement." In *Quintana Roo Archaeology,* edited by Justine M. Shaw and Jennifer P. Mathews, 127–43. Tucson: University of Arizona Press, 2005.

————. "The Archaeology of Muyil, Quintana Roo, Mexico: A Maya Site on the East Coast of the Yucatan Peninsula." PhD diss., Tulane University, 1993.

————. *Muyil, Quintana Roo, Mexico.* 2008. http://muyil.smv.org/.

Witschey, Walter R. T., and Clifford T. Brown. *Historical Dictionary of Mesoamerica.* Edited by Jon Woronoff. Historical Dictionaries of Ancient Civilizations and Historical Eras. Lanham, MD: Scarecrow Press, 2012.

Woodbury, Richard B., and Aubrey S. Trik. *The Ruins of Zaculeu, Guatemala.* Vol. 1. New York: United Fruit Co., 1953.

Wright, David R., Richard E. Terry, and Markus Eberl. "Soil Properties and Stable Carbon Isotope Analysis of Landscape Features in the Petexbatún Region of Guatemala." *Geoarchaeology* 24, no. 4: 466–91, 2009.

Wright, Lori E. "In Search of Yax Nuun Ayiin I: Revisiting the Tikal Project's Burial 10." *Ancient Mesoamerica* 16, no. 1: 89–100, 2005.

Yaeger, Jason, and David A. Hodell. "The Collapse of Maya Civilization: Assessing the Interaction of Culture, Climate, and Environment." In *El Niño, Catastrophism, and Culture Change in Ancient America*, edited by Daniel H. Sandweiss and Jeffrey Quilter, 197–251. Washington, DC: Dumbarton Oaks, 2008.

Zavala Ruiz, Roberto, Luis Millet Cámara, Ricardo Velázquez Valadez, and Roberto MacSwiney. *Guía de las grutas de Loltún, Oxkutzcab, Yucatán.* México, D.F., México: SEP, Instituto Nacional de Antropología e Historia, 1978.

Zender, Marc, Ricardo Armijo Torres, and Miriam Judith Gallegos Gómora. "Vida y Obra de Aj Pakal Tahn, un Sacerdote del Siglo VIII en Comalcalco, Tabasco, Mexico." *Los Investigadores de la Cultura Maya. Universidad Autónoma de Campeche* 9, no. 2: 386–98, 2001.

Zender, Marc Uwe. "A Study of Classic Maya Priesthood." PhD diss., University of Calgary, 2004.

INDEX TO INVESTIGATORS AND EXPLORERS

INDEX TO THE ENCYCLOPEDIA

Pages which refer to, or also refer to, a map or figure are italicized. See also the Index to Investigators and Explorers above.

ABOUT THE EDITOR AND CONTRIBUTORS

THE EDITOR

Walter R. T. Witschey is Research Professor of Anthropology and Geography at Longwood University, past president of the Virginia Academy of Science, and Director Emeritus of the Science Museum of Virginia. His research interest is Maya settlement patterns, and he is co-PI with Clifford T. Brown of the *Electronic Atlas of Ancient Maya Sites*. Brown and Witschey coauthored *The Historical Dictionary of Ancient Mesoamerica*.

THE CONTRIBUTORS

E. Wyllys Andrews is Professor Emeritus of Anthropology at Tulane University, New Orleans, Louisiana, and was Director of the Middle American Research Institute at Tulane from 1975 to 2009.

Kazuo Aoyama is Professor of Anthropology at Ibaraki University, Japan.

Wendy Ashmore is Professor of Anthropology at the University of California, Riverside.

Anthony F. Aveni is the Russell Colgate Distinguished University Professor of Astronomy and Anthropology and Native American Studies at Colgate University, Hamilton, New York.

Maya Azarova is a graduate of Moscow State University and a PhD student at the University of California, San Diego.

Christopher S. Balzotti is research faculty in the Plant and Wildlife Sciences Department at Brigham Young University.

Antonio Benavides C. is an archaeologist at Centro INAH Campeche, Campeche, Mexico.

George J. Bey III is Professor of Anthropology and holds the Chisholm Chair of Arts and Sciences at Millsaps College, Jackson, Mississippi.

Erik Boot is an anthropologist with a PhD from Leiden University, specializing in the study of Maya epigraphy, iconography, and cultural history.

Justin Bracken is a graduate student at the CUNY Graduate Center and an Adjunct Professor at Queens College, both located in New York, New York.

James E. Brady is Professor of Anthropology at California State University, Los Angeles.

Geoffrey E. Braswell is Professor of Anthropology at the University of California, San Diego, and the coeditor of *Latin American Antiquity*.

Mark Brenner is Professor of Geological Sciences and Director of the Land Use and Environmental Change Institute (LUECI) at the University of Florida, Gainesville, Florida.

Nicholas Brokaw is Professor of Environmental Science at The University of Puerto Rico–Río Piedras, San Juan, Puerto Rico.

Bryce M. Brown is a senior majoring in environmental science at Brigham Young University, Salt Lake City, Utah.

Clifford T. Brown is an Associate Professor in the Department of Anthropology at Florida Atlantic University in Boca Raton, Florida.

Leslie G. Cecil is an Associate Professor of Anthropology at Stephen F. Austin State University, Nacogdoches, Texas.

Arlen F. Chase is a Pegasus Professor and Associate Dean in the College of Sciences at the University of Central Florida, Orlando, Florida.

Diane Z. Chase is a Pegasus Professor and Interim Provost at the University of Central Florida, Orlando, Florida.

Oswaldo Chinchilla Mazariegos is Assistant Professor of Anthropology in the Department of Anthropology, Yale University.

Flora S. Clancy (d.) was Professor Emerita in Art History at the University of New Mexico in Albuquerque.

Rafael Cobos is Professor of Anthropology and Archaeology at the Universidad Autónoma de Yucatán, México.

Nicholas Dunning is Professor of Geography at the University of Cincinnati, Cincinnati, Ohio.

Rachel Egan is an anthropology PhD student at The University of Colorado at Boulder.

Jerald D. Ek is a Lecturer of Anthropology at Western Washington University.

Alberto G. Flores Colin has a degree in archaeology from Mexico's Escuela Nacional de Antropología e Historia (ENAH). He is field director of the Cochuah Regional Archaeological Survey Project in Quintana Roo.

Anabel Ford is the Director of the MesoAmerican Research Center at the University of California Santa Barbara and President of Exploring Solutions Past ~ The Maya Forest Alliance.

Amy Frappier is Assistant Professor of Geosciences at Skidmore College.

Tomás Gallareta Negrón is a research associate at Centro INAH Yucatán, Mexico.

Toni Gonzalez is a graduate student in the Department of Anthropology at California State University, Los Angeles.

Elizabeth Graham is Professor of Mesoamerican Archaeology, Institute of Archaeology, University College, London.

Joel D. Gunn is in the Department of Anthropology at the University of North Carolina at Greensboro.

Alexandria Halmbacher is an anthropology graduate student at The University of Colorado at Boulder.

Ashley Hampton is an anthropology graduate student at Florida Atlantic University.

Jessica Harrison is a PhD student in the Department of Anthropology at the University of Illinois at Urbana-Champaign.

David R. Hixson teaches anthropology and geography at Shepherd University, West Virginia, and is a research associate with the Maya Exploration Center, Austin, Texas.

John Hoopes is Professor of Anthropology at the University of Kansas in Lawrence, Kansas.

Justin Kerr is a leading photographer of pre-Columbian artifacts and provides a photographic archive of roll-outs of more than 750 Classic Maya polychromes.

Jeff Kowalski is Emeritus Professor, School of Art, Northern Illinois University.

Edward B. Kurjack (d.) was Professor Emeritus from the Department of Sociology and Anthropology, Western Illinois University.

Michael Love is Professor of Anthropology at California State University–Northside.

Sheryl Luzzadder-Beach is Professor and Chair of Geography and the Environment, and Fellow of the C. B. Smith Sr. Centennial Chair in U.S.-Mexico Relations, at The University of Texas at Austin.

Jessica MacLellan is a PhD candidate in the School of Anthropology at the University of Arizona.

Rubén Maldonado Cardenas is an investigator at the Centro Regional de Yucatán, Instituto Nacional de Antropología e Historia in Mexico.

Marilyn Masson is Associate Professor of Anthropology at the University of Albany, State University of New York.

Jennifer P. Mathews is a Professor of Anthropology at Trinity University, San Antonio, Texas.

Judith M. Maxwell is Louise Rebecca Schawe and Williedell Schawe Professor in the Department of Anthropology, Tulane University, New Orleans, Louisiana.

Heather McKillop is Doris Z. Stone Professor of Latin American Studies at Louisiana State University, Baton Rouge.

Mary Miller is Sterling Professor in the Department of the History of Art, Yale University.

Johan Normark, PhD, is researcher at the Department of Historical Studies, University of Gothenburg, Sweden.

Liseth Pérez is a Research Associate in the Institute of Geology at the Universidad Nacional Autónoma de México (UNAM), México City, D.F., México.

Kendra L. Philmon is an archaeologist for the Kalispel Tribe of Indians in Usk, Washington.

Timothy W. Pugh is Professor of Anthropology at Queens College and the Graduate Center of the City University of New York.

Kathryn Reese-Taylor is Associate Professor and Graduate Program Director in the Department of Anthropology and Archaeology, University of Calgary, Canada.

Matthew Restall is Sparks Professor of Latin American History at the Pennsylvania State University.

William M. Ringle is Professor and Chair of Anthropology at Davidson College, Davidson, North Carolina.

Francis Robicsek, MD, PhD, is Chairman Emeritus, Department of Thoracic and Cardiovascular Surgery, University of North Carolina at Chapel Hill and Vice President for International Medical Outreach at the Carolinas Medical Center, Charlotte, North Carolina.

Eugenia J. Robinson is Professor of Anthropology at Montgomery College, Rockville, Maryland.

Melanie P. Saldana is a graduate student in the Department of Anthropology at California State University, Los Angeles.

David Martin Schele is an architect with Felder Group Architects.

Elaine Day Schele is Adjunct Assistant Professor at Austin Community College.

Justine M. Shaw is Professor of Anthropology and History at College of the Redwoods in Eureka, California, and a research associate at Humboldt State University in Arcata, California.

Payson Sheets is College Professor of Distinction at the University of Colorado, Boulder.

Yuko Shiratori is a PhD candidate in anthropology at The Graduate Center, City University of New York.

Michael P. Smyth is President of the Foundation for Americas Research, Inc., The University at Buffalo, Winter Springs, Florida.

Amara Solari is Associate Professor of Pre-Columbian and Latin American Art History at the Pennsylvania State University.

Ivan Šprajc is Head and Research Advisor at the Institute of Anthropological and Spatial Studies or ZRC-SAZU, the Research Centre of the Slovenian Academy of Sciences and Arts.

David Stuart is the Linda and David Schele Professor of Mesoamerican Art and Writing in the Department of Art and Art History at the University of Texas–Austin.

George E. Stuart (d.) was for 40 years staff archaeologist, editor, and Vice President for Research and Exploration at the National Geographic Society.

Carolyn E. Tate is Professor of Art History in the School of Art at Texas Tech University.

Richard E. Terry is Professor of Soil Science in the Plant and Wildlife Sciences department at Brigham Young University.

Erin Kennedy Thornton is Assistant Professor of Anthropology at Washington State University, Pullman, Washington.

Austin Ulmer is a master of science student in the Plant and Wildlife Sciences department at Brigham Young University

Gabrielle Vail holds a research and teaching position at New College of Florida in Sarasota.

Mark Van Stone is Professor of Art History at Southwestern College, Chula Vista, California.

Dirk Van Tuerenhout is Curator of Anthropology at the Houston Museum of Natural Science.

Cristina Verdugo is a graduate student in the Department of Anthropology at University of California, Santa Cruz.

Beniamino Volta is a PhD candidate in anthropology at the University of California, San Diego.

Christopher L. von Nagy teaches as Adjunct Graduate Faculty at the University of Nevada, Reno.

Debra S. Walker is Research Curator at the Florida Museum of Natural History, University of Florida, Gainesville.

Sheila E. Ward is Director of Mahogany for the Future, Inc.